●●●● Special Pedagogical Features

Popular **Model Student Activities** are ready to be used or adapted in the classroom.

MODEL STUDENT ACTIVITY

Where Would You Locate Your City?

Overview

The object of this activity is to determine whether students will change their original decision in light of new information.

Procedure

Provide students with a copy of Map 1. Ask where, with just the information they have, they would locate a city if they were prospective settlers. Assume that the area is otherwise uninhabited. Permit students to discuss their choices in small groups, and then have each group present its choice to the entire class. Then provide each group with copies of Maps 2, 3, and 4 (see page 347), one at a time, permitting discussion and explanations (as warranted) after each map is distributed.

Sources/Variation

Making the maps for this activity used to be a major undertaking. However, for any teacher with access to the computer programs referred to earlier (*PC-Globe, PC-USA, USA Atlas, World Atlas,* and *Microsoft Encarta*), it is now a simple process, and the areas that students deal with are real. The computer programs will usually print whichever maps you need. However, it is usually necessary to remove the name of the area manually, using typewriter white-out, tape, or some other method, if you wish it to remain anonymous. After students have decided where to locate their cities, you can provide them with a computer-generated map showing the actual location of major cities.

Map 1

Scale: 1 inch = 50 miles

⎓⎓ sea water

▷ rivers

◗ lakes

(continued)

Literary Mapping. You may remember reading Mark Twain's *The Adventures of Huckleberry Finn*, in which Huck and his comrades travel to various places along the Mississippi? Most of the places Huck visits are real, and most can be located on a map of the area. As your class is reading *Huck Finn* wouldn't it make sense to trace Huck's travels on a map?

There is a wealth of children's literature in which the settings are real places and, thus, locatable on a map. There is still more literature in which the set-

---

Model Student Activities include:

- Who is Qualified for the Presidency?
- Who Is Best Suited for Which Jobs?
- Holly and the Cat in the Tree– Procedure for Young Children
- Heinz and the Druggist
- Taba's Concept-Formation Strategy
- A Sample Unit Plan: Super Burger Unit
- "The Wearin' of the Green"– A Group Investigation
- The Lunch Policy
- Nation X– Using a Fact Sheet
- Returning from the Crusades
- Pumpkin Geography
- Where Would You Locate Your City?
- Constructing a Table
- Linear Charting
- Current Events: "And Now a Word from Our _____ Desk."

Resource Handbook Contents

RESOURCE HANDBOOK

D1468535

An end-of-text **Resource Handbook** includes instructional materials, planning aids, instructional resources, and annotated bibliographies of children's literature.

Children and Their World

Strategies for Teaching Social Studies

8th Edition

•••• **David A. Welton**

Professor Emeritus
Texas Tech University

Houghton Mifflin Company   **Boston New York**

To. . . .

David Jr., Stephen, Christopher, Lynda, and Shawn

. . . . as they encounter their world.

Editor in Chief: Pat Coryell
Senior Sponsoring Editor: Sue Pulvermacher-Alt
Senior Development Editor: Lisa Mafrici
Editorial Associate: Sara Hauschildt
Senior Project Editor: Florence Kilgo
Art and Design Coordinator: Jill Haber
Photo Editor: Jennifer Meyer-Dare
Composition Buyer: Sarah Ambrose
Designer: Henry Rachlin
Senior Manufacturing Coordinator: Priscilla Bailey
Marketing Manager: Jane Potter
Marketing Assistant: Erin Lane

Cover photo © Zigy Kaluzny/Getty Images/Stone

Printed in the U.S.A.

Library of Congress Catalog Card Number: 2003110105

ISBN: 0-618-37644-5

2 3 4 5 6 7 8 9-DOC-09 08 07 06 05 04

Brief Contents

Contents

7 Social Studies: Gateway to Literacy 172

11 Nurturing Critical and Reflective Thinking   303

12 Helping Students Understand Maps, Globes, and Graphics

Preface

For almost two hundred years, education has been guided by the belief that teaching should be aimed at preparing children for the future. Today, however, the world is changing so rapidly that predicting the future with any certainty is risky business. Until children gain a perspective on the past, the world they wake up to each morning is undoubtedly their normal everyday world, very much like the world they experienced yesterday. If their world is changing rapidly, that too is probably its normal state for children, and certainly not something they need to be concerned about. Yet, each time I prepare a new edition of *Children and Their World* I wonder whether the title should be changed to better reflect the many worlds of childhood—the adult world, the television world, the peer world, the fantasy world, and so forth. Instead of changing the title, I have opted to make clear that the children's world—"their world"—is indeed many worlds.

The teacher's world is changing, too, and at a pace that is almost breathtaking. Teachers dare not ignore the ever-changing technology, the influences of teaching standards, and the increasingly diverse children they greet in their classrooms each day. When the first edition of this book was published almost thirty years ago, the technology was fairly mundane. At the time, filmstrips were still "hot stuff," whereas television, which was hyped as the tool for a vastly improved education—a potential it never realized—was used very little until teachers learned to hook it up to a VCR or DVD player. No longer must most teachers schedule audiovisual equipment weeks in advance. At the same time, back in the mid-1970s, the idea of standards was at least a decade in the future, while diversity got little more than a passing glance. In this edition, the strong emphasis on diversity (two chapters) has been maintained, and like technology and standards, it emerges in themes that reappear at various points throughout the book. These themes are indicated by special marginal icons: a ☼ for technology, a ✔ for standards, and a ♟ for diversity.

In the constantly changing world of teaching social studies there are some constants. The Battle of Hastings, for example, was fought in 1066, and thanks to the nature of history, that's not going to change. What *could* change, however, is whether children will be expected to learn about the Battle of Hastings and many other topics. Also a constant is the common and often self-imposed belief among beginning teachers that they must know all the content they will be expected to teach before they begin teaching, when in reality no one does. Desirable as it might seem to have everything mastered beforehand, beginning teachers will discover that having to make decisions about subject matter is a potent motivation for learning.

● ● ● ● Underlying Assumptions of This Book

This book reflects some underlying premises about social studies, about teaching, and about social studies methods books. Here, in summary form, are some of the fundamental ideas that are basic to this edition.

- The world of teaching elementary- and middle-school social studies is not a world of gimmicks and recipes for teaching activities. Neither is it a chaotic world that somehow becomes clear and understandable if only students are given predetermined bits of information—that Robert E. Lee's horse was named Traveler, for example—or given sets of prescriptive ideas.

- Children come in many different sizes, shapes, forms, and cultural packages. From birth onward, they live in a number of competing worlds and learn countless lessons not taught in classrooms. Much of what occurs in classrooms involves the social and cultural contexts that children bring to school.

- Teaching and learning are social activities.

- Social studies is complex partly because of the nature of its field of knowledge, and partly because some of its purposes may be in conflict. Consider that social studies is the only subject area in the school curriculum that publicly ascribes to citizenship education an educational goal. Sometimes physical education is said to build health and character, but citizenship education is almost never mentioned in the context of mathematics, science, or English.

- Teaching elementary- and middle-school social studies sometimes demands a willingness to live with a degree of bewilderment, even confusion.

Audience and Purpose

Children and Their World: Strategies for Teaching Social Studies, eighth edition, is intended for preservice and in-service students taking a first course in teaching elementary- and middle-school social studies. The goal was to make this edition compatible with the growing number of field-based courses where students' time is often at a premium. At the same time, in-service and graduate students should continue to find this edition as useful, or even more so, than previous editions.

A continuing purpose of this book is to help prospective and in-service teachers understand the complex nature of elementary- and middle-school social studies. I, like others, take exception to the conventional contention that "anyone can teach social studies." That contention too often ignores the complexities of a subject area that bridges the social sciences and the humanities. I also advocate a hands-on approach to teaching social studies, but only up to a point. Teachers who adopt a hands-on approach simplistically, and who, for example, have their students spend two weeks building igloos out of sugar cubes, may need to reexamine their priorities. The intent here is to help prospective teachers build a perspective for judging the appropriateness of social studies teaching activities, a perspective that recognizes the uniqueness and potential of the underlying subject matter.

This book also is based on the premise that learning is an active, constructivist process. That premise is hardly new or earthshaking—indeed, it's an approach the late Hilda Taba advocated almost four decades ago (though she called it a "spiral" curriculum)—yet it applies equally to students in elementary- or middle-school classrooms and to the preservice students who read this book. For prospective teachers especially, I argue that teaching social studies successfully depends primarily on the teacher's ability to manage the triumvirate of teaching: the ability to correlate (1) social studies content, (2) teaching methods, and (3) the application of content and methods in classrooms. Content and methods are certainly essential, but the key to effective instruction lies in *application,* in being able to relate subject-matter content with teaching methods, and teaching theory with classroom practice.

● Revisions in This Edition

The entire text has been extensively revised and updated to incorporate the most recent research in social studies education and to reflect emerging practices and emphases in the field.

Part Organization and Coverage

This edition still has three parts. Part 1, "Building a Framework for Social Studies," focuses on the "what is" of social studies. It explores (1) the dynamic nature of social studies teaching, (2) how social studies reflects the scholarly disciplines that it derives from, and (3) how traditional and alternative social studies programs are organized.

Part 2, "Contexts for Teaching Social Studies," considers factors that impinge on teaching social studies and constitute a context in which it is taught. Consistent with the current emphasis on diversity, this edition has two chapters, one dealing with cultural/multicultural diversity, and the other with educational/instructional diversity. Other chapters in this section focus on developing character and using social studies to enhance students' literacy skills.

The last section, Part 3, "Instruction," which is also the largest, focuses on the nuts and bolts of teaching social studies. Chapters in this section examine planning, assessment, teaching strategies for hands-on learning, teaching critical and reflective thinking, helping students use maps and globes, and, finally, a chapter on instructional tools and resources.

Significant Changes and New Coverage

New and expanded coverage in this edition include the following:

- *The number of chapters has been reduced* from fourteen to thirteen. This was accomplished by consolidating the teaching strategies and the activities chapters into one.

- *The chapter opening pedagogy has been improved.* The "Key Questions" sections remain, but the "Key Ideas" have been integrated into the text and appear as occasional sectional summaries.

- *Increased currency* by updating research in every chapter.

- The inclusion of a major new section on *service learning* in Chapter 6, including a new section on *constructivism* in Chapter 1, and in Chapter 4, expanded treatment of students with *limited English proficiency.*

- *The planning chapter (Chapter 8) has been reconceptualized and refocused.* Instead of canned corn, it now includes a new sample unit plan that focuses on a hamburger not unlike the Whopper.

- *The Suggested Activities sections have been moved* from ends of chapters. Individual activities now appear in the margin next to relevant text or have been relocated to the Instructor's Resource Manual or the Student Website, as appropriate.

- *New and updated Model Student Activities,* such as the new "And Now a Word from Our (Berlin, Tokyo, London, etc.) Desk" activity for current events. The "Who Is Qualified for the Presidency?" model student activity has been updated. The historical figures remain but Eleanor Roosevelt and Cesar Chavez have been replaced by Hillary Clinton and Henry Cisneros.

- The *Bibliography of Children's Literature* in the Resource Handbook at the end of the book has been significantly updated with the addition of more than 150 new children's books.

- Coverage related to *technology, standards, and diversity* are highlighted by *redesigned icons* in the margins of relevant sections of all chapters.

Other Current Features

Several major emphases from previous editions also appear in this edition. These include the following:

- *Exemplary Classroom Practices.* Vignettes of exemplary classroom practices are, in effect, mini-case studies of how real (or composite) teachers elect to approach social studies in their classrooms. For example, the literacy chapter (Chapter 7) begins with a vignette of how a second-grade teacher in Arizona integrates social studies and language experiences with her students, for many of whom English is their second language. Other vignettes illustrate how teachers can use historical documents as a springboard, how they use technology, and how they use a K-W-L chart with their students.

- *Integrating Children's Literature.* Opportunities for integrating children's literature into social studies have been expanded throughout this edition. The same is true for the bibliography of children's fiction and nonfiction books presented in the Resource Handbook, as noted earlier.

Special Pedagogical Aids

To make this text easy to study, appealing to use, and a valuable teaching resource, the following features are included:

- *Key Questions* at the beginning of each chapter that serve as advance organizers for the content to be covered.

- *Key Ideas* highlighted throughout the text that serve as section summaries.

- *Introductions* that provide an overview of what is to come.

- *Technology Updates* that provide technological resources for contemporary social studies programs.

- *Model Student Activities* that illustrate model lesson formats that can be adapted to other social studies topics or content.

- *Commentaries* in which I offer a point of view on various problems and issues.

- *Vignettes of exemplary practice* that demonstrate how various teachers approach social studies with their students.

- *Marginal notes* that highlight key ideas within the text.

- *Marginal icons* that call out key coverage of diversity, technology, and standards.

- *Summaries* that synthesize the major concepts presented in each chapter.

- *Suggested Activities* that are designed to stimulate further thought or provide opportunities for students to apply the concepts treated within the chapter.

- *Suggested Readings and Resources* that list, with annotations, additional print and Internet sources for students to locate detailed information on topics considered with the chapter.

- A *Resource Handbook* that provides additional sources and materials related to social studies teaching. The four parts of the Handbook include: (1) instructional materials relating to text activities, (2) planning aids, (3) additional instructional resources, and (4) annotated bibliographies of children's books that are keyed to common social studies topics.

- *Web site support* that provides additional resources for students and instructors alike, featuring student self-tests for each chapter, additional examples of social studies teaching activities, such as a WebQuest, and links to other resources.

Acknowledgments

I am keenly aware of my indebtedness to the many people who helped to make this book possible. Among the most important are the countless elementary- and middle-school students who have helped me understand what it means to teach a subject like social studies. Equally important are the college students and in-service teachers with whom I have been privileged to work, and whose questions (and responses to our answers) have indicated directions in which I needed to go and areas where I needed to be clearer than I was.

I gratefully acknowledge the contributions of the following reviewers for the thoughtful advice and criticism they offered at various stages in the development of this book: Peter L. Higgs, Central Michigan University; Rene A. Pico II, Carlow College; and the others who offered their helpful comments and criticisms.

I also extend special thanks to my talented developmental editor, Sara Hauschildt, whose comments and criticism were more on target than I sometimes care to admit. I also extend thanks to my wonderful production editor, Florence Kilgo; and to the rest of the editorial staff at Houghton Mifflin who were my partners in this endeavor.

Finally, I continue to owe special acknowledgment to Kathy Welton, who, after thirty some years, has come to understand the trials and joys associated with producing a book such as this. Together we were able to complete an extensive home renovation and this new edition, both with satisfying results.

DAVID A. WELTON
Winston-Salem, North Carolina

Prologue:
Reflecting on What's Ahead

● ● ● ● ● Introduction

Some things about social studies you may remember fondly, and others you've long since forgotten. From time to time you may have asked yourself why you needed to learn certain things, like the states and capitals (assuming you know them), when that information is readily available elsewhere. There are a variety of reasons, some valid and others questionable, why things like the states and capitals are often taught in social studies, reasons we will explore throughout this book.

The Joan of Arc Syndrome

You may be aware that portions of the social studies you studied might not have been taught at all were it not for the "Joan of Arc" syndrome. In this phenomenon, which is illustrated in the following conversation, the only qualification is that at least one of the speakers has spent time studying about Joan of Arc, the national heroine of France.

"I've heard they're taking Joan of Arc out of social studies. Children won't be studying her anymore."

"What! What are they doing that for?"

"I guess it's because they can't figure out why they should keep her in."

"You gotta be kidding! Why they should keep her in? I mean isn't it obvious?

I learned about Joan of Arc—you did too. She's someone everyone should know about. . . . I mean, well. . . look what it's done for us! We'd never be where we

© Gary Walts / The Image Works

are today if we hadn't learned the stuff that everybody needs to know—including Joan of Arc."

"You're saying that because *we* learned it when we were in school, students today should learn it too."

"Exactly! We learned it, they should learn it too!"

There's probably a little Joan of Arc in each of us—a reluctance to reflect on some of the things we have done in the past. This is not to suggest that everything about the past is "bad" or outdated, or that every new idea that comes along is worthwhile and is the kind of thing that schools should move toward immediately. The point is that tradition, which is what the Joan of Arc syndrome represents, is such a potent force that trying to remove almost any topic from the school curriculum can elicit howls of protest. In many cases, the protesters may not remember much about the topic—whether it's Joan of Arc or whatever—all they must remember is having studied it. As long as people perceive certain topics as useful, those topics tend to remain in the curriculum, which then grows larger and larger with every passing day.

Tradition plays a role in keeping the curriculum as large as it is, but there is another side to this coin: that is, there are some things that could be included in the curriculum but usually are not. For example, you may recall some questions that arose during your school experience that you thought were important, but that were almost never considered at school. These may have included questions like the following:

The questions kids ask

Is it OK to lie sometimes? If so, when?
How do other people feel about me, and how can I know for sure?
If cooperation is so important, why don't you get graded on it?
Why are the best movies almost always rated "R"?
Must I like everybody? What happens if I don't?
Why doesn't everyone have all the money he or she needs?

Underlying questions like these are genuine human and social concerns. Some people argue that such questions involve things that students will learn—or should learn—from their parents or from everyday life. They also argue that for schools to get involved in such matters, is either unnecessary or an invasion of parental rights and responsibilities, sometimes both. Although questions and concerns cannot and indeed should not be the sole basis for elementary and middle-school social studies programs, we will explore some legitimate roles they can play.

● ● ● ● An Inquiry

After spending a dozen or so years watching social studies teachers in action, you already have some beliefs, assumptions, and impressions about what social studies is and about why it is taught. In the next section, you have the opportunity to clarify what you believe about elementary- and middle-school social studies and then compare our beliefs. It is not important that we agree on everything, because the purpose is simply to establish a point of departure.

A Social Studies Inventory

Select the response that best reflects your impressions of your elementary and middle-school social studies experience by circling the appropriate number.

		Agree	*Uncertain*	*Disagree*
Comparing beliefs about social studies	1. Social studies is too often dull and boring.	1	2	3
	2. What children learn in social studies is useful in their everyday lives.	1	2	3
	3. Teaching social studies is not as important as teaching reading or mathematics.	1	2	3
	4. The main purpose of social studies is teaching history and geography.	1	2	3
	5. Most social studies teachers put about the right emphasis on teaching thinking skills.	1	2	3
	6. Many social studies teachers place too much emphasis on textbooks.	1	2	3
	7. Social studies involves everyday classroom behaviors, such as lining up properly to walk through the hall or learning to obey classroom rules.	1	2	3
	8. Small-group work in social studies often uses time that could be better spent learning things that are really important.	1	2	3

Responses

The responses in this section are geared to traditional social studies programs, and not to one-of-a-kind programs you rarely encounter.

1. *Social studies is too often dull and boring.* Response: Agree.

   Content that deals with people—which is what social studies focuses on—should never be dull and boring, yet too often that's what seems to happen. For example, as Alter and Denworth noted in 1990 (p. 3), "History itself isn't boring; it's just taught that way." As much as one may be inclined to agree with Alter and Denworth, some related problems play a role here. First, many textbooks present materials in ways that are—well—less than thrilling. Second, the vast amounts of material that teachers (and textbooks) are expected to cover during a year can be almost overwhelming. One could argue that a major part of the problem here is the so-called survey course. Sixth-grade teachers, for example, are often expected to teach a span of history that covers prehistoric times to the atomic age—roughly five thousand years. The scope is so broad that they and their students are forced to rush through historic eras so quickly that students often have difficulty differentiating one era

The coverage problem

from another. Trying to cover so much material in a 180-day school year inevitably results in superficial exposure, not in-depth understanding. The paradox here is that teachers at other grade levels may spend the entire year on social studies topics that may not require that much time. For example, the traditional curriculum focus for second grade is the neighborhood. Spending 180 days on the neighborhood is more than some second-grade teachers want or need and often leads to situations where they teach social studies only once a week, and that is only *if* they get to it.

"Less is more"

More and more teachers and even some states have begun to address the problems associated with survey courses by adopting an approach that is sometimes referred to as "less is more." The premise is that by studying fewer ("less") topics in greater depth, teachers can spend the time necessary to develop ("more") in-depth understanding. This approach may help reduce the extent to which social studies may have been dull and boring in the past.

2. *What children learn in social studies is useful in their everyday lives.* Response: Uncertain.

Relevance

Because the relevance of social studies often hinges on how teachers approach it, it is difficult to generalize here. Some portions of social studies—especially history—are taught because they represent bodies of knowledge that children are expected to learn and know, regardless of any direct relevance to their day-to-day lives. Still other segments of social studies can be taught in ways that have immediate relevance to children and to their actions as future citizens.

3. *Teaching social studies is not as important as teaching reading* or *mathematics.* Response: Disagree.

Priorities

The conventional wisdom in many schools holds that teaching reading and mathematics is more important than almost everything else. This book reflects the position that thought-provoking social studies programs will incorporate elements that are just as important as reading and mathematics, possibly more so.

4. *The main purpose of social studies is teaching history and geography.* Response: Disagree.

History and geography are so prominent in many social studies programs that the other social sciences, like anthropology, often fade into the background. Then, too, many people think that social studies is simply another name for history and geography. Common as such thinking is, it is much too limited. Social studies deals with the human experience, with human beings and human behavior in every sense of those terms.

Goal: To produce good citizens

The main purpose for teaching social studies is to produce thoughtful, competent, well-informed, and responsible citizens. In other words, the purpose for teaching social studies parallels the purpose for which schools exist—to produce good citizens. Not every child will become an engineer, a doctor, or a scientist, but everyone will be a citizen; it's an office that every one of us occupies.

© Fredrick D. Bodin/Stock Boston

There is no question that social studies is not always taught well. Nevertheless, it is the only place in the school curriculum where students might engage in the formal study of democratic practices and ideals. It is where students can encounter models of civic courage, such as Abraham Lincoln and Rosa Parks, and where they can study the struggles and problems associated with achieving "liberty and justice for all." And, when social studies is taught well, it is where the youth of this nation can experience the problems, the pitfalls, and the decision making that are among their responsibilities as citizens in a democratic society.

5. *Most social studies teachers put about the right emphasis on teaching thinking skills.* Response: Disagree.

Many traditional social studies programs place too much emphasis on learning names, dates, and other information and too little emphasis on using social studies as a vehicle for teaching critical thinking and problem solving. Throughout this book the emphasis is on *using* social studies content—the stuff of which history, geography, and other social sciences are made—for a variety of teaching purposes. Among the most important of those purposes is helping students to become skillful thinkers.

6. *Many social studies teachers place too much emphasis on textbooks.* Response: Agree.

Text as tools

Some teachers apparently feel that skipping one or more chapters in a textbook will leave irreparable gaps in their students' education. Such teachers may rely on textbooks exclusively, perhaps because they are not aware of how to use alternative data sources. Still other teachers feel compelled to emphasize the textbook because of state or school board mandates or other forces beyond their control. All of this notwithstanding, consider an approach to social studies in which textbooks are used as teaching tools but do not become the program itself.

7. *Social studies involves everyday classroom behaviors, such as lining up properly to walk through the hall or learning to obey classroom rules.* Response: Uncertain.

Classrooms as caring communities

This response is not weaseling out or avoiding the issue here because everything depends on the context in which the behaviors take place. In schools and classrooms that employ "developmental discipline" (see Schaps and Solomon, 1990), where students are treated as valued and participating members of a learning community, behaviors such as lining up to go to the cafeteria can be an integral part of social studies. However, this occurs only when students play an active role in classroom governance and decision making. That role includes participating in the development of classroom rules—through which students begin to understand what rules are for—and working collaboratively with teachers to solve problems. Classrooms and schools that function as caring democratic communities—as microcosms of the larger society in which students actually "do" democracy—can provide a vital part of citizenship education (see Garrison, 2003). We disagree with people who claim that training children to walk down the hall properly is necessarily a vital part of social studies. Training students to conform to expected behaviors through the imposition of adult authority is obviously one approach to classroom management—and classroom management is clearly something that every teacher must be concerned with. Nevertheless, one can question whether teachers who adopt this approach are actually teaching social studies.

8. *Small-group work in social studies often uses time that could be better spent learning things that are really important.*   Response: Agree.

Group work

Small-group work in many social studies programs sometimes seems to be included as a respite from normal classroom routines, almost as a way to make the regular work more palatable. At the same time, the most common reason that people are fired from their jobs is their inability to get along with others in the workplace. Social studies can provide a context for small-group work, which helps children learn to work effectively with one another.

The key to small-group work and most of the other items on this inventory is how teachers use them. Small-group work can be a raging success, a disaster, or something in between. Likewise, you've had teachers who could somehow make the dullest, most lifeless material become interesting and worthwhile. Clearly, teachers hold the key to vibrant and appealing social studies programs.

Building on what children already know

The other key ingredient is the children. Some of the problems that children experience with social studies—like confusing cities, states, and countries—are simply a result of their lack of experience with the world as we know it. Young children are prone to view their world from a highly personal perspective that, even in this age of advanced technology, may not extend beyond their immediate neighborhood. At the same time, young children are often fascinated with our world and the people who inhabit it. The purpose throughout this book is to provide the basis for developing elementary- and middle-school social studies programs that can capitalize on children's inherent interest in their world and that will add depth and richness to what they already know.

Building a Framework
for Social Studies

PART
1

Part 1 examines three elements that make up the framework for teaching social studies. The first of these is the nature of social studies itself and the purposes for which it is taught, both of which are the focus of Chapter 1, The Dynamics of Social Studies. The second element of that framework is the knowledge base from which social studies is drawn—history and the social sciences— which is the focus in Chapter 2, History and the Social Sciences: The Knowledge Base for Social Studies. The third element of the framework in Chapter 3, How Social Studies Programs Are Organized, explores how social studies is organized for teaching purposes.

The overarching purpose for teaching social studies, which is the focus in Chapter 1, can be captured in two words: citizenship education. That purpose has remained constant for almost one hundred years, but as our society continues to change, the demands of contemporary citizenship education have also changed. In a society made up of overlapping cultures—national, regional, ethnic, and so forth—citizens are apt to face conflicting demands and allegiances. In addition to the ability to read and write, everyone in our society needs to become conversant in at least three complementary literacies of citizenship: multicultural literacy, civic literacy, and community literacy.

Chapter 2, History and the Social Sciences: The Knowledge Base for Social Studies, surveys the disciplines from which social studies is drawn. Because history often plays a major role in social studies programs, special attention focuses on the demands that teaching history imposes on teachers.

There are literally hundreds of ways in which you could organize and teach social studies, but as Chapter 3, How Social Studies Programs Are Organized, explains this variety is seldom evident in most textbook-based programs. Chapter 3 focuses on the most common social studies programs—especially the expanding-environments approach, the most common program of all. For balance, several alternative program formats, both past and present, are also examined.

1

The Dynamics of Social Studies

KEY QUESTIONS

● **What is social studies, and why is it an integral part of elementary- and middle-school programs?**

● **What is citizenship education?**

● **How does social studies lend itself to multiple objectives?**

● ● ● ● Introduction: Teaching Social Studies in a Technological Age

An old adage holds that you need only three things to teach social studies successfully: an atlas, a globe, and a map—preferably one mounted on a roller. Textbooks might be useful too, of course, but according to the adage they are not essential.

In this context it may be useful to visit Ramirez Elementary, one of several schools we will revisit from time to time throughout this book. Ramirez was built about thirty years ago, which is fairly recent for an inner-city school, and as such has been around long enough that it still has some atlases, globes, and wall maps. It's not that Ramirez's teachers have bought into the old adage; rather, many of them believe that they've identified some better ways to teach social studies—which is why they are featured here.

DIVERSITY

Ramirez Elementary is a predominantly (90%+) Hispanic school located in a midsize city in the Southwest. Over 95 percent of the Ramirez students are eligible for free breakfast and lunch, the commonly used indicator for the socio-economic status of the neighborhood the school serves. The mobility rate at Ramirez is more than 50 percent, which means that over half its student population will either enter or leave the school during a given year. This also means that some teachers' classes have an almost completely different student population at the end of the year than they began with. Note, however, that this situation is not unique to Ramirez; many inner-city schools share similar demographic profiles.

TECHNOLOGY

What sets Ramirez Elementary apart from most of its counterparts is the technology available to its teachers and students. Every classroom has at least five computers, each networked to a color printer and equipped with CD-ROMs, Internet capability, sound systems, and the ability to import and transmit images

New computers in
regular classrooms

from digital cameras or camcorders. With this kind of hardware, you are correct to assume that these are neither bargain-basement computers nor the ancient Apple 2e machines that are still found in some schools today. As Ramirez's principal, Lucy Guiterrez Brown says, "We put the new computers in classrooms where teachers can use them, and put the old computers in the computer lab where we teach keyboarding skills." For a detailed description of how an inner-city school is able to purchase so many new computers, see Welton (1999). A description of how Ramirez students use authoring software to produce animated "books" of "Colonial Occupations" appears in the Technology Update on page 187.

TECHNOLOGY

Some of Ramirez's teachers prefer to use atlases and maps (and textbooks), but others use computer-based atlas and encyclopedia programs, such as Microsoft's Encarta, which permit them to access an almost infinite range of maps and other data. The key component is having the hardware those programs require. And using that technology, Ramirez students do some remarkable activities. For example, sixth graders typically use information from the Internet to identify the locations (latitude and longitude) of the previous day's earthquakes. They then plot the locations of the earthquakes on an oversize world map (detailed instructions for this activity appear in the Technology Update on pages 340–341).

The fifth graders at Ramirez correspond via E-mail, both individually and collectively, with fifth graders elsewhere around the world. At the beginning of the year, neither Ramirez nor the "foreign" fifth graders know where each other are—although teachers know this of course. And during their first month of E-mailing, both groups of students are restricted to asking questions that can be answered by either yes or no—no explanations are permitted. This means that students must learn to phrase their questions very precisely. Yet in less time than you might imagine, the students in both nations will have identified their correspondent's school and location—maybe not exactly, but close. Thereafter, they are free to interact without restrictions—and interact they do!

One clue that students use to identify their partner school's location usually occurs when they notice that their correspondent's E-mail messages were dated "Tuesday," for example, when it is still "Monday" here—and vice versa. Because even very young students know you cannot jump ahead in time, their first conclusion is that there's a glitch in the E-mail program. However, after teachers assure them the dates are correct, for many students the situation creates a "need to know," the desire for an explanation. Teachers from both countries indicate that their students often *insist* they teach them how time zones "work"—and let's do it now, not sometime later in the year!

Teaching about time zones, which necessarily means that students need to understand latitude and longitude, especially longitude, is a common challenge for most elementary- and middle-school teachers; it's part of most fifth- and sixth-grade programs. But having their students ask them to explain time zones is something teachers rarely encounter; it's what is sometimes called having reached a "teachable moment."

Several clarifications to this illustration are in order. First, the "foreign" students are located in New Zealand, where, because they too speak English, both student groups can use E-mail without translators. Second, and with the cooperation of

SUGGESTED ACTIVITY

The teachers at Ramirez often wait until after students have asked about time zones before explaining how they work. Knowing that students are likely to have a problem with time zones, wouldn't it be preferable if teachers simply explained the concept prior to students' requests? Is anything gained by waiting?

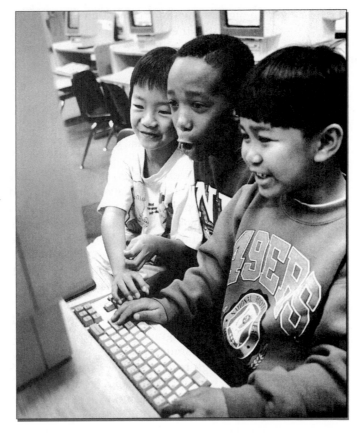

Even young students
can master elements of
computer technology.
(© Susie Fitzhugh)

TECHNOLOGY

nearby universities, teachers here and in New Zealand were able to arrange an interactive videoconference as a capstone experience for their students. Interactive video is a two-way system that permits participants to view and hear each other simultaneously. Interactive videoconferences that rely on satellites are ridiculously expensive. There is the technical equipment, including satellite dishes to upload and download the signal as well as per-minute transmission charges. Although the videoconferencing aspects of the activity were not essential to the overall project, the American and New Zealand teachers obtained funding for this special event by soliciting small contributions from numerous service groups (e.g., Rotary clubs) and local foundations.

Thanks to continuing advances in technology, the Ramirez teachers are no longer forced to appeal to community groups for contributions. Their computers are now equipped with simple "eyeball" cameras and inexpensive microphones (and the appropriate software), which, along with the Internet, enables Ramirez students to connect with peers around the world. An elementary school in Saint Cloud, Florida, has a similar program (see McGoogan, 2002). It uses two computer stations, one with a global, well-protected connection that allows school-to-school communication and the other station that provides a secured chatroom in which ten students can participate simultaneously.

**Simpler, less
expensive equipment**

The time differences between the United States and nations elsewhere make it necessary to adjust schedules accordingly. For Ramirez students, the eleven-hour time difference between New Zealand and the United States (here are those time zones again) means that they had to be at school at 7:30 P.M. while the students in New Zealand had to be at their TV studio at 6:30 A.M. For the St. Cloud students, their program culminates in a twenty-four-hour "Big Night" where students actually spend the entire night at school—with appropriate sleeping accommodations and additional parental supervision, of course.

Identifying partner schools

Locating another class or school somewhere around the globe to partner with is seldom the problem it might seem. You simply make Internet contact with an organization such as the Global Schools Network (http://www.mdc.com.my/smart/gsn/pages/fullframe.htm) that specializes in matching schools. The final decision is always up to the participating schools. Details are in the "Suggested Readings and Resources" section at the end of the chapter. There's no guarantee that your experience will be as successful or elaborate as those we have described here. Then, too, there should also be no question that what the Ramirez and Florida students experienced is a far cry from answering the questions at the end of the chapter in a textbook.

STANDARDS ✔️

Before personal computers and the Internet became such an integral part of our lives, the Canadian media scholar Marshall McLuhan predicted that the world would become a global village—a place of almost instantaneous communication. Accurate as McLuhan's prediction has proven to be, it's doubtful that even he anticipated all the effects the information age would have on our lives. As suggested in this introduction, technology has had a profound effect on how some teachers approach teaching social studies. Yet technology is not the only element that teachers must address. You are surely aware of the movement, at the state level especially, that focuses on the question "How well are schools performing?" During the 1990s, state-mandated tests designed to determine how well students can perform in reading, mathematics, and other subject areas proliferated, seemingly faster even than technology. If this were not enough, teachers also are confronted with performance standards that identify what students should be expected to know in the various subject areas. The Ramirez teachers were caught up in these expectations as much as teachers elsewhere, especially because the school would become eligible for additional state funds if students did well on the state-mandated tests but could face a variety of sanctions if students performed poorly.

Does the activity address the standards?

The skill of writing E-mail messages (to students in another nation) is not on most state-mandated tests, so you can be sure the Ramirez teachers had to wrestle with the question of whether the activity was worth the time it takes. Ultimately they decided that in addition to the interest the activity aroused in students, the E-mail correspondence involved creating "real" messages as opposed to an "out-of-the-book" assignment. And as some teachers told their students, "You've got to write clear E-mail messages that have good grammar and correct spelling. You're gonna look dumb if you make lots of errors." So the Ramirez teachers justified the E-mail activity in terms of the opportunities it provided to teach composing skills, including grammar and spelling, all of which are covered on the state tests.

Technology, subject-matter standards, and mandated testing are three elements

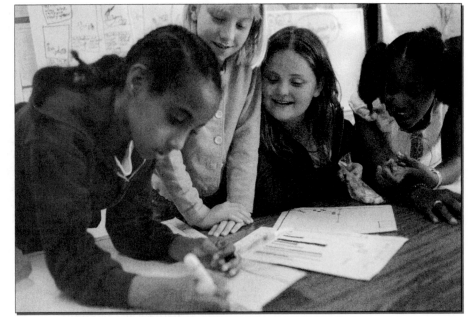

Students in democratic classrooms share responsibility for maintaining safe and caring learning environments.
(© Susie Fitzhugh)

that teachers today cannot ignore. These elements also have become part of the dynamics of teaching social studies, which is the focus of the balance of this chapter (and throughout this book).

● ● ● ● Dynamic Social Studies: The Continuing Debates

The next section of a chapter usually doesn't begin with another teaching vignette after such a lengthy example as this chapter's introduction. Notice that I said "usually." Instead of presenting a list of the emerging practices in teaching social studies, for example, it is better practice to provide students (and readers) with one or more concrete examples that provide a context for the summary list of generalizations that will follow later. In other words, the premise is that "experience should precede abstraction"—an instructional tactic that will reappear from time to time.

Experiences should precede abstraction

· · · ·

Teaching Vignette: Using Cooperative Biographies with Jigsaw Grouping

· · · ·

Tarry Lindquist teaches fifth grade at the Lakeridge Elementary School, which is located in the San Juan Islands immediately across Puget Sound from Seattle, Washington. Ms. Linquist is the focus of a vignette because (a) her teaching is truly exemplary, and (b) she writes (or coauthors) wonderful books about her teaching experiences. These include *Seeing the Whole Through Social Studies* (1995), *Ways That Work: Putting Social Studies Standards into Practice* (1997), and *Social Studies at the Center* (with Douglas Selwyn, 2000), all of which are outstanding.

Writing books cooperatively

Ms. Lindquist warrants our attention here because she devotes five weeks of class time to having her fifth graders write cooperative biographies of Abraham Lincoln. Cooperative biographies are books that students write together—that is, cooperatively. Having said this, back up for a moment and consider how much time this activity consumes. Of the thirty-six weeks in a typical school year, Ms. Lindquist has elected to devote at least five of them to a cooperative writing project on just one aspect of American history. By allotting so much time to one historical personage, imagine all the history that Ms. Lindquist doesn't have time to cover! Thus, a basic question here is: How can she justify spending so much classroom time on just one activity/person? Before addressing that question directly, you need to be aware of the activities the children engage in as they produce those biographies.

Getting Started.   Writing cooperative biographies is such a time-consuming project that students write only one of them during the year. And, because most students have never experienced a writing project of this magnitude, Ms. Lindquist predetermines some elements that make it less overwhelming. One restriction—that all biographies are on the same person, Abraham Lincoln—enables groups of students to work together as they encounter problems. It also simplifies the background information that Ms. Lindquist must provide. Ms. Lindquist also predetermines that (1) each writing group will have five members

Laying the ground work

and (2) each biography will have five chapters (the number of chapters or the size of groups can vary depending on the number of students in the class each year). This procedure means that one student in each group will be responsible for one chapter of the final biography. A third ground rule is that there must be a balance among the chapters—no fifty-page chapters on Lincoln's early life, for example. This limitation may not seem important at first, but its importance often grows as the project progresses.

You may be asking yourself how Ms. Lindquist knew what to predetermine and what decisions she should leave up to the children. Ms. Lindquist credits Myra Zarnowski's (1990) book, *Learning About Biographies: A Reading and Writing Approach for Children,* a joint publication of the National Council for Teachers of English and the National Council for the Social Studies, as an invaluable resource. If you are thinking that a cooperative biography project might be too ambitious for you or your students, read Zarnowski before you decide.

One of the first questions the writing groups must decide is: what will each chapter be about? Students cannot make this decision until they know something about their subject, and it is also useful to see how previous Lincoln biographers organized their work. At this point, Ms. Lindquist spends several days providing background information—some as read-alouds and others as minilectures— which highlight different aspects of Lincoln's life. Meanwhile, students are doing independent research. The students and Ms. Lindquist then brainstorm significant events in Lincoln's life, after which they try to categorize and organize their

SUGGESTED ACTIVITY

Ms. Lindquist predetermined several elements of this activity, including group size and the required number of chapters. Do you think Ms. Lindquist was justified in imposing these requirements, or would it have been better had she left these decisions up to the groups?

FIGURE 1.1 Jigsaw Grouping

brainstorming ideas into chapter topics—Lincoln's early life, his presidency, and so on. Eventually they decide on the focus for each of the five chapters.

Jigsaw Technique.   Ms. Lindquist also uses a *jigsaw* technique where the students from each writing group who are responsible for Chapter 1 (or 2, or 3) meet together as task-alike groups to share what they are planning to include in their chapter. This technique is shown in Figure 1.1. After the Chapter 1 (and Chapters 2 and 3) people have returned to their original working group, they spend at least one class discussing how they will organize their respective biographies.

Once the chapter topics have been determined, students engage in more independent research. But this time, and because they know that Chapter 1, for example, will be about Lincoln's early life, their research is more focused. This is where students may encounter another problem—having too much information. To maintain a balance between their chapters (ground rule 3), some students find they need to cut some "really good stuff" from their chapter. Less often, authors may need to beef up their chapters. The overly long chapters may lead to lengthy meetings as group members help the author wrestle with deciding what to cut. The recognition that real-world authors are sometimes forced to omit perfectly good but excessively lengthy materials is one that many fifth graders accept reluctantly—usually very reluctantly.

Fine-tuning

Before each cooperative biography is printed, students compose a brief dedication page and an equally brief biography of each author, along with an introduction and a table of contents. These elements are not essential, of course, but when students discover that many biographies of Lincoln contain them, they see no reason theirs should not have them, too.

Completing the Biographies.   Word processing programs greatly simplify the final production of the completed biographies. Usually the writing group goes over the rough draft very carefully. Spelling checkers and grammar programs also get a workout, but the finished product invariably looks good. Some tasks still remain however, such as (1) making covers, and then (2) printing extra copies for parents, grandparents, other family members, and (3) finally, making and autographing one copy that will go into the school library. An original cooperative biography written by Ms. Lindquist's students appears on pages 114–131 in her book, *Ways That Work* (Heinemann, 1997).

TECHNOLOGY

Adding the finishing touches

Ms. Lindquist's "To Do" list and her time allotments for the cooperative biography project include the following (1997):

1. Content packing (5 periods). Ms. Lindquist reads aloud from various works on Lincoln while students take notes.
2. Content stacking (5 periods). Students read and research independently.
3. Brainstorming key events in Lincoln's life (1 period). A whole-class activity.
4. Categorizing the events identified during brainstorming (1 period). A whole-class activity.
5. Independent writing (3–5 periods). An individual activity.

Time allotments

6. Creating jigsaw groups for sharing by chapter (1–3 periods). Small-group work.
7. Rewriting and refining (1–2 periods). An individual or small-group activity.
8. Book groups meet together and share (1–2 periods). A small-group activity.
9. Revising and refining (1–3 periods). A small-group activity.
10. Creating and adding dedications, the introduction, the table of contents, the bibliography, a cover, and other related elements (3–4 periods). A small-group activity.
11. Publishing and distributing (1–2 periods). A small-group activity.
12. Reading, evaluating, and sharing (1–2 periods). An individual and whole-class activity.
(13.) Phew!

Analysis.   Consider for a moment the variety of activities that Tarry Lindquist's students engaged in as they produced their cooperative biographies.

Activities associated with cooperative biographies

- Based on their independent research (along with some help from Ms. Lindquist), they worked actively and cooperatively with their groups to produce an original (authentic) document they would share with others.

- They engaged in realistic *decision-making* activities, such as making choices about what their chapters would focus on, and what materials they would include or need to cut.

- They engaged in *critical thinking* activities, such as comparing how other authors organized their biographies.

- They worked on a single topic—Abraham Lincoln—for five weeks. Clearly this was an *in-depth* effort, not a superficial survey.

Certain terms in the preceding list are highlighted because they appear frequently in at least two places: (1) the National Council for Social Studies (NCSS) publication *Expectations of Excellence: Curriculum Standards for Social Studies* (1994), which is often referred to as the NCSS standards document, and (2) throughout this book. This is not sheer coincidence!

• • • •
Relationship of Cooperative Biographies to the NCSS Standards
• • • •

The NCSS standards are one of several sets of standards that apply to social studies. Additional standards have been established by professional organizations associated with social studies—including the history standards, the geography standards, and so forth. This section examines how Ms. Lindquist's cooperative biography activity meshes with the NCSS standards.

STANDARDS ✔   The introduction to the NCSS standards publication (*Expectations of Excellence*) identifies four skills that students should gain from an effective social studies program. The following material maintains the language of the NCSS standards but their form has been modified to create a checklist for assessing the cooperative biography project. On the following form, check the appropriate space ("Yes," "No," or "Possibly") to reflect the extent to which you think that the cooperative biography activity addresses each element.

Does the cooperative biography project reflect the following learning skills?

Yes	No	Possibly	Did the cooperative biography project enable students to
Learning skills ___	___	___	1. acquire information and manipulate data?
___	___	___	2. develop and present policies, arguments, and stories?
___	___	___	3. construct new knowledge?
___	___	___	4. participate in groups?

The cooperative biography activity clearly involved students in the acquisition and manipulation of information as well as in participation in group activities. Thus the answers to numbers 1 and 4 are yes. In addition, because the finished biographies reflect information that had never existed in that form previously, it

"New knowledge"—for whom?   probably qualifies for another yes for number 3, "constructing new knowledge." It's true that the knowledge students created was not new to the world—as it might be for scientists who unlock the secrets of DNA, for example. Yet very few professionals, to say nothing of eleven-year-olds, will ever have that opportunity. Thus, it seems appropriate to interpret this item in its narrower sense, that the knowledge Ms. Lindquist's students gained about Abraham Lincoln was new to them.

One criterion that could be a little "iffy" relates to number 2, "developing and presenting policies, arguments, and stories." Because this expectation indicates three formats that students should be able to deal with, it is necessarily more global than the others. However, the standard does not say that all three elements must be dealt with simultaneously. Over a school year or possibly even a school career, it's reasonable to expect teachers to provide activities in which students "develop and present policies, arguments, and stories," but not necessarily in a single activity. In summary, the cooperative biography project incorporates the four NCSS skill criteria, although with some limitations for number 2.

In addition to the skill areas just noted, the NCSS standards also identify characteristics that "powerful" social studies activities should reflect. Decide whether the cooperative biography activity reflects these characteristics.

Does the cooperative biography activity reflect the following characteristics of powerful social studies lessons and activities?

Characteristics of powerful social studies activities

Yes	No	Possibly	
___	___	___	meaningful
___	___	___	integrative (involving multiple disciplines or subject areas)
___	___	___	value-based (where students must make judgments about what is or is not important, useful, etc.)
___	___	___	challenging
___	___	___	active (*Note:* This characteristic relates to students' hands and minds, to their interest and involvement, not simply a manipulative activity.)

Analysis

The cooperative biography project rates as high or even higher on these "powerful" characteristics than it did on the previous criteria. The activity clearly had meaning for students, even if not at first. It was also integrative in that students had to apply skills from other subject areas, primarily writing and composing. There was also a value base as, for example, when students had to decide what should or should not be included in their chapters. Likewise, producing a historically accurate biography was certainly challenging for fifth graders, as it would be for many adults. Finally, the activity involved students actively as opposed to passively. For example, students were not simply listening to Ms. Lindquist as she provided background information on Lincoln, but were also involved in taking notes and determining what information they would or would not use in their chapter.

● ● ● ●
The Question of Time
● ● ● ●

Justifying such a lengthy activity

Regardless of how well the cooperative biography project meets the NCSS standards, there is still the question of how a teacher can justify spending five weeks on this kind of activity. Consider first that no teacher can hope to cover the entire range of American history, or world history, or whatever, especially if he or she commits five weeks to an activity like this. Consider second that no teacher can cover the entire range of American history, or world history, or whatever, even if he or she does *not* commit five weeks to a cooperative biography project. In almost any traditional social studies program, there is simply more history, more geography, more economics, and so on, than it is possible to teach effectively in any given year. There are occasional exceptions, however. In California, for example, the sixth-grade curriculum does not cover all of world history, as is common in most social studies programs. Rather, the California curriculum for

● ● ● ● ● **COMMENTARY** **But Is This Social Studies?**

Is the Abraham Lincoln cooperative biography activity a social studies project that draws heavily on language arts? Or is it a language arts activity that draws on social studies content? Or does its subject classification really matter?

Most students are not much beyond kindergarten before they learn there are apparently clear demarcations between subject areas. It begins with "OK, children, put away your science books, it's time for social studies," and continues on from there. Perhaps most people don't realize (or necessarily care) that when scholars created separate disciplines of knowledge, they did so for convenience, clarity, and perhaps even a little self-interest. In other words, to be considered an expert (or scholar) in something, it was necessary to have a defined area of knowledge—a discipline—in which to demonstrate one's expertise. It's the phenomenon that practitioners in medicine have made into an art form.

Dividing the immense body of knowledge into smaller chunks, called disciplines, makes it more manageable and, in some instances, easier to understand. But in everyday life, most of the problems we deal with—like deciding what to have for lunch—resist easy classification. For example, suggesting that the decision about what to have for lunch is a sociobiological question seems to border on the absurd.

The point is that in the compartmentalized world we live in today, classification dilemmas sometimes arise. So whether the cooperative biography project is a social studies or a language arts activity is the kind of question that some people ponder. Actually, it's an activity that integrates both language arts and social studies. Pursuing the classification matter further—as in "Well, it's mainly a language arts activity"—is probably not very fruitful. The more significant questions concern whether the teaching activities are authentic and useful to children.

Grade 6 focuses on ancient civilizations through A.D. 500; the Grade 7 program begins at A.D. 500 and carries through to the Middle Ages.

The California program reflects one state's effort to reduce to more manageable proportions the tremendous time periods that most teachers are expected to cover—a topic examined in more detail in Chapter 3. At the same time, consider that over the past century the 180-day school year has remained largely unchanged. However, over the same period we have acquired another one hundred years of history. As one wit put it, "history just keeps rollin' along." The result: teachers must face the prospect of squeezing an ever-growing body of historical knowledge into a relatively fixed time period.

The coverage problem   Dealing with the expectation that they will somehow "cover" social studies is something all teachers must face. And, yes, it's possible to achieve coverage. But there is a price to be paid in trying to do so. It is not surprising to hear students say things like "Oh, yeah, I've heard of the Redcoats . . . they were British, I think. . . . Or were they French? We didn't have much time to talk about them." Zemelman, Daniels, and Hyde (1998) suggest that trying to achieve coverage in social studies typically yields superficiality and is like "painting a room—covering plenty of square feet but only one-thousandth of an inch thick" (p. 139).

As you might expect from a teacher who devotes five weeks to the cooperative biography project, Tarry Lindquist rejects the expectation that she try to "cover" everything. As Ms. Lindquist (2002) says, "Social studies is an enormous discipline. . . . It is not possible to teach everything that has ever happened, so it becomes of paramount importance for us to identify themes and concepts that allow the students to at least begin to understand how to learn about the world" (p. 4).

"Less is more"   Ms. Lindquist ranks among the growing number of teachers who have adopted the "less is more" concept noted in the prologue. In practice, this idea means going into detail on selected topics so that students can build in-depth understandings—a practice also called *postholing*, or as Zemelman, Daniels, and Hyde (1998) suggest, "post-holing." Whichever way you spell it, postholing reflects the notion that if you elect to dig one hundred postholes, each one inch deep, your fence is likely to fall over. But if you dig just ten postholes, each ten inches deep, your fence could remain standing for a long time. The basic question that you and every other social studies teacher must consider concerns whether you will settle for an essentially useless fence that is really long but so shallow that it falls over, or one that is planted deep enough to remain standing for years—but may be just a little short. In other words, it's a tradeoff.

Options   One dynamic of teaching social studies involves deciding how you will deal with the problem of coverage and the superficiality that too often goes with it. This is not entirely an either-or matter because there are some intermediate positions. For example, you could try for a balance between the two positions by spending parts of the year knowing that you are simply "covering" the subject, and the balance of the year going into greater depth. Whatever you elect to do, know that there is not one "approved" way of proceeding.

The next section examines how social studies has evolved as a subject area, and the characteristics that have led to the continuing debates about how it should be organized and taught.

● ● ● ● Social Studies: Its Nature and Origins

· · · · A Social Studies Parable

In the beginning there was history. People had to be around before there could be history, of course, and the stories of the past that those individuals created were much more personal than the formalized record most of us know today. Nevertheless, history began soon after our ancestors became aware of their past.

How social studies evolved   History was followed almost immediately by geography. It wasn't called "geography" until much later, and it was really rudimentary, focusing on things like locating the good hunting and fishing areas, and avoiding places where the water sources dried up in hot weather. Yet knowing the geography of the area—what resources were available and where they were in the immediate environment—was often essential to survival.

The history and geography that our ancestors dealt with were basic and important. Their history helped them identify who they were, individually and collectively, and where they had come from. Their geography helped them survive what otherwise had to have been a harrowing existence. Yet an equally important aspect of our ancestors' lives dealt with determining how they would conduct relationships between and among themselves. They had to decide things like whether it was OK to take another family's food or belongings against their wishes, simply because someone felt the urge to do so. Safe and orderly societies cannot exist when everyone is free to "do his or her own thing," so they also had to decide what would happen to those who violated the "rules." Without clear moral and ethical standards, daily life would be chaotic, and the survival of individuals and the society itself would be questionable. In almost every respect, creating a moral code to live by was as important to our ancestors' survival as was their knowledge of history and geography—sometimes more so.

Creating a code of moral conduct

Our ancestors obviously learned to cope with their physical and social environments, or we wouldn't be here today. Likewise, when some of our ancestors grew skilled enough that they no longer needed to spend every waking minute worrying about their survival, they were able to formalize their history, expand their geographical horizons, and codify their moral and ethical principles as laws. And so it went through various civilizations—the ancient Egyptians, the Greeks, the Romans, and so forth. Adults in these societies passed on their histories, their geographies, and their codes of ethics to their children so that they too would become aware of their heritage and their responsibilities to others—a challenge that remains to this day.

The emergence of the social sciences

Once they had satisfied their survival needs, some of our ancestors began to examine specialized aspects of human behavior. For example, some individuals began to explore why corn and wheat were more costly when rainfall was scarce, and cheaper when rainfall was plentiful. Investigations such as these marked the beginning of what eventually became the discipline of economics. Other specialized studies followed. Some people began to study cultures, both past and present, thus providing the beginnings of anthropology. Others began to explore how societies govern themselves, which provided the basis for political science (or government). Still others investigated how groups of people interact, which ultimately led to the discipline of sociology. Even more recently, individuals began to examine everyday human behaviors, such as how we learn and how we develop our beliefs and attitudes, which are part of the discipline of psychology.

From these beginnings, the school subject called social studies was created. History is a major component of social studies, as are the social science disciplines of geography, economics, political science, anthropology, sociology, and psychology. Morals and ethics, which we include as part of philosophy, also play a role in social studies, as do elements from the humanities and the fine arts. These components and others are reflected in the National Council for the Social Studies's (NCSS, 1994) definition of social studies. It states:

Social studies defined

> Social studies is the *integrated study* of the social sciences and humanities to promote civic competence. Within the social program, social studies provides coordinated, systematic study drawing upon such disciplines as anthropology, archaeology, economics, geography, history, philosophy, political science, psychology, religion, and sociology, as well as appropriate content from the humanities, mathematics, and natural sciences. [Emphasis added]

The common focus of social studies is human behavior. In one form or another, the components of social studies deal with how we humans interact with each other, both past and present, how we interact with our environment, and on the myriad ways in which we organize, govern, and trade among ourselves. That focus on human (social) behavior led John Dewey (1938) to suggest the shortest definition for social studies that we know of. He said: "Social studies is the study of things social."

• • • •

The Continuing Debates

• • •

You may have asked yourself why the subject was called "social studies" when you were in elementary and middle school, but after you got to high school and college, you almost never heard the term. Secondary schools and colleges almost always teach discipline-based courses. In the sciences, for example, you studied subjects like botany, biology, physics, and so forth, and in the social sciences you studied history, geography, political science, and so on. Each course focused on a recognized discipline in its respective field. In all likelihood, your high school and college courses were taught by individuals who identified themselves with discipline-based titles such as historian, botanist, and geographer. Be advised that there are any number of people who go the next step and say that how high schools and colleges organize their courses is the way they should be organized in elementary and middle schools. And this contention has remained at the crux of an ongoing debate almost since social studies was created in the early years of the twentieth century.

Multidiscipline vs. single-discipline subjects

It is easy to skim over the term "integrated study" in NCSS's definition for social studies without recognizing that some people object—sometimes strongly—to that idea. Their concerns often reflect the following: "What do you mean you select things from several disciplines and then unify them in something called 'social studies'? By doing that you're destroying the purity of these time-honored disciplines." Enter then a social studies advocate who is likely to argue that "teaching the so-called pure academic disciplines to young children is a form of academic arrogance, because all the disciplines focus on the same thing—different aspects of social behavior. By teaching these elements in unified courses we can help children focus on the world they really live in, and everybody knows the world is not neatly divided into the history section, the geography section, the political science section, and so on. Besides, we need to help children understand interrelationships among the various disciplines that they would not see if they were taught separately."

Studying the disciplines separately or as a unified subject

Multidisciplinary studies

In many parts of the world, there is no debate about whether schools should teach the social science disciplines separately or as unified social studies. This is because the notion of unified or *multidisciplinary* social studies is limited to three nations primarily: the United States, Canada, and Australia. People almost everywhere study history, geography, and the other social sciences, but in most parts of the world these are taught as separate subjects. This is why students in England, for example, usually study English history and English geography separately.

The practice of intermingling separate disciplines into a single course of study, which is usually referred to as a unified or *multidisciplinary studies* approach to curriculum, is common in American (and Canadian and Australian) elementary- and middle-school programs. Most language arts, science, and social studies programs

Social studies is a multidisciplinary school subject based primarily on history and the social science disciplines.

are organized on this basis. A typical elementary science program, for example, will have separate chapters on plants (botany), animals (zoology), the earth's crust (geology), insects (entomology), and weather (meteorology), each of which reflects a separate discipline in its own right. Language arts and social studies also follow a similar pattern, although the specific disciplines are different.

Other multidisciplinary subjects

Contemporary Implications

In the course of the debates between the unified studies and separate-discipline advocates, some individuals who favor teaching the disciplines separately referred to social studies as a kind of "social stew," a subject closely akin to the "mystery meats" sometimes served in school cafeterias. Individuals who favored the unified approach to social studies would sometimes accuse the separate-discipline advocates of trying to turn young children into miniature historians and geographers, which wasn't necessarily helpful for teaching children to live in modern society. As the debates continued in academic circles, most teachers found they could close their classroom doors with relative assurance that the debates would have little impact on their daily activities. But then, in the 1990s, came the standards.

STANDARDS ✔

Nominations for the organizations that would create the national standards for the subjects taught in American schools came largely from the Department of Education and were submitted to the U.S. Congress for its approval. During this period, some key individuals in the Department of Education happened to be strong advocates for teaching the disciplines separately. When Congress approved the nominations in 1993, there were to be standards for science, mathematics, history, geography, economics, and so forth, but standards for unified social studies programs were nowhere to be found. The NCSS was understandably appalled. How could Congress fail to recognize social studies?

How the standards evolved

While the nominees began developing their proposed standards, the NCSS began a belated effort to (1) create standards for teaching social studies, and (2) have Congress recognize social studies as a subject area unto itself. That undertaking was undoubtedly assisted by a fortuitous turn of events (depending on your perspective, of course). When the draft version of the proposed history standards were submitted for approval, even some separate discipline supporters objected to them. Apparently the proposed standards devoted (1) too much attention to African-Americans, Native Americans, and other minorities and (2) far too much attention to failures and atrocities committed over the course of U.S. history (Zemelman, Daniels, & Hyde, 1998). For example, most history texts traditionally treat the topic of the westward expansion of the United States under subtitles such as "How the West Was Won." The idea of changing to a perspective more sympathetic to Native Americans—"How the West Was Lost" (or Stolen)—apparently irritated quite a few people, including some members of Congress and some individuals in the Department of Education. Questions

Problems!

involving "Who is right here?" or "Who should be offended?" became moot when the U.S. Senate voted 99 to 1 to reject the draft version of the proposed history standards.

Congress ultimately approved both the NCSS standards for social studies and the separate standards for the social science disciplines—history (revised), geography, economics, and so forth. As a result, social studies teachers have an array of standards to inform their teaching.

Because all the standards focus on different aspects of social behavior, it is reasonable to ask whether there is much duplication. The general answer is no. For the most part, the historians, geographers, economists, and so on were very discipline specific. For example, the history standards identify five standards for Historical Thinking (which are included in the Resource Handbook at the end of this book), but these are quite different from the five themes of Geography, (which are included in Chapter 2). So instead of duplication, there is often great specificity—lists of hundreds of facts and topics deemed essential for student competence in the discipline. The NCSS materials and the standards from the separate disciplines resulted in an impressive stack of documents approaching the size of an unabridged dictionary.

A wealth of standards

Social studies is the only subject taught in elementary and middle schools that has such a wealth of standards. In addition to the NCSS standards for social studies and the standards for history and the social science disciplines developed by other organizations, there are also standards (sometimes called "outcomes") that were developed by the states and are often referenced to state-mandated tests. With so many standards to choose from, the pertinent question becomes: Where does a teacher begin?

STANDARDS ✔

The NCSS recommends that teachers use the social studies standards, which are organized around ten broad themes, to address overall curriculum design and comprehensive student performance expectations. Teachers can then use standards for the individual disciplines (for civics and government, economics, geography, and history) to provide focused content for grade-level strands and specific courses. Sometimes a discipline such as history will take the lead, while other disciplines, such as geography and economics will play supporting roles. At other times, separate disciplines such as history, geography, and economics will be equally involved, thus reflecting the multidisciplinary nature of social studies.

The NCSS Themes

The ten themes from the NCSS standards (as detailed in the Resource Handbook) are as follows:

1. Culture
2. Time, Continuity, and Change
3. People, Places, and Environment
4. Individual Development and Identity

   5. Individuals, Groups, and Institutions
   6. Power, Authority, and Governance
   7. Production, Distribution, and Consumption
   8. Science, Technology, and Society
   9. Global Connections
   10. Civic Ideals and Practices

STANDARDS 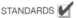 The complete NCSS standards are available on-line at the Internet address listed in both the following Technology Update and in the "Suggested Readings and Resources" section at the end of the chapter.

Performance Expectations

What children are expected to do

Performance expectations for each of the NCSS themes are presented in three clusters: (1) for the early grades, (2) for the middle grades, and (3) for high

---

T E C H N O L O G Y   U P D A T E

Standards for Social Studies, History, and Social Sciences

This is the first Technology Update, each of which is keyed to the content of the chapters in this book. Most Updates require access to the Internet and will direct you to additional resources and materials related to teaching elementary- and middle-school social studies. In this instance, we provide more detailed sources for standards that apply to teaching social studies.

Note that Internet addresses sometimes change or cease operation. In the event that a listed address fails to work correctly, you can use a standard search engine to locate a new address.

The three best sources for standards-related materials are:

1. The Home Page maintained by The National Council for Social Studies (NCSS), at:
   http://www.ncss.org

   This site has the complete NCSS standards on-line along with many other social studies–related sites and materials.

2. Resources for Social Studies Teachers at:
   http://www.csun.edu/~hcedu013/

This site, maintained by Dr. Marty Levin, at California State University, Northridge, includes standards among a wealth of other social studies–related materials.

3. Putwest BOCES at:
   http://putwest.boces.org/StSu/Library.html

   In addition to the various national standards, this site also links to states that have adopted standards or standards-related materials.

Most of these sites have links that enable you to reach the other sites without having to enter the full address. They also provide links to standards-related materials from other organizations including:

The American Historical Association at:
   http://web.gmu.edu/chnm/aha

The Center for Civic Education at:
   http://www.informall.org:80/showcase/civnet/partners/center/center.html

The National Center for History in the School at:
   http://www.sscnet.ucla.edu/nchs

school. The following example for the early grades reflects the performance expectations for the theme Culture.

Social studies programs should include experiences that provide for the study of culture and cultural diversity, so that the learner can

a. explore and describe similarities and differences in the ways groups, societies, and cultures address similar human needs and concerns.

b. give examples of how experiences may be interpreted differently by people from diverse cultural perspectives and frames of reference.

c. describe ways in which language, stories, folktales, music, and artistic creations serve as expressions of culture and influence the behavior of people living in a particular culture.

d. compare ways in which people from different cultures think about and deal with their physical environment and social conditions.

e. give examples and describe the importance of cultural unity and diversity within and across groups.

Classroom Examples

Most standards documents include examples of classroom activities illustrating how learning experiences can be designed to help students meet performance expectations. For example, an exemplary classroom activity for the NCSS theme of culture describes the experiences of Carlene Jackson, a teacher who uses a new program to develop geographic understanding among students in her first-grade class. Upon examining her class list (before the first day of school), Ms. Jackson determines that she might have students of Mexican, Vietnamese, and Korean ancestry, as well as of African-American and European-American backgrounds. Jackson and her students decide to study how families meet their basic needs of food, clothing, and shelter in five places: their own community; Juarez, Mexico; Hanoi, Vietnam; Lagos, Nigeria; and Frankfurt, Germany. The students read books and stories, look at photos and slides, watch videos, and talk to speakers from their cities. Students sharpen their reading, writing, and speaking skills and learn new geography skills such as map reading. For each city, they read and discuss something about its location, climate, region, and people. This activity addresses performance expectations a, b, and d.[1]

An example, continued

The following Model Student Activity is the first of many model activities in this book. In this instance the activity shows how historically accurate materials can serve as the basis for realistic decision making. Note also that all the model activities in this book are presented as models, that is, as exemplary lesson formats that can be adapted for other topics or content areas.

[1]Abridged from the Executive Summary, *Expect Excellence: Curriculum Standards for Social Studies.* Copyright 1994 by the National Council for the Social Studies. Reprinted by permission.

MODEL STUDENT ACTIVITY

Who Is Qualified for the Presidency?

Overview

In this activity you are asked to identify which one of seven potential candidates is the best qualified and which is the least qualified to be president of the United States. The biographical data on the candidates are presented on separate cards—a procedure usually referred to as a Q-sort. All the candidates are (or were) real people who meet (or met) the three constitutional qualifications for the presidency; that is, they (1) are natural-born citizens, (2) are at least thirty-five years old, and (3) have resided in the United States for at least fourteen years prior to a presidential election. To ensure that the candidates are judged on their qualifications—and not your prior knowledge of them—their names and gender have been omitted. The candidates' identities appear in the Resource Handbook.

Recommended Procedure

Phases One and Two of this activity should be done in small groups. The discussion questions in Phase Three can also be considered in small groups and then summarized in a large-group discussion.

Phase One—Additional Qualifications

Before considering the candidates, identify any additional qualifications (beyond those identified in the Constitution) that you think a president of the United States should possess. For example, should a president be a college graduate? Should he or she have had prior political experience?

Phase Two—Selection

Use the data cards to select the two individuals, one of whom you feel would be (1) best qualified and the other (2) least qualified to be president of the United States.

[Note: "Age as of this date" on the data cards refers to the point in each candidate's career at which he or she had accomplished all the activities listed on the card. For the candidates who actually served as president, the date used was just prior to their election to office.]

CARD 1

College Attended: None

Religion: Protestant

Career (Major Occupations): Investor, Druggist, Bookseller, Brigadier General in U.S. Army

Married: 1st spouse: 5 years until spouse's death, 2nd spouse: 1 year   **Children:** 3 by first marriage

Age as of This Date: 38

CARD 2

Colleges Attended: Harvard University, Columbia University

Religion: Protestant

Career (Major Occupations): Farmer, Lawyer, State senator, Assistant Secretary of Navy, Governor, Vice-Presidential candidate

Married: 27 years   **Children:** 6

Age as of This Date: 50

CARD 3

Colleges Attended: Morehouse College, A.B. and L.H.D.; Crozer Theological Seminary, B.D.; University of Pennsylvania; Boston University, Ph.D., D.D.; Harvard University, L.L.D.; Central State College; Morgan State College

Religion: Protestant

Career (Major Occupations): Protestant minister, Teacher of Philosophy at Harvard, President of a civil rights organization, 1 of 10 outstanding men for the year according to *Time* magazine, Nobel Prize winner, Noted public speaker

Married: 15 years   **Children:** 4

Age as of This Date: 37

CARD 4

College Attended: Columbia University

Religion: No specific denomination

Career (Major Occupations): Writer, Served as Lieutenant Colonel in Army, Lawyer, Member of a congress, Member to a constitutional convention, Secretary of the Treasury

Married: 24 years   **Children:** 8

Age as of This Date: 47

CARD 5

College Attended: Wellesley, A.B.; Yale Law School, J.D.

Religion: Protestant

Career (Major Occupations): Adviser to the Children's Defense Fund; Member of the Legal Staff, Judiciary Committee, House of Representatives; Lawyer; Law School Faculty member; Member of the Board of Directors for various organizations (e.g., a children's hospital, the Children's Defense Fund, etc.); Author of a weekly newspaper column and two books; United States senator.

Married: 27 years   **Children:** 1

Age as of This Date: 55

CARD 6

College Attended: Texas A&M, B.A., M.A.; Harvard, M.A. (in Public Administration); George Washington University, PH.D. (in Public Administration).

Religion: Roman Catholic

Career (Major Occupations): Assistant to the City Manager; City Councilperson; Elected to four terms as mayor of one of the ten largest cities in the U.S.; President of the National League of Cities; Chairman of an asset management company, Host of a one-hour television show; Board member, Federal Reserve Bank of Dallas and the Rockefeller Foundation

Married: 32 years   **Children:** 3

Age as of This Date: 52

CARD 7

College Attended: None

Religion: No specific denomination

Career (Major Occupations): Postmaster, Lawyer, U.S. Representative, Store owner, State congressman, Served as Captain in U.S. Army, Noted public speaker

Married: 19 years   **Children:** 4

Age as of This Date: 51

Phase Three—Summary

Questions:

1. To what extent did your choices reflect the qualifications you listed in Phase One? Would you modify your list in any way?

2. Determine whether any of the following factors should be considered in selecting a presidential candidate.

2.1. Age	2.7. Previous occupation
2.2. Religion	2.8. Personal appearance
2.3. Gender	2.9. Personality
2.4. Educational background	2.10. Ethnic background
2.5. Number of children	2.11. Marital status
2.6. Character	2.12. Physical health

3. Should any other factors be considered?

4. How did your group decide what qualifications were most important? Least important?

Optional Extending Activities

1. Examine the candidate's identities as shown in the Resource Handbook. Would you change your selection? Why or why not? Does the new information influence your conclusions about the necessary qualifications?

2. Do your qualifications reflect the beliefs of most individuals in your community? in your class? Identify a plan for determining how you could find out.

Source: Adapted and updated from Marsha Hobin, "Clarifying What Is Important," in Allan O. Kownslar, Ed., *Teaching American History: The Quest for Relevancy.* Copyright 1974 by National Council for the Social Studies. Reprinted by permission of Allan O. Kownslar and NCSS.

● ● ● ● COMMENTARY **On Using Model Activities with Children**

A key question for "Who Is Qualified for the Presidency?" or any instructional activity is: "What should students learn from having done it?" It's doubtful, for example, that students will remember much about the constitutional qualifications for the presidency, primarily because that information is almost incidental to the activity. On the other hand, students are likely to remember some of the biographical information about the candidates because the format of the activity requires them to work with that information. However, expecting students to commit the biographical information to memory, such as which college Alexander Hamilton attended, seems very questionable at best. The biographical information serves a legitimate and necessary purpose in the activity, but in the sweep of human events it is on the same level as the name of Robert E. Lee's horse (Traveler): historical trivia.

The biographical information in the "Presidency" activity serves as a vehicle to help students consider factors that influence the election of a president. In that context, an appropriate learner objective for the *content focus* of this activity would be: "Upon completion of this activity, learners will identify at least seven factors that could influence voters in their decisions about a candidate's qualifications for the presidency."

In the activity, students are also asked to identify the best- and least-qualified presidential candidate, and then reach group consensus about their choices. The students' involvement in a group decision-making process, as well as their responses to questions like "What process did the group use in reaching its decision?" and "Did some factors weigh more heavily in that decision than others?" are just as instructionally significant as whichever candidates the group selects. The point is that the group's decision-making process reflects a *process/skills* focus for this activity that deserves as much attention as their final decisions. A sample learner objective for the process/skills emphasis of the activity would be: "Given the constitutional qualifications for president, students will (a) identify additional qualifications (for the presidency) that they feel are appropriate, (b) determine if these qualifications are acceptable to a group of peers, and (c) defend or modify the selection of potential candidates to reach group consensus." In other words, the "Presidency" activity could serve as a vehicle for (1) identifying and learning about factors that may influence the selection and election of a presidential candidate, which is its content focus, and for (2) analyzing and learning about a group decision-making process, which is its process focus.

● ● ● ● ● The Continuing Debates: Constructivist Learning

Consider an instance where two fourth-grade teachers are considering using the "Who is Qualified for the Presidency?" activity with their students. Teacher A is concerned that his students lack the background knowledge to understand some of the candidates' qualifications, so he thinks about spending two days going over items that might pose problems. These include the differences between Republicans and Democrats, and between Catholics and Protestants. Teacher B, on the other hand, feels that being able to describe the differences between Republicans and Democrats—which some adults have difficulty doing—or a Catholic and a Protestant, is not critical to the overall thrust of the activity. In addition, Teacher B believes that trying to conduct discussions about any of these topics prior to students having seen the candidates' qualifications would be a clear case of decontextualized teaching, that is, instruction apparently unrelated to students' concerns. It would be one thing if students were already concerned with how Republicans and Democrats (or Catholics and Protestants) differ, because that would provide a context for having such a discussion. In this setting, however, and if Teacher A's students were to ask him why they are dealing with this topic, he might resort to "You are going to need to know this" or perhaps its corollary, "It's going to be on the test."

Decontextualized teaching

Consider that giving a drawn-out (two-day) introduction to "Who Is Qualified for the Presidency?" could severely limit what is otherwise an interesting and effective activity. The preliminary discussions could actually take longer than the entire activity. On the other hand, many fourth graders are unable to distinguish between Republicans and Democrats, or Catholics and Protestants. The key question here is: is this an appropriate time to deal with those distinctions? I think not.

When children come to school, their minds are not blank slates. All of them have a wealth of experiences with their world, and all of them have acted on those experiences in various ways, some of which are undoubtedly unique to them. Some children's ideas may be consistent with what most adults believe, which is what educational psychologist Jerome Bruner (1996) refers to as our "cultural toolkit." Other ideas will be unique.

A wealth of prior experiences

All of us develop "toolkits" of common understandings, beliefs, and ideas—sometimes referred to as "common knowledge"—that enable us to function in society. This means that in normal discourse you could use the expressions "Christmas" or "Thanksgiving," for example, without having to go into long explanations of what Christmas and Thanksgiving are. It also means that you can use expressions like "She was madder than a wet hen" or "It came out of the blue" without having to tell the listener that you are using an adage.

Building cultural toolkits

Constructing a cultural toolkit is a lifelong task. Children who are still constructing theirs may act on their experiences in ways that are inventive. The children's ideas may make perfect sense to them, even if those ideas are naive or inaccurate by adult standards. For example, consider what can happen when you ask first graders to complete the second half of some common adages:

"Never underestimate the power of . . . . . . termites."
"An idle mind is . . . . the best way to relax."

"Where there's smoke there's . . . . pollution."
"If at first you don't succeed . . . . get new batteries."

All of the children's responses are plausible. They did not go out into left field somewhere to find an answer. Yet their completed adages are clearly nonstandard. Whether the responses should be considered "wrong" is another matter entirely. The basic point here is that children, indeed all of us, are sense-making creatures. We look at events occurring around us and try to make sense of them based on our prior knowledge and experiences, both of which can differ considerably from one person to the next. The essence of *constructivism* lies in the belief that we, children or adults, make sense of new experiences by examining and interpreting them in light of our previous experiences. In some instances it may be necessary to create new ideas that help us make sense of ideas and experiences that don't otherwise fit our existing mental schemes.

Building new ideas based on prior experiences

Perhaps the reason so many children dislike textbook-based social studies is because there is seldom anything to explain. There's lots of stuff to remember—gobs of it to be sure—but in a textbook it's all laid out for you. The children's major task is not to construct ideas but to act as a kind of blank slate that will enable them to remember all that information in roughly the same form as it exists in the text.

There are multiple ways to learn things, of course. Some of those ways are more effective and some less effective than others. For example, you may remember using flash cards to learn your multiplication tables (e.g., $9 \times 6 = 54$).

Behaviorist teaching

In behaviorist learning theory, the flash card (9×6) was the stimulus, and your answer, hopefully 54, was the desired response. The so-called new math was designed to help children understand why $9 \times 6 = 54$ (and $8 \times 6 = 48$, etc.), but many children today still resort to memorization (or rote learning) to deal with multiplication facts. It is still an effective system for certain kinds of material. You may have also used rote learning to memorize the Preamble to the Constitution or the presidents of the United States, in order. However, unless you were called on to demonstrate that proficiency from time to time, you've probably forgotten that information (along with your lines in the fifth- or sixth-grade class play).

Many teachers still use those beloved or hated—depending on your point of view—worksheets as follow-ups to social studies lessons. In an attempt to use behaviorist theory to justify worksheets, teachers sometimes make statements about needing to reinforce what their students learned in the prior lesson. On

Is it really reinforcement?

one hand, one sometimes wonders if worksheets are not designed to give the teacher some quiet time after a lesson. If so, there are other ways to do this. On the other hand, you know what too often happens with worksheets. They are returned perhaps two days after you turned them in, and they have been marked and graded. First, the idea of grading worksheets that are supposedly intended for reinforcement or practice suggests some confusion as to their purpose. Worksheets with grades on them look very much like tests, but then tests are not intended for reinforcement—at least according to the theory. Second, in behaviorist theory the reinforcement must occur reasonably close to the original stimulus. Doing a worksheet immediately after a lesson would seem to fit the requirements. However, for genuine reinforcement to occur, the child needs immediate feedback. You can avoid some of the common problems with worksheets by doing them as a group activity or permitting students to complete the worksheets in small groups; either technique can provide immediate feedback. **Options** Graded worksheets that are returned two days (or more) after a lesson are unlikely to reinforce anything. You know what students will do; they will look at the grade, possibly skim over the items they missed, and then shove the worksheet into their social studies folder without further thought.

• • • •

Experience Before Analysis

• • • •

In using instructional activities with children, consider providing enough procedural information so the activity can occur smoothly, but save nonessential information and analysis until after the activity is completed. In shorthand form, the rule of thumb is that experience should precede analysis. Actually doing an activity such as "Who Is Qualified for the Presidency?" provides students with a common experience that serves as the basis for subsequent analysis and interpretation. In the postactivity follow-up, consider creating with students a prioritized list of desirable characteristics for presidential candidates. Prioritizing the listing will prove difficult and may lead to the conclusion that different people will prioritize the listing differently. But recognize that creating such a list prior to the students actually doing the Presidency activity would be almost impossible. Remember: experience precedes analysis.

Social Studies and Citizenship Education

Our democracy was still in its infancy when the French observer, Alexis de Tocqueville (1947), wrote, "The Americans are hardly more virtuous than others, but they are infinitely better educated (I speak for the masses) than any other people of my acquaintance." De Tocqueville went on to say that an educated citizenry "the mass of those possessing an understanding of public affairs, a knowledge of laws and precedents, a feeling for the best interest of the nation, and a faculty of understanding them, is greater in America than any other place in the world." De Tocqueville wrote these words almost two centuries ago, when it was unusual for students to attend school through the eighth grade, and even more unusual for students to attend a college or university. It was also a time when democracies were rare and most of the world was ruled by kings and emperors.

Democracy demands an educated citizen When governing power is vested in a single individual, such as an absolute monarch, there is little need to educate the masses; the monarchs make all the decisions and the people simply follow. But when governing power is vested in the people, as in a democracy, and when people participate in determining whether something is or is not for the common good, new expectations arise. The citizens in a democracy have a right—even a duty—to expect their citizen colleagues to be knowledgeable, to deal morally and ethically with others, to challenge and critically question ideas and proposals, to make good and defensible decisions, and to be concerned about the welfare of others and the common good (see Ravitch, 2002). The first point here is that democratic forms of government impose responsibilities on everyday citizens that were virtually unknown when De Tocqueville wrote his immortal words. A second but closely related point is that schools—along with the family and the church—were charged with making students knowledgeable and responsible enough that they could handle the duties of citizenship just described.

The purpose of social studies: citizenship education

The main point here is that schools in general and social studies in particular share the common goal of training the young to be responsible citizens, which, in a more condensed form, is referred to as *citizenship education*. The schools' mission of citizenship education is broad and encompassing, whereas social studies shares a somewhat smaller piece of the action. The relationship between social studies and citizenship is reflected in the NCSS's (1994) definition of social studies, which states that a major purpose of social studies is "to help young people develop the ability to make informed and reasoned choices as citizens of a culturally diverse, democratic society in an interdependent world" (p. 2).

KEY IDEA

The overarching aim of social studies is citizenship education, but how this relates to the selection and use of content in instruction has not been settled.

Almost everything students learn in schools can help to make them more knowledgeable, and, thus, good (or perhaps better) decision makers and citizens. But there is more to citizenship that simply subject-matter knowledge. Citizens in a democracy must also be conversant with the attitudes and predispositions that are essential parts of the literacies of citizenship.

The Literacies of Citizenship

At one time, *literacy* referred almost exclusively to the ability to read, write, speak, and use language effectively. Today it can refer to a variety of aptitudes, including cultural literacy, historical literacy, scientific literacy, mathematical literacy, and so forth. This section focuses on three literacies, multicultural, civic, and community, that seem both essential and unique to citizens who live in a democracy.

Multicultural Literacy.   This form of literacy reflects the unique nature of American society. As MacIntyre (1990) suggested in "How to Be a North American," we who live in a nation of immigrants must be able to deal effectively with two cultures simultaneously: one based on our common "American" heritage, and the other based on the particular ethnicities from which we derive. All of us contribute to the common American culture, and, as MacIntyre points out, if we were to lose the contributions that our ethnicities afford us, we would have nothing to bring and nothing to give. However, MacIntyre also warns that "if each of us dwells too much, or even exclusively, upon his or her own ethnic particularity, then we are in danger of fragmenting or even destroying the common life" (p. 5). More recently, Salinas (1997) warned that if we as a nation are unable to maintain a reasonable balance between our competing loyalties, first to our individual ethnicities, and second to the larger American culture, we will join the ranks of the world's other multiethnic nations—the Bosnias and Serbias of the world—as a battleground of perpetual ethnic discord.

We live in several cultures simultaneously

DIVERSITY

The goal of multicultural literacy is to develop citizens who have the knowledge and ability to understand events and experiences from different perspectives. This "understanding" derives from the ancient Greeks, who, according to Arendt (1961), "sought not to understand one another as individual persons, but to look upon the same world from another's standpoint, to see the same in very different and frequently opposing aspects" (p. 51). In this context, for example, it is as important for white, Anglo students to understand how slavery was viewed from the perspective of an enslaved person, as it is for African-American students to understand how slavery was viewed from the perspective of white persons living in the seventeenth and eighteenth centuries, and much of the nineteenth century. Those two views will obviously be quite different. A second but vitally important element of multicultural literacy—the willingness to suspend judgment—may be even more difficult to achieve. In the context of slavery, for example, it is one thing to say that "1 understand where they (either slaves or slave owners) were coming from." However, it is quite another to accuse contemporary Americans of being "wrong" because they reflect the ethnicity of either slave or slave owner. It is also one thing to judge the rightness or wrongness of activities in their historical perspective, but another to transfer those judgments to modern-day activities.

Willingness to suspend judgment

Multicultural literacy should be the end product of a *multicultural education*. Both concepts share a common goal: enabling students to view concepts and issues from multiple ethnic perspectives, and from the points of view of the cultural, ethnic, and racial groups that were most intimately involved in the event or issue (see Banks, 1997). It is not essential that students understand every possible point of view on every possible issue, nor is it essential that they accept or adopt a divergent view. But everyone needs to understand that any question or issue has at least two sides.

Viewing events from different perspectives

The concept of multicultural education has been around for at least two decades, but it—like most topics in this chapter—is still a matter of continuing debate. For example, some people argue that there is no common American culture, and hence no beliefs that unite us; rather, there is just a common American society in which all of us live. Others argue that the current curriculum is too biased toward the European origins of American culture—or what is sometimes called a "Eurocentric" curriculum.

Bias in the curriculum

There is a Eurocentric bias in the existing curriculum. As just one example, too many Americans are unaware that Sante Fe (New Mexico) was a thriving community before the Pilgrims ever stepped onto Plymouth Rock (and despite the fact that the Spanish who controlled Mexico at the time were of European origin). The unresolved question here is: Should a curriculum that is biased in one direction be replaced by curriculum biased in another direction? Other potentials associated with multicultural education are considered in more detail in Chapter 4, but from this limited treatment it should be clear that most schools do not yet have a multicultural curriculum that effectively addresses the goals of multicultural literacy.

Civic Literacy.   Civic literacy refers to a form of political socialization that ensures that future citizens develop the knowledge, attitudes, and values that are consistent with the society's political system. This is obviously a much smaller body of information than multicultural literacy. Developing civic literacy is something that many schools already do, at least up to a point. It involves understanding the following:

Elements of civil literacy

- The political principles on which our government is founded
- Our political system and how it *really* works
- The functions of government, both real and perceived
- That a democracy places more responsibilities on citizens than do most other forms of government
- That political liberty hinges on the level and quality of civic and civil discourse, which also depends largely on the extent to which citizens participate and are willing to reason together

The students you encounter, including even kindergartners, will have already begun to acquire some of the attitudes and values associated with civic literacy. For example, most young children usually have a highly developed sense of "fair play." At the same time, other attitudes, like "the government is responsible for taking care of everyone," will be simplistic and perhaps even inconsistent with democratic citizenship. It can be difficult to determine where the citizen's responsibilities end and the government's take over, as in matters related to welfare or health care. Developing civic literacy means that citizens are aware of the different points of view on issues, not that they adopt a liberal or conservative stance.

A long-term enterprise

Many younger children will neither care about nor be able to understand some of the elements just listed, especially theoretical or complex explanations of the role and functions of government. Once again, the development of civic literacy extends throughout the entire school (K–12) experience and beyond.

Civic literacy extends beyond the narrower notion of "government" that most of us were exposed to in schools—such as the idea that there are 435 members of the House of Representatives—and focuses on helping children understand and develop the abilities that will be expected of them as citizens. This can mean helping children understand the need for rules and laws, and how the two are different. It also extends to helping children understand those things for which they as individuals are responsible, which includes the respect of self and others, as well as things for which the government is responsible, such as defense from foreign invasion. It also extends to elements for which the individual and the government share mutual responsibility, such as the safety of the neighborhood.

Community Literacy.   In some areas of the country, people are virtual prisoners in their own homes. Some of them keep their window shades down at all times and dare not sit on their porches for fear of being injured in a drive-by shooting or drug-related gun battle. In this kind of environment, it is heartening to read about

The "spirit of community": acting together

neighbors who band together in a spirit of community to rid their neighborhoods of criminal elements. Those neighbors' efforts do not reflect a return to the days of vigilante justice, because they almost always work in cooperation with the police. Important as it is to rid neighborhoods of criminal elements, the key here is to ensure living situations for all people that do not compromise the quality of daily life. All of us depend on each other to provide positive and supportive living environments, and by working together in a spirit of community, citizens in a democracy can influence the moral, social, and physical environments in which they live.

Reciprocal relationships

The community in a democracy (and in community literacy) exists to provide the broadest and most effective environment for people to develop as citizens and as individuals. Our relationship with that community is reciprocal: The social environment affects the kinds of things that we as citizens can do, just as we, as individuals, influence the environment itself. The responsibility for a safe and effective social environment does not rest solely with Congress, which has passed crime bill after crime bill, nor with the city council, the police, or the schools. It is a societal responsibility that rests with all of us, as citizen members of a democratic community.

Most children and many adults are quick to point out their rights as citizens in a democracy. However, if you ask about the reciprocal—their responsibilities as citizens—they tend to have problems. Almost everyone will mention voting, of course, but thereafter the responses are few and far between. To help future citizens understand that citizenship in a democracy entails both rights and responsibilities, more and more schools and teachers—elementary, middle, and high school—are adopting *service learning* (or community service) components in their curricula and courses. In the state of Maryland, for example, all students are required to participate in service learning projects in order to graduate. The projects can and do take an endless variety of forms, usually depending on the age of the students. These include such things as volunteering at a food bank, organizing teams to assist the elderly, removing trash from the school grounds or vacant lots, or making proposals for community improvements to the city council. Ten years ago you almost never heard of service learning; today it is a rapidly growing phenomenon. The point is that citizens in a democratic society, working together in a spirit of community and for the common good, can reflect Abraham Lincoln's famous words—"government of the people, by the people, and for the people." And this, after a somewhat convoluted journey, is the goal of community literacy.

KEY IDEA

The purpose of social studies is to provide children and youth with the knowledge, skills, and dispositions that permit them to participate actively in a democratic society.

These literacies of citizenship—multicultural, civic, and community—suggest multiple goals for social studies education.

Why Teach Social Studies—Revisited

Everything schools do is, in theory at least, geared toward citizenship education. This means that social studies and all the other subject areas contribute to making an individual a responsible citizen—even algebra, literature, and physical education! Unfortunately, this line of reasoning, although accurate, is so global that it seldom provides the specific guidance some people seek. With that in mind, this section addresses more specific goals for teaching social studies. The question here is: What does social studies contribute to citizenship education?

The four basic purposes for teaching social studies are as follows:

Goals for teaching social studies

- Teaching young citizens about our collective cultural heritage—about where we as world cultures have come from, where we are, and where we may be going

- Teaching young citizens to think and process information skillfully and intelligently

- Teaching young citizens about human behavior

- Teaching young citizens to act morally and ethically in accordance with what they know

If you think that "teaching about our cultural heritage" is simply a longer way of saying "learning history," you are partially correct. The problem is that history tends not to include the other social science disciplines—archaeology, anthropology, geography, and so forth—all of which can contribute to understanding how we got to be the way we are. Our cultural heritage extends to the origins of **Transmitting the human story** human civilization, the development of cultures throughout the world, literary and technological achievements, and the different ways we humans have devised for explaining our place in the universe. One of the main purposes for teaching social studies is to transmit that "story"—that knowledge and its associated attitudes and values—to students.

"Teaching children to think skillfully" is a phrase that educators are often fond of, even though it seldom communicates especially well. Nevertheless, if you examine most state-mandated tests, you will find that one aspect they almost **Teaching thinking** always focus on may be referred to by a variety of names, including *critical thinking, reflective thinking, problem solving*, or, simply, *inquiry*. There are subtle differences between these terms, but they are more similar than they are different; all of them involve doing something with information. At the risk of burdening you with even more vocabulary, we think the expression "information-processing skills" is more descriptive of what people actually do when they think and thus have adopted it throughout this book.

Information-processing skills refer to what people do with information—how they mentally manipulate and process various pieces of data. These include skills such as hypothesizing, identifying relevant and irrelevant information, hypothesis testing, and generalizing. Consider, for example, that when the children's tale of *Hansel and Gretel* is told in Africa, the wicked witch's house is made of salt, not candy (as in Europeanized versions.) Upon learning this, you may find yourself saying "something is wrong here." You may also find yourself trying to explain why the two tales are so different. Could it be that in parts of Africa, salt is more highly prized than candy? Or that candy is so foreign to some cultures that the children would be unable to understand why Hansel and Gretel found it so attractive? The underlying phenomenon here reflects the fact that some African cultures value salt more highly than gold (or candy).

"Fit" You may have found yourself comparing one or more pieces of information from the preceding example to determine whether they "fit." That is one aspect of teaching information-processing skills: determining whether the various pieces of information agree and are logically related to one another. Another aspect of processing information includes creating possible explanations or hypotheses that might explain a situation. Helping children to process information—otherwise known as thinking—is one of the purposes for teaching social studies.

The goal of "teaching children about human behavior" may sound like it's shorthand for "teaching psychology," but it is actually broader than that. Each of the social science disciplines focuses on a different aspect of human behavior, but history, and to a lesser extent geography, so dominate most social studies pro-

Studying findings and processes

grams that some students never study anthropology, sociology, or the other lesser known social sciences. And even when students take courses in these disciplines, their emphasis sometimes focuses on findings in the field—such as when certain products are scarce, the price tends to increase—as opposed to the techniques the disciplines use to identify patterns in human behavior. The concern here is that too often courses in the social science disciplines focus almost exclusively on the findings of previous social scientists, and with relatively little emphasis on the processes they used to discover the tendencies in human behavior.

The last goal, "teaching young citizens to act morally and ethically in accordance with what they know," was an oft-cited purpose of schools (and social studies) at the turn of the last century. At the time, it was called character education, a

The return of character education

movement that fell out of favor in the middle of the twentieth century, for reasons detailed in Chapter 6. Since the mid-1990s, however, schools at all socioeconomic levels were increasingly besieged by irresponsible and sometimes immoral behaviors. Long-cherished values such as honesty, responsibility, and treating others with mutual respect were being replaced by new codes of conduct. These included behaviors such as lying whenever it serves your purpose (especially if you don't get caught), and treating other individuals any way you want to. The corollary here is that if someone doesn't like how they are being treated, as in "He's lookin' at me," a fight could result. Even more extreme situations have been widely reported in the press and occur when students bring weapons to school and open fire on their fellow students or teachers. Since the mid-1990s character education has enjoyed a rapid rebirth as more and more schools adopt character education programs. This complex issue is the focus in Chapter 6.

KEY IDEA

Social studies is characterized by multiple goals and purposes, some of which it shares with other subject areas.

✳ Promoting Democracy in the Classroom

Someone once said that democracy is something you live, not something you teach. The parallel here is that if the purpose of schools and social studies is to prepare youth of the society for democratic citizenship, they need experiences with democratic process and ideals prior to graduation. In this section, we explore how teachers can begin to "do" democracy in their classrooms.

Students cannot learn the responsibilities of democratic citizenship while sitting in classrooms run by dictators. The two formats are incompatible. At the same time, however, everyone knows that teachers must deal with a host of constraints that operate against the creation of a pure classroom democracy. First,

"Doing" democracy in the classroom

teachers have legal and ethical responsibilities for the safety, welfare, and learning of their students, and thus they cannot relinquish their overall authority as teachers. In addition, and because teachers seldom have had much experience with democratic classrooms as students, we suspect that "doing democracy" in the classroom is something that evolves over time, as opposed to something that teachers jump into immediately.

A key element in moving toward a democratic classroom is your students' prior classroom experience. Most of them will not have experienced many of the responsibilities that the role of classroom citizen demands. Some students may find that it is easier to be a spectator or a follower, which requires only simple obedience, than to participate in self-governance. Be advised also that helping students become accustomed to the more demanding role of participant can be fraught with problems.

Children play a real role in classroom governance

A growing body of research suggests that it is impossible to teach children the moral and ethical behaviors associated with democratic citizenship—things like respecting the right of others to voice their opinions even if they differ from yours—in twenty-minute lessons taught on every other Thursday. Likewise, teaching ethics, morals, and values should be part of a whole-school enterprise, not something that individual teachers do in isolation.

The common good

A final element critical to operating a democratic classroom is the need to maintain an unswerving focus on the common good. No matter how much individual students may wish to follow their whims and impulses, the criterion for determining whether or not behavior is acceptable is the extent to which it reflects a shared conception of justice based on the common good. It is not your responsibility as teacher to be the sole determiner of the common good, even though that may be the case from time to time; all students should participate in that determination. In group situations, our right to do our own thing must be tempered by a concern for others, by the common good. It is one of the primary rights and responsibilities of democratic citizenship.

SUMMARY

Social studies is a composite subject created for teaching purposes that draws its content from history and the social science disciplines—geography, sociology, political science, economics, anthropology, and psychology—and to a lesser extent from philosophy, religion, and the fine arts. The main purposes for teaching social studies include (1) teaching children about our cultural heritage, (2) teaching children to think skillfully, (3) teaching about human (social) behavior, and (4) teaching children to act morally and ethically according to what they know. Because these purposes are not mutually exclusive, teachers will often deal with two or more of them simultaneously.

The overarching goal of social studies is citizenship education: that is, training students to be effective participants in a democratic society. Because educating responsible citizens is the major responsibility of schools everywhere, so citizenship education is an all-school enterprise, not the responsibility of social studies alone. Citizens in democratic societies have special responsibilities that are often denied their counterparts in totalitarian societies, where leaders make the decisions and citizens merely follow. For example, citizens in democratic societies must be able to strike a balance between the common heritage that all of us enjoy and the contributions that individual ethnicities make to our cultural mosaic. This is the essence of multiethnic literacy. At the same time, citizens in a democratic society must recognize their responsibilities for maintaining a civic environment that welcomes their voice in determining how government will function—in other words, civic literacy. And finally, citizens in a democratic society must recognize their responsibilities for maintaining secure living environments that ensure the continuing safety of one's family and community, yet still enable individuals to achieve their aspirations—or community literacy. These literacies of citizenship are essential to nurturing and maintaining a representative democracy, and as such, reflect an ongoing challenge that all of us share.

SUGGESTED READINGS AND RESOURCES

Introductory Note: This section contains both print and electronic resources and is organized by categories that correlate with major topics in the chapter. The resources located under the heading "General," for example, expand on the overall focus of the chapter, and additional resources are included under their respective headings.

Print Resources

GENERAL RESOURCES

Robert D. Barr, James L. Barth, & S. Samuel Shermis. (1977). *Defining the social studies.* Bulletin 51. Washington, DC: National Council for the Social Studies. This classic book is one of the standard works for clarifying the competing philosophies of social studies.

Jere Brophy & Bruce VanSledright. (1997). *Teaching and learning history in the elementary schools.* New York: Teachers College Press. Most of this book focuses on the very different techniques that three fifth-grade teachers use to teach fifth-grade American history. However, the first two chapters also present an excellent overview of recent research.

S. G. Grant & Bruce VanSledright. (2001) *Constructing a powerful approach to teaching and learning in elementary social studies.* Boston: Houghton Mifflin. The "powerful" approach reflected in the title is a reference to the NCSS Standards that use the same term. The text also uses a four-component framework based on the commonplaces of education.

SOCIAL STUDIES STANDARDS

Mary E. Haas & Margaret A. Laughlin. (1997). *Meeting the standards: Social studies readings for K-6 educators.* Washington, DC: National Council for the Social Studies. This is a useful collection of readings.

DeAn M. Krey. (1998). *Children's literature in social studies: Teaching to the standards.* Bulletin 95. Washington, D.C.: National Council for the Social Studies. This book is filled with annotated lists of children's books published during the 1990s that are keyed to the ten NCSS thematic strands. Very useful.

Margaret A. Laughlin & H. Michael Hartoonian. (1997). *Succeed with the standards in your social studies classroom.* Portland, ME: J. Weston Walch. This book contains ready-to-use reproducible activities for the ten NCSS themes.

Tarry Lindquist. (1997). *Ways that work: Putting social studies standards into practice.* Portsmouth, NH: Heinemann.

T. Lindquist & D. Selwyn. (2000). *Social studies at the center.* Portsmouth, NH: Heinemann. Lindquist and Selwyn provide lots of examples of good social studies teaching and then show how these reflect the standards. Highly recommended.

National Council for the Social Studies. (1994). *Expectations of excellence: Curriculum standards for social studies.* Washington, DC: National Council for the Social Studies. This is a well-written compendium.

MULTIETHNIC LITERACY

Peter D. Salinas. (1997). *Assimilation, American style.* New York: Basic Books. In this short but brilliant work, Salinas argues that in the past thirty years we have moved toward a policy of enhancing ethnic consciousness, but at the expense of America's historic commitment to assimilation. If you read Salinas, you should also read Nathan Glazer's (1997) *We Are All Multiculturalists Now* (Cambridge, MA: Harvard University Press), to get the other side of the coin.

COOPERATIVE BIOGRAPHIES

M. Zarnowski. (1990). *Learning about biographies: A reading-and-writing approach for children.* Urbana, IL: National Council for Teachers of English and the National Council for the Social Studies. We agree with Tarry Lindquist that this little book is an invaluable resource for teachers thinking about doing a biography project with their students.

Internet Resources

Introductory Note: Web sites sometimes change Internet addresses or cease operating entirely. All the addresses supplied here were operating when this book was printed, but should any of them fail to work properly we suggest you enter the topic or target organization in any standard search engine.

The National Council for the Social Studies

http://www.ncss.org/online/home.html

This site, maintained by the largest professional association for social studies, is an excellent place to begin. Contains a wide variety of materials, including information about social studies, teaching techniques, lesson plans, networks, and information about professional development and travel opportunities.

ERIC Clearinghouse for Social Studies/Social Science Education ERIC/Chess

http://www.indiana.edu/-ssdc/eric-chess.html

This site is maintained by the national clearinghouse for social studies materials, including curriculum guides, teaching units, journal articles, and bibliographies.

Social Studies Sources

http://education.indiana.edu/~socialst/

This site is maintained by Indiana University and links to a variety of topics including American and world history, government, geography, news groups, and other sources.

CSS Journal

http://www.cssjournal.com/journal/sites.html

This site offers links to hundreds of social studies sites on the web.

Social Studies Around the Web

http://www.li.net/~ndonohue/ssus.html

Created by a teacher, Nancy Donohue, this site links to hundreds of topics. Well organized and easy to navigate.

Resources for Social Studies Teachers

http://www.csun.edu/~hced013/

This site, which is maintained by Dr. Marty Levine, California State University, Northridge, was one of the first and remains one of the most useful resources for anyone planning to teach social studies.

ePALS Classroom Exchange

http://www.epals.com/index.html

The ePALS Web site encourages teachers and students to share educational experiences through the classroom exchange. This site boasts an E-mail membership of over fifteen thousand classrooms in more than one hundred countries. Each participating teacher provides a brief introduction as well as information on grade level and class size.

Partner Schools

Intercultural E-Mail Classroom Connections

http://www.stolaf.edu/network/iecc/

This free service is offered by St. Olaf College in Minnesota.

Developing Educational Standards

http://edStandards.org/Standards.html

If you are looking for information on standards, this site has it. It provides access to the educational standards for fifteen subjects, all fifty states, the U.S. government, and a few other nations.

History and the Social Sciences: The Knowledge Base for Social Studies

KEY QUESTIONS

● **What is the academic knowledge base for social studies?**

● **How has the human experience influenced what we think, do, and value?**

● **How do the social sciences differ from history?**

● **On what areas of the human experience do the social science disciplines focus?**

● **How does one teach history and the social sciences to young children?**

● ● ● ● Introduction: On Waiting in Line

Have you ever found yourself waiting in line at a bank, post office, or super-market, only to discover that all the other lines are moving faster than yours? Which of the following describes your reaction when this happens?

a. Do you think about changing lines?
b. Do you scowl at the person causing the delay?
c. Do you continue waiting impatiently until it is your turn?
d. Do you do all of the above?

In these situations, my response would be "All of the above." To avoid these kinds of responses, many businesses—airports, banks, and fast-food restaurants especially—have shifted to "snake lines." This is where all the windows or sta-tions are served from a single-file line. Snake lines are no more efficient than separate lines, but they are much fairer, because you cannot get stuck in a line that's moving slower than all the others.

Snake lines

In some nations, waiting in line is referred to as "queuing up." New Yorkers call it "waiting on line." Yet regardless of what it is called, social scientists have found that "queuing up" is part of a complex social system that involves culturally spe-cific principles of fairness and justice. For those of us who live in the Western world, this means that the people from some cultures seem to know how to line up "properly" and others don't. For example, when the Walt Disney Corporation

Lining up is culturally related

opened Euro-Disney in France, they had expected ticket buyers to line up in the same orderly way they do at Disney locations in California and Florida. But to Disney's dismay, the lines for both rides and tickets at Euro-Disney were chaotic. Disney's experience was consistent with what social scientists had noted previously: the more a society values equality, the more fairly its members will queue up.

How perceptions influence reality

Social scientists have found that it's not how long people actually wait in line that matters, but their *perception* of how long they *think* they had to wait. People often felt that they had waited 30 percent longer than they actually had. A similar phenomenon occurred when high-rise office buildings and hotels were first constructed and workers began complaining about long waits for the elevators. The researchers suspected that instead of installing more new elevators or speeding up the existing ones, there might be a less costly solution: provide something for the people to do that would influence their perception of the time they spent waiting. The researcher's recommendation was to install mirrors in the elevator lobbies. The complaints declined markedly. The next time you're in a major hotel or high-rise office building, take notice of the decor in the elevator lobbies.

Significance?

Researching how we humans respond to waiting in line may seem like pretty banal stuff. You might even want to ask, "Shouldn't those researchers be studying something more significant?" But imagine that you are the architect of a high-rise building and you are confronted by an angry chief executive officer (CEO) who says, "Look at all these complaints! You didn't install enough elevators." Do you install more elevators, which is an expensive proposition? Or tell the CEO to ignore the complaints? If you are aware of the social science findings, you could propose a far less expensive alternative that CEOs and many other people would probably never think of: mirrors.

Most of us are not architects (or CEOs) who might reap direct benefits from this research. So the next question is: Should students be expected to study these findings as a part of social studies? In addition to offering some insights into human behavior, the findings about waiting in line could reflect persistent behavior patterns that may emerge in other settings. Students could investigate questions such as: In what ways (besides waiting in line) does perception influence our view of reality? Or, in what other ways besides waiting in line do cultures that place less value on equality differ from ours? The waiting-in-line findings are insignificant and almost trivial by themselves, yet they could serve as a vehicle for reaching other more significant ideas about human behavior. How information can serve as a vehicle for developing ideas in other contexts is explained throughout the balance of this book.

Chapter organization

This chapter focuses on history and the social sciences, both of which reflect the largest portion of the knowledge base from which social studies is drawn. First we consider history as a field of study and look at some of the problems associated with teaching history to young children. We then examine the individual social science disciplines and what it means to be historically, geographically, and politically literate. Finally, we turn to what all of this means in terms of those portions of the human experience that we as teachers pass on to the young in the form of social studies.

History and the Human Experience

Many of the things that affect our lives today are of comparatively recent origin, historically speaking. Laptop computers, pagers, and cellular phones are just a few that come to mind, but consider that, in the perspective of historical time, even the printing press is a relatively recent innovation. This becomes especially evident when historical time is depicted through the metaphor of a clock. Imagine the face of a clock on which every minute represents fifty years—a substantial part of anyone's lifetime. On that basis, the entire clock face represents three thousand years—or from about 1000 B.C.E. (before the Christian Era) to A.D. 2000 (see Figure 2.1). (Portions of this material are based on Postman and Weingartner [1969].) On this scale, the printing press would have been invented only ten minutes ago, television about a minute ago, and fax machines and cellular phones in the last second or two. In the field of medicine, it would have only been about three minutes ago that doctors began curing more people than they harmed. Likewise, it has also been only seconds since medicine achieved some of its most significant developments—organ transplants, laser surgery, synthetic drugs, and many other things we take for granted today.

The clock metaphor illustrates that life today is much faster paced than it was in years past. An hour is still sixty minutes long, of course, but changes and innovations—particularly technological innovations—have become an accepted and even expected part of modern life. Yet as quickly as changes are occurring today, history shows that change was also a facet of life in the past, although the pace was much slower.

A historical clock

TECHNOLOGY

FIGURE 2.1 The Sequence of Inventions

One minute = 50 years

How we view ourselves

Two areas that have changed significantly over time are in how we look at ourselves as human beings, and how we regard the world in which we live. It's been only recently that we have understood our historical past well enough to realize that how we think of ourselves as human beings can differ from how members of other cultures view and think of themselves. And only recently have we come to understand that our definition of what it means to be human has changed over time. The information in Table 2.1 is oversimplified, but it reveals some of those changes.

History and the World Children Know

History as understanding

One of the values in teaching and studying history is the extent to which it can help young citizens view the human experience in its broader context and understand events from different perspectives (Arendt, 1961). The phenomenon of slavery can illustrate how this occurs.

It is widely known that during the seventeenth and eighteenth centuries and portions of the nineteenth century, thousands of African-Americans were enslaved and brought to this country against their will. It is less widely known that during the same period slavery was also practiced elsewhere in the world, especially in parts of Asia and North Africa. Most women in harems, for example, were not there of their own free will. Even today, parents in some parts of Southeast Asia sell their daughters into virtual slavery working in the brothels of larger cities like Bangkok.

Three-corner trade

Shift now to your twenty-first-century classroom. You have reached the section of every American history textbook that deals with the three-corner (or triangular) trade. This was where American ships would haul cargoes of naval stores (lumber, pitch, etc.) or other products from New England to southern Europe— the first leg of the triangle. The ships then sailed to North Africa, where the captains would purchase cargoes of slaves. The enslaved people would then be transported to ports in the southern United States or the Caribbean, where they were sold. To complete the triangle, the ships would pick up cargoes of agricultural products—often rum, cotton, and sugar—and transport them back to New England, where their voyage had begun originally. It was a lucrative trade that made many shipowners wealthy.

Against this background, consider one of your fifth graders who asks: "How could those people buy and sell human beings? Don't they know it's wrong? Don't they have a conscience?" The student's questions are reasonable, and common. How will you respond? (presentism)

Different ways of viewing the world

In developing your response, consider that your students are products of twentieth-century thinking, and, as suggested in Table 2.1, are likely to believe in self-determination. They are also likely to believe (as your student has already indicated) that buying and selling human beings or keeping them in bondage is immoral and illegal. It has probably never occurred to most children that people in other times and places, including the seventeenth and eighteenth centuries, looked at their world quite differently than today's children do.

TABLE 2.1   What It Means to Be Human: A Western Historical Perspective

When	Conceptual Framework	Implications
Ancient Times	Without necessarily making any reference to the real world about them, human beings were believed to be able to use their unique mind to reason about their condition.	The world was what human beings said it was. Humans were unique and set apart from the rest of the world. The concept of science at this time was the application of reason to morality and virtue.
Early Christian Era	Religious frameworks found men and women to be part of a larger scheme and to serve purposes for existence that transcended their earthly experience. The application of the human mind and reasoning ability found rational reasons for following reasoned authority and authorities.	Mind was pure and good and physical needs and desires were viewed as evil. Humans were seen as having two dimensions—the soul and the body. Men and women were born in sin, and human effort was directed toward redemption and the "other world."
Renaissance	The political framework found men and women recognizing social realities found in existing social conditions. Power, control, leadership, and forms of social organization were based on political realities. Machiavelli's precepts emerge. Note: some argue that Machiavelli was the first political *scientist*—a scientist because he built his framework by observing and generalizing from the real world.	Beginning of the nation-state and nourishment of loyalty to earthly concerns now ran parallel to religious ideals. Beginning to use observed and observable information upon which to build ideas, people started to become increasingly aware of the complexity of their world. This movement modified their "way of knowing."
18th and 19th Centuries	The economic framework emerged. The human condition began to focus on industrializing, on ideological justifications for property, and the accumulation and distribution of wealth. The industrial revolution was under way. Adam Smith, Karl Marx, and others observed and interpreted the human experience as basically economic. Economic activity was part of the "natural" world. Human behavior was subject to "laws" just as the natural world was.	There was a definite relationship between people's "daily bread" and their larger conceptual frameworks of politics and religion. Class distinctions emerged, and economic mobility was related to social mobility. The organization and rules for economic activity fed nation-state rivalry, the need for justifying imperialism, and the need for explaining differing economic "levels." Natural laws pertaining to government, economics, and social class emerged as "right" when viewed as a larger, observed pattern of human experience. This led to a view of natural progress that human beings couldn't control.
Early 20th Century	The psychoanalytic conceptual framework found men and women at the mercy of their subconscious and deterministically	The primary focus appeared to be on the individual, and this seemed compatible with political and economic world-views that

TABLE 2.1   **What It Means to Be Human: A Western Historical Perspective (*continued*)**

When	Conceptual Framework	Implications
Early 20th Century	influenced by experiences. The framework reintroduced the individual and raised concern with the ego, superego, and id. Each individual was a product of his or her environment—especially the early environment that acted in screening subsequent experiences. Freud's interpretation helped sharpen this framework.	seemed to carry weight. Emphasis was *not* on the individual deliberately interacting with experience but on the impact of early experiences that "conditioned" the psychological sets that an individual carried through life. Stress was on the inner person and the psychological impact one's life history carried.
Middle 20th Century	The physical sciences had struggled into maturity. The social sciences commenced to scientifically (empirically) study human behavior. Instead of emerging with set and unchanging "laws" of human behavior, the social sciences, through systematic research, came up with findings stated in "if-then" terms—findings stated in probability rather than certainty. Aspects of human behavior became the provinces of specific disciplines, as potential sources for understanding and explaining the human condition. The proper study of humans was humans. Previous conceptual frameworks that focused on external absolutes became challenged through the application of a maturing science to the area of human behavior.	The social science concept of human beings freed people from any sort of absolute determinism. It portrayed human beings as organisms interacting with artificial and natural environments. Rational applications of social science findings again brought focus to *Homo sapiens* as a learning/teaching and valuing species. Social concern moved from "other-worldliness" to the human condition on this planet. Ways of "knowing" shifted from logic and reason to observable human phenomena. In a continuing struggle, men and women assumed responsibility for their life choices. As John Dewey maintained, the purpose of life is life. Social science provided different information with which to help adapt and control. The choices, difficult as they are, are ours to make.
Turn of the 21st Century	Traditional ways of knowing, including the natural epistemology provided by science, as well as the notions of objectivity and rational rules for evidence, are being challenged in the academic community. The turn of the century is a time of ferment as the conceptual framework seems to be moving from a form of rationalism—rooted partly in the Enlightenment and based on the canons of science—to a form of intellectual relativism that accommodates multiple methods and procedures for knowing.	The implications of competing ways of knowing are not entirely clear. However, it appears there will no longer be a single standard for measuring and judging what one knows and how one knows. What this will mean for the structure and nature of the school curriculum and the academic disciplines is not clear. Also unclear is the mechanism—other than sheer numbers and power—that societies will use to resolve social conflicts, or whether the courts will need to establish new rules for handling evidence. The implications are substantial.

The problem of helping children understand different views of the world is compounded because elementary textbooks seldom deal with different views. This means that you are essentially on your own. In this context, the first time you say "natural laws," you are apt to get some bewildered looks from students. Nevertheless, people in the seventeenth and eighteenth centuries who considered themselves moral individuals were able to rationalize the practice of slavery on the basis of one or more so-called laws of nature, or "natural laws." The natural law that applied to slavery was based on the notion that some human groups were ranked as "higher" or "lower" than others, usually along racial lines. By virtue of their ranking, members of lower groups were considered eligible for domination, subservience, and even enslavement. Note that such thinking was common throughout the world, not just in the United States.

"natural laws"   Unless you are willing to explain how people in the seventeenth and eighteenth centuries viewed the world, including the concept of natural law, providing intelligible responses to your student's question will be difficult. An adequate though not very comforting compromise is to say something like "What those people did was wrong by our standards today. I'm not trying to excuse what they did, but people at that time didn't look at their world in the same way we do." If you think that the last line is too much, you could ignore it. However, unless you've laid some preliminary groundwork with your students, they won't understand the notion of worldview any more than the notion of natural laws.

* * * *
Helping Young Children Connect with the Past
* * * *

Part of the dilemma arises because of the way history is often presented in schools. From your experience, you know that most history courses are organized as chronological surveys in which you begin somewhere in the past and then work slowly toward modern times. But, as Levstik and Barton (1997) noted, "Too often, history instruction is simply a march through time that never quite con-

Chronological surveys   nects to the present" (p. 1). When history survey courses finally get to the present day—if they do—it is typically in a hurried treatment that occurs during the last week of May, when most students are looking forward to the end of school.

You may also recall that when history is taught chronologically, one event usually leads up to, or is said to "cause," a later event. The Boston Tea Party, for example, is often presented as a cause that led to the Revolutionary War, just as slavery and states' rights are usually identified as causes of the Civil War. In this context, ask yourself whether the colonists who participated in the Boston Tea Party were saying to themselves, "We are causing the Revolutionary War!" Even if most colonists wanted a war with England, which some of them did, they could not say they were causing the Revolutionary War—at least not until the war itself actually occurred. Likewise, the first enslaved person arrived in this country in 1619, but the Civil War did not occur until 1861, almost 250 years later. Is it possible that a cause existed for five generations? What actually happened, of course, is that beliefs changed over those 250 years, and the natural laws that had once made enslavement a tolerable practice were gradually replaced by even stronger beliefs in self-determination for all people. The first point here is that slavery

> **⚙ SUGGESTED ACTIVITY**
> Consider how things would be different if history were taught in reverse chronological order, begining with the present and moving back to the past.

became a cause of the Civil War, even though it didn't start out that way. The second point is that historians can look at past events, such as the Revolutionary or Civil wars, and then, with the hindsight that history permits, go back to identify what caused those events. Despite the image that many textbooks convey, children need to understand that the cause-effect nature of history always occurs after the fact. The third point is that although historians can rightfully focus on explaining the past, they cannot predict the future. Even after analyzing events that are occurring today, no reasonable historian would say: "These events *will* cause the Caribbean War of 2021." Forecasting is the business of meteorologists, not historians.

History looks back, not forward

Yet another factor that influences how young children understand history is the way they perceive the passage of time. Very young children often think of time in terms of tonight, tomorrow, and perhaps next week. If you have any doubt about this, recall those holiday eves from your childhood when you wondered if it would *ever* get dark? Perhaps you've also noticed that your birthdays (and possibly the holiday seasons) come around more quickly than they used to. As adults, we know that time has not speeded up; rather it's our perception that changes. The time that once crept along so slowly when we were children somehow speeds up as we get older. The point here is that for young children who measure time past by the number of "longs" they attach to "ago"—as in "It happened a long, long time ago"—trying to instill precise historical dating is probably an exercise in futility. All of us eventually develop the ability to deal with the past, including the distant past, but expecting young children who have lived a decade or less to understand historical time is probably a case of imposing adult views onto children who look at their world quite differently.

How children perceive time

Two additional factors, one peculiar to history and the other pertaining to how we as adults expect children to deal with history and the other subjects they study, also have a bearing here. The distinguished historian Arnaldo Momigliano (1982) noted that although history has existed as a research and literary activity for at least twenty-five centuries, it has been a subject taught in schools and universities for only two or three centuries. Momigliano went on to note that in the two thousand years before it became a school subject, "history was written for *adult* minds" (p. 245). Although young children can deal with history, teachers need to be sensitive to (1) how they approach it as a subject, and (2) the kinds of expectations that they impose on children who are expected to learn it.

History was originally for adults

• • • •

History for Young Children

• • • •

A growing body of research (see Brophy & VanSledright, 1997; and Levstik & Barton, 1997) indicates that young children can deal with history quite readily. However, teachers must approach history in ways that accommodate young children's abilities and prior experiences. Sometimes this can mean avoiding certain practices. For example, when history was first introduced as a school subject, the prevailing educational view was that children were "miniature adults"—individuals who needed only proper guidance and training to function effectively as adults. At that time, the dominant educational technique for providing that training was called "mental discipline" or "mind training." From this perspective, the mind was regarded as a muscle that would "strengthen" and respond to exercise, just as skeletal muscles do. The usual procedure for training children's minds, and thus building mental discipline, was by providing children with long and often onerous mental exercises—things like memorizing the presidents *and* vice presidents of the United States, in order. History and geography provided ideal subject matter for the advocates of mental discipline—just look at all the facts children could be expected to memorize.

The "mental discipline" notion has died a lingering death, as did the conception of children as "miniature adults." Despite the huge body of research (e.g., Piaget, 1950; Egan, 1979; Elkind, 1982) that shows that young children do not think and reason as adults do, at least not initially, some parents today still dress their children in designer clothing and otherwise put the trappings of adulthood onto their children.

How then should you approach history with young children? Here is a brief summary of practices that are based on a growing body of research (see Brophy & VanSledright, 1997; Bruer, 1993; Bruner, 1986; Caine & Caine, 1994; Gardner, 1991; Good & Brophy, 1994; Levstik & Barton, 1997).

Recommended practices

- Avoid trying to cover long periods of time very quickly. Try focusing instead on one historical era, and then providing in-depth narrative accounts for that period. Better yet, let your students become involved in those detailed accounts. With a teacher's help, young children can often make sense of the original source materials found in journals, diaries, biographies, pictures, and historical documents.

"Particular" history

- Avoid broad and sweeping statements such as "Reconstruction was a time of turmoil," at least until students have had the experiences that will permit them to know what such statements mean. Instead of painting history with a "broad brush," try focusing instead on *particular* history, that is, on narrative accounts where *a* person (or small group of persons) deals with *a* particular problem in *a* particular place at *a* particular time, and under *a* particular set of circumstances. Especially useful in this respect are fictionalized diaries based on original sources but that avoid the archaic language that can sometimes cause problems for young children. Two examples in this genre are Kristiana Gregory's *The Winter of the Red Snow: The Revolutionary War Diary of Abigail Jane Stewart* (1996) and *Across the Wide and Lonesome Prairie: The Oregon Trail Diary of Hattie Campbell* (1997). The red snow in the title of the Revolutionary War diary refers to the bloody footprints left by George Washington's troops as they marched bootless in the ice and snow en route to their camp at Valley Forge over the winter of 1777–78. Likewise, the Oregon Trail diary does a wonderful job conveying the hardships and the occasional joys that occurred during that arduous eight-month journey from Missouri to Oregon. Note also that although the Gregory diaries are written from the perspective of girls between eleven and thirteen years old, most boys find them as engrossing as girls. The

Fictionalized diaries

Living history museums can
offer wonderful opportunities
for stepping back into the past.
(© Joel Gordon)

point here is that in teaching history to young children, use materials that will
personalize events and make them real.

- Avoid using outlines as an introductory activity. If you remember making an
  outline after you wrote your report (on whatever the topic), as noted in the prologue, don't expect your students to approach outlines any differently. Outlines
  of historical events that children have not yet studied are simply lists—often
  disjointed lists. Outlines (and timelines) are excellent devices for organizing
  preexisting information and are especially useful as concluding or synthesizing activities. On the other hand, neither you nor your students can organize
  information that you do not have (which may explain why you wrote your outline after you had written your report!)

Time and specificity   The research (see Levstik & Barton, 1997) suggests that two keys to teaching
history to young children successfully are *time* and *specificity*. For example, let's
assume that you want your students to understand the role that the Underground Railroad played before the Civil War. You could probably convey this
information in a ten- to fifteen-minute minilecture, or you could have students spend several days reading a biography of someone who lived through
that period, possibly Harriet Tubman. Which would you do? Despite the time it
takes, the biography would personalize events surrounding the Underground
Railroad in ways that children can relate to, and it would also permit you to *scaf-
fold,* that is, to build on students' prior knowledge and experiences. In the

absence of scaffolding, children may be forced to treat new knowledge as separate and, thus, highly perishable pieces of information. A final but not insignificant reason to use the Harriet Tubman biography specifically is that most students love it.

Coverage vs. specificity

The issue here is not whether you could "cover the material" in less time via other means, but whether you could do it with the specificity, immediacy, and poignancy that most biographies, diaries, and primary source materials do. This is essentially the same "less is more" issue that we considered in Chapter 1. In addition, and although these guidelines are applicable to teaching history to very young children, they are also applicable to older children, even adults.

Where do social studies textbooks fit in here? Many teachers, expecially beginning teachers, use textbooks as their main organizer and then supplement the text with primary source materials. It is not unusual for some primary source materials to be included as part of a total textbook package. In other instances, teachers (such as Tarry Lindquist from Chapter 1) organize most of their teaching around primary source documents and then use textbooks to help their students pull everything together.

History and the Social Sciences

This section explains why most social studies educators use the expression "history and the social sciences," instead of lumping the two together. It then examines the social science disciplines, how they are organized, and areas of the human experience they usually focus on.

History

History is not a social science discipline, which is why the expression "history and the social sciences" is used throughout this book. History actually falls into a gray area that lies between the social sciences and the humanities. This is not a defect or deficiency; it simply reflects the nature of that vast and wonderful discipline.

Why history is not a social science

History differs from the social sciences in at least two significant ways. First, historians focus on the past—which is not exactly a revelation, I'm sure. However, because the events of history are in the past, it is physically impossible for historians to move backward in time to control and reproduce historical events experimentally in the same way scientists can control events in a laboratory. This is why historians cannot predict future events with a reasonable degree of accuracy. Historians often reconstruct events from historical documents, but this too can pose other problems: Historians cannot be certain they have all the pertinent documentation. Neither can they be certain that whatever documentation they have reflects an unbiased account of the events in question. In times of war, for example, the losing side's records are often destroyed or lost, sometimes intentionally. This situation is what possibly led the noted historian Henry Steele Commager (Commager and Muessig, 1980) to comment that, over the centuries, history is typically written by the victors, not the vanquished.

In most social studies programs, history is treated as a social science discipline, even though it does not meet all the procedural requirements of a science. At the factual level—the names, places, and dates that we typically associate with history—there is probably no problem in treating it that way. But we cannot expect history to answer questions about the purpose of life or about the shape of the future.

Historical viewpoints and objectivity

Elementary- and middle-school students typically believe that everything in their history textbook is fact, an agreed-upon and unquestioningly true record of the past. It wasn't until we majored in history in college that we discovered that historians may interpret the same events very differently. The point is that no historical account is entirely objective. Events of history are always interpreted through human eyes, and everyone knows that if six different people observe the same event, you can get six different accounts of what occurred. Historians must decide which (of those six or more) accounts are the most plausible, and even then there is always a lingering doubt. Did the historians miss something, or overemphasize one account at the expense of others? Such questions simply reflect the often incomplete and interpretive nature of history. This also suggests why history's niche among the branches of knowledge is often more closely associated with the humanities than the sciences.

Selected Focal Areas of History

Civilization	Change	Continuity	Progress
Chronology	Bias	Invention	Leadership
Colonization	Perfectability	Historical records	Exploration

Geography

Geography is the science of place and space. Geography's two major areas of study are (1) places on the earth, and (2) the interaction between places and the people who live in them. These areas are the focus of geography's two major subdisciplines: *physical geography* and *cultural geography*.

The components of geography

Physical geography, which is one of the oldest of the social sciences, focuses on the physical characteristics of place. Physical geographers study place location, landforms, climate, resources, and the other facets of our habitats on earth. When you learned about the capital of Belgium (Brussels), the mountains that separate France and Spain (the Pyrenees), or the major American river that flows into the Gulf of Mexico (the Mississippi), you were studying physical geography.

Cultural geography focuses on the interaction between peoples and their environments, or, in other words, how people use the spaces in which they live. Cultural geographers look mainly at the effects of human intervention on the environment. These include how people are distributed on the earth's surface, how they use resources, how they develop transportation and communication systems, and so forth. If you remember studying how the scarcity of usable land forced farmers in the Orient to build terraces on the steep hillsides, you were dealing with cultural geography.

A third subdivision of geography is *cartography*—mapmaking. Maps and aerial or satellite photographs (from which most maps are made) are among geographers' most important tools for displaying and analyzing the phenomena they study.

Geographic Literacy.   Although geography is second only to history as a mainstay of the social studies curriculum, most of the geography that students study occurs in elementary and middle schools, primarily in Grades 3 through 7.

Complementary subjects   Rather than having students take additional courses in "pure" geography, the emerging view is that geography and history are complementary subjects that are best taught together in the social studies curriculum (see Bednarz, 1997). When you think about it, every event in history occurred somewhere on earth, and sometimes where the event occurred influenced its outcome. As Bednarz noted, there are good geographic reasons why the Revolutionary War "Battle of Bunker Hill" was actually fought on nearby Breed's Hill (p. 140).

In the past, most efforts to assess geographic literacy were based almost solely on the student's knowledge of physical geography. This means that students were

Place-name geography   expected to answer questions such as "What is the capital of the Philippines?" and "What are the five major rivers of Africa?" Information of this kind is sometimes derisively referred to as "place-name geography," but it still plays a role in many social studies programs and as a component of geographic literacy. Contemporary measures of geographic literacy often include aspects of place-name geography but in many instances have been broadened to include elements of critical and creative thinking and the use of geographic resources. These dimensions are reflected in the following exemplary geographic literacy tasks designed for fourth-grade students:

● Locate the seven continents and four oceans on a world map.

● Locate specific geographic features, such as the Ozark Plateau or the Susquehanna River, on a map of North America.

● Tell a story about what it is like to travel to or live in another region of the country or world.

Performance standards   ● Find answers to questions, such as "What are the five largest cities in your state?" by using an encyclopedia, atlas, gazetteer, computer database, or other resources.

● Measure the distance between two places on an interstate highway map.

● Describe the relative location of your local community in terms of its situation in your state and region, such as "My town is halfway between the state capital and the largest city in the state" (Henry, 1994, p. 4D).

Selected Focal Areas of Geography

Landforms	Location	Areal specialization	Demographics
Region	Migration	Habitat	Population density
Resources	Ecosystem	Climate	Spatial interaction

TECHNOLOGY UPDATE

G.I.S.: Geographical Information Systems

G.I.S., or Geographical Information Systems, refers to powerful computer software that can store and display a variety of geographical information. G.I.S. programs such as the *Mapmaker's Toolkit* (Tom Snyder Productions) and *Mapping the USA* (ERIM International) are suites of databases, including maps and photographs—both current and historical—that are integrated or geo-referenced. This means the materials are designed so that two or more pieces of information will fit together and can be displayed simultaneously. If you have ever tried to compare two maps of the same area, both in different scales, you know what a problem that can be. And if you have never tried doing this, what may sound like a simple matter can easily prove otherwise.

A brief example based on an older technology may help to clarify how a teacher could use G.I.S. software effectively. Imagine if you will that you have made overhead transparencies of three different maps, all in the same scale, of southern California from San Diego to the Los Angeles area. The first transparency shows population density, which in the Los Angeles and San Diego metropolitan areas is dense indeed but is significantly sparser in desert regions. On top of this map you overlay a second transparency (map) that shows the yearly rainfall. By projecting the two maps simultaneously, your students should be able to see that people tend *not* to live in areas that get less than ten inches of rainfall—the geographical definition of a desert—each year. But again, trying to locate maps in the same scale and that contain just this information—population den-

sity and rainfall—*and* that are not cluttered with additional details, such as city names and roadways, is an almost impossible task. If you don't have access to G.I.S. software, you may want to visit Atlapedia Online at **http://www.atlapedia.com/index.html,** where you can download maps and up-to-date statistical information about every country in the world.

Once children have determined where people tend to live (and where they don't), you might then remove the rainfall map and place your third transparency—a map of the roadways in the area—on the overhead projector. It should quickly become apparent that highway systems in the San Diego–Los Angeles areas are far more complex than in a desert community like Needles, California, where roads are few and far between.

Teachers in technologically advanced schools need not endure the time-consuming hassle of locating and making the necessary maps and overhead transparencies; rather, they need only punch a few keys on their G.I.S-equipped computer. Whether you use the older technology (overhead transparencies) or the G.I.S. programs, the activity can lead to at least two powerful geographic ideas: that people tend *not* to live in areas that receive less than ten inches of rain a year, and that as the population density increases, highway systems tend to become more complex. The G.I.S. software greatly simplifies the process of selecting and layering maps that show only the geographic features a teacher wants to display. To paraphrase the housekeeping guru, Martha Stewart, G.I.S. is a good thing.

Five Fundamental Themes of Geography

The Joint Committee on Geographic Education (1984, pp. 3–7) identified five fundamental themes that are intended to capture the essence of geography and serve as guidelines for geographic education in the schools.

Location

THEME ONE: *Location: Position on the Earth's Surface*

Absolute and relative location are two ways of describing the positions of people and places on the earth's surface.

Place

THEME TWO: *Place: Physical and Human Characteristics*

All places on earth have distinctive tangible and intangible characteristics that give them meaning and character and distinguish them from other places. Geographers generally describe places by their physical or human characteristics.

Relationships

THEME THREE: *Relationships Within Places: Humans and Environments*

All places on the earth have advantages and disadvantages for human settlement. High population densities have developed on floodplains, for example, where people could take advantage of fertile soils, water resources, and opportunities for river transportation. However, floodplains are periodically subjected to severe damage. By comparison, population densities are usually low in deserts, yet some desert areas, such as Israel, have been modified to support large populations.

Movement

THEME FOUR: *Movement: Humans Interacting on the Earth*

Human beings occupy places unevenly across the face of the earth. Yet these people interact with each other; that is, they travel from one place to another, they communicate with each other, or they rely upon products, information, and ideas that come from beyond their immediate environment.

Regions

THEME FIVE: *Regions: How They Form and Change*

The basic unit of geographic study is the region, an area that displays unity in terms of selected criteria. We are all familiar with regions showing the extent of political power, such as nations, provinces, countries, or cities, yet there are almost countless ways to define meaningful regions, depending on the problems being considered. For example, Indiana as a state is a governmental region, Latin America as an area where Spanish and Portuguese are major languages can be a linguistic region, and the Rocky Mountains as a mountain range is a landform region.

Anthropology

A focus on culture

Anthropology is the study of culture—the different ways of being human. Using artifacts, written and oral accounts, and on-site observations, anthropologists strive to develop profiles of cultures around the world. Anthropologists often use maps in their studies, but among their most important tools are cameras or camcorders, tape recorders, field notebooks, and laptop computers.

The components of anthropology

The discipline of anthropology is organized much like geography: its two major subdisciplines are *physical anthropology* and *cultural anthropology*. Physical anthropology focuses on the physical characteristics of humans and, in some cases, animals. The fact that one branch of physical anthropology, *primatology,* focuses on the behavior of nonhuman primates—apes, baboons, and gorillas—harkens back to a time when anthropology was considered a subdiscipline of biology. Anthropologists who focus on studying fossils (instead of living beings) reflect a subspeciality known as *paleoanthropology* or *paleontology*.

Cultural anthropology (or social anthropology) is the broad descriptor for the study of culture. Some cultural anthropologists employ a "cross-cultural

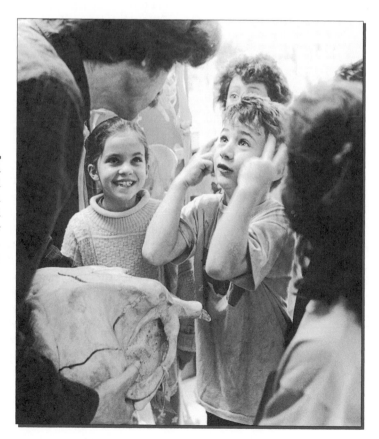

Historical and archaeological artifacts can bring the real world into the classroom.
(© Susie Fitzhugh)

perspective" to study the behaviors of past or present cultures. Others narrow their study to a single culture or ethnic group, such as the Hopi, the Maori of New Zealand, or former Puerto Ricans who now live in the Spanish Harlem neighborhood of New York City. Anthropologists who study single ethnic groups are called *ethnographers,* or literally, "individuals who map an ethnic (or culture)."

The power of language

Anthropological linguistics or *linguistic anthropology*—the two terms are interchangeable—focuses on the study of language and its use in social contexts. Most anthropologists agree that the creation and use of language is one of the key elements of human adaptation. As a result, linguistic anthropologists study the structure of a group's language, how they acquire it, and what it shows about their relationship to other groups.

Archaeology reflects a subspeciality of anthropology that focuses on the study of remains from lost or past civilizations. The materials could be a single piece of broken pottery or the contents of an entire city, as in Pompeii, Italy; but they usually fall somewhere in between. By studying these remains, the archaeologist's goal is to discern the way of life of the peoples who used them.

Selected Focal Areas of Anthropology

Culture	Acculturation	Diffusion	Customs
Ethnology	Tradition	Language	Kinship patterns
Rituals	Enculturation	Innovation	Tools

Political Science

Government and political behavior

Political science is the study of how human beings think, organize, and act politically (Brody, 1989). However, some totalitarian societies, such as China, do not recognize political science as a legitimate area of study (Theroux, 1997). Specializations in political science include public administration, international relations, political theory, and the study of policymaking and political behavior.

All societies develop ways to maintain social order, which are usually called governments, and most societies endow their governments with power and authority over members of the society. The form of government may be very simple—a chief and a council of elders or sometimes just a chief who acts unilaterally—or it can be more complex, as in the executive, legislative, and judicial branches of the U.S. government. The authority of government may be reflected by rules, which when written are called *laws* or when unwritten are called *mores* or, more simply, *tradition.*

In our society, decisions about whether someone has violated the law are vested in the judicial branch of government. In other societies, those decisions may be vested in the same bodies or persons who make the laws—a chief, a council, or some similar individual or group. In our society, the legislative, executive, and judicial branches of government are separate, at least theoretically. Ongoing issues like the abortion question have refocused attention on the way in which the Supreme Court interprets the law, thus determining what is or is not lawful behavior.

Civics emphasis

Political science appears in most elementary- and middle-school social studies as *government* (or *civics*). The major emphasis is on the law-making process and the form and structure of government at the local, state, and national levels. A second emphasis emerges at the upper-elementary- and middle-school grades when students study the historical evolution of the American government—from colony to confederacy to republic.

Selected Focal Areas of Political Science

Government	Authority	Power	Monarchy
Citizenship	Democracy	Fascism	Judiciary
Socialism	Federalism	Communism	Due process

Sociology

Many of us voluntarily join a variety of groups—school groups, the PTA perhaps, religious groups, or social or service groups such as the Lions Club or the Rotary. At the same time, all of us are members of other groups—cultural, ethnic, or age groups, such as teenagers, "yuppies," or seasoned citizens—simply because of who we are. Whether one is a teenager, a young adult, or a Golden Ager is not a matter of choice. But sociologically speaking, all of the groups to which you belong influence your behavior, just as you influence the behavior of the group itself.

The study of group behavior

Sociology is the study of human groups, how they form, and how they function. During the 1800s, sociology was very broadly defined as the study of all aspects of human life and social activity (Dawson, 1929). Almost everything "social" was subsumed under either sociology or history. However, as the other social science disciplines began to carve their niches from the human experience, people tended to drop the generic "sociology" and refer to the more specialized disciplines, such as political science. *Sociology* has been retained as a term, but its focus has narrowed to the discipline concerned with the study of group behavior.

Sociology has an array of subdisciplines. Some of these include economic, organizational, political, rural, and urban sociology; the sociologies of knowledge, law, religion, and medicine; human ecology; the history of social thought; sociometry and other small-group research; survey research; and special fields such as criminology and demography.

How disciplines may overlap

Sociology's focus on groups sometimes overlaps with other social science disciplines, mainly anthropology and political science, which also deal with human behavior in group settings. At times, the question becomes one of who is overlapping whom. Sociology and political science typically focus on modern, industrialized societies, whereas anthropology usually focuses on preliterate societies. Yet when sociologists, anthropologists, and political scientists all focus on a contemporary society, some overlap is probably unavoidable. However, each discipline typically examines phenomena from a different perspective and, in so doing, adds richness and depth to what we know about the human condition.

Selected Focal Areas of Sociology

Groups	Socialization	Discrimination	Stratification
Social class	Social status	Society	Norms
Role expectations	Segregation	Social mobility	Power

Economics

The "science" of scarcity

Economics is the study of systems for producing, distributing, exchanging, and consuming goods and services. The economy of a society may be based on trading grain or beads or tobacco or money, but regardless of its medium of exchange, an economy underlies every society. Subdisciplines in economics include economic history, agricultural economics, industrial economics, international economics, public finance, and certain aspects of business management.

Allocating resources

Scarcity is the engine that drives economies everywhere. If we lived in a utopian world where everyone had everything that they could ever want or need, scarcity would not exist and an economy would be unnecessary. In the real world, there are more things we want and need (or think we need) than there are resources available to satisfy them. Thus we must allocate resources to balance our wants and needs with the resources available to us. In the process, we may be forced to settle for a compact Ford or Chevrolet instead of the Corvette we always dreamed of. Economics is sometimes called the science of scarcity because of the central role it plays in every economy.

One of the two major areas of study within economics is *microeconomics,* which focuses on specific segments of the larger economy. These segments may include individual consumers or households, or businesses that serve a particular segment of the market, such as retail sales or medical services. The other major area of economics, *macroeconomics,* studies the economy as a whole. Macroeconomists typically study the complex web of relationships among such things as the money supply, the inflation rate, business and industrial inventories, and the unemployment rate.

Intervening in the economy

The findings of macroeconomists often provide the basis for governmental intervention in the economy, whether it be to maintain lower interest rates or low inflation, or to reduce unemployment. Strictly speaking, actions designed to maintain low interest rates, low inflation, and full employment are matters of social policy, *not* economics per se. Economists do not intervene in the economy; rather, they provide the data that enable social planners—who are usually employed by government—to do the actual intervention.

Macroeconomics focuses on economic elements, like inflation and the gross national product, that can have a profound influence on consumers. At the same time, macroeconomics can seem dry, dense, and removed from day-to-day living. As Schug et al. (2003) note, teachers often have to work at making economics interesting. Few of us, for example, may pay much attention to changes in the interest rate until it becomes so high that we can't afford taking out a loan to purchase something. Likewise, trying to understand abstract concepts such as inflation, much less what causes it, can be frustrating for young children and adults alike. Inflation is an abstraction that no one has ever seen, although we do see its effects in higher prices. In place of abstract concepts like inflation, the economic components of elementary- and middle-school social studies programs usually focus on *consumer economics*, which aims at helping children become informed consumers. Most social studies programs also deal with basic concepts of microeconomics, such as resources, wants and needs, production, consumption, and exchange.

Consumer economics emphasis

Selected Focal Areas of Economics

Goods	Services	Production	Exchange
Resources	Profit	Scarcity	Supply and demand
Consumer	Labor	Needs and wants	Price

Psychology

Psychology is the study of behavior—animal or human, instinctive and learned. The psychologists who study rats in a maze or chickens pecking at buttons to obtain food may be interested solely in the animals' behavior or may be searching for clues to human behavior, or both. Humans are infinitely more complex than rats or chickens, of course, which is why findings based on animal behavior don't always transfer to human beings. The point is that psychology is the study of behavior, broadly speaking, not human behavior alone.

Behavior is a tremendously complex and varied subject, and so is the discipline that studies it. Some subdisciplines of psychology use procedures more common to medicine and the natural sciences, such as treating disturbing or abnormal conditions, including mental illnesses. Still others focus almost exclusively on human behavior and are clearly social sciences.

The study of behavior

The fields of psychology most pertinent to the social studies include social psychology, which focuses on the behavior of humans in groups and group settings; cognitive psychology, which focuses on intellectual functions such as memory, perception, learning, and reasoning; and developmental psychology, which deals with the development of human behavior over the lifetime. Other related subdisciplines include personality psychology, which deals with the nature and development of personality, and psycholinguistics, which examines the development of language and language skills.

KEY IDEA

History and the various social sciences study different aspects of the human experience. Collectively they are sources of content for social studies programs.

Content drawn from psychology is common in elementary and middle schools, but it is more often part of the health curriculum, not social studies. Most health programs consider topics such as the nature of thinking and learning, the stages of human development, and the influences of heredity and the environment on human behavior, all of which derive from psychology. Also common to schools is what could be called "applied psychology." This is reflected by teachers' efforts to help students (1) build their self-concept and self-esteem, (2) deal with possible feelings of inadequacy, (3) cope with physical or verbal abuse, and (4) maintain good relationships with adults and peers. Although the elements of "applied psychology" are an inescapable part of teaching, they seldom occur as a formal subject. Whether psychology is treated as health or social studies, it remains a fertile source of social content.

Selected Focal Areas of Psychology

Learning	Personality	Motives	Self-concept
Perception	Aggression	Attitudes	Traits
Instinct	Conditioning	Punishment	Reinforcement

Related Disciplines

Other fields of study besides the social science disciplines apply the processes of science to social phenomena. For example, the field of psychiatry, which we normally think of as part of medicine, could be considered a social science (see below). The following are related disciplines that may be incorporated into social studies programs:

Related fields of study

Law—including jurisprudence, the major legal systems, legal theory, and the relation of law to the other social sciences.

Psychiatry—including theories and descriptions of the principal mental disorders and methods of diagnosis and treatment.

Statistics—including theoretical statistics, the design of experiments, sampling errors, sample surveys, governmental statistics, and the use of statistical methods in social science research. Note that statistics are mathematical tools that scientists use to determine the probability that the phenomenon they observed in a sample of the population is an accurate reflection of the entire population. In other words, scientists use statistics to test the probability that their findings are valid and not simply random or chance occurrences.

Natural Sciences—including biology, geology, and environmental sciences.

KEY IDEA

History has a history, as do each of the social science disciplines. The parts of the human experience that these disciplines study, as well as how they study it, have changed over time.

Major Findings from the Social Sciences

indings from the social science disciplines can take many different forms. Sometimes they are presented as generalizable statements that apply at all times and in all places. For example, all cultures develop a means for social control—that is, for governing the conduct of their members. This means that all cultures hold certain expectations of how their members should behave.

Generalizations

Other social science findings are presented in the "if-then" format that describe how people will tend to behave. Thus, for example, the members of a group will tend to perceive the group's collective opinion as closer to their own than it really is. Such findings provide a basis for anticipating and interpreting the behavior of others, but because they are based on tendencies, not absolutes, the behaviors they predict will not always occur.

In many (some will say too many) cases, data from the social sciences consist of factual, uninterpreted, documentary information. You could, for example, find out how many acres of farmland were harvested in 1957 or how many bushels of wheat were produced in Kansas in 2002—assuming that you needed that kind of information. In still other instances, social science findings can reflect reinterpretations of previously existing information. This might include a reconsideration of the role that slavery played as a cause of the Civil War, or a new explanation for why the food problem in India might be further complicated if the Hindus were to eat their sacred cows.

Raw (uninterpreted) data

An ever-growing body of knowledge

Regardless of the form the data take, social scientists are continually adding to the fund of knowledge. That's why social studies books get thicker, not thinner. The efforts of individual social scientists are usually systematic and well organized, but because there is no systematic way of managing all the information they produce, their findings are scattered throughout hundreds of sources—journals, magazines, even the Internet. Some of them, like the findings about waiting in line, eventually appear in textbooks.

The following sample generalizations, which are stated in nonacademic language, are based on history and the social sciences. They apply to human activities regardless of social situation, cultural background, or geographic location and could serve as a foundation (or part of one) for social studies programs.

- Human beings learn to behave the way they do.

Most behavior is learned

- Most human beings learn social habits, many of which they perform automatically and without thought. These patterns of behavior can help others predict how people will behave.

- Most people think that their ways of thinking and doing things are natural and right.

- All people can learn from past experience and can accept or change their ways of living.

- A change in one part of a person's life often requires changes in other parts of their life.

- Most people live in several different group settings simultaneously. This may cause conflict for the person if the groups expect different kinds of behavior.

Most human behavior is purposeful

- Most groups in which people live are dependent upon other groups (in which they don't live). This can lead to cooperation or conflict.
- Most human behavior is aimed toward satisfying some purpose or achieving certain goals.
- People living in the same group tend to share values and behaviors that are similar.
- Every human group has ways of handling how people work, how resources are used and distributed, and how the group's "wealth" is to be managed.
- How people use their physical environment depends on what is available, what is wanted, and how the group manages itself.

All societies have rules they live by

- All human groups develop ways for handling disagreements.
- Most groups of people believe in myths and legends that help them interpret and make sense of their world.

These findings could become the major ideas—the content—around which social studies instruction is organized. In this instance, content refers to two different but mutually supporting ideas: (1) the information and ideas contained in a particular subject area, such as social studies, and (2) the subjects or topics that matter in a specific field of study. If you consider the two different meanings, a significant aspect of social studies teaching may emerge: being a teacher is different from being a scholar. Teachers must identify and use specific information and ideas to ensure that their students learn to identify and use information and ideas. Scholars, on the other hand, usually identify information and ideas to be used in developing more content and more effective modes of inquiry. This is not to suggest that scholars can't teach, or that teachers cannot also be scholars. The point is that although teachers have some dependency upon the scholars' work, teachers and scholars may view content from different perspectives.

KEY IDEA

Findings from the social sciences are usually stated as tendencies or probabilities, not absolutes.

The knowledge base for social studies

The social science disciplines were originally created to aid in the scholarly pursuit of knowledge. Yet the content and findings from history and the social sciences furnish the raw materials—the knowledge base—upon which social studies programs are built. How one chooses to select, organize, and use these raw materials will determine the nature of the program, which is the focus of Chapter 3.

• • • • **COMMENTARY**   Social Studies or Social Science Education

When most of us were in elementary and middle schools, we studied social studies, not social science. We learned the names, dates, and places of history and geography, and we occasionally sampled some of the other social science disciplines. What we did not study much about was how scientists work with information and how they validate their findings. Occasionally we put information into chart and graph form, but it was usually decontextualized data—stuff like graphing the amount of wheat grown in Kansas from 1970 to the present. Some of us may have experienced the problems associated with polling or conducting a survey to determine the most popular soft drink or peanut butter, and whether students' taste for such products change from kindergarten to sixth grade, but such activities may have been the exception, not the rule.

When the knowledge base of history and the social sciences is drawn on to produce a social studies program, what often gets omitted are the processes of science. In other words, most social studies programs leave out the "science" part of social science. We are not suggesting that we need to put science back into social studies, because for the most part it was never there to begin with. We do suggest, however, that the information processes of science should be part of every social studies program. Helping students to gather, process, and evaluate information would be useful in its own right and would also help move from traditional social studies toward social science education.

SUMMARY

The human experience is that colossus from which all social studies stem. Our collective knowledge of the human experience is so all-encompassing that scholars created smaller, more manageable bodies of knowledge to organize what we know. Yet even these smaller bodies of knowledge, like geography and biology and medicine, have grown to massive proportions.

Somewhere in the human experience, scholars began referring to the smaller branches of knowledge as *disciplines*. At another point in the human experience, scholars who specialized in certain disciplines adopted rigorous (disciplined) processes and procedures, called *science*, for adding new knowledge to their fields of study. Consequently, the social science disciplines today represent organized bodies of knowledge in which scholars employ the processes of science to study selected aspects of the human experience.

The fields of study most pertinent to social studies are history and the social science disciplines of geography, political science, economics, anthropology, sociology, and psychology. Because some aspects of psychology are affiliated with the natural sciences, and others are closer to the social sciences, psychology—like history—can fall into a gray area. Psychology can provide a kind of bridge between the natural and social sciences, whereas history provides a bridge between the social sciences and the humanities. The point is that how curriculum developers and others classify the various disciplines that focus on the human experience can influence the topics that are included in a social studies program.

Recent research suggests that even young children are often able to study history and historical events, but they must do so in ways that accommodate their limited range of experiences. The key element in presenting historical events to young children is to make them as personalized and specific as possible. This means that sweeping statements, such as "The Reconstruction period (after the Civil War) was a difficult time for many people," will probably be meaningless to young children unless they have had prior experiences with the problems that people actually faced during that era. Historical narratives, including historical fiction in which someone does something to someone, can often provide the immediacy and involvement that young children require. Young children must be able to see how history relates to their lives, but the same principle is also appropriate for older students—even adults.

SUGGESTED READINGS AND RESOURCES

Print Resources

GENERAL RESOURCES

Linda S. Levstik & Keith C. Barton. (1997). *Doing history: Investigating with children in elementary and middle schools.* Mahwah, NJ: Lawrence Erlbaum Associates. This engaging book is packed with countless examples of appropriate classroom practice on teaching history to young children. It belongs on your "must read" list.

Raymond H. Muessig (Ed). (1980). *Study and teaching of social science series.* Columbus: Charles Merrill. Each of the 100-page volumes of this aging but still useful series focuses on a social science discipline. The authors and volume titles are as follows: Henry Steele Commager & Raymond H. Muessig. *The study and teaching of history.* Jan O. M. Broek, Henry Hunker, Raymond H. Muessig, and Joseph M. Cirrincione. *The study and teaching of geography.* Pertti J. Pelto & Raymond H. Muessig. *The study and teaching of anthropology.* Roman F. Warnke, Raymond H. Muessig, & Stephen L. Miller. *The study and teaching of economics.* John A. Straayer & Raymond H. Muessig. *The study and teaching of political science.* James A. Kitchens & Raymond H. Muessig. *The study and teaching of sociology.*

Patrica L. Roberts. (1997). *Literature-based history: Activities for children, grades 1–3,* and (1996). *Literature-based history: Activities for children, grades 4–8.* Boston: Allyn & Bacon. Both of these books offer abundant teaching ideas and activities as well as supplementary children's books that can make history come alive for young children. An excellent teaching resource.

ECONOMICS

Mark Shug and Richard Western (eds). (2003). *Social Education,* 67 (March) This special theme issue has useful articles for various grade levels by Allan Greenspan and economic education specialists.

CHILDREN'S LITERATURE

Kristiana Gregory. (1996). *The Winter of the Red Snow: The Revolutionary War Diary of Abigail Jane Stewart,* and (1997). *Across the Wide and Lonesome Prarie: The Oregon Trail Diary of Hattie Campbell.* New York: Scholastic. These slender volumes capture the joys and tribulations of the winter of 1777–78 at Valley Forge and the eight-month journey from Missouri to Oregon. Excellent for reading aloud. Highly recommended.

Internet Resources

Introductory Note: Internet sites related to teaching history and the social science disciplines are so extensive that to keep this section manageable we have presented only a partial listing here. The focus here are sites maintained by social studies–related professional organizations. Finally, Web sites sometimes change their Internet addresses or cease operating entirely. All the addresses supplied here were operating when this book was printed, but if any of them fails to work properly, we suggest that you enter the topic or target organization in any standard search engine.

HISTORY

National Council for History Education

http://www.history.org/nche/main.html

The organization promotes the study of history in the schools and offers links to other Web sites pertaining to teaching history.

The National Center for History in the Schools

http://www.sscnet.ucla.edu/nchs

This site is the home of the history standards.

Library of Congress—American Memory

http://rs6.loc.gov/amhome.html

This outstanding site contains a wide range of downloadable history-related resources including photographs, and audio and video materials. Highly recommended.

GEOGRAPHY

National Council on Geographic Education

http://multimedia2.freac.fsu.edu/ncge/

The National Council on Geographic Education provides excellent resources related to teaching geography.

National Standards for Geography

http://www.nationalgeographic.com/xpeditions/main.html

This site, which is maintained by the National Geographic Society, contains the eighteen national standards for geography (titled "Geography for Life") and a wealth of other teaching resources—lesson plans, maps, and so on.

GEOGRAPHY LESSON PLANS

http://www.eduplace.com/ss/autoact/ss-l.html

This site, maintained by Houghton Mifflin, offers a collection of geography lesson plans for Grades K–6.

POLITICAL SCIENCE/GOVERNMENT

Center for Civic Education

http://www.civiced.org/stds.html

This site is maintained by the Center for Civic Education and contains the complete *National Standards for Civics and Government* document. In addition to other links, this site also provides an executive summary of *Civitas: A Framework for Civic Education,* a program for improving teaching about democratic government practices (at: http://www.civiced.org/civitasexec.html).

ECONOMICS

National Council on Economic Education

http://www.nationalcouncil.org/

This site is maintained by the largest professional organization for promoting economic education in the schools and offers a variety of information and curriculum materials for K–12 economics programs.

EcEdWeb

http://ecedweb.unomaha.edu/ec-cncps.htm

This site, maintained by the economics education center at the University of Nebraska at Omaha, offers curriculum guidelines, program information, and other economic education materials of interest to elementary and middle-school teachers.

SOCIOLOGY

Teaching and Academic Resources—Sociology

http://www.asanet.org/teaching.htm

At this site the American Sociological Association provides information on sociology-related teaching approaches and curriculum. Primarily aimed at college and university faculties.

ANTHROPOLOGY

American Anthropological Association

http://www.ameranthassn.org/resinet.htm

At this site the American Anthropological Association offers a wide range of information and links to other sites related to teaching anthropology.

PSYCHOLOGY

American Psychological Association

http://www.apa.org/ and **http://www.apa.org/psychnet/**

This site, maintained by the American Psychological Association, offers wide-ranging information related to the general subject of psychology. Adding "psychnet" to the original address will take you to links to other psychology-related Web sites.

How Social Studies Programs Are Organized

3

KEY QUESTIONS

- What topics are typically taught in social studies, and when?
- What are common patterns for organizing social studies programs?
- How important is sequence to a social studies program?
- How does the nature of social studies influence the creation of social studies programs?

● ● ● ● Introduction: On Framing the Constitution

New York is one of almost twenty states, including California, Texas, and Virginia, where social studies programs are determined primarily at the state level. This sometimes means that what gets included in, or is omitted from, the state's social studies curriculum may depend on how successfully individuals or groups can lobby for their cause at the state level.

This phenomenon became apparent when the New York Board of Regents (the state board of education) was considering the adoption of a new, multicultural social studies program. As one aspect of the proposed program, students would be expected to learn that the framers of the U.S. Constitution were inspired by two factors: the European Enlightenment, and the Iroquois Confederation—the alliance of seven tribes of indigenous people from New York and nearby areas.

New York State experience

Most historians readily acknowledge the Enlightenment's impact on the framers of our constitution. The Enlightenment reflected the belief that common people were capable of deciding the common good. However, it is rare to find a social studies program that includes the Iroquois Confederacy as a contributing factor to the Constitution. Some people in New York apparently questioned this also and began asking, "How does anything—not just the Iroquois Confederation—get into the (state-mandated) social studies program?"

Jack Weatherford contends in his book *Indian Givers* (1988) that the Iroquois helped the colonists resolve the dilemma of how to join the thirteen colonies into one country without each one giving up its powers. A confederacy, which is a voluntary association of separate states, does that. The United States actually operated under the Articles of Confederation between the Revolutionary War in

1776 and when the Constitution was ratified in 1789. However, in 1988, Congress passed a joint resolution acknowledging the historical debt that the United States owed "to the Iroquois Confederacy and other Indian nations for their demonstration of enlightened democratic principles of Government."

Whose history?

Whether the Iroquois Confederacy did or did not influence the framers of the Constitution was one aspect of an often heated debate in New York between supporters of the new curriculum and others who argued that history was being rewritten to serve political purposes. The controversy grew even more heated when people learned that the Iroquois's contributions to the Constitution were included in the New York social studies program after a delegation of contemporary Iroquois had visited the state's commissioner of education. Armed with the congressional resolution, the Iroquois apparently convinced the commissioner that New York's social studies program should be changed—a decision that would affect countless teachers and the 2.5 million schoolchildren who live in that state.

The issue here is: Is failing to include the alleged Iroquois contribution to the Constitution a glaring omission that should be changed (in New York and elsewhere), or is this an instance where certain predisposed individuals are attempting to rewrite history to make it come out the way they want it to? World history is replete with examples where dictators had their nation's histories rewritten to make them come out the way they wanted them to. I mean no disrespect to the

A growing trend

Iroquois; the point here is that decisions about the social studies that you will be expected to teach are increasingly being made at the state level, and not in local school districts as was once the case. This incident in New York is not an exception, because similar situations (usually involving different content) have occurred elsewhere (see Cornbleth & Waugh, 1995).

This chapter examines the organization of contemporary elementary- and middle-school social studies programs and factors that often influence them. Throughout the chapter, the terms *program* and *curriculum* are used interchangeably. Authorities sometimes distinguish between the two, usually using *curriculum* to indicate the broad framework within which teachers may develop their own *programs,* yet in many schools today you will hear expressions such as "our social studies program" or "our map skills program." Because *program* seems to be edging out *curriculum* in common usage, I follow that convention in this chapter.

The next section presents the predominant curriculum pattern for elementary- and middle-school social studies programs. Following that is an examination of several alternative curriculum patterns and a sampling of factors that can influence how social studies programs are organized.

● ● ● ● The Dominant Curriculum Pattern: Expanding Environments

Figure 3.1 illustrates the organizational approach to social studies that was created in the mid-1920s, became increasingly popular during the 1940s and 1950s, and continues to dominate programs throughout the country today. You may find occasional variations on the *expanding-environments* approach to social

FIGURE 3.1 Expanding-Environments Approach to Social Studies (K–6)

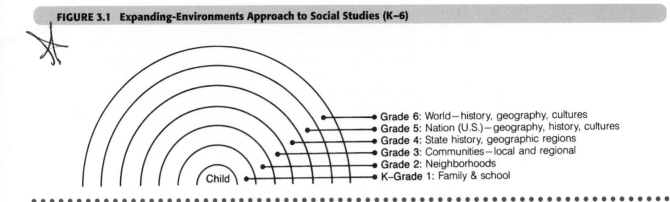

Grade 6: World—history, geography, cultures
Grade 5: Nation (U.S.)—geography, history, cultures
Grade 4: State history, geographic regions
Grade 3: Communities—local and regional
Grade 2: Neighborhoods
K–Grade 1: Family & school

Child

studies, some of which are described later in this chapter, but for all practical purposes it is a national curriculum. This organizational pattern is also known as *expanding horizons, widening horizons,* or the *expanding communities of man.*

The organizing principle The organizing principle for the expanding-environments approach as shown in Figure 3.1 is a mixture of physical and conceptual distance. The sequence begins with the environments (or communities) that are physically closest to the child, such as the home, school, and neighborhood. It then progresses through environments that are successively more distant: the local community, the state (or region), the nation, and finally the world. All of us live in these environments simultaneously, of course, so the assignment of certain environments to certain grade levels is done for instructional simplicity and convenience.

A Composite K–8 Program

When the expanding-environments principle is translated into an actual curriculum, the result is similar to the composite program shown in Table 3.1. The table, which reflects the topics commonly found in widely used textbook series, shows the common topics, the typical sequence of units, and the social studies disciplines emphasized within the units.

Scope and Sequence Summarized

Focus: Self and School **Kindergarten.** Most social studies programs for kindergarten are designed to familiarize children with their developing selves and their new environment—the school. No social science discipline predominates in kindergarten programs, and the sequence of topics has no particular logic. And although the "Special Days" or holidays unit is listed last in kindergarten (and in Grades 1 and 2), teachers often draw on it extensively throughout the year, in what is sometimes referred to as the "holiday curriculum."

TABLE 3.1 Composite Social Studies Curriculum (K–8)

Grade	Focus/Title	Typical Sequence/Unit Topics	Dominant Discipline
K	*Getting Started*	Learning About My World	The social science disciplines are integrated throughout all units.
		Families/Community Helpers	
		Transportation and Communication	
		Special Days	None
1	*Families, Homes, and Neighborhoods*	Our Earth	Geography/Map Skills
		Families Meet Their Needs: Food, Clothing, Shelter	The social science disciplines are integrated throughout all units.
		Families at Work	
		The Neighborhood	
		Holidays Around the World	
2	*Neighborhoods and Communities*	Exploring Our Earth	Geography/Map Skills
		Urban, Suburban, and Farm Communities	The social science disciplines are integrated throughout all units.
		Communities—Today and Yesterday	
		Transportation and Communication	
		Communities Celebrate Holidays	
3	*Communities and Resources, Here and There*	Map and Globe Skills	Geography/Map Skills
		Living in Different Communities	Integrated
		Governing Communities	Political Science
		How Communities Change	Integrated
		Farm and Ranch Communities	Integrated
		Communities Around the World	Geography/History
4	*Regions Near and Far*	Our Earth	Geography/Map Skills
		Regional Studies Emphasis: Units on Forest, Plains, Mountain, and Desert Regions, e.g., The Pacific Northwest, etc.	Geography
		Working Together Around the World	Economics
		State History Emphasis: Major Resources and Land Forms	Geography
		Early Settlements	History
		Governing Our State	Political Science
		Our State Today	None/Integrated

(continued)

TABLE 3.1 **Composite Social Studies Curriculum (K–8)** (*continued*)

Grade	Focus/Title	Typical Sequence/Unit Topics	Dominant Discipline
5	*Our United States*	Map and Globe Skills	Geography/Map Skills
		Founding the New World	History
		Building a Nation	History
		Establishing a Government	History/Political Science
		A Divided Nation (Civil War)	History
		Our Nation Expands Westward	History
		Our Nation Today	History
		Regional Geography of the United States: Units on New England, the Mountain States, the Pacific States, etc.	Geography Geography/History
		Map, Globe, and Graph Skills	Geography
6	*Our World Today*	**World History Emphasis:** Classical Civilizations: Egypt, Greece, Rome	History
		The Industrial Revolution through the Twentieth Century	History
		Eastern Hemisphere Emphasis: Our World Today: Units on Europe, Africa and the Middle East, Asia, and Australia	Geography and history are integrated in all units.
		Western Hemisphere Emphasis: Our Neighbors to the South: Units on Mexico, South and Central American nations	History and geography are integrated in all units.
		Our Neighbors to the North: Units on the Canadian Provinces, etc.	History and geography are integrated in all units.
7	*State History, World History, or World Geography*	Early Times to the Present	History
		Selected Civilizations	History
		Regions of the World	Geography
8	*U.S. History*	See Grade 5 except for the geography	History

Focus: School and family

Grade 1.   First-grade programs typically focus on the family, the school, and the neighborhood. The social science disciplines are usually integrated throughout, although consumer economics often gets more attention than the others. The emphasis on holidays also continues.

Focus: Neighborhoods

Grade 2.   Second-grade programs traditionally focus on neighborhoods, but this focus is often broadened to include communities and "community helpers." This broadening has occurred, in part, because of how neighborhoods have changed. Fifty years ago, the residents of a neighborhood were often ethnically similar (Polish, Italian, Chinese, etc.), and many neighborhoods had stable populations and well-established social systems; often a person was born, got married, and eventually died in the same neighborhood. As the U.S. population has become increasingly mobile, the stability of many neighborhoods—along with the social control and cohesiveness that they once enjoyed—has largely disappeared. Most neighborhoods today are no longer cultural enclaves but rather places where one resides.

Second-grade programs usually deal with different types of neighborhoods and communities—rural, urban, and suburban. Identifying connections between the students' local community and communities elsewhere in the nation or world is often the focus of the last unit.

Focus: Communities

Grade 3.   After an obligatory first unit on maps and globes, most third-grade programs turn to communities in the generic sense of the term. Initially the focus is on communities in different geographic environments, and then shifts to emphasize the political, economic, and social aspects of community life. Selected cities, both contemporary and historic (e.g., Washington, D.C., Williamsburg, Virginia), are often presented as case studies.

Focus: Regions/the state

Grade 4.   Most fourth-grade social studies programs focus on the geographic regions of the United States, which are often compared with similar regions elsewhere in the world. Geography—physical, social, and economic geography—is the dominant social science discipline. However, some states, including California and Texas, have either supplemented or replaced the regional geography emphasis with a first course in state history and geography.

Focus: U.S. history and geography

Grade 5.   Fifth-grade programs have a strong historical emphasis, as shown in Table 3.1, as well as a geographical emphasis in those areas where the Grade 4 program focuses on state history. Grade 5 is also the level where the problem of coverage usually becomes apparent. It is difficult to deal with American history in one year, but if you are also responsible for teaching regional geography, it becomes almost impossible. Opting to do a five-week, cooperative biography project on Abe Lincoln, as Ms. Lindquist's students do, would be out of the question. Some states have responded to this content-overload problem in Grades 5 and 6 by adopting the "less is more" approach noted earlier. For example, in the California program (illustrated in more detail shortly), fifth-grade history ends at 1850. Recent American history is not picked up again until Grade 8.

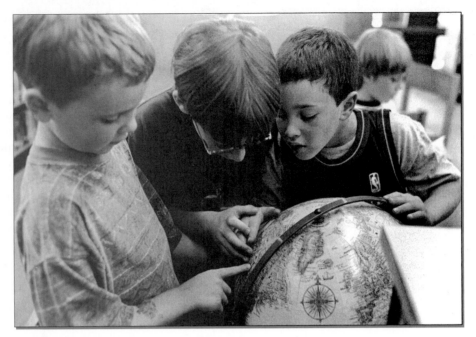

Map and globe skills are part of most social studies programs from Grade 2 onward.
(© Susie Fitzhugh)

Focus: World history and geography

Grade 6.   The scope of many sixth-grade programs is often even broader than for fifth grade. A common pattern is to devote the first semester to a survey of world history and the second semester to a study of the geography of nations in the Eastern Hemisphere.

If there is one grade where there is too much content to teach effectively, this is it. It is almost impossible to do justice to world history in a typical ninety-day semester, much less the geography of nations of the Eastern Hemisphere in a second ninety-day semester. This is why some states have split the course into two or more segments. In the California program referred to earlier, the sixth-grade program is limited to ancient civilizations prior to A.D. 500.

Focus: Varies considerably

Grade 7.   The guiding principle of the expanding-environments approach exhausts itself at Grade 6; it is strictly an elementary (K–6) program. The grade-to-grade sequence in secondary (7–12) social studies programs is topical, but there is no apparent guiding principle for organizing or sequencing courses or topics.

Social studies programs for Grade 7 seem to have more variability than at any other grade level. Some seventh graders will study either world geography or world history, which are extensions of what they studied in Grade 6. Others will study state history, which is theoretically an extension of what they studied in Grade 4 but often has significant repetition. In still other areas, seventh-grade programs will combine both elements: one semester of world geography and one semester of state history.

KEY IDEA

The predominant organizational pattern for elementary social studies programs (K–6) is based on the expanding-environments approach. Middle schools (Grades 7 and 8) typically use the topical approach common in secondary schools.

Focus: U.S. history **Grade 8.**   In Grade 8, the study of American history is almost universal. Significant deviations occur in schools where American history is treated over a two-year period. In those cases, the eighth-grade program may focus on American history through 1850, 1860, 1877, or another convenient date, and the "second half" is treated at another grade level (usually Grade 9 or 11).

Selected Program Features

This section presents selected features from all levels of the composite program illustrated in Table 3.1.

Scope   1. *Large increases in the scope of the program from grade to grade*—Primary-level social studies programs are sometimes faulted for dealing with a very limited range of material. At the same time, the scope of intermediate-grade (4–6) programs is often extremely broad.

Map and globe skills   2. *Separate units on map and globe skills at most grade levels*—Map and globe skills are vital components of social studies programs, but when they are presented in isolation, they are often decontextualized and seemingly without purpose. Instead of teaching map and globe skills as a separate unit, we recommend integrating these skills into lessons throughout the year in contexts where those skills provide information that your students can actually use.

A global emphasis   3. *An emphasis on developing a global view*—This emphasis is reflected by units or chapters that have an "our world" perspective in their titles. The intent is to help students understand that many problems, such as providing food and shelter and maintaining world peace, are common to people around the globe.

Holidays   4. *The continuing presence of the "holiday" curriculum*—Much of the primary (K–3) curriculum is devoted to observing and celebrating holidays and festivals throughout the year. This long-standing practice has added life and color to classrooms and has been the reason for holding countless parties. A note of caution is warranted here, because in some classrooms the "holiday" curriculum gets so much emphasis that it overwhelms everything else.

5. *Multidisciplinary social studies tends to diminish at the higher grades.* The multidisciplinary nature of primary social studies programs is evident in Table 3.1. Also evident, however, is the emphasis on single disciplines that begins in Grade 4 and continues through the middle (and high) school years.

Expanding Environments Reconsidered

The organizing principle for the expanding-environments approach—studying nearby environments before more distant environments—seems to make eminent sense. Each environment seems to build on the previously studied environment, and in a logical sequence that's readily evident to most adults.

The expanding-environments pattern also seemingly reflects the educational principle of "beginning with the concrete and moving to the abstract." Families (Grade 1) and neighborhoods (Grade 2) are certainly more concrete and real

● ● ● ● ● **COMMENTARY** **Teaching About Birthday Parties?**

In a scathing review of four primary-level social studies text-book series, Larkins, Hawkins, and Gilmore (1987) argue that "adherence to the sequence of family, neighborhood, community is in part responsible for the trivialization of social studies in the first three grades" (p. 301). The authors cite many examples that support their contention, but one involving the study of birthday parties is especially illustrative:

[The textbook publisher] is also convinced that children must be taught about birthday parties. A Chinese-American family is shown with a birthday cake. An American-Indian family is shown with a birthday cake. And a nonminority American family is shown with a birthday cake. A superficial dribble of noninformation about the differing cultural backgrounds of the three families is thrown in to help fill out the ten pages devoted to birthday parties. Danny's Chinese-American

grandmother tells him how birthdays are celebrated in China. Unfortunately, neither she nor Danny share that information with the reader. Maria's father tells her about birthdays on the Chippewa reservation, but neglects to tell us. And Jane's mother tells her, but not us, about what it was like to grow up in West Virginia. (p. 304)

Had these texts told us how birthdays are celebrated in China, on the Chippewa reservation, or even in West Virginia, that ten-page section might have been salvaged. In the absence of such information, I find myself wondering (1) what it is about birthday parties that children need to learn in school, and (2) is this not the kind of knowledge children will learn without instruction? Larkins, Hawkins, and Gilmore's concern about the damage such treatments can do to children's, teachers', and the public's perception of the importance of social studies is clearly warranted.

Conceptual versus physical distance

for most children than are states (Grade 4) or the nation (Grade 5). When third graders are studying their community, they are learning about something fairly concrete, something most of them have experienced simply by having lived in a community. However, when children study "the state" in fourth grade, they move to something that is often beyond their immediate view of the world. States have physical dimensions—boundaries, a capital, and so on—of course, but the state is a phenomenon of political organization; it is lines on a map that can't be seen anywhere else.

Although states are smaller and less-distant environments than the nation (which children study in fifth grade), and although children do indeed live in a state, these factors do not make the state any less an abstraction. Likewise, fifth-grade children cannot "see" the United States, except by looking at a map that is itself an abstract representation of the country. Eventually most children gain the experience that enables them to deal with the different worlds in which they live. The point here is that abstraction is determined by conceptual distance—the extent to which a phenomenon is within or beyond a child's realm of experience—*not by physical distance*. From this perspective, the expanding-environments approach is not so much a logical progression from concrete to abstract as a quantum leap that occurs after third grade.

Role of sequence

The sequence in which children study different environments is neither as rigid nor as important as it might seem. In more practical terms, this means that it is not necessary for primary-level children to study their families (or *the* family) before they study the (their) neighborhood, for example. Neither is it necessary for children to study the American family prior to studying Russian families or any other family around the globe. Rather, an appropriate way to study the family is by examining various families in the neighborhood and in other nations.

Despite its continuing popularity, the expanding-environments approach is not without some other problems. For example, most kindergarten and first-grade children are not aware of, nor do they necessarily understand or care about, the sequence of environments they will study over the next six years. They almost never concern themselves with the "whole," with how one topic relates to other topics they will study; rather, their concern is with what they are studying today. For most young children, the future—next week perhaps—is so distant that they hardly even think about it. At the other end of the program, it is not clear whether sixth, seventh, or eighth graders necessarily understand the organizational pattern of social studies that they've been exposed to. But then, perhaps children don't need to understand the overall pattern of what they study; that's a question researchers have yet to investigate. One thing is clear, however: social studies consistently ranks among the least-liked subjects children study in school.

An important consideration in organizing any instructional program rests on the nature of the underlying subject areas. Although the expanding-environments pattern makes it seem otherwise, social studies does not have the same kind of inherent structure or prerequisites as does a discipline like mathematics. In teaching arithmetic, for example, you must begin with counting, addition, and subtraction, for these are legitimate prerequisites for other arithmetic processes. In social studies, on the other hand, it is not necessary for children to know anything about families in order to study communities, nor is it necessary for them to have studied American history before they study the history of ancient civilizations. The point is that the mathlike sequence of the expanding-environments pattern makes social studies appear to be an inherently structured subject based on prerequisite learnings when, in fact, a social studies program can be assembled in many different ways.

You could, for example, teach first graders a unit on the Stone Age, instead of waiting until Grade 6 as called for by the expanding-environments approach. You would need to make adjustments for the children's limited reading ability, but there is nothing so inherently complex about the Stone Age as to be beyond a first grader's comprehension. Or you could use chronology as your organizer and begin teaching first graders about ancient civilizations (Egypt, Greece, etc.) as many European nations do. The single exception to everything said here is the area of map skills. This is because most map skills, especially latitude and longitude, are based in mathematics, as illustrated in Chapter 13. Some alternatives to the expanding-environments pattern appear later in this chapter.

Do children see a forest or just the trees?

SUGGESTED ACTIVITY

Review the assumptions on which the expanding-environments approach to social studies is based—for example, that children should be exposed to the world by Grade 6. Then, in small groups, outline the characteristics of a K–8 studies program that follows alternative assumptions of your choosing.

KEY IDEA

Social studies does not have the inherent structure (hierarchy) of a subject like mathematics; as a consequence, teachers often have more flexibility in designing a social studies program than they may realize.

● ● ● ● **COMMENTARY** **The Power of Contrast**

It may seem to be common sense to begin studying nearby environments—like the family, home, and school—before tackling more distant environments. This is also one of the basic premises of the traditional expanding-environments approach to social studies. But this is one time when common sense may fail us. Studying things that we are extremely familiar with and close to, such as our families, our language, and ourselves, is often difficult, simply because we are too familiar with them. Our families, for example, are so much a part of our everyday lives that we often take them for granted. Likewise, each of us has a vast body of feelings and information about families in general and about our own family in particular, but because of our upbringing and prior cultural experiences, most of us (including children) have developed perceptual blinders that keep us from thinking about families objec-

tively. Common sense notwithstanding, things that are more physically distant from us are often easier to study objectively.

When first graders study "the family," you sometimes find them studying Japanese families. They are not doing this because there are things about Japanese families that everyone should know, but because information about (or from) other cultures can provide a basis for *contrast,* that is, a way to relate the unfamiliar with phenomena that we know well. In other words, first graders can study Japanese families as a vehicle for studying American families, for learning how they are alike and how they are different. When first graders discover that Japanese children do not celebrate their birthdays every year, they simultaneously discover something about themselves and about their own culture.

● ● ● ● Alternative Organizational Patterns

From time to time, various groups and individuals have proposed alternative elementary programs. Most of them are variations on the expanding-environments approach, but in other instances, they ignore the expanding-environments pattern entirely. This difference is the basis for this section's organization.

● ● ● ●

Variations on the Expanding-Environments Pattern

● ● ● ●

NCSS alternatives

The National Council for the Social Studies (NCSS) has endorsed three alternative curriculum models for social studies, one of which is shown in Table 3.2. Although this proposal is not a radical departure from the expanding-environments approach, it claims different motives. Those motives, along with the other two recommended models, are included in the Resource Handbook.

Most state social studies programs are similar to the composite program presented earlier (see Table 3.1). However, the California History–Social Science Framework represents an exception to the rule. It attempts to (1) incorporate appropriate children's literature at each grade, (2) incorporate more multicultural and historical content than do most traditional programs, at the primary grades especially, and (3) at the same time reduce the scope of the history covered at the intermediate level. Table 3.3 shows the major topics and selected children's literature for each grade in the California program.

TABLE 3.2 NCSS Proposed Social Studies Program

Grade Level	Content
Kindergarten	Awareness of Self in a Social Setting Socialization experiences to bridge home life with life in schools
Grade 1	The Individual in Primary Social Groups: Understanding School and Family Life Specialized roles, family structure, interdependence, the need for rules and laws
Grade 2	Meeting Basic Needs in Nearby Social Groups: The Neighborhood Social functions including education, production, consumption, communication, and transportation within a neighborhood context
Grade 3	Sharing Earth Space with Others: The Community Same social functions of Grade 2 except in the context of the community in a global setting
Grade 4	Human Life in Varied Environments: The Region Geographic and cultural regions; the state as a political region, as may be required
Grade 5	People of the Americas: The United States and Its Close Neighbors Emphasis on the development of the United States, core values, significant individuals, history and geography of Canada and Mexico
Grade 6	People and Cultures: The Eastern Hemisphere Major geographical regions, historic and economic development, political and value systems

Source: NCSS Task Force on Scope and Sequence, "In Search of Scope and Sequence for Social Studies." Reprinted by permission from National Council for the Social Studies' *Social Education,* April 1984.

• • • • COMMENTARY How States Affect Textbooks, and Vice Versa

Whenever states opt to change their social studies programs, they risk creating something that doesn't fit any of the current textbooks. This was potentially the case when California decided to limit its sixth-grade program to ancient civilizations prior to A.D. 500. In years past, when there were literally dozens of textbook publishers, you had to hope that one of the smaller houses would risk publishing "the maverick" program. Today, however—thanks to countless mergers and buyouts—there are only four major textbook publishers (Toppo, 2003). This means that a publisher's willingness to go with a maverick may depend on other factors, not the least of which is the size of the potential market. In states as large as California, New York, and Texas, the textbook market at every grade level is so huge that most publishers will design materials to fit the state's programs. But smaller states, such as North Dakota or New Hampshire, may need to settle for a more generic text that is marketed nationwide. It is a matter of economics. Should you encounter a new fifth-grade text that goes only to 1850, it is fairly safe to assume the book was designed for another state's program, in this case, California.

TABLE 3.3   Selected Children's Literature Used in the California Social Studies Program (Abridged)

Grade	Topic	Children's Literature
K	Learning and Working, Now and Long Ago	*Jack and the Beanstalk, Goldilocks, Aesop's Fables*
1	A Child's Place in Time and Space	*Little Toot, Little Red Lighthouse, Mike Mulligan and His Steam Shovel*
2	People Who Make a Difference	*Johnny Appleseed* Other myths, folktales, and legends
3	Understanding Continuity and Change	*White Stallion, Wagon Wheels, The Drinking Gourd*
4	California: A Changing State	
5	The Making of a New Nation, to 1850	*Immigrant Kids* *Waiting for Mama*
6	Ancient Civilizations, to A.D. 500	Selections from Greek and Roman literature and the Bible
7	The Medieval World, A.D. 500 to 1789	*Pillow Book, Song of Roland* *Tale of Genji*
8	U. S. History, 1783–1914	*Huckleberry Finn, My Ántonia*

• • • •

A Distinctive Variation: The CORE Curriculum

• • • •

The CORE Knowledge Program

For many years, most variations to traditional social studies programs were produced by states, like the California program just considered. However, in 1991, a group of educators who were inspired by E. D. Hirsch's book *Cultural Literacy* (1988), decided to use it as the basis for an elementary curriculum that would have national circulation. The last section of *Cultural Literacy* contained a listing of five thousand names, dates, phrases, and concepts ranging from names such as Aaron (Hank), through colloquial sayings such as "A stitch in time saves nine" to places around the globe, such as Zurich (Switzerland), that Hirsch believed reflected the "core" knowledge that everyone should know to be considered "culturally literate." However, Hirsch did not identify his criteria for selecting the five thousand items, and this reluctance has remained a bone of contention among his critics. Nevertheless, the educators organized those random elements into an instructional program.

CORE is not an acronym

The product of the group's effort is called the CORE Curriculum. In this instance, CORE is not an acronym; rather, it refers to the "core" of fundamental knowledge that was referred to above. The CORE Curriculum is a comprehensive program that covers all subject areas except reading, and is designed to comprise 50 to 60 percent of an elementary curriculum. A second distinguishing feature of the CORE Curriculum is its content specificity; it lays out exactly what teachers are expected to teach in each subject and at each grade level. The Core Knowledge Foundation makes teacher-developed sample units available at its Web site (**http://www.coreknowledge.org**), but it does not otherwise specify how teachers should teach the material.

E. D. Hirsch, Jr., is among the individuals we identified in Chapter 1 as critics of multidisciplinary social studies. He argues that multidisciplinary social studies does not allow children to study history and geography in enough depth to enable them to become historically and geographically literate. Because of Hirsch's position, it should be no surprise that the words *social studies* do not appear in the CORE materials. Instead, the CORE Curriculum's "social studies" component is organized around three strands: World Civilizations, which focuses primarily on world history; American Civilizations, which includes U.S. history and studies of western cultures including Central and South America; and Geography. Table 3.4 shows how the "social studies" component of the CORE Curriculum differs from a traditional social studies program.

In place of the expanding-environments pattern, the CORE program reflects an organizing principle that has been used for years throughout Europe: historical chronology. In practice, this means that students study older civilizations before they study modern civilizations. This seemingly modest change has some far-reaching consequences because it means, for example, that first graders study ancient Egypt, and second graders study ancient Rome, both topics that are far removed from the family, school, and neighborhood focus of traditional programs at those grade levels. At the same time, spreading the study of world and American civilizations across the grades (from K through 6) means that instead of having to consider almost all of American history at Grade 5 and almost all of world history at Grade 6, as is the case in traditional social studies programs, both teachers and children have opportunities to examine these areas in greater depth than would otherwise be the case.

Since the CORE Curriculum was created in 1991 it has been adopted by more than a thousand schools across the country (Whitmire, 2000). This acceptance has been fairly rapid, especially considering that none of the currently available textbook series are geared to it. Teachers sometimes use one of seven books that accompany the program, variously titled *What Your Kindergartner* (First Grader, Second Grader, etc.) *Needs to Know* (Hirsch, 1991–1993), which highlight the topics taught at each grade level. In place of regular textbooks, CORE teachers usually make extensive use of informational books and whatever other resources they can lay their hands on. It almost goes without saying that the CORE Curriculum places a heavy burden on teachers, especially during their first year using the program.

Does the CORE Knowledge Program work? It seems to, but until recently, the data on student performance has been limited. Information provided by the Core Knowledge Foundation (Marshall, 1996) indicated that administrators in CORE schools credit the program with improving students' performance on standardized tests. More recently, in a rigorous study conducted in Oklahoma City (Whitmire, 2000), three hundred students from CORE Knowledge schools were matched on five criteria with a comparison group of three hundred

History and geography are treated separately

The organizing principle: chronology

No textbook, per se

Recent research

TABLE 3.4   Comparison of Traditional Social Studies and CORE Curriculum

Grade	Traditional Program Topics	CORE Curriculum Strands		
		World Civilizations	**American Civilizations**	**Geography**
K	Family and School	Seven Continents	American Geography Native Americans Columbus/Mayflower	Maps and globes
1	Family and Community	Early Civilizations: Egypt, etc. World Religions Mexico	Early Civilizations: Mayas, Incas, Aztecs Early Colonies to Independence	Place location for topics at left
2	Neighborhood	Ancient Civilizations: India, China, Greece Modern Civilizations: Japan	The Constitution Westward Expansion Civil War	Geography of the Americas and World Civilizations
3	Community	Ancient Rome Byzantine Civilizations	Earliest Americans The 13 Colonies	Geography of the Mediterranean
4	The State	The Middle Ages Islam and Holy Wars Medieval Africa and China	American Revolution The Constitution Presidents and Heroes	Mountains Geography of Africa
5	The Nation (U.S. History)	Meso-Americans: Mayas, Aztecs European Exploration Renaissance English Revolution Russia	Westward Expansion The Civil War Reconstruction	The Political Geography of Europe Geography of topics at left
6	The World (World History)	Lasting Ideas from Ancient Civilizations: Judaism and Christianity, Greece and Rome, Capitalism and Socialism Latin America	Immigration, Industrialization, Urbanization America as a World Power	Geography of topics at left

students from traditional (non-CORE Knowledge) schools. The matching criteria included: age, grade level, race, sex, income level, and students' scores on the (standardized) Iowa Test of Basic Skills. To be included in the study, each student had to match on all five criteria. The results? After one year, almost all the CORE Knowledge students scored higher than the non-CORE Knowledge students— not on average, but individually! Researchers are currently following up on this study to determine whether other factors may have played a role, such as more motivated teachers among the CORE Knowledge group.

What the Critics Say About CORE Knowledge.   Criticisms of the CORE Knowledge Program typically focus on three elements: (1) concerns that the program is developmentally inappropriate, (2) concerns that the program is essentially a nineteenth-century course of study repackaged for the twenty-first century, and (3) concerns about how its elements were identified for inclusion. It is oversimplified but essentially correct to say that concerns about the developmental appropriateness (or inappropriateness) of the CORE stem from individuals' beliefs about what kinds of experiences are within (or beyond) a child's realm of experiences, and thus, what he or she is "ready for." Some critics cite the expectation that first graders will study ancient Egypt as an example of developmentally inappropriate subject matter. And when you think about it, few things might seem further removed from a seven-year-old's life than ancient Egypt. On the other hand, if you talk to first-grade CORE Knowledge teachers, they are likely to tell you that although they initially had concerns about the developmental appropriateness of topics like ancient Egypt, those concerns vanished when they saw how enthusiastically their students responded.

Developmental appropriateness?

A second and perhaps more fundamental criticism involves the question of whether traditional knowledge—what some critics refer to as nineteenth-century knowledge—is what students need to live in the twenty-first century. A colleague, for example, refers to CORE Knowledge as "the curriculum based on dead white males." CORE supporters usually respond that much of the core of common knowledge on which cultural literacy is based is indeed rooted in the past. A related criticism has focused on the strong Euro-American bias in the literary selections. For example, Peterson (1995) noted that over 80 percent of the poetry and literature selections are Euro-American, and over one-third of the non-European selections have animals as the main characters. This, Peterson argues, sends a not-so-subtle message that stories about non-European cultures are not as serious. Then, too, the inclusion of classic tales, such as Snow White and Cinderella, where passive females are rescued by handsome princes, have raised questions about gender equity. Still other critics have chastized E. D. Hirsch for his reluctance to identify the criteria he used for selecting the five thousand elements of "cultural literacy" (see Apple, 1993).

A nineteenth-century program?

Sexist literature?

The Core Knowledge Program is a distinctive variation from traditional social studies programs that requires much more teacher planning than do most traditional programs. Other approaches that teachers can take to create distinctive variations include using a thematic-unit approach or developing a concept-based social studies program. We consider these variations in the next section.

● ● ● ● Developing Social Studies Programs

You probably don't plan to design an entire social studies program in the next week or so, but this section provides an overview of program development elements that teachers and program developers should consider.

Basic Program Design Elements

The essential aspects of creating any instructional program are captured in four little words: *what, why, when,* and *how. What* am I expected to teach? *Why* am I expected to teach "this" instead of "that"? *When* in the year am I expected to teach something? And *how* am I supposed to do that? These are the basic questions of curriculum planning that teachers usually refer to as their "scope and sequence."

Scope.   The first decision in determining a social studies program involves scope. In other words, what segments of the universe of social studies knowledge

What to study   will be taught? In more practical terms, the question is one of whether a unit on "the farm" or "desert communities," for example, will or will not be included in a social studies program.

Concerns related to scope, or the *what* you plan to teach, must always be considered in relation to the question of *why* (or *why not*). Answering a question like Why should we include a unit on the farm?, for example, gets into matters of the program's rationale.

Why study it?   **Rationale.**   The question *why* ("this" topic instead of "that" topic) is a request for a rationale—a reasoned statement of justification about why children should be taught and expected to learn certain subject matter.

The curriculum guides that most new teachers receive seldom provide a justification for why the selected topics are worth being studied. Somewhere along the line, whoever created the program had to address that question, but the reasons why certain content was selected and other content ignored are seldom conveyed to teachers. As a result, you may find yourself wondering why you are expected to be teaching something. And if you aren't sure why you are supposed to be teaching something, it probably won't be long before your students are asking the same question.

In what order and   **Sequence.**   After determining what topics should be taught, and why, it then
at what grade?   becomes necessary to decide *when*—at what time and in what order, or sequence—to teach them.

Sequencing subject matter has two dimensions: a "between-grades" dimension and a "within-grade" dimension. First, it's necessary to determine at which grade level something will be taught. For example, having decided that a unit on "the farm" should be included in a program, the between-grade question is, At which grade level should "the farm" be taught? Once that question has been answered, the second element involves determining when (at what time during the year) it should be taught within that grade level.

The within-grade-level question concerns the sequencing of units within a grade level. For example, having determined that Greece, Rome, and ancient Egypt should be taught at a certain grade level (probably Grade 6), the next decision is to determine the order in which those topics will be taught. Sometimes that sequence may be based on a logical progression, such as from simple to complex; in other cases it may be arbitrary. When history is involved, as in this example, the sequence is invariably based on chronology. On that basis, you will teach ancient Egypt first. But which will come next—Greece or Rome?

Synthesis. How will everything be pulled together into a whole that is meaningful to students? There probably isn't any one best basis for sequencing a social studies program, but the program needs to be organized around something. To illustrate the importance of the synthesis, consider a third-grade social studies program that asks you to teach the following sequence of topics:

Making it meaningful

1. explorers
2. the geography of Australia
3. community helpers
4. transportation
5. the Civil War

If there is something—a theme, an approach, anything—that can pull these topics together so that they make sense, it isn't apparent. However, young children may not care about the sequence of topics they study as long as they are interesting. In some respects, sequencing may be more of a problem for adults than for children.

SUGGESTED ACTIVITY

Do you think it is important for children to understand the logic (the *why*) of what they are studying? In math? In social studies? In anything?

. . . .
Subject-Matter Considerations
. . . .

Social studies seldom imposes the kind of prerequisite prior learnings that you might associate with a subject such as mathematics. Children's vocabulary and reading ability may limit what you can teach, but this holds true for almost every subject area. The absence of a hierarchy or predetermined sequence in which history or social studies must be taught means that teachers have more latitude to use other factors, such as students' interests and abilities, as a basis for selecting content.

No hierarchy = more flexibility

There are many possible entry points to studying about the human experience, and some of these possibilities are illustrated in Table 3.5. By mixing and matching items from the various columns of Table 3.5, it is possible to create hundreds of alternative configurations for social studies. Each of these will reflect a different orientation and a different blending of content and instructional purpose. When we suggested that social studies could be approached in many different ways, we doubt that you anticipated quite this many possibilities!

Alternative entry points

TABLE 3.5   Alternative Menus for Social Studies

Objects of Study	Disciplines	Major Findings and Ways of Knowing	Instructional Purposes
The community	Anthropology	Value statements	Miniature scholars
Native Americans	Economics	Descriptions	Cognitive skill development
Area studies	Geography	Nonempirically based feelings	Accumulation of knowledge
The United States	History	Principles (analytic or empirical)	Concept development and testing
Non-Western civilization	Philosophy	Generalizations based on observations and probability	Creative use of individual and collective experience
The environment	Political science		Indoctrination
Change processes	Psychology		Social control
Minorities	Sociology		
Local, state, and national government			
Citizenship			
Consumer economics			

· · · ·
Developmental Considerations
· · · ·

Creating a viable social studies program must also consider young children's abilities to deal with elements like time, space, and distance.

Children's concepts of time

Time.   It isn't entirely clear how children develop a sense of time, especially historical time. Apparently children's conceptions of time—including personal time, social time, and historical time—develop at different rates and so gradually that children are unaware of what is taking place.

When young children enter elementary school, they have a fairly secure conception of "yesterday." But events that happened to them prior to yesterday—two weeks, two months, or two years ago—are usually thought of as happening "a long time ago," somewhere in a vast and undifferentiated past. However, because young children sometimes have difficulty differentiating the time span of past events does *not* mean that they have forgotten what happened. Children can often describe past events—vacations, birthday parties, or other experiences—in excruciating detail. They can tell *what* happened, but they may be unable to provide an accurate time frame for *when* the events took place.

TECHNOLOGY UPDATE

So All Can See

Asking your class to crowd around one 14-inch computer screen is probably inviting problems. Someone is almost sure to step on someone else's foot, whether intentionally or not. How then do you use computer-based technology so that everyone can see, but without having to crowd around a single monitor?

There are at least four possible solutions to this problem. One is to use a liquid crystal display (LCD) device that fits on an overhead projector and that projects the computer-driven image on a screen. The image is not always as bright as you might hope for, and special overhead projectors that don't produce too much heat are required.

A second option is to get a device that projects the computer-driven image on a screen. Computer projectors are becoming less expensive than they once were ($250 and up), and they permit large groups to view the image simultaneously. A third option is to get one of the "black boxes" that will project computer images through a TV set. This is a less costly option ($100 or so) than the others because most schools already have the TVs available. A fourth option is to download the files onto a disk and then allow children to view them when it is their turn to use the computer. The disk option is the least costly, but it does not permit the entire class to view the images simultaneously. Nevertheless, it is a plausible alternative as schools acquire the resources to use computer-based technology effectively.

At about age ten or eleven, children's conceptions of time apparently permit them to feel an awareness (but not a complete understanding) of the historical past. All of this does *not* mean that history is out of the question for younger children, however. Even very young children can often relate vicariously to the individuals and events of history, particularly if those events are presented in narrative (story) form.

Children's views of space and distance

Space and Distance.   Children's conceptions of space—how they fit into their environment—and distance (physical remoteness) seem to develop in ways similar to their conception of time. Initially, distance is measured by the number of *fars* they attach to *away*. As any young child can tell you, "far, far away" is much farther than "far away."

KEY IDEA

The organization of social studies programs is (or should be) influenced by developmental considerations, including how children develop concepts of time, space, and distance.

Eventually everyone develops conceptions of time and space. It's something all of us do, simply through the process of living. Thus we question whether trying to speed up processes that will occur normally is a good investment of our time. Instead of trying to accelerate the way your students perceive time, space, or distance, you can teach educationally valuable things that do not require them to alter the way they view their world.

• • • •

Organizational Considerations

• • • •

This section presents two distinctive ways to organize subject matter for a social studies program. These include: (1) thematic units, which integrate elements from several subject areas, and (2) a concept-based approach, which provides a way for children to organize what might otherwise be isolated facts.

Thematic and Topical Units.   The whole-language approach to reading and language arts has come under fire in some parts of the country. Nevertheless, the underlying belief that the components of language—reading, writing, spelling, handwriting, and so on—are best learned and taught in contextualized settings instead of as separate subjects makes intuitive sense. Teachers in whole-language classrooms often provide those settings by organizing units around a theme or topic, such as "desert environments," "time," or even "bears" or "dinosaurs."

Fusion   More and more teachers are recognizing that it is possible to integrate elements from several subject areas into what are sometimes called *transdisciplinary units*. It is needlessly redundant, for example, to study a unit on desert environments in science at one point in the year, and then study a unit on desert communities in social studies later in the year. By carefully selecting themes and topics, and by identifying learning experiences that seem to cluster together, it is possible and often desirable to integrate across subject areas.

The key question: Is it worth learning?   Before you spend hours developing a thematic unit, be certain that the theme you select is worth studying. Children might very well enjoy a three-week unit on bears, for example, but you need to ask yourself just how much about bears children need to know. And does a unit on bears have enough substance and learning potential to warrant spending three weeks on it? Second, as more and more teachers develop thematic units on their "pet" topics, the chances increase for children to study essentially the same topics over two or more grade levels. Thematic units on "rainforests" are apt candidates for such problems (see Hirsch, 2001). Despite the fact that rainforests offer an opportunity for some spectacular classroom displays, and despite the fact that such units usually focus on animals, which most children find inherently interesting, you need to ask yourself how much about rainforests children need to know. Separate thematic units on rainforests or similar topics in Grades 2, 3, and 4 are likely to be repetitious at best.

Figure 3.2 shows an abridgement of a web for a thematic approach to time that was developed by Pappas, Kiefer, and Levstik (1995). The original of this figure fills two 8½-by-11-inch printed pages.

Figure 3.2 shows that the overall theme of time was divided into several subthemes, including "Changes over Time," "Personal Time," and "Measuring Time." Instructional activities and relevant works of children's literature were then identified for each subtheme. Titles of the children's books for each subtheme are shown in italics, and complete citations are provided in the references for this chapter.

Concept-Based Approaches.   In most traditional social studies programs, the emphasis is on learning the information associated with whatever topic is the focus. If the topic was Holland, for example, you probably learned about tulips, and chocolate, and cheese. If the topic was China, you probably studied things associated with the geography and climate of China, China's government, China's resources, and other aspects of life in that nation. If the next unit was

FIGURE 3.2   Partial Web for Thematic Unit: Time

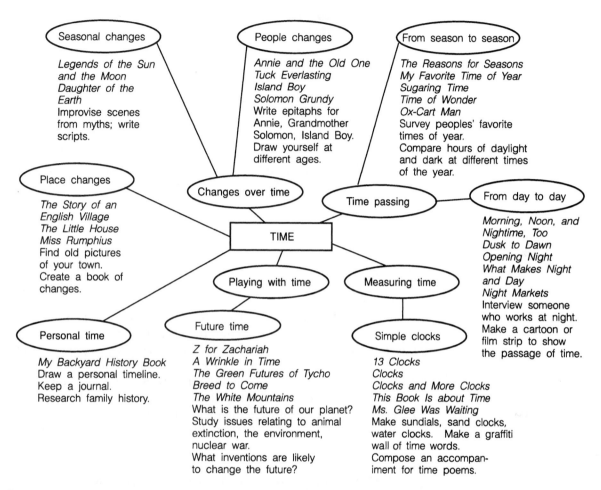

Source: From *An Integrated Language Perspective in the Elementary School: Theory into Action* by Christine C. Pappas, Barbara Z. Kiefer, and Linda S. Levstik. Copyright © 1995, 1990 by Longman Publishing Group. Reprinted with permission.

Japan, you went through the same process again, this time studying Japanese agriculture, the climate of Japan, and so forth. This topic-by-topic approach is illustrated in Figure 3.3.

Topical vs. concept-based approaches

A quite different approach is based on following a single concept or idea through several different applications. In other words, the concept-based approach is based on the idea that it is not necessary to study every country in the world to be able to say something about how nations organize their governments, practice agriculture, or use their resources, and so on. By studying only selected nations (instead of the entire universe of nations) it is possible to identify patterns

FIGURE 3.3   A Traditional Topic-by-Topic Approach

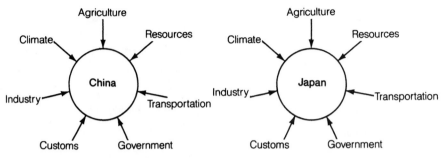

Source: *Teacher's Handbook for Elementary Social Studies* by Hilda Taba, Mary C. Durkin, Anthony H. McNaughton, and Jack R. Fraenkel. © 1967 by Addison-Wesley Publishing Company. Used by permission of Pearson Education, Inc.

among nations. Figure 3.4 illustrates that it is possible to identify *patterns* in agricultural practices by studying agriculture in China, India, Japan, Russia, and the United States.

In traditional programs, students often become so concerned with the "parts"—the climate, the government, the customs, and so on—that they may not see the "whole." By focusing on agricultural practices in Thailand, in Laos, in China, and in Japan, children tend to treat each nation separately, and in that process may miss the point of agricultural practices that are common to heavily populated areas in the Pacific Rim or elsewhere.

An emphasis on the whole   In a concept-based approach, the focus shifts from the parts to the "whole." This parts/whole emphasis is illustrated by the questions associated with each

FIGURE 3.4   A Concept-Based (Selected-Dimensions) Approach

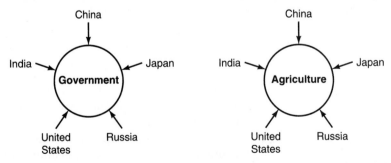

Source: *Teacher's Handbook for Elementary Social Studies* by Hilda Taba, Mary C. Durkin, Anthony H. McNaughton, and Jack R. Fraenkel. © 1967 by Addison-Wesley Publishing Company. Used by permission of Pearson Education, Inc.

approach. In a topic-by-topic approach, at least seven questions are generated, all of which follow this general form: "What is Chinese (agriculture, transportation, etc.) like?" The same questions are then asked about Japan. The result may be fourteen or so pieces of discrete data. In a concept-based approach, however, such an examination has fewer questions, and each is studied in greater depth.

When to use which approach

A concept-based approach can help students become aware of patterns that exist among cultures, but it is not appropriate for some elements, especially truly unique elements such as a culture's customs and rituals. For example, if your interest is in Japanese customs, it will be necessary to study Japan. On the other hand, if you are interested in determining whether some customs are common to nations in the Far East, you would need to study several Far Eastern nations to decide.

Perhaps one reason that concept-based instruction has not been more widely accepted is that most teachers lack familiarity with it. Not having experienced concept-based instruction as students, they will tend to use the topic-by-topic approach with which they are more familiar. In a concept-based program, for example, the children might study the sixteenth- and seventeenth-century Spanish monarchs, the Mayflower Compact, and the Inuit (Eskimos). From a traditional perspective, these would be seen as three separate and unrelated topics, but as Figure 3.5 illustrates, the focus for all three is the concept "social control."

A concept-based approach to social control

You may recall that the Mayflower Compact was produced by the travelers on the good ship *Mayflower*, who agreed in writing to govern (control) themselves for the common good. The Inuit on the other hand govern themselves by elaborate but unwritten laws and traditions. The Spanish monarchy serves as an exemplar of absolute control based on the divine right of kings. The differences among these forms of social control provide the basis for contrast.

Concept-based programs may sometimes seem a little piecemeal, especially to individuals who are familiar with traditional topic-based approaches. As a result, some teachers occasionally provide in-depth case studies of a single culture, subculture, or nation. However, a concept-based approach to social studies allows children to learn about human behavior in general, as opposed to learning unrelated ideas about many different subjects.

KEY IDEA

Traditional social studies programs usually examine various facets of a topic, whereas alternative social studies programs usually examine various facets of a concept or an idea.

FIGURE 3.5 An Approach to the Concept *Social Control*

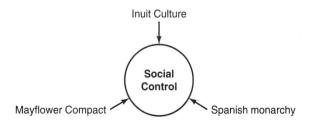

SUMMARY

Traditional K–6 social studies programs are based on the expanding-environments (or expanding-horizons) approach, where children progress from environments they are close to—such as the home, family, school, and neighborhood—in the primary grades, to more distant environments—the state, the nation, and the world—at the intermediate grades. The organizing principle for expanding environments exhausts itself at the end of Grade 6 (what do you study after you have examined the world?), so middle-school programs at Grades 7 and 8 typically repeat elements that students studied at the elementary grades. Grade 7 programs often focus on state history, or world geography, while Grade 8 programs usually deal with American history, but without the geography elements common in most elementary programs.

The CORE Knowledge Program is a recent and distinctive variation to traditional K-8 programs, especially in the area of social studies. Because of E. D. Hirsch's philosophical belief that multidisciplinary social studies does not permit students to study subjects in depth, the social studies component of the CORE Knowledge Program focuses on three strands that students study at each grade level: World Civilizations (world history and geography), American civilizations (history and geography), and geography. The organizing principle for the "social studies" portion of the CORE Knowledge Program is historical chronology. This means that children in the early grades study ancient civilizations, such as Egypt, Greece, and Rome, instead of waiting until Grade 6, as is more common in traditional programs.

Other variations to traditional social studies programs include: (1) the thematic unit approach, in which content from several subject areas is integrated around a topic such as "the desert," or "time"; and (2) a concept-based approach, in which children examine patterns among cultures, such as how they organize their governments, practice agriculture, or exercise control over their citizens.

SUGGESTED READINGS AND RESOURCES

Print Resources

E. D. Hirsh, Jr. (Ed). (1992). *What your third grader needs to know.* New York: Doubleday. This is one book from the Core Knowledge series edited by the author of *Cultural Literacy;* other books have similar titles for different grade levels, for example, *What your first grader needs to know.* Various sections cover language arts, American and world civilization, fine arts, mathematics, and the natural sciences.

Catherine Cornbleth & Dexter Waugh. (1995). *The great speckled bird: Multicultural politics and educational policy-making.* New York: St. Martin's Press. If you are interested in exploring how political pressures can influence the curriculum, this book is where you should begin.

Stephanie Steffy & Wendy J. Hood (Eds.). (1994). *If this is social studies, why isn't it boring?* York, ME: Stenhouse. This book is just as delightful as its title. It contains fifteen first-person essays by teachers and others describing how they brought new life to social studies classes by integrating different kinds of literature.

Internet Resources

Introductory Note: Web sites sometimes change their Internet addresses or cease operating entirely. All the addresses supplied here were operating when this book was printed, but if any of them fails to work properly, enter the name of the target organization in any standard search engine.

CORE Knowledge Program

http://www.coreknowledge.org

Information on this program is available at this Web site or from the CORE Knowledge Foundation, 801 East High Street, Charlottesville, VA 22902; 804-977-7550. A periodic newsletter, *Common Knowledge,* is also available.

H-Net, Humanities and Social Studies Online

http://www.h-net.msu.edu/

This site contains the Michigan State University collection of discussion networks and information on a wide range of subjects. A useful site for making contact with others interested in teaching social studies.

The Resource Center of the Americas

http://www.americas.org

This Web site offers innovative and challenging curricula designed to build bridges between people throughout the Americas. The Center also offers a huge lending library of books, periodicals, and videos on the Americas.

The Social Studies Curriculum: Conceptual Teaching

http://www.sasked.gov.sk.ca/docs/midlsoc/gr6/ g6currss.html

This highly recommended Web site is maintained by the provincial Department of Education in Saskatchewan and offers useful information about the grade-level placement of concepts and associated social studies skills.

Contexts for Teaching
• •
Social Studies

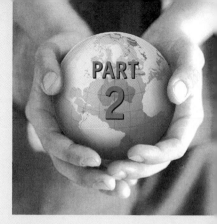

Part 2 examines the factors that furnish a context for teaching social studies— or any subject—in schools today.

The first two chapters are devoted to the increasingly culturally and educationally diverse student audiences in schools everywhere. A significant portion of Chapter 4, The Dimensions of Cultural Diversity, focuses on multicultural education as a means for addressing cultural diversity. Other sections of Chapter 4 address the diversity that students from specific cultural and ethnic groups may reflect. Chapter 5, The Dimensions of Instructional Diversity, focuses on meeting the needs of students who may be physically or emotionally challenged, display learning disabilities, or have preferred learning styles.

In turn-of-the-century schools, character education was used to describe efforts to mold children into responsible citizens. Over the years the term "character" fell into disfavor, for reasons described in Chapter 6, Developing Character and Values. Devoting a major section of this chapter to building character, as well as the inclusion of the term *Character* in the title, reflect changes in the broader society that are imposing new demands on what schools and teachers do.

Chapter 7, Social Studies: Gateway to Literacy, focuses on language literacy and children's ability to encounter social studies. This does not mean that social studies should be taught as reading, especially the type where children open their textbooks and begin reading aloud. Rather, the emphasis is on using social studies to enhance children's literacy skills without doing a disservice to either social studies or literacy.

4

The Dimensions of Cultural Diversity

KEY QUESTIONS

- **What kinds of diversity should you anticipate in your classroom?**
- **How do you accommodate diverse students' interests and abilities?**
- **How can teachers avoid cultural and gender bias?**
- **How can teachers approach multicultural education?**

Introduction: On Mottoes and Metaphors

DIVERSITY

The eagle on the Great Seal of the United States, which is on the back of a dollar bill, is holding a ribbon or scroll in its beak. Inscribed there is our national motto: *e pluribus unum*—"Out of many, one." The notion of *E pluribus unum* is such a dominant theme in the multicultural education literature that it seemed to provide an appropriate introduction to this chapter on diversity.

Are we one? or many? or both?

The current interest in *E pluribus unum* focuses not on "the many," for we are indeed a nation of immigrants, but on *unum*—the "one." The question today is, Is the United States *one*—a nation with a common culture that binds us together? Or would our national character be better described by *E pluribus pluribus*—out of many, many? As Barber (1992) suggested, the diversity of America is at once a virtue, a source of pride, a brave boast, a troubling reality, and an unsettling problem that muddles what it means to be an American.

When people try to describe the American character, they sometimes turn to metaphors. For example, our society, and schools especially, were once described as a "melting pot" from which recently arrived immigrants were expected to emerge as "Americans." Regardless of an individual's prior ethnicities—whether they were Italian-Americans, African-Americans, or Chinese-Americans—the idea was to get rid of that hyphen and make everyone fully qualified members of the mainstream American culture.

Changing metaphors

The problem with most metaphors is that they seldom "fit" perfectly. Many people's problem with the melting pot image stemmed from the belief that America is not a single culture but a multitude of cultures, each with traits and characteristics that contribute to the larger society. The longer hyphenated descriptors—European-American, African-American, and so on—may reflect an effort to capture this notion. Nevertheless, when the melting pot notion fell into disfavor, some people turned to a "salad bowl" metaphor, in which each ethnicity retains its separate identity but still contributes to the whole. Describing America as a salad bowl was an improvement over the melting pot, but this metaphor too has problems. Among other things, it's too easy to overemphasize the ingredients in the salad and neglect the importance of the bowl—which represents the beliefs and values that all Americans have in common.

Instead of a food-related metaphor, consider describing American society as a mosaic—a work of art when it is assembled, but simply a collection of individual pieces before it is put together. The parts-whole relationship of a mosaic also captures the duality of *cultural pluralism* noted in Chapter 1. This is because all of us must deal with at least two cultures, sometimes simultaneously: the common American culture that everyone shares, and our individual ethnicities that set each of us apart from other people. If you question whether there are beliefs and values that all of us share, consider what would likely happen if the people who argue that we have no common values were denied their right to state that position. Phrases like "freedom of speech" and "the Bill of Rights" would probably appear as if out of nowhere.

> **⊗ SUGGESTED ACTIVITY**
>
> Design a poster or bulletin board that uses a metaphor to desribe our multicultural society. Consider pizza as a possibility, but do not restrict yourself to food-related products. Then determine in what respects your description might be distorted.

Why Diversity Has Become a Concern

The diversity that you and every teacher must deal with has grown tremendously in the last twenty or so years. One reason for this is *desegregation,* in the broadest sense of that term. *Brown v. Topeka Board of Education* (1954) marked the beginning of the end of racially segregated schools, although the effects of the Supreme Court's ruling were by no means immediate. In addition, and after years of progress, there are growing concerns that the end of busing has led to schools that are becoming re-segregated. According to Orfield, Frakenberg, and Lee (2003), the average Latino student attends a school where the majority of students are Latinos. Likewise, in 1957 President Eisenhower had to call out the National Guard to enroll the first nine African-American students in Central High School in Little Rock, Arkansas. Today, the majority population of Central High is African-American.

Why classrooms are more diverse today

The end of overt racial segregation has accounted for some of the increased diversity in classrooms today, but the end of another more subtle form of segregation also had a discernible impact. The Individuals with Disabilities Education Act of 1990, which extended Public Law 94-142, continued to reduce the number of physically and educationally disabled students who were formerly segregated into separate, often special education, classrooms. The legislation did not abolish separate classes entirely, but it did require that students be placed in the *least restrictive environment:* that is, environments that best met the student's needs. That environment might be a regular classroom, a regular classroom plus special services in separate classrooms (which are known as pull-out programs), placement in a totally separate classroom, or, in the most extreme cases, institutionalization. The key point is that one effect of PL 94-142 and subsequent legislation was to increase substantially the diversity in regular classrooms.

Other factors

Three other factors also account for the increased diversity in classrooms today: (1) demographic changes resulting from new immigration, (2) increasing minority populations, and (3) an increased recognition of the ethnicities of all students, many of whom had been in classrooms all along. For example, there is an elementary school in San Francisco where students may speak one or more of twenty-seven different languages in their homes. This situation, both in California and elsewhere, has resulted largely from increased immigration—primarily from Mexico, Central America, and the Pacific Rim. As a consequence, in many of the large school districts in America, the majority of students are currently nonwhite or soon will be.

When the melting pot was the prevailing metaphor, the dominant belief was that the faster newly arrived students dropped the hyphen and began thinking of themselves as "Americans," the better. But if you think about it, expecting people to submerge their ethnicities was tantamount to asking them to deny their heritage. It was a nearly impossible expectation to begin with, as many third- or fourth-generation, American-born offspring of immigrants and enslaved peoples will readily attest. It is also an expectation that diminishes one of the qualities on which our nation of immigrants was built. Instead of denigrating or trying to erase individual ethnicities, many people today prize them for the contributions they make to the mosaic of life in America. Some people are reinserting that infamous hyphen to describe themselves as African-Americans or European-Americans, even though it has been centuries since their ancestors came from either Africa or **Honoring one's heritage** Europe. It's the heritage that matters, not the time span.

This chapter examines the educational impact that the increasingly diverse American culture has and will have on those of us who teach its future citizens. To provide a context, a profile of a classroom that reflects some of the different kinds of diversity you are likely to encounter in your own classroom is presented. The focus then turns to ways in which you can address some forms of diversity, including cultural, racial, gender, and religious differences. Chapter 5 follows up with the various physical, emotional, and learning disorders that may exist regardless of race and ethnicity. For lack of a better term, the latter group is referred to as reflecting educational or "instructional" diversity.

● ● ● ● A Classroom Profile

The following vignette illustrates the diversity you are apt to encounter wherever you teach. This vignette describes a fourth-grade classroom at Roscoe Hunt Elementary School, a racially and ethnically mixed magnet school located in a lower-middle-class neighborhood. Hunt Elementary serves neighborhood children as well as students from other parts of the city who want to take advantage of its enhanced programs in math and science.

Mary Jane Blanchard is in her third year of teaching fourth graders. She has between twenty-two and twenty-six students in her class—the number changes almost weekly. Every so often a student will leave and a new student will arrive or a former student will return. For example, one former student, Tyrone, has recently returned after spending three months living with his aunt in Chicago.

Only seventeen of the twenty-four currently enrolled students began the year with Ms. Blanchard.

Students may reflect multiple forms of diversity

The mobility of students in Mary Jane's classroom is high, but not as high as at Ramirez Elementary, the school featured in Chapter 1. Likewise, the diversity in Mary Jane's students is common, although she, like any teacher, has several students who are exceptions to the rule. Note also that although the following list looks long, this is because some students reflect multiple forms of diversity or exceptionality. Some of Ms. Blanchard's students include the following:

Academic considerations

- Five students—Tyrone, Trisha, Jesus, Miguel, and Maria—whose reading skills are *at least* one-half year below grade level; all of them spend a part of each day in the Resource Room, where they receive special tutoring in academic skills. Two of these students, Trisha and Miguel, have difficulty remembering what they read.

- Six students—Juan, LaShawna, Melissa, Gina, Richard, and Chen Lee—who, although they are fourth graders, have reading, math, and language skills that are at the sixth-grade level or above.

- Tyrone, Richard, and Christi—who have illegible handwriting, despite all Ms. Blanchard's efforts otherwise.

- Three other students—Jesus, Miguel, and Maria—who come from homes where Spanish is the dominant language.

- One student, Trang, who spoke no English at the beginning of the year (and no one in the school spoke Vietnamese).

Emotional considerations

- One student, Heather—a girl with apparently normal intelligence who spends her day huddled in her seat with her coat pulled over her head, almost as if she were withdrawing from the world.

- One gifted student, Chen Lee, who is a very hard worker and who places extraordinary emphasis on memorization. In math, for example, she memorizes the answers *and* the problems.

- One student, James, who has muscular dystrophy and is confined to a wheelchair.

- Another student, Jason, who takes the drug Ritalin to calm his hyperactivity.

Religious diversity

- Two students, Amy and Melissa, whose parents have requested that their children be excused from any lessons involving witches, ghosts, goblins, or other supernatural beings, all of which are offensive to their religious beliefs. In addition, Melissa's parents have requested that she be excused from saying the Pledge of Allegiance during the opening exercises, again because of the family's religious convictions.

- Six students—Tyrone, LaShawna, Patrick, James, DeLeon, and Charles—who come from single-parent homes. Four students live with their mother, one lives with his grandmother, and Charles lives with his father.

Mary Jane Blanchard's class is *not* an uncommon example. If you have any doubts about this, consider the kinds of diversity she does not have in her classroom—at least not this year. She does *not* have students who

- have limited vision or hearing,
- are cognitively disadvantaged,
- are absent from school more than three days every week,
- have infant alcohol or "crack baby" syndrome,
- have known tobacco, drug, or alcohol addictions, or
- are abused.

All classrooms are diverse, some more so and some less so than Mary Jane Blanchard's. This means that all teachers must adapt their teaching in ways that accommodate their students' needs. Some forms of diversity may require major instructional changes, like accommodating Trang's limited ability with English or Trisha's lack of reading skills. Other forms of exceptionality, such as making sure that Jason gets his medication on schedule, don't require instructional modifications, but they are things that a teacher must keep in mind.

The forms of diversity and exceptionality that are considered in this section include

Cultural diversity summarized

- cultural and ethnic diversity. Mary Jane's class currently has mainstream Anglo, Latino, African-American, Cuban-American, Mexican-American, mixed Anglo–Mexican American, and Haitian-American students. In addition, she teaches a variety of Asian-Americans, including students whose ancestry includes China, Taiwan, Vietnam, Laos, and Japan.

- religious diversity, especially as reflected by Amy and Melissa.

In the following sections, we look at how teachers can accommodate cultural, ethnic, and religious diversity.

KEY IDEA

Diversity is a normal part of life in classrooms today. The range of diversity in any classroom can be astounding—religious, cultural, physical, intellectual, and social.

● ● ● ● Responding to Cultural and Ethnic Diversity

The Three Little Pigs Revisited

Hidden messages

Remember "The Three Little Pigs," that tale filled with delightful opportunities for huffing, puffing and "blo-o-wing" the house down." As is often the case for children's stories, it is useful to look beneath the surface for hidden messages. For example, doesn't the "Three Little Pigs" extol the virtues of brick homes and, by implication, the people who build them? And isn't one of its underlying messages that hardworking people should build brick houses—homes that can withstand adversity? In addition to "brick is best," the story also seems to belittle homes made of straw and wood (sticks), as well as the "lazy types" who build them. It seems to say that "If those people would take some initiative and were willing to work a little harder, they could build themselves a good (brick) house too!" Then consider the countless thousands of people in the world who don't have a brick kiln nearby and who probably couldn't afford to buy bricks even if they did. They are likely to build their homes from inexpensive and readily accessible materials, like adobe, or stone, or logs. In very warm climates, some people's homes may consist of raised bamboo platforms that are open to the cooling breezes. Certainly such homes would not meet the standard set in "The Three Little Pigs." The question here is whether a home—any home—that is not built from bricks is necessarily inferior.

Teaching Implications

It would be easy to overstate the effects of inaccurate and possibly hurtful stereotyping in children's tales like "The Three Little Pigs." But should teachers ignore it entirely? Or should they stop using such stories because of the questionable stereotyping they contain? On one hand, most children seem readily able to handle fantasy, including pigs that talk and wolves that huff and puff. In addition, you don't want to be seen as someone who consistently denounces or takes all the fun out of classic stories. But from a social studies perspective, "The Three Little Pigs" and stories of similar ilk can furnish the basis for some brief lessons that counter the lightly disguised stereotyping they contain. For example, you could

- conduct a brief, follow-up examination of housing in different parts of the world, perhaps accompanied by pictures downloaded from the Internet. Be sure to include a picture of an English cottage with a thatched roof to show that straw (actually reeds) is still used for roofing material in some parts of the world. The overall idea here would be to show that housing often reflects the availability of materials.

- conduct a discussion of the "hidden messages" the "Three Little Pigs" contains. Do we know that people who live in brick houses are necessarily more industrious and harder working than people who live in other kinds of housing?

"The Three Little Pigs" is not alone among materials that can foster a particular worldview in the young (see Christiansen, 1994). The contemporary media is filled with programming that often generates stereotypes that are only slightly more open and varied than media of thirty-five to forty years ago. Individuals have only limited power to alter the stereotyping presented in the media, of course, but as teachers we can select the media we use with students and thereby control at least to some extent the intentional and unintentional racial and gender bias that might otherwise occur.

Cultural Diversity

Lisa Delpit (1995), in *Other People's Children,* writes about teachers who, when facing a multiracial class, sometimes say things like "I don't see color, I only see children" (p. 177). Would you consider this a situation where to acknowledge children's color is to insult them? Or is it a matter of fairness, of treating all

Children of color   children alike, regardless of race, color, or creed? Or is it a matter of taking a standard for fairness too far? Delpit questions the real message that this otherwise well-intentioned statement sends. Does it suggest that there's something wrong with being black or brown, and that it should *not* be noticed? Delpit argues, on the other hand, that if one does not see color, then one does not really see children.

Maintaining consistent standards of fairness and respect that apply to all students is something most teachers strive for. But Delpit suggests that carrying the fairness standard too far could have unintended consequences. For example, when some Native American students are called on to answer questions, they will remain silent—even when they know the answer. Such behavior may have led to the stereotype of the "nonverbal Native American." It may also cause some teachers to avoid calling on Native American students in large-group activities so as not

Cultural patterns   to embarrass them publicly. Unlike white, middle-class society, where everyone's contribution is valued, many Native American parents (as well as parents from Asian-American cultures) expect their children to sit quietly and observe—to be seen but not heard. The matter is further complicated by the fact that quick responses from Native American children are likely to be considered rude or disrespectful (Stokes, 1997). The first point here is that Native American children, who are usually as verbal as children anywhere *in small-group settings,* may find themselves caught between the differing expectations of two cultures. The second point is that although teachers are sometimes aware of some aspects of Native American cultures—such as their close relationship with the land and nature—teachers may not be aware of the differences in child-rearing practices, differences that can lead to erroneous conclusions and unintentional stereotyping. A third point concerns teachers who claim that to succeed in our culture, Native American children must (among other things) overcome their reluctance to talk in front of large groups. Part of that argument is surely valid, although it is not a foregone conclusion that Native American children will necessarily opt for success in the larger society. The

Intangible penalties   other side of the coin is that members of most minority groups will face intangible penalties if they seek to leave the warmth and support of their familiar culture so as to affiliate with and achieve "success" in a less familiar culture. In other words, not everyone wants to look like Vanna White and sound like Dan Rather, no matter how highly those personae may be valued in the dominant culture.

Even if you anticipate teaching in an area where there are few Native American students, children from other cultures may have equally unique ways of responding to the events around them. At the risk of overgeneralizing, some of these cultural differences that are particularly relevant to social studies are summarized here:

- Children from cultures that have strong, group storytelling traditions—which includes some Native American, Inuit, and Native Hawaiian groups—often prefer activities that demand lots of talking and small-group activities. As you might expect, students from these cultures often become frustrated with worksheet activities that they must complete individually and silently.

Cultural traditions   - Many students of Asian origins are reluctant to ask questions and express personal opinions because doing so may be considered rude and disrespectful to adults. In Korean and Japanese cultures especially, the idea that students must ask questions implies that the teacher did such a poor job in the initial teaching that additional questions were necessary. In other words, asking questions is not necessarily a way for students to clarify things they do not understand, but rather becomes a subtle way to attack the teacher.

● Many Latino and Hispanic *male* students will often look you boldly in the eye when you talk with them, regardless of whether you are male or female. However, many Latino and Hispanic *female* students (and some males) are trained to avoid looking directly at adults, especially males. They will sometimes look at the ceiling, or more often the floor, but they will avoid looking at some adults even if the adult says, "Look at me when I am talking to you." What we may interpret as disrespectful behavior may in fact be the ultimate sign of respect in cultures where one does *not* look into the eyes of someone older, someone you respect. Whenever you experience such behavior, it can take some getting used to.

Polar opposites

● Students from other cultures will sometimes display culturally defined behaviors that are polar opposites from what we consider appropriate. For example, individuals from some Oriental cultures indicate sympathy by laughing (usually while covering their mouth with their hands). This can be disconcerting for an uninformed teacher who, for example, announces to the class that he or she was absent to attend a relative's funeral, and then finds that some of their Oriental-American students cover their mouths and laugh. Instead of taking offense and saying, "This is not a laughing matter," a more culturally appropriate response would be a simple "Thank you."

Culturally defined expectations

● African-American students sometimes respond to teachers' questions in ways similar to the Native American students noted earlier. They may give short answers, flippant responses, or none at all. In traditional African-American communities, children are (1) seldom expected to contribute to adult discussions or (2) to ask direct questions (Shade & New, 1993). In addition, African-American students are likely to follow the "rules" that govern conversation in their native cultures or homes, rules that often differ considerably from the more restrained and laid-back conventions that govern conversations among Anglos. These differences are often reflected in the (1) passion, (2) animation (gestures), (3) pacing (fast) and (4) volume (often loud) of conversations among African-American speakers.

Muslim students

● In the aftermath of 9/11, Muslim students attending American schools have encountered even more problems than they did previously (Elnour & Bashir-ali, 2003). This is especially true of Muslim girls who follow Islamic dress codes, which require that their entire body except for their faces, hands, and feet must be covered. With such readily identifiable dress, it is difficult not to notice a female Muslim student. Nevertheless, they are culturally conditioned to stay separated from the whole group, and they often seat themselves in the back of the classroom, hoping they will blend into the woodwork. If they interact with anyone, it will most likely be other Muslim girls, but certainly not males—Muslim or otherwise. It is as if their goal is to be invisible.

From a social studies perspective, how Muslims are treated in the curriculum can pose problems for males and females alike. For example, when Christian teachers teach about the Crusades, it is too easy for the Muslims to be cast as the "bad guys" and the Christians as the "good guys"—despite the fact that the Christians were the invading force. When most of the class reflects the Judeo-Christian heritage, you can well imagine the hateful looks (or worse) that may be directed toward Muslim students—for events that occurred hundreds of years ago. Because it isn't easy to be seen as "the enemy," teachers must be especially cautious about how they cast the events of history.

• • • •
Teaching Implications
• • • •

Children from most non-Western cultures will seldom voluntarily tell you, for example, that "I don't ask questions because you'll think I'm rude." This means that identifying the cause for apparently troubling behaviors can become a form of "discovery" learning for teachers. Perhaps the easiest way to deal with this is to ask **Seeking underlying causes** the child directly about your concerns—in private and in the least threatening way possible. If the child says, "Yes, talking in front of the group really bothers me (for whatever reason)," the next question concerns whether this is something children will need to live with, or whether you are willing to use an alternative strategy that does not place students in an embarrassing position or leave them open to ridicule. Teachers may also need to clarify their motives by asking themselves why they are conducting question-and-answer sessions in a large-group format. Because it's convenient? Because they haven't really thought about it? Or do they believe that children will learn from and remember the other students' responses? Unless you can satisfy yourself that there are good reasons for using a whole-group, question-and-answer activity—sometimes erroneously referred to as a "discussion"—consider using a strategy where students respond to your questions in small groups. You then appoint one group member to report the group's findings to the larger group. This minor procedural change will (1) permit more students to participate simultaneously and (2) change the student's role from being "an answerer" to that of "a reporter." Such a subtle shift can eliminate many of the pressures that can cause problems for nonwhite students, especially students from Oriental and Native American cultures.

Many of the considerations that apply to nonwhite students also apply equally to African-American students, who are also obviously nonwhite. The research suggests that African-American students do better in school when teachers provide opportunities for them to think out loud and talk with their classmates in **Alternate strategies** informal, conversational settings, all of which are usually most feasible in small-group settings. The research also suggests that African-American students benefit from highly participatory activities, including role-playing and dramatic play, and by having teachers present materials auditorily, through music, chants, and rhyme (Gay, 1991, 1997; Delpit, 1995; Shade & New, 1993).

Role-playing and dramatic play are treated in Chapter 11, but consider a brief example of how you might incorporate an auditory approach to fifth-grade

American history. Assume that the class has been studying the origins of the Revolutionary War, and you want students to understand that the British Parliament already knew the American colonists were in ferment. After creating small groups, you randomly assign each group the task of summarizing and then presenting either the American or the British prewar position to the entire class. In addition, each group's report must be presented as a "rap." Because the grammar in many raps is purposefully atrocious, you might offer extra credit for raps that use good grammar (as would certainly be the case for Parliament's message to the colonists).

Does Everybody Really Know?

The first point here is that children from other cultures often react to everyday classroom situations in ways that are traditional and wholly acceptable in their respective cultures. The second and perhaps more important point is that children from other cultures often assume that you understand and accept their responses to situations. Their notions for how they should demonstrate respect and express sympathy, for example, much less for what are the "correct and appropriate" ways to respond to situations, are behavior patterns they have grown up with. Such children are often inclined to believe that "everybody knows" about them. This means that your students may be quite unaware of why you reacted so strongly when they refused to look you directly in the eye or used laughter to express their sympathy. They are likely to assume that everybody understands that laughter is a perfectly appropriate expression of sympathy—as it is in their culture—or that one should not look directly at a person he or she respects. The students may be equally unaware that their behavior is culturally determined, just as you may be unaware of the basis for their seemingly aberrant behavior. Because most children are not inherently mean-spirited, when encountering behaviors that you cannot explain, consider stopping for a moment, taking a deep breath, and then saying something like "OK" in as accepting a way as you can. Because it would be unfair to the children to drop matters at this point, you should probably talk with the child privately. You may also want to make inquiries about the children's behaviors among people you know and trust, preferably people with immediate knowledge of the cultures in question.

Exploring a different perspective

Teaching Implications

In developing social studies lessons and units, try to incorporate multiple perspectives—the "other side of the coin" if you will. For example, if you plan to teach about the Revolutionary War you should make every effort to present the British point of view as well as the colonial perspective. And if the Civil War is the focus, be certain that you include both the Union and Confederate perspectives. To deal with one perspective without the other could do a disservice to such studies.

In developing social studies lessons and units that focus on other cultures, try to include a component on child-rearing practices, or, if you prefer, "family life." As noted earlier, children in many cultures are expected to be seen but not heard. In still other cultures, girls are routinely expected to provide child care for their younger siblings and are strongly discouraged from interacting with boys outside the family. If you place girls from these cultures into work groups that also include boys, the girls may be very uncomfortable and may effectively withdraw from participation. The point here is that parental expectations for children probably have a more significant impact on a culture's way of life than do the foods they eat or the clothes they wear.

Cultural expectations

● ● ● ● Racism and Ethnic Diversity

· · · ·
"Being Bad Is the Way We Are"
· · · ·

Marc Elrich (1994) teaches in a school on the outskirts of Washington, D.C. All but two of the twenty-nine students in his sixth-grade class are African-American or Hispanic, and most of them are of low socioeconomic status—in other words, they are poor. In some respects, Marc doesn't face the range of diversity that Mary Jane Blanchard must deal with, but he faces some difficult problems nonetheless.

Marc teaches in a school that offers a range of programs that are meant to teach children to celebrate and prize their diversity. Yet despite the school's programs, many of Marc's students have such low self-esteem and low expectations for themselves that by the age of ten or eleven, many of them have opted out of the educational system.

Another classroom example

On one occasion Marc showed a film that he hoped would provoke a discussion of self-esteem. The film was based on a Langston Hughes story about an African-American youth who attempts to steal the purse of an elderly African-American lady. The youth fails, and the woman takes him into her home, where she applies a generous amount of love and understanding. The messages: love is a powerful medicine, and, with love, all of us can become better people.

In the postfilm discussion, it quickly became apparent that Marc's students hadn't bought the message. For example, one student said, "As soon as you see a black boy, you know he's gonna do something bad!" Marc's question: "Just because he's black, he's bad?" Student: "Everybody knows that black people are bad. That's the way we are." Marc: "Do you mean 'bad' like 'cool' or 'tough' or 'hot,' or do you mean 'bad' as in 'not good' or 'evil'?" (p. 12). The student meant the latter.

As the discussion continued, a disturbing picture began to emerge. Marc's students were nearly unanimous about the following comments:

Students' self-images and prejudices

- "Black people don't like to work hard."

- "Black boys expect to die young and unnaturally."

- "White people are smart and have money."

- "Asians are smart and have money."
- "Asians don't like blacks or Hispanics."
- "Hispanics are more like blacks than whites. They can't be white so they try to be black."
- "Hispanics are poor and don't try hard because, like blacks, they know it doesn't matter." (pp. 12–13)

Good at being bad

In subsequent discussions, Marc's students indicated that people who can afford the material goods associated with the "good life" get their money through guns and dealing in drugs. They also believed that wimps die young and live in fear, whereas tough guys die young but are proud. Likewise, bosses are white and workers are black, and black people don't do important things, except in school books. "But," Marc also indicated, "my students don't lack for pride. They are, in fact, quite proud of what they are. They were good at being bad, some were excellent at it, and the badder they were, the greater their social status" (p. 14).

Somewhere along the line, Marc Elrich's students had obviously learned some powerful lessons, perhaps not what we might have wanted and hopefully not in school, but powerful nonetheless. In reflecting on his experience, Marc indicated:

Students' responses to special programs

I gave a lot of thought to how we teach students to value diversity. The thoughts and words of my students make a mockery of our [school's] celebrations. Setting aside a month for black history or women's history seems strange and artificial to most students regardless of color. These children aren't naive. What are the other months: White Male History Months? History needs to be inclusionary, but it also needs to be natural so children come to see that there's nothing strange or odd about black people or women achieving success. I have begun to fear that singling out groups for special attention does more to foster suspicion, jealousy, and cynicism, than it does to promote understanding, empathy, and community. (p. 14)

Children are perceptive observers of their world, and for one to believe that teachers can change those views by teaching occasional lessons on successful African-Americans, Asian-Americans, or whatever, may be naive. As Elrich noted, ". . . children form their own impressions early on, and they sense the dissonance between the reality of life and the pretty pictures offered in school. If we are concerned with our children genuinely valuing diversity and with all children developing high self-esteem, then we have to offer our children genuine knowledge and insight into the world in which they live. I don't think we do" (p. 15).

Whether schools can single-handedly eliminate the kinds of stereotyping that Marc Elrich's students reflect is debatable. The fact that streetwise children may consider the examples of successful minorities that appear in textbooks—the Jackie Robinsons and the Martin Luther King Jrs.—as exceptions, as people far removed from the life they know, suggests that some of the underlying problems associated with racism extend beyond what schools can influence on their own.

Powerful lessons

Multicultural education programs (considered later in this chapter) may be able to address some of these problems, but for this to occur, students, teachers, and communities that the schools serve must regard multicultural education as an integral part of the school program, not simply an add-on designed to placate (or mislead) minority children.

● ● ● ● ● Sexism and Gender Equity Education

Sexist stereotyping

The first illustration in a first-grade social studies book from the 1960s shows a neatly dressed woman (possibly Beaver Cleaver's mother) standing on the front steps waving good-bye to her children as they board the school bus. Several pages later, a briefcase-carrying male arrives home from work (according to the text) and is shown, his feet on the ottoman, reading the newspaper while the woman (who we know by then is the wife and mother) is shown preparing dinner in the kitchen. When the family goes on trips—which families do often in first-grade books—guess who drives?

After over a decade of enhanced awareness of the need for more gender-equitable treatments, the messages that such illustrations can convey to children should hardly be lost on any of us. They begin with "A woman's place is in the home" and go on from there. Such messages are simplistic and sexist, and they inaccurately depict the roles and responsibilities of both women and men in modern society. Current social studies textbooks are far less guilty of such treatments, and typically show single-parent families, women in roles traditionally viewed as male, and men in roles traditionally viewed as female. However, recent studies suggest that instructional materials sometimes insert pictures of females, but say nothing about their substantive contributions (Kames, 2000). An annotated bibliography of women's contributions throughout history is included in the Resource Handbook.

Failing at Fairness

In a now-classic report that was published as *Failing at Fairness: How American Schools Cheat Girls* (1994), Myra and David Sadker analyzed a large group of social

TECHNOLOGY UPDATE

Multicultural Resources on the World Wide Web

The Internet offers an almost mind-boggling array of resources for diversity-related topics. Listings in addition to those highlighted here are contained in the Suggested Readings and Resources section at the end of the chapter.

An excellent source for multicultural/ethnic studies materials is the **Balch Institute for Ethnic Studies** at:

http://www.balchinstitute.org

This site has extensive listings of materials related to multicultural issues, many of which are downloadable. It also contains samples of historical materials that reflect stereotyped images of various ethnic and cultural groups.

The Montgomery County Maryland Public Schools maintains an outstanding program titled **"Making Multicultural Connections Through Trade Books"** at:

http://www.mcps.k12.md.us/curriculum/socialstd/MBD/Books_Begin.html

In addition to providing an extensive database of children's trade books for specific cultures, this site also identifies (a) relevant technology and (b) how that technology can be used with specific books. For example, Patricia Polacco's delightful stories, Chicken Sunday (New York: Scholastic, 1992) and Rechenka's Eggs (New York, Putnam and Gosset, 1998), both involve intricately designed, Ukranian (Easter) eggs—which are also known as "Pysanky" eggs. The program identifies relevant children's books and then links to software, in this instance Kid Pix Studio (Broderbund), and the Kid Pix Around the World Activity Book by Barbara Chan (Addison Wesley, 1994), which children can use to make their own Pysanky eggs.

A female pilot in the classroom can speak volumes about the increasing equity among individuals of either gender.
(© Michael Zide)

studies text materials and found that females were seriously underrepresented. In one sixth-grade, world history text, for example, only eleven female names were mentioned, and none of them were adult American women. As further evidence of the male-dominated curriculum, the Sadkers asked students at all levels of schooling to identify twenty famous American women from history who were not athletes or entertainers. The majority of students flunked miserably—most had difficulty identifying ten women, even though some of them had included names like Aunt Jemima and Betty Crocker to beef up their lists.

Thanks in part to efforts by the Sadkers and others, current texts are less guilty of slighting women than was true just ten years ago. African-American women, for example, such as Sojourner Truth (a former slave) and Harriet Tubman are presented more prominently than in the past. Yet other contemporary materials may still be guilty of promoting gender bias. For example, Bigelow (1996) suggests that the popular computer simulation *Oregon Trail* (MECC) can contribute to gender bias because even if students elect to play a female character, which is a selection they make at the beginning of the simulation, most subsequent decisions they are asked to make were usually made by males, not females. This does not mean *Oregon Trail* is unsuitable for children, but it does mean that some of the cautions that apply to classic fairy tales also apply to contemporary materials.

Current materials may reflect subtle gender bias

Guidelines for identifying sexism and racism in children's books are presented in Figure 4.1 on pages 108 to 109.

The immediate goal of gender equity education involves the equal treatment of people regardless of gender, but it is part of a broader goal that encompasses the inclusion of individuals regardless of gender, race, age, religion, or economic

FIGURE 4.1 Guidelines for Analyzing Children's Books for Racism and Sexism

Racism and sexism in children's books range on a continuum from blatant and intentional to subtle and inconsequential. The following are elements to consider.

1. The Illustrations

—— **Look for Stereotyping.** Stereotypes are over-simplified generalizations about a particular group, race, or sex, and usually carry derogatory implications. Look for instances where characters are ridiculed or demeaned because of their race or sex.

—— **Look for Tokenism.** Do the nonwhite characters look just like whites except for being tinted or colored in? Are minority faces depicted with distinctive features?

—— **Look at Who's Doing What?** Are minorities depicted in subservient and passive roles or in leadership and action roles? Are males shown as the "doers" and females as the observers?

2. Check the Story Line

The following checklist suggests some subtle forms of bias to watch for.

—— **Standard for Success.** Must people of color adopt "white" behavior standards to get ahead? Is "making it" in the dominant white society projected as the only ideal? Must people of color exhibit extraordinary qualities—excel in sports, get A's, and so on—to gain acceptance and approval? In friendships between white children and children of color, is it the child of color who does most of the understanding and forgiving?

—— **Resolution of Problems.** How are problems presented, conceived, and resolved in the story? Are people of color considered to be "the problem"? Are oppressions faced by women and people of color represented as causally related to an unjust society? Are the reasons for poverty and oppression explained or presented as inevitable? Does the story line encourage passive accept-ance or active resistance? Are the problems faced by a person of color resolved through the benevolent intervention of a white person?

—— **Role of Women.** Are the achievements of girls and women based on their initiative and intelligence, or are they due to their good looks or their relationship with boys? Are sex roles incidental or critical to characterization and plot? Could the same story be told if the sex roles were reversed?

—— **Use of Loaded Words.** Loaded words have insulting overtones and include examples such as *savage, primitive, conniving, lazy, superstitious, treacherous, wily, crafty, inscrutable, docile,* and *backward.* Look for sexist language and adjectives that exclude or ridicule women, or use the male pronoun to refer to both males and females.

3. Look at the Lifestyles

Are people of color and their settings depicted in ways that contrast unfavorably with the unstated norm of white middle-class suburbia? If the non-white group is depicted as "different," are negative value judgments also implied? Are people of color depicted exclusively in ghettos, barrios, or migrant camps? In depicting another culture, do the illustrations and text offer genuine insights into another lifestyle? Look for inaccuracy and inappropriateness in the depiction of other cultures. Be wary of the "quaint-natives-in-costume" syndrome, which is usually most noticeable in areas like clothing and customs, but can extend to behavior and personality traits as well.

FIGURE 4.1   Guidelines for Analyzing Children's Books for Racism and Sexism (*continued*)

4. Weigh the Relationships Between People

—— **Power.** Do the whites in the story possess the power, take the leadership, and make all the important decisions? Do people of color and females function in essentially supporting roles?

—— **Family Relationships.** In African-American families, is the mother always dominant? In Latino families, are there always lots of children? If the family is separated, are societal conditions—unemployment, poverty—cited among the reasons for the separation?

5. Note the Heroes

The key question to ask here is: "Whose interest is a particular character serving?" Are minority heroes (when they appear) admired for the same qualities that have made white heroes famous, or because what they have done has benefited white people?

6. Consider the Effects on a Child's Self-Image

Are norms established that limit a child's aspirations and self-concepts? Are African-American children continuously bombarded with images of the color white as the ultimate in beauty, cleanliness, virtue, and so on, and the color black as evil, dirty, menacing, and so on? Does the book counteract or reinforce exclusively positive associations with the color white and negative associations with black?

Do individuals of one sex perform all of the brave and important deeds? Are individuals of either sex denigrated because they are not fair-skinned or slim of body? Are there one or more characters with whom children of color can readily identify to positive and constructive ends?

7. Author's (or Illustrator's) Background, Qualifications, and Perspective

Analyze the biographical material (on the jacket flap or the back of the book) to determine whether the author(s) or illustrator(s) seem qualified to deal with the subject. If the author and illustrator are not members of the group being written about, is there anything in their background that would recommend them as the creators of this book? The same criteria apply to books that deal with the feelings and insights of females. Look carefully to determine whether the author's perspective substantially weakens or strengthens the value of his/her written work. Are omissions and distortions central to the overall character or "message" of the book?

8. Look at the Copyright Date

Only recently has the children's book world begun to reflect the realities of a multiracial society and the concerns of feminists. Copyright dates can be a clue as to how likely the book is to be overtly racist or sexist, even though recent dates are no guarantee of a book's relevance or sensitivity.

Abridged and adapted from the Council on Interracial Books for Children, "10 Quick Ways to Analyze Children's Books for Racism and Sexism."

The goal: inclusion

position. Gender equity education focuses primarily on helping children develop a perspective—a way of looking at the world and how individuals are treated within that world—not on learning a body of information. You can play a key role in that process, especially by selecting teaching materials in which the gender role treatment is balanced and equitable (Flynn & Chambers, 1994). You

MODEL STUDENT ACTIVITY

Who Is Best Suited for Which Jobs?

Introductory Note: Lessons like the one that follows can sometimes be problematic if parents perceive that you are trying to instill a particular point of view in their children. Therefore, make certain that this lesson corresponds closely with the curriculum for your grade level.

Grades:

3 through 8

Overview

This lesson is based on a survey of your students regarding which gender—male, female, or both—is best suited to certain jobs or tasks.

Objectives

1. The teacher will determine the extent to which students have stereotyped expectations about who should hold various jobs.

2. Students will show that they understand the word stereotype by correctly identifying certain expectations about jobs as stereotypical.

Procedure

1. Discuss the vocabulary important to this lesson: stereotype, bias, opinion.

2. Before you give the questionnaire to students, make sure they understand that you want honest opinions. Stress that there are no right or wrong answers and that you are not testing them on facts. Make it clear that they don't need to put their names on the questionnaires.

3. Divide the class into small groups (to facilitate tallying the results later). Hand out the questionnaires and allow students up to thirty minutes to complete them (individually).

4. Collect the questionnaires from each group and then give each group's responses to another group for tallying. Provide groups with blank questionnaires that they can use for summarizing the responses.

5. Use an overhead transparency of the questionnaire to summarize the small-group's tallies.

6. Lead a group discussion. Possible topics include:

   ● What are the occupations that mostly men go into? Why do you think so?

   ● What are the occupations that mostly women go into? Why do you think so?

   ● Can both men and women hold those jobs? Why do you think so?

   ● What job would you like to have? Give several reasons.

7. Be ready to counter stereotypical ideas with information about women astronauts, women scientists, male librarians, male secretaries, and male nurses. Ask students for examples from their own experience or from TV, magazines, or the Internet.

Who Should?

Part I. For each of the jobs listed below, decide whether you think it should be done by a man, a woman, or could be done equally well by both. Circle 1 under MAN if you think only a man should do the job; circle 2 under WOMAN if you think only a woman should do the job; or circle 3 under BOTH if you think both a man and woman should do the job. Circle only one answer for each job.

	MAN	WOMAN	BOTH
1. airplane pilot	1	2	3
2. astronaut	1	2	3
3. carpenter	1	2	3
4. chef	1	2	3
5. doctor	1	2	3
6. lawyer	1	2	3
7. librarian	1	2	3
8. lifeguard	1	2	3
9. nurse	1	2	3
10. president of USA	1	2	3

11. race-car driver	1	2	3
12. secretary	1	2	3
13. telephone operator	1	2	3
14. truck driver	1	2	3
15. nursery school teacher	1	2	3

Part II. When there are class jobs to be done, who do you think should do them? Circle a number to show your answer.

	BOY	GIRL	BOTH
16. messenger	1	2	3
17. class president	1	2	3
18. eraser cleaner	1	2	3
19. class secretary	1	2	3
20. class treasurer	1	2	3

Part III. Now what about things at home? Circle a number to show your answer.

	MAN	WOMAN	BOTH
21. When children misbehave, who should correct them?	1	2	3
22. Who should teach good manners?	1	2	3
23. Who should take care of a sick child?	1	2	3
24. Who should teach children right from wrong?	1	2	3

Part IV. Here is a list of jobs that people do at home. Circle who you think should do the job.

	MAN	WOMAN	BOTH
25. washing dishes	1	2	3
26. taking out the trash	1	2	3
27. grocery shopping	1	2	3
28. paying bills	1	2	3
29. cooking	1	2	3
30. fixing things	1	2	3
31. dusting furniture	1	2	3
32. scrubbing floors	1	2	3
33. sewing	1	2	3
34. working in the yard	1	2	3
35. moving furniture	1	2	3
36. doing the laundry	1	2	3

Part V. Here is a list of spare-time activities. Circle who should do them: a man, woman, or both.

	MAN	WOMAN	BOTH
37. playing football	1	2	3
38. swimming	1	2	3
39. playing the piano	1	2	3
40. going to sports events (like baseball games)	1	2	3
41. working out in a gym	1	2	3
42. helping in a hospital every week	1	2	3

The "Who Should?" survey was abridged and adapted from material originally developed by the Highline School District, Project Equality, Seattle, WA 98166.

This activity was abridged and adapted from "Awareness of Sex Bias and Equity" originally developed by Carol Hankinson, Waiahole Elementary School, Hawaii, and Amy Okumura, Beverly J. Pu, and Yuriko Wellington, Hana High and Elementary, Hawaii, and appearing in Oceans of Options: Sex Equity Lessons for the Classroom, which was published by the Far West Laboratory for Educational Research and Development, 730 Harrison Street, San Francisco, CA 94107.

can also call attention to the inequitable treatment of individuals of either gender in whatever situations or materials the children encounter.

• • • •

Racism and Sexism: Institutional or Personal?

• • • •

Unconscious bias

In situations involving perceived racism or sexism, two questions usually apply. One, is the apparent racism or sexism personal or institutional? And, two, is it conscious or unconscious? The majority of teachers we meet are fair and caring people who go out of their way to avoid intentionally racist or sexist behavior. Most of them, for example, would not refer to a black male student as "boy," for doing so could be perceived as consciously racist. But the same teachers may unconsciously engage in what are perceived as racist or sexists acts by, for example, assigning only boys when heavy things need to be carried to the office or library, or by apparently using a double standard to judge the behaviors of boys and girls—"Boys will be boys, you know." On the other hand, a teacher who, after becoming aware of a textbook that distorts the images or contributions of people of color, decides to use it anyway—without saying anything or providing opportunities for students to investigate the bias—could be considered to have committed a consciously racist act.

Institutional bias Institutional racism and sexism are usually more difficult to see and, thus, avoid. For example, many people may not be aware that there are more males than females in administrative positions in public schools, especially at the superintendent level—where the proportion of women is tiny. In still other instances, school practices that are designed to serve one purpose can sometimes have the effect of being racist or sexist. Homogenous grouping (or tracking) is one example. Some people argue that when schools group their students by ability, teachers are (a) better able to target individual needs and (b) students will learn more. Others argue that although homogeneous grouping "works" for high-ability students, it can have discriminatory consequences for students in the lower tracks, especially for the poor and minority students who tend to inhabit these tracks. Not only are students in the lower tracks often seen as less able, but some students come to see themselves as less able—"well, we are the lower group, you know, we're not supposed to 'get' this stuff."

Conscious institutional racism and sexism is very difficult to combat on an individual basis. The same is true of conscious personal racism and sexism. In either case, individuals or groups are knowingly supporting a particular agenda.

Raising one's awareness Unconscious racism and sexism is a different matter, because it lacks conscious motivation—it may simply be the effect of actions that someone hasn't thought about. Combating unconscious racism and sexism is largely a matter of bringing the effects of the actions to a conscious level. As opposed to comments such as "You're being a racist (or sexist)," which can be construed as a personal attack that raises one's defense mechanisms, consider focusing on the actions, not the individuals. A question such as "I wonder if some people think that (the action) is racist (or sexist)?" may be sufficient to bring an unconscious action to the conscious level where it can be dealt with.

KEY IDEA

Racism and sexism can be either personal or institutional, and conscious or unconscious.

● ● ● ● Multicultural Education

There is no single, agreed-upon definition for *multicultural education*. Some individuals prefer a stronger descriptor. For example, Enid Lee (1994) prefers "anti-racist education." Whatever descriptor you elect to use, multicultural education and cultural pluralism reflect the notion that the richness of our society is rooted in every nook and cranny on the globe. This means that all peoples must be treated in ways that recognize and respect their inherent dignity and their **Goal** contributions to society. The basic goal of multicultural education is to help all children—regardless of ethnicity, gender, disabilities, or social class—understand and appreciate events and people from various points of view. Those points of view may reflect cultural and ethnic similarities and differences, as well as identify alternative choices for people regardless of their situation.

The literature on multicultural education is vast, and some of it reflects attempts by individuals to push a particular agenda. For example, consider the following survey of cultural awareness (Grant & Sleeter, 1989) in which you are asked to match the following individuals with their occupations. The answers are at the end of the chapter.*

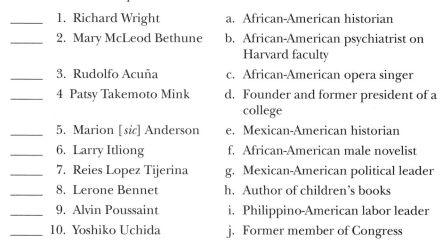

Multicultural awareness?

_____	1. Richard Wright	a.	African-American historian
_____	2. Mary McLeod Bethune	b.	African-American psychiatrist on Harvard faculty
_____	3. Rudolfo Acuña	c.	African-American opera singer
_____	4 Patsy Takemoto Mink	d.	Founder and former president of a college
_____	5. Marion [*sic*] Anderson	e.	Mexican-American historian
_____	6. Larry Itliong	f.	African-American male novelist
_____	7. Reies Lopez Tijerina	g.	Mexican-American political leader
_____	8. Lerone Bennet	h.	Author of children's books
_____	9. Alvin Poussaint	i.	Philippino-American labor leader
_____	10. Yoshiko Uchida	j.	Former member of Congress

Some people breathe a sigh of relief when they get to Marian Anderson, the acclaimed African-American opera singer. Often this is the first entry they recognize. In desperation, they sometimes turn to a process of elimination based on the perceived ethnicity of the individual's last name. They might also ask where was Ella Fitzgerald, Ernie Banks, Kathleen Battle, Joycelyn Elders, Henry B. Gonzales, and Cesar Chavez—people they had heard of.

With due respect to Grant and Sleeter, one might question whether this is a legitimate survey of cultural awareness. Or perhaps it was designed to heighten one's awareness of what one does not know. The point is that the goal of multicultural education is *not* to replace Eurocentric trivia with a different kind of more politically correct trivia. Rather, multicultural education is intended to de- **Building mutual respect** velop the knowledge, perspectives, and frames of reference that build *mutual respect* between and among all peoples.

● ● ● ●
Approaches to Multicultural Education
● ● ● ●

Multicultural education can be embraced in different ways, some more and some less effective than others. One of the ways to look at this is to think of multicultural education as a continuum that ranges from discrete activities that teachers occasionally employ to a broadly comprehensive program where multicultural

*Source: From *Turning on Learning: Five Approaches for Multicultural Teaching* by Grant/Sleeter. Copyright 1989. Reprinted by permission of Prentice-Hall.

elements are integrated into the program on an ongoing basis. (Note that portions of this treatment are based on Banks, 1989). Various phases of such a continuum, each more comprehensive than the one that precedes it, include:

1. **Contributions Approach.** Examples include the addition of discrete activities and units that focus on heroes, holidays, and unique cultural phenomena.

2. **Additive Approach.** Examples include the addition of content and themes, such as incorporating works of African-American literature into an existing American history course. At this stage, the curriculum is added to but remains otherwise unchanged.

3. **Transformational Approach.** At this level, the structure of the curriculum is changed to focus on issues and events from the perspective of different cultural and ethnic groups.

4. **Social Action Approach.** At this most comprehensive level, the curriculum is restructured to focus on important social issues, with the clear expectation that students will engage in actions to help resolve them.

Each of these approaches is examined in more detail below.

Contributions Approach. This approach to multicultural education is one of the more common, especially in schools where teachers elect to approach multicultural curriculum on their own. Special culturally oriented events such as "Black History Month" or "African- or Native-American Heritage Day" characterize this approach, as do insertions of special lessons on ethnic heroes such as Crispus Attucks (the first African-American to die in the Battle of Concord), Cesar Chavez (the organizer of Mexican-American farm workers), or even Rosa Parks (who initiated the Montgomery bus boycott).

Stage one: Contributions

CAUTIONS AND LIMITATIONS

The contributions approach to multicultural education has some limitations, not the least of which is that children will see it as a curriculum add-on designed to appeal to a certain population. If there is a question about this, consider the responses of Marc Elrich's students to the inclusion of certain African-American heroes in their textbooks.

Limitations and liabilities

A second and perhaps more serious limitation of the contributions approach is that well-intentioned activities can sometimes do as much harm as good. The special days set aside to honor certain cultural or ethnic groups, or the eating of ethnic foods that Elrich (Banks and many others) referred to, can unintentionally convey inaccurate information and create negative stereotypes.

For example, I thought that, when our youngest son went to camp, where a sizable contingent of his fellow campers would be from countries in Eastern Europe and Russia, the experience would be useful to him. What better way to get to know people from other cultures than to live with them for a week? He returned from camp asserting that Russians stank! They didn't wash or take showers, he said.

While I knew that people from some cultures in Eastern Europe did not bathe as often as many Americans, and that some of them regard deodorants as feminine, I was not prepared for the vehemence of my son's reaction, nor could I temper his conclusion. To this day, and with no experience to the contrary, my son still believes that Russians stink.

CRAFT ACTIVITIES

Arts and crafts activities must also be treated carefully, or they too can sometimes be misleading. On one occasion, for example, I visited a kindergarten social studies class in which the children were studying Native Americans. They had dyed elbow macaroni with red, orange, yellow, green, and blue food coloring. After the macaroni had dried and was strung on strings, the children proudly displayed their "Indian necklaces." The teacher's motives were well intended; she wanted a hands-on activity that related to the unit, preferably one the students could complete quickly. The problem here was with what the children learned from the activity: that Native Americans wear necklaces made from colored macaroni—which no self-respecting Native Americans do.

The context is important

Having students create a macaroni necklace can be an engaging craft activity that may be worth doing on that basis alone. However, problems can arise if the teacher introduces it with "Today, boys and girls, we are going to make necklaces like the Native Americans used to wear." Justifying activities on a multicultural basis can easily become misleading, and can provide learnings that go beyond what the teacher intended. Multicultural education is an area where otherwise well-intended activities, like the African-American History Month that Marc El-rich referred to, could be regarded as an insult.

Adding new elements to the existing curriculum.

Additive Approach.   The additive approach to multicultural education involves the inclusion of books, units, or courses that add to the existing curriculum but do not change it substantially. It would also be reflected by a teacher who, for example, decides to teach a unit on the internment of Japanese-Americans in special camps during World War II—a topic often omitted from textbooks. The teacher might base the unit on Yoshiko Uchida's *Journey to Topaz: A Story of the Japanese-American Evacuation* (1971) and Ken Mochizuki's (1993) *Baseball Saved Us,* an easy book that traces how Japanese-Americans imprisoned in a desert internment camp built a baseball field to relieve the monotony.

Limitations of the add-on approach

The add-on approach is a legitimate stage in the development of a truly multicultural curriculum, particularly for teachers working on their own. However, it has some limitations. For example, Banks (1989) noted that students may see the units as appendages rather than as an integral part of the overall course of study. Occasional add-on units can provide different cultural perspectives, but they are unlikely to show how the histories and cultures of various groups are interwoven over time.

Transformational Approach.   This approach focuses on transforming the existing curriculum within and across subject areas by "the infusion of various perspectives, frames of reference, and content from various groups that will extend students' understanding of the nature, development and complexity of U.S. society" (Banks, 1989, p. 203). In other words, the transformational approach involves

Multicultural activities should be an ongoing part of social studies. (© Marc W. Bernsau/The Image Works)

restructuring the existing curriculum so that it routinely provides a variety of cultural perspectives.

Transforming the existing curriculum

A transformed curriculum should, in Banks's (1989) view, reflect the process of *multiple acculturation*. Instead of focusing simply on contributions per se, the "emphasis should be on how the common U.S. culture and society emerged from a complex synthesis and interaction of the diverse cultural elements that originated within the various cultural, racial, ethnic, and religious groups that make up U.S. society" (p. 161).

Social Action Approach. This approach builds on the transformational approach by adding dimensions that ask students to make decisions and take appropriate actions in light of their decisions. Banks (1989) contends that traditional schooling often fosters political passivity and socializes students to accept existing ideologies and practices rather than helping them to become skilled participants in social change. As Banks states, "to participate effectively in democratic social change, students must be taught social criticism and must be helped to understand the inconsistency between our ideals and social realities, the work that must be done to close this gap, and how students can, as individuals and groups, influence the social and political systems in U.S. society" (p. 205).

Moving from knowledge to social action

· · · ·

Assessing Multicultural Activities

· · · ·

The four approaches to multicultural curriculum that Banks described reflect one way of looking at multicultural literacy. The key element in all of them involves the nature of culture itself.

The layers of culture

The Cultural Pyramid.
Artifacts, relics, and foodstuffs are among the most visible and readily available aspects of a culture. At the same time, they are among the *least* significant aspects of the total cultural mosaic. Figure 4.2 shows that the basis of every culture rests in its fundamental beliefs and attitudes—in its cosmology or worldview. A second component is reflected by the way the culture has organized itself—the organizational layer—and by the customs and practices the culture follows. Those customs and practices usually reflect the group's underlying beliefs. At the top of the cultural pyramid are the materials and artifacts the culture uses, including the foods it considers suitable for consumption.

Consider, for example, that Jews who follow the kosher tradition do not serve meat and dairy products on the same dish. This practice reflects the organizational layer—the middle layer—of the cultural pyramid. The reason for serving meat and dairy products separately is rooted in the Jewish faith, in the belief layer of culture. Because of their beliefs, kosher Jewish families have two sets of china and kitchen utensils, one used exclusively for dairy products and another for meat and other foods. The dishes themselves reflect the artifacts and materials layer of culture.

Establishing a cultural context

Considered in isolation, the two sets of china in kosher Jewish families or the practice of serving meat and dairy products separately may seem nothing more than quaint customs or cultural oddities. The same would be true of the Amish's refusal to use electrically powered appliances or to drive automobiles. In any multicultural activity, it is essential that students understand how a culture's artifacts, customs, and practices are related to the underlying basis in belief. If those relationships and connections are *not* made, children could easily regard unfamiliar groups as cultural eccentrics.

FIGURE 4.2   The Pyramid of Culture

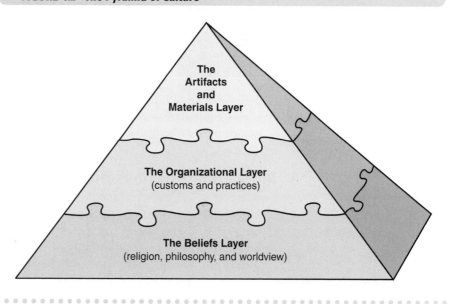

The
Artifacts
and
Materials Layer

The Organizational Layer
(customs and practices)

The Beliefs Layer
(religion, philosophy, and worldview)

Multicultural Activities with Substance

Despite some questionable activities that are passed off as multicultural education, there are legitimate and educationally defensible ways to deal with some of
them. For example, teachers who have their students build a tepee or models of
other cultural artifacts must make certain that students clearly understand that
they are re-creating historical or cultural events, and imperfectly at that. For
food-related activities, recognize that in many cultures the preparation and presentation of food is often more important than eating. For tortillas or Indian corn
bread, for example, let students experience what it is like to grind the corn into
flour—as some people in Mexico and some Native Americans still do today. Be
More than meets the eye
advised, however, that grinding corn by hand is boring and tedious; and it takes a
long time to grind enough corn to make a single tortilla. Students may become
frustrated at their lack of progress, but with that frustration may come a new appreciation of what some people must do to obtain food.

Likewise, instead of serving canned spaghetti, consider having your students
make spaghetti from scratch, as many Italian-Americans do. All it requires is
some flour, an egg, and perhaps a little water kneaded together on a clean surface, like a clean desktop. No bowls or utensils are needed except for a rolling
pin, a knife to cut the dough into thin strips, and a large pot of water in which to
cook it. (Note that homemade spaghetti is flat, not round like the commercially
Include research
prepared product.) While their pasta is drying, one group of students can research the recipe and then prepare a tomato-based sauce characteristic of southern Italy. Another group can research and make a clear or cream-based sauce
like those served in northern Italy. In this activity, cookbooks—the Time-Life
series is wonderful for this—can become reference books.
There is a world of difference between what children can learn
from the spaghetti activity described here, and what they can
learn from heating and eating canned spaghetti.

Food-related activities is an area that has a high potential
for abuse. The rule of thumb should be: if you wish to use
food-related multicultural activities, do them in educationally
defensible ways. If that takes too much time—and such activities can require lots
of classroom time—then don't do them at all. Multicultural education clearly demands unusual sensitivity to and respect for the peoples of all cultures.

KEY IDEA
Multicultural activities must be
authentic; otherwise they can lead
to inaccurate stereotyping.

Respecting Religious Diversity

Some public school teachers mistakenly believe that they cannot mention
religion in their classrooms (see Ayers, 2003). If that were the case, it would
be impossible to teach about any of the world's religions—Islam, Hinduism,
Buddhism, and so forth. Not only have the courts sustained teachers' (and
Teaching religion vs. teaching
***about* religion**
schools') rights to teach *about* religion, but they have also indicated that information about religion is necessary to a good education. This means that you could
do an in-depth analysis of Christian and non-Christian religions if you wished

to, as long as it is relevant to the course of study. It also means that teaching about religion should be handled as objectively as possible, and without any suggestion that teachers are attempting to sway their students' beliefs in a particular direction.

Guidelines for Teaching About Religion

The following guidelines help to establish the distinction between teaching about religion and the teaching of religion.

- The approach to religion should be academic, not devotional.
- The goal is to seek student awareness of religions, but not acceptance of any religion.
- The school sponsors the study about religion, not the practice of religion.
- The intent is to expose students to a diversity of religious views and beliefs, but not to impose conformity to any particular view.
- The approach should not promote or denigrate religion.

Excerpted and adapted from Haynes, C. C., & Thomas, O. (2000). *Finding common ground: A guide to religious liberty in public schools.* Freedom Forum, 75–76, appearing in Douglass, S. L. (2002). Teaching about religion. *Educational Leadership*, 60, 32–37.

You may recall that because of their religious beliefs, the parents of two students in Mary Jane Blanchard's class had requested that their children be excused from Halloween activities involving witches and goblins. In addition, Melissa's parents had requested that she be excused from saying the Pledge of Allegiance during morning exercises. In both instances, the underlying issue involves the parents' and children's rights to the free exercise of their religious beliefs under the First Amendment.

Respecting First Amendment Rights

How did Mary Jane Blanchard handle the parental requests? In the case of Halloween observations, the school board had previously passed a policy banning black cats, witches, and symbols of the occult from all school-based activities, including Halloween. Such policies are often extensions of actions originally intended to curb gang-related activities. In any event, the Board policy effectively eliminated both the activities in question and the need to excuse Amy and Melissa; Ms. Blanchard adjusted activities for her entire class accordingly. More and more schools are adopting similar policies, but in schools that do not have

Investigate existing procedures

them, honoring the parent's request is recommended. For other matters, especially attempts to censor certain books, most schools have established procedures for determining whether the protested content or activities serve an overriding and compelling educational purpose.

At one level, the request to excuse Melissa from saying the Pledge of Allegiance became a kind of nonissue. Over fifty years ago the Supreme Court ruled

● ● ● ● **COMMENTARY** **The Scope of Diversity**

Among the myths in education is the notion that diversity occurs only in classrooms inhabited mainly by African-Americans. However, plenty of diversity exists in suburbia too.

When I first accepted the offer to teach sixth grade in the Quaker Ridge School in Scarsdale, New York—one of the wealthiest school districts in the country—I could not help but think what a delight it would be to teach those "smart little rich kids." I had from twenty-seven to thirty-six students in the classes I had taught previously in rural Ohio, but in Scarsdale, my largest class had nineteen students and the smallest, nine. This, I thought, was going to be a teacher's dream.

You can probably see where this is leading. It wasn't long into the school year before I found that some of my preconceived notions were incorrect. The idea that these students were "smart little rich kids" was one of the first to fall by the wayside. None of my children's parents were on welfare, and the free lunch program was nonexistent. However, I soon discovered that in wealthy communities like Scarsdale, many parents send their children to private schools. Although most of my students lived in comfortable homes, almost half of them were the children of housekeepers, chauffeurs, maids, and cooks and were often restricted to cramped "help's quarters" within the larger homes. Even though many of my students came from the higher end of the economic spectrum, an almost equal number came from the lower end; there were few middle-class students, economically speaking. In addition, and even though most of my students didn't need to worry where their next meal was coming from, they were neither smarter nor any less intelligent than the students I had taught previously.

In three years of teaching in rural Ohio, I had not encountered an African-American or an Asian-American student. This was not the case in Scarsdale. Three African-American students and four Asian-American students were among that sea of fifty or so shining faces I saw each day. One African-American student whom I especially remember was Clarence, whose parents were both prominent physicians. Clarence was among the brightest students I have ever encountered, but homework was a lost cause with him; he didn't think he needed it, and based on his performance without it, I eventually agreed.

My four Asian-American students performed as the stereotype says they will: they worked harder and more conscientiously than most of the other students that I dealt with that year. At one point I asked one of them if she ever relaxed, but her blank look suggested that I didn't understand her cultural mores.

Yet another incident indicated how provincial my perspective on diversity had been. While teaching in Ohio, I had the unenviable task of organizing the school's assemblies. We sang patriotic songs at Thanksgiving, Christmas carols at Christmas, and so forth. Upon moving to Scarsdale, I made the mistake of mentioning my prior experience handling assemblies, and they once again became my responsibility. The Thanksgiving program went as well as such programs usually do, but when I sat down with the music teacher (and pianist) to select the carols for the Christmas program, I was informed that (1) we were planning a "Winter Holiday Program," and (2) my old list of carols—which included "Oh Come All Ye Faithful" and the like—would be inappropriate in a largely Jewish community. We quickly discarded the religious carols and sang "Winter Wonderland" and "Santa Claus Is Coming to Town" instead. However, this incident caused me to reflect on how many non-Christian families in Ohio I may have unintentionally offended.

Every classroom and school reflects diversity, even when you may not expect it (or should know better).

Court rulings

that students cannot be compelled to say the Pledge of Allegiance. But for questions about whether teachers can ask students to stand during the Pledge (even if they do not say it)—where standing can be regarded as a means for honoring something—or whether teachers can permit the student to leave the classroom during the Pledge, the answer is: it depends. The Supreme Court has not ruled on either question, but many federal circuit and state courts have. The problem according to my school law specialist is that the various courts have not ruled consistently one way or the other. This effectively means that what is or is not legal depends on the rulings (or absence of rulings or local policies) in the legal jurisdiction where you teach.

Excusing Melissa from saying the Pledge was problematic for Ms. Blanchard in the sense that she pondered long about how she would present Melissa's non-participation to the rest of the class. She finally decided to tell them "The Pledge of Allegiance is a way of showing our respect for the flag and what it stands for, but some people's religious beliefs—like Melissa's—do not permit them to say the Pledge. We are going to respect Melissa's beliefs too." It turned out that what Mary Jane had worried about was a bigger problem for her than for her students. Melissa stood for the Pledge without being asked to, but she did not speak the words. For Melissa's classmates, this procedure had been going on since they were in kindergarten and was nothing out of the ordinary.

Respecting cultural diversity

The basic requirement for dealing with the ethnic, religious, and cultural diversity in classrooms today is a healthy respect for each individual's heritage, including the teacher's, and for the deeply held beliefs associated with that heritage. For those of us who teach, diversity in all of its forms demands that we demonstrate an honest and supportive sensitivity to what individuals bring with them to the classroom.

SUMMARY

Four factors have contributed to the phenomenal diversity in classrooms today: (1) desegregation, (2) increased immigration, (3) rapidly growing minority populations, and (4) growing recognition of the ethnicity of students who were in classrooms all along. Of these factors, the end of segregation has two dimensions; the first dimension involves ending the practice of segregating schools along racial lines, and the other involves removing students with handicapping conditions from separate classrooms and returning them to the mainstream of public education—regular classrooms.

This chapter has focused primarily on cultural and ethnic diversity. Children from the various cultures that make up the American mosaic often bring with them different and sometimes unique ways for addressing common situations. As a consequence, some children avoid looking adults in the eye when they are talking to them; to do otherwise would be considered disrespectful. Likewise, children from some cultures avoid asking (and sometimes answering) a teacher's questions so as not to be what, in their culture, would be considered rude. The idea that schools should act as melting pots that will eradicate cultural practices so as to "Americanize" children has fallen into disfavor, but traces of it still exist. For example, suggesting to a child that "we do it differently here" can be interpreted in different ways. The key is the teacher's implicit message, which, admittedly, is not easy to determine out of context. Is the teacher's real message, "Don't do that anymore," or is it "I'm just telling you this so you know there's another way you could do that"? One statement is obviously a put-down, and the other is intended for the child's information, and most children are skilled enough observers of human behavior to recognize the difference between the two.

This chapter also focused on forms of racism and sexism that are perpetuated in the media and educational materials. The popular media has broadened its once narrowly defined definition of "hero" to (occasionally) include individuals other than handsome, white males, but the classic tales that parents and teachers read to children often contain a healthy dose of racial and/or sex-role stereotyping. Parents who read stories to their children at bedtime are at a disadvantage, because they cannot engage in a discussion with their sleeping child about whether people who, for example, build their houses of sticks or straw are less worthy than people who build their homes from bricks. Most teachers don't face those limitations and are probably remiss if they permit such blatant stereotyping to go without comment. People should not "ruin a classic story with excessive analysis," of course, but neither should a teacher perpetuate cultural, racial, or sexist myths by saying nothing about them. This is not an "all or nothing" matter, but rather one of assessing whether the perspectives depicted in classic tales correspond with the prevailing views in contemporary society.

Multicultural education has become the major means for recognizing the multiple cultures and ethnicities that exist in almost every classroom. Multicultural education is a multifaceted effort aimed primarily at helping all children, regardless of ethnicity, gender, disabilities, or social class, to understand and appreciate events and people from various points of view.

SUGGESTED READINGS AND RESOURCES

Print Resources

GENERAL RESOURCES

Bill Bigelow, L. Christensen, L, S. Karp, B. Miner, & B. Petersen. (1994). *Rethinking our classrooms: Teaching for equity and justice.* Milwaukee: Rethinking Schools. The title of this thought-provoking collection of articles and teaching activities says it all. Developed by a group of teachers from Milwaukee (WI), this volume also includes contributions from noted authorities in the field. Excellent.

MULTICULTURAL EDUCATION

James A. Banks. (1997). *Educating citizens in a multicultural society.* New York: Teachers College Press. This paperback reflects Banks's latest contribution to the multicultural education literature and directs special attention to the relationship between multicultural education and citizenship education.

Eugene Garcia. (2002). *Student cultural diversity: Understanding and meeting the challenge.* Boston: Houghton Mifflin. This book provides excellent treatments of the different types of diversity in classrooms today and ways in which teachers can respond appropriately to them.

Enid Lee, Deborah Menkart, & Margo Okazawa-Rey (Eds.). (1998). *Beyond heroes and holidays: A practical guide to K–12 anti-racist, multicultural education, and staff development.* Washington, DC: Network Educators on the Americas. This is an excellent collection of articles by a remarkable range of authors.

Nancy Schniedewind & Ellen Davidson. (1998). *Open minds to equality: A sourcebook of learning activities to affirm diversity and promote equity* (2nd ed). Boston: Allyn & Bacon. This excellent and wide-ranging collection includes brief background materials and a variety of learning activities, many of which are ready for duplication.

WOMEN'S HISTORY/GENDER-EQUITY

Not all of the books listed here are intended for young children, but all of them provide an inclusive history. They include:

Joy Hakim. (1999). A *history of US.* New York: Oxford University Press Children's Books, ten volumes.

Christine Lunardini. (1994). *What every American should know about women's history.* Holbrook, MA: Bob Adams.

Wilma Mankiller, Gwendolyn Mink, Marysa Navarro, Barbara Smith, & Gloria Steinem (Eds.). (1998). *The reader's companion to U.S. women's history.* Boston, MA: Houghton Mifflin.

M. M. Merryfield and M. S. Crocco. (Eds.). (2003). Women of the world. *Social Education,* 67 (January/February). This special theme edition of *Social Education* offers a balanced perspective on women's lives across the globe.

Howard Zinn. (1995). *A people's history of the United States: 1492 to the present.* New York: Harper Perennial Library.

_____. (1998). *The twentieth century: A people's history.* New York: Harper Perennial Library.

GENDER EQUITY LESSON MATERIALS

Oceans of options: Sex equity lessons for the classroom. Far West Laboratory for Educational Research and Development, 1855 Folsom St., San Francisco, CA 94103. This is an interesting collection of sample lessons.

Internet Resources

Introductory Note: Web sites sometimes change their Internet addresses or cease operating entirely. All the addresses supplied here were operating when this book was printed, but if any of them fails to work properly, enter the name of the target organization in any standard search engine.

MULTICULTURAL/ETHNIC INTERNET RESOURCES

National Association for Multicultural Education

http://www.nameorg.org

This site is maintained by the National Association for Multicultural Education and includes references to multicultural reference materials, promising classroom practices, and sources of teaching materials.

The Resource Center of the Americas

http://www.americas.org

This organization focuses on creating innovative curricula that build bridges between people throughout the Americas. It also offers a lending library of thousands of books, periodicals, and videos. Periodic E-mail updates of new resources can be found at **bookstore@americas.org.**

Resources for Afro-American History

http://www.libraries.rutgers.edu/rul/rr_gateway/ research_guides/history/afrores.shtml

This site provides extensive listings of resources related to African-Americans.

GENDER EQUITY–RELATED INTERNET RESOURCES

Conexiones

http://conexiones.asu.edu/gender.html

This site, sponsored by the University of Arizona, offers a selected lsiting of "some of the best" Internet sites that deal with gender equity.

Women's Studies

http://www.hist.unt.edu/09w-amm6.htm

This site offers an extensive collection of links related to women's studies, including resources, guides and programs, history, great women, and women in the professions.

Answers to Cultural Awareness Activity

1. f   His most well-known novel is *Native Son.*
2. d   The college was called the Daytona Educational and Industrial School; it was for African-American girls.
3. e   Best-known book is *Occupied America.*
4. j   She was a representative from Hawaii; the only Asian-American woman to serve in Congress.
5. c   (No answer provided in original.)
6. i   Helped organize the grape boycott with Cesar Chavez.
7. g   Fought state and federal authorities for land grants to Hispanics, which were legally protected by the Treaty of Guadalupe.
8. a   Best known for his book, *Before the Mayflower.*
9. b   Publishes widely in both scholarly and popular literature, such as *Ebony.*
10. h   Former Japanese-American internment camp prisoner who has published numerous stories.

5

The Dimensions of Instructional Diversity

KEY QUESTIONS

- **What is instructional diversity?**
- **How do physical and emotional disabilities influence instruction?**
- **How do teachers adapt instruction to meet individual needs and still keep their sanity?**
- **What is learning style, and how does it affect the ways in which students learn?**

⬤ ⬤ ⬤ ⬤ Introduction: On "Falling Through the Cracks"

DIVERSITY 👥

In the not too distant past, when schooling was a "one-size-fits-all" enterprise, some students invariably "fell through the cracks." Sometimes they failed in certain subjects, sometimes they got poor grades or had work habits that left much to be desired, and sometimes they just had problems learning. Some of those kids dropped out of school as soon as they could; some still do. You can almost bet that many students who "fell through the cracks" were at least a half-grade level or more behind in reading. And some of them may have been auditory learners who rely heavily on listening, as opposed to more visually oriented learners—which includes most teachers—who rely on how things look.

How do you learn best?

For a quick test of your learning preference, think about how you deal with situations when you are writing something and encounter a word that you are not sure how to spell. Using the dictionary is always an option, of course, but after ten minutes looking up *pneumonia* under the letter "N," you may turn to another strategy. Do you (1) sound out the word and go with the result, (2) change to a different word that you know how to spell, or (3) write the word three different ways and then pick the one that "looks right"? Auditory (hearing-oriented) learners are more likely to use techniques 1 and 2, whereas visual learners more often rely on technique 3. Because auditory learners may lack an accurate visual image of words, they often encounter problems with words containing silent letters (like *pneumonia*) and words like *nickel* and *pickle*, where there are no sound cues as to whether the word ends with "el" or "le." But then, even ardent visual learners are not above using technique 2—changing to a different word—especially if the teacher or reader has a "thing" about spelling.

Non-English speakers

It is also likely that some students who "fell through the cracks" were nonnative speakers of English, usually known as English as a Second Language (ESL) students. It is not the students' fault that they were born into families where the native language is Spanish, Vietnamese, Laotian, or any of hundreds of others. Likewise, there's no question that ESL students must become proficient in English. The problem for most ESL students is making the transition to English, and the insensitivity they occasionally encounter along the way.

Mandated testing closes some of the "cracks"

STANDARDS ✔

Mandated competency testing has put students who might otherwise have fallen through the cracks into a different light. The focus today is on how *all* students perform, not just those who have traditionally done well. Under clearly defined circumstances, some students can be exempted from state-mandated tests, but the process typically involves more paperwork than you would believe—paperwork designed to prevent students from slipping through the system untested. This means that making provisions for ESL students or other students who are experiencing problems has become significantly more important than was true in the past. Even small groups of low-performing students can affect a school's overall performance rating, which can bring with it unfavorable publicity, the prospect of reduced funding, or even more dire consequences. The point is that mandated testing programs have made it increasingly difficult for schools to use selective testing to conceal the performance of students who, in the past, might have slipped by unnoticed. It also means that students encountering problems are more likely to get the kind of assistance they require. Ignoring learning problems in the hope that they will go away of their own accord or that the students can slip through unnoticed is not an option.

SUGGESTED ACTIVITY

Some people believe that schooling should be the same for all students, and that providing special programs for exceptional students is somehow undemocratic. This belief often conflicts with the principle that every child has the right to an education appropriate to his or her needs and abilities. How do you reconcile this conflict?

A second related point is that the practice of shipping students with disabilities to special education classrooms was limited even before competency testing became as popular as it is today. As noted in Chapter 4, the Individuals with Disabilities Education Act of 1990 reduced the number of physically and educationally disabled students who were formerly segregated into separate, often special education, classrooms (Turnbull, Turnbull, Shank, & Leal, 1999). The *least restrictive environment* provision of that legislation permits students to be placed in special education classrooms full time only if their needs cannot be met in either (1) a regular classroom or (2) a regular classroom combined with a program of special services (what are known as pull-out programs).

KEY IDEA

Instructional diversity includes academic and linguistic diversity, and students with physical and emotional disabilities.

The overarching point is that two elements—mandated competency testing, combined with the disabilities legislation—have had profound effects on what it means to be a "regular" classroom teacher. Every teacher must be able to adjust his or her instruction to accommodate the needs of educationally diverse students.

 Classroom Profile, Part Two

DIVERSITY

The previous chapter provided a preliminary profile of the students in Mary Jane Blanchard's fourth-grade class at Roscoe Hunt Elementary. As we revisit the same classroom in this chapter the focus is on educationally diverse students.

The students whose diversity falls within the scope of this chapter include:

Instructional diversity
- Five students—Tyrone, Trisha, Jesus, Miguel, and Maria—whose reading skills are *at least* one-half year below grade level; all of them spend a part of each day in the Resource Room, where they receive special tutoring in academic skills. Two of these students, Trisha and Miguel, have difficulty remembering what they read but can remember—almost verbatim—things that they hear.

Gifted and talented
- Six students—Juan, LaShawna, Melissa, Gina, Richard, and Chen Lee—who have reading, math, and language skills that are at the sixth-grade level or above. LaShawna, Chen Lee, and Richard are considered gifted.

- Three students—Tyrone, Richard, and Christi—who have illegible handwriting, despite all of Ms. Blanchard's efforts otherwise.

- Three students—Jesus, Miguel, and Maria—who come from homes where Spanish is the dominant language.

- One student, Trang, who spoke no English at the beginning of the year (and no one in the school spoke Vietnamese). With no English skills to speak of, Trang was unable to perform school tasks successfully at the beginning of the year. However, with some accommodations Ms. Blanchard made, and thanks to Trang's desire to overcome his language barrier, he has made remarkable progress.

Emotional considerations
- One student, Heather, is a girl with apparently normal intelligence and physical development. Heather can do fourth-grade work but apparently prefers not to. Instead, she spends her day huddled in her seat with her coat pulled over her head, almost as if she is withdrawing from the world. Heather will answer direct questions from Ms. Blanchard, but her responses are monosyllabic and barely audible; she will not look at the teacher, even when asked to do so. Heather has not uttered a complete sentence all year and avoids interacting with other students as much as possible. Heather has no real friends in the class, but neither does she have any enemies. The other students are patiently tolerant of Heather, and some are almost protective of her.

Need for structure
- One gifted student, Chen Lee, is an extremely hard worker who places extraordinary emphasis on memorization. In math, for example, she memorizes the answers *and* the problems. Chen Lee also has "high structure needs"; that is, she has difficulty dealing with independent problem solving and unstructured or open-ended activities. Chen Lee often became frustrated when Ms. Blanchard gave topical assignments, such as "read the next section in the text." This is no longer the problem it once was, because to accommodate Chen Lee's need for structure, Mary Jane now provides page numbers for all assignments.

- One student, James, who has muscular dystrophy and is confined to a wheelchair. The school district provides a full-time aide who assists James and helps him get from place to place. Because James is unable to write, he dictates all written assignments to his aide.

Disabling conditions
- Another student, Jason, who takes the drug Ritalin to calm his hyperactivity. The difference between Jason's pre-Ritalin behavior and his behavior today is like night and day. Jason's parents have given Mary Jane permission to administer Jason's midday dose of Ritalin; in fact, they have asked that he take it at 11:30 sharp, so that he will be ready for his evening dose when he gets home from school. Both Jason and Ms. Blanchard sometimes get involved in activi-

ties and forget about Jason's medication schedule, but Richard has volunteered to remind them.

- Finally there is Gina, a Type 1 (early onset) diabetic. Gina wears an insulin pump and usually manages her condition without assistance. However, about once every six weeks, her blood glucose level gets too low and she slips into a diabetic coma. If this occurs on one of the three days a week when the school nurse is at Roscoe Hunt, she will administer a potentially life-saving glucose injection. If coma occurs when the nurse is not present, Ms. Blanchard administers the injection.

We'll examine each of these students in the balance of this chapter.

● ● ● ● ● Responding to Physical and Emotional Diversity

Responding to physical impairments

Mary Jane Blanchard does not have sight- or hearing-impaired students in her class this year, but if she did, there are some no-cost, commonsense things that she could do to make life easier for them. These include things like seating sight- and hearing-impaired students toward the front of the classroom. Ms. Blanchard also offered James, the wheelchair-bound student, a seat near the door; that way he wouldn't have to thread his way through a roundabout route to reach his desk. However, James felt that his aide would be distracting to the rest of the class if they were in the front of the room, so he opted for a seat near the rear. Based on James's decision, Ms. Blanchard now keeps an extra-wide aisle on one side of the room. Such seemingly minor accommodations can have important consequences for children with physical impairments.

Diversity is the norm in most classrooms today. (© Richard Hutchings/PHOTO EDIT)

Once you move beyond the simple, no-cost accommodations, making provisions for students with physical impairments typically requires additional funding, which necessarily means some form of administrative involvement. A key element for children with physical disabilities—although not those with emotional disabilities—lies

Removing barriers

in removing the barriers that hinder their physical access to buildings, classrooms, and other ancillary services. Stairways, drinking fountains, and restroom facilities can still pose problems for children with physically disabling conditions, but most schools have already modified their facilities to accommodate them.

Emotional Impairments

In talking with Ms. Blanchard about Heather, the student with the (apparent) emotionally disabling condition, Mary Jane said, "I just didn't know what to do about Heather. At first I tried creating special assignments for her—really interesting activities, you know—but she still just sat there with her coat pulled over

Seeking help

her head. I got so frustrated that I finally called the school district's Diagnostic and Counseling Center. They came out and observed her and agreed they would work with her for an hour every week. After three weeks, nothing had changed, so I complained again. Then the counselors began working with her for an hour every day, but there was still no change in her behavior. They were finally able to obtain some medical testing, which indicated that Heather had a chemical imbalance that causes a form of depression. It took a while for them to get her medications adjusted correctly, but today she acts like a perfectly normal fourth grader."

Helping students with emotionally disabling conditions (including, in Heather's case, an underlying medical problem) is often difficult, in part because few teachers have the training needed to cope with severe emotional disabilities. Once Heather was properly diagnosed, her disability responded quickly to treatment. But the outlook is not so optimistic (or quick) for students with purely emotional

Troubling problems

disorders. These situations can become more complicated if the children's problems are caused by child abuse or, more commonly and seemingly less offensive, a divorce in the family. Not all learning disabilities result from abuse, emotional problems, or divorce, of course, but sudden changes in academic performance are often symptoms of underlying emotional (or sometimes physical) problems. Because there are so few instructional options that a teacher can use, the key lies in identifying and orchestrating school and community support services that can deal with emotional disabilities, as Ms. Blanchard did for Heather. Also, when you encounter children with emotional disabilities, you will undoubtedly be reminded of how complex and fragile our emotions really are.

Accommodating Educational Diversity

You are almost certain to encounter students, like those in Mary Jane Blanchard's class, who are *at least* one-half year below grade level in one or more

Diversity that can be expected

subjects or who have limited proficiency in English. You may also have students who excel academically and are considered gifted, but who quickly become bored with routine schoolwork. You are just as likely to have one or more students who

● ● ● ● COMMENTARY   **Health Care: How Far Should Teachers Go?**

Not long ago, over five hundred staff members—including the teachers, administrators, clerical and custodial personnel, and school bus drivers—in a 28,000-student school district in Virginia were trained to administer glucose injections to students like Gina, the diabetic student from Ms. Blanchard's class. In other instances, teachers may find themselves responsible for performing urinary catheterizations, suctioning a child's trachea, or feeding a student through a stomach tube (Temple, 2000). Although such students represent only a tiny fraction of the students that teachers encounter during a year, being responsible for performing such medical procedures can seem a little daunting. Nowhere in my training did anyone suggest that I would be responsible for suctioning a child's tracheotomy tube, for example, nor was I trained how to do it.

Both the National Education Association and the American Federation of Teachers strongly oppose holding teachers responsible for tending to students' health needs. On the other hand, parents of children with physical infirmities typically claim that their child's disability is a 24-hour-a-day condition, not something that ends when they enter a classroom. To make their point, a growing number of parents (and the courts) are invoking the provisions of some fairly old, federal legislation—the 1977 Individuals with Disabilities Education Act (IDEA), and the Vocational Rehabilitation Act of 1973, which prohibit discrimination against the disabled in any federally funded programs. In most instances, the courts seem to have supported the parents' position.

Determining who should perform medically related procedures is a matter of dispute in some areas. Asking teachers to assume responsibility for such tasks is, for the school district at least, a no-cost option. Whether there is an emotional cost to the teachers who assume those responsibilities is another matter, of course. Some school districts have banned teachers from such health-related tasks and have hired nurses and aides to tend to children with health-related disabilities. Unfortunately, this seemingly obvious solution is complicated by several factors, not the least of which is the serious shortage of nurses in most parts of the country. When you combine this with the fact that the salaries for nurses working in hospitals or private practice can equal or exceed a principal's salary, whereas school district salaries are typically one-third to one-half of what nurses could earn elsewhere, you see other dimensions of the problem.

It is politically expedient for most school districts to keep their tax rates as low as possible. Yet despite this I believe they should (1) offer and pay for appropriate training for whatever medical procedures teachers may be required to perform, *and* (2) provide liability insurance for teachers who are asked to accept such responsibilities. Consider also that some school boards pay for a superintendent's professional liability insurance (or increase their salary accordingly) for what are seldom life-and-death matters. Thus it seems reasonable and just for school boards to indemnify teachers for what could really become life-or-death matters.

---

have "high structure needs," and thus have difficulty dealing with independent problem solving and unstructured or open-ended activities. You are also likely to have students who abhor small-group work, and still others who thrive on it.

Educational diversity includes students who have nonethnic and nonculturally related conditions or preferences that influence what and how they learn. These conditions can influence the kind of instruction a teacher offers, the form in which he or she offers that instruction, and the way in which students respond to it.

● ● ● ●

The Learning Disabled (LD)

● ● ● ●

Responding to students with learning disabilities

Learning Outside the Lines (2000) is a remarkable book by two remarkable authors, Jonathon Mooney, who and David Cole. Mooney, who was diagnosed as learning disabled in elementary school, didn't learn to read until he was twelve, still can't spell, and dropped out of school for a while when he was in the sixth grade. Mooney recently graduated magna cum laude from Brown University with a degree in English literature. David Cole, also a recent honors graduate from Brown, was diagnosed with attention deficit hyperactivity disorder (ADHD) in first grade and was taking the drug Ritalin before he entered second grade.

Students who don't "fit" the system

Much of *Learning Outside the Lines* focuses on the anguish that Mooney and Cole experienced in school. Their problems, and those of learning disabled students elsewhere, may result at least in part from the fact that they don't "fit" the system. It is not a matter of conscious rebelliousness or desire to "do their own thing"; they just could not accommodate the system. Jonathon Mooney, for example, spent most of second grade sitting in the hallway for disrupting class. By third grade, Mooney's inability to read had become almost unbearable, and he spent countless hours wondering "what's wrong with me." He also learned to hide in the bathroom to escape reading out loud.

Frustration all around

According to Mooney, a psychological turning point occurred when his mother read him *Leo the Late Bloomer* (Kraus, 1998), a story about a lion who couldn't read. After hearing about Leo, Jonathon was more willing to accept the fact that he was not a "weird klutz." Nevertheless, his writing and spelling were atrocious, and even in Grade 3, he did not have the ability to look at words to determine what they meant. As Margaret King-Sears (cited in Allen, 2003) described it, LD students see textbook chapters as "80 zillion pieces of information flying around in the air" but are unable to determine what is or is not important. Because Mooney was unable to read, he had no idea what the symbols represented nor could he decipher which words were spelled correctly. Jonathon sometimes erupted in fits of temper, and his teachers occasionally (and understandably) responded in a similar fashion—"Here I am trying to help you, and you 'blow your top' at me." Jonathon was frustrated and so were his teachers.

Coping with feelings of inadequacy

Learning disabled students are often bright and otherwise capable individuals. For example, David Cole's IQ was so high that despite his disability he was permitted to skip grades. In some instances, LD students can excel athletically, and most of them get along well socially, as long as they, like Jonathan Mooney, can cope with their feelings of inadequacy. In most instances, LD students would love to read and spell well, but no matter how hard they try they just can't. Such ongoing academic problems can lead to what Dr. Mel Levine, noted author and director of the Center for the Study of Development and Learning at the University of North Carolina Medical School (cited in Thomas, 2000) calls "chronic success deprivation." Levine suggests that most of us need to be successful at something—no matter how small or insignificant—and that ongoing failures can lead to the feelings of despondency and desperation that Mooney described earlier.

Success despite the odds

Students with learning disabilities can often cope successfully after they leave school, despite their inadequacies in certain academic areas. The literature is filled with examples of people—like Charles Schwab, the stock broker, and John Chambers, the CEO of high-tech Cisco Systems—both of whom have severe learning disabilities, and both of whom are multimillionaires today. Perhaps the ultimate irony is that the place where most LD students cannot succeed is in school.

Performance issues

Two issues that are almost always associated with LD students involve performance standards and the related issue of fairness. Here's how Jonathon Mooney describes one aspect of the problem. "I'd think 'I've got to write, but I can't spell, so they won't know what I'm trying to say.' So I dumb down my writing to not get busted on spelling. How stupid is that?" He remembers not the teachers in the resource room who tirelessly and unsuccessfully tried to teach him to spell, but the teachers who "bent" the rules to accommodate his disabilities—like the (few) teachers who said they wouldn't "count his spelling." Computer-based spelling checkers can sometimes help here, but even with such aids, the words in question need to be reasonably close.

Fairness   The standards issue for LD students includes questions such as: How important is it that every word be spelled correctly? And, how important is it that the paper be written? Would a report on tape be equally acceptable? The fairness issue arises if the answers to these questions are different for students who are not learning disabled—and if the LD students feel that things are being "dumbed down" just for them.

Teaching Implications.   In teaching social studies to LD students, there is no "perfect solution" that can address all the problems at once. Rather, the task is to employ alternatives, each of which addresses a part of the problem. One major hurdle to overcome is helping students to gain access to the textbook. Traditional techniques for teaching reading seldom have the kind of short-term impact that will immediately give students access to the text, so consider instead a strategy that eliminates reading entirely—textbooks on tape. Most publishers **Books on tape**   market their books on tape, and most schools have special education money that can be used to purchase those materials. If you follow this option, be certain that your listening center has multiple sets of earphones because you are almost certain to have other students who can benefit from listening to the text on tape. If purchasing the tapes is not an option, consider getting the teachers on your grade level together for a taping party and then make enough copies for each social studies teacher. (Teachers of other subjects may want texts on tape for their classes, too, and the tapes can be reused until a new text series is adopted.)

As students listen to the text on tape, have them follow along in their books by pointing their index finger at the words as they are read. The idea is for children to see the visual image of the words as they listen to them being read. This can be especially helpful for ESL and LEP (Limited English Proficiency) students whose native language is Spanish, and in which certain letters, such as /j/ and /l/ have alternative pronunciations or are not pronounced at all. The city of La Jolla, California, for example, is pronounced La Hoya.

Avoid outlines   Resist your temptation to provide students with an outline of historical events *prior to study*. The reasoning for this is explained in more detail in Chapter 7, but essentially the idea is that, prior to study, an outline is simply a list of events about which students may know virtually nothing. On the other hand, using an outline after studying a historical period—when students are more aware of what they are dealing with—offers a useful organizing tool.

The LD Dilemma.   Accommodating LD students can be among the most frustrating and heart-wrenching problems in teaching—for students and teachers alike. Being stern and hard-nosed usually doesn't work, because most LD students really do try. Encouraging them to "try harder" seldom works, because they are often trying as hard as they can, and they just don't know what to do differently. Giving LD students poor grades usually doesn't work, because they've been that route before. What LD students really seem to need is success—just a tiny bit of success—to offset all the failures with which they are all too familiar.

• • • •
Language Diversity
• • • •

Bilingual students are conversant in two or more languages. In everyday terms this means that they are proficient enough in a second language to engage in face-to-face conversations as well as deal with the specialized vocabulary involved in learning subject matter in that language.

Bilingual defined

Teachers occasionally encounter bilingual students, but unlike many European cultures where people learn to communicate in two or three languages from birth onward, English is usually the student's second language. In other words, they are apt to have learned their languages elsewhere. Many Americans admire individuals who are bilingual at the same time that they are reluctant to learn a second language themselves. This may contribute, in part, to some of the opposition to bilingual education programs, where instruction is conducted in a language other than English. I suspect that common phrases such as "We are Americans here, and we speak English!" are uttered by people who have never experienced the problems and joys associated with learning a second language.

Currently, the majority of students in Texas are of Hispanic origin. Likewise, the proportion of Hispanic students in other states, especially in the Southwest, is growing rapidly. For large numbers of these students, their native language is Spanish, as is the language of the home. Some Hispanic students are truly bilingual—they are fluent in Spanish and English—but they more commonly fall into one of two categories, educationally speaking. The determining factor here is fluency in English. Students who come to school speaking a main language other than English are referred to, as mentioned earlier, as English as a Second Language (ESL) students. But among ESL students is a large subgroup who are not yet proficient enough in English to perform everyday school tasks successfully. Students in this group are referred to as *Limited English Proficiency* (or LEP).

Fluency in English

Trang, the Vietnamese student in Ms. Blanchard's class, who had virtually no English skills at the beginning of the year, would clearly be classified as LEP. However, being able to properly label Trang (or any other LEP students) does nothing to address the more significant issue here: determining how to help Trang (and others) to communicate effectively in English. Trang's situation was further complicated because there was no one in the school who spoke Vietnamese. Trang's parents were unable to do much for him because their English skills were similar to Trang's, a situation common to many LEP students. Most schools have the funds to pay for *language assistants,* and even a part-time language assistant can be of significant help. In some areas of the country there are pools of Vietnamese speakers who, if they are otherwise qualified and are seeking employment, could serve as language assistants. Unfortunately this was not the case in the city where Roscoe Hunt Elementary is located. The pool of Spanish speakers was far larger, but of course that solution was not appropriate to Trang's problem.

Alternatives for LEP students

The absence of a Vietnamese speaker in both the classroom and the school meant that Trang was effectively denied a bilingual education program. By default, he learned English using the process that some opponents of bilingual education favor: *submersion* or immersion in an English-only environment. There's no question that the "sink or swim" approach eventually works, but the significant question is: at what cost to Trang? It is one thing to learn the English words for common objects—a pencil, a desk, a book, and so on—but quite another to learn the kinds of abstract concepts—for example, economy, democracy, region—associated with social studies.

"Language buddies"

Several students in Ms. Blanchard's class volunteered to help Trang—even though communication would be difficult at best. This was a variation on an approach called *language buddies*. A language buddy is typically an English-speaking classmate who also speaks the native language, and who explains, models, and otherwise assists the LEP student. In classes with several LEP students who speak the same first language, it is not unusual to have other students who are fluent in both the native language and English. Because both students share a common language, the "buddy" can help explain concepts to the LEP student in the native language. In Trang's case, however, the fact that none of the volunteers spoke Vietnamese posed a serious problem. Ms. Blanchard explained the situation to the volunteers, but they indicated they wanted to try it anyhow. Without many other alternatives at her disposal, Ms. Blanchard agreed that they would see how it went—for two weeks at least. At the end of that time, the volunteers and Trang had created a modified sign language—which was a far cry from the sign language used by the Deaf—that involved a lot of finger-pointing while simultaneously saying the word in English. And Trang, who was normally shy and quiet, was jubilant. No longer was he forced to sit by himself, and he was suddenly the focus of considerable peer attention.

Things went well until one afternoon when Ms. Blanchard heard one of the volunteer boys casually use a strange word that had the intonation of an expletive. When she asked the volunteer what he had said, he refused to say the word or tell her what it meant. It was, he said, a kind of code. This piqued Ms. Blanchard's curiosity, and upon further investigation, she discovered that in return for teaching him English, Trang was teaching the boys how to swear in Vietnamese. Ms. Blanchard then got the male volunteers together and pointed out rather forcefully that cursing was cursing—even if people who overheard you didn't know what the word meant. This, she emphasized, was not appropriate behavior in their classroom. Whether Trang ceased his role as teacher of Vietnamese is unknown.

Language loyalty

Trang's efforts to learn English were successful, due in large measure to his relaxed attitude, his willingness to learn a new language, and his "help" from his language buddies. Note that even if the language buddies had not helped Trang learn a word of English, the impact on his self-esteem was remarkable. But such successes are by no means universal. One of the more difficult hurdles in this area involves working with children who are so reluctant to leave the comfort and familiarity of their native language—*my* language, as they put it—that they simply go through the motions of learning a new language. This phenomenon may reflect what is sometimes called language loyalty (see Spolsky, 1998). Language loyalty is a relative measure of one's affinity and attachment to his or her native language. Many Europeans, for example, are bilingual, trilingual, or more. The French, however, tend to be an exception here, which is why Americans abroad sometimes regard them as arrogant or haughty. The French (in France) expect people to speak French in much the same way that Americans expect people to speak English.

Most Europeans have a preferred language that they use in the home, but they otherwise (except for the French) have low language loyalty. Americans, on the other hand, typically have a very high language loyalty and implicitly expect people who come here to be able to converse in English. In most instances there is little need for Americans to learn another language, and you can probably count on one hand the number of Americans you know who are bilingual. Yet Americans who go abroad are often more inclined to expect natives to have learned English rather than for Americans to have learned the native language.

Perceptions of the need to learn a second language

Many Hispanics, like most Americans, have a high affinity for their native language. In some instances Hispanic adults will speak Spanish—where they are admittedly more comfortable—even when they are proficient in English. Likewise, among Hispanic students who are not fluent in English, you may encounter a subtle undertone that says, "You can't make me learn English!" Again, we are not talking about outright rebellion here, because many Hispanics prefer not to confront an adversary publicly. Rather, they tend to rely on the "silent treatment"; they do nothing. If you have difficulty following the logic here, it is probably because we are dealing with a situation that is largely emotional.

The power of conformity

Why then did Trang respond so positively to efforts to teach him English? In most Asian-American cultures, conformity is highly desirable. Among the worst thing Asian-Americans can do in their native cultures is draw attention to themselves; they simply transfer that premise to their new environment. In other words, for many Asian-Americans, "fitting in" is their objective, and learning English is clearly one way to do that.

Teaching Techniques.   Two additional techniques to consider using with LEP students are (1) environmental print and (2) literature in the native language.

ENVIRONMENTAL PRINT.

Putting up signs

Environmental print refers to those signs you may have seen on objects in primary classrooms that label whatever you are viewing. The file cabinet will have a sign, often a large Post-it note, that says "File" on it, and the table will have a similar sign. What's different in a classroom with LEP students is that each label has two words on it, one in English and the other in the target LEP language.

Mary Jane Blanchard did not use the environmental print technique for Trang because Vietnamese is an ideographic language. Even after purchasing a Vietnamese-English dictionary Ms. Blanchard found that she had difficulty creating the symbols in the Vietnamese language. Until she could find someone competent in Vietnamese, she decided to limit the technique to English and Spanish (for her Hispanic LEP students).

CULTURALLY RELEVANT LITERATURE.

Ms. Blanchard didn't know whether Trang was a competent reader of stories written in Vietnamese, but she decided to give it a try. The librarian looked at Ms. Blanchard suspiciously—"No, we have never had a call for stories written in

Vietnamese," and "No, we have nothing that remotely resembles what you are asking for."

"Can you get some?" Ms. Blanchard asked. The librarian promised to check on the availability of books in Trang's native language, and several weeks later three stories written in Vietnamese appeared in Mrs. Blanchard's box.

The key question here is: Why should students learning English be supplied with literature in their native language? The answer lies in the fact that bilingual children must become proficient in at least one language. Until they can become proficient in English, ESL students will often find themselves translating English into their native language. In other words, they think in their native language, not in English. Until they reach the point where they are comfortable thinking in English, they must continue to develop their native language at the same time they are learning English. If they don't, they are apt to have mediocre vocabularies in *both* English and the second language. Giving LEP students literature in their native language is an attempt to stimulate children's native language skills at the same time that they are learning to cope with English. Once a child has become fluent in English, it rightfully remains his or her decision as to whether to continue working on fluency in his or her native language.

What language do they think in?

Other Teaching Implication.   Beginning teachers are sometimes at a loss as to what they can do for LEP students, especially when they do not speak that language. They need to resist the temptation to haul out the grammar worksheets, which seldom have anything to do with learning a second language. Consider that young children can communicate quite well in English even when they do not know what nouns, verbs, and adjectives are. If improper grammar is the concern ("we is," "ain't," etc.), consider that the first priority is basic communication. Once basic communication has been achieved, it is much easier for a child to learn the niceties of language.

Avoid grammar worksheets

Because basic communication in English is the main objective, some LEP students spend their entire day working with language skills. Six hours a day for five days a week of remedial drilling in basic language skills—with time out for art, music, physical education, and lunch, of course—can grow old very quickly. Some teachers also excuse LEP students from science and social studies so they can devote that time to language skills. Instead of excusing LEP students from social studies and science, try teaching a rich and varied curriculum in both areas. In addition, and wherever possible, try to integrate the language instruction into the subject areas. This can be done using a variety of art, music, drama, and construction activities. The opening vignette in Chapter 7 illustrates how a teacher from Arizona uses choral speaking and poetry to teach a social studies lesson to ESL and LEP students.

Integrate language activities into other subjects

• • • •

Learning Style

• • • •

Some people can't wait until someone quits talking so that they can read the instructions—whether they are making a cake or whatever. Others will say, "Don't bother me with that, just tell me how to do it." Another group of people will say, "Just let me do it." These examples reflect three preferred approaches to learning, or what is sometimes referred to by the generic term *learning style* (see Riding, 2002).

Preferred approaches to learning

Learning style, in abbreviated form, refers to how people would prefer to learn about things. Some people, for example, prefer to learn through reading; others prefer to learn through listening; and still others prefer to learn by manipulating objects or materials. If you are a person who prefers to learn about something through reading—or what is sometimes called a "*visual* approach to learning"— you may be able to remember where words or pictures are located on a page. Given your preference, you may find yourself becoming impatient with people who repeatedly ask for expanded verbal explanations. On the other hand, people like Mary Jane Blanchard's students, Trisha and Miguel, very much prefer *auditory* explanation and instructions. Auditory learners often have difficulty remembering what they read, but they can sometimes recall verbal explanations with the same precision that visual learners remember where words are located on a page.

Appealing to different styles

Lest it seem otherwise, education is not an ongoing battle between visual and auditory learners. The point here is that problems can arise when visually oriented teachers fail to provide the verbal explanations that sound-oriented learners rely on. As Ms. Blanchard says, "I sometimes explain stuff that seems obvious, but I know that at least some of my kids need that explanation." The fine line that teachers must determine, of course, is when they have explained something in enough depth to satisfy their auditory learners, but without boring their visual learners in the process.

Manipulative learners include students who cannot wait until everyone quits talking or reading so they can get their hands on whatever they are expected to do. The use of manipulatives is an important component in some areas of teaching, especially mathematics education, but it is not simply because hands-on techniques appeal to manipulative learners. Manipulative materials often permit students— whether visual, auditory, or manipulative learners—to see what might otherwise be abstract concepts in more concrete terms. This means that instead of having to memorize that $2 + 2 = 4$, students can actually see that when you combine one set of 2 beans with another set of 2 beans, you will have a total of 4 beans.

Using nonverbal feedback from students

You will undoubtedly have a mixture of visual, auditory, and manipulative learners in your classroom. Thus, the fine line referred to earlier will most likely lie in appealing to different learning styles, but without going overboard on any one style so that it "turns off" the others. One key here lies in closely observing your students' nonverbal communication, especially their expressions. For example, after giving a long verbal explanation, your visual learners' eyes may have begun to glaze over. This is OK so long as it doesn't go on too long. However, if your manipulative learners' eyes also begin to glaze over, you face the prospect of losing the attention of two groups—the visual and the manipulative learners. When this happens, you may wish to move quickly into the activity and then provide extra assistance individually.

Observing patterns of responses

How do you know which of your students are visual, auditory, or manipulative learners? The key here is by observing their responses to different classroom situations. Students who open a textbook (not a novel) without being told to do so are likely to be visual learners. Students who ask you a million questions, and can't seem to begin an activity without precise instructions, are probably either auditory learners or students who need lots of personal attention (perhaps both). Then you will have students who don't seem to have a clear preference one way or another. That's because learning style is a preference, not a trait etched in granite. Actually, learning style is like people's feelings about broccoli; some people love it, some hate it, and others are indifferent to it. And like most preferences, learning style can vary by degrees. Some students have strong preferences for visual, auditory, or manipulative learning, whereas other students have no real preference and can take whatever comes. Note that a sample learning style inventory is presented in Part I of the Resource Handbook.

Accommodating students' preferred learning styles may make students feel more comfortable and satisfied, but this does not mean that learning style necessarily reflects the only way a child can learn. For example, auditory learners can learn using visual and manipulative approaches, even if that is not their preferred style. Good and Brophy (2000) also note that, "accommodating students' preferences is not the same as meeting their needs" (p. 349). Good and Brophy cite several studies that suggest that although tailoring instruction to students' preferences may improve their attitudes toward learning, it can also produce *less* achievement than teaching them in other ways. The implication here is that teachers should strive for teaching activities that appeal to a variety of learning style preferences as opposed to relying extensively on activities that appeal to only one learning style. In addition to their preferred learning styles, other factors can influence how a learner learns. These include:

Attitudes vs. performance

Factors that influence learning style

- Environmental factors, including studying with music playing, in complete silence, or somewhere in between

- Sociological factors, including working alone or in groups

- Emotional factors, such as working in open-ended or highly defined assignments

- Physiological factors, such as studying while standing, sitting, or lying on the floor

- Psychological factors, such as one's preference for visual, auditory, or manipulative sources

KEY IDEA

Various strategies can be used to tailor instruction to meet students' needs.

Varying tolerances for ambiguity

Need for Structure.   A related aspect of learning style involves the extent to which students prefer open-ended activities, where they define most of the elements themselves, or—at the other end of the continuum—where they insist on having *everything* spelled out for them in advance. In this context, structure refers to how highly the teacher specifies or organizes a task in advance. Consider how you approached writing papers in the courses you have taken. Did you insist on precise instructions, perhaps including such things as the absolute minimum length of the paper, the number of footnotes, acceptable type fonts, the width of margins, and so on, or were you more willing "to go for it" until you met the assignment? You have too much experience to know that most students do not ignore factors that can play a role in grading, such as the number of references or proper font sizes, but you may also ask yourself, what is most important—the substance of the paper or its format? Such a question is unlikely to occur to students with high structure needs, because their main concern is with meeting the established expectations. They want to be certain that *everything* about their paper is within the guidelines. It may not matter that their paper says nothing, because they often hope to get a good grade simply because they met all the structural requirements. It is part of the "grading game" familiar to everyone in schools today.

An example of intolerance for ambiguity

An example of one student who faces the "structure" dilemma is Chen Lee, one of Mary Jane Blanchard's gifted students, who has "high structure needs." She is very uncomfortable in unstructured situations; she wants to know what task is to be done, exactly how that task should be done, when it must be done by, and in some instances, how to know when she is finished. Students like Chen Lee stand in contrast to students who have low structure needs, who can tolerate ambiguity in the tasks they are expected to do, and who often prefer to decide things for themselves.

A one-way relationship

Because you are likely to have both kinds of students in your classroom, two aspects about the need for structure are worth noting here. First, there appears to be no link between a child's need for structure and their intelligence (as need for structure is traditionally defined). This means that although Chen Lee is a gifted student, the same needs may appear among normal and low-ability students. A second aspect about the apparent need for "structure" is that it is a one-way relationship. Children with low structure needs may prefer open-ended and unstructured tasks, but they can also tolerate highly organized assignments, whereas students like Chen Lee are often frustrated with open-ended tasks. Therefore, if you are going to err, do so in favor of providing more structure, not less, to the tasks you assign.

Implications for grouping

You may also want to use your students' structure needs as a basis for creating groups. By putting students with high structure needs in one or two groups—which will be heterogeneous in terms of sex, ethnicity, and so on—you can provide them with very specific guidance, but without stifling the creativity of your other groups who are more comfortable making decisions among themselves.

Cooperative Learning

Cooperative learning defined

Cooperative learning is an approach to instruction in which students deal with learning tasks cooperatively, usually in small groups. The extended example in Chapter 1 of how Tarry Lindquist's class writes cooperative biographies reflects one teacher's approach to cooperative learning. In general, the teacher acts as a guide and consultant and other students serve as resources. Each individual is accountable for the group's effort, and all group members must learn the material in question. Typically, everyone in the group receives a common grade. In theory, students who goof off or don't contribute to the group's effort will be subjected to intense peer pressure, but in reality, some students willingly fade into the background and let others do all the work. The cumulative research findings (Johnson & Johnson, 1998) suggest that cooperative learning can lead to higher achievement, enhanced self-esteem, and improved attitudes toward teachers, other students, and school itself.

Individual vs. group achievement

Cooperative learning provides an environment in which all students can contribute according to their abilities. However, cooperative learning necessitates some modifications in the competitive work ethic that prevails in many classrooms. In its simplest form, the work ethic is based on the notion that each student must do his or her own work, and that working with someone is tantamount to cheating. The individual work ethic effectively negates almost any kind of cooperative group enterprise. This necessarily means that the cooperative model should be applied to tasks where students are expected to work cooperatively, and the competitive, individualistic model should be applied to tasks that students are expected to deal with on their own. Trying to mix the two approaches can give rise to problems and probably explains why legitimate small-group work has often played second fiddle in many schools. In the final analysis, few things are more basic than working successfully with others.

The Jigsaw Method.   The *jigsaw* name for this variant form of cooperative learning derives from an analogy to a jigsaw puzzle, which is not complete until the separate pieces are reassembled back in place. It is the technique that Ms. Lindquist used in the cooperative biography project described in Chapter 1. You may recall that Ms. Lindquist created five working groups, each with the task of producing a biography of Abe Lincoln. The individual members of each group were responsible for producing one chapter—one student would create the chapter on Lincoln's early life, another the chapter on Lincoln as president, and so on. The jigsaw comes into play when members leave their original (working) group and meet together in a new, task-alike group—the students responsible for the chapter on Lincoln's early life meet together as a group, the students responsible for Lincoln's presidency meet together, and so on. You may wish to reexamine Figure 1.1 in Chapter 1 to see a visual depiction of how jigsaw groups are organized.

Mary Jane Blanchard also uses the jigsaw method on occasion. In one instance, she organized her twenty-five-member class into five heterogeneous working groups of five students each. Each working group gets the same assignment: to produce a pictorial collage that shows examples of, and clearly distinguishes among, goods and services in five different areas—health, food, transportation, housing, and education. Each working group member is responsible for one area (or puzzle piece). For example, Student A on each team has health, Student B has food, and so forth. The working groups meet initially to clarify their assignment and assign topics. Then the working groups disband temporarily and reconvene in task-alike groups. In this case, all the students working with health-related goods and services meet together, all food-related members meet as a group, and so forth. The task-alike groups work together to consider such things as the kinds of pictures that would show their respective areas, and whether a picture of a nurse, for example, would show a good or a service. Once the task-alike group members are certain what they are after, they can reassemble as their original working groups. In this instance, they work individually to collect pictures from magazines. Mary Jane provides guidance and support throughout the activity, because cooperative learning is not intended as a technique in which students must work totally on their own. After the team members have completed their tasks, the original working team members reassemble to develop their collages. The problem the working teams must deal with now, if they have not done so already, is to figure out how they can present their information so that the goods and services for each area are displayed clearly and separately from the other areas. The complete collages are hung around the room and shared during the

Using working groups and task-alike groups

The jigsaw in practice

debriefing. Also considered during the debriefing are the problems that the teams encountered in completing their tasks and how they dealt with them.

An alternative   A less-structured alternative to the jigsaw technique involves assigning projects to small teams of students and then allowing the teams to work out their own procedures, thus eliminating the task-alike groups. Regardless of which approach a teacher takes, the problems that students encounter as they work together must be considered together with whatever content they learn.

Multiple Intelligences

Just as some of us have preferred learning styles, so some of us are also artistically, musically, or athletically inclined and others of us are not. Ask yourself why some people can play a musical instrument without lessons, whereas for others of us it is a lifelong struggle. These abilities or inclinations have become the focus of a growing body of theory and research related to multiple intelligences.

An expanded view of intelligence   Intelligence has traditionally been thought of as a single, inherited entity that enabled people to learn almost anything, provided it was presented in an appropriate way (see Gardner, 2000). Anyone who has taken traditional intelligence (IQ) tests knows that those instruments place a premium on one's ability to manipulate words—what Gardner calls "linguistic intelligence"—and on one's ability to solve logical or mathematical problems—what Gardner calls "logical-mathematical" intelligence. All of us know that schools recognize other talents, especially athletic skills, and in high schools at least, offer classes like band, choir, art, and shop where students can apply those talents. But most people will agree that this is an area where not all things are valued equally. Telling your mother that you flunked shop, for example, is usually a less serious crime than flunking English. The point is that most schools focus on linguistic and logical-mathematical intelligence.

The eight intelligences   A growing number of authorities believe that multiple intelligences are each quite independent of each other and that each has its own strengths and constraints. In addition to linguistic and logical-mathematical intelligence, which he originally suggested, Gardner has identified six other intelligences: musical, spatial, bodily-kinetic, interpersonal, intrapersonal, and naturalistic. Gardner's most recent addition, *naturalist intelligence* (see Gardner & Checkley, 1997) refers to an individual's ability to identify patterns in nature and discriminate among living things. Some individuals, for example, can discriminate between animals that are OK to hunt, and those that are better to run away from lest they kill you before you can kill them. Likewise some individuals can readily distinguish between varieties of wild mushrooms that are safe to eat, and others that cause dire consequences if you eat them.

Reviving an old idea   Some people think that Howard Gardner created the notion of multiple intelligences, but he actually popularized and expanded on an ancient idea. Over two millennia ago, the ancient Greeks viewed intelligence as a multifaceted phenomenon that included shrewd intelligence, analytic intelligence, aesthetic intelligence, spiritual intelligence, and others (Rosenthal, 1971). The first point here is that although the concept of multiple intelligences has been around for over a thousand years, it was largely ignored (or minimized) until recently. The second point is that differences in individuals' learning style could reflect differences in their underlying intelligences. The third point is that the diversity reflected in multiple intelligences could mean that there are multiple ways to teach something.

As researchers continue to explore multiple intelligences and learning styles, it is becoming ever more apparent that the two concepts are related. This is reflected in Table 5.1, which correlates the two notions. Table 5.1 also indicates potential activities that appeal to different intelligences. However, if you examine those activities closely, many of them seem very appealing, the kinds of things that most children would enjoy. Clearly, multiple intelligences and learning styles are areas where there is still much to be learned.

TABLE 5.1   Multiple Intelligences and Learning Styles

Children Who Are Strongly	Think	Love	Need
Linguistic	in words	reading, writing, telling stories, playing word games, etc.	books, tapes, writing tools, paper diaries, dialogue, discussions, debates, stories, etc.
Logical-Mathematical	by reasoning	experimenting, questioning, figuring out logical puzzles, calculating, etc.	things to explore and think about, science materials, manipulatives, trips to the planetarium and science museum, etc.
Spatial	in images and pictures, doodling, etc.	designing, drawing, visualizing, imagination games, mazes, etc.	art, LEGOs, videos, movies, slides, puzzles, illustrated books, trips to art museums, etc.
Bodily-Kinesthetic	through sonintic sensations	dancing, running, jumping, building, touching, gesturing, etc.	role play, drama, movement, things to build, sports and physical games, tactile experiences, hands-on learning, etc.
Musical	via rhythms and melodies	singing, whistling, humming, tapping feet and hands, listening, etc.	sing-along time, trips to concerts, music playing at home and school, musical instruments, etc.
Interpersonal	by bouncing ideas off other people	leading, organizing, relating, manipulating, mediating, partying, etc.	friends, group games, social gatherings, community events, clubs, mentors/apprenticeships, etc.
Intrapersonal	deeply inside of themselves	setting goals, meditating, dreaming, being quiet, planning, etc.	secret places, time alone, self-paced projects, choices, etc.

Source: Based on Harold Gardner. (2000). *Intelligence reframed: Multiple intelligence for the 21st century.* New York: Basic Books.

SUMMARY

In this chapter, several issues related to the instructional diversity you will face in your classroom were examined, not the least of which is the difficulty that schools face in moving away from a one-size-fits-all educational model. Just the thought of providing instruction geared to divergent learning styles or a particular intelligence, for example, may panic some people. History suggests that in movements of this kind, there will be a series of refinements, each of which offers more specific guidance to classroom teachers. However, history also suggests that there will be some gross errors, some backtracking, and some people who go overboard or use the movement to serve their own ends. As a teacher, you will be pushed and pulled in various directions and will be told that you should do this instead of that. Surviving in this environment probably requires two things above all others: healthy doses of (1) thoughtfulness and (2) common sense.

SUGGESTED READINGS AND RESOURCES

Print Resources

Howard Gardner. (1983). *Frames of mind.* New York: Harper-Collins Basic Books. This is the book that sparked the interest in multiple intelligences.

Daniel Hallahan & James Kauffman. (1997). *Exceptional learners.* Boston: Allyn & Bacon. This special education text takes the position that in dealing with exceptional children, the emphasis should be on their abilities, not their handicapping conditions.

Educational Leadership. (September 1997). This highly useful theme issue focuses on teaching for multiple intelligences.

Jonathon Mooney and David Cole. (2000). *Learning outside the lines.* New York: Simon & Schuster. This book offers remarkable insights into what it is like to be learning disabled.

Internet Resources

Introductory Note: Web sites sometimes change Internet addresses or cease operating entirely. All the addresses supplied here were operating when this book was printed, but should any of them fail to work properly, enter the topic or target organization in any standard search engine.

New Horizons for Learning

http://www.newhorizons.org/

This organization focuses on how people learn. It has links to issues ranging from brain research to learning styles to lesson plans. Recommended.

ESL/BILINGUAL EDUCATION

TESOL

http://www.tesol.org/index.html

This site is maintained by TESOL, Teachers of English to Speakers of Other Languages, which focuses on helping to improve the English-language proficiency of people who are nonnative speakers of English. It has numerous links to other Web sites on ESL.

National Clearinghouse for English Language Acquisition

http://www.ncela.gwu.edu/

This recommended site contains information of interest to teachers who work with nonnative speakers of English.

Language Development Strategies

http://www.laep.org/target/SMART/sunrise/lang.html

This site focuses on materials, strategies, and sample lesson plans for assisting limited-English-proficiency students. Information pertains to English language development, second-language acquisition, and self-image and multicultural learning.

SMALL-GROUP STRATEGIES

Teachers Helping Teachers

http://www.pacificnet.net/~mandel/

This site is a resource for getting teaching ideas and information about a variety of topics of interest to teachers. Teachers share their insights with each other.

A Guide to Maximizing Learning in Small Groups

http://www.cs.kent.ac.uk/national/CSDN/edu_resources/small-group-learning.html

This site offers guidelines for working with students in small groups.

The University of Kansas Center for Research on Learning

http://www.ku-crl.org

This site offers extended treatments of student-oriented learning strategies that make up the Center's Strategic Instruction Model.

www.GraphicOrganizers.com

http://www.graphicorganizers.com/index.htm

Click on "samples" and "free downloads" to view examples of graphic organizers developed by special education professor Edwin Ellis of the University of Alabama.

Power of Two

http://www.powerof2.org

This site is designed to help teachers successfully include children with special needs in the general education classroom. It provides access to effective strategies, complete learning modules, and useful training and teaching materials.

6

Developing Character and Values

KEY QUESTIONS

- **What gives schools and teachers the right to intervene in children's values and morals?**

- **How sensitive must teachers be to parental and community expectations?**

- **What are the moral implications associated with teaching or *not* teaching values and character?**

- **What is service learning?**

●●●● Introduction: The Reemergence of Character Education

Teachers cannot avoid teaching morals and values even if they want to. Everything they say and do, everything they study and discuss in class, even how they operate their classrooms, will reflect the values and standards that guide their conduct. Simply by observing teachers' actions and deeds, their students will learn what they think is important, valuable, and worth cherishing—and what is not. Without a teacher's saying a word about respecting others, for example, students will know whether he or she respects them as individuals.

Children will not necessarily adopt your values or any teacher's values. In fact, some children's value systems may prompt them to reject what you hold dear. When that happens, it's difficult not to take the child's rejection of what you value as a rejection of you personally. It takes a strong person who, in the face of defiance and rejection, can still say to a child, "I care about you regardless of how you feel about me." At the same time, the child's out-of-school environments may also reflect a self-centered, "do your own thing" mentality that directly contradicts many of the behaviors you are trying to model. Nevertheless, for those of us who intervene in children's lives, teaching morals and values is an inescapable fact of life.

When the first edition of this book was written over twenty-five years ago, serious questions were being asked about the school's role in teaching morals and values. At the time, the nation was extracting itself from the

Values permeate everything teachers do

KEY IDEA

Every teacher teaches values and morals, whether explicitly or implicitly; it's an unavoidable fact of teaching . . . and living.

war in Vietnam, and teaching even long-cherished values like patriotism had become controversial. Antiwar riots and protests occurred on campuses and elsewhere prompted by individuals who believed that the Vietnamese conflict was an unjust war that the United States should get out of as quickly as possible. Many of those protesters also believed that the traditional notion of patriotism as "Our country, right or wrong," was itself wrong, and that expecting them to support an unjust war was immoral. Such antiwar views often clashed with the views of other Americans who believed that the nation was obliged to support its armed forces, regardless of whether they personally supported or opposed the war. Those were troubling times indeed.

Troubling times   When the United States was involved in the Korean conflict in the early 1950s, similar protests did not occur. In the time between the two wars, the moral climate had changed dramatically. Beginning after World War II and continuing into the 1960s, more and more people in America (and around the world) began to embrace a rampant form of individualism that was divorced from notions of social responsibility. Also emerging at that time was a movement toward *logical positivism:* that is, the tendency to distinguish between facts, which were scientifically verifiable, and matters involving morals and values, which were regarded as expressions of personal feelings or preferences. Thus, when someone advocated a particular course of action as "the right thing to do," the usual responses were "Says who?" and "Nobody can force me to do anything I don't want to." Values and morals were becoming personalized and privatized, and moral and value issues were increasingly seen not as matters of doing the right thing, but as matters of personal judgment. For many Americans, morality was becoming a matter of "doing one's own thing."

Individualism and the personalization of morals

The Rise of Personalism

Lickona (1993) suggests that the era between the Korean and Vietnam wars and into the 1970s, 80s, and 90s was marked by a worldwide rise in *personalism.* This was and is a social movement that celebrates the autonomy of individuals, and their individual rights and freedoms. As Lickona stated, "Personalism rightly protested societal oppression and injustice, but it also delegitimized moral authority, . . . turned people inward toward self-fulfillment, weakened social commitments (for example, to marriage and parenting), and fueled the socially destabilizing sexual revolution" (p. 6).

Questioning the school's role in teaching values   President Theodore Roosevelt once said, "To educate a person in mind and not in morals is to educate a menace to society." Nevertheless, the legitimacy of teaching morals and values in schools began to be questioned during the 1970s and 1980s. In the process, many schools and teachers began consciously avoiding explicit instruction in moral and ethical principles, at least to the extent they could. In place of the school's traditional role in character education, they began focusing almost exclusively on the knowledge component of education—on transmitting "smartness."

The concerns for self-fulfillment and individual rights continued through the 1980s and into the 1990s, but disheartening signs arose on the horizon. Many families were no longer the stabilizing force in society they once were; crime and corruption were increasing; everyday life was becoming increasingly uncivil.

Calls for returning to teaching morals and values

By the mid-1980s, some authorities had begun to call for a return to the school's former role of providing explicit instruction in morals and values. For example, Ryan (1993) contended that by *not* treating values explicitly, the schools were doing only half their job.

Character education

By the mid-1990s, the occasional voices suggesting that our society was facing a growing number of problems had become a chorus. Some individuals, like William Kilpatrick (1992), suggested that in addition to persistent educational problems—like Johnny's inability to read well—an even more serious problem is that Johnny doesn't seem to know the difference between right and wrong. The contention among many observers was that schools could not remain morally and ethically neutral, but must return to their traditional role of teaching character education. In the late 1990s, and into the twenty-first century, character education was returning to many schools, in some cases with a vengeance.

Schools mirror the society

The schools had some valid reasons for backing off from traditional character education in the 1960s and 1970s. How, for example, could teachers continue to teach about "doing the right thing" when the larger society said, in effect, "It's OK to do your own thing"? Schools always tend to mirror the larger society, so to whatever extent the society says "we are going in this direction," the schools inevitably follow. When society effectively said "Back off on teaching values as moral absolutes, " schools did. Today, however, more and more people are turning to schools to do something about the problems facing our society. Unfortunately there is no clear consensus on (1) how schools should accomplish the task, or (2) whether schools have the tools and skills necessary to remedy moral problems.

Can schools do the job?

The first part of this chapter examines some current attempts to reestablish character education in the schools. The following sections explore alternative approaches for dealing with value issues.

● ● ● ● Terminology Clarified

The area of morals and values can easily become a morass of vague terms, so the following definitions are included:

Ethics defined, from the Greek

Ethics comes from the Greek *ethikos* and refers to norms and standards for judging behaviors as right and good or wrong and bad. In popular usage, ethics is typically used in connection with how we conduct our relationships with others; for example, persons who act unethically always do so in relationship to someone else.

Morals defined, from Latin

Morals is the Latin version of the Greek *ethikos* and carries the same meaning. In popular usage, *morals* often refers to the norms and standards that guide behavior.

Values defined

Values are ideas that serve as standards of conduct, beauty, efficiency, or worth. No one has seen an individual's values because they, like all ideas, are mental constructs. But we can observe how people behave, which indicates what they value.

Ethics and aesthetics

The standards we use for determining beauty are usually treated separately from standards of conduct, efficiency, and worth. For example, what we enjoy and find beautiful, such as a spectacular sunset, is said to reflect *aesthetics*. Aesthetic matters, such as whether you like or dislike modern art or classical music, seldom involve moral or ethical considerations. One way to think of this is that morality and ethics deal with "right" and "wrong," whereas aesthetics deals with what we think of as good or bad, beautiful or ugly.

Virtue defined

Virtue, a term popular in the Victorian era, is enjoying a rebirth (see Bennett, 1994; Doyle, 1997; Himmelfarb, 1995). It refers to qualities that all individuals should strive for, such as honesty, truthfulness, self-respect, and self-reliance. Himmelfarb suggests that the need to distinguish between virtues and values has come about because values in popular usage can refer to "beliefs, opinions, attitudes, feelings, habits, conventions, preferences, even idiosyncrasies—whatever any individual, group or society happens to value, at any time and for any reason" (p. 3). Some authorities use the term *core values* to set the virtues noted above apart from other values.

KEY IDEA

The key components of character education are (1) values themselves and (2) a process of valuing.

Character

Character refers to virtuous behavior—behavior that conforms to valued norms and customs.

Building Character

When one of the school's missions was to "melt" newly arrived immigrants into the mainstream society, the teaching of values and morals was usually called *character education*. That term has enjoyed a rebirth, but you will sometimes hear it called *values education* or *moral education*. All three terms refer to what schools do to help children become ethically mature adults who are capable of practicing moral thought and action in democratic ways.

What to teach, exactly?

Teaching character is clearly a more complex enterprise than teaching content-oriented lessons. For example, what exactly would you teach if you wanted your students to demonstrate respect for others? There is some excellent children's literature that you could use, but unlike conventional subjects, character traits do not have easily defined content. You might resort to preaching platitudes like "Be nice to others," but the research indicates that such exhortations, as well as various codes and pledges, are unlikely to have any lasting effects on students' character (see Leming, 1993).

What Is Good Character?

The purpose of character education is to develop good character in the young. One authority, Thomas Lickona, suggests that "good character consists of knowing the good, desiring the good, and doing the good" (1993, p. 9). Lickona's definition, broad as it is, highlights a major difference between character and conventional knowledge-based subjects. In addition to a cognitive (or knowledge) dimension that character traits share with conventional subjects, character also has an attitudinal (or feeling) dimension and a psychomotor (or behavioral) dimension that conventional subjects usually lack. Many children already

The multidimensional nature of character

Is this the future of teaching in the age of technology?

(© 1997 Wm. Hoest Enterprises, Inc. Reprinted courtesy of Bunny Hoest and PARADE Magazine.)

"Keep your eyes on your own monitor, and don't e-mail anyone."

know about values like honesty and truthfulness, for example, but nobody needs to tell you that some children (and adults) will be dishonest or lie whenever it suits their purpose. What they may lack is an attitude, a disposition, a conscience if you will, that disposes them to do the right thing regardless of its ultimate effect on them. The affective, or dispositional, component of character provides an essential bridge between character's cognitive (or knowing) dimensions and a person's actions. The cognitive, affective, and behavioral dimensions of character, as identified by Lickona (1993), are summarized in Table 6.1.

Simply knowing about character is inadequate

A bridge between what people know and do

Which Values Should Be Taught?

Parents who oppose character education usually do so out of fear that schools will try to indoctrinate their children about gay rights, abortion, premarital sex, and similar matters. The issue is compounded because of individuals who want schools to deal explicitly with such issues. The issue is even further compounded by one segment of the character education movement that defines character very narrowly—as helping adolescents avoid premarital pregnancy. Most character education programs, however, focus on developing core values, or virtues, that are (1) basic to morality and (2) that almost no one opposes. These virtues (or core values) include respect, the dignity of the individual, personal and civic responsibility, honesty, trustworthiness, fairness, caring, and courage. (All these values are elements of the community literacy referred to in Chapter 1.)

A focus on virtues (core values)

TABLE 6.1   The Moral Components of Character

Dimension	Trait
Cognitive	1. Awareness of the moral dimensions of a situation
	2. Knowing moral values, like truthfulness, and what they require in concrete cases
	3. Perspective taking, the ability to look at situations from various perspectives
	4. Moral reasoning, the ability to differentiate among different rationales and motives for behaving in certain ways
	5. Thoughtful decision making, the ability to assess alternative courses of action
	6. Moral self-knowledge
Affective	1. Conscience, the felt obligation to do what one judges is right
	2. Self-respect
	3. Empathy
	4. Love of the good
	5. Self-control
	6. Humility, a willingness to recognize and correct our moral failings
Behavioral	1. Competence, skills such as listening, communication, and cooperating
	2. Will, which mobilizes judgment and energy
	3. Moral habit, a reliable disposition to respond to situations in morally good ways

Source: Abridged from Thomas Lickona, "The Return of Character Education," *Educational Leadership,* 51 (1993), 10.

Different labels Some schools integrate elements of character education into their programs without using an explicit label, like *character education,* whereas other schools may use terms such as *positive conflict resolution.* One expression you commonly hear in schools today is "character counts," a sentiment I agree with entirely. However, it is also the name of a popular, commercially available character education program. Regardless of how they refer to character education, most schools involve parents in meetings that focus on the values they intend to promote. Almost never do those schools encounter anyone who argues, for example, that lying is better than telling the truth.

KEY IDEA

Community expectations concerning values education are seldom consistent, nor are they necessarily known in advance.

· · · ·

The Movement Toward Caring Schools

· · · ·

As more and more educators have discovered, teaching character can require some far-reaching changes in the school itself. You might try modeling desired behaviors to your students, but if you teach in a school organized on a marine boot camp model, the environment could effectively undo everything you are trying to accomplish.

Concern for the school environment

You cannot build trusting relationships or teach respect in an environment—be it a classroom or school—where disrespect and incivility are rampant. The atmosphere in the larger environment is just too contradictory. When students feel that no one cares about them or that they are nameless cogs in a huge bureaucracy, they are unlikely to assert themselves or to voluntarily accept responsibility for the common good. Individual teachers are sometimes able to foster civility and respect in their classrooms, but the idea of the caring school extends those efforts to the larger environment.

According to Olweus (2003), caring schools reflect the following characteristics:

- Warmth, positive interest, and involvement from adults

- Firm limits on unacceptable behavior

- Consistent application of nonpunitive, nonphysical sanctions for unacceptable behavior or violation of rules

- Adults who consistently act as authorities and positive role models

Caring vs. noncaring

The movement toward caring schools should not be construed as resulting from the failure of character education, because both caring schools and character education address related problems. In some respects, both phenomena are attempts to combat the steady rise in greed, disrespect, and incivility in the larger society. Finally, the notion of a caring school can unfortunately connote that if a school does not bill itself as caring, it is necessarily a "noncaring" school. Caring schools have a degree of warmth and vibrancy that you can feel when you walk into the building, but under no circumstances should other schools be construed as noncaring.

Schools that wish to adopt the caring school concept must be willing to subject their entire operation to scrutiny. Two elements that invariably receive close examination are (1) the hidden curriculum and (2) classroom management practices.

Dealing with the Hidden Curriculum.   The *hidden curriculum* refers to what students learn from day-to-day schooling pratices that students experience but that are not part of the formal school curriculum. Consider, for example, teachers who talk about the need to respect one another, but who routinely put down certain students. Or who talk about the importance of cooperation but then set up instructional programs in which students must compete for every reward. Or who show entertainment videos every Friday. On one occasion, an adult in a noncaring school stopped a student in the hallway and said, "Do you have the time?" The student said, "It's 10:46." Instead of a simple thank-you, the adult replied, "That's correct." Individually, such activities may seem insignificant, but collectively they send powerful messages.

KEY IDEA

The "hidden curriculum" is a powerful instrument of instruction.

Classroom Management Practices.   The hallmark of many classroom management programs, such as Assertive Discipline and others like it, is a series of system-

Rewarding good conduct

atic consequences for students who misbehave. For a first offense, the student's name goes on the board; for a second offense, the student must stay after school, and so forth. The key to such programs is recognizing and rewarding students when they behave appropriately or, as Canter (1989) suggests, "catching them being good." Rewarding students for good behavior might seem an appropriate balance for negative consequences, but Kohn (1997) has pointed out that this aspect of management plans can sometimes undermine a character education program. Regardless of the specific management plan that teachers use, the key concern is how they reward good behavior. Providing students with tangible rewards can be an effective technique in the short run but could have negligible or negative long-run effects. Kohn suggests that questionable reward systems include (1) providing "bonus bucks" (or punching tickets or putting marbles into a jar) that can be redeemed for an ice cream or pizza party and (2) rewarding children with a leaf to hang on the "Forest of Virtue" bulletin board. Equally questionable, according to Kohn, are activities such as targeting a certain value on a particular day of the week—"If it's Thursday, this must be Respect Day"—and then rewarding children for demonstrating that day's value. One could ask, "What's wrong with respecting others on Mondays, or any other day of the week?" Even worse than tangible rewards, in Kohn's view, are awards that are so limited that only a few children can get them: "This week's winner of the Hard Worker Award is. . . ." Such awards—assuming children really value them—force children to compete with their peers and thus to regard their classmates as potential obstacles to success.

SUGGESTED ACTIVITY
Providing tangible rewards to students for demonstrating good behavior may be successful in the short run, but over time it can undermine a child's intrinsic motivation. Determine how you might resolve this apparent dilemma.

Extrinsic vs. intrinsic motivation

Using tangible rewards for virtuous conduct is a form of extrinsic motivation that can undermine intrinsic motivation. What children can learn from such practices is not that virtuous behavior is good, desirable, and something worth doing on its own merits, but that the purpose of "being good" is to earn rewards. Frequent rewards for children who demonstrate virtuous behavior can make them *less* likely than other children to continue demonstrating those behaviors (Fabes et al., 1989; Grusec, 1991, cited in Kohn, 1997).

An alternative to tangible rewards

Should you find yourself teaching in a school that has adopted Assertive Discipline, or a similar management plan, your options are necessarily limited. Because ignoring the school's plan would probably be unwise, you should consider modifying the plan, especially to the extent to which you provide tangible rewards for desired behaviors. In place of tangible rewards, consider offering free time or using classroom meetings as they are described in William Glasser's *The Quality School* (1990) and his earlier works. From time to time, you might want to conduct classroom meetings that focus on whether it is "right" to reward people for doing what they ought to do anyhow. The basic point here is that the hidden curriculum and classroom management practices must complement, or at least not contradict, everything else that schools and teachers do.

Ongoing Activities for Character Education

A variety of activities can support character education. Some of these can be part of a comprehensive and schoolwide effort, whereas others are techniques that teachers can use on occasion in their classrooms.

National Schools of Character

National Schools of Character are the recipients of rewards of excellence from the Character Education Partnership (CEP), a national organization based in Washington, D.C., that supports effective character education programs in schools. The CEP produces a quarterly newsletter, hosts an annual conference and a website (www.character.org), and offers other resources for conducting character education programs. The CEP address is 1025 Connecticut Ave., NW, Suite 1011, Washington, DC 20036. Telephone 1-800-988-8081.

Eleven principles

The CEP recognizes that although there is no single script for effective character education, there are eleven basic principles that should be reflected in programs. These include:

Principle 1   Promoting core ethical values as the basis of good character.

Principle 2   Defining "character" comprehensively to include thinking, feeling, and behavior.

Principle 3   Using a comprehensive, intentional, proactive, and effective approach to character development.

Principle 4   Creating a caring school community.

Principle 5   Providing students with opportunities for moral action.

Principle 6   Including a meaningful and challenging academic curriculum that respects all learners, develops their character, and helps them to succeed.

Principle 7   Striving to foster students' self motivation.

Principle 8   Engaging the school staff as a learning and moral community that shares responsibility for character education and attempts to adhere to the same core values that guide the education of students.

Principle 9   Fostering shared moral leadership and long range support in the character-building effort.

Principle 10 Engaging families and community members as partners in the character-building effort.

Principle 11 Evaluating the character of the school, the school staff's functioning as character educators, and the extent to which students manifest good character.

Lickona (1993) recommends the following as activities that individual teachers can use in their classrooms:

Things teachers can do

- *Acting as caregiver, model, and mentor.* Treating students with love and respect, setting a good example, supporting positive social behavior, and correcting hurtful actions through one-on-one guidance and whole-class discussions

- *Practicing moral discipline.* Using the creation and enforcement of rules as opportunities to foster moral reasoning, voluntary compliance with rules, and a respect for others

- *Creating a democratic classroom environment.* Involving students in decision making and sharing the responsibility for making the classroom a good place to be and learn

- *Teaching values through the curriculum.* Using ethically rich content of academic subjects (such as literature, history, and science) as well as outstanding programs, such as the Heartwood Ethics Curriculum for Children (which is described shortly)

- *Using cooperative learning.* To develop students' appreciation of others, perspective taking, and ability to work with others toward common goals

- *Developing the "conscience of craft."* By fostering students' appreciation of learning, capacity for hard work, commitment to excellence, and sense of work as affecting the lives of others

- *Encouraging moral reflection.* Through reading, research, essay writing, journal keeping, discussion and debate

- *Teaching conflict resolution.* To help students acquire the essential moral skills of solving conflicts fairly and without force

A moral imperative

The movement toward reestablishing character education will undoubtedly be challenging. If nothing else, many teachers today grew up in a cultural milieu that encouraged the personalization and privatization of moral values. Also, many questions exist for which there are no clear answers. Why, for example, do some people consistently act in morally responsible ways and others don't? And, can schools provide the same kind of moral anchors that families have provided in the past? Despite the unanswered questions, the consensus in the literature is that character education has become a moral imperative.

● ● ● ● Service Learning and Responsible Citizenship

I never pictured myself doing community service, and now I can. I did extra days at the soup kitchen because I had fun the first time, and I liked the feeling I got from helping people.

—Kayla M.

Now I have had the experience of helping others, and it made me feel so good about myself. Sometimes it's hard to see people who are not as lucky as you and sometimes you just feel like crying. It's not fair!

—Alix F.

The preceding are responses from middle-school students about their service-learning activity (cited in Bloom, 2003, pp. M4, M5).

Service learning defined

Service learning in its narrow sense refers to what students learn from having participated in school or community service on a regular basis. In its broader sense, service learning refers to the inclusion of service to the school or, preferably, the community, as a part of the school program. Whatever service the students render should be related to their program of studies and appropriate to their age. Having students volunteer as candy stripers at a local hospital is one possibility, assuming they can meet the hospital's requirements for volunteers. On the other hand, the candy striper role is an example of pure volunteerism and could be difficult to justify in relation to the curriculum. In a different sense, having second graders pick up trash along the highway (in states that have an "Adopt a Highway" program) could also render a valuable service. However, the

Safety potential safety hazards of such an activity could make it unsuitable for young children.

Service-learning activities are especially relevant to social studies because of their relationship to social studies' overall mission of citizenship education (see Boyle-Baise, 2003; Morris, 2003). That relationship is captured in the phrase "the

Rights *and* responsibilities rights and responsibilities of citizens in a democratic society." Most children, even the very young, are highly attuned to their rights and will quickly point out anything that is not in their opinion fair and just. But if you ask them about their responsibilities as citizens, you will usually get a puzzled look. Even adults some-

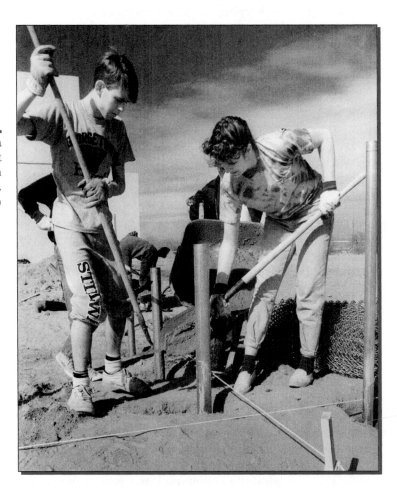

Many schools are including a community service component in their character education programs.
(© Jonathan A. Meyers)

times have problems identifying the responsibilities of citizenship. Given enough time, students (and adults) usually say something like, "I need to vote"; unfortunately, they may have problems identifying other responsibilities. And almost never do they mention that public schools, which are paid for by all citizens, were created to ensure an informed citizenry; that is, a population that is able to understand the issues they will be asked to vote on, and who can do so thoughtfully and deliberatively. Informed citizens have the responsibility to look beyond mere self-interest so as to judge issues in terms of their impact on the common good. The main points here are that (1) democracies would be in tough shape if voting were the extent of a citizen's responsibilities and (2) a goal of service learning is to enhance students' willingness to participate actively in civic life.

Active participation in public life

Service Learning and Character Education

If you are curious why service learning appears in a chapter on character education, it's because the research suggests that service learning tends to be more effective than many of the alternative character education techniques that are presented later in this chapter. Educators have long known, for example, that teaching children to be responsible by talking (lecturing) at them about personal responsibility is unlikely to be successful. At the same time, the concern among parents and teachers alike about increasing instances of bullying in elementary and middle schools (see Olweus, 2003 and Cooper & Snell, 2003) could not be ignored. Nevertheless, the bullying phenomenon seemed to be immune to existing techniques for helping children learn to respect the rights and opinions of others. As one teacher put it, "I've tried everything but I can't get through to the students (the bullyers) who need it most." In other words, after almost a decade of focused attention on problems and attitudes related to character education, the situation did not seem to be improving as it should.

Prior lack of success

Many educators came to realize that "talk was indeed cheap." Big signs in the hallways that said, "Respect Others," and "Responsibility," which are part of some character education programs, as well as teachers who talked about the need to care about others apparently had little impact on students who satisfied their needs by continuing to demonstrate superiority and acting out against other students. Parents of the victims and parents of the perpetrators were concerned, as were parents who wondered, "will my child be next?"

It became apparent that students needed to experience situations where, instead of just talking about attitudes and values at an abstract level, they would be called on to demonstrate them. A good possibility here was service learning. Students doing service-learning work in animal shelters, for example, would quickly recognize that the animals under their care would not be fed unless they fed them. In other words, the animals were depending on them. And students working on a stream beautification project in one community learned that nothing was likely to happen unless they got behind the project and made a case for it. Students who find themselves in positions of responsibility are much more likely to accept that responsibility and then act accordingly than students being told that they need to act responsibly.

Hands-on experiences

Effectiveness.   Findings on the outcomes of service learning are encouraging. In one of the most thorough analyses of service learning projects, Bellig (2000) described the findings as compelling. She found that participation in service-learning activities often led to the following outcomes:

- A positive effect on students' personal and social development

- Moderate to strong gains on achievement tests

Outcomes - A greater likelihood to treat others kindly and to help one another

- Increased self-esteem and fewer behavioral problems, especially among boys

- Better ability to trust and be trusted by others, to be reliable, and to accept responsibility for their actions

Getting Started.   Service-learning activities need not be ongoing, at least not at first, and not at the lower grade levels (Allen, 2003). Rather, they can occur as occasional in-school projects, such as organizing a food drive or a campus beautification project. Even small projects have a way of growing into more involved activities.

Students are not simply the source of labor for service learning. If they begin grumbling about feeling put upon or suggesting that they "would rather be doing math than 'this'," you may want to reflect on how the activity was presented to them—as a finished project, that is, almost another assignment—or whether they were involved in the planning phases too. Admittedly you could probably organize the activity much more quickly and efficiently by yourself, but then it *Ownership* would be your project, not theirs. The key element here is ownership. Consider holding class meetings where students brainstorm responses to the question: How could we improve life around here? You will get plenty of responses, including some you never thought of and others you might best avoid (e.g., "Hire a new cafeteria director," etc.) At subsequent meetings the class could work on identifying ideas that are doable. But before making any final decisions, make certain you have visited with the principal and other members of the administration to let them know what is going on. It isn't necessary that you get their wholehearted support—after all, you will be talking about a proposal, not a finished product—but their active opposition could be the kiss of death. Likewise, be certain to let *Keep parents involved* parents know what is going on. Many parents and members of the public are wedded to the notion that when children are in school, they should be sitting at their desks, pen or pencil in hand, doing "legitimate" schoolwork. Recognize also that parents sometimes feel that picking up trash on the school grounds or working in a soup kitchen, for example, are inappropriate tasks for their sons and daughters. Such feelings are less likely to emerge if students are participating in a project that they had a hand in creating. Remember also that service learning is not a school version of household chores—like taking out the trash. The goal of service learning is to enhance the students' willingness to participate in civic life.

Service-learning activities will increase your workload. The amount of time *More work for you* spent making placements and coordinating activities can be significant—particularly if it is your first time to organize such a project. Recognize also that many students will not welcome service-learning activities with open arms. Complaints,

Expect grumbling at first.

grumbling, and sometimes outright negativism are common, especially at first. These usually pass when students discover that there is nothing fearful or necessarily onerous about service-learning activities; on the contrary, they are more likely to be interesting and self-fulfilling. However, if the grumbling continues beyond the first few weeks, investigate promptly. Pay special attention to the tasks the students are doing. It is one thing to work on the serving line of a soup kitchen, for example, but quite another to spend three hours every Thursday scouring dirty pots in the kitchen.

KEY IDEA

The goals of service learning are (1) to provide experiences that will enhance students' willingness to participate actively in civic life and (2) to help students understand that the responsibilities of citizenship are the reciprocal of the rights of being a citizen.

Reflection. A key component of service learning is periodic reflection, preferably in group settings, under a teacher's guidance. As Billig (2000) noted, "reflection should include elements that help students make meaning of their experience and draw connections to the roots of the community's needs. . . . When teachers facilitate discussions that help students to see deeper meaning, such as understanding and valuing cultural background, students are more apt to identify and retain the outcomes for a longer time" (p. 8). Depending on the students' age, you may want to require a written paper, a class presentation, or a journal or log that documents the service-learning activity, but these elements should be in addition to, not instead of, time for active reflection.

Other Approaches to Values Education

Amenable to moral and ethical issues

Most of the approaches to values education dealt with in this section are amenable to ethical questions or to issues involving the moral and ethical standards that influence one's behavior.

TABLE 6.2   Recommendations for Service Learning

....

- Find out what service-learning opportunities are available in your community. Good places to start include environmental projects, established volunteer programs, hospitals, nursing homes, and especially animal shelters.

- Don't forget to explore the possibility of working with the elderly or the disabled.

- Be sure to ask students for ideas.

- Get your principal on board from the beginning.

- Talk up your program wherever you go. You will be surprised at the ideas and assistance people will offer (but don't be surprised if some of them think it's too novel an idea).

- Involve parents from the beginning, even to the extent of offering them opportunities to participate.

- After the project has firmed up, develop and distribute a written explanation of it. Be sure to include how you will ensure each child's safety. Also include how the service-learning project will be part of your grading system.

Inculcation

Throughout human history, *inculcation* (or exhortation) has been a common technique for molding human behavior. It refers to the process of making an impression on the mind through frequent repetition, insistent urging, or modeling. Inculcation, like brainwashing, is based on the premise that if you show or tell people something often enough, eventually they will behave accordingly.

Repeated telling

Whenever you hear parents (or teachers) saying things like "Good girls (or boys) don't do *that* kind of thing, " they are using inculcation. Somewhere along the line, the parents identify the desired behavior, such as "Children should respect their elders. " Then, over the years, they provide appropriate reinforcement—a nod or smile of approval when children demonstrate the desired behavior and a gentle reminder when they don't.

For centuries parents have successfully inculcated desired values and behaviors in their children, although recent polls (Peterson, 2002) suggest that they are beginning to doubt their effectiveness. Nevertheless, children will usually behave as they are expected, at least when their parents are present. Even though many parents have used inculcation successfully, research suggests that it does not work equally well for teachers. The research doesn't indicate why this is so, but it most likely has to do with contact time. Parents can consistently reinforce desired behaviors in their children from their birth onward. Teachers, on the other hand, have only a 180-day school year in which to accomplish the same thing. And children know that, come each September, they will have a different teacher who will probably hold different expectations.

Literature-Based Techniques

Literacy springboard to teaching values

Most children have heard the famous lines "1 think I can, I think I can, I think I can," and "1 thought I could, I thought I could, I thought I could." They are from Watty Piper's (1930/1978) children's classic, *The Little Engine That Could.* Through diligence, perseverance, and a lot of effort, a little switch engine is able to pull a trainload of Christmas food and toys to the children who live on the other side of the mountain. If some of your students have heard the story, you can still read it again—even students familiar with the story will enjoy it another time. Children's stories like *The Little Engine That Could* can provide the basis for a follow-up discussion of how diligence, perseverance, and patience, combined with a positive attitude, can often overcome overwhelming obstacles. The children can also talk about times when positive attitudes have helped them complete challenging tasks or do things that they were afraid to do.

Other examples

If you want to focus on behaving responsibly, you might consider reading Chris Van Allsburg's (1988) delightful tale, *Two Bad Ants.* This story focuses on an ant colony that sets out to retrieve a huge mound of delicious crystals (sugar) their scouts have located. But instead of returning to the colony with all the other ants, the two bad ants decide to remain and feast for a while. The crystal pile soon becomes a dangerous place, and the two ants eventually end up in a coffee cup, are put down into the garbage disposal, and even get blown out of an electrical outlet where they are trying to hide. Needless to say, the ants suffer severe consequences for their actions.

Still in the context of responsible behavior, older students will enjoy Kate McMullan's (1991) *The Great Eggspectations of Lila Fenwick.* In this story, a librarian tries to teach sixth graders about responsibility by having them care for a hard-boiled egg as if it were a newborn baby. Lila discovers that many of her usually great ideas backfire on her as she tries to care for her egg.

So many literary works can serve as springboards for values-oriented discussions and activities that an extended listing of children's stories is included in the Resource Handbook. These stories are organized by the main values they focus on—sharing, responsibility, and so on.

A literature-based approach to values education can be as organized (or unorganized) as you wish to make it. The basic procedure is to read the story to your students and then conduct a follow-up discussion or share-and-tell session. The discussion period should be regarded as a time to talk with children about the values in question, and not an opportunity to moralize.

Other literature-based programs

Two character education programs that make use of children's literature warrant special mention here. They are the Heartwood Ethics Curriculum and the Exploring Ethics through Children's Literature Program. The Heartwood program was developed by an attorney from Pittsburgh who was appalled by the lack of remorse among the young defendants she represented in court, as well as by some retired teachers from the Pittsburgh area. The Heartwood materials are based on Newbery award-winning, multicultural books (stories) that address core values such as courage, loyalty, justice, respect, hope, honest, and love. The Exploring Ethics through Children's Literature Program follows a similar format.

Values Clarification

Clarifying what our values are

Values clarification is one of the rare techniques whose title describes exactly what it tries to do: help individuals *clarify* what their values really are. The underlying premise is that most individuals are not clear about what their values are until they are confronted by situations that cause them to examine their values.

Values clarification is a value-neutral approach that was created in the mid-1970s when the explicit teaching of values was declining. Rather than trying to instill or impose certain values, values clarification is based on a seven-phase valuing process, as follows:

Choosing

The valuing process

1. Encourage children to make choices, and to make them freely.
2. Help them *discover alternatives* when faced with choices.
3. Help children weigh alternatives thoughtfully, reflecting on the *consequences* of each.

Prizing

4. Encourage children to consider what it is that they prize and *cherish.*
5. Give them opportunities to *affirm their* choices to others.

Acting

6. Encourage children to act, *behave,* and live *in accordance with their choices.*
7. Help them be aware of repeated behaviors or patterns in their life *[emphasis added]* (Raths, Harmin, & Simon, 1978, pp. 28, 38).

The Clarifying Response. A key element of values clarification is the clarifying response. This refers to how teachers respond to students, either individually or as a class, to help them identify what is important and desirable. In many instances, the exact form of the clarifying response will be situational and may take the form of a question, as illustrated in the following exchange:

TEACHER: Bruce, don't you want to go outside and play on the playground?

STUDENT: I dunno. I suppose so.

The clarifying response   TEACHER: Is there something that you would rather do?

STUDENT: I dunno. Nothing much.

TEACHER: You don't seem much to care, Bruce. Is that right?

STUDENT: I suppose so.

TEACHER: And mostly anything we do will be all right with you?

STUDENT: I suppose so. Well, not anything, I guess.

TEACHER: Well, Bruce, we'd better go out with the others now. You let me know sometime if you think of something you would like to do. (Dialogue adapted from Raths et al., 1978, p. 55.)

Clarifying responses should encourage students to examine their ideas, but without the teacher moralizing, criticizing, evaluating, or otherwise suggesting that they have a "right answer" in mind.

Productive clarifying response questions include the following:

Suggested clarifying responses   Is this important to you?
Are you happy about that?
Would you really do that or are you just talking?
What other possibilities are there?

What Critics Say About Values Clarification. The criticisms of values clarification usually focus on four areas: (1) values clarification activities may place students in situations that can jeopardize their right to privacy, (2) the approach can require teachers to respond to situations as trained counselors would, (3) the approach makes no distinction between moral and nonmoral issues, and (4) the approach tends to support the position that all value beliefs are equally valid (ethical relativism).

Consider the consequences of asking children to identify the meanest person they know or who in their family causes them the greatest sadness. Both questions are clearly "loaded," and asking either of them publicly will put students in a situation where they are highly likely to disclose personal information about themselves or their relationships with others—including their families. In addition, related questions (e.g., "Is this important to you?") that are intended to help the child clarify his or her response will be much like those a trained counselor and psychologist might use in group therapy and might lead to situations where teachers could easily find themselves in over their heads.

Values clarification activities have also been criticized for failing to distinguish between moral (ethical) and nonmoral (aesthetic) value issues. There is obviously nothing immoral about asking students to identify their favorite foods or how they would spend their allowance, both of which are a matter of personal priorities. However, a popular values clarification activity called "The Bomb Shelter" asks students to select which six of ten candidates—which include a doctor, a violinist, a police officer, and so forth—should be permitted to enter the shelter. Candidates who are not admitted will presumably die. Asking children to determine which individuals should be permitted to live and which should die, or whether doctors make greater contributions to society than do violinists, are far different matters from asking about a students' favorite flavor of ice cream, which is purely a judgment call. So ask yourself if it is appropriate to place children in situations where they must (1) make life-or-death decisions or (2) judge the relative merits of different occupations.

A final and perhaps the most serious criticism of the values clarification approach is that it tends to promote *ethical relativism*. This means that instead of using overarching moral principles, such as the dignity of the individual and the sanctity of human life—principles that should apply in all situations—the values

Should children be asked to make life-death decisions?

Ethical relativism

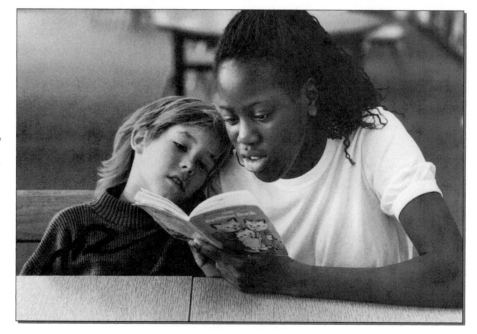

When students help each other both may gain from the experience. (© Jean-Claude Lejeune)

clarification approach seems to suggest that individuals' actions should be governed by the situations in which they find themselves, and by what is practical or expedient. This criticism arises, in part, because there is no justification phase in the seven-step valuing process shown on pages 159–160. Because students are not asked to justify or defend their decisions, they could come away with the impression that one person's views are as good as anyone else's, regardless of the situation.

Questionable effectiveness

In 1985, Leming reviewed over seventy-five studies involving values clarification and found that they seldom produced the attitudinal or behavioral changes that the researchers had anticipated. Nevertheless, at that time one of the books on which values clarification is based, *Values Clarification: A Handbook of Practical Strategies for Teachers and Students* by Simon, Howe, and Kirschenbaum (1972), was the all-time, best-selling book in professional education. Leming therefore suggested that the lingering popularity of vlaues clarification activities resulted, in part, from their widespread availability for classroom use.

● ● ● ●
Moral Reasoning
● ● ● ●

The *moral-reasoning* approach to values education is closely associated with the work of the late Harvard psychologist Lawrence Kohlberg and his associates. Kohlberg first developed a theory that dealt with how children learn to reason morally and then developed a teaching strategy to help children improve the quality of their moral reasoning. To determine what makes one kind of moral reasoning "better" than another, it's necessary to understand the moral development theory on which Kohlberg's teaching strategy is based.

Moral Development. Kohlberg's research focused on the question "How do individuals develop the ability to reason morally (to justify their actions)?" After investigating moral reasoning among individuals of various ages and from various cultures, Kohlberg identified a developmental sequence, which is shown in Table 6.3. (At one time the developmental sequence had six stages, but Kohlberg redefined his model so that Stage 5 now incorporates what was formerly in Stage 6.)

Implications

In Jean Piaget's scheme for cognitive development, sooner or later almost everyone reaches the last stage, formal operations: the ability to think and reason abstractly. However, Kohlberg found that fewer than 25 percent of American adults ever reach Stage 5 (Principled level) in the development of their moral reasoning. If you consider that the moral basis of the Bill of Rights reflects Stage 5 reasoning, Kohlberg's findings suggest that many citizens may neither understand nor appreciate the fundamental moral principles upon which the nation was founded. This also helps to explain why many fifth- and eighth-grade teachers get frustrated teaching a required unit on "the Constitution"; the majority of their students may be operating at Stage 3, the level at which their primary interest is in gaining the social approval of others, as opposed to the Stage 5 reasoning on which the Constitution is based.

In Kohlberg's developmental scheme, each stage serves as a basis for the next. But unlike developmental schemes that link children of certain ages with particular stages, Kohlberg found that the age-stage relationship is less evident

TABLE 6.3 Kohlberg's Stages of Moral Development

Level	Stage	Characteristics
Principled: Concern for fidelity to self-chosen moral principles	5	*Motivator:* Internal commitment to principles of "conscience"; respect for the rights, life, and dignity of all persons. *Awareness:* Particular moral/social rules are social contracts, arrived at through democratic reconciliation of differing viewpoints and open to change. *Assumption:* Moral principles have universal validity; law derives from morality, not vice versa.
Conventional: Concern for meeting external social expectations	4	*Motivator:* Sense of duty or obligation to live up to socially defined role and maintain existing social order for good of all. *Awareness:* There is a larger social "system" that regulates the behavior of individuals within it. *Assumption:* Authority or the social order is the source of morality.
	3	*Motivator:* Desire for social approval by living up to good boy/good girl stereotype; meeting expectations of others. *Awareness:* Need to consider intentions and feelings of others; cooperation means ideal reciprocity (golden rule). *Assumption:* Good behavior equals social conformity.
Preconventional: Concern for external, concrete consequences to self	2	*Motivator:* Self-interest: What's in it for me? *Awareness:* Human relations are governed by concrete reciprocity; let's make a deal; You scratch my back, I'll scratch yours. *Assumption:* Have to look out for self; obligated only to those who help you; each person has own needs and viewpoints.
	1	*Motivator:* Fear of getting caught; desire to avoid punishment by authority. *Awareness:* There are rules and consequences of breaking them. *Assumption:* Might makes right; what's regarded by those in power is "good"; what's punished is "bad."

Source: Excerpted and adapted from Thomas Lickona, "How to Encourage Moral Development," *Learning,* 5 (March 1977), 37–42. Reprinted with permission.

in moral reasoning. As Lickona has noted, "In general . . . Stages 1 and 2 dominate in the primary school years and persist in some individuals long beyond that. Stage 3 gains ground during the upper elementary grades and often remains the major orientation through the end of high school. Stage 4 begins to emerge in

MODEL STUDENT ACTIVITY

Holly and the Cat in the Tree—Procedure for Young Children

Introduce the Situation

TEACHER: One day, a little girl named Holly was walking down the street.

Role-Playing

TEACHER: We need someone to play Holly and the little boy.

(Two students, Rosemary and James, role-play a possible solution for the incident.)

1. Minidiscussion

TEACHER: Did they manage to solve the problem?

(Brief discussion follows. If a child wants to suggest a different solution, move to part 2 immediately. If not, the teacher suggests another solution, secures new role players, and the incident is reenacted again.)

2. Role-play another alternative.

   Continue (1) and (2) until children are satisfied they have identified the possible alternatives.

Debriefing

1. Review briefly.

TEACHER: Let's see. In the first incident, Holly disobeyed her daddy and climbed the tree. In the second, she went to get somebody else to help. What happened in the third incident?

LOUISE: Holly made the boy get someone else to help.

TEACHER: Thanks, Louise. Then in the fourth incident . . .

2. Evaluate alternatives.

TEACHER: Were some solutions better than others? And do you think Holly's father should punish her for disobeying?

(Students' responses will vary.)

TEACHER: (Summarizing) It's good to help a person in need, but we should obey our parents too. Sometimes we need to look for a way to do both things. It's hard, sometimes, isn't it? (More discussion may follow.)

The debriefing is not an opportunity for the teacher to moralize or present "right" answers, Rather, the pluses and minuses of each alternative should be summarized.

---

75 percent don't reach Stage 5

adolescence. Only one in four persons moves on in later adolescence or adulthood to Stage 5" (1977, p. 39). Note also that individuals who can reason at higher levels may sometimes use lower-level reasoning to justify their actions.

Using Moral Dilemmas.   Kohlberg's research suggests that students will be stimulated to move to the next stage of moral development upon repeated exposure to higher levels of moral reasoning. Such exposure can be gained by helping students work with moral dilemmas. These are stories or situations that involve conflicting moral principles and in which students must identify and evaluate alternative courses of action. Dilemmas necessarily involve situations in which the alternative courses of action are either desirable or undesirable, but **Dilemmas involve conflicting** not both. When the two elements are mixed, there is no dilemma; the individual **moral principles** merely follows the most desirable course of action.

   A simple moral dilemma suitable for younger children might involve a seven-year-old girl named Holly who comes upon a small boy whose kitten is stranded in a tree. Tears stream down the boy's cheeks as he pleads with Holly to rescue his kitten. Although Holly is sympathetic, the last time she climbed a tree she fell

MODEL STUDENT ACTIVITY

Heinz and the Druggist

In Europe, a woman was near death from a special kind of cancer. There was one drug that the doctors thought might save her. It was a form of radium that a druggist in the same town had recently discovered. The drug was expensive to make, but the druggist was charging ten times what the drug cost him to make. He paid $200 for the radium and charged $2,000 for a small dose of the drug.

The sick woman's husband, Heinz, went to everyone he knew to borrow the money, but he could only get together about $1,000, which is half what it cost. He told the druggist that his wife was dying and asked him to sell the drug cheaper or let him pay for it later. But the druggist said, "No, I discovered the drug and I'm going to make money from it." So Heinz gets desperate and considers breaking into the man's store to steal the drug for his wife.

Question: Should Heinz steal the drug?

Procedure

1. Ask students to identify what should be done and why. "What should Heinz do?"

2. Divide the class into small groups, either in terms of those who support a particular course of action or at random. Ask them to discuss their reasons and justify the course of action they have chosen. "Why should Heinz do what you think he should do?"

3. Permit groups to summarize and clarify their positions.

4. Ask additional probing questions:

   ● Is the welfare of one's relatives more important than the welfare of others?

   ● Should Heinz steal the drug for a stranger? For a pet that he loves?

   ● It is against the law for Heinz to steal. Does that make it morally wrong? Why or why not?

Students should be encouraged to express reasonable value positions, though it is not necessary that they arrive at consensus.

Source: From *Models of Moral Education: An Appraisal* by R. H. Hersh, J. P. Miller, and G. D. Fielding. Copyright 1980 by Longman Publishers. Reprinted with permission.

and sprained her wrist. After that incident Holly promised her father she wouldn't climb any more trees. What should Holly do? (Lickona, 1977, p. 37.)

Holly could do many things, including trying to get help from an adult or breaking her promise to her father. By exploring such alternatives in group settings, moral dilemmas are intended to expose students to different and, it is hoped, higher stages of moral reasoning. For younger children, the dilemmas should involve relatively few characters and moral principles (obedience to authority versus helping a friend in need, for instance). Note also that changing just one element in the kitten moral dilemma, such as changing the kitten in a tree to a kitten trapped on a telephone pole, can alter the situation dramatically.

Exposure to higher levels of reasoning

The Model Student Activity above is designed for older students. It is based on a classic moral dilemma involving a husband's attempt to secure a drug for his sick wife. How students justify what Heinz should or should not do will identify their level of moral reasoning, as illustrated in the following:

Stage level reasoning

● *Stage 1:* Heinz should not steal the drug because he will be severely punished if he does.

- *Stage 2:* Heinz has the right to steal for his wife *if he wants to;* besides, a judge would understand and wouldn't punish him.

- *Stage 3:* Heinz has an obligation to help his wife, even if it means stealing for her. Besides, the druggist is being cruel and selfish; doesn't he have a heart?

- *Stage 4:* Heinz has an obligation to obey the law; by stealing the drug and thus breaking the law, he will be harming the society.

- *Stage 5:* Stealing and the law are not issues. Heinz should work to see that scarce drugs are distributed fairly, but even if that fails, the sanctity of human life exceeds everything else.

Designing simple dilemmas

The small-group decision making and the extended discussion of complex issues associated with moral dilemmas can demand a level of experience and sophistication that some younger children cannot handle. "Heinz and the Druggist," for example, involves too many elements for young children to deal with simultaneously.

What Critics Say About Moral Reasoning.

Adequacy

Much of the criticism directed toward the moral-reasoning approach has questioned either the adequacy of Kohlberg's theory or the contention that higher-stage reasoning is necessarily better than lower-stage reasoning. Harvard psychologist Carol Gilligan (1977, 1982), for example, contends that women tend to score lower than men on

Gender differences

Kohlberg's scale, not because of deficiencies in women's moral reasoning, but because women often use a different basis—an ethic based on interpersonal caring—for determining morality.

Earlier questions about whether discussing moral dilemmas results in movement from one stage to the next have largely been resolved. Leming (1985) states that "unlike the values-clarification approach, the weight of the evidence supports the claim . . . that the discussion of moral dilemmas can stimulate development through the stages of moral reasoning" (p. 131). For this to occur, however, moral-dilemma discussions must take place regularly, not just once or twice during a semester.

Caring: An Alternative Ethic for Moral Reasoning.

The moral-reasoning approach is based on the ethical ideal of justice. In that context, the most prized values are the equality of human rights and the dignity of human beings. On the

Justice is one aspect of morality

other hand, some authorities (Gilligan, 1977, 1982; Kohn 1997) argue that although nothing is wrong with justice as an ethic, using it as the sole defining standard for morality is too limiting. Those authorities (and others) argue that justice does not adequately reflect the caring and supportive behaviors on which human relationships should be based.

As an example of this, Brogmann (1992) suggests that the "Heinz and the Druggist" episode reflects the main point of contention between the masculine and feminine moral voice. Brogmann argues that the masculine way is to rest one's case on the universal principle that life comes before property, which means that Heinz should steal the drug. The feminine approach, Brogmann contends, is to consider the consequences that stealing would have on Heinz and his wife, and to explore alternatives to stealing; such as borrowing the money or seeing an understanding between Heinz and the druggist (see also Gilligan,

1982). The point here is that justice is only one of the bases that can be used to resolve this dilemma.

The following dilemma reflects elements inherent in an ethic of caring.

An example of caring

Bob, a top high school swimmer, was asked to teach young children with physical disabilities to swim. This would help strengthen their legs, possibly enabling them to walk. Bob was the only one in town who had the life-saving and teaching experience to do this job well. But helping these children would take most of Bob's free time after work and school, time that Bob would otherwise use to practice for some important, upcoming swimming contests. If Bob did not use his free time to practice, his chances of winning the contests, and possibly receiving a college scholarship, would be greatly lessened.

Should Bob agree to teach the disabled children? Why or why not? (Adapted from Mussen & Eisenberg-Berg, 1977, p. 121)

Prosocial behaviors

Integral to an ethic of caring are *prosocial behaviors:* that is, actions that aid other people without the expectation of direct rewards. Prosocial behaviors, such as that illustrated in the preceding dilemma, can sometimes involve personal costs or sacrifices. Prosocial behaviors, such as sharing, helping, sacrificing, and giving, are motivated by empathy, altruism, respect, sensitivity, nurturing, and a sense of caring.

- - - ●
Values Analysis
- - - ●

"Should students be permitted to go outside on the playground for recess, weather permitting?" This may seem like an innocuous question, but as more and more schools remove their playground equipment and do not permit students to leave the building during recess, it's being debated in many communities. When children ask it, it's the kind of question that also lends itself to values analysis.

Analyzing the values in an issue or question

The values-analysis approach to values education emphasizes careful, deliberate, discriminating analysis. The idea is to examine value questions as rationally and unemotionally as possible and then arrive at a decision. In contrast to moral reasoning, where students take a position and then justify it, values analysis would have students refrain from taking a position until they have analyzed the issues involved.

The phases of values analysis

The following tasks are essential to the analysis of the recess question or any value question or issue:

What are the value issues?

1. *Identifying the issue.* The underlying issues in allowing children to go out onto the playground for recess usually involve one or more of the following: (a) the children's safety, (b) the legal liability and costs that the school may face in the event of injury, and (c) teachers' distaste for playground supervision responsibilities. The issue also may involve whether the recess policy is districtwide or whether each school can establish its own.

2. *Clarifying the value question.* Dealing with this element is not as easy as it appears. Ostensibly the value question is whether children's safety is more important than their need for physical exercise. However, whether safety, the avoidance of legal liability, or some other factor or combination of factors is the main motivation must be determined.

Do we have the data we need?

3. *Gathering and organizing evidence.* See Step 4 below.

Are our data accurate and relevant?

4. *Assessing the accuracy and relevance of the evidence.* For the recess question, Steps 3 and 4 of values analysis can occur simultaneously. To facilitate this, the teacher could place the following on the board or in a more permanent location in the classroom:

Reasons for Children to Go Outside for Recess

1. Need for physical activity
2. Need for a change of scene

Reasons for Children to Stay Inside for Recess

1. Safety
2. Lawsuits
3. Other??

The visual display helps children keep track of what portion of the issue they are dealing with. Various individuals can be invited to give their views: an attorney knowledgeable about school litigation, a school board member, the principal, a telephone interview with a principal whose students go outside for recess, and so on. Students could also survey teachers in the school for their opinions.

What are the alternatives?

5. *Identifying potential solutions.* The key question here is, What are the options? Are there other means for providing a break and physical activity for children?

Do our "solutions" create other problems?

6. *Identifying and assessing the possible consequences for each solution.* The children need to consider questions such as: Would running around in a crowded gym be any safer than going outside? What if the gym is already scheduled? If legal liability is the problem, can insurance cover this? And if so, is there money to pay for such insurance? And, if insurance were possible, would the administration permit going outside?

7. *Choosing among the alternatives.* Determining viable alternatives will hinge on the assessment done in Step 6 above.

What is the best course of action?

8. *Deciding and taking appropriate action.* The latter phases of value analysis depend on what happens in the earlier steps. In the recess question, students may decide to petition the principal to review the current policy. This kind of action is only appropriate if the students have determined it is the kind of issue on which the principal or another administrator can act. Students may find that, in today's world, their health and safety cannot be compromised.

As the preceding example illustrates, values analysis is not a "quickie" process. It need not be as elaborate as described here, yet some steps in values analysis, including gathering and assessing evidence, can require considerable time to do well. The overall intent is to wean students from the teacher's influence so that they can follow the processes on their own.

What Critics Say About Values Analysis.   Values analysis has many supporters and few critics. Nevertheless, because some elements of values analysis are similar to the other approaches to values education, some of the same cautions may be in order. For example, elements of values analysis rely heavily on teachers asking a series of questions. Sometimes a single student may respond to

KEY IDEA

Alternative approaches to values education include (1) service learning, (2) inculcation, (3) literature-based techniques, (4) values clarification, (5) moral reasoning, and (6) values analysis.

a sequence of three or four questions (or more if elaboration is required). In a class of twenty-five students, a teacher could find herself engaged in a dialogue with one student. Hopefully the other twenty-four children will be interested enough to pay attention, but the longer the minidialogues go on, the more likely young children are to become disinterested. In light of this, several cautions seem prudent:

1. Teachers should be especially sensitive to the interest level of students who are not participating actively.
2. When possible, the approaches should be used in a small-group format.
3. When student interest begins to sag, summarize and move on to something else.
4. For values analysis especially, do not begin unless the issue is sufficiently involving *and* time is available to see the matter through to resolution.

SUMMARY

Values underlie *everything* teachers do. It is simply impossible to sterilize lessons to make them value-free. In the 1970s and 1980s, when schools were retreating from their traditional role in building good character, moral education tended to be a hit-or-miss proposition. Teachers might have occasionally employed one or more of the approaches presented in this chapter, but there was seldom a coherent program. To varying degrees, the approaches tend to be value-neutral; that is, they help individuals to explore what they *might* do, but they usually refrain from saying what the individual *ought* to do. This value-neutral stance was and is consistent with the privatization and personalization of values and morals that has occurred in the last half of the last century.

In view of the myriad social problems the United States is facing today, and especially the inability of some children to act in morally responsible and acceptable ways, a growing number of schools have reestablished character education programs. Their common goal is to produce students with good character: that is, students who know the good and feel disposed to act accordingly.

Character education is a comprehensive, schoolwide effort that focuses on teaching core ethical values such as

honesty, respect, responsibility, and truthfulness—values that are essential to the society's continuing survival and that almost no one opposes. Character education also extends to the hidden curriculum, the day-to-day schooling practices that can sometimes contradict, even neutralize, the values that schools and teachers espouse.

Character education is an overarching movement that sometimes incorporates one or more of the alternative strategies identified in this chapter. Those strategies can provide excellent vehicles for raising moral and ethical questions. However, some of the alternative moral education strategies, especially values clarification, must be approached cautiously.

Character education is the focus of intense interest across the country, in part because of the growing recognition that transmitting knowledge—making students smart—does not ensure that children will act in morally acceptable ways. But whether schools can become caring moral communities remains to be seen. Equally unknown at this point is whether schools can provide moral anchors for children from families that are unable to do so. Until we get answers to such questions, the final chapter on character education cannot be written.

SUGGESTED READINGS AND RESOURCES

Print Resources

GENERAL RESOURCES

William J. Bennett. (1993). *The book of virtues: A treasury of great moral stories.* New York: Simon & Schuster. This

book, which was a popular Christmas gift a few years ago, contains classic literary pieces—poems and stories—arranged around ten virtues and sequenced from simple to more complex. For example, the section on Responsibility begins with simple poems for young children, then includes such classics as Tennyson's "The Charge of the Light Brigade," and concludes with a section by Plato, and public documents by Jefferson, Madison, Frederick Douglas, Abraham Lincoln, and Martin Luther King, Jr. The other virtues documented include self-discipline, compassion, friendship, work, courage, perseverance, honesty, loyalty, and faith.

Edward F. DeRoche & Mary M. Williams. (1998). *Educating hearts and minds: A comprehensive character education framework.* Thousand Oaks, CA: Corwin Press. This book offers a nine-component model for a comprehensive character education program. The components include vision, standards, expectations, criteria to guide program development, the role of leadership, necessary resources, training, partnerships, and assessment.

Gertrude Himmelfarb. (1995). *The demoralization of society: From Victorian virtues to modern values.* New York: Alfred A. Knopf. This insightful and sometimes acerbic book by a distinguished historian is not yet another diatribe on what has gone wrong with America. Rather, it is a well-researched history of the Victorian period and focuses on Victorian virtues including hard work, thrift, cleanliness, self-reliance, self-respect, neighborliness, and patriotism.

Alfie Kohn. (1997). How not to teach values. *Phi Delta Kappan, 78,* 429–439. This article provides an in-depth analysis of techniques that are purported to teach values, but probably don't.

Thomas Lickona. (1991). *Educating for character: How our schools can teach respect and responsibility.* New York: Bantam Books. Lickona argues that if we care about the future of our society and our children, educating for character is a moral imperative.

Alex Molnar. (Ed.). (1997). *The construction of children's character: The ninety-sixth yearbook of the National Society for the Study of Education.* Chicago: University of Chicago Press. This book presents a current overview and critical assessment of the theory and practice of contemporary approaches to character education in the schools. Individual chapters by noted authorities provide an excellent cross section of opinion in the field.

Madonna M. Murphy. (1998). *Character education in America's blue ribbon schools: Best practices for meeting the challenge.* Lancaster, PA: Technomic Publishing. This book is full of useful information and succinct evaluations of commonly implemented character education programs, including Here's Looking at You, Quest, and Second Step. It also reviews materials from major character education curriculum development institutes, including the

Character Education Institute, The Heartwood Curriculum, and CIVITAS.

Nel Noddings. (1986). *Caring: A feminine approach to ethics and moral education.* Berkeley: University of California Press. Noddings makes the case for human caring as the foundation of ethical responsiveness. She argues that although men often base their ethical decisions on universal principles (à la Kohlberg), women are more likely to base their decisions on feelings, needs, and impressions. Noddings claims that morality should be based on a reciprocity between the person doing the caring (e.g., mother, teacher) and the one being cared for.

Edward Wynne & Kevin Ryan. (1997). *Reclaiming our schools: A handbook on teaching character, academics and discipline.* New York: Merrill. This widely acclaimed book is by perhaps the best known character education proponents in the country. Individual chapters focus on teaching character and discipline, teachers as moral educators, the curriculum as a moral educator, and leadership in moral schools.

OTHER RESOURCES

Information on the Heartwood Ethics Curriculum is available from The Heartwood Institute, 12300 Perry Highway, Wexford, PA 15090 (412-934-1777).

Information on the Exploring Ethics through Children's Literature Program is available from the Critical Thinking Press & Software, PO Box 448, Pacific Grove, CA 93950-0448 (1-800-458-4849).

Internet Resources

Introductory Note: Web sites sometimes change their Internet addresses or cease operating entirely. All the addresses supplied here were operating when this book was printed, but if any of them fail to work properly, try entering the topic or target organization in any standard search engine. Note also that if you enter "character education" into most search engines, you will get hundreds of listings, many of which are for organizations that are trying to market various books and materials. The following are noncommercial sources.

ERIC Clearinghouse

http://www.indiana.edu/~eric_rec/chared/index.html

The ERIC Clearinghouses were created long before the Internet existed, but they still offer excellent sources of information. This one could be subtitled, "more than you want to know about character education."

Two states, California and Utah, offer useful Web sites for character education. They are:

California Character Education Clearinghouse

http://www.cde.ca.gov/character

This site, maintained by the California Department of Education's Character Education Project, offers a variety of resources including reviews of character education materials, information about model programs and professional development, an excellent annotated bibliography, and links to other character education Web sites.

Utah Character Education Project

http://www.usoe.k12.ut.us/curr/char_ed/

This useful site offers many links and resources, very few of which are specific to the state of Utah.

Virtuous Stories

http://www.pbskids.org/adventures

This site features on-line versions of some stories that appear in William Bennett's *Book of Virtues*. The idea is worthwhile, but some of the stories are so abbreviated that PBS's execution leaves something to be desired.

Internet Resources for Service Learning

www.mssa.sailorsite.net/curric2.html

This site presents Maryland's service-learning curricula and curriculum materials.

www.ehhs.cmich.edu/ins/serv

This site offers definitions, descriptions, and a source book for service learning.

www.learningindeed.org/index_mac_ie.html

This is a web tool that can help teachers become informed about and more involved in service learning.

www.nationalservice.org

This site examines how the Corporation for National and Community Service engages Americans of all ages and backgrounds in service activities.

www.learnandserve.org

This site offers information about service learning.

www.nhusd.k12.ca.us/Instruction/St_handbook/links. html

(and)

www.nhusd.k12.ca.us/Instructions/St_handbook/SL-index.html

This site offers a description and examples of service learning as well as links to various service-learning Web sites.

7

Social Studies: Gateway to Literacy

KEY QUESTIONS

- What are the different forms of literacy?
- How can social studies serve as a gateway to literacy, and vice versa?
- What role does oral language play in building literacy?
- How do children (and adults) construct meaning?

● ● ● ● Introduction: People, People, People

DIVERSITY

For the last fourteen years, Ms. Lynda Esparza has taught second graders at Mesa Verde Elementary School in southern Arizona. Over 80 percent of her students are Hispanic. A few recently arrived from Mexico, some arrived three or four years ago, and others are native-born citizens of the United States. Another 10 percent of Lynda's students are Native American, and the balance are Anglo- and African-American.

I visited Ms. Esparza on a warm November afternoon as she and her class were beginning a social studies unit on community helpers. To find out what her children already knew about communities and community services, Ms. Esparza gathered everyone in the carpeted area. Seated on a low chair and using an overhead projector on a low cart, Lynda told her second graders, "Today, we're going to share ideas about people who work in communities. Remember our rules for brainstorming—everybody gets a chance to speak. After I put down everyone's ideas, we'll go back and work on them." The children nodded; they had apparently done brainstorming activities before. "OK, what different jobs do people in communities do?"

Working with ESL students

Brainstorming

Hands shot up. Carlos suggested, "police." Lynda recorded it on the transparency. Maria suggested, "store people," and Lynda asked, "What do you mean, Maria?"

"People who work in stores."

"What about 'mall people'?" asked Armondo. "Lots of people work at the mall."

Lynda turned to the class and said, "Let's decide whether we should describe some people by where they work, or whether we should list specific jobs, like clerks or cashiers." The class decided that either way was OK.

Determining prior knowledge

Gracie then suggested "mail people." Because the homophone for *mail* could be confusing for some students, Lynda asked, "Do you mean people like letter carriers, people who work for the post office?"

"Yeah, people like that," Gracie replied.

"Let's put that down as 'postal people,' and then put *mail* in parentheses just so we're sure," Lynda said, demonstrating what parentheses were as she did so. Soon the transparency was filled with a listing of various occupations, some public and some private employees, and some people listed in terms of where they worked. Lynda said, "All these people work in communities, and some of them work for communities. Right now, let's make a 'Beans' poem from our brainstorming."

From the children's expressions, it was clear that they knew what a "Beans" poem was, and that they enjoyed doing it. A "Beans" poem is a form of structured poetry based on "Beans," by Lucia and James Hymes (1960) (shown in Figure 7.1).

Lynda rose from her chair and dragged an easel filled with large chart paper to an area where everyone could see it. She flipped back the cover sheet to reveal the "Beans" poem format that she had drawn previously, but with blanks where the words had been. Taking a marker, she then said, "Because our poem will be about people, I'm going to put the word *people* where *beans* used to be. She quickly wrote "people" in the appropriate spaces, as shown in Figure 7.2.

Deciding on an ending

Lynda then said, "Remember that when we make a 'Beans' poem, one of the first things we decide is how we're going to end it. Let's think about what would make a good last line." Lynda and her students talked about different endings, and finally settled on "I like all people." Lynda then handed the marker to Maria,

---

FIGURE 7.1   Beans

Beans,
Beans,
Beans.
Butter beans,
Baked beans,
Big fat lima beans,
Long thin string beans—
Those are just a few.
Green beans,
Black beans,
Big fat kidney beans,
Red hot chili beans,
Jumping beans too.
Pea beans,
Pinto beans,
Don't forget shelly beans.
Last of all, best of all,
I like jelly beans!

Source: Hymes, Jr. *HOORAY FOR CHOCOLATE,* poem, "Beans, Beans, Beans" (pp. 34–35), © 1960 by Lucia and James L. Hymes, Jr. Reprinted by permission of Pearson Education, Inc. publishing as Pearson Addison Wesley.

FIGURE 7.2 A Writing Pattern Based on "Beans"

People ,
People ,
People ,

_____ *people* ,
_____ *people* ,

_____ _____ _____ *people* ,
_____ *people* ,

Those are just a few.

_____ *people* ,
_____ *people* ,

_____ _____ _____ *people* ,
_____ *people* ,

_____ *people* too.
_____ *people* ,
_____ *people* ,

Don't forget _____ _____ *people* .

Last of all, best of all,

I like _____ _____ *people* !

and said, "Why don't you write this for us?" Maria jumped up, took the marker, and filled in "i like all" in the spaces on the last line before "people." Half a dozen hands went up. Lynda nodded to Placido, who said, "I think Maria needs a capital *I*." Turning to Maria, Lynda asked, "What do you think, Maria?" Maria thought for a moment and said, "Yes, I should have made a capital *I*." She then took her marker and neatly transformed the lowercase *i* into a capital letter.

Interactive writing

With the ending decided, Lynda and the class then began filling in the other blanks. Lynda suggested that they put people who work for the government in the top half of the poem, and people who work in the community in the lower half. For example, when Carlos suggested "fire people," Lynda asked, "Should this go in the top half or the bottom?" Carlos responded that "fire people are city workers, so they belong in the top half." Lynda handed Carlos the marker and he wrote "Fire" in one of the empty spaces. When Armondo was writing "electricity," he spelled it "electrisity." To change the *s* to a *c*, Lynda reached for her roll of correction tape, which is similar to Post-it Notes, and handed a small piece to Armondo, who pasted it over his errant *s*, and then wrote the *c* where it belonged. The result was a product with correct spelling and grammar. If there are a lot of spelling errors or other changes, all the correction tape can create a speckled appearance on the final chart.

When all the blanks were filled in, Lynda asked, "What should we do now?"

Choral speaking

"We chorus it!" her students responded in unison. Lynda picked up a pointer with her right hand and began quietly snapping the fingers of her left hand to establish a rhythm. The students quickly joined in. In unison, and as Lynda pointed to each word, they began chorusing, "People, people, people. . . ."

When the first chorusing was completed, Lynda asked, "Let's see if there is anything we want to change?" Several students offered suggestions, including changing the last line to "*We* like all people." The group debated each suggestion, using more correction tape to make the necessary changes, until the final poem was as shown in Figure 7.3.

Adding variations

After chorusing the revised poem another time, Lynda suggested, "Let's orchestrate this poem—any ideas?" Jason's hand waved vigorously, but his actions violated a rule the class had agreed on previously: A raised hand is sufficient to get attention. If you wave your hand too vigorously or call out "Me, me," you won't get called on. Lynda raised an eyebrow as she looked at Jason, and then called on Lucinda, who suggested, "Let's let the girls be 'people' people, and the boys say the other parts; then we can switch."

Lynda responded, "Shall we try it?" The children nodded. Lynda continued, "The boys and I will say the words until we get to the word *people*. Then we'll stop

FIGURE 7.3   People, People, People

People,
People,
People,
Police people,
Fire people,
Electricity and water people,
Friendly, helpful postal people,
Those are just a few.
Teacher people,
Principal people,
Library and cafeteria people,
Doctor and nurse people,
TV people too.
Delivery people,
Store people,
Don't forget McDonald's people.
But last of all, best of all,
We like all people!

and our 'people' people (the girls) will say their word." With the same finger-snapping rhythm they had used previously, a chorus of girls' voices began, "People, people, people." A chorus of boys' voices then chimed in with "Police," "Fire." . . . Later, the boys chorused "People, people, people . . ." and the girls added the specifics. After a second time through the poem with the boys as "people" people, Lynda said, "Let's give all our choristers a round of applause." It was a fitting ending for an activity the children had clearly enjoyed.

KEY IDEA

Language literacy is the ability to read, write, and speak the language fluently and effectively in different situations.

Developing fluency

Ms. Esparza's students had participated in an activity that enhanced their oral fluency and that could ultimately enhance their ability to deal with language in different contexts. Lynda was also satisfied that her students already knew about many of the jobs available in the community. Whether the students could organize and classify the different occupations they had listed would become the focus for another lesson.

● ● ● ● Oral Language and Listening: Bases for Literacy

When Lynda Esparza and her second graders created and then chorused the "People" poem, that activity was more than a cute way to end a social studies lesson. A large body of research (see Button, Johnson, & Ferguson, 1996; Cooper, 2003; Flood & Lapp, 1987; Pinnell & McCarrier, 1994) indicates that both reading and writing depend, at least initially, on children's facility with speaking and listening. Children who have poor oral language and listening

Planning should encompass what you as a teacher will do and what your students will be doing. (© Michael Zide)

skills are also likely to have poor reading and writing skills. This also means that many students, especially those for whom English is their second language, can benefit from experiences in speaking and using language fluently, comfortably, and confidently.

Prior language learnings

By the time most five- and six-year-old children arrive in school, they have already acquired a vast knowledge of language, most of which they learned without formal instruction. In that process, they will have learned to distinguish separate units of sound (*phonemes*) and meaning (*morphemes*), to discover patterns and rules by which units of phonemes and morphemes are combined into sentences (*syntax, grammar,* etc.), and can identify context clues (*semantics*) that guide the social aspects of dialogue. Children don't use the kinds of labels we have here, of course, but when most of them enter school, they already have what linguists call a "fully formed grammar and language system." It matters not whether the children speak standard English, a regional dialect, Black English, or a mixture of English and another language; they will have acquired whatever language they speak through listening and observing, and then by experimenting with their language in social situations.

How do children use listening, speaking, and observing as they acquire language? Were you to observe young children over time, you would likely see them do the following:

- They rely on listening and speaking as the main channels for learning language (which is obviously true for children who are unable to read or write).

Building and testing theories about language

- They actively reflect on and analyze what they observe and hear.

- Based on what they hear and observe, children usually form theories about language and then test those theories in real situations. For example, most children learn that by adding the (bound) morpheme *ed* to certain words, they can talk about things that happened in the past. They test their theory about *ed* by using it in different situations, such as "I walked to the store." However, having discovered the marvelous power that *ed* gives them to talk about things that happened in the past, many children overgeneralize its application

Overgeneralizing

by adding *ed* to verbs of any tense, including *go* or *went*. Thus, it's common to hear young children make statements like "We *goed* to Burger King" or "I *runned* around the track." Eventually, most children discover that their new rule doesn't work all the time. They learn these language patterns without asking questions such as, "When do you add *ed* to a word or use a different word—when do you use *ran* instead of *runned*? Instead they typically look for patterns in the language to identify words that are exceptions to that rule.

The role of prior experience

- When children lack the correct words for describing something, they usually select from the words that they already know. This is why, upon meeting an elderly man with deep wrinkles, a child might ask, "Why does that man have *paths* all over his face?" (Morrow, 1989). It makes sense, at least from a child's point of view.

Constructivist learning

Children do not develop their ability to use language passively; they continually construct or reconstruct language as they learn it. How children learn to use language correctly also transfers to the ways in which they learn (as opposed to memorize) anything. Children (and even adults) construct knowledge by over-generalizing, by identifying and refining ideas, by testing ideas that may or may not fit their prior experiences, and then by going back through the cycle again.

Helping Children Develop Fluency in Standard English

Children bring their language from home

Most children come to school fluent in the language of the home. That language may be standard English, the language of schools and textbooks, but it will often reflect at least a regional or ethnic dialect, sometimes both. Most of us are so attuned to the language we grew up with that we notice almost immediately if someone speaks in a different regional or ethnic dialect. To hear someone talk with a southern drawl, perhaps, or say "Hush" instead of "Quiet," is sometimes regarded as quaint, especially at first. But upon hearing someone repeatedly pronounce *especially* with an "x," as *expecially*," for example, it probably won't be long before speakers of standard English begin to make judgments about the speaker's intelligence—or lack thereof. In still other cases, the primary language of the home may be something other than English. Thus these children will be learning English as a second language. Either situation can pose problems for children who are becoming fluent in standard English.

English as a Second Language (ESL).   I suspect that only people who are truly bilingual can appreciate the problems associated with becoming proficient in two languages simultaneously. Children who are learning English as a second language face challenges that native English speakers seldom encounter. For example, all the children in Lynda Esparza's class know their alphabet, but students whose native language is Spanish tend to pronounce the vowels differently than English-speaking children. What English speakers say as /a/, /e/, /i/, /o/, /u/ are pronounced in Spanish as /ah/, /ey/, /ee/, /o/, /oo/. As a result, native Spanish speakers may have difficulty distinguishing between words like *cut, cat,* and *cot* (see Hennings, 2002).

Problems of second-language learners

DIVERSITY

Even native English speakers sometimes encounter problems when they first see familiar words in written form. Because English has so many silent letters, what children know and say as /rit/, for example, seems to take on extra letters when it is written as *write*. However, because English-speaking children's pronunciation of the word does not change, their problem is primarily one of recognizing the word in its written form. For Spanish-speaking children, however, the problems are compounded because, except for *h,* all the written letters in Spanish are sounded. Thus, upon encountering a word like *write* in its written form, a native Spanish speaker will want to pronounce it as a two-syllable word, /wreetey/, which is something they have never heard before, even if they're familiar with the English word *write* in its spoken form. In such situations, an ESL child's ability to use context clues becomes even more important than it is for native English speakers.

Language differences

In some parts of the country, Spanish-language textbooks may be available for social studies and other subjects. However, these texts typically reflect Castilian

● ● ● ● **COMMENTARY**   **On Speaking the "Cash Language"**

There is a subtle and often unspoken bias against people who—regardless of whatever language they speak in their homes—are unwilling or unable to speak or write standard English. Several years ago, some entrepreneurs noticed that individuals who represented major corporations based in Texas and the Southwest sometimes had difficulty dealing with their colleagues in corporations based in the East. Upon further investigation, these individuals concluded that a big part of the problem involved how people from southwestern (and southern) regions talked. For example, talking "Texan"—with its lazy drawl and the tendency to say "Y'all"—was often essential to doing business in parts of the Southwest. But the same dialect became a liability in the East. It is difficult to convince someone from the northeastern United States (New York, Boston, etc.) that the pace of his or her speech is fast—in part, because everybody talks "this way." Likewise, it is equally difficult to convince people who talk at a much slower pace and use regional dialects that people elsewhere may perceive of them as intellectually challenged. Perhaps this is why in the South and Southwest, people who talk rapidly are often regarded with suspicion. On the other hand, people in the Northeast may perceive slow talkers as dimwitted and unable to express themselves with speed and precision. The point here is that the entrepreneurs noted earlier eventually established a school in Dallas to which corporations throughout the South and Southwest send people so they can learn to speak standard English in ways that do not subtly offend people in other parts of the country.

Do people resist changing the speech patterns they grew up with? Of course. Our speech patterns, even those we are not aware of, are integral to who we are.

A second brief example may illustrate this point. Whenever you have the opportunity, close your eyes as you listen to a pregame show on the ESPN cable network. Focus your attention on the sportscasters, not the ex-athletes or former coaches—some former athletes sound as if they just came in from feeding the animals (as do some coaches). Until you open your eyes, it's unlikely that you will be able to determine the ethnicity of the sportscasters. Some of them are obviously African-American, some are Anglo, and some are Hispanic, but most of them speak flawless standard English.

Some individuals may claim that asking someone to replace a regional or ethnic dialect with standard English is tantamount to asking them to deny their heritage. Still others regard it as a matter of chasing after dollars or of selling out to the Anglos. Regardless of which position you accept, consider the Reverend Jesse Jackson's position (see Christiansen, 1998). Jackson argues that when people are at home, they are free to speak however they want to. But when anyone wants to communicate to and be accepted by a larger audience, they can eliminate several hurdles by speaking standard English—what the Reverend Jackson calls the "cash language."

Spanish, which can be quite different from regional Spanish dialects, like Tex-Mex, that the children are accustomed to hearing in the home. This can mean that, in addition to basic structural differences in the languages, ESL students must often overcome dialectical differences. If the ESL child's native language is neither English nor Spanish, finding appropriate text materials will be almost impossible.

Dialectically Different Children.   Anyone who speaks a regional or social-group dialect exclusively can be regarded as dialectically different. For example, children from New England often add an /r/ to words that end in *a*. Thus, *Cuba* (the country) is usually pronounced /cuber/. On the other hand, children from New York City tend to drop the /r/, as in /pak da cah/ (park the car).

Dialectically related usages are different from standard English, but they are not substandard forms. Children from Appalachia who say /warsh/ for *wash* or

Regional and cultural dialects

"I done it," for example, are simply repeating the speech patterns they hear and use in their homes and neighborhoods. As different as their pronunciations may be, they are not doing anything "wrong." Teachers who insist on "correcting" such usages in children's oral language may very well send the message that there is something "wrong" with a language form that children feel comfortable with. As Hennings notes, "Children who are made to believe there is something wrong with their speech may stop speaking in school, which is counterproductive" (2002, p. 59).

The problems that dialectically different children encounter learning standard English are similar to the problems that ESL students face but are less serious. For a child from Appalachia to discover that there is no *r* in *wash,* for example, is hardly as serious as learning that descriptive adjectives in English go before the noun, not afterwards as in Spanish.

Developing Fluency.   The techniques for helping children become fluent and effective users of standard English are similar to the techniques that children use to learn language in the first place (which is why I went into such detail on that earlier). Children need opportunities to "play" with language. They need oral activities that enable them to build on, transform, expand on, and interpret standard English sentence patterns. They also need to experience the rhythms of standard English, which is one of the reasons that Lynda Esparza had her students chorus the "People" poem in different ways. Children also need to hear standard English used in realistic settings. You may have noticed that Lynda Esparza used the word *shall* correctly during her lesson, and she did so naturally and without making a "big deal" about it. Although even some proficient users of standard English cannot distinguish between when to use *shall* or *will,* Lynda effectively modeled a usage that was not likely to be in many of her children's everyday language repertoires.

Additional suggestions for handling oral language and listening activities include the following:

- Model correct, standard English speech and writing to the best of your ability to do so.

- As you model the language, do it in ways that say to children, "I accept you (and the way you speak) as you are."

- Recognize that the goal is to help children use standard English effectively and fluently, *not* to denigrate the child's (and the family's) existing dialect. Literacy is not a crusade to stamp out regional or social dialects.

- Permit children to use whatever dialects they are most comfortable with in class discussions, storytelling, and creative dramatics.

- React to the message the child is trying to convey and not to the form of speech. Cursing and obscene language are obviously unacceptable.

- Resist the impulse to interrupt children to correct their vocabulary or sentence structure. Constantly interrupting and correcting students in front of their peers is embarrassing and uncomfortable for most students. In such situations it's questionable whether they will be focused on either the language

Playing with language

Recommended practices

 SUGGESTED ACTIVITY

Children's grammar errors often reflect speech patterns common in their home environment. Indeed, the entire family may use nonstandard expressions such as "I done seen him." What would you recommend as a preferred course of action for teachers?

that led to the interruption or the correction. As Hennings (2002) notes, students may find such situations discomforting.

• • • •

Listening Activities

• • • •

The nature of listening

Listening is a combination of what you hear, what you expect to hear, what you observe, and what you recall from your previous experiences. Effective listeners are aware of factors that influence listening. These include (1) thinking ahead of the reader or talker and anticipating the direction of the discourse; (2) assessing **Factors that influence** the kind(s) of evidence the reader or talker is using; (3) periodically reviewing the **effective listening** author's or speaker's main points; (4) "listening between the words"; (5) constructing ideas instead of just picking up facts; and (6) withholding evaluation of the message until after the reader or speaker is through talking.

Like other language-related activities, listening is probably best approached as part of other ongoing activities. One of the best activities for this is reading aloud to children. What you read aloud should not be restricted to children's literature or limited to the primary grades. Sharing *brief* passages of informational content with older students can be equally appropriate.

Whenever you are reading aloud or it is possible to stop someone who is talking to the class, you might interrupt with *one* of the following questions:

1. What do you think will happen next?

2. What has the author/speaker said up to this point?

3. What is the author's/speaker's main idea?

4. What things [kind(s) of evidence] has the author/speaker used to get us to believe what he or she is saying?

5. Which parts of what the author/speaker said were opinion?

6. How would you have said what the author/speaker said?

Because students (or anyone) may resent the intrusion when their train of thought is interrupted, you must use your judgment about when such questions are appropriate. If students are bored, they probably won't mind the interruption, but then they may not have been listening well enough to answer your questions.

"Hearing" a supermarket

Cassette tape recorders have made it possible to develop homemade listening-oriented activities. By taking a tape recorder with you as you travel, for instance, you can gather interesting materials for listening activities. Consider developing a three-minute tape of sounds at a busy intersection, a shopping mall, or a supermarket. The idea, initially, is to have students *describe what they hear,* not guess what they're hearing. If a child says, "I hear a supermarket," for example, he or she is inferring something rather than describing the sounds. Inferring is a logical extension of describing—usually an inevitable extension—but the students' first focus should be on describing the sounds themselves.

KEY IDEA

Oral language and listening provide the basis for subsequent reading and writing.

● ● ● ● Reading, Writing, and Social Studies

This section is based on two simple yet powerful ideas: Children learn to read by reading, and they learn to write by writing. Reading is that marvelous process by which children gain meaning by decoding written symbols. If children do not understand what they are decoding, they are merely *word-calling*, not reading.

The focus is meaning

Writing is the process of encoding thought and speech into written symbols. Because meaning is inherent in our every thought or utterance, we simply don't think meaningless thoughts. As a result, almost all writing is inherently meaningful, at least to the writer. Unfortunately, what some students do in school might look like writing but is likely to be *pseudowriting*. Certainly you remember reports and term papers that you largely copied from encyclopedias or other sources. That's pseudowriting.

A different perspective on rules

Even the most basic conventions of writing can make sense to children if they are approached from the perspective of writers (or authors) who are trying to convey meaning to readers, instead of as decontextualized rules that writers must follow. Consider: How do writers tell their readers that they've come to the end of an idea? They use a period. How do writers tell their readers that they're beginning a new idea? They begin with a capital letter. How do writers tell readers that they are finished with one cluster of ideas and are ready to move on to a new cluster? A new paragraph.

From thinking thoughts to writing sentences

There are surely millions of students across the country learning rules like "Always end a sentence with a period." Those students really need to understand that a sentence is a thought, an idea in written form, and that the period simply marks the end of the idea. Unfortunately, schools sometimes complicate matters by teaching rules that involve multiple abstractions. Remember, for example, the countless hours you spent drawing one line under the subjects and two lines under the predicates of sample sentences? Ask yourself when was the last time you thought about predicates. The subject-predicate business may be useful if you want to talk about sentences, but you might also ask yourself how often you need to talk about sentences. Most people don't think in terms of nouns, verbs, subjects, or predicates—they think whole thoughts.

Clear thinking leads to clear writing

The points here are several. All of us think in terms of thoughts and ideas that have meaning to us. And when we convert an idea into spoken form, it becomes a statement. When we put a thought or idea into written form, we produce a sentence. However, if decontextualized rules and labels are introduced in the context of writing, the effect can be to make writing more difficult than it really is. All writers must deal with many things as they write, including spelling, punctuation, intended audience, tone, and organization. Yet, to the extent that writing is thinking in a written form, consider that the key to helping children produce clear writing is clear thinking.

The primacy of meaning

Reading and writing are complementary processes for getting and conveying meaningful ideas. So, regardless of how you feel about the "whole" language approach to literacy, one of the main contributions of that movement may be the renewed focus it has placed on meaning in all language-related activities.

. . . .
Reading and Textbooks
. . . .

Several factors play a role in helping or hindering children from getting meaning from the materials they read, especially social studies textbooks. You could regard the subtitle for this section as: "Why Are Social Studies Textbooks So Difficult?"

Consider the following passage from a fifth-grade social studies book. As you do so, try to (1) identify the number of ideas it presents explicitly—not those that are implied—and then (2) decide which if any of these ideas is important enough that you would ask a test question about it. If an idea is important enough to be included on a test, it is something students should know and remember.

Sample textbook passage

Little by little, Canada won its freedom from Great Britain. By 1949, Canada was fully independent. Canadians control their own country. They also choose their own leaders. (McAuley & Wilson, 1985, p. 41)

The passage, which amounts to a sweeping summary of recent Canadian history, contains only four short sentences—twenty-seven words in all. Yet the number of ideas that are packed into this space is significant. Consider the following:

Few words, but many ideas

- Canada is a country that now controls itself.

- Canada got its freedom gradually.

- Canada gained its independence from Great Britain in 1949. (This idea could be considered two separate ideas: [1] independence from Great Britain and [2] independence in 1949.)

- Canada was partially independent before 1949.

- The people of Canada select their leaders.

Concept loading

This passage has more ideas than sentences. The extent to which this or any other passage contains ideas that are packed densely, sparsely, or somewhere in between is called *concept loading*. Concept loading contributes to the material's *readability*, that is, to the relative ease or difficulty of reading and gaining meaning from the material. Passages in which ideas are densely packed, and thus have a high concept load, are usually more difficult to understand than passages with a lower concept load.

There are no absolute standards for high or low concept loading, which can vary for different types of materials—novels versus textbooks, for example—so concept loading is a relative measure. However, placing ideas in short sentences does not in itself make those ideas easier to understand. Although the sentences in the sample passage are short, its concept load is fairly high.

Textbooks and Readability.   According to Chall and Conard (1991) and others, the readability level of most elementary social studies texts ranges from one to **What the research says** two grade levels above the intended grade level. For example, most fourth-grade books have a fifth- or sixth-grade reading level. This difference tends to diminish during the middle-school years, so that by eighth grade textbooks are likely to be closer to their intended grade level.

To understand the abstract concepts and terms that social studies texts often contain, most children usually need concrete examples that they can relate to. The more examples, the better. Yet this is where a confounding element, length, enters the picture. Every example in a book requires space, which adds to a book's length. The overall length of the text becomes a concern, primarily because of the way in which textbooks are perceived. If social studies textbooks were regarded more like dictionaries, as resources to be drawn upon as needed, their length would be irrelevant—except, perhaps, with respect to cost. However, because textbooks are often viewed as something students must "cover" by the end of the year, their length can become a significant factor. Dictionary-size textbooks would strike fear in the hearts of students and teachers alike, and their chances of being adopted are unlikely. Thus textbook authors and publishers are almost forced to maintain a reasonable length and, in the process, are denied the opportunity to clarify abstract concepts and ideas with multiple examples. Presenting large numbers of concepts on each page can make books more efficient, but doing so can also make them more difficult to read and understand.

The textbook author's dilemma: Adding examples without increasing the length

In response to complaints about high concept loading, most publishers have tried to simplify their materials. However, instead of attacking concept loading directly, which would mean eliminating some abstract concepts and adding examples for others, they usually attack the problem by shortening the sentences, as we saw in the textbook passage about Canada. In theory, short sentences are easier to read than longer, more complex sentences, even though that notion has been disputed by some recent research in reading. Nevertheless, the trend in textbooks is to improve readability (and thus reduce the apparent difficulty level) by reducing sentence length. Consider also that the blame for mediocre textbooks does not rest solely with the publishers, who must deal with voluminous curriculum guidelines and various other expectations that change from district to district and state to state.

Shorter sentences

- - - ●
Helping Children Understand Specialized Vocabulary
- - - ●

Every subject has its specialized vocabulary. Literature has its *sonnets* and *metaphors,* science has its *atoms* and *antennae,* and social studies has its *wings, steppes,* and a host of others. For most students, such vocabulary poses a twofold problem. Even though a simple word like *wash* is already part of most students' oral vocabulary and even though the student can probably spell the word correctly, he or she may have never heard of a dry streambed referred to as a *wash.* Likewise, *run* is a regional expression for a brook or stream. Words with multiple meanings like these are called *polysemous,* and they make up about one-third of all commonly used words (Irvin et al., 1995). They often have meanings that are specific to particular content areas—such as *antenna* in science and *wash* in geography.

Terms with multiple meanings

In many instances, polysemous words like *wing, class, bill, branch,* and *fork* are not particularly difficult for students if the teacher can build on the child's existing experiences. In the case of *wash* and *run,* the goal is to associate the word with the child's prior experiences with rivers and waterways, thus adding other terms to their repertoire. Other regional expressions that fit this category are *borough, county, parish; tote, carry; pop, soda, tonic.*

Figurative expressions and abstract concepts

Two categories of terms that can pose more perplexing problems are *figurative expressions,* such as *Fertile Crescent, dark horse, cold war, iron curtain, log rolling,* and *corn belt,* and terms associated with *abstract concepts,* such as *ethnocentrism, nationalism, culture, democracy,* and *inflation.* Even though none of us have ever seen a belt made from corn, most children already have *corn* and *belt* in their reading and oral vocabularies. Their problem usually arises because they have never encountered these familiar words in their *corn belt* configuration. Abstract terms can pose added problems because they are often not part of the child's oral and reading vocabularies and because they, like figurative expressions, refer to phenomena that are beyond the child's realm of experience. Figurative expressions and especially abstract terms often require more comprehensive teaching strategies, which are considered in detail in the last section of this chapter.

Two final categories of specialized terminology that can affect social studies teaching include the following:

- *Proper names for historically or physically remote personages and places.* Many terms in this category do not follow familiar rules for phonic analysis. Examples: pharaoh, tsar (or czar), Hwang Ho, La Jolla, San Jose.
- *Acronyms and abbreviations.* These can present problems because they are often abbreviations for organizations with which students are not familiar. Examples: OPEC, IRS, GOP, FCC.

Some terms are more important to meaning than others!

In helping children understand unfamiliar vocabulary, a key element to keep in mind is that not all terms are equally important (see Irvin et al., 1995). Students can often get the basic thrust of a passage even if they don't understand every word. For example, consider the following sentence: "With the mechanization that accompanied the agrarian revolution, farmers were able to grow more corn, wheat, oats, and barley." Many students today have never heard of barley, a grain crop used extensively in producing beer, but this word is actually incidental to understanding the text. In addition, because *barley* is presented in association with other grains that should be more familiar to students, the context of the sentence suggests that it is one of several crops that a farmer might grow. Thus, the preteaching of *barley* is not essential, although you could make certain that students understand it in postreading follow-up.

Students are very unlikely to understand the sample sentence above unless they also understand the term *mechanization.* In this instance, *mechanization* is so critical to the meaning of this passage that teachers cannot treat it in the same way they do *barley.* The key here is to anticipate potential problems before students become frustrated. The time-honored technique for doing this is to preteach the term before students read the passage. The teacher should introduce new terms that are vital to understanding the passage—not including *barley*—by writing them on the chalkboard and then defining them before students begin reading. Although this technique tends to treat the vocabulary out of context, it is often preferable to having students look up the new terms in a dictionary, which at this stage in a lesson too often becomes a ritual in word copying. Thus teachers must be familiar enough with what their students will read that they can decide between terms that are critical to understanding the passage or lesson, and thus demand preteaching, and terms that are incidental or for which context clues will be sufficient.

What Do You Do for Children Who Can't Read the Text?

A nonsolution

The commonsense solution for helping students who have reading difficulties is: get an easier textbook. Unfortunately social studies content varies so markedly from one grade level to the next that it's almost impossible to find easier texts that cover the same topics *and* are appropriate to the student's reading-skill level.

Other options

A second alternative is: don't use the book! There is a vast array of children's literature that is far more interesting than most textbooks. You are more likely to find an easier literary book, even a picture book, on almost any topic, than an easier textbook. Some children's books that you could use either in place of or in addition to the text have already been suggested, and additional annotated bibliographies are presented in the Resource Handbook.

If you feel that your students absolutely must have access to information in the text, you could use one of the following courses of action. Perhaps the least difficult and most readily available option is to read the passages to the students who are having difficulty. The management problem associated with reading to small groups lies in finding something meaningful for the other students to do. This

Still other options

can be avoided if you (1) have an aide or parent volunteer read to individual children, (2) have one student read to another, or (3) have designed a section of the room as a listening center and have recorded portions of the text available on cassette tapes.

Your third and fourth options, both of which can be time-consuming, involve having small groups of children rewrite *small* portions of the text in their own language and with illustrations after they have finished a section, or rewriting the material in simpler language yourself. If you have the children do the rewriting, be sure that you (1) explain to the children why they are doing this activity, (2) have students work cooperatively in groups but on different sections, and (3) do not use this activity too often—despite its utility, it can pose problems for younger students especially.

Rewriting materials

The feasibility of the fourth option, rewriting material yourself, often depends on the kind of material you are working with. It isn't easy to simplify *statistics*, for example. For text material, this option is further complicated because most texts are written at a very simple level to begin with. Rewriting is a more viable (and often necessary) option if you wish to use advanced material, especially from sources such as *Time, Newsweek*, or social science journals.

A longer-range course of action involves identifying the problem that's keeping the child from reading the text in the first place. No one needs to tell you that reading remains a problem for some students, and teachers everywhere are looking for answers to that problem. Until those answers are found, you will undoubtedly be forced to rely on one of the preceding alternative strategies.

TECHNOLOGY UPDATE

Computers as Writing Tools—Ramirez Elementary

Each of the twenty-four students in Mrs. Mary Llanas's combined class of fifth and sixth graders uses one of the four computers in her room to produce a "report" on an African nation. Each report is filled with pictures that students have downloaded from the Internet or reproduced from various books or other sources. When students locate a picture they want to include, they have two options. First, they can place the book or illustration on an easel and then use a video camcorder to incorporate the image into their report, an option that works best if they have large illustrations. Their second option is to use the classroom scanner, which, because they need not assemble so many separate pieces of equipment, seems to be the preferred technique.

Students sometimes use scenes as backgrounds for their written narrative with the text superimposed in a contrasting color in front of the picture. In other instances, pictures are presented with accompanying text either above or below them. In either case, the students are involved with the total visual effect their reports create, not just the words they write.

Other teachers may have their students use "presentation software" as a vehicle for writing activities. The picture below is from a book on colonial occupations that was created by Mrs. Judy Rogers's third-grade class using the *Time Trip USA* (EdMark) presentation program. Each student wrote the text for his or her occupation and then incorporated it into the animated program. The animation cannot be shown in this format, but everything movable in this scene actually moves—the horse and carriage, the people, and so on. The children even borrowed a technique from Richard Scarry's popular children's books, which include a tiny worm that peers over the activity on each page. Instead of the worm, Mrs. Rogers's children decided to include a child who pops out of a barrel, as shown in the illustration below. Such computer-based presentation programs offer an excellent medium for motivating students to write.

The town crier was a man that called out the news. The crier had to be loud so that the people could hear the news. Sometimes he had special news and he had a bell to ring or a drum to bang so that the people could hear the special news.

Source: Used by permission of Judy Rogers and Darlinda Rogers.

. . . .
The Reading-Writing Connection
. . . .

Few educational movements can match the revolution in writing instruction that has occurred over the last decade or so. Whereas writing was once regarded as drudgery, in some classrooms it now rivals recess as a preferred activity.

A growing body of research shows a clear reading-writing connection: improved writing skills can lead to improved reading skills, and vice versa. As young children write, they also come to understand that the words on a printed page were written by somebody—they didn't just magically appear there. As students begin to grasp the concept of author, they begin to realize that authors are responsible for communicating clearly and understandably to others—a responsibility that students assume whenever they write.

Reading and writing are complementary processes

The Writing Process.   One notable aspect of the ongoing revolution in teaching children to write well is the recognition that most traditional writing assignments, where children were given a topic and expected to produce a polished story in one draft, were a far cry from the way in which most authors really write. Moreover, little or no teaching was involved; rather, those assignments were actually tests of the children's existing abilities. It is now recognized that instruction in writing should more closely parallel the processes that most authors follow when they write. Many teachers now follow variations of the writing model shown in Figure 7.4.

Writing: Moving toward what authors really do

If you plan to do a lot of writing activities in your classroom—two or more structured writing activities a week, for example—the WRITE model can become almost burdensome. It is geared toward producing the "perfect" paper, and the time that novice writers spend producing such a document can be considerable. This was the problem that Maria McCoy (2003) encountered in her social studies classroom.

In reviewing her own teaching, McCoy decided that integrating writing instruction into her social studies work was taking so much clsss time that she could easily become a full-time teacher of writing, and social studies would fall by the

---

FIGURE 7.4   A Writing Model

What to write about. Decide on a topic that may be worth pursuing.

Research. Do you need to find out more about the topic?

Initial draft. Write your story.

Two revisions (may be done simultaneously). Focus on (1) content and (2) mechanics.

Extend. Share your writing with others.

wayside. Unwilling to accept this alternative, she decided (10) that not every writing activity needed to be aimed at producing works of publishable quality and (20) that she would use a variety of shorter-range writing activities during the semester. A colleague also shared with her the Targeted Writing Skills (TWS) Approach, developed by Gary Chadwell (1992).

The TWS Approach.   The TWS approach is keyed to five different levels of writing that correspond to the basic phases of the writing process—thinking, answering, creating, and so on, as shown in Figure 7.5. The targeting in TWS occurs when the teacher identifies three specific skills (and only three) that the students focus on and are graded on. The target skills must be identified specifically, for example, punctuation, spelling, capitalization, no run-on sentences, and so on. "Mechanics" per se, for example, is not allowable because there are literally thousands of ways to make mechanical errors in written papers. On the other hand, beginning every sentence with a capital letter is an acceptable target because it is narrow enough that students (and teachers) can check their papers for this element very quickly.

The TWS approach comes into play at Levels 3 through 5. Because doing the multiple revisions associated with Level 5 writing can become a chore for students, it is important that the papers serve a real purpose, not be simply another assignment. Some teachers, like Ms. McCoy, reserve Level 5 papers for the really "big" deals, such as student submissions to newspapers or essay contests. Lower-level writing activities, on the other hand, can take many forms. For example, Level 1 writing can be used to demonstrate students' prior knowledge. Before beginning a unit on the Civil War, Ms. McCoy asks students to create a list of ten things they already know about the Civil War, and then to underline the three things that they feel are most important. Level 2 writing works well to determine what students remember from previous lessons or reading assignments. For example, the teacher can ask "based on last night's reading assignment, why was it important for Union troops to control the flow of goods over the Rio Grande?" Level 3 assignments are more complex than lower-level papers, and it is here that the three-part TWS focus applies. As a writing task, Ms. McCoy asks her students to imagine that they are the son or daughter of a Confederate soldier who is away fighting with the troops. The students must write a letter to their father describing their life at home and the sacrifices they are making. The TWS approach can also help to deal with the wide spectrum of ability levels among students.

Writing Activities.   The potential for realistic writing activities in social studies is almost endless. In most cases, the possible writing activities that are described next require prior class activities or research. However, in many instances, the activities can provide a motive for doing the research.

- *"How to's"* are precise, step-by-step descriptions of how to do something. Examples:

  1. How to brand a calf
  2. How to make soap
  3. How to make a peanut butter sandwich

Targeted writing skills

Using the levels

Writing activities

FIGURE 7.5 Levels of Writing

LEVELS OF WRITING

Description: Writing that has no right or wrong answers

Level 1: Thinking Phase
Purpose: To capture ideas

Grading: Credit given for length and completion

Examples: Brainstorming, free writing, outlining, clustering, webbing, journal writing, idea generating

Description: Writing that makes a point with a definite, correct answer

Level 2: Anwering Phase
Purpose: To answer correctly

Grading: Credit based on correctness of information

Examples: Reader response, answers to specific questions over reading

Description: Single draft writing; reviewed and read aloud by the writer

Level 3: Creating Phase
Purpose: Review for TWS

Grading: Credit for content and correct use of TWS

Examples: Narrative, descriptive, informative, classificatory, and persuasive essays; poems, creative writing

Description: Writing that has been reviewed by another, and has been through two or more revisions; extensive peer and self editing

Level 4: Improving Phase
Purpose: Reviewed by peers

Grading: For content and TWS

Examples: Two or more drafts, revising and polishing a Level 3 work

Description: Publishable writing that can go outside the classroom after multiple revisions and drafts; a major project of the highest quality

Level 5: Perfecting Phase
Purpose: Publish

Grading: For all preceding TWS

Examples: A flawless, publishable version of a Level 4 work

Source: Adapted from Chadwell (1992) and McCoy (2003).

● *Diaries* or *journals,* or *anecdotes* or *stories* of real or imagined people describing a place, event, or experience. Examples:

1. A visitor to a dairy
2. A pioneer on the Santa Fe Trail
3. A photojournalist in Scotland

- *Applications* for jobs, describing qualifications for the position and reasons why you would like it. Examples:

  1. A sailor on Magellan's first voyage
  2. A firefighter
  3. The king or queen of England

- *Letters* written by students themselves or as another person, either real or imagined, containing descriptions, reactions, observations, or attempts to persuade someone to take a certain course of action. Examples:

  Letters
  1. A description of San Francisco (or Fairbanks, Alaska) during the Gold Rush
  2. A letter to the mayor asking that the community follow a particular course of action
  3. A letter (circa 1860) from a Northerner to a Southern relative explaining why the South should not secede from the Union (or vice versa)

- *Radio scripts* describing events or conditions. Examples:

  1. A "You Are There" description of the first Thanksgiving
  2. A news broadcast from Paris during the time of Joan of Arc
  3. A news bulletin from inside the Alamo (or Nagasaki, Japan, just after the atomic bomb was dropped)

- *Pamphlets* or *brochures* (with illustrations) that describe places or events. Examples:

  1. Washington, D.C.
  2. Valley Forge
  3. The school

- *Interviews* (with real or imaginary people) in which students ask and answer questions. Examples:

  What was General Lee thinking?
  1. An interview with General Lee on the eve of signing the surrender at Appomattox, Virginia, in 1865
  2. An interview with Martin Luther King, Jr., circa 1965
  3. An interview with a French fur trader, circa 1700

- *Advertisements* for inventions, places, products, and so on. Examples:

  1. The printing press
  2. The water wheel
  3. A medieval castle

- *Biographies* of imaginary children living in other times or places. Examples:

  1. A child living in ancient Sparta
  2. A child living on a plantation in Georgia in 1840
  3. A child living in Sydney, Australia, today

- *Wanted posters,* with a picture, description, crime, and so on. Examples:

  What should a wanted poster for Benedict Arnold say?
  1. Benedict Arnold
  2. Jean Lafitte (pirate)
  3. Saddam Hussein

● *Itineraries* for imaginary trips through places past or present. Examples:

1. A trip on the Underground Railroad
2. An itinerary for Marco Polo
3. A sightseeing trip through your community

Before using any of these writing activities, be certain to establish an authentic, purposeful context. Writing a descriptive brochure of Washington, D.C., or a wanted poster for Jesse James, for example, needs to serve a useful purpose. Otherwise, the activities could easily become "writing for the sake of writing."

Helping Children Construct Meaning

Consider the following conversation between a mother and her six-year-old daughter.

MOTHER: What did you learn at school today?

DAUGHTER: Oh, the teacher said we live in a democracy, but I told her that we live in an apartment.

MOTHER: That's nice.

DAUGHTER: What *is* a democracy anyway?

MOTHER: Why it's a form of government, dear.

DAUGHTER: What's a *form?*

Form is one of the polysemous (multiple-meaning) words noted earlier. Young children often know that *form* refers to the shape of something, and, after experiences like the one above, they may learn that *form* can also refer to a category or type of phenomenon. I used *construct* in the heading for this section because words and ideas (other than our own) are meaningful only to the extent that we

Relating ideas to prior experiences

can relate them to our prior experiences. For unfamiliar terms, we must rearrange the mental pigeonholes we use to organize and store our past experiences to accommodate the new ideas. That process is often called *accommodation,* although more recently the term *scaffolding,* which more clearly conveys the notion of "constructing" or "building onto," is often used.

Scaffolding

I was reminded of the scaffolding process when I encountered the Dennis the Menace cartoon shown below. I already had many ideas that I associated with Abraham Lincoln—a tall, bearded man in a stovepipe hat, the sixteenth president, teaching himself the law by candlelight, and so forth. Each of these elements reflects an *attribute* that I associated with Lincoln. Also included among those attributes are my attitudes, feelings, and impressions about Lincoln, which, though more difficult to describe, are along the lines of respect for his apparent honesty and an appreciation for the dignity and bearing with which he conducted himself.

Accommodating new ideas

Dennis the Menace suggested a new attribute that I (and perhaps you) had *not* previously associated with Abraham Lincoln. I accommodated this new attribute by adding "toys" to our existing concept. However, I have since learned that Lincoln Logs were invented by the son of Frank Lloyd Wright, the famed archi-

DENNIS THE MENACE   **By HANK KETCHAM**

"THIS IS LINCOLN'S BIRTHDAY, JOEY. YOU KNOW ...
THE GUY THEY NAMED THE LOGS AFTER."

Source: DENNIS THE MENACE reprinted with special permission of King Features Syndicate.

tect, who named them after the president who was sometimes called "the log splitter." That piece of trivia could be useful if you ever become a contestant on a TV game show, but it also suggests that the relationship between Lincoln Logs and our sixteenth president is more tangential than direct.

In the earlier example in which the daughter is puzzled by the term *form,* she will probably reconstruct her existing ideas (about *form*) to accommodate the new usage. In addition, at some time in the future she will probably test her newly constructed schema for *form* by using the word in an appropriate situation (or one that she hopes is appropriate). Such testing is a normal part of the language learning process that was referred to earlier.

The old rule of thumb—"If you don't know what a word means, you look it up in a dictionary"—is not especially productive for most polysemous terms. For example, a *wing* can refer to the thing that a bird flies with or to a part of a larger building, both of which most children already know. However, *wing* can also refer to a more or less identifiable group of people who belong to an organization, often a political group called a *party,* or it can mean any one of twenty other definitions listed in our dictionary. For children who think of "party" as a kind of celebration, the dictionary definitions for *wing* can create a situation where they must cope with multiple attributes simultaneously. There are times when using the dictionary to define new terms is appropriate, but this is not one of them.

Testing new conceptualizations

The problem with definitions

Decontextualized instruction

Helping children understand the various attributes associated with polysemous terms like *wing* is more than simply a matter of definition learning. To approach it in that way would be a classic example of decontextualized instruction—of trying to learn things in isolation and without reference to the phenomena with which they are associated. To provide a context for *wing*, teaching needs to begin with the phenomenon it is associated with, in this case, political parties. If children have only a vague notion of what political parties (or similar organizations) are, which is more than likely, then that becomes the appropriate beginning point for instruction. In other words, trying to teach children about wings when they don't understand the nature and characteristics of political parties is putting the cart before the horse.

Coping with inclusive and narrow ideas

Part of the difficulty that students face in understanding abstract ideas like *wing* or *democracy* is their breadth—they are broad concepts with many attributes. In contrast, nonpolysemous words like *barley*, or even a term like *pharaoh*, are often easier for children to handle. Although pharaohs were unique to ancient Egypt, the term reflects a narrower concept with relatively few attributes, as opposed to a broader and more inclusive concept such as *absolute monarch*. Eventually you might wish to help students build the broader concept of *absolute monarch*, but until they are comfortable with narrower concepts—like *pharaohs, kings,* and *emperors*—they may not know what you are talking about.

To summarize briefly, the process of making things meaningful for children or adults involves connecting new ideas with the individual's existing experiences, their existing frames of reference. When children have no previous experiences with the phenomenon in question, like the *wing* of a political party, teachers may need to begin from scratch and provide experiences for them. Broad ideas that have many attributes—like *freedom, democracy,* or *absolute monarch*—tend to be more difficult for children than narrower concepts like *pharaoh*, which, though they may be equally abstract, have fewer attributes that children must accommodate. There are so many broad and encompassing concepts in elementary- and middle-school social studies that it is often impossible to avoid them. If you find yourself in that situation, one of the strategies in the next section may be appropriate.

. . . .
Examples of Instruction Designed to Construct Meaning
. . . .

The following exemplars illustrate how you might go about managing the idea-building process.

Building on what students know

Vocabulary.   There are several options when students do not understand a narrow concept, such as *isthmus*. First, you can *define* it for them: "An isthmus is a narrow strip of land between two bodies of water." However, because few students will have prior experience with an isthmus, your words will mean more if you use a picture or other illustration to provide a visual image of the term. You might also use an *analogy*—for example, "An isthmus is a kind of 'land bridge,' a skinny piece of land that connects two larger land masses." That analogy could be part of a larger explanation in which you use a *simile*—for example, "An isthmus is

● ● ● ● COMMENTARY   **The Role of Details in Constructing Meaning**

Obviously, students cannot move backward in time and actually participate in the events of history—actually join Christopher Columbus on his voyage, for example. And if your students saw how tiny the *Nina, Pinta,* and *Santa Maria* actually were, they probably wouldn't want to. In lieu of real experiences, teachers can often appeal to children's imagination in ways that support their vicarious participation in events. By using literature to create vivid mental images of historical events, it's sometimes possible to engage children as if they were witnessing the events unfold. These vivid mental images are created by *details.*

Unfortunately, the role of factual details in teaching history is among the most widely misunderstood aspects of social studies instruction. For example, consider the following statements as they might appear in a textbook: "In 218 B.C.E., Hannibal led an army of over 100,000 soldiers across the Alps. He then met and defeated the Roman legions in what is now Italy." The passage is factually accurate but so bland it fails to capture the imagination. It takes details to make the passage come alive, such as the fact that Hannibal was only eighteen years old when he gathered his huge army from various parts of Africa and Europe. Hannibal's army spoke so many different languages that often his troops could not communicate with one another. In addition to the 100,000 soldiers, Hannibal's army also included thirty-seven elephants. Thirty-six of them were African "attack" elephants that had been trained to terrorize enemy soldiers by trampling on them; the elephants practiced on prisoners at the training center in Carthage. The thirty-seventh, an Indian elephant named Syrus, was probably Hannibal's personal pet.

After a harrowing journey across the Alps, Hannibal still had to get his army, its supplies, and the elephants across the Rhone River. The army "borrowed" boats, made rafts, or used anything they could get their hands on to get across the river. But getting the elephants across was another problem; they refused to go onto the rafts that had been built for them. In desperation, Hannibal's soldiers covered the rafts with pieces of sod so that they looked like extensions of the shoreline. Apparently the elephants were deceived, because they willingly walked onto the rafts. However, when boats began towing the rafts toward the opposite shore, the elephants realized something was wrong and panicked. Some reared up, trumpeted loudly, and threw their mahouts (drivers) into the river. Many of the mahouts, who were originally from Africa, had never learned how to swim and were drowned. Some of the elephants also jumped into the river, but they swam to the opposite shore and waited there for the elephants that had remained on the rafts. All the elephants made it safely across the Rhone River.

Individually and in the sweep of human experience, most details appear small and insignificant. It is not important that students come away remembering how many elephants Hannibal had, for example, even though they often do remember such information. The point is that, collectively, details play a vital role in the creation of vicarious experience and subsequent learning. Too often children must deal with test questions such as "How many elephants did Hannibal have?" Because a teacher's test questions often define what is or is not important, one must wonder how many students focus their attention on trying to learn what is actually historical trivia. Perhaps some students learn to hate history because the role of factual details continues to be misunderstood.

like a strait, except it's land instead of water." Your explanation for some concepts, such as *peninsula,* might include a description of the origin of the expression: "*Peninsula* comes from the Latin—*pene* for 'almost' plus *insula* for 'island.' In other words, a peninsula is almost an island."

Having students use a dictionary or glossary is another option for relatively narrow real-world concepts, such as *isthmus* and *peninsula.* But for abstract concepts such as *capitalism* or *imperialism,* dictionary definitions may lead to the situation noted earlier—that is, where one abstraction is defined with other abstractions.

The Taba Model.   The following idea-building strategy was developed by Hilda Taba and is based on a three-step sequence illustrated in Table 7.1 (Taba et al., 1967). In some respects, this strategy is similar to the way that Lynda Esparza began her lesson in the introduction to this chapter, although she opted not to do

An old strategy but still useful   the entire process in a single lesson. In this strategy, students are asked first to identify and enumerate items, then to find a basis for grouping or clustering the items together, and finally to identify a label for the items they have clustered. How the three phases might be conducted for a second-grade class is illustrated in the following Model Student Activity.

· · · ·

Anticipatory Strategies

· · · ·

Anticipatory strategies are teaching techniques that teachers use prior to a learning experience. Some of these strategies, like contextual redefinition and word mapping (explained next) focus on one or two words that are apt to prove troublesome for students. Other strategies, such as KWL charting and SQ3R, are usually designed to set the stage for learning, but also have follow-up components that occur after a learning experience.

Learning to use the context   **Contextual Redefinition.**   Helping students learn to use the context in which unfamiliar words appear is vital to the process of becoming an independent learner. This was illustrated in an earlier example involving the word *barley*, which I suggested was not important enough to the meaning of the passage that it demanded preteaching. Unlike the *barley* example, students will encounter

---

TABLE 7.1   Taba's Concept-Formation Strategy

Phase	Overt Activity	Operations	Questions
One	Enumeration and listing	Differentiation	What did you see? Hear? Note?
Two	Grouping	Identifying common properties, abstracting	What belongs together? On what criterion?
Three	Labeling and categorizing	Determining the hierarchical super- and subordination	What would you call these groups? What belongs under what?

Source: Teacher's Handbook for Elementary Social Studies by Hild Taba, Mary C. Durkin, Anthony H. McNaughton, & Jack R. Fraenkal. Copyright © 1967 by Addison-Wesley Publishing Company. Used by permission of Pearson Education, Inc.

MODEL STUDENT ACTIVITY

Taba's Concept-Formation Strategy

Phase 1: Enumeration and Listing

TEACHER: Let's start listing on the board the things that you would buy if you went to the store.

DAVID: Apples.

PAUL: I'd buy a steak.

RANDY: Shrimp.

DENNY: I'd buy a puppy.

TEACHER: A puppy is different, isn't it?

MICHAEL: Watermelon.

CARLA: Candy bar.

ANN: Scooter.

TEACHER: Scooter, that's something different again, isn't it?

TEACHER: We've almost filled up our board with things that we would buy. What can we do with these things? Do some of them belong together? Which ones belong together? Which ones could you find in the same place?

DENNY: You can buy a doll and scooter in the same place.

TEACHER: You would buy them in a toy shop, wouldn't you? Let's pick the ones that you might buy in a toy shop. What else would you buy in a toy shop?

RICKY: Squirt gun.

TEACHER: All right, we would buy a squirt gun in the toy shop. What else would we buy in the toy shop? (Taba et al., 1967, pp. 95–99).

Phase 2: Grouping

Students continue to suggest different (and multiple) groupings for some items, such as "steak and watermelon—things at a cookout" or "shrimp and steak, because both are meats." Students may or may not identify a "food" category for items such as apples, watermelon, steak, and shrimp.

Phase 3: Labeling and Categorizing

After the larger clusters have been identified, the teacher then moves to labeling and categorizing by asking, "What would you call these groups?" Responses may include "things you can buy in a store," "things we eat," and "things we use." As Taba and her colleagues (1967, p. 94) noted, it is important for students "to discover that any item has many different characteristics and therefore can be grouped in many different ways. Each of the multiple qualities can be used as a basis for grouping."

many passages with unfamiliar words that are critical to understanding and that must be pretaught. In such cases you can use contextual redefinition, a teaching strategy that is based on making and verifying predictions. Phases of the contextual redefinition strategy are as follows:

Selecting problem terms

- *Phase 1:* Select terms that are likely to be unfamiliar to students *and* that are critical to understanding the passage. For purposes of illustration, consider the term *civil service* (after Irvin et al., 1995).

- *Phase 2:* Using an overhead or chalkboard, present each term individually and in isolation.

- *Phase 3:* Ask students to brainstorm possible definitions for each term. Accept all suggestions, including those that are wrong or "off the wall," as in "a civil service is a wedding where everyone is polite" (Irvin et al., 1995).

Deciding on a possible meaning

- *Phase 4:* Help students reach a consensus on the most probable meaning.

• *Phase 5:* Present a sentence or cluster of sentences that illustrates the meaning of the term. For example: "Civil service was created during the T'ang dynasty in China. Using an examination system, government officials were selected based on their qualifications instead of their noble birth."

Modify as needed • *Phase 6:* Help students modify their earlier definitions if necessary.

• *Phase 7:* Ask one or two students to verify the definition in a dictionary or glossary.

Word Maps. In the example for Phase 5 above, the term *dynasty* might be troublesome for some students. An alternative strategy to contextual redefinition involves creating a word map for the unfamiliar term, in this case *dynasty*. The emphasis in this strategy is on relating unfamiliar terms to students' prior experiences. A sample word map for *dynasty* is shown in Figure 7.6.

The KWL Strategy. Portions of the KWL Strategy occur prior to a learning activity, and other portions take place after the activity. This is reflected in the following vignette, "Why Woodpeckers Don't Hurt Themselves."

VIGNETTE: WHY WOODPECKERS DON'T HURT THEMSELVES

I first met Eric Cederstrom when he was teaching at Harwell Elementary in a midsized city. He has since moved into administration, which, as he puts it, "Is

FIGURE 7.6   A Sample Word Map for *Dynasty*

Source: From J. L. Irvin, J. P. Lunstrum, C. Lynch-Brown, & M. F. Shepard, *Enhancing Social Studies Through Literary Strategies* (Washington, DC: National Council for the Social Studies, © 1995). Reprinted by permission of NCSS and J. L. Irvin, J. P. Lunstrum, C. Lynch-Brown, & M. F. Shepard.

where the money is." When I dropped by Eric's third-grade classroom one after-noon, there was a huge sheet of red paper covering one of the chalkboards. Un-der the heading "Animals," the paper was divided into three columns: (1) Know, (2) Want to Know, and (3) Learned (see Table 7.2). On that first visit, the "Learned" column was still blank.

I said, "Oh, you're using the KWL strategy." Eric replied, "I don't know whether I'm doing it or it's doing me. We're working on an animal unit, and yes-terday we brainstormed what the kids already knew about animals. Then we talked about what they wanted to know more about. The brainstorming is sup-posed to activate their prior knowledge, and the 'Want to Know' column identi-fies what they want to find out. Right now, the kids are at the library getting books on animals."

TABLE 7.2   KWL Chart for Animals

What We Know	What We Want to Know	What We Learned
1. They can be furry.	1. How do animals communicate?	1. Some lay eggs.
2. Most have four legs.	2. Can sharks jump to the sun?	2. They can have long or short tails.
3. Some animals can fly.	3. How do sharks breathe?	3. Turtles can't get out of their shells.
4. Some animals are playful.	4. Do animals have secrets?	4. Some animals are slow, some are fast.
5. Animals have insides like ours.	5. Do turtles have ears?	5. There are different types of animals.
6. Some animals are mean.	6. How do dogs bark?	6. Some animals swim a lot.
7. Some animals bite.	7. How do animals swim without hands?	7. Some eat a lot.
8. Some animals live in trees.	8. Why do animals have tails?	8. Dogs "talk" with their tails.
9. Some animals live in water or underground.	9. How do people train animals, like Flipper?	9. Some animals have hands.
10. Some animals peck.	10. Why don't woodpeckers hurt themselves?	10. Some animals don't have ears.
11. Some animals have sharp teeth.	11. How do dogs stand?	11. Kangaroos have pockets.
12. Most animals don't talk.	12. How do turtles put their head in their shell?	

Source: Courtesy of Eric J. Cederstrom's Third-Grade Class, Harwell Elementary School, Lubbock, TX.

Unexpected questions

"The 'What They Want to Know' column included a lot of stuff I really didn't expect," Eric continued, "like 'Why don't woodpeckers hurt themselves?' I don't know why woodpeckers don't hurt themselves, and when I wrote that item on the chart, I told the kids that I didn't think we'd be able to answer this one—or why animals have tails or whether they have secrets. But I also didn't get the kinds of things I really wanted to focus on either, like 'What do animals do in the winter?'"

"Maybe not," I answered, "but you got a good indication of what your kids are thinking about."

"That's true; . . . we'll see how it goes," Eric said hopefully.

Unexpected answers

Upon my return to Eric's classroom, all the columns on the KWL chart were filled in. When I asked how it went, Eric responded, "Not bad for the first time using this strategy; as I expected, they couldn't answer some of their questions, but I was also surprised about some of the items, like 'Kangaroos have pockets.' I thought almost everyone knew that."

"So, would you use this activity again?"

Making adaptations for the next time

"I think so," Eric said, "but I would do some things differently. I really need to limit the topic more, because 'animals' is way too broad. Maybe we should do reptiles and birds separately. And instead of one master chart, I'll have the kids make their own copies so they can have something to refer to. I'm also thinking about structuring the groups a little more."

Eric Cederstrom's first rendition of the KWL strategy isn't perfect, which he readily admits. However, he had already identified some things he would do differently another time around. The first point here is that the KWL strategy permits students to participate, albeit in a limited way, in clarifying what they are going to learn. A second but equally important point is that planning is an ongoing process that occurs before, during, and after instruction.

PreP (PreReading Plan).   The PreReading technique is an anticipatory strategy in which students focus on what they already know about a topic before they begin reading. In many respects, this phase is similar to the "What I already know" phase of the KWL strategy. If the topic is the Revolutionary War, for example, the teacher might ask students what comes to mind when he or she says, "the Revolutionary War." Students' responses may include "Redcoats," "the Stamp Act," or, if students have no notion of the Revolutionary War, silence (or no response).

Assessing students' prior knowledge

In an attempt to build on students' associations, the teacher may ask a question such as "What made you think of the Stamp Act?" (or whatever the student said). One problem that may arise here occurs when some students recall the Stamp Act, but other students have no idea what everyone is talking about. One purpose of this phase of the strategy is to help the teacher determine whether the students' responses show (1) significant prior knowledge, (2) some prior knowledge, or (3) no prior knowledge. Students whose facial expressions suggest they are "lost" probably belong in Category 3—no prior knowledge. Based on this information, the teacher's decision focuses on determining whether students with no prior knowledge can be successful reading the passage, or whether they need more information before attempting it. But then, if the passage explains the Stamp Act (or whatever the topic) so that readers with no prior knowledge will understand it, using the PreP technique may not be worth pursuing further. In instances where the reading passage is in a textbook, most of which assume no prior knowledge of the topic, the PreP strategy may be only marginally useful.

SQ3R/SQ4R.   The SQ3R and its slightly modified cousin, the SQ4R, are time-honored techniques (Cooper, 2003; Robinson, 1962) for helping students pose their own questions and purposes for reading. The phases of SQ3R, which are *Survey, question . . .* done in sequence, include: (1) *survey* the section of the text to get a general idea of what it is about, (2) pose a *question* that is likely to be answered in the text, (3) *read* the section until the reader can answer the question, (4) *recall* the answer to the question without referring to the text, and finally, (5) *review,* where the reader tries to recall the main points learned from the reading. The SQ4R technique follows essentially the same pattern except that it includes a *recite* phase, that is, *survey, question, read, recite, recall,* and *review.* In the *recite* phase, the reader is asked to verbalize the answer to the guiding question.

Follow-up Comprehension Strategies

Follow-up strategies, such as semantic mapping and Somebody-Wanted-But-So summary/review charts, which are described here, are designed to build upon and to enhance students' initial understandings.

Using Semantic (Concept) Maps.   Semantic (or concept) maps are similar to word maps but have a broader focus. Semantic maps are devices that (1) visually depict the attributes associated with an idea or concept, and (2) show the relationships among those elements.

Visualizing how elements are related   The process of making a semantic map is sometimes called "webbing," probably because the finished product can resemble a spider web. Semantic mapping uses elements that are similar to the Taba strategy, especially since students organize and cluster related elements. To illustrate the mapping process, consider again the textbook passage about Canada on page 183. The steps in creating a semantic map are shown below.

Existing ideas   ● *Step 1: Determining students' existing ideas.* Ask, "When someone says Canada (or whatever your map will focus on), what do you think of?" List the students' responses in key words on the board or an overhead transparency. Their responses, which will be organized in Step 2, may include attributes such as "borders the United States to the north," "is larger than the United States," "national capital is Ottawa," and "bilingual, especially in the eastern provinces, where French is commonly spoken."

Clustering   ● *Step 2: Clustering related responses.* Help students identify related elements by using symbols to show each relationship—circles around items related to language, boxes around elements related to the economy, and so forth. The purpose of this step is to organize what might otherwise be a random listing of attributes.

● *Step 3: Making a preliminary concept map.* Begin the webbing process on an overhead transparency or a blank section of the board. Place "Canada" in the center; then add elements radiating outward as shown by the solid lines in Figure 7.7. Use branching to show related elements.

- *Step 4: Adding new elements to the map.* Decide with students where new elements should be placed. In this example, the new elements come from the textbook passage noted earlier:

Canada is a country that now controls itself.

Canada got its freedom gradually.

Canada gained its independence from Great Britain in 1949.

Canada was partially independent before 1949.

The people of Canada select their leaders.

Many students will treat each fact as a separate item until they see a need or reason to organize or cluster them in a different way. To stimulate clustering, ask, "Is there any pattern to these new elements?" or "Do they fit together somehow?" Multiple categories that could accommodate these elements include history, political organization, and independence. There is no best way to organize the new items, but one way needs to be agreed upon and then added to the concept map. Our treatment is shown by the broken lines in Figure 7.7.

FIGURE 7.7 A Concept Map of Canada

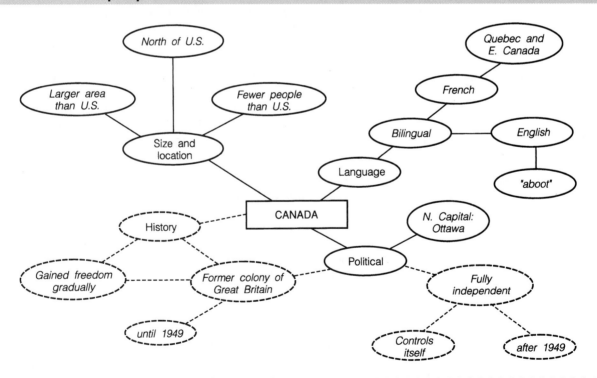

- *Step 5 (Closure): Debriefing and reflection.* This step helps students reflect on what they have done and how they did it. The idea is to get students to think about how they dealt with the problem—to think about thinking. Ask questions such as these: "How did we deal with this?" "Is there a better way we could have done this?" "What have we learned from doing this?" Responses will vary.

Thinking about thinking

Perhaps it is excessive to go to so much trouble with a four-sentence passage about Canada. In one respect, it would be simpler to ask children to remember the facts within that passage and to leave it at that. However, doing so would place the burden on the students, who *might* store the information in their short-term memory—perhaps long enough to take a test—but in six months or less it will assuredly be forgotten. Even having done all this, students are still likely to forget some specifics, such as the date of Canada's independence. Whether they should be expected to remember such information to begin with is debatable. What they should learn from this activity is a process for organizing and dealing with information in ways that are personally meaningful. Without meaning, the activity would be an academic exercise.

Questioning the Author Technique.   To help students ferret meaning from the dense and sometimes obscure prose in social studies textbooks, Beck and McKeown (2002) suggest a technique they call "questioning the author." Unlike traditional apporaches to comprehension, where students deal with the author's ideas after they have finished reading, this technique is applied as they are reading. As the students read, the teacher intervenes at selected points and poses context-specific questions that prompt students to think about what they have just read.

Deciding what children should know

The teacher has the first task in using this technique. He or she must decide what information students should take away from the text. Consider an example from a fourth grade text's unit on desert regions that focuses on the Sahara. The first section of the text describes deserts in general, and the second section describes how the Sahara long ago changed from grassland to desert. According to the text, climate changes were the major culprit here, but people are also mentioned as being partly responsible because they "worked the land too much" and "use[d] the land for too much grazing" (Macmillan, 1985, cited in Beck and McKeown). The text section ends as follows:

> Many people became nomads. Nomads are people who move from place to place to find grazing land for their animals. The nomads of the Sahara began to move about the desert. They had to find food for their sheep, goats, and camels. (p. 131)

Separating causes and effects

This section of the text is obviously trying to help children understand the meaning of *nomad.* But the section also connects the climatic conditions in the Sahara and their impact on the nomads. But because the preceding section dealt with people's overuse of the land, the text can leave the impression that the nomads created the desert conditions in the Sahara by moving their animals around to graze in different places, when in fact the nomadic lifestyle is a response to desert conditions, not the cause of them.

To apply the questioning-the-author technique, Beck and McKeown recommend stopping after the nomad section and then asking a question such as, "How does that information fit in with what the text tells us about the Sahara?"

Student's responses should be followed up with additional queries such as, "Does the text really mean to suggest that the nomads created the desert conditions in the Sahara?"

A context-specific technique

Two things should be apparent from this brief example. First, and perhaps most important, the teacher must identify what students should understand from having read the material. Second, the queries and follow-up questions of the questioning-the-author technique must be integrally related to the substance of the text passages. In other words, this is a context-specific technique, not one where you learn two or three generic questions and then have at it.

Somebody-Wanted-But-So Summary/Review Charts. To use a Somebody-Wanted-But-So summary/review chart with students, the teacher enters only the headings for the four columns, as illustrated in Figure 7.8, on large paper or an overhead transparency. Working interactively with students, the teacher then fills in the columns, from left to right, for one or more topics that the class has studied.

Summary review charts

To illustrate the utility of this technique, both social studies and language arts topics are shown in Figure 7.8. However, this summary/review activity can only be done *after* learning experiences that provide the information that students must have to complete the chart. This necessarily means that summary/review charting does not lend itself to initial teaching activities.

"Somebody," "Wanted", "But," and "So" are everyday terms that even very young children understand. However, middle-school teachers may wish to substitute the terms: "Character," "Motive," "Conflict," and "Resolution." Nonetheless, even some adults will prefer the terms "Somebody," "Wanted," "But," and "So," apparently because they are less abstract and bring everything down one level of complexity.

FIGURE 7.8 Sample Summary/Review Chart

SOMEBODY	WANTED	BUT	SO
The South (1861)	States' rights (slavery)	The North opposes slavery	Civil War breaks out
John Wilkes Boothe	To keep slavery and support the Confederacy	Lincoln (and the North) abolish slavery	He shoots Pres. Lincoln
Cinderella's Stepmother	A good life for her daughters, but not Cinderella	Fairy godmother intervenes	Drats, foiled again!
Mr. MacGregor	A nice garden	Peter Rabbit eats his vegetables	He chases Peter with a hoe

SUMMARY

This chapter has focused on helping children gain meaning from spoken or written words. The first premise is that in the absence of meaning, literacy is an impossibility. Meaning depends largely on the extent to which children can make connections between the new ideas they encounter and their existing base of experiences. Helping children to make those connections is one of the most important roles a teacher plays.

Language literacy refers to the ability to use language—to read, write, speak, and listen—fluently and effectively in different situations. Recent research has indicated that children require opportunities to talk and play with standard English, the language of textbooks and the school, in ways that mimic how they learned their language in the first place: by listening, observing, and sometimes by testing theories about how language operates in realistic and purposeful situations. Too often, children in traditional classrooms had few opportunities to practice or demonstrate their oral language skills. When researchers discovered that children with poor oral language facility also tended to be poor readers and writers, things began to change—although slowly at first. It has become increasingly apparent that the basis for literacy is the child's facility with oral language. In slightly different terms, this means that if children cannot understand the spoken word, they will be not be able to understand those ideas when they try to read them, nor will they be able to convey those ideas in written form.

SUGGESTED READINGS AND RESOURCES

Print Resources

Lucy McCormick Calkins. (1994). *The art of teaching writing.* Portsmouth, NH: Heinemann. A book with this title *must* be well written; this one is superb.

_____. (2000). *The art of teaching reading.* New York: Longman Group. Another excellent work by this talented writer.

J. D. Cooper. (1993). *Improving reading comprehension.* 2nd ed. Boston: Houghton Mifflin.

_____. (2003). *Literacy: Helping children construct meaning* (4th ed.). Boston: Houghton Mifflin. An excellent resource on developing literacy skills.

Linda Christiansen. (1994). Whose standard? Teaching standard English. *Rethinking our classrooms: Teaching for equity and justice.* Milwaukee, WI: Rethinking Schools Ltd. This touching and thought-provoking article by a teacher who grew up speaking nonstandard English, describes what she went through as she learned to adapt her own language patterns to the prevailing standard in our culture today.

Leslie W. Crawford. (1993). *Language and literacy learning in multicultural classrooms.* Needham Heights, MA: Allyn & Bacon. This book is especially useful because of its focus on multicultural classrooms.

I. C. Fountas & G. S. Pinnell. (2001). *Guiding readers and writers (Grades 3–6): Teaching comprehension, genre, and content literacy.* Portsmouth, NH: Heinemann. This is an excellent companion volume to the Calkins books listed above.

Donald Graves. (1994). *A fresh look at writing.* Portsmouth, NH: Heinemann. This work is by the person who started the writing revolution in the United States.

Internet Resources

Introductory Note: Web sites sometimes change or Internet addresses cease operating entirely. All the addresses supplied here were operating when this book was printed, but should any of them they fail to work properly, try entering the desired topic or organization in any standard search engine.

Constructivist Learning

http://netra/exploratorium.mcgill.ca/fedwww/wac/intedpsych/students/lgraha/paper.html

This insightful article explains the basis for constructivist teaching and learning.

National Reading Styles Institute

http://www.nrsi.com/homepage.html

This site focuses on helping children who display different reading and learning styles: auditory, visual, analytical, tactile, and kinesthetic.

Visualizing Verbs

http://www.cypress.ne.jp/schwindt/tesol/vtnvs.htm

This site describes a technique for using colored index cards to help students, especially ESL students, visualize the complexities of the English verb system.

Reading and Writing Across the Curriculum

http://www.indiana.edu/~eric_rec/bks/wac.html

This site is sponsored by the ERIC Clearinghouse on Reading, English, and Communication and provides links to sites and materials for teaching reading and writing across the curriculum.

What Is a Thinking Curriculum?

http://www.ncrel.org/sdrs/areas/rpl_esys/thinking/html

This article focuses on metacognitive teaching and curriculum design for engaging students with content.

Instruction

8

Planning for Instruction

KEY QUESTIONS

- How does one plan social studies lessons and units?
- What are the major phases of instructional planning?
- How do teachers manage the planning process?
- How do goals and objectives differ?

Introduction

Planning, which is the focus of this chapter, and assessment, the focus of the next chapter, are ongoing elements of teaching. In everyday terms, planning is the process of determining where you (and your students) want to go, instructionally speaking, whereas assessment refers to the process of determining how well everyone got to where you had planned to go. What can make teaching and planning so psychologically demanding is its unfinished nature. Even in the middle of an activity, teachers may find themselves thinking "I should have done *that* differently" or "Next time I need a better activity"—all while simultaneously managing a group of twenty or so students.

A balancing act

In planning this chapter, I considered reprinting one or more of the countless unit and lesson plans on the Internet and in the literature. I rejected this option because completed unit plans do not reflect the decisions and the processes their developers used to create them. Neither do they indicate what the developers thought about but excluded from their final plans, an element that's as important as deciding what to include, especially if you are the one doing the including.

A unit plan is simply a chunk of instruction. It can be as long or short as meets your purposes. There must also be something that makes a unit hang together, which is usually a topic or idea. A unit that does not hang together is merely a collection of random lessons. This chapter takes you through the process of planning a freestanding (non-text-based) teaching unit. It also considers other planning-related elements, such as how you can look at social studies content and topics in different ways, and how state and national standards can influence a teacher's planning.

● ● ● ● **Planning Options**

There are probably as many different ways to plan for instruction as there are teachers. This is another way of saying that teachers often develop idiosyncratic planning techniques depending on (1) the subject matter they are expected to teach (and their familiarity with it), on (2) their students and their backgrounds and abilities, on (3) the time available, and on (4) the materials available. Planning techniques typically follow one of three approaches discussed next.

Planning Option A: Using Textbooks as the Main Organizer

Despite the bad press that textbooks sometimes get, using them as the basis for planning has surely been the salvation for thousands of beginning teachers, especially those who face the prospect of planning for six or seven different subjects every day. There is precious little time during the teaching day to plan specialized units in one subject area, much less five or six. As a consequence, and although planning teaching units in the various subjects is a worthwhile goal, realistically it is going to take some time to reach that point. Using the textbook as the basis for planning helps to ensure that units will fall into a reasonable sequence and that they are aligned with national and, in most cases, state standards.

STANDARDS ✔

Planning Option B: Going Beyond the Textbook in Selected Subjects

Departmentalized instruction refers to the practice of assigning teachers responsibility for one or two subjects, not most of the subjects as is true for self-contained classrooms. As departmentalized instruction has become increasingly popular at the intermediate and middle-school grades, it is reasonable to expect that teachers of fewer subjects will be in a better position to develop specialized units that go beyond the textbook. Unfortunately, even among departmentalized teachers it is not uncommon to see spectacular lessons in mathematics, for example, and some truly "ho-hum" lessons in social studies or science (or vice versa).

Occasional beyond-the-text units

The basic pattern for this option is to use the textbook as the overall basis for planning and then teaching beyond-the-text units from time to time throughout the year. One problem with this approach, oddly enough, can come from students. For example, imagine Ms. Lindquist's fifth graders' reaction when, after completing their five-week project on the Lincoln biographies (see Chapter 1), they face the prospect of going back to textbook-based lessons. Grumbling? Complaints? We can't know for certain how students would react because Ms. Lindquist does not use a text-based approach, but you can rest assured that students often have distinct preferences for what and how they study something.

- - - •
Planning Option C: Using Beyond-the-Text Units as the Norm
- - - •

After you have planned a series of beyond-the-book units, it usually takes just some updating and fine-tuning to be able to use them again. On the other hand, changing from one grade level to another could have far-reaching consequences, but then no one really expects teachers to create an entirely new set of units in every subject every year. Despite this, some teachers are continually modifying and creating new units.

The next section focuses on one of the more important considerations in planning and teaching; that is, how you approach social studies content. On one hand, people often think of social studies content as topics, such as slavery or the Civil War, as well as facts related to those topics—the Confederates (the Grays) fought for the South, and General Robert E. Lee's horse was named Traveler. There is no question that social studies has more facts than anyone can possibly deal with, much less be expected to remember. On the other hand, there are some techniques for helping students (or anyone else) to organize and make sense of what would otherwise be a massive collection of separate pieces of information. The next section provides some examples.

SUGGESTED ACTIVITY

Individually or in small groups, identify the assets and liabilities of the three planning options listed here.

KEY IDEA

Instructional planning is a complex activity only because of the number of elements that must be considered; it is not inherently complicated.

● ● ● ● **A Perspective on Using Social Studies Content**

You probably remember that delightful children's classic *Mike Mulligan and His Steam Shovel* (Burton, 1939), in which Mike's steam-powered shovel, Mary Anne, is nearly sent to steam-shovel heaven because the new, engine-powered shovels are getting most of the jobs. In Burton's story, Mike and Mary Anne agree to dig the cellar for the new Popperville town hall. They also agree to complete the job in just one day; otherwise they won't get paid. By digging furiously for the entire day, Mike and Mary Anne manage to finish the job—except for one thing. In their haste, Mike forgets to leave a way to get Mary Anne out of the cellar (see Figure 8.1). So there she sits, quietly belching smoke, at the bottom of the huge hole.

Henry B. Swap, a member of the Popperville town council, arrives at the construction site and argues that because Mary Anne is stuck in the cellar, the job wasn't finished within the agreed-upon time and Mike should not be paid. The day is saved when a little boy, who has been watching the whole episode, suggests that they build the new town hall around Mary Anne and make her its new furnace. And Mike? He could become the new janitor.

Creative thinking

Mike Mulligan and His Steam Shovel is not the kind of content that you would normally associate with social studies. Nevertheless, a teacher could use the story to introduce the powerful idea of structure and function. That idea reflects the notion that certain structures—like steam-powered shovels—could be used for several functions (such as a hole digger, a *very* slow form of transportation, or even

Structure and function

FIGURE 8.1   Children's Book Illustration

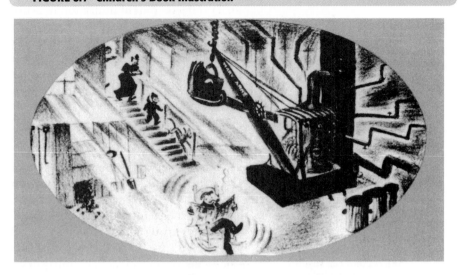

Source: *Mike Mulligan and His Steam Shovel* by Virginia Lee Burton. Copyright © 1939 and © 1967 by Virginia Lee Burton. Reprinted by permission of Houghton Mifflin Co. All rights reserved.

a furnace). Some of those functions, such as digging, are obviously more appropriate than others, yet all are potential functions for a steam-powered shovel.

Serving multiple purposes   Some teachers approach social studies subject matter as if it had only one major function, as something that "teachers teach and students are expected to know." This section shows how content can serve a variety of instructional purposes and how it can become something that teachers and students *use,* not simply something that students are expected to know.

Using content as a vehicle   *Content utilization* refers to the notion of using content (subject matter) as a *vehicle,* as a way to help teachers and students move toward educational destinations. Using content as a vehicle is not restricted to social studies, but the main focus here is on using content in teaching social studies.

Throughout this section the terms *content* and *subject matter*—the "stuff" of instruction—are used synonymously. It matters not whether you are using excerpts from a biography of Martin Luther King or Thomas Jefferson, or a textbook passage dealing with vital services in a community. A teacher could use the ideas inherent in social studies content (1) as the "stuff" children are supposed to know, (2) as a vehicle to help students identify and test hypotheses, (3) to distinguish

Multiple purposes   between facts and opinions, or (4) to teach other critical thinking skills. Students could also use the ideas inherent in social studies content as a basis for looking for recurring patterns in the human experience, to test previously identified hypotheses, as a springboard for further inquiry and research, and for many other purposes. In other words, social studies content can have a multitude of uses.

The Model Student Activity "Who Is Qualified for the Presidency?" (from Chapter 1) reflects content utilization in action. In that activity, the biographical information served as a vehicle to help students identify factors such as age, education, marital status, and the like, that might influence the selection and election of a president. It was *not* intended to teach information that students would be expected to remember about the candidates themselves. The point here is that there is a reciprocal relationship between the teachers' purposes and the kind of content they use with their students:

Purpose determines use

Purposes ◀─────────▶ Content

If a teacher's purpose is to involve children in identifying factors that influence the selection of a president, the teacher could use the "Presidency" activity to do that. However, instead of using the "Presidency" activity, other teachers might wish to have students debate the importance of a previously prepared list of factors that can influence presidential elections. Either approach is equally valid, although not necessarily equally effective.

The content can suggest potential uses

The first point here is that the relationship between purposes and content is reciprocal, or nearly so. A teacher's purposes can dictate the content she or he needs, just as certain content, like the "Presidency" activity, can suggest some purposes for which you could use it. The second point is that major curriculum goals are the dominant element in the purpose–content relationship. The "Presidency" activity (and every other Model Student Activity in this book) must fit into a larger picture. At the risk of stating the obvious, teachers should not use the "Presidency" activity in the middle of a unit on the geography of Australia if they want to maintain any sense of curricular continuity. Content vehicles can *suggest* purposes for which they can be used, but they do not *determine* what those purposes should be.

Using Unconventional Content to Teach Social Studies

Education has such a long tradition of using written or printed materials as content sources that it's easy to overlook other materials that can serve the same purposes. This section illustrates how two cans of Green Giant Niblets corn might serve as a content vehicle for social studies (and other subject areas).

Purposes clarified

Why corn? Why not something more conventional? First, using corn as a content vehicle avoids the "it's something that all children should know" syndrome. There is probably nothing about two cans of corn that students must know (see Figure 8.2). The second purpose is to illustrate how it's possible to identify and teach legitimate skills by using neutral content. A third related purpose is to illustrate that this content vehicle, mundane as it is, can also be used in subject areas other than social studies. Whether you ever elect to use this "corny" curriculum with students would depend on your purposes, of course.

The immediate task here is to use the canned corn as a vehicle for identifying potential questions and teaching activities. Besides posing possible research questions, you could identify potential instructional activities, such as "Design a new label" or "Try to figure out a more appealing color scheme for the existing label." Or you could do both. It is often useful to begin with a combination of questions and potential teaching activities because they provide a focus for pos-

FIGURE 8.2   The Basis for the Corn Curriculum

NUTRITION INFORMATION PER SERVING
Serving Size: ½ cup (solids and liquid)
Servings Per Container: 2

Calories . . . . 90 Fat 0g
Protein . . . . 2g Sodium** . . 230mg
Carbohydrate . . 20g Potassium . . 170mg
**Nutrition is calculated for liquids and solids
together. If the liquid is removed, there will be
180mg sodium.

**PERCENTAGE OF U.S. RECOMMENDED
DAILY ALLOWANCES (U.S. RDA) PER
SERVING:**

Protein . . . . . 2 Thiamine (B$_1$) .2 Calcium . . . . .*
Vitamin A . . . 2 Riboflavin (B$_2$) .4 Iron . . . .*
Vitamin C . . 10 Niacin . . . . . . .4 Phosphorus . .6
*Contains less than 2% of the U.S. RDA of these
nutrients.

Ingredients: Golden Whole Kernel Corn,
Water, Sugar, Salt.

Distributed by Green Giant Co., The Pillsbury
Company, Minneapolis, MN 55402

††Weight of corn means weight before addition of liquid necessary for processing.

NUTRITION INFORMATION PER SERVING
Serving Size: ½ cup (solids & liquid)
Servings Per Container: 4

Calories . . . . 80 Fat 0g
Protein . . . . 2g Sodium** . . . 290mg
Carbohydrate . . 18g Potassium . . 170mg
**Nutrition is calculated for liquids and solids to-
gether. If the liquid is removed, there will be 230mg
of sodium.

**PERCENTAGE OF U.S. RECOMMENDED
DAILY ALLOWANCES (U.S. RDA) PER
SERVING:**

Protein . . . . . 2 Thiamine (B$_1$) .* Calcium . . . . .*
Vitamin A . . . 8 Riboflavin (B$_2$) .2 Iron 2
Vitamin C . . . 8 Niacin . . . . . . .4 Phosphorus . .4
*Contains less than 2% of the U.S. RDA of these
nutrients.

Ingredients: Golden Whole Kernel Corn,
Water, Sugar, Salt.

Distributed by Green Giant Co., The Pillsbury
Company, Minneapolis, MN 55402

sible lessons. A question such as "How many words can be made from the word *niblets?*," for example, clearly implies a language-related activity. In presenting the task to students, it's not essential that the teacher pose the question directly. Rather, the teacher can say something such as "Let's see how many words we can make from the letters in *niblets.*" If you were to use such an activity, you could present it either as a task or as a question.

Brainstorming   Try your hand at brainstorming three or four potential research questions or teaching activities in each of the major subject areas: language arts (including reading), mathematics, science, and social studies. Some potential questions and activities are suggested to get you started. As you identify potential research questions, note that it is *not* essential that you be able to answer them in advance. Some of your best and most interesting questions will be those you can't answer immediately. For example, questions like "Why do most cans have ridges (or rings)?" or "Is there any tin in a tin can?" can serve as things to research or inquire about. Concern for answers to those questions can come later.

Language Arts

Possible activities
- Is *niblets* a real word? How could we find out?
- Write a story in which the Green Giant comes to life.
- Classify the words on the label beginning with *G* as naming words, action words, or describing words. Star the words that fit into more than one category. Then use at least some words from your list to create a cinquain poem.

Other Language Arts Questions/Activities

_____

_____

_____

Mathematics

- Identify three ways to figure out the number of kernels in the large can. Then determine which way is the most accurate.

Possible activities
- Determine how you could measure the length of the label without taking it off the can.
- Figure out three different-shaped cans that would hold the same amount of corn.

Other Math Questions/Activities

_____

_____

_____

Science

- What else is in these cans besides corn? Why would this be important to know?

Possible activities
- Does "net weight" include the liquid the corn is packed in? How could we find out?
- Are tin cans really made from tin? How could we find out?

Other Science Questions/Activities

_____

_____

_____

Social Studies

- Do most people in this class prefer canned corn or frozen corn? How could we find out?

Possible activities

- What ingredients (resources) went into growing the corn and producing the can and label?
- What role does corn play in our diet?
- What occupations are involved in getting corn from the Green Giant's valley to us?

Other Social Studies Questions/Activities

_____

_____

_____

Shifting to a process focus

A question such as "How could we find out?" shifts the focus of an activity from a concern for the answers to a concern for *finding* answers. Realistically, the answers to many of these questions, such as "What else is in these cans besides corn?" (water, salt, etc.), have little utility in a child's day-to-day life. However, their transfer value often lies in the processes that students use to arrive at their answers—processes that students can use to investigate other problems they encounter. Indeed, how can you find out what is in these cans besides corn?

Separating the grain from the chaff

The potential questions and activities identified here are a nebulous collection, nothing more. And simply because potential questions and activities have been identified doesn't mean they are worth using with students; some may have limited instructional value and should be discarded. The point is that content—even seemingly unconventional content like canned corn—can be used for a variety of teaching purposes and in different subject areas. It's all a matter of how you perceive it.

● ● ● ● Unit Planning

Teaching units vs. resource units

Planning a teaching unit, as opposed to a resource unit, is like lesson planning on a broader scale. A *teaching unit* focuses on a series of related lessons, whereas a *resource unit* is mainly a collection of materials and resources that you could draw on to create a teaching unit. Because unit plans have a broader focus than individual lessons, they can attend to broader learning outcomes than is possible with single lessons. In addition, unit planning offers a way of ensuring that the lessons you teach today will relate to the lessons you taught yesterday, and to those you will teach tomorrow. All of this reflects the fact that there is a flow to teaching and how students learn.

The Sequence of Planning Activities

Most published curriculum guides and units provide (1) a statement of the unit theme or topic, (2) a list of desired learning outcomes (goals and objectives), (3) a list of suggested student activities, (4) a list of resources and materials essential to teaching the unit, (5) potential assessment procedures or other evaluation activities, and (6) a listing of additional resources. The sequence of presentation sometimes leads prospective teachers to believe that instructional planning follows the same sequence. In most instances it probably does not. Instructional planning is a synthetic activity where all the parts must fit together when you are finished. But this does not mean that you must have every last objective etched in granite, for example, before you move on to identifying learning activities. This is because learning activities will sometimes suggest certain objectives. Then, too, if you think of a great learning activity as you are identifying unit objectives, by all means jot it down. Then come back to it when you are sequencing your learning activities.

KEY IDEA

Planning is a systematic process, as opposed to a series of discrete steps, in which each aspect interacts with every other aspect of instruction.

Almost every aspect of planning is tentative, so don't be surprised to find yourself discarding some learning activities or objectives and substituting others. This kind of ongoing editing occurs at all phases of planning.

Identifying a Unit Focus

Deciding what to focus on

The traditional focus of third-grade social studies is "communities," so we would surely be safe in developing one or more units on that topic. A unit on "community helpers" is a possibility, but I rejected this because most eight- and nine-year-olds already know to call 911 if there is an emergency and to get to a doctor or the emergency room if they are ill. In other words, a community helpers unit could have a high risk of focusing on material that most eight- and nine-year olds already know. We might also select other topics, such as "transportation," or "rainforests," or "Native Americans," especially if we have lots of teaching materials on them. The possibilities are not endless, however, because teachers are seldom free to teach anything they want to. They may be able to sneak in one or two units on their favorite topics over the course of a year, most likely in May, after the state-mandated tests are given, but most of what teachers select to teach needs to be compatible with state-mandated essential elements and national standards, especially in states that have state-mandated testing programs.

Identifying a Vehicle and Powerful Ideas

In the "Can of Corn" activity from earlier in this chapter, the idea was to use canned corn as a possible vehicle to reach some useful skills and knowledge. Selecting a vehicle is one of the first phases in planning, but the vehicle must also be compatible with the basic ideas that you intend to teach. For example, after deciding to teach about the institution of slavery, you might select the Underground Railroad as your vehicle. Or, if you wanted to teach about the geography of the Pacific Northwest, you might use a product (or products) produced in that area, for example, Red Delicious apples or Boeing airplanes.

Caution

Identifying a vehicle first and then trying to build a unit around it can lead to problems. Some of these are evident in the "bears" and "dinosaur" units that are popular today in the primary grades. Ask yourself "what ideas should a unit on bears or dinosaurs teach?" That some bears go fishing in the summer and hibernate in the winter? That the *Tyrannosaurus Rex* is a powerful meat-eating dinosaur? Children will experience new ideas from studying almost anything, of course, but the fundamental question here is, *what ideas of lasting value will the children gain from having studied these units?*

Using vehicles to teach ideas

The concept of using content as a teaching vehicle is not to teach about the vehicle itself. Rather, it is to use the vehicle to teach powerful ideas that will help children as they encounter their world. The two elements—vehicles and ideas—must go hand in hand. You cannot select a good unit vehicle until you also have a ballpark idea of the ideas that you could teach with it. A second option is to first determine the ideas you want to teach. The common problem here is that the listings of ideas, such as those found in the social studies standards, are lengthy almost to the point of being unwieldy. Many people need to narrow the field a bit so the task is more manageable. The point is that selecting a vehicle (your unit focus) and selecting the main ideas you might teach are simultaneous tasks. You're looking for the best "fit" between your vehicle and the powerful ideas you might teach. Having a potential vehicle (unit focus) in mind simply helps to narrow down the possibilities.

The uniqueness of historical studies

Selecting and using vehicles in teaching history poses some unique circumstances. Unlike the other social science disciplines, the potential vehicles amenable to teaching history are usually imbedded in the historical period in question and are unlikely to be known to students prior to instruction. If you were considering teaching about ancient Egypt, for example, the pyramids are an obvious (and excellent) potential vehicle. For the Middle Ages, the castle. For slavery in the United States, the Underground Railroad. Vehicles such as these can serve as excellent starting points for getting students involved in the period in question. But in most historical studies, you will devote some time to teaching about the vehicle itself. In other words, students cannot leave the study of slavery, for example, believing that the Underground Railroad was an actual railroad that ran under the ground or that the pyramids were built as tourist attractions.

Criteria for Identifying Potential Vehicles.   One criterion for a potential unit vehicle is that it be fairly simple, not something so complex or esoteric—like a proton accelerator, for example—that lengthy instruction would be required before most people, and students especially, would know what we were talking

The KISS principle

about. For a first planning effort it is probably advisable to stick to the KISS principle (Keep It Simple Stupid!), because even the simplest units can become complex very quickly. A second though closely related criterion is that the vehicle be common, that is, something known to most students. The second criterion is not absolutely essential, but it is consistent with the KISS principle noted. (See the Commentary on p. 218). A third related criterion is that the vehicle be something that you already know something about. An electronic keyboard, for example, might serve as an excellent vehicle for a science unit dealing with sound, but unless you already know about such instruments or are willing to research them, you may be inviting problems.

A potential vehicle for our sample unit that fits most of the criteria noted earlier is a McDonald's Big Mac™ or a Burger King Whopper™. They are well known

● ● ● ● **COMMENTARY**   **On Beginning with the Known?**

The idea that the best way to present new material to students is to connect it to what they already know is almost universally accepted among educators. It also helps to explain the continuing popularity of the expanding horizons curriculum in social studies, which ostensibly begins with the child's everyday experiences. Enter Kiernan Egan (2003), a professor at Simon Fraser University in Burnaby, British Columbia, who suggests that we consider a second principle: "asking what students can imagine." Egan asks that if children's minds are restricted to the everyday details of their social lives, why then are their minds so occupied with monsters or animals, like Peter Rabbit for example, who often speak readily understandable English yet cannot possibly exist?

Egan reminds us that storytellers seldom pay attention to the principle of starting with what children know. Rather, storytellers begin wherever they want to—in galaxies far, far away and long, long ago or somewhere in the future, whatever suits their purpose. Storytellers are also free to introduce strange characters and weird situations just as long as they build into their narrative the concepts that children understand: good/bad, brave/cowardly, anxiety/security, and so on. The connections that kids make with such stories are via metaphorical leaps, not logical progressions.

Egan emphasizes that he is not suggesting that teachers should ignore children's everyday experiences—which can sometimes be dreary—or their prior knowledge, but rather that they not ignore appealing to children's imaginations.

to most students, but, more important, they reflect the countless decisions that people had to make in order to produce them. These include ranchers who must decide whether to raise cattle (for beef) or something else, and other farmers who must decide whether they will grow lettuce, tomatoes, or possibly wheat (for the buns). Those farmers' and ranchers' decisions will be influenced by the climate, the kind of land they have available, the different kinds of equipment they must have, and the capital they need to pay for the equipment, and the necessary seed, fertilizer, and labor. In other words, a hamburger can be a tangible reflection of decisions about how resources are allocated—a primary focus of economics.

Decisions, decisions

My legal constraints

Classroom teachers could probably use an actual Big Mac™ or Whopper™ as a teaching vehicle, but to avoid infringing on these registered trademarks in a published work, I have opted to use a hybrid hamburger—called a "Super Burger"—as the vehicle for this unit. This name obviously lacks the pizzazz of the others, but when you see the term "Super Burger," picture in your mind a thick, juicy hamburger patty served on a large bun with lettuce, sliced pickles, onion, tomato slices, mayonnaise, ketchup, and mustard. If you find pickles or mayonnaise (or any of the other condiments) on a hamburger revolting, adjust accordingly. Note that I cannot use the expression "have it your way" in this context for it, too, is a registered trademark.

There is obviously nothing about a Super Burger that every child needs to know—or, perhaps, doesn't know already. The idea of course is to use the Super Burger as a way to get at more significant learnings. These will be the ideas that make what is essentially a study of hamburgers worthwhile.

What Young Children Already Know about Food.
Hamburgers are so much a part of American life that it's possible that children already know much of what this unit will deal with. In some recent research, Brophy, Alleman, and

O'Mahony (2003) set out to discover what primary-grade students (kindergarten, first, second, and third graders) actually know about food production and the origins of common foods. They found that almost all the participants knew about common food items, such as applesauce, cheese, bread, and hamburgers. For example, most of them knew that applesauce was made from apples. However, when they were asked more specific questions about hamburger—such as what is hamburger? where does it come from? and how is a hamburger patty made?—their responses showed much more variability. A typical kindergartner would respond, "from a cow or something." (Follow-up question: How does it get from the cow to the hamburger?) "I don't know." To the same questions, a typical first grader would say, "you've got two breads—one is on the bottom, one on the top, and you have lettuce inside." (How is the meat made?) "It is made out of chicken and it turns into meat." Second graders would typically say "some of them are made out of cows" (How is the meat made?) "I really don't know." A third grader would respond saying, "They kill a pig and then they take the meat from the pig and cook it and then they put it in a bun" (p. 17–18).

What do young children know about food?

Food is what you buy at a supermarket.

Based on their findings, Brophy, Alleman, and O'Mahony concluded that most primary-grade students are unaware "of the land-to-hand progressions that bring food to our tables." They went on to say that most of what children know begins with the purchase of products at the supermarket, but with "little knowledge about their essential nature (e.g., flour is milled grain, hamburger is ground beef) or the processes involved in manufacturing them" (p. 22). Based on these findings, it is highly unlikely that this Super Burger unit will deal with information already known to our target audience.

Identifying Potential Knowledge Outcomes

STANDARDS ✔

To formalize some of the powerful ideas (knowledge outcomes) that a Super Burger unit might teach, it's useful to turn to the social studies standards. You may recall from Chapter 1 that the standards are organized around ten interdisciplinary themes or threads that correspond roughly with the social science disciplines. Those thematic strands are:

I. Culture (Anthropology)
II. Time, Continuity, and Change (History)
III. People, Places, and Environments (Geography)
IV. Individual Development and Identity (Psychology)
V. Individuals, Groups, and Institutions (Psychology/Sociology)
VI. Power, Authority, and Governance (Political Science)
VII. Production, Distribution, and Consumption (Economics)
VIII. Science, Technology, and Society (Multidisciplinary)
IX. Global Connections (Multidisciplinary)
X. Civic Ideals and Practices (Political Science/Multidisciplinary)
(NCSS, 1994)

 SUGGESTED ACTIVITY

Reflect on this list of themes to determine where our potential hamburger unit might best "fit."

At this level of generality, the standards don't offer much guidance. However, each of the strands is further elaborated in statements of performance expectation.

These begin: "Social studies programs should include experiences that provide for the study of. . . ." The performance expectations for Theme VII, Production, Distribution, and Consumption, which seem particularly relevant to our embryonic unit, are shown in the following.

Performance Expectations: Social studies programs should include experiences that provide for the study of *how people organize for the production, distribution, and consumption of goods and services,* so that the learner can

Performance expectations

a. give and explain examples of ways that economic systems structure choices about how goods and services are to be produced and distributed;
b. describe the role that supply and demand, prices, incentives, and profits play in determining what is produced and distributed in a competitive market;
c. explain the difference between private and public goods and services;
d. describe a range of examples of the various institutions that make up economic systems such as households, business firms, banks, government agencies, labor unions, and corporations;
e. describe the role of specialization and exchange in the economic process;
f. explain and illustrate how values and beliefs influence different economic decisions;
g. differentiate among various forms of exchange and money;
h. compare basic economic systems according to who determines what is produced, distributed, and consumed;
i. use economic concepts to help explain historical and current developments and issues in local, national, or global contexts; and
j. use economic reasoning to compare different proposals for dealing with a contemporary social issue such as unemployment, acid rain, or high-quality education.

The national standards and the performance expectations were developed by an NCSS committee. In an apparent effort to make sure they don't omit something important, committees often produce documents that, while they are certainly complete, may also be long and convoluted. In this instance, performance expectations (knowledge outcomes) are intended to cover at least a three-year period, the middle grades. A similar situation often prevails for state mandates. What many teachers do, then, is select elements that are most relevant and ig-

Select what you need or what applies

nore the rest until another time. However, they cannot ignore entirely the expectations that are irrelevant to the unit in question, because the expectations are usually the basis for state-mandated tests.

Relationship to Other Mandated Expectations.   It is generally safe to assume that national performance expectations will encompass the state's expectations, but it does no harm to be sure of that. Several examples typical of state-mandated essential elements relevant to our emerging unit are noted next.

Goal One: *Students will practice a variety of listening, speaking, writing, and reading skills in completing social studies activities.*

STANDARDS ☑️ **Goal Two:** *Students will understand that people use natural resources to meet their basic needs and these resources must be protected and conserved.*

Goal Three: S*tudents will understand geographic concepts.*

Goal Four*: Students will understand the interplay of economics in their daily lives.*

State mandates   Goal Four could become a major focus of the Super Burger unit. This means that we will need to develop learning activities that correspond to the following objectives for Goal Four:

Objective 4.1: Define wages, prices, producer, consumer, specialization, division of labor, profit, loss, and productivity.

Objective 4.2: Identify the relationship between supply and demand and its effect on the price of a product.

Objective 4.3: Identify the natural resources that determine the types of jobs in your community in the past, present, and future.

Objective 4.4: Identify the role of profits as being a primary reason for production.

Implications.   The state-mandated competencies suggest some elements that need to be included in this unit. For example, some teaching activities should have language arts-related extensions that address components of Goal One. In one potential activity, for example, a small group could select one component of a Super Burger, such as lettuce, and then research how the product is grown and transported to market. The group can then present their findings in the form of **Activities and standards** an illustrated, first-person diary; for example, "Hi, I'm Lucy Lettuce, and I grew up in the Imperial Valley of California." Having the children keep ongoing journals would also correlate with Goal One.

    Teaching activities that involve identifying the occupations and resources that go into producing a Super Burger pertain to Goals Two and Four. More specifically, either individually or collectively, the children can create a "family tree" for a Super Burger (which is described shortly).

    Goal Three is not a major focus of this unit, but activities pertaining to crops that farmers grow will involve elements related to climate, terrain, weather conditions, and so on. The fact that some components of the Super Burger, specifically the lettuce and tomatoes, can be grown in many places in the summer but in much more restricted areas in the winter is something we will need to take into account.

● ● ● ●
Decision Point
● ● ● ●

There seems to be a reasonably good fit between our potential unit vehicle and some of the performance expectations for Theme VII of the social studies standards. The idea that will serve as the focus for this unit is: *The production of any product involves countless decisions on how resources will be used.*

    Not all units have subtitles, but to make it clear that the main interest here is in the thousands of decisions that go into producing a Super Burger—not just **Adding a subtitle** the hamburger itself—a subtitle such as "Decisions, Decisions, Decisions!" seems appropriate.

● ● ● ● Planning Tools

Two techniques that often prove useful in planning are (1) identifying key questions and (2) webbing. In addition to helping plan the unit, these techniques may also become part of teaching activities we use with students.

Using Key Questions in Planning

A key question for the Super Burger unit is: What products and resources are used in creating a Super Burger? This question and the others in this section are for planning and organizational purposes; they are not final exam questions. The goal of this unit is to help children understand the kinds of decisions and resources that go into producing a Super Burger (and other products), not to memorize a list of the ingredients for a recipe. Among other key questions are: "Why do farmers decide to grow lettuce, tomatoes, and onions, instead of cotton, soybeans, or other crops?" "Why do some farmers raise beef cattle instead of crops?" and "What human resources are involved in producing a Super Burger?"

Questions can simplify the identification of outcomes

Key questions can lend specificity and clarity to lessons. They can also be restated as learning outcomes. For example, a question such as "Why do farmers decide to grow lettuce, tomatoes, and onions instead of cotton, soybeans, or other crops?" can be restated as "Students will explain the factors that farmers consider in deciding which crops to produce." As we get further into our planning, we may generate more key questions and topics to pursue, but we are just as likely to discard some questions, especially if we cannot create reasonable teaching activities geared to them. An example of this is provided shortly.

Using Webbing as a Planning Tool

Because the relationship between Super Burgers and how people use resources may still be amorphous at this point, webbing can provide a useful technique for getting a better handle on the topic. The *webbing* process produces a kind of semantic map, similar to the one for Canada shown in Chapter 7, which shows the range and scope of relationships among related elements.

Building a web for a burger

There are several ways to begin the webbing process. One is to brainstorm (free-associate) by listing anything you can think of related to the theme or topic (the Super Burger). A second technique is to identify questions and possible teaching activities, a process that we began earlier. Or you could do either of these. Because we've already explored some aspects of our hamburger unit we'll follow up on that here.

Figure 8.3 shows a web that reflects some of the questions and potential teaching activities we considered earlier. The web and everything else noted thus far seems to confirm that the notion of resources—natural and human—offers a potentially workable direction or theme for this unit.

FIGURE 8.3 Preliminary Web for a Super Burger

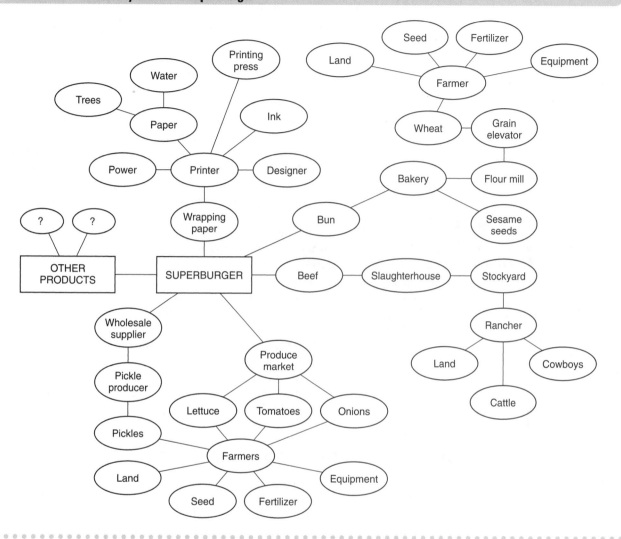

Other Elements

Refining the scope

One element we could include in our emerging unit could deal with the different forms of transportation that play a role in producing and transporting the products that go into a Super Burger. Such a topic would be within the scope of Objective 4.1, and it would also add an appealing focus to the unit, especially if we could create some interesting nonreading activities dealing with trucks, trains, and other forms of transport. On the other hand, most third graders are already aware of trucks, trains, and so on, so unless we are careful we could find ourselves conducting a lesson about how milk trucks carry milk.

Task-analyzing potential content

To pursue the transportation focus, we need to determine what *prior knowledge* children must have before they can deal with the role that transportation plays in any kind of trade. An obvious prerequisite is the need to understand the notion of trade as the exchange of goods and services. The students must also understand the notion of transportation in terms of its function—the movement of goods and people. In addition, to understand why things are transported, students must also understand why goods are traded, which involves concepts related to self-sufficiency, interdependence, and profit.

If this seemingly simple topic has become very complex, you're right. The potential ideas include *trade, transportation, self-sufficiency, interdependence, goods and services, exchange,* and *communication.* Separately, none of these is beyond the grasp of most third graders, but when it comes to helping them understand how these topics are interrelated, we have tackled something much more complicated than we bargained for, something unnecessarily complex for exemplary purposes. Instead we can treat transportation simply as the movement of goods from place to place, which adds to their cost, but not otherwise include it as a significant element in this unit. This decision illustrates a common planning phenomenon: the need to back up and either go in a different direction or, in some cases, even start over. If everything went well on the first try, planning would be less exciting and less time consuming.

KEY IDEA

Effective planning hinges on two elements: (1) determining what students should know and be able to do after instruction, and (2) creating instructional activities that enable them to reach those goals.

After considering many alternatives, we have finally laid the foundation for our unit. Our planning is far from complete, but the progress report on page 229 shows the elements identified thus far.

● ● ● ● ● A Perspective on Learning Outcomes

Outcomes should fit the time span

As teachers plan their courses, units, and lessons, the time span they are dealing with affects how they create and state their learning outcomes. For example, it's doubtful that any teacher can attain the goal of "producing effective citizens," because this is a desired outcome for an entire school experience. As such, it would represent the collective effort of teachers over a period of years. Still other outcomes, such as having students "understand the geography of the Western Hemisphere" or "understand the Civil War" will cover shorter periods, possibly a course, semester, or a unit of study. Daily lessons, on the other hand, almost always have even more specific outcomes or objectives than units or courses.

The levels of specificity for educational outcomes are shown in the following:

Goals   *Level 4: Very General.* Example: The student will be able to cope with the problems of life. (School or Lifelong Goal)
            Level 3: General. The student will understand how technology has influenced our way of life. (Course Goal)

Objectives *Level 2: Specific.* Given a limited amount of information about unknown nations, students will be able to identify two or more plausible hypotheses that describe life in those nations. (Unit or Course Objective)

Level 1: Very Explicit. Example: Given a state highway map, the student will be able to use the index to locate five towns or villages. (Specific Lesson Objective)

Objectives are stated specifically

Broadly stated goals, such as helping students "to understand the geography of the Western Hemisphere" or "to understand how humans use resources" indicate the overall direction that teaching should take. However, these outcomes are not specific enough to indicate what students who understand "the geography of the Western Hemisphere" or "how humans use resources" should know or be able to do. This is where more specifically stated outcomes, often called objectives, (or learner objectives) enter the picture. An objective, such as "name forty-five of the fifty state capitals," indicates exactly what students should know and thus lends precision and direction to what could otherwise be very general expectations. There are problems with an objective like "name forty-five of the fifty state capitals," which are considered shortly, but the overall point is that although goals and objectives play a role in teaching social studies, they serve different functions.

Goals and objectives serve different functions

Stating Outcomes in Performance Terms

Stating expectations for units or lessons often depends on the specificity of the words you use. Of the two lists of phrases shown below, determine which one uses terminology more appropriate for units and courses, and which is more applicable to daily lessons.

Goals vs. objectives

List 1	*List 2*
To grasp the significance of	To write or list
To understand	To illustrate
To recognize	To define
To appreciate or to enjoy	To predict or to suggest
To believe or to have faith in	To name or identify
To comprehend or to understand	To locate or to rate
To know (or to know thoroughly)	To restate or to tell why
To be aware of	To distinguish between or to discuss

The terms in List 1 are more often associated with units or courses, whereas the more explicit terms in List 2 are typically associated with specific lessons. Learning outcomes that use the more specific format are sometimes called *performance objectives, behavioral objectives, criterion-referenced objectives,* or *learner objectives* and typically have four components:

Characteristics of performance outcomes

1. An *object* of instruction ("state capitals")
2. A *condition* under which the behavior will be demonstrated ("from memory")
3. A *standard* (*criterion* or *performance level*) that the student must demonstrate ("forty-five of fifty")
4. An identifiable *task* or *behavior* ("to name")

Judging the Appropriateness of Objectives

Criteria for judging appropriateness

Although the sample objective "Students will be able to name forty-five of the fifty state capitals from memory" reflects all the criteria for precisely stated objectives, it still has some problems. Every objective must be judged in terms of (1) whether students can realistically achieve it, which may depend on students' grade level and maturity, (2) whether it is logically consistent with the purpose(s) to which it relates, *and* (3) whether the goal or objective pertains to something that children *should* attempt to do. Given enough time, for example, most first graders could probably memorize forty-five of the fifty state capitals. But simply because children *could* achieve that objective does not mean it is something they *should* strive for.

The "who cares?" test is one technique for judging the appropriateness of learning outcomes. For an objective such as "Students will identify from memory the number of horses that pulled Cinderella's coach," you need simply ask "who cares?" If your answer is "nobody," the objective should probably be discarded.

Creating Intermediate-Level Outcomes

Intermediate-level outcomes—a middle ground

Learning outcomes should be stated as precisely as possible, but this does not mean that *everything* must or can be stated in behavioral terms. For example, it's almost impossible to specify precise behavioral indicators for creative or open-ended group activities, especially when there are no right answers. The same situation can exist for objectives pertaining to attitudes or higher-level thinking skills, such as analysis and synthesis, and for works of children's literature. To accommodate situations like these, it is helpful to create some intermediate-level goal statements, which, although they may lack the specificity of instructional objectives, are often explicit enough to guide instruction. For example, suppose you want to use a book like Bunting's (1991) *Fly Away Home* with your students. This is the story of a homeless boy and his father who actually live in an airport. Developing precise objectives for this story, such as "The student will from memory, identify at which gate the father and son most often slept" is possible, but some of them will probably be on the same level as "How many horses pulled Cinderella's coach?" Such objectives could ask students to focus on what is essentially trivia. After using a story such as *Fly Away Home,* some acceptable intermediate-level goals might include (1) for students to appreciate what it feels like to be homeless, and (2) to be aware of the things that homeless people sometimes think about as they search for shelter. Intermediate-level goal statements can provide guidance for identifying instructional objectives, unit objectives, and even course objectives.

Goals and Objectives for Thinking and Feeling

Many elementary- and middle-school classrooms have a semipermanent poster or bulletin board that states:

Evaluation
Synthesis
Analysis
Application
Comprehension
Knowledge

The *Taxonomies*

These bulletin boards reflect the work that Benjamin Bloom and his associates did over forty years ago when they developed a system for organizing and classifying educational goals and objectives. Two major parts of this landmark work are the *Taxonomy of Educational Objectives: The Classification of Educational Goals, Handbook I: Cognitive Domain* (Bloom et al., 1956), and *Handbook II: Affective Domain* (Krathwohl et al., 1964). A revision of the original taxonomy by L. W. Anderson and David R. Krathwohl was published in 2001. Its title is *A Taxonomy for Learning, Teaching, and Assessment: A Revision of Bloom's Taxonomy of Educational Objectives. A taxonomy* is simply a hierarchical classification scheme whereby each level builds upon and is more complex than the previous level.

Cognitive domain—thinking

The *cognitive domain* refers to activities that involve different kinds of thinking and remembering. The taxonomy for the cognitive domain is organized in terms of the complexity of the thinking skills involved, as shown on the sample poster above. Thus, when you hear people refer to "higher-level thinking skills," they are in all likelihood referring to skills at the higher and more complex levels of the *Taxonomy* (application, analysis, synthesis, and evaluation).

Affective domain—feelings and attitudes

The *affective domain* includes attitudes and values, both of which involve feelings and emotions. For analytical and planning purposes, it's possible to treat the cognitive (knowing) and affective (feeling) domains separately, but in practice the two often merge together. You've seen this in instances where your teacher's attitudes and feelings about certain subject matter came across as strongly as the subject matter itself.

The challenge of affective objectives

The part of social studies directed toward the affective domain is reflected by goals such as "Develops respect for the American way of life," "Develops an appreciation for American history," or "Becomes a responsible school citizen." It is one thing to state a desired attitude, such as "being a good classroom citizen," but it is another to identify specific behavioral indicators for that notion. Although everyone might agree that a "good school citizen" is someone who pays attention, turns in work on time and so on, it soon becomes difficult to avoid stating behaviors that students should not exhibit—does not interrupt, never gets out of seat. Unfortunately, when possible affective objectives are phrased as positive statements, such as "The student will stop interrupting the teacher whenever the teacher is talking," they can take on a "Have you stopped browbeating your spouse yet?" flavor. If it is not already clear, developing affective objectives is a difficult task.

Content, Process, and Affective Outcomes.   The reason for this detour through the various kinds of instructional outcomes is to indicate why our teaching unit will have three kinds of goals or objectives. The first type is knowledge or *content objectives*, which indicate what we expect students to know from having studied this unit. For example, after studying the Super Burger unit, it is reasonable to expect students to know what resources are. Thus one of the content objectives should be that the student will describe the nature of a resource. The second type of outcome is skill or *process objectives*, which indicate how students will use data. Process objectives depend largely on the kinds of teaching activities we develop (and which we haven't done yet), but an illustrative objective is that students will generate and test three hypotheses that explain how farmers decide what crops to grow. The third type of outcome is attitudinal or *affective goals*, which indicate the attitudes and appreciations we would like students to develop from having studied this unit. There may not be many affective goals, but one example is that the student will appreciate the need to use resources wisely. We will identify additional outcomes as planning progresses.

Outcomes focus on
different elements

KEY IDEA

Learning outcomes are stated with varying levels of specificity.

TECHNOLOGY UPDATE

Teaching Units and Lesson Plans
on the Internet

So many lesson plans and units are available on the Internet that some sites have their own minisearch engines. The following is a sampling of sites that have lesson plans and units available for downloading.

Academy Social Studies Curriculum Exchange for Elementary (K–5) or Intermediate (6–8) Schools. Two sites with 130 different lesson plans. The address for elementary plans is:

> **http://ofcn.org/cyber.serv/academy/ace/soc/
> elem.html**

The address for intermediate (6–8) plans is:

> **http://ofcn.org/cyber.serv/academy/ace/soc/
> inter.html**

Columbia Education Center in Portland, Oregon. This center offers a large assortment of lesson plans for Grades K–5 and 6–8. The address for K–5 plans is:

> **http://www.col-ed.org/cur/#sst1**

For intermediate plans, substitute "#sst2" for "#sst1" (do not type the quotation marks) in the K–5 address.

Core Knowledge Lesson Plans and Units. All of the K–6 units and lessons available from this site correspond with the Core Knowledge program that we described in Chapter 3. Address:

> **http://www.coreknowledge.org/**

Publishers' plans and activities. Houghton Mifflin and McGraw-Hill are two of several publishers that have K–8 lesson plans available. The address for Houghton Mifflin is:

> **http://www.eduplace.com/activity**

The address for McGraw-Hill is:

> **http://www.mmhschool.com/teach/ss2003/in-
> dex.html**

Lesson plans and activities that correspond with television programs. Three examples in this category are the History Channel Classroom Materials, at:

> **http://www.historychannel.com/classroom/**

CNN (The Cable News Network) Lesson Plans and Multimedia Resources at:

> **http://www.turnerlearning.com/newsroom/
> specials.html**

and the Discovery Channel School at:

> **http://school.discovery.com**

Progress Report

Unit Development
Unit Title: Super Burgers: Decisions, Decisions, Decisions
Grade Level: Primary (third)
Unit Focus: Allocation and utilization of resources
Generalization: The allocation and use of human and natural resources is based on decisions.
Major vehicle: A Super Burger hamburger
Unit goals: (partial listing)

COGNITIVE

- The child will understand what makes something a resource, either natural or human.

- The child will understand that land, labor, and capital are the basis for all production decisions. (For brevity, the additional goals shown earlier are not repeated here).

AFFECTIVE

- The child will appreciate the scarcity of resources, our widespread dependency on them, and the need to use resources wisely.

Objectives (tentative):

- The child will identify, from memory, three examples of natural resources.

- The student will distinguish between a human resource and a natural resource. (For brevity, additional objectives shown earlier are not repeated. Additional objectives may also grow out of teaching activities.)
Learning activities: Yet to be determined.

● ● ● ● Identifying and Sequencing Teaching Activities

Cognitive engagement potential

The basic structure for this unit is identified, but it still lacks teaching activities and other components. In the process of selecting teaching activities, Brophy and Alleman (1991) suggest an activity's *cognitive engagement potential* as an important criterion. This refers to the likelihood that the teaching activity has the potential to engage the student cognitively—that is, get students thinking actively. Brophy and Alleman claim that many teaching activities have only limited potential to engage children intellectually. Notable here is much of the "seatwork" that students encounter—the page after page of workbook-like questions they must answer. Such activities are sometimes called "check-ups" or "skill-builders" or some other beneficial-sounding name, but it would probably be more honest to call them what they usually are: tests or busywork. Recognize that students are not likely to "build a skill" simply by answering a question that tests their prior knowledge.

Brophy and Alleman also contend that the educational value of some long-term projects, including some hands-on construction activities as well as end-of-unit or end-of-semester activities, is also suspect. For example, end-of-unit pageants or the construction of complex displays—like scale-model colonial villages—can consume vast amounts of time but have limited instructional payoff. Students may enjoy such long-term projects and even look forward to them, but their enjoyment could very well arise from the opportunity to avoid more seatwork.

With Brophy and Alleman's cautions in mind, there isn't necessarily one best way to proceed from this point. One option is to follow up on the earlier brainstorming by using the following technique.

Strategy for Identifying Instructional Activities

The following technique for identifying potential teaching activities is based on a modified brainstorming format. It is not essential that you use every category; likewise, the number of entries per category can be expanded or reduced to fit the situation. Consider treating this activity as you would a grocery list, as something you return to whenever you get a good idea.

Identifying Potential Learning Activities

Students could *read:* [List potential reading materials/activities, e.g., original source materials, etc.]

    a. _____

    b. _____

    c. _____

Students could *view:* [List potential viewing activities, e.g., videos, CD-ROMs, etc.]

    a. _____

    b. _____

    c. _____

Students could *listen to:* [List potential listening materials/activities, e.g. books for read-alouds, etc.]

    a. _____

    b. _____

    c. _____

Students could *write:* [List potential writing activities, e.g., imaginary diaries, reports, etc.]

    a. _____

    b. _____

    c. _____

Brainstorming potential learning activities that appeal to different modalities

Students might *construct:* [List potential modeling or construction activities (including art-related activities), e.g., collages, etc.]

a. _____
b. _____
c. _____

Students could *discuss* or *debate:* [List potential discussion or debate topics.]

a. _____
b. _____
c. _____

You may have more than three activities in some areas and fewer in others

Students could *research/investigate:* [List potential research activities, e.g., how steel is made, etc.]

a. _____
b. _____
c. _____

Students could *complete:* [List other potential activities not included above, e.g., worksheets, etc.]

a. _____
b. _____
c. _____

An Alternate Technique for Identifying Teaching Activities.   The preceding technique creates a pool of potential activities to select among. Another way to begin is by identifying a way to initiate the unit, preferably a way that grabs students' attention and establishes a direction for the activities that follow. Then you can go back to the activity pool and sequence things from that starting point in ways that seem to make sense.

Another technique

Creating and Initiating Activity

Among the possible ways to initiate this unit, my first decision is not to begin with a vocabulary activity. Note that throughout this section adult language is used unless otherwise noted. Definitions will eventually need to be dealt with, of course, but beginning the unit with a vocabulary lesson is not something that will grab students' attention. An alternate initiating activity that seems to have some potential is to deconstruct (take apart) a Super Burger (which means that you may need to stop at a Burger King or McDonald's take-out window before teaching this lesson). Advise students that the class is going to be studying hamburgers for the next week or so, and that when the unit is over, it is going to have Super Burgers for lunch. (If you agree here, you have just identified your culminating activity!) For the initiating

Deconstructing a burger

activity, one alternative is to generate a list of the ingredients that go into a Super Burger—I recommend using a Burger King Whopper for this. Another alternative would be to develop a simplified "family tree" for a hamburger, as illustrated in Figure 8.4.

Choosing between beginning the unit with a list of resources, a family tree activity, or something else is just one of the countless decisions that planning demands. In this instance, the family tree activity is appealing because it shows the ingredients in an unusual format. Finally, developing a family tree for a hamburger in a whole-class setting will serve as a model for subsequent activities in which small groups of students create similar family trees for each of the condiments (onions, pickles, etc.).

Factors to consider

The detail provided here is to indicate some of the factors to consider in arriving at planning decisions. If the notion of a family tree is foreign to students, a preliminary activity in which students learn to create their own family trees may be advisable. That decision necessarily hinges on an awareness of students' previous experiences with family trees, which is something teachers gain simply by working with their classes. On the other hand, you can always model the process for them.

Weighing alternatives

FIGURE 8.4   A Family Tree for a Can of Corn

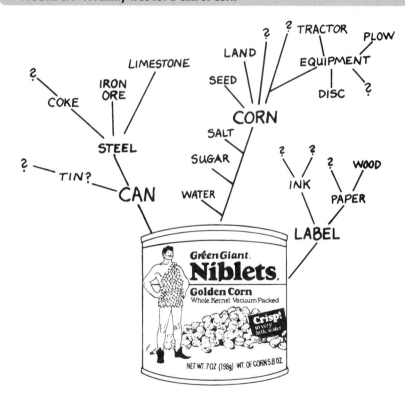

Another potential activity is to conduct a survey to determine which of the condiments are the most popular among members of the class. You might want to call this activity "It's My Burger." The idea here is to survey the class regarding their preferred condiments, and then present the findings in graphic form. This kind of activity is not really significant enough that is needs to involve the entire class (except to respond to the survey), but it could be a worthwhile small-group activity. The management issue that must be considered here involves what the other students will be doing as the small group deals with its condiment survey.

Research and small-group activities

This potential unit offers ample opportunities for teacher-led lessons, but what about research and small-group activities? It seems pointless to have the entire class research the various ingredients of a Super Burger, but this activity could be more suitable for small-group research tasks. For example, groups of approximately three students could each research and report on a different condiment—how it is made, where it is produced, and so forth. The condiment survey group can also conduct their survey at this time.

A Brief Side Trip.   To add a multicultural dimension to this unit, you may want to include a brief side trip focusing on migrant farm workers. These are the people, almost exclusively Hispanic, who harvest most of the crops that ultimately become condiments for the Super Burger. Several children's books that focus on migrant workers and would be suitable for reading aloud are as follows:

Books for a migrant-workers focus

Migrant Worker: A Boy from the Rio Grande Valley by Diane Hoyt-Goldsmith. This factual account is written from the perspective of an eleven-year-old Mexican-American migrant worker and provides a realistic look at the migrant worker's lifestyle.

Tomas and the Library Lady by Pat Mora. This picture book traces the life of Mexican-American author Tomas Rivera, who as a young boy in the 1940s travels to Iowa with his family to harvest crops. On his trip he meets a librarian who instills in him a love of books while he, in turn, teaches her Spanish.

La Mariposa by Francisco Jiménez. This book presents the problems and the intolerance that a young Mexican-American boy encounters when he attends a school in an area where his family works as migrant laborers.

Ongoing Activities

Activities that extend throughout the unit

This aspect of planning is not essential unless you will have some activities that will extend throughout the entire unit. Two potential, ongoing activities appropriate to this unit are (1) student journals and (2) the award- winning, computer-based simulation *DinoPark Tycoon* (1995), which is available from MECC. Although this engaging simulation does not address hamburgers directly, students must plan and operate a dinosaur theme park. In addition to meeting the needs of their dinosaurs, such as land, fencing, and food, students must also decide how they will staff the park and make provisions for maintenance and daily operations.

The goal in creating and selecting teaching activities is to engage students actively and intellectually. In most instances, the potential for engagement is more important than the potential for "fun."

(© Susie Fitzhugh)

Determining a Culminating Activity

Deciding how to end the unit

Finding a good culminating activity is something teachers may think about throughout the entire planning process. Also relevant here are Brophy and Alleman's earlier comments about end-of-unit activities that, although they require considerable time, often fail to engage students' thinking processes. Ideally, culminating activities should provide opportunities to apply and extend some ideas previously dealt with in different contexts.

The "Having-Super-Burgers-for-lunch" culminating activity noted earlier will be retained. Even though the activity does not stimulate students cognitively, it still makes a nice way to wrap up the unit. However, this also means that we need to seek out another culminating activity—to precede the hamburger lunch—that has a higher cognitive payoff.

By initiating the unit using the hamburger as a vehicle, we can return to it in the culminating activity in a slightly different context. Returning to the master family tree chart for hamburgers, we can ask the children to identify the main decision makers at each phase of production. They can also identify at least one alternative decision that each individual might have made in determining how he or she would use the available resources. The objective here is to call attention to all the decisions that go into the production process.

Although it is not essential to return to the family tree in the culminating activity, it seems to round things out rather nicely. It is also useful, though not essential, if the culminating activity provides a bridge to the next unit. In this

MODEL STUDENT ACTIVITY

A Sample Unit Plan:
Super Burger Unit

Grade Level: Third Grade
Introductory Note: Because many elements of this unit plan were described earlier, they have been cross-referenced to relevant pages rather than repeat them again here. In addition, the activities are described in adult terms, not necessarily as we would present them to children. In developing your units, you may wish to include key questions in the language you would use with students.

Introduction: As described on pages 229–230.
Curriculum Standards:

* **Benchmark Standard:** The Fifth Essential Element of Geography. See page RH-7.
* **Mandated Outcomes:** See pages 219–221.
* **Key Learning Outcomes:** See pages 224–228.

Ongoing Activities: (1) Journals; (2) *DynoPark Tycoon* (MECC) simulation

Activity 1: Initiating Activity

Overview: In a teacher-led lesson, the teacher will create a master family tree for a Super Burger while students will create their own copies.

Description: *Phase One:* Lead the class in identifying the basic elements of a Super Burger.
 Phase Two: Divide the class into small groups. Ask each group to identify as many "things" as possible that went into making the hamburger. Gauge the time spent on this portion of the activity by the students' interest. Five minutes or less may be sufficient.
 Phase Three: Have the various groups report their findings, listing the components on the chalkboard as each group reports. Probe, cajole, and stimulate as necessary. After the groups have gone as far as they seem able, ask if any of the items seem to go together (following the Taba concept-building procedure, pages 196–197). Note that some items may go into more than one category.

Skill Areas: Observing, analyzing, inferring, classifying,

Activity 2: Building a Family Tree

Overview: The teacher and students will develop a model "family tree" for a hamburger.

Objective: The child will explain the process for making a family tree (pedigree) chart.

Description: Working with the list of "things" previously identified, the teacher and students will locate components on a family tree chart (begun in Activity 1) similar to the one illustrated in Figure 8.4. As a group, students will identify all the "things" (not yet identified as resources) they can think of that were involved in producing the hamburger. Items the students identify should be listed on the board and may include such things as farmers, ranchers, vegetables, paper and ink (for the wrapper). Don't push too far here. For example, accept paper without going into paper's components (wood, etc.) unless the children insist on it. This will be picked up again in Activity 3.

Skill Areas: Recording data.

Activity 3: Small Group Research

Overview: The children will be divided into small groups (2–3 students each) to identify and research the resources and processes that go into producing the various components of the Super Burger. Each group should select or be assigned to one of the following components: beef, buns, lettuce and onions, pickles and catsup, mayonnaise, salt and pepper, and the wrapper (paper and ink). Advise the groups that they must present their reports to the entire class, using visuals as appropriate. Also ask each group to prepare a first-person diary for their product in the manner described earlier that will be part of their presentation.

 One small group should be assigned to "It's My Burger." That group's task is to prepare and conduct a survey of the class to determine its preference for the different condiments. The results should be presented using a large graphic.

The nature of the research group activities and the length of time they take will depend on the materials and resources available.

Possible Materials: The Internet, encyclopedias, *Explorapedia* (a children's interactive encyclopedia from Microsoft), assorted cookbooks.

Objectives:

* The student will identify a natural resource as something from our environment that people may use.

* The child will name at least five resources used in producing a hamburger.

* The student will describe the process for growing beef, the vegetables for the condiments, making the condiments, and making paper and ink (the label).

Optional Activities: Depending on the amount of time available, resource people can demonstrate how various products, including pickles, catsup, and mayonnaise, are made. The recipes and procedures for making most of these products are available in *Ball Blue Book* (revised periodically) published by the Ball Corporation, Muncie, Indiana, 47302, and from the Food Network (http://www.foodtv.com/). Students may also make paper, as explained in the Resource Handbook.

Activity 4: Small-Group Presentations

Overview: Each small group should present their findings and their diary to the class.

Activity 5: Side Trip: Migrant Farm Workers

Overview: The teacher will read aloud two of the children's books on migrant workers noted earlier (p. 233). The teacher and students will then complete a summary Venn diagram on which they identify each story's unique elements and those that are common to both.

Objectives:

* The student will describe the circumstances that lead to farmers hiring large numbers of workers for short periods of time.

* The student will explain how all members of migrant worker families (except infants and the infirm) are expected to contribute to the family's well-being.

Activity 6: Minisynthesis

Objectives:

* The student will identify at least five resources originating in the land.

* The students will distinguish between a human resource and a natural resource.

* The students will distinguish between wants and needs.

Description: Using the family tree for the Super Burger and the materials the children developed for Activity 4, develop a discussion-oriented activity. The purpose of the activity is to help children to recognize that (1) the "things" (materials) that went into making the Super Burger ultimately originated in the land, (2) all goods ultimately have their origin in the land, and (3) people are involved in every step along the way. If the occasion has not arisen previously, the term *resources* can be identified as a label for "things," and the term *goods* can be associated with objects or products produced from natural resources.

Key questions include the following: (1) Do you notice anything about those things that our Super Burger was made from? (2) Can you think of anything that does not come from the land?

Culminating Activities

Phase One

Objectives:

* The student will, from memory, (1) identify the primary decision makers (the farmer, the rancher, etc.) involved in the production of the Super Burger, and (2) identify at least one alternative decision that those individuals might have made in terms of the way they used the resources available to them.

* Given a series of pictures of people in different occupations (a machinist, a dairy farmer, a baker, etc.), the student will identify (1) the goods or services being provided and (2) the natural resources being used.

Description: As described on page 234.

Phase Two: The Super Burger Luncheon

Description: As described previously.

instance, the next unit might focus on conservation (the use and abuse of resources), the role of tools in using resources to produce goods and services, or perhaps the role of money as a medium for allocating resources.

Reviewing the Unit for Completeness and Consistency

In planning this unit, several stages were left partially completed. Once the unit has taken on a clearer form and direction, it is time to go back and fill in the holes. A Unit Plan Checklist that can be useful for this task is shown in Figure 8.5.

FIGURE 8.5 Unit Plan Checklist

General Elements

Yes	No	Goals
_____	_____	Does it identify what students should know at the end of this unit?
_____	_____	Does it identify the skills that students should be able to demonstrate at the end of this unit?
_____	_____	Does it identify affective goals for this unit?
_____	_____	Does it identify what should be done for students who cannot demonstrate what is indicated above?
_____	_____	Does it identify cognitive and affective objectives for this unit?

Specific Elements

Yes	No	
_____	_____	Does it identify a vehicle or focus for the unit?
_____	_____	Does it identify a main idea or generalization for the unit?
_____	_____	Does it task-analyze the elements of this unit in terms of prerequisite understandings?
_____	_____	Does it state instructional objectives in performance terms?
_____	_____	Does it identify and sequence learning activities?
_____	_____	Does it identify guiding (key) questions?
_____	_____	a. For planning purposes?
_____	_____	b. For instructional use with students?
_____	_____	Does it identify teaching materials and resources?
_____	_____	Does it identify a way to initiate the unit?
_____	_____	Does it identify the means for student evaluation?
_____	_____	Does it identify a way to bring closure to the unit?
_____	_____	Does it devise a means for evaluating the unit for internal and external consistency (such as this checklist)?
_____	_____	a. Do the various sections of the unit "fit together" — for example, no "hidden objectives" (internal consistency)?
_____	_____	b. Is the unit, as a whole, justifiable? Can it be defended as worthy of being studied (external consistency)?

The final test of any unit plan comes when you teach it with students. In the process, you will discover those activities that work well and those that don't and will make the necessary adaptations for the next time you teach it.

Lesson Planning

Multiple purposes?

Detailed unit plans often eliminate the need for separate daily lesson plans. However, many prospective teachers' lesson plans are vehicles to communicate with cooperating teachers, college supervisors, and sometimes even principals (some of whom collect weekly lesson plans). As a result, your daily lesson plans may be more detailed than they would otherwise need to be for effective teaching. Thus the length and scope of your lesson plans may be a function of the dual purpose they serve: (1) as a plan for the students you teach and (2) to convey your intent to those who observe you.

Figure 8.6 shows a template you can use to write daily lesson plans.

FIGURE 8.6 Template for Daily Lesson Plans

Put the title of the lesson here

I. Introduction/Overview

Write a brief overview of the lesson, including why it is something students should experience or learn.
Also indicate how you intend to introduce (or set the stage) for the lesson.

II. Entry-Level Knowledge/Skills

Briefly describe what learners will need to know prior to this lesson (that they cannot pick up in the course of the lesson).

III. State the Task (Objectives)

Describe clearly what the end result of the learners' activities will be — answer a series of questions, solve a problem, summarize what they have learned, etc.

IV. Resources/Advanced Preparation

List the specific physical resources you need to teach this lesson. Do not include materials common to classrooms, such as chalkboard, overhead projector, etc. Attach copies of worksheets, charts, or other materials you plan to use with students.

V. The Process

Describe the basic steps the learners will experience as they go through the lesson. These may include the following:

1. How you will make connections with the students' previous learning (review)
2. How you will make students aware of the objectives for the lesson
3. How you will introduce and/or model the content/skills
4. How you will provide guided practice (if applicable)

VI. Assessment/Evaluation

Describe how you will assess or evaluate students' performance or understanding.

VII. Conclusion/Closure

Briefly describe how you will bring this lesson to a close.

VIII. Follow-up Activities

Briefly describe other activities or lessons that logically follow from this lesson, or how you would integrate the "big ideas" from this lesson into other subject areas.

SUMMARY

For most teachers, planning is a never-ending process. It continues even as teachers are teaching, usually in the form of day-to-day adjustments. Additional planning often occurs after instruction as teachers decide what should be changed, deleted, and added to the unit when (and if) they teach it again.

This chapter identified the components of planning and illustrated how those components fit together. Goals are statements of intent that show the general direction teaching should take. A sample goal for the affective domain, which pertains to feelings and attitudes, is: "Students will appreciate the contribution of American patriots." A sample goal for the cognitive domain, which pertains to different types of thinking, is: "Students will understand the impact of technology on contemporary life." Objectives, on the other hand, describe specific behaviors that students are expected to demonstrate at the end of an instructional activity. Outcomes such as "The student will, from memory, identify three factors that led to the Civil War" and "Given a list of statements, the student will tell which are facts and which reflect opinions" reflect instructional (behaviorally stated or performance) objectives.

Simply because objectives are phrased in performance terms does not necessarily mean that they are good and worthy of instruction. Rather, teachers must evaluate potential objectives—no matter how they are stated—in terms of (1) their students' ability to achieve them, (2) the goals to which they relate, and (3) their appropriateness.

After you have identified your purpose and your instructional intent, instructional planning becomes a systematic, interactive process—as opposed to a sequence of discrete steps that one must follow. For example, objectives may imply or suggest certain teaching activities, just as activities may suggest or imply certain objectives. In most instances, the unit planning process moves from the "whole," the unit, to one or more of the specific "parts,"—the resources, the teaching activities, or assessment—and then moves back to the "whole."

SUGGESTED READINGS AND RESOURCES

Print Resources

Linda L. Levstick & Keith C. Barton. (1997). *Doing history: Investigating with children in elementary and middle schools.* Mahwah, NJ: Lawrence Erlbaum. This book provides detailed examples of activities that engage children in historically related activities.

Stephanie Steffy & Wendy Hood. (1994). *If this is social studies, why isn't it boring?* York, ME: Stenhouse. This collection of first-person vignettes details how fourteen teachers were able to depart from traditional text-based teaching.

Internet Resources

Introductory Note: Web sites sometimes change their Internet addresses or cease operating entirely. All the addresses supplied here were operating when this book was printed, but if any of them fails to work properly, try entering the name of the target organization in any standard search engine.

AskERIC Lesson Plans

http://askeric.org/Virtual/Lessons

This highly recommended site provides an array of detailed lesson plans that are organized by school subjects, including social studies. It also has links to other Web sites that feature lesson plans.

Connections+

http://www.mcrel.com

This site is maintained by the Mid-continent Regional Education Laboratory and focuses mainly on standards and benchmarks, and associated lesson plans. Lesson plans are listed by subject/topic, and each contains a link that details a related content standard. This site offers excellent resources for connecting lessons to standards and benchmarks.

The Copernicus Education Gateway

http://www.edgate.com.

This highly recommended site is maintained by the Learning Channel with the cooperation of, and with links to, other prominent organizations including *Encyclopaedia Britannica*. With continuous updating and an amazing variety of resources, to say nothing of lesson plans that are linked to standards, this should be among the top ten sites on your Internet list. **Bookmark quality.** Subscription: $11.95/yr.

Education World

http://www.education-world.com

This highly recommended site contains an astounding array of resources for teachers, including lesson plans. If you are an Internet novice, this is an excellent place to begin—it links to everything!

Lesson Plans Library

http://ali.apple.com/edres/ellesson/elem-menu.shtml

This site links to lesson plans prepared by the Apple K–12 education program. You first select your area of interest—elementary, middle school, or high school—and then select the desired subject area.

SCORE History/Social Science Online Resources

http://score.rims.k12.ca.us

This site is maintained by SCORE, the acronym for Schools of California Online Resources for Educators. Although geared primarily to California's curriculum and standards, it offers resources and lesson plans that are useful to teachers anywhere.

Teacher Explorer Center

http://ss.uno.edu/SS/homePages/SSLib.html

This site was created by the University of New Orleans and offers links to resources in the following five categories: content resources, lesson plans, teaching with technology, teacher resources, and research theory.

The New York Times Learning Network

http://www.nytimes.com/learning

If you are seeking lesson plans that are oriented toward current events, this is a recommended site for you. In addition to summaries of current (and past) news events, the site offers standards-based lesson plans, a lesson plan archive, and ideas for interdisciplinary lessons.

Social Studies Lesson Plans

http://askeric.org/cgi-bin/print.cgi/Resources/Subjects/Social_Studies/Lesson_Plans.html

This is an excellent site for social studies lesson plans designed for elementary- and middle-school classrooms.

Assessing Learning

9

KEY QUESTIONS

- **Where does assessment fit into the instructional cycle?**
- **How do norm-referenced and criterion-referenced assessment differ?**
- **What is authentic assessment?**
- **How does one evaluate higher-level cognitive skills?**
- **What is the relationship between objectives and test questions?**

● ● ● ● Introduction: An Alternative Assessment Strategy

For twenty-six years, Janet Jacobsen has been teaching fifth grade in the same classroom in the Yakima Valley in south central Washington State. When she began teaching, the building was a K–8 elementary, but is now a departmentalized 5–8 middle school. Mrs. Jacobsen is the head teacher for the fifth-grade teaching team and the building coordinator for social studies.

When I met Mrs. Jacobsen for the first time, she explained her approach to teaching social studies. "When I began," she said, "I went pretty much by the book. But it always seemed that we were rushing to finish one chapter so we could get to the next one. That got 'old' after a while, for both the kids and me, so I began to cut out things—things we'd skip. I wasn't sure how I'd like it, or how the kids would react, but I've become a believer in studying fewer things in more depth."

"Less is more" in practice

"What did you leave out?" I asked.

"The War of 1812 was the first thing to go, because the kids have trouble understanding who we were fighting and what we were fighting for. I also began to leave out the Mexican War, the Spanish American War . . . and things like the Depression of the 1930s.

"But I think the biggest change," Janet continued, "was when I decided to modify my role as teacher and help my kids become more responsible for their own learning. How do you say it—I shifted from being a 'sage on the stage'—the person with all the information—to a 'guide by the side.'"

Changing roles

Basically, Mrs. Jacobsen shifted to a modified cooperative-group investigation approach that is similar to how Tarry Lindquist organized her students as they created their cooperative biographies of Abraham Lincoln (as described in

Chapter 1). The main difference between the two approaches is that in Ms. Lindquist's class, each group worked on the same topic—their biography of Lincoln—whereas in Mrs. Jacobsen's class, individuals and groups work on different topics.

The teaching strategies I observed on my first visit to Mrs. Jacobsen's classroom appear at the beginning of Chapter 10. If you don't mind skipping ahead to Chapter 10 now, you'll have a better context for understanding why Mrs. Jacobsen had to develop an alternative approach to assessment, which is the focus here. In a classroom where no two students are necessarily doing or learning the same thing, it could be very unfair if Mrs. Jacobsen tried to use paper-and-pencil tests. So she created an approach to assessment that fit her new situation.

Mrs. Jacobsen began to explain her assessment techniques by walking over to a bookshelf and picking up a quarter-inch-thick booklet in an orange binder. "This is Jamie Button's report," she said proudly. "Take a look at it."

What a dedication!

On the title page, in large bold type, it read: "How to Make (Mint) Money by Jamie Button." The next page, half-filled with print, was a combination dedication/copyright page. A portion of it said: "This book is dedicated with pride to my father, Craig Button, who helped me with some of the graphics and illustrations; to my sister Katy, who gave me time on the computer so I could finish this report; to my grandfather, Benton J. (B. J.) Burns (he's my mom's father), who showed me his collection of old coins; and . . ." It was as if Jamie had thanked half the people in the area! I looked quizzically at Janet, who said, "My kids feel this is one of the most important pages in their report, and I'm not about to argue with them."

Grouping patterns

"Sometimes my students work in pairs, and occasionally I have one or two threesomes, but no larger—bigger groups spend too much time figuring out who is going to do what," Janet noted, "and all of them produced creditable reports, not something they copied out of an encyclopedia." She then added, "The children's reports were on topics like: 'Pirates in Puritan Times,' 'A Comparison of Hawthorne's Written Works,' 'How Do You Make Change in Old English Money?' [where a shilling is one-twentieth of a pound sterling, and a shilling contains twelve pence], and a bunch of others. Everybody did visually based presentations, too. The kids were excited and involved, and they learned more from this activity than I ever imagined. And then," Janet added somewhat dispiritedly, "comes evaluation and grading."

In some cases, grading seems to drive everything else

"In a lot of schools, grading seems to overwhelm everything," I indicated.

"I know," Janet said, nodding in agreement. "Assessment and grading were the hardest things I had to deal with." Then she added, "And I have both extremes in this class: kids who won't do anything unless it's for a grade, and kids whom grades don't motivate in the least.

Dealing with district policies

"One of the first things I had to deal with," she continued, "was the school district's policy. It mandated that all teachers must have at least two grades each week in every subject for each grading period. That policy was O.K. when we used those 'skill builder' worksheets, which we graded and recorded as if they were tests, but the district policy is still based on a lot of simplistic assumptions about how learning occurs. Learning is incremental, it doesn't always inch upward, bit by bit; sometimes it grows by leaps and bounds—like when you can see a light bulb go on in a child's expression that tells you, 'Yeah, I understand this!'

The policy also forced me to spend a lot of time on testing and grading that I could have used for teaching."

"So what did you do?"

Doubling up

Janet responded, "Well, sometimes if we did an activity that involved both social studies and language arts, for example, I would record the same grade twice, once in each subject area, but these were coping strategies for what I think was a questionable policy to begin with."

"So what did you do?" I asked.

"I began working to get the district's grading policy changed," Janet responded. "I got my colleagues to begin talking about the policy in their grade-level meetings. Most of them agreed that the policy was often difficult to comply

Policy changes

with and that it seemed geared to helping administrators and teachers cover themselves if questions were raised."

"Were you successful?"

Her response was, "Yes . . . and no. What they did was permit exceptions to the policy for teachers who filed an alternative evaluation and grading plan. That was fine with me, except that I had to figure out exactly how I would assess the kids—and this was new territory for me. But then I decided that if I couldn't defend what I wanted to do, and if I couldn't assess my students fairly, I probably shouldn't be doing it.

"With the kids studying different aspects of events like the 'Pine Tree Shillings' incident, I couldn't very well give them a knowledge-based test—most of the kids were learning different things. And then, it wasn't just knowledge that

Goals

I was after. I wanted the children to begin taking some responsibility for their own learning, to learn how to inquire about things—to become experienced in using the inquiry process. And I wanted them to become skillful in organizing, interpreting, and presenting information. And I wanted to reward the kids who showed progress in developing those skills, not just give good grades to the kids who already had well-developed skills."

"That's an imposing agenda," I said.

"The more I thought about it, the more I began to wonder what I was getting into," Janet continued. "It's a lot easier to give kids the prepared tests that come with the textbooks series, and let it go at that . . . but I was determined."

A revised strategy

"So then . . . ?" I asked.

"I decided to follow my instincts and develop an assessment strategy that reflected my goals." Janet opened a file folder and said, "Remember I'm a novice at this," and gave us a one-page form (shown in Figure 9.1).

"How do you use this?" I asked.

"At the beginning of the year I give the kids a copy, and we talk about what it means. Then at the end of each grading period, I have a five- or six-minute assessment conference with each student. They complete a copy of the form that they bring to our conference, along with everything they've done in

Conferences

social studies for the period—what I loosely refer to as 'their portfolio.' If they've lost stuff—and some of them always do—that's too bad. I also bring a preliminary copy of the form that I've filled in, based on my anecdotal notes on each child, and then we talk. Together, we complete the form and agree on a grade. The district uses computerized, fill-in-the-bubble grading forms that I fill

FIGURE 9.1 Social Studies Assessment/Progress Report

	Unsatisfactory	Satisfactory	Excellent

1. Responsibility for Learning:
1.1 Demonstrates responsibility for learning.
1.2 Progress in taking responsibility for learning.

Comments: _____

_____

2. Subject Matter Knowledge:
2.1 Demonstrates subject matter knowledge.
2.2 Progress in mastering subject matter.

Comments: _____

_____

3. The Inquiry Process:
3.1 Ability to use the inquiry process.
3.2 Progress in using the inquiry process.

Comments: _____

_____

4. Organizing and Interpreting Information:
4.1 Ability to organize and interpret information.
4.2 Progress in organizing and interpreting information.

Comments: _____

_____

5. Sharing/Presentation Skills:
5.1 Ability to present information.
5.2 Progress in presenting information.

Comments: _____

out for the report cards, but also I send the assessment forms home with the students."

"Do you weight each of the elements equally?"

"No," Janet answered. "I almost never give equal weight to the presentation skills, because some kids are naturally shy and some of them are less verbal than others. And sometimes the weightings change based on what we are doing. For example, during the six-week period just before we give the Iowa Test of Basic Skills [a standardized achievement test] we drop the inquiry format and do a teacher-directed overview of the parts of history that we won't get to. It's pretty much awareness-level stuff, but the kids need to be aware of it to do well on the tests. I even give old-fashioned tests, just like I used to. During that period, we use only the 'Subject-Matter Knowledge' criterion, because, well, that's all we focus on."

"Doesn't it take forever to have conferences with every child?"

"Sometimes it seems like it," she responded, "but it only takes three class sessions to do everyone in each of my four classes. But," she continued, "I *really* have

Weightings change depending on activities

Time considerations

to watch my time—five or six minutes per student, no more, otherwise I'd be conferencing all the time."

"What do your other students do while you are conferencing?" I asked.

Optional activities

"Usually I try to schedule them so students are in the research phase of an activity," Janet indicated, "but it almost never works out right. So I give the kids options. While some of us are conferencing they can work on their projects, go to one of the centers I set up around the room, or they can read almost anything their hearts desire. Historical biographies and books like Jean Fritz's *Shh! We're Writing the Constitution* (1987) are really popular. But I will not give my students busywork activities, because that would violate my rule of doing something productive with their time."

"It sounds like you're happy with your assessment system," I observed.

An imperfect system

"It's not perfect," Janet responded, "but it's better than what I used to use. And I keep fiddling with it every year to improve it."

"What impresses me about your system is the way you've blended objective and subjective elements and involved your students in the conferencing process. Have you thought about writing this up for a journal article?"

Janet Jacobsen looked at me a little sheepishly and said, "Maybe when it's perfect."

There is no perfect assessment and grading system, period! Yet, Mrs. Jacobsen's assessment system includes some notable aspects: (1) she uses a variety of different (nontest) data forms, including her anecdotal notes and the students' "portfolios," and (2) her assessment process is ongoing, even though the conference itself occurs near the end of the grading period. Too many people hold the mistaken notions that (1) assessment is something that occurs only at the end of the instructional cycle, and (2) the terms *evaluation, testing,* and *grading* are synonymous. Although evaluation, testing, and grading often go hand in hand, they are separate processes—at least in theory—as explained in this chapter.

Mistaken assumptions

> **KEY IDEA**
>
> Assessment focuses on determining what students know and are able to do—before, after, or during instruction—whereas evaluation focuses on how well students can demonstrate a particular behavior or skill.

From a student's point view, evaluation is something teachers do—often involving paper-and-pencil testing and most commonly at the end of an instructional episode—that ultimately results in a grade. From the teacher's point of view, evaluation usually focuses on judging how well students have progressed toward desired educational objectives. Unfortunately, this process is complicated by the fact that with grading, the student's performance on several criteria tend to be mingled together in ways that cause their performance on any one criterion to get lost in the crowd.

Assessment focuses primarily on discovering what students know and are able to do prior to, during, or after instruction. In other words, in assessment the major emphasis is on whether students can demonstrate certain behaviors/knowledges, and secondarily on how well they can demonstrate them. Because *assessment* has largely replaced *evaluation* in the literature today, I will follow that convention here.

The first part of this chapter considers the roles that assessment can play in the instructional cycle. This is followed by several strategies for gathering assessment information.

● ● ● ● Assessment and the Instructional Cycle

Assessment is a natural and ongoing part of the instructional cycle, which is shown in Figure 9.2. As noted in Chapter 8, you decide where you and your students want to go, instructionally speaking, by identifying learning outcomes. Your focus then shifts to the creation of teaching activities and experiences that will help you and your students move toward the outcomes you identified earlier. Finally, the focus shifts again, this time to determining whether your students have gotten to where you wanted to get to.

Figure 9.2 makes the instructional cycle look as if it is a series of discrete steps that teachers follow in sequence. In actuality, the instructional cycle is a series of overlapping and interacting categories. This means that you really cannot deal with one aspect in isolation from the other aspects. This was evident in Chapter 8 where we began planning for assessment at the same time that we were determining our learning outcomes. Likewise, we tried to assess how much our students already knew about Super Burgers before we even got into the unit. The main point is that assessment is not an add-on or an afterthought that comes at the end of an instructional episode; it should be done before, during, and after instruction.

KEY IDEA

Assessment is the reciprocal of planning.

● ● ● ● Forms of Assessment

Slightly different forms of assessment apply to the different phases of the instructional cycle. Consider, for example, a situation where you want students to be able to identify at least four of the five Great Lakes, or to distinguish statements of facts from statements of opinion with at least 80 percent accuracy. In

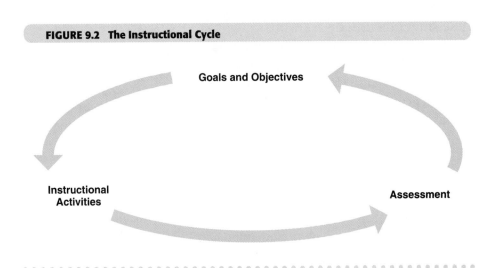

FIGURE 9.2 The Instructional Cycle

Goals and Objectives

Instructional Activities

Assessment

SUGGESTED ACTIVITY

Assume that you were considering teaching a unit on Christmas in other lands for kindergarten to second-grade children. What are the merits and limitations of using the prompt "Has anyone ever heard of Santa Claus?" for diagnostic assessment?

both cases, your assessment criteria are already established (four of five, or 80%). What you don't know is whether your students can already demonstrate these behaviors—prior to any instruction. If they can, you could be wasting your time and theirs by retracing familiar territory. On the other hand, if they cannot demonstrate these behaviors, additional instruction may be warranted. Or you could simply assume that first or second graders have no knowledge of this material and proceed as you had planned to earlier.

One way to deal with this situation is to use *diagnostic assessment;* that is, assessment conducted before instruction. In many instances, diagnostic assessment need not be an involved or drawn-out affair. Students need some kind of prompt to respond to, such as "Have you ever heard of the Great Lakes?" It probably isn't necessary that students write out their answers, thus creating another set of papers for you to read. Simply observing how the children react (or fail to react) to your question may provide the information you are after. The prompt for distinguishing between facts and opinions would be different, of course, but the basic technique could remain the same.

Assessment that occurs during instruction is referred to as *formative assessment;* it takes place as the instruction is "forming up." For example, assume that you have just taught a lengthy lesson about using latitude and longitude to identify locations, and you have now provided students a worksheet that asks them to identify the latitude and longitude of several major cities—Moscow, London, and so on. You are concerned about moving ahead too quickly and decide that a formative assessment might be appropriate. You have several options: (1) collect and grade the students' worksheets, (2) assume that some students are likely to have had problems and decide to review the lesson again tomorrow, or (3) carefully observe students as they work on their worksheets.

Be careful that you don't change the ostensible purposes of a practice worksheet by grading it and thus using it as a lightly concealed test. Some students, especially those who don't understand the underlying concept but are also hung up about grades, could be resentful—"You said this was for practice!" Second, you should be able to determine how things are going by simply observing the general tenor of the room and watching students as they complete their worksheets. Third, if you notice that some students are floundering, consider stopping the worksheet activity and announcing that they can work on the practice worksheets in small groups. As an alternative, you could announce that you will review the lesson with them tomorrow. However, if things seem to be going along merrily, you might opt to carry on as you had planned originally.

What distinguishes formative assessment from the assessment that often occurs spontaneously during teaching is its planned nature. In using formative assessment, teachers consciously plan to (1) pause periodically to assess how things are going and then (2) use the criteria provided by their objectives to evaluate the situation. In this way, formative assessment provides useful information to supplement your intuitive sense of how things are going.

Formative assessment is one of several forms of assessment, each of which serves a different purpose. The appropriate type of assessment is determined by the kind of information, and the kinds of questions, that you want answers to. The types and phases of assessment are reflected in Table 9.1.

Formative assessment: a form of feedback

TABLE 9.1   Types and Phases of Assessment as Reflected by Teachers/Questions

Information Desired (Teachers' Questions)	Type of Programs	Phase of Instruction When Used	Typical Form of Assessment	Comments
"Can the student perform a designated task? Demonstrate a desired behavior?"	Criterion-referenced	Anytime	Teacher-made tests Standardized tests Observations Portfolios	Used to determine a student's skill proficiency. Sole focus is on individual performance.
"How does this student's performance compare with the class's performance as a whole?" or: "How does the performance of my students compare with that of similar students across the state or country?"	Norm-referenced	Anytime	Standardized tests	Used to compare an individual's performance with that of a group, or one group's performance with that of another group.
"How well are students moving toward our goals and objectives?" (How are we doing?)	Formative	During	Observations Journals Student comments	Used to determine progress during instruction.
"How am I doing as a teacher? As a student?"	Self-assessment	Anytime	Varies	Criteria and results are usually private.
"All things considered, how does the student's overall performance rate?"	Summative	After	Varied measures	May be norm-referenced, criterion-referenced, specific or global, or some combination of all elements.
"Can the student exhibit mastery of important understandings as they apply to real-life problems or challenges?"	Authentic (Applied)	After	Demonstrated performances	Used to demonstrate performance in tasks related to real-life problems or expectations.

Criterion-Referenced Assessment

Criterion-referenced assessment is "referenced," or keyed, to specified knowledge or skills, each of which serves as a criterion that students are expected to demonstrate. If you have decided that each of your students should be able to identify the location of the United States on a world map, for example, that becomes a referencing criterion. But what happens if some of your students are unable to meet that objective? If you use *mastery learning* in your classroom, students who do not meet the criterion must work through additional instructional activities until they can demonstrate mastery. Once your students meet the objective, they (and you) can move on to other objectives and teaching activities. In instances where mastery learning is not used, the student will probably receive a lower grade and then move on to other things.

Evaluation and mastery learning

Criterion-referenced assessment can be used at any point in the instructional cycle. It can be used (1) as a pretest prior to instruction, (2) to determine student progress during instruction, and (3) to find out whether students have mastered the expected behaviors after instruction.

Alternative criteria

If mastery learning were adhered to in its purest form, students would be expected to answer every question on a test correctly. By doing so, they would be demonstrating mastery of the desired behaviors. However, when several desired competencies are clustered together on a test, the performance standard or criterion is often established as a percentage of questions that must be answered correctly. Thus, to demonstrate mastery, students might be expected to complete at least 80 percent (or another percentage) of the test items correctly.

KEY IDEA

Every test question has an underlying objective, either implicit or explicit.

Every question on every test should reflect a corresponding learning outcome. For example, if you expect students to identify the year in which the Magna Carta was signed (1215), you need to have a test question or use some other means to assess that they know that information. Common sense suggests that if a teacher doesn't care whether students know when the Magna Carta was signed, a test question to that effect should not be on the test. However, students sometimes don't discover what they are supposed to know until they actually take the test. This situation may occur because some teachers wait until the night before the test to pore over the textbook or some other source, looking for test questions. Only then, *after* they've made the test, do the teachers' real expectations (objectives) become known—to themselves and, later, to students. Testing is not necessarily the preferred way to evaluate one's objectives, but by identifying clear objectives in the planning phase of instruction, teachers can reduce much of the mystique that is often associated with testing and assessment.

Testing defined

Vagueness about a teacher's expectations may explain why some students ask that proverbial question, "Will this be on the test?" At other times, the question is simply part of the grading game. In either case, the unfortunate implication is that if something isn't going to be on the test, it's not worth learning. In theory, *testing* is simply a technique for gathering assessment information. Yet no one needs to tell you that, in practice, testing is often a much more potent force.

Let's return for a moment to Janet Jacobsen's assessment strategy. Does she use criterion-referenced assessment? Because each of her students was investigating different aspects of the "Pine Tree Shillings" incident (see Chapter 10), and thus was learning different things, Janet did not establish knowledge objectives that applied to everyone. Then too, subject-matter knowledge was only one of five goals that Janet and her students were working toward. Although each of her goals serves as a kind of criterion, each was stated too globally to meet the strict definition of criterion-referenced assessment.

Norm-Referenced Assessment

Norm referenced: comparing students against a norm

Norm-referenced assessment focuses on comparing one student's performance in relation to that of other students. The *norm* in norm-referenced assessment is usually the average of students' performance—the class average—or, in the case of standardized tests, the performance of students across the school district, the state, or the country. Regardless of how the norm is determined, the purpose is to rate a student's performance relative to the norm.

Norm-referenced assessment permits you to say, for instance, that "Johnny did better than 31 percent of the third graders who took this test on map skills." In this instance, Johnny's performance probably isn't very good—indeed, it may be awful—but unless you shifted to criterion-referenced evaluation and analyzed Johnny's performance on each test item, it's doubtful whether you could determine what problems caused Johnny to perform as he did.

Caution

The results of norm-referenced assessment are always stated comparatively—that is, in relation to whatever norm is being used. Thus, to learn that Maria got a 95 on her test might seem impressive at first, especially if you assume it was a 100-item test. However, if it was a 200-item test and the average score was 161, your impression of Maria's performance will probably change considerably. Your impression might change even more when you find that Maria is an average eight-year-old whose native language is Spanish, who has been in this country less than a year, and whose score of 95 was on a test of English vocabulary (or American history). Unless the group that Maria is being compared with (the norm) shares Maria's characteristics (age, linguistic background, etc.), the results of normative assessment could be misleading.

DIVERSITY 👥

Different ends and different means

Norm-referenced assessment and criterion-referenced assessment serve different purposes, so it is pointless to say that one is better than the other. In many respects, the comparative nature of norm-referenced assessment has become one of the conventions of American schooling. But from a purely instructional point of view, criterion-referenced assessment can provide the information that teachers must have to target instruction toward the specific needs of individual students.

Summative Assessment and Grading

For all practical purposes, *summative assessment* and *grading* are synonymous. Summative assessment, which always occurs at the end of an instructional

Grading defined

episode, "summarizes" the changes that have occurred as a result of instruction, usually in the form of a grade. Grading, in its technical sense, refers to the process of judging whether someone (or something) belongs in a particular category. The key elements of grading are (1) determining the characteristics of the categories to be used for reporting purposes and then (2) deciding whether the person or object reflects those characteristics. Yet the basic question in both summative assessment and grading is: All things considered, how would you judge the quality of a student's performance (or product)?

You already know that in most schools grading is usually reflected by letters (A, B, C, D, F), numbers, descriptive expressions ("Satisfactory," "Excellent," etc.), or some combination of these. The labels we've got! What we lack are consistent descriptions of the categories to which they apply. As a result, almost everyone knows that one teacher's A can be another teacher's B, C, or even worse.

Grading on the curve

Some teachers use norm-referenced evaluation for grading purposes; that is, the student's grade is based on the individual's performance relative to the class's performance as a whole. That procedure is commonly called "grading on the curve" and is well known to most college students. Other teachers identify grading categories by using a criterion-referenced format. In those instances, the standards—such as "scores of 90 or more are an A"—are commonly established in advance. Things usually work out adequately *if* the preestablished standards are appropriate and *if* there are a limited number of elements that grades are based on. But when teachers say things like "In determining your grade, I'm going to 'count' your test scores, homework, class participation, and group work," expectations can become fuzzy. Other teachers use mathematical formulas (e.g.,

Elaborate formulas do not make grading objective

"Class participation counts one-fifth") in an apparent effort to make grading more objective. However, the mathematical manipulation of scores does not

---

● ● ● ● **COMMENTARY** **Self-Assessment and Grading**

I have not dealt with self-assessment in this chapter because it is among the most private forms of evaluation; the criteria are usually private, as are the results—unless, of course, you choose to make them public.

Self-assessment demands a considerable degree of self-awareness and self-direction. To help my students develop these qualities, I decided on one occasion to permit them to give themselves their citizenship grades. To be certain that everyone used similar grading criteria, I spent much time talking about what constituted "good citizenship." However, when the children turned in their grades, almost without exception, their grades were one to two grades lower than I would have given. Upon more investigation, I discovered that what I had considered trivial incidents, such as the failure to complete a homework paper on time, were blown out of proportion, and students had downgraded themselves accordingly. I ended up spending

even more time helping the children to examine their conduct in a broader perspective and trying to convince them that they were being overly harsh on themselves.

On another occasion I permitted college students to use self-assessment as one element for determining their course grade. Once again, we attempted to identify mutually agreeable criteria. This time the results were very different; all thirty-four students gave themselves an A.

My elementary students had taken self-assessment more seriously than I had anticipated, but by the college level the connection between grading and self-assessment had apparently become tenuous at best. Interestingly, some students at both levels objected vehemently to basing their grades on self-assessment. They claimed that grading was the teacher's responsibility, whereas self-assessment was a private matter—one that should remain private.

KEY IDEA
Subjectivity is inherent in all assessment; the goal is to limit and control its influence.

necessarily make grading more objective, and teachers who use such devices may be doing little more than objectively manipulating subjectively selected data.

Judgment and subjectivity are an integral part of summative assessment and grading. Subjectivity can be controlled, of course, which explains much of the emphasis on performance outcomes and on establishing clear expectations for students (as well as for teachers, who are also subject to periodic evaluations). To make assessment and grading even more reliable, and thus avoid the wide discrepancies in grading from one teacher to the next, more and more teachers are developing assessment rubrics. These are devices that more clearly and consistently identify the characteristics of performances that fit into existing grading categories. The development of rubrics is part of the movement toward authentic assessment, the focus of the next section.

● ● ● ● ● Authentic Assessment

A retired British educator of my acquaintance is fond of claiming that American schools are "test-driven." "Everything in your schools," he claims, "is geared to testing—weekly tests, six-week tests, final examinations; and then there is standardized testing several times a year. You Americans spend so much time on testing, it's a wonder the students ever have time to learn anything."

There's no question that testing in American schools is a time-consuming business. However, there is also growing recognition that many tests fail to measure learning in important and authentic ways. The problem, as Wiggins (1989) suggests, is that many tests are standardized, but they are not *standard setting*—that is, much of the learning that tests supposedly measure is neither realistic nor is it necessarily worth striving for. Instead, much testing is a perfunctory, bureaucratic checkup designed to put marks in a gradebook instead of posing authentic, challenging tasks that are related to real-life problems and expectations (Parker, 1991).

If much of the testing in schools today is inauthentic, even trivial, it's reasonable to ask what authentic assessment, or what is sometimes called "performance assessment" would look like. Most authorities suggest that students engage in periodic performances (hence the term *performance assessment*) that reflect important understandings and abilities (Spady, 1994). Parker (1991, p. 88) recommends the following as attributes of authentic assessments:

Characteristics of authentic assessment tasks

1. Tasks that go to the heart of essential learnings; that is, they ask for exhibitions of understandings and abilities that matter.

2. Tasks that resemble interdisciplinary real-life challenges, not schoolish busywork that is artificially neat, fragmented, and easy to grade.

3. Tasks that are standard setting and that point students toward higher, richer levels of knowing.

4. Tasks that are worth striving toward and practicing for.

5. Tasks that are few in number and known to students well in advance.

6. Tasks that strike teachers as worthwhile.

7. Tasks that generally involve higher-order challenges and that ask students to go beyond the routine use of previously learned information.

8. Tasks that are attempted by all students.

The movement toward more authentic assessment is increasingly working its way into schools. For example, Larry Lewin, a teacher in Eugene, Oregon, described how he uses performance tasks to help students in his U.S. History/English class understand the events of 1492 (O'Neil, 1996). Larry's students spend several weeks preparing for and writing a short story from the point of view of either a Spanish sailor or a Taino Indian. The story, although fictional, must reveal the student's understanding of historical events.

KEY IDEA

Authentic assessment is intended to more closely reflect the tasks that students might encounter in real life.

The target audience for the stories that Larry's students write is fifth graders, who are also studying 1492. The students'

Preparation

stories are judged on how realistically they present their fictional characters, the setting, and the other events that occur. In preparation for their assignment, students in Larry's class read several selections of historical fiction to help them understand the genre. Before beginning their final story, they must also write a short expository piece on "A Sailor's Life." The point is that students are not given a performance task and then turned loose to "sink or swim"; several miniperformances serve as building blocks for their final story.

The Use of Rubrics.   When Larry Lewin assesses his students' final stories, he uses a rubric similar to the one shown in Figure 9.3. A *rubric* is a device that per-

Rubrics are an assessment tool

mits teachers to rate the characteristics of students' performances at various proficiency levels (see also O'Neil, 1994). The sample rubric shown in Figure 9.3 was designed to assess students' writing ability.

A rubric itself does not eliminate teacher bias. For example, some teachers have difficulty giving a "4" rating to students' stories that contain only one or two mechanical problems, even though the criterion states "Grammatical or mechanical errors are hardly noticeable." Obviously what is "hardly noticeable" to one teacher can be a major problem to another.

The development of assessment rubrics reflects a movement to describe students' performance with more precision than is possible with traditional letter grading. In addition, giving students the rubric in advance and then using it as the

Rubrics can serve as diagnostic tools

basis for a student-teacher conference can indicate where students are encountering problems and can serve as the basis for additional instruction. In other words, rubrics can sometimes serve as diagnostic tools, not simply grading devices.

Designing assessment rubrics can be a challenging task. Danielson (cited in ASCD, 1996) suggests the following standards:

Rubric design recommendations

1. Use a four-point scale (as shown in our sample) as opposed to a five- or six-point scale. A five-point scale corresponds more closely to the A-B-C-D-F grading system, but the larger number of points can make it more difficult for people to distinguish between the different levels.

2. Use equal distances between levels, as opposed to giant leaps.

FIGURE 9.3 Rubric for Assessing Students' Writing

Rating 4 = Excellent Response

Organization: Well-organized paper with a clear beginning and ending. Transitions are smooth and clear. Content is logically structured.

Clarity: All information is clearly explained.

Content: Information is thorough enough to provide a clear explanation.

Mechanics: Grammatical or mechanical errors are slight and hardly noticeable.

Rating 3 = Adequate Response

Organization: Paper is organized with a beginning and ending. The structure is logical, and there are no major problems in reading.

Clarity: Most of the information is clearly explained.

Content: There is sufficient information to explain the subject.

Mechanics: The grammatical and mechanical errors that may exist do not detract from the explanation.

Rating 2 = Less Than Adequate Response

Organization: Paper is not organized. It may lack a clear beginning and ending. The reader has difficulty moving from one idea to another.

Clarity: Parts of the paper are difficult to understand.

Content: Information is insufficient to provide a clear explanation; some unnecessary information is included.

Mechanics: Grammatical and mechanical errors are frequent enough to create problems for the reader.

Rating 1 = Inadequate Response

Organization: Paper has very little sense of organization. It has no clear beginning and ending. The reader has major difficulties following the explanation.

Clarity: Most of the information is difficult to understand.

Content: Information does not explain the topic. Much irrelevant information is included.

Mechanics: Numerous grammatical and mechanical errors make the information difficult to understand.

3. Use examples of student work at each level. These provide concrete examples of performances at each level.

Proposals for more authentic assessment—and less testing—are consistent with the renewed emphases on active participation in social studies and on being certain that students can perform the tasks required of informed citizens. It is

Technology affords opportunities for multimedia presentations by teachers and students. (© Michael Zide)

In place of, not on top of   important that authentic assessment replace much of the norm-referenced testing that goes on in schools today, and not become simply another layer that is added on to, and possibly dwarfed by, existing testing programs.

Gathering Assessment Information

The keys to gathering useful assessment information are, first, identifying the kind of information you want and, second, using an appropriate means to gather that information. The kind of information needed to evaluate social studies usually relates to (1) what children know and are able to do (cognitive domain) and (2) what children believe and how they respond to what they believe and feel (affective domain). Assessment in the cognitive and affective domains is examined in the following sections.

Assessing Cognitive Knowledge and Skills

The most common technique for assessing cognitive knowledge and skills involves a teacher's oral questions. A second common technique involves paper-and-pencil testing. In this section I examine questions posed in test form.

Evaluation instruments   *Instrument* is the technical name for an assessment technique or scale. There are three major categories of instruments: (1) nationally standardized tests and scales; (2) achievement tests developed by local, regional, or state agencies; and (3) tests constructed by teachers themselves.

Standardized Tests.   Standardized achievement tests are often used as part of statewide or schoolwide testing programs. For examples of standardized test items, see the graph for population growth of two cities in this chapter (p. 265), and the Pleasure Island Activity (Figure 12.6), which assesses map skills. The key element about standardized test items is that they almost always provide information for children to work with, a principle that should also be reflected in teacher-made tests for higher-level thinking skills. Consider how you would respond if you were asked to draw a graph of the corn production in Iowa between 1987 and 1997. Drawing a graph is not too difficult, but asking you to memorize Iowa's corn production for a ten-year period would probably elicit justifiable howls of protest. The example may seem extreme, but the point is that, when testing a student's ability to process information, the necessary data should be provided.

Provide data for students to work with

KEY IDEA

Skills-based assessment almost always provides students with the necessary data to work with.

"Standardizing Authentic Assessment."   Efforts to combine elements of authentic assessment and traditional standardized testing have met with mixed results. Instead of mainly multiple-choice questions—the format for traditional standardized tests—the "more authentic" tests typically present fewer questions and more varied tasks. This phenomenon is evident on the sample performance assessment of fifth-grade students' knowledge about the European origins of exploration, a familiar topic in American history courses, as shown in Figure 9.4.

Fewer questions, more varied tasks

ANALYSIS

Part I of the sample assessment asks students to provide open-ended definitions for vocabulary related to exploration. On a typical standardized test, students would be asked to select a multiple-choice item that best describes a "smallpox epidemic" or any of the other items. The students' answer sheets would typically be run through a test-scoring scanner. However, the open-ended-question format, as in this example, means that an evaluator must read each response to determine if it is acceptable. A similar situation exists for Parts II and III. There are multiple possible relationships between the elements for both of these questions, and the only way these can be evaluated accurately is by having someone analyze the child's thinking. The concern here is not that the sample questions are "bad"—for most of them are an improvement over traditional assessment instruments—but rather in the time it takes to evaluate the answers. If classroom teachers pose assessment tasks like these to their students, they should anticipate evaluating their students' responses, regardless of how long it takes. But assessing students' responses to standardized tests is a different animal. The cost of preparing, administering, and evaluating the more authentic standardized assessment tests can be significantly higher than traditional tests. Such increased costs are certain to cause schools to reflect on whether they can afford to use large-scale authentic testing.

Machine scoring is problematic

FIGURE 9.4 Selected Examples of Authentic Standardized Test Questions

All of the following questions pertain to European exploration of the New World.

I. Short Answer

Directions: Write a short answer that explains what each of the following words mean and why the word was important in history. Try to write something for each word.

Vocabulary items

1. Colony

_____

_____

2. Christopher Columbus

_____

_____

Other words that follow this format (with spaces provided to respond) include: 3, New World, 4. Slavery, 5. Smallpox epidemic, 6. Trans-Atlantic route to Asia, 7. Indentured servant.

Demonstrating understanding

II. Comprehension

Directions: Your teacher has asked that you teach what you know about European exploration to some new students in your class. Think about everything you know about European exploration, including things you've learned from your friends and family, TV, and other sources. Then on the lines below, write what you will tell the new students. You can make drawings to help explain your ideas if you wish. *[Several pages of lined paper follow.]*

III. Problem Solving (Creative Thinking)

Directions: Imagine that it is the year 2020, and the earth is overcrowded. There is a shortage of food and energy resources (such as oil). The United States wants to send astronauts to distant planets to explore for new resources. Scientists think one of the distant planets may have valuable resources, and that some unknown kind of "beings" have homes there.

As an expert on exploration, the President asks you to advise her planning team. She understands that there are some similarities between what the astronauts will try to do and what happened when European explorers like Columbus explored the New World. Your knowledge of what happened in the past will be useful in planning what to do in the future.

Answer the following questions to prepare for advising the President.

Identifying similarities

1. What are some of the *similarities* (things that are the same) between this situation and what you know about what happened when European explorers like Columbus came to the New World? Describe at least two

(continued)

FIGURE 9.4 Selected Examples of Authentic Standardized Test Questions *(continued)*

similarities, but write more if you can think of them. Use specific facts or events from history to support your ideas.

_____

_____

[Additional lines are provided for this and subsequent questions.]

Identifying differences

2. **What are some of the *differences* between this situation and European exploration of the New World? Describe at least two differences, but write more if you can think of them.**

_____

_____

Identifying possible goals

3. **What are the *main goals or positive things* the explorers should be trying to accomplish on this mission? Describe at least two goals for Earth and two that could benefit the other planet, but write more if you can think of them.**

_____

_____

Identifying possible problems

4. **What are some possible *problems* that the explorers should try to avoid or minimize? Describe at least two problems for Earth and two for the other planet, but write more if you can think of them. If possible, give specific facts or events from history that support why you think these problems are likely.**

_____

_____

Identifying other elements

5. **What are some other *ideas or other things to consider* in making a good plan?**

_____

_____

Identifying a course of action

6. **Keeping in mind what you know about Columbus and other explorers in history, what do you think the president and astronauts *should plan or do* to make this new exploration as successful as possible?**

_____

_____

Writing good questions is more difficult than it may appear

Teacher-Made Tests.   Developing good test questions may seem easy enough, but appearances can be deceptive. For example, it is not at all difficult to write a question such as "Abraham Lincoln was born in ___," but this apparently straightforward question places an unfair burden on students, who must figure out which of a multitude of possible answers (place? month? year?) the teacher has in mind. In such cases they may not be able to demonstrate what they know about Lincoln's birth.

VALIDITY

Clarifying your intent

Validity refers to the extent to which test questions measure what they are intended to measure. If there is any doubt, the validity of the Lincoln question is very low.

The validity of test items can often be improved by adding information that clarifies the intent of the question. To do this, teachers must first eliminate any fuzziness from their original objectives about what they expect of students. Thus an objective such as "From memory, the student will identify something about Abraham Lincoln" is inadequate, because the word *something* is too vague. Depending on what the teacher really expects students to know, the objective could be "From memory, the student will identify the place (state) in which Lincoln was born." In this instance, a short-answer test item could then be stated as follows: "Abraham Lincoln was born in the state of _____."

Changing the form of the question

The clarity of test questions can sometimes be improved by changing the form of the question itself. For example, instead of using a short-answer format, the sample Lincoln item could be presented as a multiple-choice or true-false question. In multiple-choice form, the question could be stated as follows:

_____ Abraham Lincoln was born in
   a. Illinois
 *b. Kentucky
   c. Indiana
   d. Washington, D.C.

As a true-false item, the question could be phrased as

_____ Abraham Lincoln was born in Indiana. (F)

Considerations

Both examples clearly reflect the underlying objective, which pertains to identifying the state in which Lincoln was born. At the same time, changing to a multiple-choice or true-false format can also compromise validity somewhat because it introduces a larger "chance" (or guessing) factor than was true for the short-answer (completion) format. For true-false questions, students have a fifty-fifty chance of guessing the correct answer. This doesn't mean that you should forgo using true-false or multiple-choice test questions but that you cannot be as confident that they validly measure what you are trying to measure.

APPROPRIATENESS

Regardless of the form in which the Lincoln test item is asked, a crucial question remains: Should students be expected to recall such information from memory? Is it a worthwhile question that everyone should be expected to answer, or does it deal with trivia?

Is it worth knowing?

A test question such as "List the fifty states in order of their admission to the Union" can be perfectly valid, but it (and the underlying objective it reflects) must be judged in terms of its appropriateness—by whether it tests something that is worth knowing. Unless test items (and the objectives they reflect) are reasonable, appropriate, and worth knowing, validity doesn't even enter the picture. To avoid such problems and to be certain that your assessment is consistent with your objectives, consider identifying potential test questions during planning, even if you don't plan to use testing as an assessment technique. The test questions offer a way for you to cross-check the clarity of your objectives, and your students may be impressed that you know what you want them to know.

Sample Test Items

The sample test items that follow illustrate some of the common problems teachers encounter in writing test questions. After each "poor" question are ways in which it might be improved.

A Fifth Grade Nontest—European Exploration of the Americas

Completion/Short Answer

Fill in the blanks with the correct answer.

Place blank at the end of the sentence . . .

1. *Poor:* The _____ _____ were among the first people to trade with the _____ inhabitants of the Caribbean islands. (Spanish/explorers/native [or orginal])

   Better: The first people to trade with the native inhabitants on the Caribbean islands were the _____ _____. Or: The first people to trade with the native inhabitants of the Caribbean islands were explorers from what country? _____

   Analysis: Ordinarily only one or two key words should be omitted, and ordinarily the omitted words should be near the end of the sentence, so that students need not continually reread the sentence to figure out the subject. In addition, the blank lines where students write their responses should be of approximately equal length so as not to provide clues to the desired answer.

Or use a question

   Short-answer test items are often clearer if they are phrased as direct questions instead of as sentence-completion items. This is particularly true if the questions contain multiple elements. Thus an alternative short-answer format for this test item is:

   What was the nationality of the first explorers to trade with the original inhabitants of the Caribbean islands? _____

2. *Poor:* The Spanish explorers landed on _____ _____ on _____ _____, _____. (Santa Domingo) (October 11, 1492)

   Better: None.

Omitting words from textbooks encourages memorization

   Analysis: This test item has at least five problems. The first of these concerns whether children will understand that the desired responses include the name of the island and the date, which is not otherwise indicated. The second problem concerns the appropriateness of the underlying objective; that is, of expecting children to remember the name of the island and the month, day, and year of Columbus's landing. Third, the question resembles a sentence you might find in a social studies textbook, and from which a few words were deleted. Omitting key words from sentences in a textbook and then using them as test questions encourages memorization, not understanding. The fourth problem involves the number of blanks; there are so many that students are likely to spend a lot of time trying to figure out what the question is really asking. Finally, the form of the question answers the previous question.

Does one question answer another?

One school of thought believes that if children can answer a test question correctly, they should get credit for it. I agree, except in instances where one question provides the answer to other questions. Whenever this occurs, the validity of the item is highly questionable. An equally important concern relates to the underlying objective. How precisely must students remember the date of Columbus's landfall? In other words, does asking students to remember the month, date, and year of Columbus's landfall amount to trivia? If you believe the objective is valid, consider asking two short-answer questions: On what island did Columbus land? And on what date did Columbus land?

True-False (Alternative Response)

Use + for true and 0 for false unless directed otherwise. (Capital T's and capital F's can look very much alike—sometimes intentionally so.)

3. *Poor:* _____ The Catholic religion was best suited to the lands that Columbus explored.

   Better: None.

Avoid opinions

Analysis: The question asks the student to make a value judgment in the absence of clearly defined criteria. Avoid absolute terms wherever possible.

4. *Poor:* _____ The original inhabitants never helped Columbus or his crew.

   Better: None.

Use absolute terms cautiously

Analysis: Absolute terms such as *none, never,* and *always,* which tend to be associated with false statements, should be avoided in true-false questions *unless you are dealing with situations where they are appropriate*—for example, "Assessment always requires the identification of criteria."

5. *Poor:* _____ When Columbus first journeyed to the New World in 1491, his ships were the *Nina, Pinta,* and the *Santa Maria.*

   Better: _____ Columbus first journeyed to the New World in 1491.

Be sure that the intent of the question is clear

Analysis: The "poor" question is misleading because the false element, the date, is subordinate to the main thrust of the question. True-false questions should avoid statements where false items are buried in an otherwise true statement.

An alternative (and probably better) technique for handling true-false questions that involve multiple elements is illustrated below:

Columbus's ships included

1. (+) the *Nina*
2. (0) the *Titanic*
3. (+) the *Santa Maria*
4. (+) the *Pinta*
5. (0) *Old Ironsides*

Multiple-Choice Questions

Select the best answer and write the letter in the space provided.

6. *Poor:* _____ A red-orange root plant grown by the native inhabitants was (a) corn, (b) yam, (c) bananas, (d) mangoes.

   Better: As multiple choice, none; if used at all, the question could be asked in a completion or true-false format.

   Analysis: All distractors for multiple-choice items must be plausible. In this instance, only one root plant is listed. In addition, this item could discriminate against children who may have never seen a mango or mango tree, or who do not know that corn is indigenous to continental North America.

The distractors should be plausible

 SUGGESTED ACTIVITY

Obtain a copy of one of the standardized tests that deals with elementary social studies (your psychology department should have copies if your education department doesn't). First, take the test so that your attention is not distracted by the content of the questions. Then analyze the items in terms of the skills they are really testing.

Distractors should be similar in style and length

7. *Poor:* Explorers to the New World _____ .
   a. were seeking places to avoid religious persecution.
   b. were seeking a new route to the Far East.
   c. were hoping to claim new lands for their sponsors, including King Ferdinand and Queen Isabella of Spain, King George of England, and King Louis of France.
   d. were hoping to become involved in fur trading.

   Better: Explorers to the New World _____ .
   a. were seeking places to avoid religious persecution.
   b. were seeking a new route to the Far East.
   c. were hoping to claim new lands for their sponsors.
   d. All of the above

   Analysis: Where possible, most of the statement should be presented in the introduction, or stem, of the question. In addition, all answers should be plausible, and in the same style and of approximately the same length as the correct answer, and, most of all, include the correct answer. The poor question does not meet these criteria, especially response c, which adds three elements that could further confound this question. Note also that this question would be inappropriate unless children have studied the exploration of North America in some depth.

8. *Poor:* _____ Which of the following explorers sailed for Spain?
   a. Jacques La Salle b. Henry Hudson c. Montreal

   Better: _____ Which of the following explorers did not sail for Spain?
   a. Ponce De Leon. b. Christopher Columbus c. Henry Hudson d. De Soto

   Analysis: Multiple-choice questions should have a minimum of three and preferably four or five alternative answers, which are called foils. The fewer the foils, the higher is the probability that students may guess the right answer. More important, the correct alternative response must be provided (it is not provided in the "poor" form of this question). Further, alternative answers should be of the same general type—the names of people, the names of places, statements, and so on. Mixing different types of alternative responses or providing obviously false foils should be avoided. Also to be avoided are multiple-choice questions in which the correct answer is revealed by clues in the item itself, such as "Many colonial families used a (a) axe, (b) apple peeler, (c) candle mold, (d) ox." Only item c is grammatically correct. Such questions should be reserved for grammar tests.

Don't use the same answer
too often

You may have noted that the correct answer for the sample multiple-choice questions was usually item c. Because test-wise students often look for such a pattern, the position of correct responses should be distributed randomly throughout the test.

Matching
Write the letter from Column II in the space provided in front of the correct term in Column I.

9. *Poor:*

Column I	Column II
_____ 1. Patroon	a. the Native American word for corn
_____ 2. Maize	b. a Dutch system for landholding along the Hudson River
_____ 3. Mayflower	c. one of the middle colonies
_____ 4. Delaware	d. a ship

Better: Instructions: In the space provided, write the letter for the occupation (described in Column II) in the space provided in front of the term associated with that occupation (Column I).

Column I	Column II
1. _____ blacksmith	a. barrelmaker
2. _____ chandler	b. hatmaker
3. _____ cooper	c. wheelmaker
4. _____ deacon	d. iron worker
5. _____ teamster	e. ship's supplier
6. _____ wheelwright	f. wagon driver
	g. church official

Matching questions should not
"match" perfectly

Analysis: The items in the "poor" example are so few and so dissimilar that almost anyone could complete the exercise, even if they know nothing about "patroons." In addition, guessing is facilitated because Columns I and II have the same number of items. Guessing on matching questions is minimized if one column contains more items than are required or contains responses that are used more than once.

Whenever your tests begin to look like the "poor" examples, you've got problems. Not only will the form of your test items be questionable, but you may also be guilty of emphasizing the kind of trivia that has given social studies a bad reputation—one that in this case is justly deserved.

. . . .
Assessing Critical Thinking Skills
. . . .

Assessing a student's information-processing skills is not inherently more difficult than knowledge-level evaluation, but it is different. For example, assessing critical thinking typically requires fewer evaluation questions or tasks. Instead of a fifty-item test, for example, two or three questions are often sufficient.

Essay Questions.   Essay testing can permit teachers to gain insight into how students think and process information. At the same time, essay testing is an

---

SUGGESTED ACTIVITY
It has been argued that creativity, evaluation, and grading are incompatible, that you can't have one as long as you have any of the others. What do you think? Is it possible to reconcile creativity, evaluation, and grading?

impossibility if students are not mature enough to **express themselves effectively in writing**. Because of this limitation, essay tests are not widely used in the primary grades. Some problems associated with essay test items are shown next.

Sample Essay Test Items

Write a good essay on one of the following questions.

1. *Poor:* What islands did Columbus's expedition visit?

   Better: None.

   Analysis: Essay questions should ask students to do more than simply reproduce information. In this instance, the question lends itself to a list, not an essay. A short-answer (completion) question would probably be better (e.g., "List three of the islands Columbus visited), but the appropriateness of the underlying objective is still questionable.

Questions should lend themselves to an essay

2. *Poor:* Discuss the explorers.

   Better: Describe, with examples, three ways in which the explorers to the New World were similar.

   Analysis: "Discuss the explorers" is so broad that it is difficult to know (a) where to begin and (b) what the intent of the question is. The improved question clearly conveys what the student is to do and also implies criteria by which the response will be judged.

Clear criteria for correct responses are required

3. *Poor:* Tell all you know about why people should always be brave and thankful.

   Better: None.

   Analysis: The task in the "poor" question is clear enough, but establishing valid criteria for evaluating students' responses would be almost impossible. This is a common problem in attempting to evaluate students' attitudes, which is what this question seems geared toward. Of course, teachers could gain insight into their students' attitudes by asking them to respond to questions such as "Why do you think some people are thankful?" But using those responses for grading purposes would be inappropriate. Some of the observational techniques suggested later in this chapter may prove to be more valid indicators of students' attitudes than direct or written questions like the ones illustrated here.

As noted earlier, another difference that separates thinking-skill test items from their knowledge-level cousins is their presentation of information to be interpreted and analyzed. In assessing critical thinking skills, the key element is the student's ability to transfer a process for manipulating information from whatever data they have worked with previously to the information presented on a test.

Provide data for children to use

The following are examples of what we are talking about. Note that in Example 1 the information from *The Works of James I* was rewritten at a lower reading level.

Example 1

Skill Area: Analysis and interpretation of data.

Instructions: Read the following quotations. Explain what they show about the responsibility of individuals and how they control themselves.

Sample 1

Kings are like God. If you think of what God can do, you can think of what a king can do. For example, a king can do anything with his people. He can make them a success or make them a failure. He can judge whether or not what people do is right. But no person shall judge the king. A king's people are like chess pieces and the king is like a chess player. He decides the moves. He decides what the pieces will do. The people should serve the king. No person is to change the government. The government is the king's responsibility.

(Adapted from *The Works of James I* [1603])

Sample 2

Having taken this trip for the glory of God and to help the Christian faith, we agree to work together for the Glory and the Faith.

(From *The Mayflower Compact* [1620])

Example 2

This example shows how a portion of the previous question can be tested in multiple-choice format.

Skill Area: Translation and comprehension.

Comprehension

Which of the following statements best shows the main idea of Sample 1 (in the preceding question)? _____

a. People in a democracy have the right to participate in the government.
b. Kings rely on the people's support for everything they do.
c. The people keep a king in power.
d. Kings can do almost anything they want to.*

Example 3

Question 1. Skill area: Interpreting data.

Interpreting data

Instructions: Use the data in the table about population growth to answer the following questions. (True-False: Use + for true, 0 for false.)

1. _____ City A has always been larger than City B. (0)
2. _____ City A has grown faster than City B. (+)
3. _____ City A was larger than City B in 1975. (+)
4. _____ City A is likely to have more city employees than City B. (+)
5. _____ City B is likely to have more schools than City A. (0)

Population Growth of Two Cities Between 1875 and 1975

Date	City A	City B
1875	111	72
1900	192	220
1925	1,621	400
1950	11,006	1,890
1975	24,000	2,773

Alternative Assessment Strategies

esting too often overshadows other equally useful assessment techniques that are dealt with in this section.

"I Learned" Statements

An obvious and commonsense way to find out what students have learned is to ask them. Parents have done this for years. Unfortunately, parents often get less-than-satisfactory answers from children who have learned that a response like "Nothin'" can avoid the additional questions that are sure to follow.

Limit the focus to something manageable

Teachers who use "I learned" statements usually have much better results. The key is to limit the focus that students must deal with. Instead of asking about an entire day or week, teachers can pose the "I learned" question after a single lesson or series of lessons. The question "What did you learn?" forces students to reflect on their experience, and it permits them to self-select the elements of the lesson they think are important.

Children can respond to "I learned" statements in either oral or written form. Teachers of younger children can summarize "I learned" responses on the board or on large chart paper, or they can simply respond to children orally. Teachers of older children may request "I learned" statements in writing or make them a part of ongoing journal-writing activities or what are sometimes called "learning logs." Consider the following example taken from a child's journal:

> Now I understand why Great-Grampa thought ice cream was so special. His ice box was not cold enough to keep the ice cream from melting, so they had to make it fresh.

No matter how teachers gather "I learned" statements, asking students to pause and reflect on a lesson is clearly superior to the common alternative: "Okay, children, put away your books and get ready to go to lunch," and so on.

Portfolios

The work of artists, photographers, and architects cannot be judged solely by objective criteria. So when those individuals apply for new commissions, they typically take a portfolio of their previous work with them. The samples in the portfolio show the variety and quality of their work—usually their best work—as well as how that work has changed over time. Samples of their poorer work are

Putting your best foot forward

left behind in the studio, probably chalked up to experience.

When you think about it, a fundamental purpose of teaching is to help students grow and change, socially and intellectually. Grades are one way to reflect growth and change, but grades are only generalized symbols. When a student's grades improve, the area of performance where the improvement occurred is seldom apparent, even to the teacher.

Consider using a portfolio, as Janet Jacobsen (from the earlier example) does, that contains representative samples of the student's best work as a basis for assessment. Every student develops a portfolio, which could include projects, papers, homework, tests, assignments, or anything representative of the quality of the student's work. The overall quality of their "best work" would vary from student to student, of course. Each student must also decide which material to include in the portfolio, and be prepared to explain why it is best.

Portfolios use real work, not symbols

From time to time, the teacher and student (and parents) can review the portfolio together, discussing the quality of the latest work and how it may be different from earlier work. Portfolio reviews are based on tangible samples, not on abstract symbols. Instead of making vague exhortations such as "You need to work on your grades," a teacher might point to several sample assignments and say "Sarah, you seem to have trouble with the last part of your assignments, like you're rushing to get them finished and don't care what you put down. Tell me about it." Portfolios need not replace the grading ritual so common in schools today but they would certainly be effective complements to it.

Permit specific feedback

Interviewing and Observing

Finding out what students know or are able to do by talking with them or watching them is hardly a new idea. Even Socrates did more than just ask questions! But observing and talking with students has traditionally been a casual affair. When students were obviously having difficulty, for example, teachers just as obviously walked over and talked with them about the problem. What distinguishes interviewing and observing from their more casual cousins is their systematic quality. An interview is systematic, though not rigidly so, and it is conducted for a particular purpose: to find out what students know about something and how they feel about it. In other words, the interview, like testing, is an information-gathering technique. The interview is not an opportunity to correct children's misconceptions or to teach them something.

KEY IDEA

The materials and strategies used to assess higher-level thinking skills may closely resemble the materials and strategies used to teach those skills initially.

Interviews and conferences are systematic

Time demands

A major deterrent to interviewing is the amount of time it can take, as Janet Jacobsen's conferencing illustrated in the introduction to this chapter. A clear and sometimes preferable alternative to individual interviews is group interviews. Group sessions permit several students to share the teacher's attention.

Suggested interview procedures include the following:

Recommended procedures

- Identify sets of similar questions on whatever it is you want to find out so that you don't always ask exactly the same questions.

- Keep your facial expression as "interested" but as unevaluative as possible.

- Do not be put off by an immediate response such as "I don't know." Often it's just the way children gain time while they think about something. Give them time to think; then probe.

● ● ● ● Assessing Attitudes and Values

Special strategies are usually not needed

To assess students' cognitive skills, they must do something to demonstrate their ability. This could involve taking a test, participating in an interview, or otherwise proving what they can do. Students' attitudes and values, on the other hand, are typically expressed in the course of their day-to-day activities. Simply by observing students' activities over time, it is possible to infer what their attitudes and values are. Evaluators need to know what they are looking for, but attitudinal evaluation usually doesn't require any special behavior on the student's part. In many instances, students' behaviors may more accurately reflect their underlying beliefs and values if students *don't* know they are being observed; that way they're less likely to behave in ways they think are expected of them. The point is that observation is an excellent technique for gathering information on students' (or anyone's) attitudes and values.

A major difficulty in assessing students' attitudes and values lies in identifying precise behavioral indicators for tolerance, respect, or whatever attitudes and values you want to focus on. It is equally difficult to identify attitudinal indicators that do not tread on people's personal liberties. For example, as long as someone's behavior doesn't interfere with another person's rights, the individual has the right to believe whatever he or she wants to believe and to like or dislike whatever (or whomever) he or she chooses.

No precise behavioral indicators

The difficulties involved in identifying and stating precise behavioral indicators for an attitude or value, combined with an unwillingness to infringe on personal liberties, may explain why attitudes and values are usually expressed as goals (instead of as behavioral objectives). This lack of precision may also account for the absence of formal instruments to measure the development of attitudes and values. Despite this limitation, when attitudinal measures are used in conjunction with other techniques, they can provide information and a point of departure that would otherwise be denied the teacher. The following sections examine several techniques for assessing attitudes and values.

● ● ● ● Attitude Scales

Conventional tests usually have correct answers; attitude scales do not. An *attitude scale* is composed of a set of questions or statements, such as "Students should willingly share ideas and materials with others" or "I think cats are smarter than dogs," to which individuals are then asked to respond in terms of their beliefs or preferences. Because those beliefs are personal, even if not always "politically correct," there are no previously established "right" answers on most attitude scales.

How will you use the information and for what purposes?

Attitude scales usually include several items that pertain to a particular attitude or belief. The individual responds to the items using a scale such as "Strongly Agree," "Agree," "Undecided," "Disagree," and "Strongly Disagree." By analyzing the pattern of responses, it becomes possible to infer the individual's attitude or belief toward the topic in question. The key decision in dealing with attitude scales occurs before you administer one, namely, deciding what you intend to do with the information once you've gathered it.

Questionnaires and Inventories

Open-ended questions

Questionnaires often deal with a wide range of topics, whereas interest inventories are usually restricted to what an individual likes or dislikes. Questions like "What do you like to do in your spare time?" or the familiar "What subjects do you like best (or least) in school?" are typical.

Questionnaires and inventories are easy to develop. You simply identify open-ended questions to which the respondent supplies a response. In interview settings, the students' responses are oral. Regardless of how you administer the questionnaire or interest inventory, you once again need to determine what you intend to do with the information after you've obtained it. Determining what your students do in their spare time, for example, can provide insight into your students and the activities they pursue. But only you can decide whether such information will affect the kind of teaching you provide, and whether collecting it is worth the time it takes.

Checklists and Rating Scales

Checklists consist of a series of descriptive statements, such as "Works willingly with others" or "Participates in class discussions," next to which an evaluator makes a check mark to reflect the frequency of how often an item is observed. On rating scales, the evaluator typically writes a number or some other indicator to reflect the frequency or quality of the student's performance on the behavior in question. There are no restrictions on who should use a checklist or rating scale; it could be the teacher, other students, or, as in self-assessment, individual students themselves.

Rating scales require qualitative judgments

Checklists and rating scales often have very similar formats, as shown in Figure 9.5. The difference between the two formats usually lies in the kind of marking system employed. On a checklist, the evaluator marks a category to indicate how often the characteristic is observed, usually using descriptors such as *often, sometimes,* or *almost never.* On a rating scale, the evaluator usually writes a qualitative rating in the space provided to indicate the individual's performance.

Figure 9.5 illustrates how rating scales and checklists can be used either by external evaluators or by students and requires only minor modifications, primarily in terms of how the criterion behaviors are phrased, to fit either circumstance. Rating scales and checklists designed for external evaluators tend to use pronouns such as *he* or *she,* whereas materials designed for self-assessment are more likely to use the personal pronoun *I.*

Focus mainly on behaviors, not causes for behaviors

Once the target behaviors are identified, checklists and rating scales are fairly easy to develop and use. If problems arise, it is more likely to be in interpreting the results. For example, if a checklist or rating scale shows that certain children do not contribute regularly in class discussions, this may simply validate what you already suspect—that certain children do not participate in class discussions. It is rare for checklists or rating scales to identify the underlying causes for that behavior. A shy child's lack of participation in group discussions, for example, may

FIGURE 9.5   Sample Rating Scale/Self-Assessment Checklist for Contributions to Discussions

Focus: How well does he or she (do I) work with peers?	Rating		Checklist Criteria		
			Always	Usually	Seldom
He or she cooperates with others as they work toward group goals. (I cooperate with others as we work toward our group's goals.)					
He or she keeps on task. (I keep on task.)					
He or she contributes new ideas. (I contribute new ideas.)					
He or she makes constructive suggestions when asked for help. (I make constructive suggestions when asked for help.) He or she encourages others. (I give others encouragement.)					
For rating scale, use: Outstanding = 4; Above Average = 3; Satisfactory = 2; and Needs Improvement = 1.					

be based on factors far removed from the evaluation itself. The point here is that while checklists and rating scales can sometimes confirm what an observant teacher already suspects, they are unlikely to indicate why children behave as they do. Remember, too, that what observers report may be colored by their perceptions, and by the fact that students' responses may reflect what they think you want to hear, not how they really feel about a topic or issue. And, finally, remember that assessing students' attitudes and values, or even their class participation, can be more involved than it appears.

SUMMARY

Teachers have long used assessment as more than just a basis for grading. However, grading is such a powerful phenomenon it can overshadow everything else. Most teachers know that *assessment* and *testing* are not synonymous with *grading*, but they don't always act that way. Quite unintentionally, they may find themselves stressing "a very important test on Friday," thereby perpetuating the evaluation-grading mystique.

Assessment, like planning, is an ongoing process.

Just as teachers' goals and objectives help to identify *what* they are attempting to do, assessment and evaluation help them identify *how well* they (and their students) are actually doing it. Testing sometimes becomes a confounding variable, even though simply an information-gathering process, nothing more. Testing, like observations, interviews, checklists, portfolios, attitude scales, interest inventories, and rating scales, is a way of gathering information.

The assessment process consists of (1) identifying (or accepting) assessment criteria, the standards against which evaluative judgments are made; (2) measuring an individual's performance, behavior, or products in relation to those standards; and (3) making judgments about the individual's performance. The form that assessment takes is largely determined by the teacher's purpose. If you wish to assess whether a student can demonstrate a certain skill or knowledge, you will undoubtedly turn to *criterion-referenced assessment*. However, if you wish to compare your students' performance with that of another group, you will turn to *norm-referenced assessment*. In instances when you are interested in determining how things are going during an instructional episode, you may turn to *formative assess-*

ment. If you are interested in determining the overall quality of a student's performance or product at the end of an instructional period, you will turn to *summative assessment*. Finally, if your purpose is to figure out how well you are doing, you will undoubtedly turn to *self-assessment*.

The growing interest in using portfolios for assessment purposes is a reflection of the broader move toward authentic assessment. Although much of the assessment in schools today pertains to the knowledge and skills required to get through school, it often has little bearing on what it takes to be successful in life beyond schools. Authentic assessment does that; it seeks to assess performance through worthwhile and realistic activities that students will encounter in real life.

SUGGESTED READINGS AND RESOURCES

Print Resources

J. Alleman & J. Brophy. (1998). Assessment in a social constructivist classroom. *Social Education, 62,* 32–42. This excellent article by two leading authorities in the field includes useful examples of rating scales and checklists.

D. Adams & M. Hamm. (1992). Portfolio assessment and social studies: Collection, selecting, and reflecting on what is significant. *Social Education 56,* 103–105. This article is noteworthy in this special issue of *Social Education* devoted to assessment.

P. Nickell. (Ed.) (1999). Authentic assessment in social studies. *Social Education, 63.* This theme issue of *Social Education* approaches authentic assessment from a variety of perspectives.

Weissberg, R., Resnik H., Payton, J., & O'Brien, M. (March, 2003). Evaluating social and emotional learning programs. *Educational Leadership, 60,* 46–50. This article describes and assesses comprehensive, long-term approaches to social and emotional learning.

Allen, R. (August 2003). Different starting points: Initial efforts to understand student abilities, interests essential. *Education Update* (a periodic publication of the Association for Supervision and Curriculum Development), 45, 1–7. This article offers insight and practical suggestions for doing formative assessment.

Internet Resources

Introductory Note: Web sites sometimes change their Internet addresses or cease operating entirely. All the addresses supplied here were operating when this book was printed, but if any of them fails to work properly, enter the name of the target organization in any standard search engine.

ERIC Clearinghouse on Assessment and Evaluation

http://ericae.net/main.htm

I spent hours on this site just getting ready to update this chapter. It contains an amazing variety of resources. Highly recommended.

Alternative Assessment in the Social Sciences

http://www.coe.ilstu.edu/jabraun/socialstudies/assess/socsci

This site is loaded with examples of authentic assessment activities associated with the Illinois Goal Assessment Program for geography and social science. Among its most useful elements are sample evaluation rubrics and examples of students' work.

Authentic Assessment

http://www.nwrel.org/

This site, supported by the Northwest Regional Laboratory, offers links to Web sites and materials that focus on authentic assessment. Topics of interest include electronic portfolios, evaluating problem-solving processes, and creating assessment rubrics.

Alternative Assessment

http://cresst96.cse.ucla.edu/

This site is supported by the Center for the Study of Evaluation at the University of California at Los Angeles and provides excellent examples of alternative assessment strategies.

10

Strategies and Activities for Effective Teaching

KEY QUESTIONS

● **What teaching strategies work best for which objectives?**

● **What's the difference between teacher-directed and student-centered teaching strategies?**

● **How do teachers manage small-group activities?**

● **Why involve students in role-playing?**

● **How do teachers manage decision-making activities?**

● ● ● ● Introduction: The "Pine Tree Shillings" Activity

Changing roles

Janet Jacobsen is the fifth-grade teacher from the Yakima Valley region of Washington State whom you met in Chapter 9. You may recall that in her years of teaching Mrs. Jacobsen has shifted from a traditional "coverage" approach to American history to a "less is more" approach. This means that her students study fewer topics but in greater depth. She also shifted from a heavily teacher-directed to a much more student-centered approach to social studies.

Mrs. Jacobsen indicated that "I now use a modified cooperative-group investigation approach where the kids focus on researching and answering questions they've raised." She then walked over to her filing cabinet and pulled out a one-page handout. "Here's an example of how I get things started," she said. "This is about the 'Pine Tree Shillings' incident that I took from an old reader." Janet pointed to an obviously old book, *Stories of Our Country* (Johonnot, 1887). "I got it for 50 cents at the Salvation Army store. This is my springboard."

Pine Tree Shillings

A springboard for inquiry

The Puritan colony of Massachusetts assigned John Hull to be the mint master. Using silver from old tableware, buccaneer bullion, and old European coins, he cast thousands of shillings, sixpence, and threepence. Each coin had an image of a pine tree on one side and the date 1652 on the other.

Sometime after Captain Hull had made his fortune minting coins, his plump daughter, Betsy, attracted a suitor, the young Sam Sewell. Captain Hull, recognizing that Sewell sought love and not a dowry, granted Betsy's hand in marriage.

Just after the wedding, Captain Hull instructed his servants to bring in a large set of scales. He directed his daughter to get on one side and then instructed his men to balance the scale. The servants scooped up handfuls of bright silver Pine Tree shillings into the other pan.

"There, son Sewell!" cried the honest mint master. "Take these shillings for my daughter's portion. It is not every wife that's worth her weight in silver!"

—Hawthorne

(Johonnot, p. 81, cited in Lauritzen & Jaeger, 1994, p. 582)

Cognitive dissonance

The term *buccaneer bullion* in the second line caught my attention. Buccaneers were pirates, of course, but pirates in New England? This was puzzling. After deciding to pursue it later I said, "This just says 'Hawthorne.' Is this *the* Nathaniel Hawthorne?"

"That's a question the kids ask," Janet responded, "except most of them don't know about Nathaniel Hawthorne, so they ask, 'Who was Hawthorne?' After we've read the vignette, I invite questions about it. Look," she said, as she pulled three overhead transparencies from the file. "I save these from year to year to remind me what I'm getting into. The kids have literally hundreds of questions."

A few of the children's questions are shown here.

Children's questions

What is a mint master?
How did a mint master make coins?
How did Captain Hull get the silver to make coins?
Did people donate the old silverware? Why?
What is bullion? What is buccaneer bullion?
What is a shilling? A sixpence? A threepence? A pence?
Why was 1652 on the coins?
How "plump" was Betsy?
What was Betsy really worth?
Is this a true story? Are the people real?
Who was Hawthorne?
What is a dowry? Do we still have dowries today? Were they common in Puritan times?

"I invite students to follow up on their most compelling questions," Janet added. "I forewarn the librarian before we get into this, and she gets a lot of books ready for us."

TECHNOLOGY

"Even more than the books," Janet continued, "my kids love using the Internet. I can't tell you how impressed they are when they get an E-mail answer to one of their questions. When some of them deal with English money, like shillings and pence, they sometimes get E-mail responses from England; it's fabulous."

I told Janet, "Whenever I tried this kind of inquiry approach, there were always a few kids who wouldn't get involved. They'd say there was nothing they wanted to investigate. Do you ever encounter this?"

"Sure," Janet replied. "I always have a couple of students who need some prodding, but I never realized how powerful computers are as motivational tools. For the kids who won't get involved, I tell them that they must be doing something productive; they can't just sit there and do nothing."

Computers as motivators

Investigating different facets of the incident

"Most of my students," Janet continued, "read books on colonial times to research the personalities; some of them go to the coin shop in the mall and look at examples of colonial coinage; some of them study the literature of Nathaniel Hawthorne to determine if it is similar to the 'Pine Tree' story; and some of them experiment with different models for testing how many coins Sam Sewell received in the dowry. The kids also record their findings in their journals, including the feelings that this inquiry evokes."

Sharing findings

"It usually takes a week or more to deal with this activity, usually more like two to three weeks when you add in the sharing time, because some of the kids really get into it. And because everyone's following a different line of inquiry, the sharing aspect of this unit is *really* important. I have one, and only one, rule for sharing: show us, don't just tell us. Every student makes some kind of visual presentation that describes his or her investigation. To eliminate duplicate reports, we sometimes team up for the sharing time."

"O.K., you've hooked me," I said. "Did any of the 'Pine Tree Shillings' stuff really happen?"

The real story

"Oh, yes," Janet replied. "Captain John Hull minted Pine Tree shillings in Massachusetts Bay colony in the mid- to late-1600s. However, all the Pine Tree shillings made after 1652 carried the same date. That was because when Charles II was restored to the English throne in 1652, the Massachusetts Bay colony lost the right to mint its own coins. Despite the new regulations, the Bay colony continued to mint its own coins for the next twenty years or so, and to avoid raising Charles II's suspicions, every coin was dated 1652. A clever ploy, don't you think?"

Using different strategies for different purposes

This chapter focuses on teaching strategies, those patterns of daily lessons and activities that teachers design to enable their students to reach desired learning outcomes. At one time Mrs. Jacobsen supplemented the textbook with additional activities. However, she began moving toward a more student-centered, small-group investigative approach to instruction. Mrs. Jacobsen also told me (as described in the introduction to Chapter 9) that during the six-week period just before her students take standardized tests, she moves back to a very teacher-directed approach. During that time, she covers a large body of information that her students will be responsible for on the test. The point here is that Mrs. Jacobsen, and all teachers, have a range of teaching strategies at their disposal, as shown in Figure 10.1.

Chapter organization

When Mrs. Jacobsen is working with her students on an activity like the "Pine Tree Shillings," her basic orientation is toward the right-hand side of the range. Then, when she moves into her pretest review mode, she shifts toward the left-hand side of the range. Some of the options and activities associated with each of these teaching orientations are examined in the first part of this chapter. We then turn to the skills necessary for working successfully with small groups. And finally, we'll examine a variety of teaching and decision-making activities that are designed to actively involve students.

FIGURE 10.1   A Range of Teaching Strategies

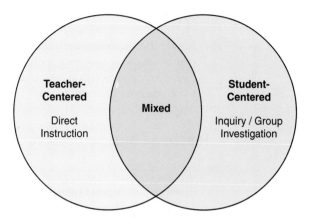

Teaching Strategies Defined

Strategy defined   The term *strategy* can sometimes have manipulative overtones, but a teaching strategy is simply a series of activities designed to help students reach desired learning outcomes. Individual teaching techniques—such as lecturing, modeling, role-playing, conducting group discussions, videos, possibly computer-based simulations, and others—must somehow fit together to constitute a teaching strategy. The relationship between a teaching strategy and the individual teaching techniques is shown in Figure 10.2.

FIGURE 10.2   Components of a Teaching Strategy

A teaching strategy is created from various combinations of short-term techniques, such as

discussion

modeling

role-playing

lecturing

group projects

individual reports

case studies

simulations

decision making

mapping

etc.

● ● ● ● Identifying Teaching Strategies

Teaching strategies range from almost complete teacher domination at one extreme to almost complete student involvement at the other (refer again to Figure 10.1). Few teachers are at either extreme, because most of them use a combination of teaching techniques and thus fall into a "mixed" strategy. Then, too, every classroom is teacher-directed to some extent at least, because that's what teachers are paid to do.

● ● ● ● Teacher-Centered Instruction
● ● ● ●

Teacher-centered instruction is usually characterized by a "telling" or "explaining" orientation. Many teacher-centered strategies are variations on a Read-Recite-Lecture-Test format. The recitation phase, which is typically an oral test of retained information, is sometimes omitted, especially at the college level. Occa-

Goal: to present information

sionally the teacher may talk about material prior to having students read it, while on other occasions, additional elements may be added, such as videos, discussions, demonstrations, or student reports. Despite such variations, the goal of most teacher-centered strategies is to present information to students as quickly and as efficiently as possible.

When teachers conduct question-and-answer sessions to determine how well students have retained information, they sometimes mistakenly refer to those

The difference between discussion and recitation

sessions as discussions. The distinction between *discussion* and *recitation* is based on the purpose of the activity. Discussions can serve multiple purposes, including sharing different points of view on an issue, motivating students or developing interest in a topic, generating ideas, synthesizing ideas, or providing closure to an activity. The purpose of recitation is to test (orally) how well students have understood and retained prior information.

Despite the bad reputation sometimes associated with teacher-centered strategies, there are times when lecturing (or telling or explaining) and especially teacher modeling are both desirable and useful. For example, recall the Lincoln cooperative biography example for Tarry Lindquist's class from Chapter 1. Although most of that activity was devoted to student research and writing, Ms.

Don't overlook direct instruction

Lindquist devoted the first five days to what she called "content packing." She read excerpts from various works on Lincoln while her students took notes. Her purpose was to share a common body of information about Lincoln with students. There are other less teacher-directed ways to do this, such as making copies of the materials for students to read themselves. However, the other strategies may be subject to other limitations, not the least of which is the variety of reading levels common to fifth-grade classes. With Ms. Lindquist presenting the information, she could make on-the-spot accommodations for difficult vocabulary and archaic usages while still preserving the style of the original author. Combine all of this with the fact that Ms. Lindquist was sharing information that students wanted and for which they had a felt need; hence, their willingness to take notes.

On Note Taking.

Asking elementary- and middle-school-aged children to take notes on class activities, as Ms. Lindquist did, can often be problematic. For college graduates, taking notes is often second nature, but for students in the middle grades it is often a brand-new activity. Recognize also that learning to take notes is a learned skill, not something you inherit or learn by osmosis. Middle-grade students often lack the basis for the continual decision making that note taking demands; that is, primarily deciding whether certain pieces of information are worth noting or can safely be ignored. Lacking the basis for deciding what information is (or is not) important, beginning note takers typically try to note *everything*. They, in effect, try to create a script of what the teacher said. This tendency is further compounded because some middle-grade students are excruciatingly slow writers. You can always tell when you are dealing with inexperienced note takers; they will continually interrupt to ask that you either slow down or repeat what you just said. If you find yourself continually repeating parts of a lesson so that the slower writers can get "everything," the pace of what you originally intended as an interesting lesson can come to a grinding halt. In other words, the pace of your lesson may be determined by the slowest writers in the class who are intent on creating a word-for-word account of everything you have said. On the other hand, if you ignore students' requests to "slow down," "back up," or "spell that word," they will surely become frustrated, perhaps slamming their notebooks closed as a signal that they are withdrawing from the activity. The double-edged sword here is that if you try to accommodate the slow writers, you are almost certain to test the patience of students who are not experiencing problems.

The way to resolve this apparent dilemma is to reflect on Rule One of Teaching: Be careful about making assumptions about what children know. In this instance, assuming that middle-grade students already know how to take notes may be at the root of the problem. If so, its resolution probably lies in modifying the lesson so as to teach children how and why to take notes. Recall also that Ms. Lindquist devoted five days to her "content packing/note-taking" lessons. If she does not address the problems related to note taking, and she too encounters the "notebook slammers" on the first day, you can imagine what the third, fourth and fifth days would be like.

margin note: Note-taking demands decision making

SUGGESTED ACTIVITY

Do you think that Ms. Lindquist ignored the problems that novice note takers encounter? How could you find out for sure?

Direct Instruction.

Teacher-centered instruction is sometimes referred to as *direct instruction* because teachers are doing something directly to students. In an instance where students are not fully aware of the issues associated with a topic, for example, a so-called discussion can become an exercise in shared ignorance. At other times, students may find themselves floundering because their teachers—who favor a student-centered approach to teaching—mistakenly believe that students can discover *everything* on their own. Given enough time, students might discover how to determine the distance between two cities on a map, but it is often more efficient and effective if the teacher demonstrates the technique by modeling it for students. Likewise, through minilectures or short presentations teachers can also bring fresh information to bear on any points in question. A daily diet of hourlong presentations would surely be excessive, but there are countless instances where minilectures are appropriate teaching activities.

Direct instruction often works well with subject matter that is itself highly structured and that has a learning hierarchy in which later learning depends on earlier

margin note: Direct instruction vs. discovery learning

SUGGESTED ACTIVITY

Some teachers claim that if independent (or guided) practice is good for mathematics, it should be good for other subjects as well. How would you respond to their argument?

learning. The most obvious candidate that fits these criteria is mathematics. Some portions of other subject areas are also highly structured, such as grammar in language arts and map skills in social studies, but for the majority of those subjects there is no predetermined learning hierarchy.

A notable problem in trying to apply a direct instruction model to social studies lies in the guided and independent practice phases. Some teachers feel guilty if they do not have a worksheet (or problems in a textbook) available for independent practice. Although that guilt is often well founded for mathematics-related subjects, it may be misplaced for other subject areas. Consider, for example, that you are expected to teach about Hannibal's ordeal in crossing the Alps with thirty-seven elephants and an army of ten thousand (see page 195 for more details). Hannibal's achievements were certainly unique and historically significant, but unlike areas such as fractions or geometry there is no grand scheme or hierarchy into which they fall.

Would you use the following questions on a worksheet?

Worksheet questions

1. How old was Hannibal when he led his army across the Alps?
2. How many elephants accompanied Hannibal's army?
3. What is the significance of Hannibal's achievements?

Questions 1 and 2 have the effect of drawing attention to what are effectively historical details. As noted on page 195, such details are important in helping to build a vivid mental image of Hannibal crossing the Alps. But whether they will have a bearing on the students' future conduct as effective citizens is highly doubtful.

Question 3 is a different matter. After spending thirty minutes or more of class time talking about Hannibal, it is appropriate to ask why this event is significant.

KEY IDEA

Teaching techniques—lectures, discussions, and so on—are the building blocks from which teaching strategies are created.

But should you ask it on a worksheet? In this instance, children may still be focusing on getting those elephants over the mountains, and they probably have not stood back to reflect on the significance of the event. Consider that the significance question would be a wonderful way to involve the class in a wrap-up discussion of the lesson. Used in this way, the question would take the spotlight off individual children and would make their response a composite of the group's opinion. If it were a worksheet question, students will probably resort to rereading the text to find the sentence that answers the question.

MAJOR TEACHER-CENTERED TECHNIQUES AND PURPOSES SUMMARIZED

Technique	*Purpose(s)*
Lecture	To present information
Recitation	To test, orally, retained information
Discussion	Multiple purposes:
	To motivate or generate interest
	To share points of view on an issue
	To generate ideas or identify new applications for ideas
	To synthesize ideas
	To bring closure to an activity

● ● ● ● COMMENTARY   There Is Nothing Like a Good Lecture

In some educational circles a notion prevails that lectures are inherently bad and that, should you ever lecture to your students, you will be committing a grievous sin. At the same time, you've undoubtedly witnessed some extremely good lectures during your career as a student, some of which made eight-o'clock classes worth getting up for. How then can it be that lecturing is such an evil?

Experience suggests that the quality of a lecture depends heavily on the lecturer's ability. Good lecturers demonstrate the following characteristics:

1. *They must be well versed in their subject.* Good lecturers stand at the opposite end of the continuum from students, whose reports to the class often reflect the total scope of their knowledge on a topic. Subject-matter expertise is just one qualification, however, because we've all heard nationally known specialists in their fields deliver some abominable lectures.
2. *They must be master communicators.* Good lecturers must be sensitive to timing, pacing, and the form and style of expression—when to raise their eyebrow, change their tone of voice, use humor, or ask a question. The importance of these so-called show-biz aspects of lecturing was illustrated in what has been called "The Doctor Fox Effect." To determine whether

the way a lecture was presented made any difference in how students reacted to it, two researchers hired a professional actor, whom they called Dr. Fox, to present six different types of lectures. The actor first memorized the scripts for three different lectures on the same topic. Each lecture differed in the amount of information it contained; one had a very high content, another had some content, and the third contained a lot of verbiage but little information. The actor then presented each lecture to different students in one of two ways. For one presentation of each type of lecture, Dr. Fox really hammed it up, using gestures, humor, movement, vocal inflection, and considerable enthusiasm. For the second set of lectures, all of the expressive embellishments were omitted and the actor virtually read from the prepared script.

What happened? Students who experienced the highly expressive presentations did significantly better on achievement tests than did students who experienced the less expressive presentations. In addition, the students almost always rated expressive presentations as "more effective" than the less expressive lectures, regardless of their content. The implication, then, is that even if you have little to say on a topic, you should say it with gusto!

Mixed Instruction

A blend of techniques   *Mixed* teaching strategies reflect a blend of teacher-centered and student-centered teaching techniques. Just how those techniques are blended often varies from teacher to teacher and, often, from topic to topic.

The further that teachers move away from the more clearly defined roles of the teacher-centered strategy, the more difficult it becomes to describe their behavior precisely. When the focus shifts to a student-centered teaching strategy, discussed next, the attention necessarily shifts to the teacher *and* the students, and to what the students will be doing.

Student-Centered Instruction

Goal: to process information   *Student-centered* teaching strategies typically have a problem-solving or inquiry orientation. The goal of these teaching strategies is to help students develop the ability to manipulate and process information from various sources—academic, social, and experiential. To do this, teachers act as guides to assist students in identifying problems, generating possible answers, testing those answers in the light of available data, and applying their conclusions to new data, new problems, or new situations. In other words, the focus is on the skills of inquiring and processing information. This means that student-centered teaching strategies are usually more appropriate for helping students develop information-processing skills, whereas teacher-centered strategies are more appropriate for transmitting information.

Individual and Group Investigation.   Group investigations can be conducted in one of three ways: (1) the entire class acts as a research group in which everyone investigates aspects of the same problem simultaneously; (2) individuals or small research groups investigate one aspect or dimension of a classwide problem; or (3) individual or small research groups investigate separate problems. Mrs. Jacobsen's class used the second approach to investigate different dimensions of the "Pine Tree Shillings" incident. The following Model Student Activity, "The Wearin' of the Green," shows a whole-class approach to group investigation.

Three formats

The Inquiry Process.   The procedures Ms. Fleury (see the Model Student Activity) and her students followed are common to many individual or group investigations. For example, after Ms. Fleury remarked that more intermediate than primary students would wear green the following day, this struck a discordant note with Stephen, who politely disagreed by asking his question, "Why?" The difference between Stephen's views and Ms. Fleury's was a discrepant event that ultimately became the problem that the entire class investigated. The other phases of the inquiry process are discussed next.

Cognitive dissonance

1. *Awareness of a Possible Problem.* One's awareness of a discrepant event results from a kind of mental "disturbance" called *cognitive dissonance.* This happened to us when we were visiting with Mrs. Jacobsen and encountered the phrase *buccaneer bullion,* which didn't "fit" our existing view of American history.

Problem awareness

The awareness of the problem is critical to the inquiry process. Likewise, when students don't sense dissonance—something that doesn't fit—they have nothing to explain, and nothing to research. Therefore, teachers who wish to use investigation-oriented teaching strategies may sometimes need to structure activities in which they intentionally create cognitive dissonance that provides students with a motive for inquiry. The "Pine Tree Shillings" incident served this purpose in Mrs. Jacobsen's class.

The inquiry process

2. *Defining the Problem.* Based on the discrepancy between Ms. Fleury's and Stephen's views, the problem was: Will more or fewer primary-level students wear green clothing than intermediate-grade students?

3. *Hypothesizing.* Stephen's contention that primary children were more likely to wear green on St. Patrick's Day because their mothers usually laid their clothing out for them was a hypothesis. Likewise, Ms. Fleury's contention that intermediate children would wear green because they were more sensitive to peer pressure was a second hypothesis.

MODEL STUDENT ACTIVITY

"The Wearin' of the Green"—A Group Investigation

It was the day before St. Patrick's Day when Ms. Fleury, a fourth-grade teacher, commented to her class that although some families don't celebrate St. Patrick's Day, many students were likely to wear green clothing the following day. She added that students in the intermediate grades were more likely to wear green than primary-grade children. Her comment prompted a curious "why?" from one student, Stephen.

Ms. Fleury responded by saying that intermediate students were older and more likely to wear green clothing because many other intermediate students would be wearing green. Stephen suggested that primary children wear the clothes that their mothers lay out for them and that many of those mothers would see that their children wore something green; therefore primary children would be more likely to wear green. In other words, there were two competing views, one based on peer pressure and the other based on parental influence.

Ms. Fleury recognized that the question—who was more likely to wear green—was an opportunity for the class to gather data and to determine which view was correct.

The students decided that they would observe each classroom in the building. Some students would be observers and others would stay in their classroom—the "control room"—to process the results. As their planning progressed, the principal came into the room. She asked how much green someone needed to wear to be counted and whether it needed to be solid green. The students decided that someone had to have at least a sweater, shirt, blouse, skirt, slacks, scarf, or ribbon to be counted and that the dominant color had to be green. When everything seemed in place, observers went to the different classrooms to ask permission to visit that room the next morning. The students agreed in advance to tell the teachers why they wanted to visit, but they knew that if they told each class what they were doing, it could change their results.

The next morning, the students observed their assigned classrooms and then gave the data to the student-tabulators. As Ms. Fleury had predicted, more intermediate students wore green than did primary-level students. Ms. Fleury was going to let it go at that, but one student, Christie, said she thought that there were more fourth, fifth, and sixth graders than there were students in the primary grades. This meant that there were more intermediate students who *could* wear green, and naturally they would win.

This was something Ms. Fleury hadn't anticipated. The issue involved percentages, which was something the students had not worked with yet. The talliers provided the total number of primary- and intermediate-level students and the numbers at each level who wore green, which Ms. Fleury then used to find the percentage. The new results: 76 percent of the primary children wore green clothing, compared with 64 percent of the intermediate-level children. Ms. Fleury admitted that Stephen's hypothesis seemed to be true.

Modifying hypotheses

4. *Testing Modified Hypotheses.* An interesting aspect of this investigation is that it did not investigate the validity of either Stephen's or Ms. Fleury's explanations for *why* one age level was more or less likely to wear green clothing. Rather, it was restricted to the more basic problem: the age level of children who actually wore green clothing.

5. *Gathering Data.* Ms. Fleury and her students agreed on a process for collecting the information they needed—observing in other classrooms. They also defined their terms so that everyone knew what "wearing green" meant.

6. *Concluding, Tentatively.* Based on the preliminary data, it appeared that more intermediate students had worn green clothing than had primary students.

Thus, Ms. Fleury was apparently correct, at least in terms of absolute numbers (though not in terms of the students' motivation).

7. *Testing the Conclusion.* Had there been no questions about the tentative conclusion, there would have been no need to test its applicability and it might have been accepted without further consideration. However, Christie raised the question about the number of students at each level who might potentially wear green, so it became necessary to reanalyze the data. That analysis showed that proportionately more primary students wore green than did intermediate students.

Based on this investigation, who was correct: Stephen or Ms. Fleury?

On-the-Spot Decision Making. "The Wearin' of the Green" Model Activity reflects one teacher's decision to explore an unplanned problematic situation in more detail. Ms. Fleury clearly took advantage of an opportunity, but in doing so she obviously had to put her planned program aside for a day or so. Ms. Fleury had to make some quick decisions: Was this difference of opinion worth pursuing? And would the time that students spent doing it result in something that was educationally beneficial? It's difficult to predict outcomes in advance—and this activity could very well "bomb"—but Ms. Fleury obviously decided to go with it.

Planning as you go

Another issue Ms. Fleury had to deal with sooner or later pertains to how this activity relates to the standards for social studies. In this instance, she would be forced into making an after-the-fact (as opposed to preplanned) decision. Be advised that as long as instructional activities are educationally defensible, you can usually identify one or more standards that will encompass them. In this instance, the activity would fall within the scope of Middle Grades Exemplar E of the NCSS Theme of Individuals, Groups, and Institutions: "identify and describe examples of tensions between expressions of individuality and groups or institutional efforts to promote social conformity" (NCSS, 1994).

STANDARDS ☑

● ● ● ● **COMMENTARY** **Inquiry, Discovery, and Problem Solving**

When teachers talk about student-centered instructional strategies, they sometimes say, "I use a discovery approach"; others say, "I prefer a problem-solving approach." Because universally accepted definitions for inquiry, discovery, and problem solving don't exist, you would need to visit these teachers to find out how they actually teach. Despite the different terminology, these teachers' strategies are apt to be more similar than different.

One similarity among these approaches is their emphasis on thinking processes and skills. Literally, *discovery* refers to the moment that a student perceives a relationship among various data—when the student says "Aha, I've got it!" The teacher's role in discovery teaching is creating situations and environments where students are encouraged to discover and test their ideas. In many respects, discovery is part of a larger process that is similar to the inquiry processes that we outlined earlier.

Problem solving can be confusing because the expression is used to refer to several different types of activities. One of these, probably the most common, refers to what students do as they complete the exercises in a math text, most of which have a right or desired answer. A second type of problem solving involves genuine investigative inquiry, such as Ms. Fleury's students experienced in the "Wearin' of the Green" activity. Ms. Fleury's students were investigating a real problem and no one, including Ms. Fleury, knew what they would find in advance.

The Dynamics of Group Investigation. Not all group investigations work

Deciding on a hands-on activity

out as well as the "Wearin' of the Green" activity. For example, consider what can happen when, in the course of studying the Inuit (Eskimos), you wrack your brain for some hands-on activities that students might do. You reject the idea of written reports because students have already written about the Inuit in their journals. You also decide against building harpoons because of the potential dangers associated with overly enthusiastic role-playing. You finally settle on the apparently safe idea of constructing model igloos from sugar cubes.

When you announce the igloo activity to the class, not everyone is thrilled with the prospect of model building. So you decide to not make it a requirement. Next, Clarisa wants to know what kind of glue they should use to stick the sugar cubes together. Will plain paste work? Robert asks if he can use the model airplane cement that is used for plastic models. Or should he use Elmer's?

Resolving the glue problem

You have visions of half-constructed igloos collapsing if you give the wrong information, but you really don't know what will work. So you pose the question, "How do you suppose we can find out?"

Shamus claims that Elmer's works best because, well, he just *knows* it will. Shamus is usually right about such things and you are tempted to believe him, but Janet poses the obvious answer: "Everyone bring in the kind of glue they want to use and we'll test them." You agree, willingly and thankfully.

Other problems

Once the glue crisis is resolved, still other questions are likely to arise. For example, will you permit your students to glue their sugar cubes to Styrofoam balls (cut in half) and then fill in the gaps with granulated sugar? Or will you have them cut off one edge of each cube so that it will lean inward properly to form the igloo's "roof"? Real igloos are hollow in the middle, not filled with Styrofoam, so cutting the sugar cubes to fit properly would be more realistic. On the other hand, cutting sugar cubes can be difficult and dangerous, and you begin to wonder if this activity is any safer than the harpoon-building project you discarded.

Reassessing the purpose of the activity

Thus far the igloo-building project has generated a lot of nitpicking problems, and you begin to wonder whether it is really worth it. You may also find yourself rethinking how you had originally justified the project—that by building model igloos, your students would learn about what it was like to find shelter in a land of scarce resources. You may also wonder if this activity has anything to do with life in the Arctic, or whether it is simply a lesson in construction—in learning how to cut sugar cubes without crumbling them, and in finding what kind of glue sticks them together best.

Is the activity worthwhile?

The igloo-building episode is an example of what Brophy and Alleman (1990) refer to as activities that occupy students' time but that often lack substance and fail to engage students intellectually. The moral? When you are considering group activities, such as presenting a play on Mexico or holding a Greek Olympic Day, be certain that the mechanics of collecting sombreros and serapes, making the scenery, or building chariots does not overshadow everything else.

Inquiry versus Activity. The "Wearin' of the Green" and the igloo-building activity illustrate a key difference between genuine investigations and simple activities. In the "Wearin' of the Green," the children identified questions they wanted answered, and then did the research necessary to answer their questions.

WebQuests: Tapping the Internet's Resources

A WebQuest [which is sometimes written as two words—Web Quest] is an increasingly popular, inquiry-oriented activity in which most or all of the information that students use is drawn from the Internet. Most WebQuests are based on a model developed in 1995 by Bernie Dodge at the San Diego State University.

A WebQuest usually begins with a brief introduction followed closely by the presentation of an engaging and highly doable task. In the hundreds, perhaps even thousands, of WebQuests available on the Internet, the tasks vary widely. They include such things as illustrating the process of making a mummy, journeying back in time to the colonial days, trekking the Santa Fe Trail, or planning for your survival on (or escape from) an isolated island. This is followed by (1) a description of steps (a process) for students to follow as they begin working on the task, and (2) links to predetermined resources that the student can use to complete the tasks. The intent in using predetermined links is to make sure students' time is well spent in using information as opposed to looking for it. Finally, there is an evaluation component, usually involving a rubric, and then a brief conclusion.

One of the best ways to become familiar with Web-Quests is to get on the Internet and sample a few. You will find countless examples if you enter "Web-Quests" or "Web Quests" into any search engine. The two key words above lead to separate listings, so try both of them. A WebQuest titled *A Perilous Journey,* which involves a group of Irish immigrants who join the Gold Rush in 1850, is available at the web site for this book at **college.hmco.com** (select "Education").

For information on designing WebQuests and additional sample WebQuests for different content areas and grade levels, the mother lode of WebQuest information is The WebQuest Page at: **http://edweb.sdsu.edu/webquest/webquest.html**

In other words, the inquiry process that the children followed was *purposeful and systematic.* For the igloo-building activity, however, the final product became the overriding concern, and the inquiry process got lost in the shuffle. An investigation is purposeful and systematic, whereas in a simple activity, the behavior is often not so systematic and organized.

Process vs. product

The irony of inquiries and activities is that students often "feel good" about both. The students who conducted the "Wearin' of the Green" inquiry probably felt good about what they had accomplished. But the students who made model igloos probably felt good about their efforts too, even though they didn't learn much about their topic. Understand that feeling good, by itself, is not a sufficient criterion for judging the quality of a learning experience.

The Challenge of Student-Centered Teaching.   A subtle but important consideration in moving toward student-centered instruction is students' perceptions of what it means to teach. Many children believe that teachers are actually "teaching" only when they stand in front of the entire class and do their thing—explaining, modeling, conducting a discussion, or whatever. Based on those prior experiences, children are apt to believe that teachers who use cooperative learning and small groups extensively are, as students put it, "not teaching very much."

Children's perceptions of what it means to teach

Such opinions are based primarily on the child's expectations (and often their parents' expectations) of teachers in general. Most children typically divorce how

KEY IDEA

Teacher-centered strategies tend to be more appropriate for conveying information; student-centered strategies tend to be more appropriate for developing information-processing skills.

much they are learning, if they are even aware of it, from what student-centered teachers do to see that such learnings occur. Thus, it's wise to get parents involved from the outset—at least let them know what you are up to—before students' comments create negative perceptions that are difficult to overcome.

In terms of classroom management, involving an entire class in a single investigation, as Ms. Fleury did in the "Wearin' of the Green" activity, is a difficult task. However, because the activity occurred over a short (two-day) period, it was manageable.

Managing group investigation

On the other hand, keeping an entire class involved with a single problem over a period of a week or more is difficult. Mrs. Jacobsen manages small-group investigations over a long period by having students self-select the problems they investigate. This procedure creates smaller groups that are inherently more manageable. However, having many small groups operating simultaneously also calls for some additional group-management skills that are examined in the next section.

Managing Small-Group Instruction

Helping children learn to work productively in small groups is directly related to the overall goal of social studies teaching: promoting citizenship education. It is difficult, perhaps even impossible, for students to learn to work cooperatively with others if all they experience is large-group instruction. Likewise, it's almost impossible for students to demonstrate their willingness to respect the rights and opinions of others if they seldom get the opportunity to express their opinions.

Large- versus small-group activities

Almost everything you can do with large groups (of twenty to thirty students) can also be done in small groups; you can even lecture to two students if you want to. But the reverse is not true: what you can do with small groups is not always possible with large groups. Discussions that involve twenty or more students, for example, are less likely to be successful than discussions involving groups of five to seven students, simply because participants in the larger groups must wait so long before they get a chance to speak. On the other hand, good small-group discussions don't happen just because you create small groups in your class. Some special structuring is usually required, as noted later in this section.

The perils of group work

You may remember times in the past when your small group spent thirty minutes getting organized when you could have completed the group's task yourself in half the time. Or when everyone in your group got the same grade but only one or two individuals did all the work. Or when group activities didn't make any difference because your grades were based solely on tests and individual projects. All of these experiences reflect decisions that need to be made before you undertake group work as a teacher. For example, will students' small-group work be graded and, if so, on what basis? You also need to decide how the groups will be created. Will you let children choose whom they will work with, or will you do the selecting? If you do the selecting, will you put two students who dislike each other on the same committee? Will you put a low-social-status child in the same group with high-social-status children (or vice versa)? High- and low-status children can often work successfully in the same group, but the relationship between two children who actively dislike each other is unlikely to improve if they are in the same small group, primarily because most groups don't deal with the causes of their disenchantment.

The Dynamics of Small Groups

From the moment you divide your class into small groups, the proportion of each student's responsibility to the group increases dramatically. Instead of representing one twenty-fourth of a class (of twenty-four), for example, a student could represent one-fourth of a group of four.

Characteristics of small groups

As a general rule, smaller groups have fewer problems than larger groups. But then small groups can also encounter problems. Groups of two, for example, often have a high exchange of information, but they also tend to have high tension. Likewise, one individual in a two-person group tends to be seen as the active initiator, while the other person acts as a passive controller (with a veto). In groups of three, two stronger members can overwhelm the weaker member, whereas four-person groups can easily deadlock, two against two. Groups of five seem to be the most personally satisfying, because they are small enough for participation yet large enough for stimulation. In addition, the possibility of a three-two split among members of a five-person group provides an ally for minority members.

Small groups offer opportunities for hands-on experiences and increased involvement and participation. (© Joel Gordon)

. . . .
Groups and Purposes
. . . .

Purposes for small groups

Small groups can serve any number of purposes. Four of the most common to social studies instruction are (1) to discuss issues or events, (2) to engage in decision-making exercises, (3) to provide small-group instruction, either remedial or enriched, and (4) to research or investigate problems or questions. Characteristics of these groups are summarized next.

DISCUSSION GROUPS

Purpose.   To provide children with opportunities to express and clarify their points of view on issues pertinent to their interests.

Size.   Two to six (enough children to stimulate interaction but not so many as to overwhelm or restrict the flow of discussion).

Establish clear and manageable tasks

Comment.   Because discussion groups can easily degenerate into rap sessions, consider establishing a task for the group, such as a conclusion, a verbal report, or a summary, that will be presented after the group's deliberations. Preprinted questions or other guides to help groups structure their discussion can also be useful.

DECISION-MAKING GROUPS

Purpose.   To provide children with experience in group consensus and in considering alternatives and arriving at a decision.

Size.   Three to seven.

Short duration

Comment.   The life of most decision-making groups is short, seldom exceeding an hour and typically shorter than that. Consequently, the social status of discussion-group members is less critical than it is in longer-range tutorial or research groups. Students can form their own decision-making groups, or members can be selected at random. Also be certain that you have realistic activities or other established procedures for the early finishers.

TUTORIAL GROUPS

Purpose.   To provide individual help or advanced work to a small group that might most need or benefit from it.

Size.   Two to nine.

Comment.   Tutorial groups provide opportunities for more immediate, direct feedback than is possible in large-group settings. However, the rest of the class will need meaningful activities while you work with a tutorial group.

RESEARCH GROUPS (INVESTIGATIVE)

Purpose. To provide students with opportunities to solve problems, research questions, pursue lines of inquiry, or prepare projects.

Organization is the key **Size.** Two to four.

Comment. The limitation on group size should be observed. Also, you may need to spend considerable time providing explicit instructions and helping the group organize itself.

. . . .

Characteristics of Effective Teacher Feedback

. . . .

Dealing effectively with students in small groups, especially those who refuse to cooperate, who don't respect the rights and opinions of others, or who refuse to accept their fair share of the work, may depend in large measure on the kind of messages you provide to them. In general your feedback must be in a form that they, either individually or as groups, can do something with (or about). The three key factors here are specificity, timing, and clarity.

Specificity. Effective feedback should identify specific behaviors that the child can modify or do something about. Statements such as "You're not smart enough to be in this group" or "You two don't care about this group" are judgments, not descriptions. Besides being unnecessarily cruel, neither statement indicates what the child should do to correct the problem. On the other hand, a statement such as "Before you proceed, you need to recheck your source of information" provides information that the child can act on.

Be as descriptive as possible

Positive feedback, such as "That was a good report" or "This group is really working well together," can be music to the ears of anyone—even if it is more judgmental than descriptive. However, negative feedback is another matter entirely. To say to Jamie, a noncooperative student, "You are not a good group member," for example, is likely to evoke Jamie's ego-defense mechanisms, especially if you state it publicly. Perhaps the only time that such a statement will *not* cause problems is if Jamie values the fact that he is *not* a good group member. To avoid such consequences, feedback should be presented descriptively, nonjudgmentally, and as your reaction. Examples:

When in doubt, add description

Poor: Jamie, you are not cooperating.
Better: You did not seem to listen to what the others were saying.

Poor: This group does not work well together.
Better: This group seems to be having difficulty deciding what information you should include in your presentation.

Timing. The most useful feedback is provided immediately after the behavior in question takes place. Sometimes, of course, you may need to delay feedback until you can deal with a student individually. For example, if a student is obviously upset about something—perhaps the death of a grandparent, or almost

When to give feedback

any of a thousand other things—it is probably not the time to criticize the student's unwillingness to cooperate; he or she is thinking about other things. Likewise, if you are upset about something, the form of your feedback may serve your needs but not the student's. A sharp "You should go along with the majority" may let you vent your feelings, but it could compound the student's problem.

Clarity.   From time to time, it may be necessary to determine whether students are receiving the messages that you think you are sending: what you intend as descriptive feedback might be regarded by the children as criticism. At other times, a student may interpret a teacher's description of a group problem as if it were the student's own fault (when it is indeed a group problem). To determine that the communication is clear, the teacher can simply ask the receiver to rephrase the feedback.

Have students rephrase the feedback

Feedback that exhibits the characteristics identified here is appropriate for both small-group work and handling discipline problems in large-group settings. In other words, a statement such as "Jamie, stop misbehaving" might be more effective if it were phrased like this: "Jamie, your persistent talking is bothering me and the people around you. Please stop." The rephrased statement identifies (1) the specific behavior in question, (2) the effects that behavior is producing in others, and (3) an appropriate course of action ("stop talking") that can eliminate the problem. Such a statement is specific, descriptive, clear, and delivered with appropriate timing—all elements of effective teacher feedback.

• • • •
Small-Group Management Practices Summarized
• • • •

As you consider cooperative group work, consider the following recommendations:

Begin with short-range tasks

1. Begin long-term group work only when you feel confident that (a) you can manage several groups operating simultaneously and (b) the individuals in each group can work together with minimal problems. You can get some idea of how individuals can work together by beginning with short-range group assignments.

Preliminary decisions

2. Decide how you plan to evaluate the group work before you begin, and then make this information known to students. If you plan to grade their reports or presentations, tell them the criteria you intend to use. They will listen intently.

Clearly defined tasks

3. Identify clearly defined tasks and products (a report, a display, etc.) for each group. It may be necessary from time to time to remind the groups to focus on their tasks, and not on the final product.

4. Present common group tasks in a whole-class format. Presenting tasks to individual groups may invite problems among groups that have nothing to do until you get around to them.

Reasonable alternatives

5. Encourage alternative ways in which groups can present the results of their efforts—videos, murals, skits, plays, charts, pictures. Long oral reports can leave much to be desired.

6. Make it clear that both group-process and content-related (but not interpersonal) problems are "fair game" for discussion in small groups or by the class as a

whole, and allow time accordingly. Obviously, immediate intervention is recommended *before* a group begins to flounder.

Reasonable deadlines

7. Establish reasonable deadlines; you can always extend them if necessary. Without deadlines, groups working on even the simplest tasks can drag on forever. Similarly, have something prepared for groups that finish early.

Teaching Activities for Active Learning

Re-creating reality

Many of the activities in the following sections are intended to re-create reality—or a slice of reality—in the classroom. Many of them also provide opportunities for children to "walk in someone else's shoes." Once that reality has been established, the children can then examine, analyze, and ultimately get a handle on the "real" reality they will face outside the classroom.

The next section begins with a brief examination of dramatic-play activities. The following sections explore expressive and enactive experiences—where children express themselves through drama or projects where they build things—as well as simulation and gaming.

Dramatic Play

Dramatic play involves the spontaneous acting out of real-life situations in structured settings. The settings can involve ships in a harbor, pioneers moving westward in the 1800s, or almost any other situation. Dramatic play differs from the play that children normally engage in because it (1) occurs in a structured setting and (2) is designed to lead to educational outcomes.

One of the myths of dramatic play is that all a teacher needs to do is toss out a few toys and blocks and then let the kids "have at it." Actually, the time and materials required to structure the room environment for dramatic play can be considerable. For example, dramatic play involving ships and ports might involve

More than meets the eye

some the following:

- Fill a large bulletin board with pictures of ships, and with the printed caption "What do these ships carry?"
- Use a smaller bulletin board to display a chart showing signal flags. Below the chart you hang four or five flags that you made from scraps of fabric. On a small table below the bulletin board are several piles of scrap cloth, preferably felt, in different colors.
- Cover a library table with books—picture books mainly—about ships and the sea.
- Hang a picture of a lighthouse above the science table. On the table you place a set of instructions on how to build a lighthouse, along with batteries, wood, wire, tacks, bulbs, and the tools required to make one.
- Place a small wooden ship (that you have built) into a large aquarium that is set on the sink counter. You also leave two or three metal ships nearby, as well as a small tagboard strip that says "Why do metal boats float?"

• • • • COMMENTARY   On Structuring the Environment

Sarah Ancell teaches third grade at Bozeman Elementary School in a city in the Southwest. She's part of a three-teacher team, who plan together, correlate their units, and occasionally trade classes for various activities.

All teachers on the team—Kippy Broderson, Sharon Newsom, and Sarah—agree that third grade is the upper limit for dramatic-play activities, and even then it's borderline. Some third graders take well to dramatic play, but often the children who don't like it make fun of those who do. As Kippy says, "At this grade level, we don't think it's worth the risk." "But," Sarah adds quickly, "we think the classroom environment is *really* important, regardless of how old the kids are."

It's impossible to describe all the different ways that Sarah and the Bozeman team arrange their classroom environments, so one example will have to suffice. When the students come down the hallway one morning, they find a huge tree—made from brown and tan colored paper and covering what used to be a pillar—its branches extending most of the way across the hallway ceiling. You can tell the tree is made from paper but it is still fairly realistic.

At first the tree's branches are bare, but a couple of days later, the branches are covered with pink blossoms. The children aren't too surprised because they made the flowers in art class. A few days later, green leaves appear among the blossoms; then the blossoms disappear and

only the leaves remain. The "branches" that hang down from the classroom ceilings mimic the changes in the tree in the hallway. Soon, tiny green apples appear, then larger green apples, and finally red apples. After a day when everyone has had an apple for a snack, both the apples and the green leaves disappear, replaced by yellow, gold, and red leaves. A few days later, the colored leaves disappear, and the tree returns to its original barren state.

As the tree and the classroom go through their various stages, children record the events in their journals. The students also do an assortment of activities related to plants, trees, and apples. They determine the average number of seeds in an apple in math; they make applesauce—after which they write the directions for "How to Make Applesauce"; they read the story of Johnny Appleseed (Kellogg, 1988) and plot his travels on a map; they study—what kinds of trees grow where, what kinds of trees lose their leaves, and what kinds keep their leaves in winter; they study products made from wood; and they read Shel Silverstein's *The Giving Tree* (1964).

Lest there be any question about it, the social environment in those classrooms is as warm and supportive as the physical environment is spectacular. But are all the decorations worth the tremendous amount of time and the considerable expense they require? Obviously, Sarah Ancell and her colleagues think so.

- Pin a six- to eight-foot piece of butcher paper (that will take tempera paint) to the wall in one corner of the room. Place cans of paint and brushes nearby. Above the paper is a picture of a port, and on the floor below the paper you place enough scraps of lumber so the children can build breakwaters, docks, and so on.

Rotating activities

The items in the preceding list should be regarded as a minimum. If you have a very small classroom, you could add one or two activities each day (and remove one or more of the existing ones). Doing dramatic play well requires that there be enough materials in different parts of the room so that all students are not crowded into one corner.

On the first day of the activity, give the class time to (a) explore their new environment and (b) whet their appetites for what is to come. After ten to fifteen minutes, you could call all the children together, divide the class into four groups, then send two groups off as "players" and keep the other two groups together as "watchers." After another fifteen to twenty minutes, you could rotate the groups. After everyone has had a chance to experience at least one

KEY IDEA

The debriefings that follow group activities are often as important as the activities themselves.

element/activity of the new environment, it is appropriate to help the group reflect on what they have seen and done.

Limitations and Outcomes. Dramatic-play activities are best suited to children who also engage in real-play activities. This means that dramatic-play activities are restricted largely to the lower elementary grades. If you were to use the activity described here with fifth or sixth graders, expect to be accused of treating them like babies. On the other hand, dramatic activities—minus the "play" components—often work well with older students.

Dramatic play requires extensive preplanning, a significant amount of varied materials, and ideally a large classroom. Dramatic play can also be done in small classrooms, but the management tasks become a bigger issue. In summary, well-planned dramatic play can have the following outcomes:

Possible outcomes

- Stimulates questions that children can then research
- Provides a means for children to use and understand concepts and symbols
- Reveals needs that can be addressed in subsequent instruction
- Stimulates other expressive activities (painting, models, etc.)
- Reveals new information and understandings the children have gained

Role-Playing

In role-playing activities, one child might role-play a father or mother, another child might play an author, and still others might play any one of a variety of different roles. In dramatic-play activities, several children may play a particular role, sometimes simultaneously. Likewise, in dramatic play there is usually no audience and everyone is involved in the "play." In role-playing activities, one or more students reenact a situation while the rest of the class acts as observers. In some role-playing situations, such as the "author's chair" example that follows, the audience may be invited to participate.

The Author's Chair Example

Setting. An empty armchair, designated as the "author's chair," has been placed in the front of Janet Jacobsen's classroom. Sometimes student authors sit in the chair when they share their writings with the class. At other times, students who have studied the works of a particular author sit in the chair and role-play the author as other students interview them. On this day a fifth grader, Becky Rodgers [alias Nathaniel Hawthorne], is sitting in the chair.

BECKY: I'm pleased to be with you today.

MRS. JACOBSEN [interrupting Jason who was about to speak]: On behalf of our entire class I want to welcome you here today, Mr. Hawthorne.

JASON: Yeah. And are you the one who wrote our "Pine Tree Shillings" thing?

BECKY: What makes you ask that, sir?

JASON: 'Cuz that sheet Mrs. Jacobsen gave us said "Hawthorne" on it.

BECKY: Well, I've written many things, like *The Scarlet Letter, Twice Told Tales, The House of Seven Gables,* and lots of others. And yes, the "Pine Tree Shillings" is from something I wrote.

Interviewing the "author"

AARON: Did you really see them put Becky Hull on the scales and match her weight in silver?

BECKY: No, that happened 150 years before I was born. When I was a student at Bowdoin College, I used to write articles that I sold to newspapers and magazines. That's how I got my spending money. And that's when I wrote the "Pine Tree Shillings" article.

AARON: Oh!

CINDI: You mean people back then really paid people to marry their daughters?

BECKY: Yes, ma'am. Some traditions the Puritans brought with them from England continued while they were here.

CINDI: I thought that those people came here to have . . . what do you call it, religious freedom?

BECKY (patronizingly): I think you may be confusing the Puritans and the Pilgrims, my dear.

CINDI: Oh!

> ### ☀ SUGGESTED ACTIVITY
> Decide the extent to which attention to the environment, such as Sarah and her colleagues (see the Commentary, "On Structuring the Environment") establish in their classrooms, is essential, desirable, or simply a frill.

The intent in dramatic play is to re-create an experience so that as the children play they will get a vicarious feel for that experience and raise questions that lead to further research and investigation. The intent in role-playing is to provide children with opportunities to experience and *analyze a problem situation.* There is not much of a problematic nature associated with ships in a harbor, for example, as opposed to, say, a situation in which a pioneer family is moving west and, because of space restrictions, must decide between taking the family Bible or a set of heirloom china. The Bible-china question *might* arise during a dramatic play involving pioneers moving westward, but as a rule, role-playing situations are more narrowly defined. To this extent, role-playing is somewhat more structured and teacher-directed than dramatic play.

Analyzing alternatives

In role-playing activities one or more students reenact a situation while the rest of the class acts as observers. How a role-playing group resolves a problem becomes the focus for discussion and analysis after the enactment is completed. However, unlike plays in which the actors follow a script, role-playing situations are open-ended, and the role players must decide how to resolve the situation.

Role of the audience

Walking in someone else's shoes

Role-playing activities are sometimes used to help students develop a sense of social consciousness—to help them experience what it is like to "walk in another person's moccasins," that is, to view an issue or problem from another person's perspective. Role-playing can also help sensitize students to the idea that maintaining a win-lose posture, one in which "I am right and they are wrong," often serves only to perpetuate a problem.

The goal of most role-playing activities is to help children say, "This is where he or she seems to be coming from." When that is said, the basis for consensus building and resolving problems may have been laid.

Procedure. The typical procedures for handling role-playing activities are as follows:

Role-playing procedures

1. "Warming up" the group (confronting the problem)
2. Identifying the role-playing participants
3. Setting the task for the observers (the audience)
4. Setting the stage
5. The actual role-playing (enactment)
6. Follow-up
   6.1 Discussing the enactment
   6.2 Possible modification of the situation by revising the roles, suggesting next steps, or exploring alternative possibilities, all of which may lead to further enactment
   6.3 Further discussion/more enactments
   6.4 Sharing reactions to the overall experience and further debriefing

Role-Playing and Decision Making

Format

Role-playing is often a part of decision-making activities. Depending on the way you arrange the activity, you can emphasize either the role-playing dimension or the decision-making dimension. The format for role-playing and decision-making activities is illustrated in the Model Student Activity entitled "The Lunch Policy." It involves (1) an open-ended problematic situation and (2) roles for the students to play.

Unstructured Role-Playing

In all role-playing activities, students must deal with a problematic situation. Teachers must identify the role players and be certain that everyone understands the situation. In other words, there is a certain amount of teacher direction in all role-playing activities, as well as a certain amount of spontaneity.

Unstructured: Limited teacher direction

Most of the role-playing examples presented thus far are unstructured; that is, the role players define their roles without specific teacher direction. In "The Lunch Policy," the teacher may have no idea how the situation will be resolved or whether the role players will become aware of all the factors that might influence the decision. In unstructured role-playing, teachers cannot be certain that a specific issue (such as safety in crossing the street) will emerge from the role-playing enactment. Of course, a teacher could introduce a neglected issue (such as the safety element) in the follow-up discussion, but teachers who want to be certain that specific issues are considered in the role-playing enactment can use a structured role-playing format.

MODEL STUDENT ACTIVITY

The Lunch Policy

Provide the following information to students.

A fast-food restaurant (e.g., McDonald's or Burger King) is to open next week across the street from Meridian Elementary School. Some students have requested permission to eat lunch there. Currently students must eat at school, or they may go home for lunch if they bring a signed permission slip from their parents. The principal has called a meeting with the following people:

- A parent
- A student
- A cafeteria director
- A teacher

Tell students that the group must decide what to do.

Procedure

Role-Playing Option

Identify students to play each of the roles, and have them try to arrive at a decision agreeable to everyone. The rest of the class should discuss and evaluate both their decision and the procedures they used in arriving at it.

Decision-Making Option

Divide the class into small groups with each student taking a role. When all groups have made their decisions, they should be reported and evaluated by the class as a whole.

· · · ·

Structured Role-Playing

· · · ·

Structured: Includes roles and sample positions

The element that distinguishes structured from unstructured role-playing is the addition of positions or points of view that the role players must incorporate into their enactments. For example, if you are concerned that students will not know how a cafeteria director might feel about the lunch policy question, you could structure the activity by adding position statements to the roles in the previous Model Student Activity, as illustrated below:

1. A parent wants her children eating well-balanced meals, not hamburgers every day.
2. A student feels that the school should not dictate eating habits.
3. The cafeteria director needs a full cafeteria to meet operating expenses.
4. The teacher doesn't want to be bothered with permission slips and feels it is up to the parents and children to decide where lunch will be eaten.

Modified model

The modified model for structured role-playing activities reflects the following elements:

1. an open-ended problematic situation,
2. roles for the individuals involved, and
3. position statements for each role player.

You are obviously free to add other roles or positions. Or you might use a mixture of each, specifying positions for some roles while leaving others open so that players can operate according to their convictions. Your procedure should be dictated by your objectives. If you wish to heighten the sense of drama and add an element of mystery, you can distribute the role positions on separate slips of paper so that, initially, only the role players know who they are. This approach tends to heighten interest at the outset of role-playing.

Providing Background Information.   For structured role-playing activities such as "The Lunch Policy," providing simple position statements is usually adequate. In other instances, however, and especially in historical situations, such as having the class role-play a negotiating session between the American colonists and the British to avoid the Revolutionary War, matters are best not left simply to your students' imaginations. Rather, the role players will need enough information so they can address the situation intelligently and accurately.

Historical settings

There are basically two ways to handle the background-information requirement for structured role-playing activities. One option is to treat the role-playing as a culminating activity that occurs *after* the class has studied the historical period or situation. Even then, some intensive review may be necessary. A second option is to provide role players with background information that you have written or otherwise duplicated from a suitable source for them. The second option can be time-consuming, especially when you consider that the role players need sufficient time, perhaps even overnight, to digest the information you give them. The main point here is that the amount of advanced preparation necessary for structured role-playing activities will vary with the complexity of the situations your students will be focusing on.

Options

Handling Conflict.   If you choose to use role-playing activities with conflicting role positions, you must be prepared to help the group cope with the disputes that are almost guaranteed to occur. Many of us have been taught that conflict is bad, something to be avoided, yet in many real-life situations, conflict is unavoidable. Acting as if conflict does not exist does not make it disappear. Students need to view conflict as a reality of human life. However, they also need to understand that conflict can be managed if it is addressed directly, and the process of doing that can often yield creative and mutually agreeable solutions to problems. In other words, part of the purpose of some role-playing activities can be to explore ways in which conflict-based win-lose situations can be converted into consensus-building win-win situations.

Helping students deal with conflict

● ● ● ● Simulation and Gaming

Simulations are instructional activities in which elements from the real world are re-created (or simulated) in the classroom. For example, after an experience in which the classroom is turned into a miniature factory to mass-produce valentine cards (see Resource Handbook), students have an opportunity to discuss what it is like to perform a task over and over again, as one would on a real assembly line. Likewise, in the computer simulation *Oregon Trail*, students have an opportunity to experience the tribulations of traveling west in a covered wagon during the nineteenth century. If students playing *Oregon Trail* do not plan properly, they may die before reaching their destination—as real pioneers sometimes did. If death occurs, they can try to do better in the next round.

Real-world models

The real world provides the model on which almost all simulations and many games are based. If you drive around Atlantic City, New Jersey, you will encounter street names such as Baltic Avenue, St. James Place, and Park Place, and the Boardwalk. Even the socioeconomic levels of the various neighborhoods roughly parallel the property values on a Monopoly board—or they did when the game of Monopoly was developed in the 1920s. That's because the model for Monopoly is based on real estate transactions in Atlantic City, New Jersey. But, to make a game of it, the Monopoly developers had to take some liberties with reality by adding more chance factors than are found in the real world. For example, you cannot buy property in Monopoly unless you land on the property, and where you land depends on the roll of the dice. Other chance factors include "Community Chest" and "Chance" cards, "Go to Jail," "Luxury Tax," and "Income Tax." All these make Monopoly fun to play, because you never know what will happen next, but the chance factor in Monopoly so exceeds reality that you can't use the game to teach the principles of real estate investment and development.

Situations usually have outcomes, but not winners

Many games are simply contests in which winning is determined by a combination of prior knowledge, luck, and skill. These include those old classroom standbys, spelling bees and Twenty Questions, and the takeoffs on TV game shows like *Jeopardy!* Most simulations, on the other hand, lack the contest quality of games. All simulations have an outcome—a result—but these usually lack the clear flavor of winning or losing that is typical of most games. In addition, because the chance or luck factor in simulations is usually lower than in most games, simulations tend to be more realistic.

● ● ● ●

Computer-Based Simulations

● ● ● ●

Computer-based simulations usually have the ability to reflect more real-world complexities than are possible through nontechnological means. For example, as pioneers journeyed westward during the nineteenth century, they encountered one set of problems as they crossed the plains and different problems as they crossed the deserts and the mountains. In the *Oregon Trail* simulation that was noted earlier, computers make it possible to replicate conditions that pioneers faced at various points on their journey. A somewhat similar situation prevails for the computer-based simulation *The Golden Spike* (National Geographic Society), in which players are involved in building the transcontinental railroad. If players spend too much money purchasing rails and ties and don't allocate enough money for food and wages for workers, they too must beware. Thus computer-based simulations can take information from a player's prior decisions and incorporate it into the next decision that the player must make.

Computer-based simulations incorporate many variables

TECHNOLOGY

Some computer-based simulations provide excellent opportunities for children to use map skills. In the simulation *Geography Search* (McGraw-Hill), players must make navigation decisions as they sail to the New World. The computer then provides them with the precise location of their ship. Likewise, in the simulation

SimCity 2000, players must become the planner, designer, and mayor of one or more cities.

Limitations. The number of computer-based simulations for social studies is increasing, but there are still very few for primary-level children. The fact that children must be able to read the instructions on the monitor is often a limitation for very young students. In addition, some programs may require knowledge that students do not have. For example, the simulation *Rails West* is about building the transcontinental railroad. It requires prior knowledge about financial markets (stocks, bonds, and debentures) that even adults can find taxing. Far less difficult is the simulation *Railroad Tycoon,* in which students can watch their locomotives chugging across the landscape.

May require prior knowledge

Many simulations (noncomputer-based) are designed or can be adapted for an entire class. However, unless you have access to a local area network, computer-based simulations are usually limited to one or two participants. The length of time it takes for an entire class to experience a particular simulation depends on the number of computers available, of course, but restrictions on the number of players are sometimes another limitation.

Limited number of players at one time

Steps for Designing a Simulation or Game

Designing a simulation or game begins with an idea. After that, it requires some materials, a little creativity, and often more time than you might imagine. The steps for designing a simulation or game are as follows:

Helpful procedures

1. Identify the process or system that you want to simulate.

2. Identify the specific characteristics of the system or process. These include the various stages in the process or system and any human components that are involved. It may be necessary to narrow your focus; for example, simulating only part of the nineteenth-century factory system, not the entire system.

3. Decide which characteristics of the system or process you wish to emphasize and which you are willing to omit.

4. Decide which format—simulation or game—is best suited to the topic.

5. Decide what the players will be doing. Will they be making something, playing a role, moving tokens around a board, or what?

6. Decide on an outcome. When will the simulation or game end—after the players have reached a decision, been reelected, reached "home," made the most points, or after time expires?

7. Decide how you will introduce the chance element (to make the activity more interesting). Make certain that negative and positive chance factors are equally balanced.

8. Simulations only: Decide how you will get information to the players. Will each player get different roles? Separate instructions?

9. Decide if everything you have decided on thus far "fits" together. If it does, begin developing or collecting whatever materials you will need.

TECHNOLOGY UPDATE

Using Interactive CD-ROMs

The year is 1492. Your monitor is displaying an animation of Queen Isabella and King Ferdinand's throne room in Spain. The king and queen are there, along with Queen Isabella's confessor, a brown-robed Franciscan monk named Francisco Jimenez de Cisneros, and a young adventurer, Christopher Columbus, who is pleading with Ferdinand and Isabella to allow him to find a new route to the Orient. After Ferdinand and Isabella agree to fund Columbus's voyage, the scene shifts to a view from a ship just offshore from a Caribbean island. Occasionally the scene also shifts to Columbus talking with one of his officers about what they might find on the island. If you move the cursor to the brush along the island's shoreline, you can view a closeup of what Columbus and his crew will encounter when they come ashore. Depending on where you place the cursor, you may see more junglelike terrain, and sometimes you will discover natives huddled in the underbrush. If you don't place the cursor on the different locations, you will simply follow Columbus as he lands on the island. The materials on this CD-ROM are called "interactive" because they permit viewers to examine elements they want to look at in more detail.

The above scenario is a segment from a CD-ROM called "Explorers of the New World" (Learning Company,

$49). Christopher Columbus is one of several fifteenth-through seventeenth-century explorers, including Magellan, De Soto, and Henry Hudson, whose voyages are chronicled on this software. The explorers are fully animated, and some of them occasionally share their hopes and concerns with viewers. The actor who portrays Columbus reads accounts from the real journals of Columbus's voyages to the New World.

Just as impressive as "Explorers" is the CD-ROM "The Alamo: Victory or Death" (Archimedia Interactive, $140). Narrated by people like newscaster Dan Rather and with music of the period performed by contemporary country music stars like Johnny Cash and Mel Tellis, this two CD-ROM set presents more information than any teacher and class can possibly cover. Highlights include an interactive tour of the Alamo as it was before Santa Anna's attack, a re-creation of the siege of the Alamo as seen from a bird's-eye view, and detailed views of weapons and materials from the period. One notable segment shows viewers how to load a flintlock musket, and then viewers practice shooting at a rabbit that runs across the screen. Because most muskets were not very accurate, the rabbit usually makes it across the screen safely.

10. Prepare a preliminary set of written rules or directions.

11. Try out the simulation or game on a small group of "guinea pigs." (This is one of the most essential steps in the entire process—you'll be amazed at what you forgot to consider.)

12. Make necessary adjustments as indicated by the field test.

● ● ● ● Expressive and Enactive Experiences

Terms defined

Expressive experiences are activities in which children have an opportunity to express themselves through drama—plays, skits, pageants, and so on—or through dramatic play, music, role-playing, or other forms of sociodrama. *Enactive experiences*, which are sometimes called *projects*, are activities in which students build or create something, such as models or murals. Opportunities for children to express their creative or artistic talents are common to both experiences.

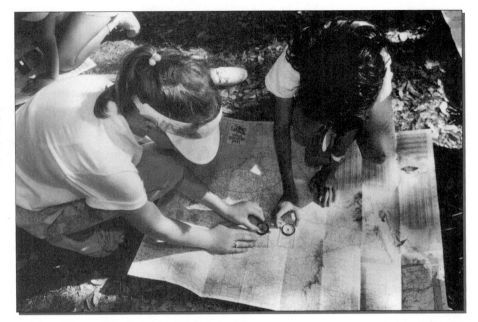

Many hands-on activities require that students apply what they know in problem-solving situations.
(©Bob Daemmrich/The Image Works)

Include research or problem solving

Most worthwhile enactive experiences incorporate a *research* or *problem-solving* dimension. For example, before boiling the first grain of rice for a Japanese meal, students should have identified what might be served at such a meal, what ingredients are used in the various dishes, how the foods are prepared and served, and on what occasions they are eaten. In other words, the guiding question here is, What are the components of a typical Japanese meal? Similarly, before building a model dairy farm, students should have compared a series of pictures of dairy farms (or visited dairy farms, if that is feasible) to identify their common characteristics. And before cooking that pioneer meal, students should have researched the foods available to the pioneers—for example, see *The Little House Cookbook* (Walker, 1979).

SUMMARY

Teaching strategies are the ways in which teachers orchestrate a variety of day-to-day teaching techniques—such as discussions, minilectures, case studies, and student projects—to achieve desired learning goals. How teachers do this will vary according to their philosophy of teaching and their instructional purposes. Teachers whose purpose is to convey information to students are likely to adopt a teacher-directed "telling" or expository orientation, whereas teachers who want to foster their students' ability to engage in independent inquiry are more likely to adopt a student-centered orientation. However, many teachers adopt a mixed orientation: sometimes they play

the primary role, and at other times the students play the active role.

The distinction between teacher-directed and student-directed teaching strategies highlights two different teaching orientations. Unfortunately, some people mistakenly assume that the term *student-centered* means that the teacher designs a few activities and then lets students take over. Students in a student-centered classroom often have considerable responsibility for what they are learning, and in some cases, not all students will be learning the same things (as was evident in Janet Jacobsen's classroom at the beginning of this chapter). Yet despite the inherent appeal of being a student-centered teacher, there are countless times when teacher-directed instruction is wholly appropriate. It is largely a question of purpose, not simply a matter of style.

Some teaching activities that highlight student involvement include dramatic play, role-playing, simulations and games, and a variety of expressive and enactive experiences. In some instances, teachers can organize these activities in ways that range from highly structured, such as providing step-by-step instructions, to very loosely structured, as in giving students a task and then leaving how they proceed totally up to them. The basic rule here

is that the more teachers structure an activity, the more they may lose spontaneity and creativity. The associated tradeoff is that what is lost in spontaneity may be offset by greater assurance that students will consider the issues and questions that were built into a more structured activity. Whatever kind of group-based strategy you opt to use—structured or unstructured, expressive or enactive—will ultimately depend on your purposes for developing the activity in the first place. Yet regardless of which type of activity you use, a key element in all of them is debriefing students afterward.

SUGGESTED READINGS AND RESOURCES

Print Resources

Bill Bigelow. (1994). Role plays: Show, don't tell. In *Rethinking our classrooms: Teaching for equity and justice*. Milwaukee, WI: Rethinking Schools, 114–115. In this brief article on developing role-playing activities, Bigelow suggests that this strategy consistently brings students to life.

Bruce Joyce, Marsha Weil, & Emily Calhoun. (2003). *Models of teaching* (7th ed.). Boston: Pearson Allyn & Bacon. This volume ranks among the landmark texts in education because it was one of the first to reduce the mountain of literature dealing with teaching strategies to manageable terms.

Stephanie Steffy & Wendy J. Hood. (Eds.). (1994). *If this is social studies, why isn't it boring?* York, ME: Stenhouse. The fifteen, first-person vignettes in this book describe how teachers and others modified the ways in which they taught social studies to make it more student-centered.

Internet Resources

Introductory Note: Web sites sometimes change their Internet addresses or cease operating entirely. All the addresses supplied here were operating when this book was printed, but if any of them fails to work properly, enter the desired topic into any standard search engine.

Teaching Strategies

http://www.ca.sandia.gov/outreach/2020/2020/Tstrat.html

This site is maintained by the Mid-Atlantic Association for Cooperation in Education and offers everything you ever wanted to know about cooperative learning and other student-centered teaching strategies. *Bookmark quality.*

AskERIC

http://ericir.syr.edu

This site contains thousands of lesson plans and other resources on a variety of topics.

Constructivist Project Guide

http://www.ilt.columbia.edu/k12/1ivetextnf/webcurr.html

This site, based at Columbia University, offers assistance on developing cooperative learning units.

Teachers Helping Teachers

http://www.pacificnet.net/-mandel/

Although this site focuses on teachers sharing their insights with others, it also offers resources and information on a variety of topics.

Maximizing Learning in Small Groups

http://www.CS.ukc.ac.uk/national/CSDN/html/EDUres/small-group-learning.html

This British site offers useful guidelines for using small-group instruction.

Role Playing: Tea at the White House

http://ericir.syr.edu/Virtual/Lessons/Social-St/US-history/USHOOO3.html

This site offers detailed lesson plans that use role-playing techniques.

American Revolution Simulation

http://ericir.syr.edu/Virtual/lessons/Social-St/US-history/USHOO27.html

This entry reflects one of the middle-grade lesson plans available at this site that uses simulation techniques to help students understand why the American colonies declared their independence.

Applications of Role Playing

http://www.nova.edu/~aed/horizons/vol9n1

and

http://gis.joensuu.fi/research/openuniv/ openuniv2.html

These sites illustrate how role-playing strategies have been applied to distance learning and international education.

Nurturing Critical and Reflective Thinking

KEY QUESTIONS

- **How does one teach students to process information critically and reflectively?**

- **What kinds of materials and activities do teachers use to teach reflective thinking?**

- **What is decision making, and how does it relate to reflective thinking?**

- **How do teachers decide which questions to ask, and when to ask them?**

● ● ● ● Introduction: Reading Between the Lines

Going beyond the printed word

"Reading between the lines" sounds innocent enough, but explaining it to young children can be challenging. Part of the problem is that even beginning readers know that the spaces between the lines on a page are blank. The situation is complicated further because "reading between the lines" is a figurative expression, like "it's raining cats and dogs." Even children who realize that you are speaking figuratively may still have no idea what you are talking about. Of course, you could explain that "reading between the lines" involves taking two or more pieces of information and then relating them in some way to produce a third idea that goes beyond the original information, but don't be surprised if your students still look puzzled.

Modeling is the key

Despite the complexity of its definition, "reading between the lines" is not that difficult to do, especially if the children have some previous experiences with it. However, instead of beginning with questions like "What is the author really saying?" or "What does the author really mean?," you could begin by saying something like "Let's see if we can figure out what this author is really saying," and then systematically modeling (demonstrating) your thinking processes for the children. In other words, questioning alone does not teach children the process. Most questioning strategies are primarily a test of children's existing ability. Reading between the lines and most other reflective thinking skills are best taught through techniques other than questioning. These include: (1) modeling the desired behaviors, including talking out loud as you think through the problem, (2) accompanying the modeling with clear explanations,

KEY IDEA

Teachers and students can model their thinking processes by talking out loud with each other.

Goals

(3) working with students as they practice the skills on related information, and then (4) talking (reflecting) with students about these experiences.

This chapter addresses three goals. The first is to help you identify the thinking skills that students should develop, including metacognition, or thinking about thinking. The second is to illustrate how reflective thinking skills are part of a family of interrelated skills, and the third is to present some exemplary teaching activities that can help students process information efficiently and effectively.

● ● ● ● ● How Critical Thinking Differs from Other Kinds of Thinking: Terminology Clarified

When people talk about thinking—that largely unseen process that goes on in a person's mind—they risk encountering a morass of confusing terminology. Some people talk about critical thinking, others talk about creative thinking, and still others talk about problem solving and decision making, or other related terms. These are not different terms for the same thing.

One of the enduring guides for making sense of the terminology and mental processes related to thinking is Bloom's (Bloom et al, 1956) landmark work, *The Taxonomy of Educational Objectives: Cognitive Domain.* Commonly referred to as the *Taxonomy,* the original work has recently been revised (see Anderson & Krathwohl, 2001). Nevertheless, Bloom's work still remains the standard in the field. The six-stage *Taxonomy* is often posted in an abbreviated form in many classrooms across the country. Briefly, the major classifications of the *Taxonomy,* in order, are (1) Knowledge, (2) Comprehension, (3) Application, (4) Analysis, (5) Synthesis, and (6) Evaluation.

Lower-level thinking

The first two levels of the *Taxonomy,* Knowledge and Comprehension, are fairly straightforward. Knowledge refers to remembering previously learned material, whereas comprehension refers to grasping the meaning of (or understanding) certain material. The distinction between these categories is illustrated by young children who can recite the Pledge of Allegiance perfectly, but who have no idea what "one nation, indivisible" means.

Levels Three through Six of the *Taxonomy* become increasingly complex, as do the examples. Application, Level Three, refers to the ability to apply previously learned material in new situations. For example: Los Angeles is located (approximately) 60 degrees west of Boston. When it is noon in Boston, what time is it in Los Angeles? The student must remember that the earth rotates about fifteen degrees in an hour, and then apply that information to the problem. Level Four, Analysis, refers to the ability to break material down into its component parts so as to identify possible relationships between and among the various parts. For example, consider two statements such as "Judy has not eaten for over a day. She must be hungry." Upon analyzing these statements, the person should be able to distinguish between the fact (Judy not eating) and the inference (being hungry). The person should also be able to determine whether a third fact, such as the height of the world's tallest building, is relevant to the two prior statements (No—unless Judy happens to be trapped on the 107th floor!).

Higher-level thinking

Levels Five and Six of the *Taxonomy*, Synthesis and Evaluation, are more complex than the lower levels and thus resist simple examples such as those provided thus far. Synthesis refers to the ability to take existing parts and put them together in ways that create a new whole. Examples at this level include: writing a well-organized theme or speech, and creating a new scheme for classifying objects (events, or ideas). Consider the possibility of creating (or asking students to create) a scheme for classifying the various actions that have preceded the outbreak of war over the last three centuries. Certain actions, such as the Boston Tea Party, for example, might be considered antagonistic. Other actions could well be conciliatory.

Level Six, Evaluation, is the most complex level of the *Taxonomy*, but ironically it is also one of the easiest to misinterpret. Evaluation refers to making judgments about the value of certain materials in relation to *definite and previously identified criteria*. The criteria may be either internal, as in judging the organization of a speech or theme, or external, as in judging whether a speech or theme is relevant to a proposed topic or position. At this level, the evaluator must describe the relationship between the speech, theme, or whatever, and the previously identified

Evaluation is *not* a matter of personal opinion

criteria. Thus, for an evaluator to say, for example, "I liked it," is *not* acceptable at this level. To be acceptable, the evaluator must explain the explicit and previously identified criteria that he or she used to arrive at the decision. Everyone is entitled to their personal opinion, of course, but feelings and impressions based on private (personal) criteria are not acceptable according to the standards for this category. It is a matter of private versus public criteria. To fit this category, the evaluation criteria must be both public and identified beforehand, which necessarily excludes personal opinions.

In the next section, the foregoing explanation of the *Taxonomy* is used as a basis for examining thinking, creative thinking, critical thinking, and problem solving.

Thinking

Many of us may recall hearing our teachers say, "OK boys and girls, Let's put our 'thinking caps' on." Although you could debate whether anyone can take their "thinking cap" off, such requests are more likely to reflect efforts to forewarn children that a "tough one"—a question, problem, or whatever—is coming.

"Thinking" is a global term

Thinking encompasses such a wide range of cognitive activities that asking children "to put their thinking caps on" is probably meaningless to most of them. On the other hand, such requests may reflect a subtle way of saying "pay attention." Other global requests, such as "I want you to think about this one," probably have the same effect. Such requests probably do little to influence a child's ability to think, but then they probably do no harm either.

Creative Thinking

Focuses on new or novel approaches

When teachers ask students to think creatively, they are in effect asking children to create new or novel approaches to a problem. In other words, the teachers are asking children to create, devise, plan, or generate—all terms associated with

Level Five, Synthesis, of the *Taxonomy*—ways to combat a problem. Hunger, for example, is obviously a very real problem in some areas around the world, so asking children to identify ways to combat world hunger would be an appropriate focus for creative thinking. The process of identifying such possibilities is usually referred to as *brainstorming.* Brainstorming generates a pool of possible solutions to a problem, but without evaluating individual recommendations until the entire pool has been created.

Shifts from synthesis to evaluation After suggestions for new ideas for combating world hunger have slowed down considerably (but before students become bored), the focus of creative thinking shifts from Synthesis—the creation of novel ideas—to Level Six, Evaluation. The ultimate question at this level is "Which of these suggestions is best?" However, the more basic question, consistent with the *Taxonomy,* is "How should we evaluate these suggestions?" The purpose here is to identify the criteria for separating workable suggestions from the unworkable and whimsical. In other words, before deciding whether sending additional food to the needy is a good solution to the problem of world hunger, criteria must be identified for distinguishing between more workable and less workable solutions.

Critical Thinking

Critical thinking Critical thinking differs from its other thinking cousins by its focus on working with information, especially primary source or uninterpreted information. The main elements of critical thinking include *analyzing and interpreting information (data) in ways that lead to* one or more of the following:

- Hypothesizing about differences and similarities across examples
- Evaluating explanatory hypotheses in light of additional data or examples
- Making plausible inferences that can be tested with additional data or examples
- Drawing conclusions and/or generalizing based on the data or examples

KEY IDEA

Critical and reflective thinking skills are part of an interactive system of mental activities that we use to interpret and assess different kinds of information and experience.

The "Nation X" Model Student Activity that appears later in this chapter illustrates the elements of critical thinking, as does The American Farmer Fact Sheet that appears on page 350.

Problem Solving

There are essentially two types of problem solving. The first and probably most common is what students do in math class when they work through sets of problems to identify the right (or correct) answer. The second type of problem solving involves situations (not usually found in math classes) where there are "best," **What kind of problem is it?** "more appropriate," or even multiple solutions. The "Where Would You Locate Your City?" Model Student Activity, which appears on pages 346 and 347, is an example of the second type of problem solving. Briefly, students are provided with different kinds of maps (topographical, rainfall, vegetation, etc.) of an area that they use to identify where (in the area) they will locate their city. Because different factors can influence their decision, there is not a single "right" answer, but rather several "better" answers, all equally defensible. The "Who Is Qualified for the Presidency?" Model Student Activity in Chapter 1 also reflects the second type of problem solving. As you may recall, in that activity the student's "problem" is determining which candidates are best and least qualified to hold that office. Once again, different groups of students may arrive at different solutions.

● ● ● ● ● Metacognition: Thinking About Thinking

Helping students become proficient thinkers and decision makers involves providing them with opportunities to process various kinds of information and experience. However, teaching students how to think critically will not necessarily make them self-directed, independent thinkers. The information-processing skills dealt with in this chapter will certainly provide the basis for independent, self-directed thinking and decision making, but actually helping students to consciously direct their thinking requires going a step further.

Helping students become conscious of what thinking involves

The goal is to help students reach the highest and most sophisticated level of thinking—consciously controlling and directing their own thinking. This means that individuals must think about *how* they are thinking while they think. For example, when you are considering a problem and you say to yourself something like, "I really ought to consider some alternative solutions," you are monitoring or exercising control over how you are thinking. Doing this—thinking about how one is thinking—is called *metacognition*.

KEY IDEA

Metacognition involves thinking about one's thinking processes.

Most authorities (Beyer, 1987) agree that metacognition develops slowly, apparently paralleling students' ability to think abstractly. Although Beyer suggests that "it is doubtful that most older students will engage in metacognition by the time they leave school" (p. 195), there are still things teachers can do to foster readiness for metacognition. These include

A thinking environment

maintaining a learning environment where thinking (as opposed to memorization and rote learning) is encouraged and valued. Also important is directing explicit attention to the components of thinking and problem solving as you model and use them with children. For example, asking "Does it look like we are getting anywhere?" or saying "Let's think about some other possibilities" can stimulate students' awareness of metacognitive behavior.

Other activities to stimulate readiness for metacognition, cited by Beyer (1987, pp. 196–197), include the following:

Activities to stimulate metacognition

1. *Conscious choosing.* Whenever students have an opportunity to make a choice—determining what to do next in class or what to do for recess, and so on—have them identify at least two options and then identify some possible consequences of each option. By reflecting aloud on the consequences, students can articulate criteria for making the choice and extend their thinking beyond the here and now to the anticipation of future events or ideas.

2. *Categorizing with multiple criteria.* Whenever students have an opportunity to discuss their actions or choices, have them make at least two categories, such as useful/not useful or like/not like or fun/not fun, and so on. Like the preceding activity, this activity extends student thinking and requires thinking about another thinking act.

Paraphrasing

3. *Paraphrasing what is heard.* Have students restate, put in their own words, or elaborate one another's plans and actions as they engage in them or observe their peers engaging in them. This may take the form of having students state goals, suggest ways to accomplish them, and try to outline exactly what would have to be done to carry out their "plan." They can also restate or paraphrase directions, or rate and discuss their own understanding of something. [Author's note: This activity and those that follow can be done orally, but they are also excellent topics for students to include in their journals.]

4. *Reflecting on how an answer was derived.* Have the students, on occasion, stop in the middle of a thinking task to discuss whether they are doing it correctly, exactly where they are in the process, whether they skipped anything and/or what to do next (and why) once they resume the process. Students can also predict the results of a thinking task and, when finished with it, reflect on and discuss the extent to which their prediction was accurate, whether or not anything occurred to alter it, and so on.

"I think" activities

5. *Engaging in "I think" activities.* After or before engaging in a thinking task, students can write a short paragraph describing how they were thinking about it. At first, such writing may be a disjointed stream of consciousness, but students can focus eventually on reporting how and why they did or planned to do a task in a specific way.

6. *Making plans.* Students can plan classroom activities and assignments in terms of goals, sequence of activities, and anticipated obstacles; list the plan on the board; and refer to it as they execute it. Upon concluding the activity or assignment, they can evaluate their plan as well as the success of their activity.

To Beyer's list I am inclined to add a seventh element: "Limitation: Despite everything that we think we know, we also recognize that there are things we need to know more about, and that we might also be wrong somewhere along the way."

Modeling attitudes of reflective thinking

Modeling the desired behaviors is the key to teaching readiness for metacognition or any critical thinking skill. Among those behaviors are the beliefs and attitudes that help to create the environment within which any kind of thinking takes place. For example, teachers who try to provide positive reinforcement by always responding to correct answers with an immediate "That's right! Great answer!" may unwittingly be creating an environment that actually undermines reflective thinking. A simple "Thank you, let's think about that" could still provide the desired reinforcement, but without the negative side effect. The point is that attitudes and dispositions such as the willingness to suspend judgment, to consider alternative solutions or points of view, and to revise one's opinions in light of new evidence are essential to teaching rational thinking and decision making.

●　●　●　● Teaching Reflective Thinking

When confronted with a genuine problem, most of us follow some variation of the inquiry/problem-solving process described in Chapter 10. Briefly, we identify and clarify the problem, identify and gather the necessary data, identify possible solutions (hypotheses), evaluate the alternative solutions to decide which one best fits the situation, and then act appropriately. During that process, we may employ one or more of the following skills:

Information-processing skills

1. describing	7. deducing
2. estimating	8. hypothesizing (predicting)
3. classifying/categorizing	9. analyzing
4. evaluating (judging)	10. experimenting
5. interpreting	11. planning and designing
6. inferring	12. generalizing

The preceding list of thinking skills may seem imposing, but all of them can be taught in some form to elementary- and middle-school children. It is not unusual to find children who lack the vocabulary or prior experiences to handle complex forms of analysis, synthesis, or evaluation, yet most children can indicate, for example, if something in a story "fits" or if "something seems wrong." **Using language that fits children** The key often lies in how you present the task to them, and more specifically, in the language you use.

Skills that involve measuring, observing, and describing seldom pose unusual problems for students, but you will probably need to translate other skills into simpler language. Your exact translation will depend on the kind of data or experiences you're using, of course, but some examples are illustrated in Table 11.1.

The balance of this section is organized to reflect the holistic ways in which we use thinking skills—that is, in relation to the inquiry (problem-solving) process. For example, before students "do" anything with information, they must sense the existence of a problem; they must have something to inquire about. Thus we first examine how teachers can help students identify problems. Following this are techniques for helping students identify hypotheses and make inferences, for

---

●　●　●　● COMMENTARY　　What We Know About Thinking

Some of the research on thinking suggests the following:

- Students' performance in classrooms is often more dependent on the strategies they use to get and use information than on IQ.
- Novice thinkers often try to memorize and recall isolated bits of information, whereas more proficient thinkers tend to look for larger patterns and relationships within the information.

- Learning thinking skills often involves repetition and practice as well as reworking, organizing, and elaborating on the information.
- Thinking involves intuitive, inductive, inferential, and sometimes even illogical components.
- A key element of thinking involves learning how to apply and use what is known.

TABLE 11.1   **Translating Tasks into Children's Language**

Task	Adult's Language	Child's Language
Classifying	Classify these into two categories.	Let's see if some of these go together.
	Can you classify these in different ways?	Can we group these together in different ways?
Hypothesizing and inferring	Develop two hypotheses that might explain this.	How can we explain this? Let's look for some other reasons why this happens.
	Given data, develop three hypotheses.	What is _____ really like?
Analyzing	Given two sources of data, identify possible contradictions.	Let's see if we can find anything "wrong" or unusual (about these data).
		Is there anything here that doesn't seem to "fit" right?
	Identify relevant or irrelevant information.	Is there information here that we don't need?
		Which information is most helpful?
Inductive reasoning	Given two or more data sources, develop an inductive generalization.	Let's find an idea that "fits" all these examples.
Deductive reasoning	Given an idea, can you test its validity?	Given this idea, let's think of other examples that it applies to, or examples where it does not apply.
Evaluating	Identify criteria to support your judgment.	Let's figure out why we think one criterion is better than another.

helping students gather information and then do something with it, and, finally, for helping students to generalize beyond their immediate experience.

◦ ◦ ◦ ◦

Identifying Problems

◦ ◦ ◦ ◦

Fact: When the story of Hansel and Gretel is told in some parts of Africa, the witch's house is made of salt, not candy.

When American children hear about how the tale of Hansel and Gretel is told in Africa, they may sense that somebody has been messing around with a story they know well. For some children at least, the change in the witch's house from candy to salt can be a *discrepant event* that leads to cognitive dissonance—that is, something that doesn't "fit" the world as they've come to know it.

Dissonance—when things don't fit

Sensing that a problem exists is the first stage of problem solving. If children choose not to pursue the matter, the process can end there—with an awareness of a possible problem. The turning point comes when a child is sufficiently concerned to say something such as "I wonder why they changed the story of Hansel and Gretel." At that point, the child's awareness of a possible problem is converted into a *real* problem for which they want an answer.

Hypothesizing

If you are sufficiently interested in why some people in Africa use a different version of "Hansel and Gretel," you've probably moved to the next step of problem solving: speculating (hypothesizing) on possible reasons for an action. In the event you want more information, consider that some groups in Africa measure wealth by the number of cattle or wives or the amount of salt one has (or some combination thereof).

To reach the hypothesizing stage with your students, you may need to provide activities in which you intentionally create cognitive dissonance, thus providing them with motives for further inquiry. Unfortunately, it is often difficult to translate traditional social studies content into problems that really engage students. Traditional requests such as "Identify the capitals of the Middle Atlantic states" or "Trace the sequence of Roman emperors" are usually teachers' problems that may or may not become the students' problems.

Techniques for creating dissonance

Even within a fixed curriculum, teachers can use some techniques to enhance their students' involvement and create the feeling that they are dealing with *their* problems. These techniques include (1) creating mystery-type situations, where students must work with unknown elements, (2) providing only limited information at the outset of an activity, from which students try to "fill in the holes," and (3) using speculative-heuristic questions, such as "What if you were the fire chief?"

Limiting the information available

Creating mystery-type situations that evoke a sense of "problem" sometimes involves limiting the amount of information available to students *at the beginning of an activity*. This limitation on information holds for all statistical data, regardless of what kind of situation you are trying to establish. Most children can deal with only limited amounts of statistical data at one time—seven to ten pieces or less—whereas a page or even a half-page filled with statistics can easily overwhelm them (and most adults). The limitation on information is intended to prevent information overload at the outset of a lesson, but once an activity is under way, students should obviously have access to as much information as they want or need.

Fact sheets

The following Model Student Activity (see page 312) is based on a teaching device called a *fact sheet*. A fact sheet is a sheet you provide to students that contains a few selected but uninterpreted facts. To enhance the children's interests, we've elected to add some mystery elements by concealing the name of the real country and identifying it only as "Nation X." Providing the name of Nation X, which we eventually will of course, would eliminate all traces of mystery from the problem, and students would simply rely on their prior knowledge about it. In this activity, students must use the uninterpreted facts to make inferences that describe Nation X. A minor problem here is keeping students' attention focused on *describing* Nation X, because they will want to guess which real nation Nation X is. Permitting students to make activities like this one into guessing games will restrict their usefulness.

Data Suitable for Fact Sheets. Not all "facts" are suitable for fact sheets. On one occasion, for example, some teachers modified the "Nation X" format to

MODEL STUDENT ACTIVITY

Nation X—Using a Fact Sheet

Overview

Using the following data, students are asked to describe Nation X. Like most inferences, these may be modified with additional information. How this activity ends depends on how far you wish to take it. We would follow up with culture cards (see following chapter text) that permit students to validate their inferences and provide additional information.

Procedure

1. Establishing set: "Today we are going to use just a few facts to describe a real nation. Some of our descriptions may be correct and some may be wrong; we'll know that after we get more information. So, let's see what we can tell about Nation X."

2. Display Fact Sheet 1 and pose the following task: "Using just this information, let's describe what Nation X is like. What can we tell about the people who live there?"

Fact Sheet 1

	U.S.A.	Nation X
Doctors and nurses (per 2,000 people)	15	1
Literacy (people over 15)		
Males (per 100 people)	92	55
Females (per 100 people)	92	28
Radios per 1,000 inhabitants	750	2
People living in cities (per 100 people)	66	18
Rooms in each dwelling (average number)	5	2

3. List inferences (in terms of key descriptors) on the board or overhead, or have small groups list their inferences on chart paper.

4. Summarize inferences, pointing out those that may be contradictory. For example, the data on doctors could suggest either that Nation X has poor health conditions or that Nation X needs only a few doctors.

5. You may wish to raise some questions such as, How is literacy defined? How big must a city be to be considered a city? Is it fair to say that Nation X is poor?

6. Present the class with the information in Fact Sheet 2 (on an overhead projector).

Fact Sheet 2

Life Expectancy for Males (in years)

USA	████████████████	*72*
X	██████████	*57*

Consider whether this information confirms any hypotheses about health care or the way of life in Nation X.

7. After assessing whether the inferences follow from the data, ask students what other information they think they might want. (Be prepared for a long list.)

8. Present the following information (on an overhead transparency).

Fact Sheet 3

Nation	Population	Percentage of World Population
China	1,175 million	21
Nation X	931 million	15
United States	260 million	7
Russia	148 million	6
Japan	131 million	3

Some students will use the information from Fact Sheet 3 to guess the identity of Nation X. Or they can check population figures in the atlases found at the back of most social studies texts. In any event, trying to maintain the mystery much longer could prove frustrating, so you can tell the class that Nation X is India. (Knowing that, you can now assess your *own* inferences.)

9. At this point you have the option of pursuing the India study in one of several ways. You might wish to do two things simultaneously: (a) have students use their inferences as research questions to be answered, using whatever resources or references

they can garner, and (b) pursue an inference that children often make about Nation X, namely, that it is poor. If they don't infer this, you can always build a case for it. Among reasons that will be suggested for India's poverty are its health and population problems.

10. You can pursue the poverty issue by raising questions such as: If most of the people in a country are poor, what does being poor mean? Is being poor an average condition? If so, would the average Indian be likely to define himself or herself as poor? The following information can then be presented to the class (again, using an overhead transparency may be easiest).

Fact Sheet 4

In many rural villages in India, the poorest families are those in which there are no children.

What does this statement suggest about the Indian value structure?

11. Closure: Using the original list of inferences, determine those about which students are fairly confident and those for which they need more information.

12. Follow up in future lessons with textbook-based passages or culture cards.

Source: Adapted from John T. Mallan and Richard Hersh. *NO G.O.D.s in the Classroom: Inquiry and Elementary Social Studies.* Philadelphia: W. B. Saunders, 1972.

Must use generalizable data

apply to states. Their "State X" fact sheets included data such as the state bird, the state tree, the state motto (in Latin), a picture of the state flag, the date of the state's admission to the Union, and sometimes the state insect. This kind of information was so unique and so tied to the individual states that little could be said about it. To be told that the state bird of X is the cardinal or that the state tree is the buckeye tells you that the state has birds and trees, but then all states have birds and trees. The point is that the data on a fact sheet should permit comparisons but should not reflect unique, one-of-a-kind information.

Must focus on using data

Fact sheets are devices for presenting information that the children then *use*—in this case to make inferences about Nation X. The purpose of the fact sheet is *not* to present factual information for children to memorize. Expecting students to understand that India has health care problems is one thing, but expecting them to remember that India has one doctor or nurse for every two thousand people violates the appropriateness criterion noted earlier.

You will be pleasantly surprised

Don't let your prior experiences with statistical information stand in the way of trying the fact sheet approach. Students often respond very positively to fact sheets. This is not a sales pitch for fact sheets; just consider not ruling them out until you've tried them.

Culture Cards

Many people regularly download pictures from the Internet, whereas the thought of cutting the illustrations of people and artifacts from a *National Geographic* or *The Smithsonian* is often more than they can bear. Yet both the Internet and publications like *National Geographic* and *The Smithsonian* offer wonderful instructional resources that too often go unused.

What you are after in materials from these sources are photographs and illustrations from which you remove the captions. Do not destroy the captions, because you will need them for the second phase of this activity. Removing the captions intentionally limits the amount of information available to students. As such, the captionless photographs represent uninterpreted information that students can then use as a basis for making observations and inferences about people, where they live, or whatever is the focus of the photo. When you bring back the captions (in the second phase of the activity), they offer a source of additional information that may cause students to modify their earlier interpretations.

When pictures or photographs of a culture are clustered together, they are considered *culture cards*. However, you could organize the photographs on some other basis, such as similar occupations or types of housing, and simply refer to them as *picture cards*. A key feature of culture/picture cards (less the captions) is that because they do not involve reading they can be used with students of any age or grade level, early childhood through graduate school.

Picture cards

Techniques for Using Picture and Culture Cards

1. Prior to studying a culture or area, provide the class with a set of uncaptioned pictures of the people (Inuit, the Japanese, etc.) or the region (the Ukraine, Switzerland, etc.). Using just the pictures, ask students to describe the people or region as best they can. The object is not to guess who the people are or what the region is. You can reduce students' tendency to do that by simply telling the class, "Here are some pictures of 'X' that we want to describe as best we can. How do the people live? What kind of area do they live in?"

Some descriptions (and inferences) that the students provide will be inaccurate because they are working with limited information. Inaccurate descriptions will be corrected as the students move into other materials—the texts, videos, and databases—that describe the culture or region. The students' inferences and descriptions should be treated as hypotheses to be tested as they obtain additional information.

2. After studying a culture, provide students with a set of uncaptioned cards intermingling photographs from two or three cultures. The students' task is to separate the pictures of the culture just studied from pictures of other cultures.

Classifying pictures

3. Provide students with a set of randomly assorted culture cards, and ask them to group the cards according to (a) criteria that you supply (family activities, seasons, etc.) or to (b) criteria of their choosing. This type of classifying activity is an integral part of concept building.

4. As a small-group activity, students can write their own captions for the pictures. They can then compare their captions with the original captions (which are mounted on a separate "caption card").

SUGGESTED ACTIVITY

Following the guidelines suggested in this chapter, create a set of culture cards.

- - - - •

Determining Researchable Problems

- - - - •

During most social studies activities, students will generate some questions that no amount of research can ever answer. In the previous Model Student Activity, for example, an inference that India is poor because the people are lazy will undoubtedly lead to frustration and discontent should your students attempt to

TECHNOLOGY UPDATE

Pictures Are Worth a Thousand Words

Somewhere among the Library of Congress's (LOC) 13.6 million images (photographs, pamphlets, paintings, etc.) you can surely find something that would be useful for whatever topic your students are studying. If the prospect of searching through several million images seems a little daunting, be advised that the LOC has a keyword search index that will narrow your choices considerably. Moreover, only a few thousand of the LOC's images are available for downloading on line at:

http://lcweb.loc.gov/coll/print/guide/

Many printers can make passable copies of downloaded images, but if you would rather have photoquality prints, these are available at reasonable cost from the Library's Photo Reproduction Division.

The Library of Congress is only one source of downloadable images. If your topic is more subject-specific, check out one or more of the following:

The Louvre, at:

http://www.paris.org/Musees/Louvre/

The National Museum of the American Indian, at:

http://www.si.edu/nmai/

The Gallary of the Open Frontier, at:

http://www.unl.edu/UP/gof/home.html

The U.S. Holocaust Museum, at:

http://www.ushmm.org/

The Museum of Fine Arts, at:

http://www.mfa.org/

The Library of Congress's American Memory Page, at:

http://lcweb2.loc.gov/ammem/ammemhome.html

If you are still unable to find what you are looking for, visit the Smithsonian Institution at:

http://www.si.edu/

---

research it. It's simply not a researchable question as long as *poor* and *lazy* are left undefined. The teaching implication is that you will need to help children examine the researchability of possible problems. To do otherwise could send them on a wild-goose chase.

Help students determine a problem's researchability

Some of the following statements and problems are based on Model Student Activities considered thus far. Others are not. Decide which of the following statements lend themselves to further student research or study:

Test Yourself   *Yes/No   Problems/Statements*

_____ 1. Identify the constitutional requirements for the office of president of the United States.

_____ 2. Bill Clinton and Franklin D. Roosevelt were two of the best presidents the United States ever had.

_____ 3. The Dutch are an industrious and friendly people.

_____ 4. The introduction of new technology into a culture is likely to lead to other changes.

_____ 5. American farmers today produce more food on larger, more specialized farms than did farmers ten or twenty years ago.

_____ 6. Yuppies are more patriotic than retired people.

_____ 7. Most students in *this* class like Italian food.

Remember Ms. Fleury's class from the "Wearin' of the Green" activity, where the students discovered they had to decide how much green clothing someone had to wear to be considered "wearing green"? Somewhat the same problem

Vague terminology poses problems

influences the researchability of the problems listed here. Researchable problems (hypotheses, inferences, and questions) cannot use vague terms, yet they must be specific enough that one need not spend a lifetime in the quest. As such, Statements 1, 4, 5, and 7 are researchable, but Statements 2, 3, and 6 need to be specified more precisely before students can deal with them. For Statement 3, for example, it might be possible to define *industrious* and *friendly,* but how do you define *the Dutch?* Are the Dutch only those people who live in the Netherlands? Or do they include all people of Dutch descent? This is not an impossible problem, of course, just one of the many things a teacher must think about.

. . . .

Hypothesizing and Inferring

. . . .

Based on the "Help Wanted" cartoon shown in Figure 11.1, which of the following might you reasonably infer?

Yes/No

_____ 1. Business seems to be good.
_____ 2. The cartoon depicts a scene in the United States.

Which are viable inferences?   _____ 3. The employer has a bias against women.
_____ 4. Women are not good workers.
_____ 5. The sign reflects a basic societal belief that a woman's place is in the home.
_____ 6. The cartoon depicts a scene that might take place today.

FIGURE 11.1 Cartoon for Inferencing

It's reasonable to infer that business is good; otherwise there would not be a "Help Wanted" sign. On the other hand, perhaps working conditions in the plant are so bad that employees quit after only a few days. If that were true, the management would continually need additional help just to maintain normal operations. But then perhaps all of the current employees are now women, and they want males so as to satisfy a quota. All of these are plausible inferences.

From inferences to hypotheses

If you have no intention of testing which of these inferences is valid, your inference would remain just that—a plausible inference. But when you set out to test whether business is good, at least as depicted in the cartoon, your inference then functions as a hypothesis. That is, your inference is a testable proposition: the reason the plant displays a "Help Wanted" sign is that business is good and the company therefore needs additional employees. To test your hypothesis, you clearly would need more data about the events depicted in the cartoon.

Formal hypotheses testing is public

All of us make inferences as we attempt to explain and understand events around us. Because we infer and hypothesize anyway, why then should there be such concern for formal hypothesis testing? The answer is that what we do in informal situations has application in many more formal situations and with many kinds of data sources. In informal situations we might be satisfied using impressionistic data—a hunch, a whim, or a feeling—but formal hypothesis testing requires that all elements of the process be *public*. In other words, in face-to-face relations, we can use whatever information we wish, but in more formal data-validating situations, we are expected to follow the rules of science—hence the distinction between inferences and hypotheses.

Knowns and Unknowns.   When something is known, there's not much left to hypothesize about. A statement such as "Milk comes from cows," for example, isn't likely to lead to any speculation. But if you ask, "Where does milk come from?" you can get some interesting hypotheses:

- From trucks
- From dairies
- From the supermarket

The accuracy of these responses is clearly testable, but you must also assess whether students will gain enough from testing them to make the effort worthwhile. We can test the accuracy of knowns, but we must hypothesize about things that are unknown or that can be explained only in part.

Using physical objects for hypothesizing

Physical objects can often serve as excellent vehicles for hypothesizing activities, especially when the object and its uses are unknown to students. A colonial bootjack—a forked board used to help remove one's boots—or even a butter churn can lead to creative hypothesizing activities.

Coins, stamps, buttons—almost any physical object—can provide the basis for hypothesizing and inferring activities. For coins, for example, the student's task can be stated as follows: "Given a half-dollar, a quarter, a dime, a nickel, and a penny, what do you know about the people who made them, the world they live in, and what things they seem to value?"

"Buildings seem to be important, as well as eagles."

"Except for one, all the coins have a man on them."

"They have a letter and number system."

"They have a god in whom they trust."

"They have a language we don't understand, *E Pluribus Unum.*"

Dealing with unknowns

In summary, hypothesizing and inferring activities require something that is unknown to students, because otherwise there may be nothing for children to explain. To help children hypothesize and infer, teachers can provide them with unexplained events—unknowns that, through inferring, hypothesizing, and hypothesis testing, can become knowns.

Gathering and Interpreting Data

Before anyone bothers to gather and process data, it's only common sense to have previously identified a purpose for that information. Gathering data is something we do in response to a problem, although in school settings the problems are often imposed on us.

Because students and teachers may perceive data gathering differently, teachers need to ask themselves two questions: What's my motive (as a teacher) for having students study this? and What are my students' motives for dealing with this information? Motivation, then, is a process of identifying the best possible match between your motives as a teacher and the motives of your students.

Conditions for data gathering

Successful data gathering depends on three interacting elements: (1) a precisely stated problem, (2) an awareness of the specific information needed, and (3) the ability to deal with data that are presented in different forms (narratives, charts, graphs, etc.). Among the most important of these is stating the problem precisely. This was driven home to me on one occasion when I made my sixth-grade students "ambassadors" and asked each of them to do a written report on a foreign nation. At the time, I failed to consider that a precisely stated problem

Criteria for inclusion and exclusion

provides the criteria for determining what information should be included— *and excluded.* Without those criteria, students put anything even remotely related to the country into their reports. The student who "did" Scotland, for example, brought her report to class in a huge carton. Reading the reports was a nightmare and, like it or not, grading was based on a subjective mixture of quality and weight. My students were proud of the huge stacks of information they had gathered, most of which I suspect they never read. The next year I spent considerable time narrowing the topics down to a more manageable size.

Using children's experiences

Teachers sometimes equate data gathering with "library research," as I did, and thus neglect data that can grow out of students' experiences. Even primary children can get involved in data-gathering procedures. Conducting surveys to determine children's favorite TV shows or the time at which most students go to bed, for example, are possible topics for data collection.

Using Data from Primary and Secondary Sources. Some kinds of information (or data) better lend themselves to information processing than do other forms of data. You may recall the earlier comments about information such as

Raw data provides the basis for interpretation

the state tree, state flower, and so on. When your purpose is to help children process information, your main focus should be on providing them with unprocessed information—raw data—that they can work with. As a rule that information should be presented in uninterpreted form so that students can do the interpreting.

Social studies programs that emphasize helping students work with information from primary sources often lean heavily on uninterpreted information, some of which (as for surveys) the students may gather firsthand. Note that *primary* in this sense refers to firsthand accounts, whereas *secondary* accounts relate to already interpreted information.

As a kind of self-check, decide which of the following sources are most likely to provide primary (firsthand) accounts (use a P) and which are most likely to contain secondary (previously interpreted) accounts (use an S). Use ? if you are not sure.

Data sources

_____ Aerial photographs	_____ Lectures
_____ Advertisements	_____ Letters (personal)
_____ Artifacts	_____ Magazine articles
_____ Atlases	_____ Maps
_____ Census reports	_____ Paintings
_____ Diaries	_____ Documentary photographs
_____ Directories	_____ Reports
_____ Documents	_____ Survey reports
_____ Encyclopedias	_____ Textbooks
_____ Interviews	_____ Journal articles

Secondary sources

The secondary sources on this list include encyclopedias, lectures, magazine articles (and *some* journal articles), reports, and textbooks. Some sources, such as advertisements, may be questionable, especially since the way data are used in advertisements is often questionable. Interviews might also be questionable, because interviewees sometimes give the answer they think the interviewer is anticipating. Maps could also fall into the questionable category, because someone had to transform (i.e., process) data into map form. However, for all practical purposes, it is safe to regard most maps (and the balance of the items on this list) as primary sources. You can turn to them as some of your best resources for process-based activities.

• • • •

Generalizing

• • • •

One of the more challenging aspects of teaching is helping students identify patterns or relationships among otherwise unconnected events or pieces of data. That challenge, expressed in a word, is *generalizing*.

Looking for patterns in the data

The process of making generalizations requires that students move into the realm of abstraction. Yet many students and even some adults may get so wrapped up in the specific details or the content of situations that they tend to consider those details separately. We are not talking about the need to generalize here, for that clearly exists. The concern is with some people's unwillingness to move into the realm of abstraction, which is something that adults are sometimes reluctant to do.

Working with classes of behavior

Generalizing reduces the disorder and confusion of otherwise isolated bits of experience. That reduction is achieved by organizing data or experiences into classes and categories. Generalizing, then, involves making statements about classes or categories of objects or events. Examples of how you can help children do this are provided in the next section.

Strategies for Teaching Critical Thinking Skills

Teaching strategies for helping children think reflectively typically involve (1) the teacher modeling the desired behaviors, or (2) posing a sequence of questions to the whole class or to cooperative learning groups, or a combination of the two, which is (3) followed by a period of reflection on the activity itself—on what worked and what didn't. After providing children with data to interpret, the basic teaching strategy follows a three-element pattern based on What?, Why?, and What does it mean?

To call the What-Why-What does it mean? sequence a questioning pattern could be misleading. Each element (What?, Why?, etc.) could be posed as a question, of course, but consider posing the elements in the sequence as tasks, using them as guides as you model the process. By using the sequence as a general guideline, you can then tailor specific questions that correspond to the data you are using.

Limit the data at first

The points here are several. First, to help children identify patterns among data that will then permit them to develop generalizations, they should deal with a very limited amount of information at first. At the same time, the tradeoff comes with helping children to understand that they cannot make generalizations based on limited information alone. Teachers need to be ready to provide additional data that may or may not be consistent with the original information and that students can then use to confirm the accuracy of the general statements they make. Taking exceptions into account is part of that process, and students need to understand that failing to accommodate exceptions can cast the shadow of doubt on their overgeneralizations. It is true, for example, that many major cities are lo-

● ● ● ● **COMMENTARY** **On Avoiding "Queen Bee" Questions**

From time to time, all of us have encountered teachers who ask questions such as "Who can tell me the capital of Alabama?" or "Who can tell me what a body of land surrounded by water is called?" The problem with questions like these is their phrasing; that is, both begin with "Who can tell me . . . ?" These can be referred to as "Queen Bee" questions, because they implicitly suggest that whoever answers them will impress the teacher by doing so. Both

"Who can tell me the capital of Alabama?" and "What is the capital of Alabama?" lead to the same answer: Birmingham. However, "Queen Bee" questioning tends to make impressing "me," the teacher, the focal point of the activity. The "Who can tell me?" question format may seem innocuous enough, but using it repeatedly could send powerful messages about the kind of classroom environment you are trying to maintain.

Taking exceptions into account

cated along large rivers, but saying that "all major cities are located along major rivers" is not true. To take the exceptions into account, students need to alter their original generalization by using "many" or "most" instead of "all." Closure for this activity can come when the teacher says, "Are we accurate if we say that 'many major cities grew up along large rivers because of the reliable water supplies and opportunities for trade and commerce that the rivers offered'?" In the next section some of the other purposes that questions can serve are examined.

Questioning Strategies

Everybody knows that questions are a teacher's stock in trade. Theoretically, a teacher's questions are supposed to lead to something, but this mission sometimes goes astray. For example, some teachers ask a question like "Has anyone ever been to Disneyland?," which they hope will motivate students and pique their interest. But if you are leading into an activity that you are going to do regardless of how your students respond, such questions could be irrelevant. **Is the question really relevant?** Whether such questions actually engage young students is questionable, and unless students' responses (about Disneyland) are relevant to the lesson that follows, you should consider moving into the activity immediately by saying something such as "Now, we're going to do an activity that . . . "

For Every Question There Is a Purpose

For every question teachers ask, there is (or should be) an underlying purpose, something the teacher is trying to get at. In many respects, deciding what questions to ask, deciding how to ask them, and deciding what answers you anticipate is part of every teaching strategy. The reverse of this statement is equally true—for every purpose there is a question. To illustrate this, let's use the information presented on the data card shown in Figure 11.2.

If students are not aware that the names listed on the data card (London, Boston, Moscow, etc.) are major cities, the activity could become an exercise in futility. To determine whether students already have this or any other prior knowledge in their possession, you could ask a *memory-recall* question, such as "What major city is located along the Thames River?" The main purpose of memory-recall questions is to determine if students can recall specific, factual information.

Memory-recall questions

Descriptive-interpretive questions

If your purpose is to determine whether students can identify patterns among data, you might ask students a *descriptive-interpretive* question. This category of questions asks students to describe, interpret, or otherwise explain what the cities listed on the data card have in common. In this instance, students' description or interpretation must be in their own words, not a memorized rehash of someone else's description (otherwise it becomes a memory-recall question).

Once students have concluded that the large cities shown on the data card are located along major rivers, you could follow up by asking them to speculate on

KEY IDEA

Underlying every question that teachers ask is a purpose for asking it. These purposes may be as varied as the questions.

FIGURE 11.2 Sample Data

Skill: Generalizing from data

Sample Data

Boston is on the Charles River.

Moscow is on the Volga River.

London is on the Thames River.

Cincinnati is on the Ohio River.

Paris is on the Seine River.

Application-synthesis questions

why this is the case. Was it simply the availability of water, or did other elements play a role? Although you might be asking another "Why?" question, in this instance it would be an *application-synthesis* question that requires students to identify possible relationships and draw conclusions, bringing in other information as needed. Application-synthesis questions require that students put things together (synthesize) so as to identify relationships or generalizations that go beyond specific events. Note, however, that unless application-synthesis questions are preceded by several lower-level questions, they may seem to come from nowhere.

Evaluative-judgmental questions

If you are interested in determining whether students have internalized the data-card lesson, you might ask an *evaluative-judgmental* question such as "How would you advise colonists as to the best places to locate their settlements?" Evaluative-judgmental questions always contain a "good-bad" or "better-best" element, which is what makes them judgmental. These questions require students to produce an evaluation or render a judgment. A distinguishing characteristic of evaluative-judgmental questions is that students must identify the *criteria* they will use in reaching their evaluation. Thus, an evaluative-judgmental question might be phrased more accurately as follows: "What criteria would you use to decide whether colonists had established their settlements to ensure possible growth?" Although this might seem a long-winded way to pose a question, the intent is to emphasize the need to specify clearly and in advance the criteria by which something is being judged. In the absence of such criteria, students' responses will be purely personal opinion.

Speculative-heuristic questions

Other potential questions could ask your students to speculate in a hypothetical mode. Examples of such *speculative-heuristic* questions based on our data card include "What might have happened if Boston (London, Paris, etc.) were located 100 miles upstream from its present location?" The "what-if" form illustrated in this example is characteristic of speculative-heuristic questions. Speculative-heuristic questions are excellent for generating inquiry, promoting divergent thinking, and getting students to speculate on and analyze alternative courses of action, but be cautious here; asking three "what-if" questions in a row may be enough to confuse even your most sophisticated students.

The various types of questions are summarized in Table 11.2.

Wait Time

"Whenever we have a discussion, the same kids participate all of the time and the rest of the class just sits there. Sometimes the students who talk don't have much to say, and it is all very superficial. I don't know. I'm about ready to give up on discussions."

Frustrated teachers have been echoing complaints like this for years, yet they often overlook a potential solution to their problem. The solution takes no special skills and has achieved dramatic results where it's been employed. It is: Doing nothing. Well, almost nothing.

In some now-classic research, Mary Bodd Rowe (1969) examined the relationship between a teacher's wait time and the quality of classroom discussions. Wait time refers to the period of silence between the end of a teacher's question and the teacher's next statement or question. Rowe found that many teachers

TABLE 11.2 Types of Questions by Category and Purpose

Type of Question	Purpose
Memory-recall	To determine whether students can recall previously learned information
Descriptive-interpretive	To describe, interpret, and/or explain events or actions in the student's own words, including reasons (nonspeculative) for why individuals acted as they did
Application-synthesis	To identify relationships and to form and draw reasonable conclusions that go beyond the particular action or event
Evaluative-judgmental	To render an evaluation or judgment as to actions or events in light of explicit, previously identified criteria
Speculative-heuristic	To encourage divergent thinking and to speculate on and analyze alternative courses of action

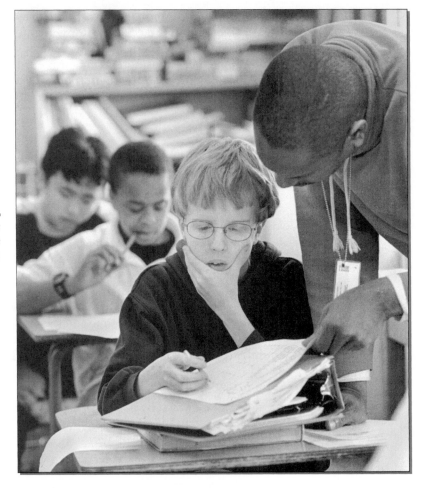

Student involvement can be enhanced if teachers increase their "wait time." (© Susie Fitzhugh)

Avoid responding too quickly

apparently have difficulty tolerating silence during a discussion; their average wait time was only nine-tenths of a second. No wonder students didn't participate! They didn't have time to think before the teacher went on with another comment or question.

After Rowe informed teachers how short their wait time was, they decided to double it—at least to two seconds. Awkwardly at first, the teachers waited the allotted two seconds, even though it sometimes seemed like an eternity. The results? The number of students participating in class discussions improved dramatically, as did the quality of their contributions. When teachers also lengthened the period of silence between a student's response and the teacher's next comment or question—what Rowe called "Wait Time II"—the results were even more impressive. Even more students responded, including some who almost never participated, and the quality of discussions also improved.

What two seconds of silence can yield

The implication is clear: if your discussions don't go well and the same students participate all the time, try lengthening your wait time. If you do that and your discussions still don't go well, you may need to reexamine the kinds of questions you are asking.

● ● ● ● Decision Making

Choosing among alternatives

Decision making is the process of making reasoned choices from among alternatives. In social studies, decision making can have two meanings, one of them broad and the other narrow. In the broad sense, *decision making* describes a total approach to social studies that incorporates all the information-processing skills. In its narrower sense, *decision making* describes instructional activities that ask students to apply decision-making skills. The concern in this section is with decision making in the narrower, "activities" sense of the term.

The Model Student Activity, "Returning from the Crusades" (see pages 325–326), illustrates a common model for decision-making activities. A heuristic (what if?) question is posed in the introduction, and students are then asked to select among the various choices provided. This is essentially the same format

MODEL STUDENT ACTIVITY

Returning from the Crusades

Introduction

The year is 1291. You are a knight who has been fighting to win back the Holy Lands—the Middle East—from the Moslems for your king and country, England. After months of fighting, you learn that the battle to win Jerusalem was lost. It has been a long and hard journey, but it is time for crusaders, like yourself, to leave the Moslem lands.

Weary and unhappy because of losing the battle, your thoughts turn toward seeing your family and loved ones once again. However, as you begin your journey back to England, you notice some abandoned Turkish villages that have different things lying about. You lost everything except the clothes on your back, so you decide to pick up some of the things the Turks have abandoned. However, between your backpack and horse you can carry only an additional 50 pounds. Even if you put some things into your pockets (instead of the backpack), your horse may not be able to carry the extra weight.

Below is a list of things you find in the foreign lands. Select the ones you would want to take back to England with you. When you have decided which items to take, rank-order these, with 1 being the most important. But remember, you can carry only 50 pounds.

Group Rank	Your Rank	
____	____	Large pouch of Turkish coins (8 lb.)
____	____	Small barrel of flour (30 lb.)
____	____	Pouch of water—2 gallons (6 lb.)
____	____	Your bow and arrows (4 lb.)
____	____	A small, live mulberry tree (9 lb.)
____	____	Large, 4-person tent (18 lb.)
____	____	20 yards of silk cloth (8 lb.)
____	____	One iron cooking pot (13 lb.)
____	____	Shovel (4 lb.)
____	____	One jar of silkworms (3 lb.)
____	____	One camel (No weight, can be led)
____	____	Persian rug (24 lb.)

(continued)

Group Rank	Your Rank	
_____	_____	Arabian math books (20 lb. for all of them)
_____	_____	10 Arabian toys (10 lb. @ 1 lb. each)
_____	_____	Food to last for the journey (33 lb.)
_____	_____	Small pouches of spices (6 lb.)
_____	_____	An elegant silk dress (4 lb.)
_____	_____	Stray puppy (6 lb.)
_____	_____	10 blown glass goblets (5 lb. @ 1/2 lb. each)
_____	_____	Fishing pole (4 lb.)
_____	_____	Small package of apricots (3 lb.)
_____	_____	Arabian artwork—1 piece (9 lb.)
_____	_____	Soap, 1 bar (1/2 lb.)
_____	_____	Other _____
		(Weight will vary)

Source: This activity was designed by and is reprinted by permission of Ms. Dena Hawley.

Procedure

1. *Individual selections:* Students should rank-order their choices of the goods they propose to take back to England.

2. *Group selections:* If you have not already done so, create small groups of about five members each. Ask each group to create a single list of items they will be taking back to England.

3. *Determining the common ground.* Ask each group to list their items on the chalkboard. Ask groups to explain their rationale for selecting the items they did, and then circle the goods that were common to all groups.

4. *Exploring the exceptions.* Explore items that were selected by only one or two groups and ask them why they selected those items.

5. *Realities:* Display (on an overhead) the following list of items that Europeans actually brought from the Middle East. These items included:

Silk cloth and silkworms

Mulberry trees (to feed the silkworms) [Note: a jar of silkworms would die en route without mulberry leaves for food.]

Blown glass objects

Apricot trees

Arabic system of numbering

Assorted spices for preserving food and for seasoning

Camels

Persian rugs

Translations of Latin and Arabic literary works

Middle Eastern styles of clothing

Nice-smelling soap

Analysis

This activity asks students to make decisions similar to those made by people over 700 years ago. At the conclusion of this activity, students should be able to see the influence that Middle Eastern nations, especially Turkey, ultimately had on Medieval European cultures. Students should also be able to consider the extent to which their decision might have "changed history," as well as explain the extent to which interchange with nations in the Middle East led to changes in what is sometimes called "the Dark Ages."

---

used in the "Who Is Qualified for Presidency?" Activity in Chapter 1. In this case, however, there are more possible choices. In this and many other decision-making activities, participants must first make decisions individually and then reach consensus in small groups. Procedurally, because most decision-making activities do not have previously identified "correct" answers, teachers often identify the common ground, or the most common choices selected by all the groups.

Identify the common ground

Developing and Using Decision-Making Activities

Applications

Decision-making activities can work well as introductions to areas of history of the world with which children are unfamiliar, particularly because the activities help to raise questions about what an area is (or was) like. Decision-making problems can be shifted to almost any area or historical period. For example, "If you were Marco Polo . . . " or "If your family was going from Connecticut to California in 1849 . . . what would you bring with you?"

Decision-making activities must be limited to problems that are both real and manageable for students; otherwise they'll have no basis for considering the alternatives. This means that for most elementary students, a question such as "Which had a better organizational basis, the League of Nations or the United Nations?" isn't a manageable problem for a decision-making format. As a rule, decision-making activities for elementary- and middle-school students should afford immediate access to the information on which their decisions will be based.

Maintain a clear focus

Decision-making activities can serve as a focus for information-processing skills. However, unless teachers continually stress rational information processing, these activities can degenerate into arguments of "My opinion is as good as yours." Attention should also be focused on the processes that students use in arriving at their decisions, not just on the decisions themselves.

Content utilization revisited

Decision-making activities require students to *use* information, as do other process-oriented activities such as fact sheets, surveys, and problem situations. Decision-making activities can be incorporated into social studies programs at every grade level on a regular basis and should not be relegated to a trivial role—as something "neat" to do on a Friday afternoon or during a rainy recess. As for all critical thinking and decision-making activities, the focus on *using* information and on rational decision making should be maintained.

 SUGGESTED ACTIVITY

Design a forced-choice format decision-making activity following the guidelines suggested in this chapter

SUMMARY

Critical and reflective thinking skills are part of a family of information-processing skills that cannot be dealt with in isolation for very long. For example, hypothesizing cannot end there; students must be able to do something with the hypotheses they have created. Otherwise, both the students and the hypotheses will be left hanging. Members of the critical thinking family work together (at least theoretically), each contributing to the overall process, be it hypothesizing, inferring, or whatever.

A key element in developing information-processing and decision-making activities for students lies in restricting the volume of information you make available at the beginning of the activity. The more you exceed ten or so pieces of information, the greater your risk of creating information overload. Once students have dealt with the

original information, you are free to add as much additional data as they can handle, just so long as you avoid an overload. A second key factor in creating critical-thinking activities involves providing students with uninterpreted information. This means that instead of describing the climate of an area as "cool" or "warm," for example, consider providing students with temperature data, which is readily available from most atlases or on *Encarta World Atlas* (Microsoft). It is a simple task to determine whether an area is warm or cool based on temperature data, but children are not going to do much interpreting if the information you provide them ("warm" or "cool") is already interpreted in advance.

The questions and tasks that teachers pose to students will often determine how they will use social studies content. The five types of questions that teachers might ask—

memory-recall, descriptive-interpretive, application-synthesis, evaluative-judgmental, and speculative-heuristic—are keyed to the thinking skills a student must employ to answer them.

Teachers who ask higher-level questions—that is, higher in terms of their level on the *Taxonomy of Educational Objectives*—are more likely to demand that their students use content. This doesn't make knowledge-level questions "bad," however, because they can be used to determine if students have essential prior information in their possession. Nevertheless, the goal in most instances is to help children move beyond the knowledge level.

SUGGESTED READINGS AND RESOURCES

Print Resources

Barry K. Beyer. (1991). *Teaching thinking skills: A handbook for elementary teachers.* Boston: Allyn & Bacon. This handbook provides an excellent overview of thinking skills as well as exemplary lessons to teach those skills. Companion volumes by Beyer include *Practical strategies for the teaching of thinking* (1987) and *Developing a thinking skills program* (1988).

Charles W. McCoy, Jr. (2002). *Why didn't I think of that? Think the unthinkable and achieve creative greatness.* Upper Saddle River, NJ: Pearson Prentice Hall. The author of this lively volume, a California judge, blends anecdotes from his experience on the bench with other sources to help you think more clearly, creatively, and comprehensively. Topics focus on perception, concentration, high-level thinking, a systematic approach, imagination, intuition, empathy, and anticipation.

M. Neil Browne & Stuart M. Keeley. (2000). *Asking the right questions: A guide to critical thinking* (6th ed.). Upper Saddle River, NJ: Pearson Prentice Hall. If you apply the lessons in this well-written volume, you could find yourself winning arguments with your friends—and perhaps alienating yourself in the process.

Internet Resources

Introductory Note: Web sites sometimes change their Internet addresses or cease operating entirely. All the addresses supplied here were operating when this book was printed, but if any of them fails to work properly, enter the desired topic or organization in any standard search engine.

The Center for Critical Thinking

http://www.criticalthinking.org/

This site is sponsored by several nonprofit organizations and offers a wealth of resources and materials for teaching critical thinking. Some sample lesson plans show excellent ways to use children's literature to foster critical thinking.

Critical Thinking on the Web

http://www.philosophy.unimelb.edu.au/reason/critical/

This Australian site offers a remarkable array of resources that are arranged into twenty-four categories. These range from on-line tutorials through language and thought, great critical thinkers, textbooks, software, and links for teachers. An excellent starting point.

Critical Reading

http://www.criticalreading.com

This excellent site, which is associated with the critical thinking site above, shows you how to recognize what a text says, what it does, and what it means.

Critical Thinking Through Writing

http://www.dartmouth.edu/~compare/faculty/ pedagogies/thinking.html

This site is maintained by Dartmouth College and shows how critical thinking skills can be improved through writing exercises.

Critical Thinking: What It Is and Why It Counts

http://www.calpress.com/pdf_files/whatandwhy.pdf

This site offers a reprint of an excellent overview of critical thinking by Peter A. Facione entitled "Critical Thinking: What It Is and Why It Counts."

Teaching Thinking Skills

http://www.nwrel.org/scpd/sirs/6/cull.html

This site, which is maintained by the Northwest Regional Educational Laboratory, offers summaries and an extensive bibliography of recent research related to thinking skills and problem solving.

Helping Students Understand Maps, Globes, and Graphics

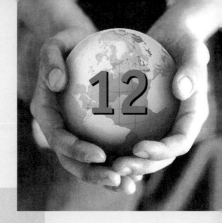

12

KEY QUESTIONS

- **How can students use maps, charts, and other forms of social studies information?**

- **How can mathematics be used in social studies?**

● ● ● ● ● Introduction: Basic Premises

Specialized ways for presenting information

Whenever someone says "social studies," many people think first of history and geography, followed closely by maps and globes. There's no question that maps, globes, and, to a lesser extent, charts and tables are integral to social studies, yet there is nothing inherently "social" about any of them. They are simply specialized ways for presenting information.

The information presented on most maps, globes, graphs, charts, and tables can almost always be presented in other forms. Aerial photographs, for example, can convey at least as much as (and probably more) information than as many landform maps. Likewise, the information on a chart or table could be presented in a written description. Although a narrative of the income tax tables would probably be hopelessly confusing, it could be done.

KEY IDEA

Maps, globes, graphs, and charts are specialized forms in which information is presented.

Reading a map, chart, or graph demands decoding skills not unlike those required to read information presented in narrative form—as you are doing now. True, the symbols are different: the dots and squares on a map, for example, usually stand for different things. Yet the process of bringing meaning to these symbols is a form of decoding.

Reading plays such an important role in gaining access to the information on maps, graphs, charts, and tables that the approach in this chapter is borrowed from the language-experience approach to teaching reading. That approach reflects the premise that if children can see their speech being encoded into written form, they will be better able to read those symbols.

How encoding and decoding are related

This chapter also reflects the premise that some students have difficulty reading maps or tables because they don't understand how the information got *into* that form. In other words, students may not understand what the information on a map is supposed to represent. Likewise, when children have difficulty decoding charts and tables, the problem may lie in their inability to understand how information

KEY IDEA

When students have difficulty gaining access to specialized forms of information, part of the problem may be their lack of understanding about how the information got into that form in the first place.

was encoded into the chart or table in the first place. This may explain why there is so much emphasis on providing encoding experiences—mapmaking, table making, and chart making—as a necessary balance for the decoding experiences—map reading, table reading, chart reading—that traditionally play important roles in social studies programs.

The first section of this chapter examines map- and globe-related skills and identifies exemplary activities you might use to teach those skills. The following sections consider experiences with tables, charts, and other graphic forms.

Maps and Globes

As the noted geographer Monmonier (1991) noted, we live in a three-dimensional world that is too rich in details to be presented on a two-dimensional map. As a result, maps typically distort the reality they depict by leaving out more information than they include and by using a variety of symbols to describe the information that is included.

The abstract nature of maps is illustrated in Figure 12.1. What to us may look like a random collection of sticks and shells can make perfect sense to mariners

FIGURE 12.1   A Mariner's Map

Source: Illustration by Paul M. Breeden, © National Geographic Society.

from the Marshall Islands. The sticks represent wave patterns, and the shells mark reefs and islands. With maps like this one, the Marshall Islanders navigated their way across empty stretches of the Pacific.

Large-area maps can pose special problems for children, who have probably never seen the real-world elements those maps depict. Many adults have difficulty interpreting Figure 12.1 because it is a model of something we have never seen and probably never will.

The abstract nature of maps is often compounded by the rapidity with which they lose one-to-one correspondence. For example, many things that children see and know to exist in their immediate environment do not appear on most maps of the area. Trees and buildings are among the first real-life elements to disappear. And as the map scale grows larger, cities often become dots or squares that look nothing like the areas they represent.

The perspective of maps: bird's-eye view

Maps also demand that we look at things from a different perspective. Very few of us have had the luxury of viewing the world while suspended in space. (Maps made from satellite photographs have helped considerably in this respect—see p. 338.) Maps require that we assume the perspective of "looking down on" or what, in children's terms, can be described as a bird's-eye view. Because that perspective is not one that most children have much experience with, you could provide activities in which young children look at or draw objects from a bird's-eye view. Here are some suggestions:

1. Draw a picture of your shoe. (If the heel is visible, it's not a bird's-eye view.)

2. Hold a "bird's-eye view contest." Place small objects in a paper bag, where they cannot be seen by others, and have students draw and identify pictures of the objects as they would be seen from a bird's-eye view. Note that doll house furniture works well for this activity.

Map-related activities

3. Follow the activity above by having students draw larger objects from their environment from a bird's-eye view. Some examples are pictured in Figure 12.2.

4. In working with children's stories, draw hypothetical bird's-eye view maps of the area. For a story like Robert McCloskey's (1941) *Make Way for Ducklings,* for example, you could make a map of the area as seen from a duck's-eye view.

FIGURE 12.2 Common Objects Seen from a Bird's-Eye View

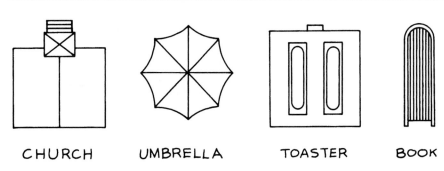

CHURCH   UMBRELLA   TOASTER   BOOK

· · · ●
Mapmaking
· · · ●

Map copying is not mapmaking

Mapmaking refers to activities in which children actually produce a map. This excludes a variety of map-copying activities (even though they are sometimes called "mapmaking") in which children color in and correctly label outline maps. Copying existing maps may be useful in helping to fix areas in a child's mind, but it teaches little about what maps are or the purposes they serve. In addition, map-copying lessons too often focus on the artistic dimensions of mapping, especially if students use colored glitter or other unusual materials to depict the different areas. Such maps should probably be judged as works of art rather than as ways for displaying information.

Children seldom omit any details

Mapmaking in the encoding sense requires an area to be mapped. Beginning with bird's-eye views of various objects, students can move to increasingly larger areas, such as their living room or bedroom, their classroom, the school building, the neighborhood around the school, or other areas of the community. Figure 12.3 shows a third grader's map of his home and yard. The map is detailed and accurate, except that the cardinal directions are incorrect (the front of the house faces to the east). The backyard, which looks like a swimming pool, is really grass surrounded by a concrete walkway—to keep the grass from going

FIGURE 12.3   Third Grader's Map of His House and Yard

into the shrubbery. The child has maintained a high level of one-to-one correspondence by showing things that he knows are present in the environment, including the piano keys, the boat in the side yard, and the jungle gym/swing set, which is made from ladders, in the backyard. About the only things not drawn strictly from a bird's-eye view are the trees, which is wholly expected for children of this age. Note that students who live in multistory apartments or houses are usually baffled by the prospect of showing several floors simultaneously; they should map each floor separately.

Specific objectives

Objectives for initial mapmaking activities include (1) helping children to visualize their immediate environment from a bird's-eye (or spatial) perspective and (2) helping them to understand that when anything is reduced in size—as maps are in relation to the areas they depict—some things must be omitted. Children should consider on what basis some things are kept in and others left out.

KEY IDEA

All maps omit certain information; if they didn't, the information they do present would be lost in a fog of detail (which is also true of other data forms).

Relief Maps.   If your school is located on the plains of west Texas, making a relief map of the area is probably pointless; much of the terrain is as flat as a tabletop. In other areas of the country, relief maps can show hills and valleys, thus illustrating yet another type of mapmaking. But beware! Making relief maps can be a time-consuming and often messy process.

Moving from two dimensions to three

Making Relief Maps.   To build relief maps of small areas such as the neighborhood around a school, you might have students actually measure the changes in elevation. However, because doing that is more difficult than it may seem, consider using topographical maps from the U.S. Geological Survey, or downloaded from **www.topzone.com,** which offers maps in three scales. Topographical maps can be less abstract for children than other maps because in addition to changes in elevation they show buildings and other features.

Relief maps can be constructed from a variety of materials. The least messy but most costly is clay—pound after pound of clay. Several recipes for other relief-map-making materials are included in the Resource Handbook.

Computer-Based Maps.   Instead of constructing relief maps, you may wish to use the maps included in computer database programs such as *Encarta World Atlas.* Most such programs contain a variety of maps and other data for any given area: relief maps, political maps, landform maps, population distribution maps, major cities, highways, rainfall—you name it. Most programs also permit you to print the maps.

TECHNOLOGY

The *Atlas* software is notable for its ability to focus on small areas of a larger map, creating exploded views. Used with a computer projection system, it permits students to see map details that were previously difficult to see even on large wall maps.

Scale.   In most mapmaking activities, the question often arises as to whether maps should be drawn to scale. For primary-grade children, the answer is generally no; neatly drawn but not-to-scale drawings will usually suffice. For the intermediate grades, the answer depends on the math program your students are using. The notion of scale, like latitude and longitude, is mathematically based. And scale, perhaps better than anything else, reflects the zenith of representational thought. In this case, one thing is said to equal something else. For younger elementary students, the notion that one inch can equal one foot (or one mile or ten miles) can present some of the same difficulties that algebra students encounter when they find that *x* can equal anything.

Representational thought

Scale is so integral to maps and mapmaking that it should not be dealt with casually. Be sure to check how your textbook series treats map skills because this is one area where many texts excel. A common treatment is to show a low-altitude aerial photograph of a school, with trees, fences, playgrounds, and so on, clearly visible. This is followed by a sequence of photos taken from higher and higher altitudes in which the school building gets smaller and smaller until it finally disappears.

By the end of the intermediate grades, children should have experienced some of the following ideas related to scale:

- Scale is the ratio between the actual distance between two objects on the ground and the distance as shown on a map.

- Maps that are drawn to a large scale can show many details about a small area.

- Maps that are drawn to a small scale can show large areas but with fewer details.

- Scale permits the measurement of the distance between any two points on the earth's surface.

- Scale on inset maps may be different from the scale of the larger map.

Correlate scale with your math program

You may have to be satisfied when most of your students can use the scale on a map to calculate the distance between two points. However, many math programs introduce representational thought, and even the notion of scale, much earlier than they used to. Therefore, consider correlating your mapmaking activities with your math program.

Translation Mapping. *Translation,* a major subdivision of the *Taxonomy of Educational Objectives,* is defined as changing data from one form to another. This is what mapmaking is all about—depicting three-dimensional reality in a two-dimensional map form. The following map-related activities involve different kinds of translation. Although some of them may not seem especially exciting, they are educational.

Scope and sequence

- Produce a written description of information contained on a chart or table (educational, but not too thrilling).

- Produce a map of a nation, such as Japan, from a written or oral description. (This activity is more interesting than it may seem and produces some very interesting maps—inaccurate but interesting.)

- Produce and translate a map. (In this activity, one group of students produces a map and another group uses it to locate an object—interesting, though the instructions are more complex than the activity.) The class is divided into teams of two. Each team places an object somewhere around the school grounds

Adding three-dimensional models may help children better undertand two-dimensional maps.

(© Mary Lang/ Positive Images)

(lavatories are off-limits), returns to the classroom, and provides an oral description to the second team, which produces a map from that description. Finally, the maps are given to yet a third team, which must retrieve the object. As a follow-up, share the various problems the teams encountered in either making or using the maps.

When Should Map and Globe Skills Be Taught?

SUGGESTED ACTIVITY

Compare two social studies textbooks for the same grade level in terms of the map-reading skills and quantitative data skills, if any, that they require of students.

There is no single established sequence for map and globe skills for the elementary- and middle-school grades. Sometimes first graders are expected to know and locate the major continents and oceans, for example, but in other instances, this may not be covered until Grade 2 or later.

From time to time, individuals and groups have identified a desirable scope and sequence for teaching map and globe skills. A sample scope and sequence for map and globe skills developed by the Joint Committee on Geographic Education of the National Council for Geographic Education and the Association of American Geographers (1984) appears in Table 12.1.

Using Maps and Globes

Satellite Maps. Satellite photography has made it possible to illustrate the earth in a manner previously possible only with a globe. Satellites from several

TABLE 12.1   Suggested Scope and Sequence for Elementary Map and Globe Skills

Grade Level	Recommended Learning Outcomes
Kindergarten	1. Knows and uses terms related to location, direction, and distance (*up/down, left/right, here/there, near/far*). 2. Recognizes a globe as a model of the earth. 3. Recognizes and uses terms that express relative size and shape (*big/little, large/small, round/square*). 4. Identifies school and local community by name. 5. Recognizes and uses models and symbols to represent real things.
Grade 1	1. Knows geographic location of home in relation to school and neighborhood. 2. Knows the layout of the school campus. 3. Uses simple classroom maps to locate objects. 4. Identifies state and nation by name. 5. Follows and gives verbal directions (*here/there, left/right*). 6. Distinguishes between land and water symbols on globes and maps. 7. Relates locations on maps and globes to locations on Earth. 8. Observes, describes, and builds simple models and maps of the local environment.
Grade 2	1. Makes and uses simple maps of school and home neighborhoods. 2. Interprets map symbols using a legend. 3. Knows and uses cardinal directions. 4. Locates one's community, state, and nation on maps and globes. 5. Identifies local landforms. 6. Differentiates between maps and globes. 7. Locates other neighborhoods studied on maps. 8. Traces routes within and between neighborhoods using a variety of maps and models. 9. Compares pictures and maps of the same area.
Grade 3	1. Uses distance, direction, scale, and map symbols. 2. Compares own community with other communities. 3. Compares urban and rural environments.
Grade 4	1. Interprets pictures, graphs, charts, and tables. 2. Works with distance, direction, scale, and map symbols. 3. Relates similarities and differences between maps and globes. 4. Uses maps of different scales and themes.

(continued)

TABLE 12.1   Suggested Scope and Sequence for Elementary Map and Globe Skills

Grade Level	Recommended Learning Outcomes
	5. Recognizes the common characteristics of map grid systems (map projections).
	6. Compares and contrasts regions on a state, national, or world basis.
Grade 5	1. Recognizes distance, direction, scale, map symbols, and the relationship of maps and globes.
	2. Works with longitude and latitude.
	3. Uses maps, charts, graphs, and tables to display data.
	4. Discusses location in terms of *where* and *why*.
	5. Maps the correspondence between resources and industry.
	6. Maps physical and cultural regions in North America.
Grade 6	1. Improves understanding of location, relative location, and the importance of location.
	2. Uses maps, globes, charts, and graphs.
	3. Readily uses latitude, longitude, map symbols, time zones, and basic Earth-Sun relationships.
	4. Gains insight about the interaction of climate, landforms, natural vegetation, and other interactions in physical regions.
	5. Maps trade routes, particularly those connecting developed and developing nations.
	6. Plots distributions of population and key resources on regional maps.

Source: Abridged and adapted from Joint Committee on Georgraphic Education (1984).

government agencies currently circle the earth and send back color photographs of remarkable clarity, such as that of the New York City area shown in Figure 12.4. Although our sample is reproduced in black and white, it should give you some idea of the potential this innovation has for map-related instruction. Satellite maps are available from the Educational Programs Office, NASA Goddard Flight Center, Greenbelt, MD 20771.

Globes.   The globe remains one of the most accurate tools for helping children orient themselves to the earth. It can help to distinguish between land and water areas, and it can help to correct the common but mistaken notion that

The merits of globes   "up" on a map is north and "down" is south. With a globe, students understand that up is away from the center of the earth and down is the reverse.

Locating specific places on the globe sometimes poses two problems. To avoid having students line up and file past the globe, more and more schools purchase classroom sets of eight- to twelve-inch globes, which may be kept on a cart and

FIGURE 12.4   Satellite Map of New York City, Long Island, and the New Jersey Coast

Source: Courtesy of Community and Education Services Branch, Public Affairs Division, National Aeronautics and Space Administration.

Size limits the amount of detail

wheeled from classroom to classroom as needed. The second common problem is a function of the size of the globe. On a twelve-inch globe, for example, the United States measures approximately four inches from west to east. The average wall map of the United States measures approximately four feet from west to east, thus permitting the presentation of much more detail. Some schools have purchased very large, thirty-six-inch globes—which often serve as focal points for libraries or learning centers—but even such large globes are limited in the amount of detail they can present. Globes are excellent geographic tools, but when it comes to detail, you'll probably need to turn to a wall map.

Wall Maps.   Getting a round Earth to fit onto a flat map has perplexed cartographers for centuries. The classic example of peeling an orange and then trying to make the peel lie flat illustrates the essence of the problem. In cartographic terms, it is a question of "projection." Projecting rounded surfaces onto a flat map in different ways can yield the images shown in Figure 12.5.

Misleading impressions   The distortion on most wall maps is greatest at the high latitudes and is largely responsible for the question children commonly ask: "Why is Australia a continent but Greenland isn't?" It's a logical question, because on many maps, such as the Mereator projection shown on page 341, Greenland appears to be two to three times the size of Australia. Using a globe, students will find that Australia is three times larger than Greenland—Australia has 2,975,000 square miles versus Greenland's 840,000 square miles. Explaining to students how some maps make small things appear larger than they really are is no small feat! For very small areas, the distortion created by different map projections is usually negligible, but for large land masses, consider using a globe in conjunction with wall maps.

Large-scale maps   To avoid the "north is up" phenomenon, you might occasionally lay wall maps on the floor. Some schools have gone even further; they paint huge outline maps on the school parking lot or playground. Such large-scale maps should be accurate in direction and as accurate as possible in scale.

FIGURE 12.5 Distortions Created by Different Map Projections

Van der Grinten's Projection

Mercator's Projection

TECHNOLOGY UPDATE

Plotting Earthquakes

Many people do not know that earthquakes of varying magnitudes are daily events around the globe. Some earthquakes are so weak you can barely feel them, and others are so powerful they cause widespread destruction. Two key questions are: (1) Are some places in the world more prone to earthquakes than others, and (2) if so, where?

Overview: This problem-solving activity uses latitude and longitude to plot the location of recent earthquakes on an oversized map of the world. The completed map should resemble the one shown in Exhibit B.

Materials

1. A *really* large outline map of the world. (Suggestion: Make an overhead transparency of an appropriate world map by (a) mounting large paper on the wall and then (b) projecting the enlarged image onto the paper. Then (c) have children trace the outlines of continents and countries with markers. They should (d) use small dots to locate the location of parallels of latitude and meridians of longitude. After they (e) remove the map from the wall and lay it on the floor, students can use yardsticks and fine-point markers to draw in the latitude and longitude. Once this is done, they can (f) label the completed map and remount it on the wall.)

2. Earthquake locators. These are 1- by 1-inch squares of clear overhead transparency material with an X drawn on them. (Suggestion: Make a sheet of neatly drawn Xs, and then make three or four transparencies. Cut the individual Xs apart. Since there are many earthquakes, you will need many Xs; start with at least fifty).

3. Download the earthquake locations from the Internet at either:

> **http://home.synapse.ru/cgi-bin/eq/**
> **http://wwwneic.cr.usgs.gov/neis/bulletin**

The data will be similar to the data in Exhibit A.

Exhibit A

Introductory Note: There are often six to nine earthquakes every day that are above 3.5 on the Richter scale, and countless more tremors of lesser magnitude (Mag). The selected earthquakes shown below were in excess of 5 magnitude and often caused significant damage and deaths. Because of the large number of earthquakes each day, consider mapping only those that exceed a threshold of 3.5 or 4 on the Richter scale; otherwise your map will become cluttered very quickly.

	Date	Time	Latitude	Longitude	Mag.	Region/Comments
1997	May 10	07:57	33.83 N	59.81 E	7.3	Northern Iran: Over 1,500 deaths, 2,300 injured, and 10,500 homes destroyed.
	May 13	05:38	31.82 N	130.28 E	5.7	Kyushu, Japan: 34 injured.
	June 23	19:13	47.60 N	122.57 W	5.0	Washington, Puget Sound Region: Slight damage.
	July 9	19:24	10.59 N	63.48 W	6.6	Near the Coast of Venezuela: Over 80 deaths and 500 injured; extensive damage.
	Oct. 14	09:53	22.10 S	176.77 W	6.7	South of Fuji Islands
	Oct. 15	01:03	30.93 S	71.22 W	6.8	Off the Coast of Chile: Over six deaths, 300 injured, and 5,000 homes destroyed.
	Nov. 21	11:23	22.21 N	92.70 E	5.9	India-Bangladesh Border Region: 23 deaths and 200 injured.
1998	Jan. 30	16:09	23.51 S	69.83 W	6.4	Northern Chile
	Feb. 4	14:33	37.07 N	70.20 E	6.1	Afghanistan-Tajikistan Border Region: 3,000 to 5,000 deaths and thousands injured and homeless.

(continued)

4. Attach the earthquake locators on the map at the correct locations by using small loops of clear Scotch tape.

5. Identify patterns of the earthquake-prone areas around the world. Follow up with research on what sets these areas apart from other areas.

Exhibit B

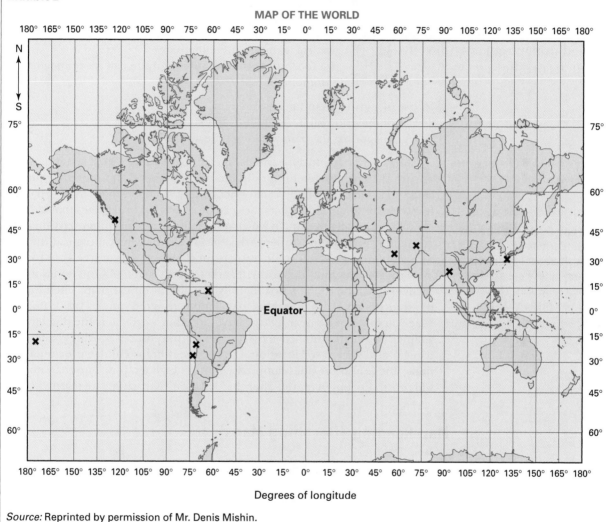

MAP OF THE WORLD

Degrees of longitude

Source: Reprinted by permission of Mr. Denis Mishin.

• • • •

Latitude, Longitude, and Other Grid Systems

• • • •

Latitude and longitude   Most map and globe skill programs from fourth grade upward call for instruction in latitude and longitude. Among the more difficult ideas for children to grasp is the fact that although most parallels of latitude are imaginary lines that appear only on a map, 90 north latitude and 90 south latitude are not lines but are points (or, in mathematical terms, poles). Also difficult is the idea that although the meridians of longitude are of equal length, the parallels of latitude get shorter as one moves away from the equator. One reason that children may find these ideas so hard to grasp is because latitude and longitude are often taught as arbitrary systems rather than as part of circular or spherical measurement. The Model Student Activity, "Pumpkin Geography," shows one way to deal with this difficult topic.

KEY IDEA

Some map and globe skills—specifically, latitude, longitude, and scale—are founded in mathematics and should be treated accordingly.

Teaching latitude and longitude can be reduced to three components:

1. Use of a grid system (any grid system)
2. Use of the grid system (longitude and latitude)
3. Understanding the basis for longitude and latitude

Grid-based map games

Even primary children can become adept at using a grid system, especially one involving a combination of letters and numbers. Math texts frequently include an assortment of grid-related activities, sometimes more than social studies texts. Also, many gridding activities can be converted into games that kids love to play. A classic is Battleship, in which a student locates his or her navy on a simple grid and then another student tries to sink the navy by calling out the various squares on the grid. You could also obtain classroom sets of free state road maps from the state highway department and create a version of Cops and Robbers. In small groups, the robbers first identify a quadrant on the map. Then the rest of the students ask them questions that can be answered only by yes or no, such as "Are you in a square near a large city?" In other words, it is the detective game adapted to a map. This activity serves several purposes: it provides experience in using a grid system for locational purposes; it helps children formulate questions; and it also provides familiarity with state geography. The road map game will prove very popular even after the skills you're teaching are learned.

 SUGGESTED ACTIVITY

Some people claim that even though teachers often make a "big deal" about latitude and longitude, these are skills that anyone rarely uses. How would you respond to this argument?

- - - -

Map Reading (Decoding Maps)

- - - -

Encoding complements decoding

Students who have had rich and varied mapmaking (encoding) experiences are likely to find that map reading is considerably easier to cope with. Realistically, however, children will be expected to read a wider range of maps than most of them will have had experience making.

Map skills

By the time students leave elementary or middle school, they generally are expected to be able to answer the questions on pages 344–345, which are based on the map shown in Figure 12.6. The questions are similar to those found on standardized achievement tests. This is doing two things: (1) illustrating how map and globe skills are likely to be tested and (2) identifying what those skills are. Accordingly, you should (1) try to answer the questions and (2) identify, in the space provided, the skill or skills required to answer the questions. You may want to use the scope and sequence presented in Table 12.1 as a guide for identifying the skills needed.

MODEL STUDENT ACTIVITY

Pumpkin Geography

The following illustrations show how you can use pumpkins to teach geography.
Set A: Shows hemispheres, the equator, and the prime meridian.

Set B: Shows how circular measurement is translated into latitude and longitude.

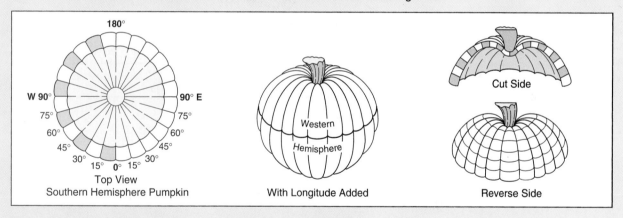

Set C: A pumpkin globe with latitude, longitude, and continental shapes drawn on.

Note: Use fine-point permanent markers to draw features on the pumpkin.

FIGURE 12.6 Pleasure Island Map

Questions

1. What is the northernmost city on Pleasure Island?
   A. Beta   B. Alpha   C. Gamma   D. Zeta
   Skill: _____

2. How far is it from Delta to Rho?
   A. 250 miles   B. 550 miles   C. 750 miles   D. 900 miles
   Skill: _____

3. Which river flows toward the northeast?
   A. Long River   B. Blue River   C. Black River   D. Red River
   Skill: _____

4. What is the busiest port city on Pleasure Island?
   A. Beta   B. Gamma   C. Omega   D. Phi
   Skill: _____

5. What city probably gets the least rainfall?
   A. Beta   B. Gamma   C. Delta   D. Can't tell
   Skill: _____

6. What city lies closest to the equator?
   A. Beta   B. Alpha   C. Rho   D. Can't tell
   Skill: _____

7. In what hemisphere is most of Pleasure Island located?
   A. Northern   B. Eastern   C. Southern   D. Can't tell
   Skill: _____

(*Answers:* 1. B; 2. B; 3. D; 4. C; 5. B; 6. A; 7. C)

Task Analysis.   Most map skills are complex chains of steps that must be followed in sequence. For example, to identify the hemisphere in which Pleasure
Island is located (see preceding Question 7), the student must know that the
equator is at 0° latitude, and that as one moves southward the degrees of latitude
increase in number until one reaches 90° south latitude at the South Pole. The
student must then apply this knowledge to the information provided on the
map. As a further example of this, identify what you must know to determine
whether Pleasure Island is in the Eastern or Western Hemisphere.

The mathlike nature of map skills makes it possible to determine precisely what
students must know and do to achieve success. For example, to determine the distance from Delta to Rho (Question 2), the student must know that (1) all maps
have a scale; (2) the scale indicates real distances in shortened form; (3) by using a
measuring device (a ruler, etc.), one can convert the distance on a map to the real
distance; and so forth. All of these elements must be brought to bear on the problem in the correct sequence or the student will most certainly have problems.

Some students just don't "get" the idea of map skills. When this occurs, which
it will, consider planning lessons in which you model the use of the skill in question. For example, to help students find the distance from Delta to Rho, make an
overhead transparency of Figure 12.6, and then model the process in a simple,
step-by-step fashion. No elaborate questioning procedure is necessary. Most map
and globe skills yield a single correct answer (such as determining the distance
between two cities); showing students an efficient process for finding that answer
will not inhibit their creativity in the least.

Most skills are a sequence of steps

Model the process

• • • •
Map-Related Activities
• • • •

Some effective and interesting map-related student activities begin with a heuristic question such as "If you were the town council, where would you build the
new incinerator (or park, or shopping center, or apartment complex)?" and use
maps as the main data source.

Another type of map-based activity involves presenting students with a sequence of maps, each of which adds specialized information. In the following
Model Student Activity, students are asked where they would locate a city on a
mythical island. Then, in succession, additional information on terrain (landforms), vegetation, and rainfall is provided, each on a separate map.

SUGGESTED ACTIVITY

Design a map-based decision-
making activity that deals with
a problem currently con-
fronting either the community
in which you are living or a
hypothetical community.

MODEL STUDENT ACTIVITY

Where Would You Locate Your City?

Overview

The object of this activity is to determine whether students will change their original decision in light of new information.

Procedure

Provide students with a copy of Map 1. Ask where, with just the information they have, they would locate a city if they were prospective settlers. Assume that the area is otherwise uninhabited. Permit students to discuss their choices in small groups, and then have each group present its choice to the entire class. Then provide each group with copies of Maps 2, 3, and 4 (see page 347), one at a time, permitting discussion and explanations (as warranted) after each map is distributed.

Sources/Variation

Making the maps for this activity used to be a major undertaking. However, for any teacher with access to the computer programs referred to earlier (*PC-Globe, PC-USA, USA Atlas, World Atlas,* and *Microsoft Encarta*), it is now a simple process, and the areas that students deal with are real. The computer programs will usually print whichever maps you need. However, it is usually necessary to remove the name of the area manually, using typewriter white-out, tape, or some other method, if you wish it to remain anonymous. After students have decided where to locate their cities, you can provide them with a computer-generated map showing the actual location of major cities.

Map 1

Scale: 1 inch = 50 miles

☰ sea water

▱ rivers

◼ lakes

N

(continued)

Literary Mapping.   You may remember reading Mark Twain's *The Adventures of Huckleberry Finn,* in which Huck and his comrades travel to various places along the Mississippi? Most of the places Huck visits are real, and most can be located on a map of the area. As your class is reading *Huck Finn* wouldn't it make sense to trace Huck's travels on a map?

There is a wealth of children's literature in which the settings are real places and, thus, locatable on a map. There is still more literature in which the set-

Map 2: Landforms

⛰ mountains or mountainous areas

⛰ hills and hilly areas

▭ plains or flat areas

LANDFORMS

Map 3: Vegetation

grass

hardwood trees (beech, oak, etc.)

tropical trees (palms, etc.)

shrubs or no vegetation at all

VEGETATION

Map 4: Rainfall (average yearly amounts)

less than 10 inches

between 20 and 40 inches

between 40 and 60 inches

between 60 and 80 inches

more that 100 inches

RAINFALL

Mapping hypothetical areas   tings are fictional but are described in enough detail that it's possible to create a map of the area. Think about Beatrix Potter's *Peter Rabbit* for a moment. The cardinal directions might be amiss, but it is possible to map the relative location of major elements in *Peter Rabbit*—the tool shed, Mr. McGregor's garden, the fence, the watering can in which Peter hides, and so forth. Each child's map might be different, but the idea is to create a tangible map of an idealized literary location. Other children's literature that lends itself to mapmaking includes *Little Black Bear Goes for a Walk,* by Beatrice Freschet (1977); *Rosie's Walk,* by Pat Hutchins (1968); Robert McCloskey's (1941) classic *Make Way for Ducklings,* which was referred to earlier, and *Henry Explores the Jungle,* by Mark Taylor (1968).

Sandra Pritchard (1989) expanded on the notion of using children's literature for teaching geography and map skills by identifying story-related activities that correlate with the five themes for geographic education (Joint Committee on Geographic Education, 1984) that were presented in detail in Chapter 2. Following is an abridgement of some of Pritchard's recommended geography-related activities for Virginia Lee Burton's (1943) *Katy and the Big Snow.*

Location: Position on the Earth's Surface

Activities correlating literature and the five geography themes

- Locate buildings and streets on a map.
- Identify and locate cardinal directions.
- Determine in which direction Katy went from the school to the railroad station, from the police station to the fire station, etc.
- Describe the location of buildings in relation to other buildings and streets.

Place: Physical and Human Characteristics

STANDARDS ✔

- Discuss seasonal changes in the little town, and how those changes affect people.
- Describe a walk along First or Third Street.

Relationships Within Places: Human-Environment Interaction

- Tell how the snow affects the lives of people in the town.
- Tell what might happen if Katy had not been able to plow out the town.

Movement: Humans Interacting on the Earth

- Identify and describe the various forms of transportation in the story and on the map.
- Identify and describe the various forms of communication.
- Find symbols for buildings, roads, and airports on various maps.

Region/Neighborhoods: How They Form and Change

- Identify different kinds of neighborhoods in the little town.

Making maps of idealized locations from children's literature may help sensitize students to the ways in which authors describe the physical setting in which stories are set, especially if you call attention to it. Such a purpose may lack clear relevance to social studies, of course, but by giving tangible meaning to a literary element such as "the setting of the story," it could show up in subsequent stories that children write.

● ● ● ● Working with Other Graphic Forms

Some teachers and students seem to regard graphs, tables, and charts as one of the "bad breath" areas of social studies. However, quantitative data are not difficult to deal with if they are approached from a "use" perspective—that is, if students actually do something with the information on a chart, graph, or table.

One instructionally troublesome aspect of graphs, tables, and charts is their efficiency in presenting information. They can present so much information in so little space that students can quickly suffer from information overload. Thus the earlier suggestion to limit the information you provide children at the beginning of an activity prevails here.

Avoiding information overload— limit the amount of data

A second consideration involves the way you present the numbers for statistical information. For example, there were 7,527,152,000 bushels of corn and 2,035,818,000 bushels of wheat grown in the United States in 1990. You probably had to count the number of places in numbers this large, which have been rounded some to begin with. Because large numbers can overwhelm children, consider rounding them even more—to 7.5 billion bushels of corn, for example. The idea is that the numbers provide the basis for identifying trends and relationships, such as that the United States grows about three times more corn than wheat. It isn't necessary to have numbers accurate to the last possible bushel to identify such relationships. And certainly the numbers are not something you would expect children to memorize.

Helping students deal with large numbers

Helping children deal with large numbers is largely a matter of making them as easy to understand as possible. In addition, because many children have no comprehension of how big a billion or how tremendous a trillion really is, consider using Schwartz's (1985) wonderful book, *How Much Is a Million?*, before you deal with large numbers.

● ● ● ● Fact Sheets

● ● ● ●

The fact sheet illustrated in Figure 12.7 was produced by a fourth-grade teacher who was teaching a unit on farming in the United States. Although the information on it is limited, it still proved to be too much for her students to process at one time. She then had them fold the paper so that only Part I was visible.

As she used the American Farmer Fact Sheet, the teacher alternated between modeling and questioning designed to help the children (1) read the charts and graphs and (2) determine what this information meant. For example, the teacher said, "Let's see if we can find out what has happened to the number of farms in this country." "They went down," was the chorus of responses. "Does anyone want to explain how we can figure that out?" After one student volunteered to explain the process for finding that information, the teacher then said, "To find out if the number of farms went down a lot or just a little, we have to look at the numbers." She then modeled the process for showing that the number of farms decreased by almost one-half (50%) and concluded that this seemed like a big decrease.

Testing versus teaching

Working through all the information in a similar fashion, the students concluded that although there are fewer farms in the United States, the amount of

Conclusions

FIGURE 12.7 Model Fact Sheet Format: The American Farmer

Part I

Corn Grown		Beef Produced	
1965	104 million tons	1965	17 million pounds
1995	246 million tons	1995 (est.)	24 million pounds

Wheat Grown		Eggs Produced	
1965	27 million tons	1965	5.5 million dozen
1995	72 million tons	1995 (est.)	5.9 million dozen

Part II

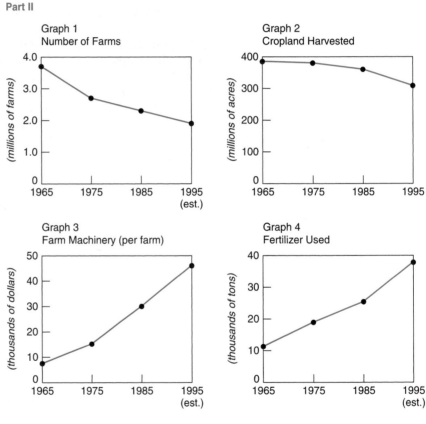

food produced on those farms has increased. They also concluded that since fewer farmers (Graph 1) were farming almost the same number of acres as in the past (Graph 2), the average size of a farm is larger today than it was in the past. Furthermore, the students concluded that fewer farmers can grow more food because of the increased use of machinery (Graph 3) and fertilizer (Graph 4). They also suggested that there could be other reasons for this (better weather, etc.), but that they didn't have enough information to be certain of these causes.

KEY IDEA

So that students do not suffer information overload, always limit the amount (number of pieces) of statistical data or other information at the outset of an activity. You can always add more once the students have gotten into it.

Using just the information on the American Farmer Fact Sheet, students developed their own conclusions about the changing nature of American farming. Of course, a teacher could approach the topic by having students read a section in the textbook. That section, in all likelihood, would begin like this: "American farms today are larger than they used to be. Farmers also use more machinery and . . ." In this instance, however, students would be reading *someone else's conclusions* about farming instead of using information to build their own.

• • • •
Encoding Quantitative Data
• • • •

Before children can use the information on a graph, table, or chart, they must be able to handle that information at the literal level. For example, if children cannot read Graph 1 on the American Farmer Fact Sheet, then it may be necessary to back up and show them how the information was translated (or encoded) into graph form.

Begin with simple encoding experiences

As a general rule, encoding experiences for primary-level students should involve simple examples and small quantities. They can be as simple as tallying the number of girls and boys in a classroom, as illustrated in Figure 12.8. Until students are able to think representationally, it is probably wisest to maintain one-to-one correspondence—that is, where one symbol on a table represents something the child can see in reality. In Figure 12.8, each symbol stands for one classmate. As students grow progressively more able to handle representational thought—as when one symbol equals five classmates, for example—their encoding experiences can become increasingly complex.

Simple surveys can provide a wealth of information for encoding activities. That's what one teacher used when her students had graph-reading problems. Small groups of students surveyed the traffic passing by the school at different

FIGURE 12.8 Sample Table Encoded by Students

Boys and Girls in Ms. James's Classroom October, 1997		
Boys	⚤ ⚤ ⚤ ⚤ ⚤ ⚤ ⚤ ⚤ ⚤ ⚤ ⚤	11
Girls	⚤ ⚤ ⚤ ⚤ ⚤ ⚤ ⚤ ⚤ ⚤ ⚤ ⚤ ⚤ ⚤ ⚤	14
⚤ Boy ⚤ Girl		25

Graphing data from surveys

times of day. They counted the number of cars and trucks, the number of pickup trucks and minivans, and the number of people who waved back at them. Then, with the teacher's help, the groups put their information onto bar graphs, which were hung around the room to provide a basis for comparison. The result of one group's efforts is illustrated in Figure 12.9.

Making Tables.   Once data have been gathered, they must be presented in a readily understandable form. One such form, a table, is intended to communicate the relationships between the data. General considerations for constructing tables (and graphs) include the following:

Four characteristics of tables

- Tables should be self-sufficient. That is, a table should give a complete and understandable message: what is being related, the form in which the relationship is established, the source of the information—everything needed to help readers make their own interpretations.

- All rows and columns must have clear headings that follow an identifiable pattern—for example, high to low, alphabetical, geographic—and, where appropriate, indicate the measure being used—percentages, thousands, square miles, and so on.

- The source of the data should be included in a footnote.

- The table title should make clear what information is being related and in what terms.

The Model Student Activity, "Constructing a Table," follows these guidelines for table (and graph) construction.

FIGURE 12.9 Summary of Traffic Survey

MODEL STUDENT ACTIVITY

Constructing a Table

Sample Data

Temperature and Snow Report, Week of January 9–15

- Monday's high temperature was 30°. Tuesday's high was 25°. Wednesday's high was 28°, followed by 32° on Thursday, 35° on Friday, 37° on Saturday, and 30° on Sunday. The average high temperature for the week was 31°.

- The snowfall for the week totaled 14 inches. It did not snow on Wednesday, Friday, or Saturday. It snowed 4 inches on Monday and 7 inches on Tuesday, for a total of 11 inches for the first two days. Average snowfall was 2 inches a day for the week.

These data were converted into table form, as shown in the next column.

Source: Personal measurements

Temperature and Snow Report, Week of January 9–15		
Day	High Temperature (F)	Snow (Inches)
Monday	30	4
Tuesday	25	7
Wednesday	28	0
Thursday	32	1
Friday	35	0
Saturday	37	0
Sunday	30	2
Average high 31		Total snowfall 14
		Average daily snowfall 2

Decoding Graphs and Tables

Task analysis

Before children can do anything with the information on a graph or in a table, they must gain access to that information. Fortunately, the process of decoding information presented on a graph or in a table is amenable to task analysis. Probably the easiest way to go about this is to ask yourself two related questions: (1) what must the student know (and in what sequence) to gain access to the information? and (2) at what points might students experience problems?

Indirect or discovery strategies for teaching the procedures associated with table or graph reading are not recommended. There are just too many points at which students might encounter problems. Thus this is another instance where modeling and step-by-step teacher-directed instruction, followed by guided prac-

Modeling is the key

tice, are wholly appropriate.

Charts

In the days before overhead projectors and copiers became widely available, chart making was probably more common than it is today. With current technology, it is a simple process to make an overhead transparency of a small chart that will be readily visible to everyone in the class.

MODEL STUDENT ACTIVITY
Linear Charting

This technique, called *linear charting,* consists of having students attach pictures or short descriptions of a process in the correct sequence on a piece of string or yarn. A linear chart for the production of bread is illustrated below.

This may not sound like an exciting activity, but actually doing it often proves otherwise. Consider that linear charting can also be used for more than just social studies activities. For example, instead of book reports, students might illustrate the significant scenes or events in a story and then attach those pictures, in the correct sequence, to a piece of yarn. When students present their reports, the rest of the class can refer to a visual representation of the book's events instead of listening to a strictly oral presentation.

Charts, like maps, omit details

All charts summarize whatever they depict. They are like most maps and outlines in that they highlight major points or phrases while omitting details. However, the need to summarize information can be an asset when you have students engage in chart making, because summarizing forces them to identify the main ideas that they should put on their chart. In this context, chart making can be an effective culminating activity for small-group work.

Linear Charting. An alternative form of charting that uses pictures attached to a piece of string or yarn is shown in the Model Student Activity above. This procedure is also useful for highlighting the main elements of a story, in which case it is sometimes called "story mapping."

SUMMARY

This chapter has suggested several approaches for helping children gain access to specialized forms of information—namely, maps, globes, graphs, and tabular data. For each of these forms, encoding experiences—which include map, graph, table, and chart making—can help children understand how information gets into a particular form. Such encoding experiences may provide students with a good basis for decoding or gaining access to information displayed on maps, graphs, tables, and charts.

Unlike some of the other areas that social studies encompasses, map, table, and graph reading (decoding) involves an identifiable sequence of the knowledge and skills necessary for gaining access to information. If any step is omitted, or if the sequence of steps is confused, the student is likely to fail. To avoid failure and the sense of frustration that can accompany it, "task-analyze" what the student is being asked to do by identifying the knowledge and skills required to complete the task. This analysis can provide the basis for step-by-step instruction as you guide your students through the decoding process.

Once students have gained access to information, the next phase is a "natural": they need to do something with it. It becomes almost a circular process when you recognize that what students do with information can provide a reason for them to get (and want) access to it.

SUGGESTED READINGS AND RESOURCES

Print Resources

Lloyd A. Brown. (1980). *The story of maps.* Mineola, NY: Dover. Originally published in 1949, this authoritative history of both maps and mapmakers is a classic work in the field of cartography.

A. K. Ellis. (1997). *Teaching and learning elementary social studies* (6th ed.). Boston: Allyn & Bacon. This text contains an excellent chapter on making and interpreting maps.

Massachusetts Geographic Alliance. (1990). *Global geography: Activities for teaching the five themes of geography.* Boulder, CO: Social Science Education Consortium. I recommend this collection of activities, all of which come with the necessary teaching materials.

Mark Monmonier. (1991). *How to lie with maps.* Chicago: University of Chicago Press. Monmonier explains why "a good map tells a multitude of little white lies" (p. 25).

John N. Wilford. (2001). *The mapmakers* (revised ed.). New York: Vintage Publications. This classic text by a two-time Pulitzer Prize winner traces the history of cartography from antiquity to the space age. This edition includes the impact of new technologies that brings the story up to the present day.

Internet Resources

Introductory Note: Web sites sometimes change their Internet addresses or cease operating entirely. All the addresses supplied here were operating when this book was printed, but if any of them fails to work properly, enter the desired topic or organization in any standard search engine.

Map Machine

http://www.nationalgeographic.com/resources/ngo/maps/

The National Geographic Society provides downloadable maps, information about each country in the world, and a variety of other map-related information.

Mapmaker, Mapmaker, Make Me a Map

http://ur.utenn.edu/ut2kids/maps/map.html

This University of Tennessee site provides a tutorial on mapmaking and links to a variety of other map-related sources.

U.S. Geological Survey

http://www.usgs.gov/

This site contains an abundance of learning resources on working with maps.

Map Collection

http://www.lib.utexas.edu/Libs/PCL/Map_collection/map_collection.html

This University of Texas collection is just one of many collections available on the Internet.

How Far Is It?

http://www.indo.com/distance/

This site calculates the latitude, longitude, and distance between any two cities. It also allows you to generate maps of the two places.

U.S. Bureau of the Census

http://www.census.gov/

This site offers more statistical information than you would believe, as well as TIGER maps that you can use for transparencies and overlays.

The World Wide Web Virtual Library: Geography

http://geography.pinetree.org

The site offers a variety of maps and map-related tools.

Topographic Maps

http://www.topozone.com

This wonderful site offers free and downloadable topographic maps, in color and your choice of three different scales, of any area in the United States or Puerto Rico. **Bookmark quality.**

13 Using Instructional Tools: Print, Multimedia, and Community Resources

KEY QUESTIONS

● **What resources are available for teaching social studies?**

● **What considerations are involved in using those resources?**

● **What do teachers do when schools lack the resources they want?**

● ● ● ● Introduction: Teaching in the Electronic Age

An abstraction has become real

TECHNOLOGY

As schools gain better and faster access to the Internet, the resources for teaching social studies have grown exponentially. For years everyone heard about how the reservoir of knowledge was growing by leaps and bounds, but because most of us had no way to tap into the vastness of that reservoir, the so-called information explosion was largely an abstraction. Today the Internet, combined with other forms of electronic technology, provides access to more resources than most of us can ever use. The information explosion has become very real.

Thanks to computer-based resources, teachers need no longer rely solely on textbooks, maps, and atlases. Many teachers also recognize that, although the Internet makes available a large amount of information, it does not teach children how to interpret and use that information.

Computerized resources for teaching social studies, along with some older resources like overhead projectors, share a common characteristic: they plug into electrical outlets. However, there is still a wide array of nonelectrical resources available, especially if you know what you are looking for. For example, something as mundane as the Yellow Pages of the telephone directory could provide the basis for a variety of social studies activities:

● For identifying the government services available in the local community.

● For identifying alternative ways in which the Yellow Pages could be organized, and then considering what those organizational patterns would mean for (1) users, (2) advertisers, and (3) the telephone company.

● For finding out what it costs, if anything, to be listed in the Yellow Pages. Is it free? And if charges do apply, speculating on how they are determined and why businesses might pay to be listed. When schools are listed in the Yellow Pages, do you suppose they pay? Or are some listings free and others must be paid for?

● For an activity in which students use the Yellow Pages from the 1960s or 1970s and a current directory to find the location of selected businesses, such as laundromats, florists, hardware stores, or video rental outlets (which did not exist in the 1960s), and movie theaters. They then plot the location of each business on a city map, and determine how the number and locations of businesses have changed over time.

KEY IDEA

Instructional tools may lurk in unlikely places.

The balance of this chapter is organized in an arbitrary and somewhat eclectic way; it covers print materials and computers, nonprint and visual resources, and finally community resources. Addresses for the teaching resources noted here are included in the Resource Handbook.

● ● ● ● Textbooks

Almost all schools have textbooks, and some classes have access to several different texts. However, some schools—even those with ample financial resources—have elected not to use social studies textbooks. Still other schools may not have enough copies of a single text for all students in the class, but this is usually intentional. Sometimes the number of texts will be limited to no more than ten copies of a particular book. Because there may be as many as forty or fifty social studies texts in a given classroom, it's technically incorrect to say that teachers don't have any textbooks. Teachers in those schools are probably using a *multitext* approach, in which they select elements from different books as they need them. This approach reduces the pressure that teachers sometimes feel to cover every chapter in a book.

Some schools use a multitext approach

Generalizing about social studies textbooks can be risky, but here goes:

● Social studies textbooks for elementary and middle schools today are more similar than they are different, especially in states that have mandated curriculums.

● You can get usable teaching ideas from every social studies textbook or accompanying teacher's guide—no matter how old or decrepit.

● Textbooks have a way of becoming the basis for social studies programs, not a resource to be used with them.

Texts as tools

For teachers who wish to depart from textbook-dominated programs, the first step is to reflect on their perception of the textbook. When they come to regard a text as a tool, as something to use when it suits their purposes, they will have begun the transition from treating the text as a body of information to be learned to treating it as a resource to be used as it is needed.

The following are some alternative ways in which you might use textbooks:

Alternative uses for textbooks

● As a source of background information that students read either (1) prior to studying a topic or concept or (2) after the need for the information has been established.

● As something students read when they need additional information on a topic.

● As a source of potential in-class activities (or test questions).

- As a contrasting point of view or as a source of data for further analysis.

- As a means to confirm or challenge certain hypotheses after group discussion—for example, "India is a 'poor' nation."

- As a vehicle for identifying the main idea of several related paragraphs.

- As a source for establishing the meaning of various terms (so that they need not be dealt with in class).

- As a way of placating people who think that a course isn't worthwhile unless it has a textbook associated with it.

- As an object of study (to determine how the text was organized and constructed).

Supplementary Print Materials

The supplementary print materials available to social studies teachers range from periodicals and current events newspapers through an unbelievable assortment of trade books (children's books) to self-contained teaching kits on almost any topic you can name. Supplementary print materials are considered in terms of these categories.

Current Events Publications

If your elementary school was like my elementary school, some of your teachers used a weekly or monthly affairs periodical. These include publications such as *My Weekly Reader, Let's Find Out* (kindergarten), *Scholastic News* (Grades 1–6), or *Junior Review* (Grades 6–9). These publications are still available.

With the Internet, additional materials have become available. One of the best is *Time for Kids,* a production of *Time Magazine,* which is available at **http://www.timeforkids.com/TFK.** This material, like the non-Internet publications, comes in three versions: the Big Picture edition for K–1, the Big Scoop edition for Grades 2 and 3, and the World Report edition for Grades 4 through 7. Be advised, however, that none of these materials are free. Subscriptions for *Time for Kids,* for example, are available at $3.95 per student, a rate comparable with the other current events publications.

Beware of articles selected at random

Instead of current events periodicals, which must be purchased separately, your teachers may have relied more heavily on daily newspapers. From time to time, they may have asked you to bring in a newspaper article to share with the class for current events time. But unless they put limitations on the kind of clipping you could bring in, a typical assortment might deal with topics such as last Saturday's Little League game or a robbery in northeastern Nevada. Seldom do child-selected articles focus on proposed constitutional amendments, changing views of morality, or the problems of international diplomacy—unless a teacher

The current events problem

insists on it. Even then, many children will be unable to understand or interpret the significance of such events. Such an assignment reflects the current events problem: much as we might like children to be interested in and aware of events and issues going on around the world that may influence their lives, many of those events and issues can go beyond their current level of comprehension and concern. The fact that some teachers have difficulty explaining things such as inflation or why the Palestine Liberation Organization and Israel have traditionally been at odds illustrates another dimension of the problem. Helping children to understand what is going on in the world at any particular moment is only part of the problem; they also need to understand why these events are occurring.

Current Events or Current Affairs?   As a teacher, you have at least two options for keeping students abreast of happenings going on around them. One option is to maintain an ongoing current events program. In this context, an *event* is anything that has happened or is happening, either trivial or potentially significant. Unfortunately, the current events approach has a tendency to become piecemeal—a little of this and a little of that—almost a warmed-over version of the nightly news. On the other hand, many children are not bothered in the least by a piecemeal approach.

Current affairs focus on ongoing issues

● ● ● ● **COMMENTARY**   *Helping Children Deal with Terrorism*

In the immediate aftermath of 9/11/2001, teachers across the country—including even rural areas where the likelihood of an attack is almost nonexistent—have had to deal with some distraught and very worried children. It also has become obvious that teachers can no longer tell children that "terrorism occurs in places that are far far away" and that "such events can't happen here." So what, then, is a teacher to do?

Linda Ellerbee (1995) and Fern Reiss (2001) offer the following suggestions:

● Forget about telling children that their chances of being involved in a terrorist attack are less than 1 in 100 million. Such information seldom offers comfort to young children.

● Let children talk about terrorist events, and let them know it is okay to feel sad or confused or even scared. However, do so in ways that respect the child's privacy; some children cope by not talking.

● Remind children that it is unfair to judge large groups of people by the actions of a few. You may wish to use words like *cowardly, sneaky,* and *unacceptable* to reinforce the notion that violence is not the way to get what you want.

● Understand that in the immediate aftermath of terrorist attacks, many children are more fearful about their parents' safety than their own. It can be helpful to maintain normal routines to take children's minds off the event and to convey the idea that the whole world has not been turned upside down.

● Don't lie to your children. Answer questions truthfully, even telling them that you are angry and saddened, too, but don't go overboard and volunteer detailed information unless they ask you.

● Be attentive to minor medical complaints about scrapes, bruises, and so forth, that you would normally pass over. Such complaints may be how young children express complicated emotions that they have trouble verbalizing otherwise.

● Point out the reassuring things that often happen in the aftermath of terrorist incidents: the rescuers who risk their lives to save others, the communities near and far who lend supplies and support, and the massive outpouring of sympathy for the victims and rage at the perpetrators. People do indeed care about others.

Sources: Ellerbee, L. (1995). What shall we tell the kids? *Liberal Opinion Week,* 6 (May 1), p. 7; Reiss, F. (2001). *Terrorism and kids.* Boston: Peanut and Jelly Press.

A second option is to establish a current *affairs* program where issues and events—the environment, human rights, conflicts occurring in various parts of the world (the Middle East, Afghanistan, or Iraq), and so forth—are studied over several weeks. In a current affairs program, your focus might be on different dimensions of the farm crisis. Or you might use changes in the price (or weight) of bubble gum or candy bars as an entrée to the continuing study of rises in the cost of living. The idea of a current affairs program is to tie together the separate events of continuing problems to help students understand their significance.

Seeking common elements among separate events

Depth versus breadth

Weekly news periodicals, like *Weekly Reader* and *Scholastic,* can furnish the background information essential for interpreting current events. The broad range of events and happenings that the weekly periodicals include may compensate for their lack of in-depth coverage.

Instead of using current events publications, teachers with Internet access sometimes opt for the real thing; their students use English-language editions of newspapers from cities around the world. See the Model Student Activity on this page for details. In many instances, however, current affairs can be esoteric for young children. It is extremely difficult to capture the reasons for the animosity between the Palestinians and the Israelis, for example, much less in a publication for young children. Thus, if you teach at the primary level, you may be

MODEL STUDENT ACTIVITY

Current Events: "And Now a Word from Our _____ Desk."

Format: Working in teams of two, students role-play TV reporters who present a three-minute (maximum) report of the latest news from the electronic (English-language) editions of one of the world's international newspapers. The students who report on the *Japanese Times,* for example, would represent the "Japanese Desk."

Frequency: Once weekly.

Procedure:

1. Identify newspapers that students could use. The easiest procedure for this is to use a search engine (my favorite is Google) and type in the name of nations whose newspapers you might want to use. By typing in the nation instead of a city, for example, "Japanese newspapers" instead of "Tokyo newspapers," and so on, you will have a larger pool to select among. Also include a few U.S. newspapers, such as the *New York Times,* the *Washington Post,* the *Chicago Tribune,* and so on.

2. Decide on a procedure for creating teams. I suggest pairing a good reader with a poorer reader, but this is by no means essential. In an average class you will have eleven to thirteen teams.

3. Decide on a procedure for assigning reporters to a desk. Free choice? Drawing names from a hat?

4. Use the front page of a current daily newspaper to help students understand the focus of various articles: for example, international, state, local, sports, human interest. Indicate that the articles they decide to report on should reflect at least two categories.

5. Encourage students to use visuals in their reports, including editorial cartoons, copies of headlines, and so on. Also indicate that they are not permitted to read the article to the class. However, they need to be prepared to respond to questions when they are "interviewed" by the class after their report.

Comment: Expect that students will have difficulty with articles involving foreign trade, tariffs, and so on. Every article of this nature will be offset by other articles they can understand, some possibly involving the health benefits of soy sauce, and so on. Be prepared to rotate team members and their "desks" periodically.

better off opting for a broad coverage, current events approach. However, if you plan to teach at the intermediate or middle-school levels, the possibility of pursuing a current affairs approach becomes much more realistic. Or you can do both; you can use an affairs approach for some issues and settle for broad awareness for other issues.

Newspapers.   In some schools, teachers base much of their instructional program—social studies, math, language arts, and reading—on daily newspapers. Students do comparison shopping using the grocery ads, compute batting averages (math) using the sports page, invest (mythically) in the stock market, examine weather patterns (using the weather map and forecast), realphabetize the newspaper's directory, put scrambled headlines back together again, compare the amount of space devoted to various categories of articles (international news, national news, etc.), use small sections of the paper to compare the amount of factual data (reporting) with the amount of opinion (editorials), or compare the amount of space devoted to ads with the space devoted to news.

Using the newspaper to teach

You might give groups of students identical collections of stories clipped from several newspapers and ask them to compose a front page. They should be prepared to explain their reasons for including the articles they did. You could also remove the headlines from various articles and have children create their own based on the content of the story. They can then compare their headlines with the originals. Or they could take several days' accumulation of TV schedules and try to identify patterns in TV programming.

Newspaper-based activities

You could do other things with a daily newspaper, but the preceding examples should serve to illustrate the idea. For many newspaper-related activities, it is not necessary for children to be able to read or understand the articles in order to use the newspaper as a learning tool. As with most instructional resources, the essential idea is to consider the newspaper as a resource, as something you can teach *with*, not simply teach *about*.

Trade Books

Criteria for selecting children's books

In the publishing world, a textbook is a book designed for classroom use. Fiction or nonfiction books intended for sale to the public are *trade books. Mike Mulligan and His Steam Shovel* (Burton, 1939) is a juvenile trade book, as are Kenneth Grahame's (1908) classic, *The Wind in the Willows,* and thousands of others.

Because so many trade books are available, the National Council for the Social Studies reviews only those books considered "most notable" during a given year. Thus, unless the book (1) is written primarily for children (K–8), (2) emphasizes human relations, (3) presents an original theme or a fresh slant on a traditional topic, (4) is highly readable, and (5) includes maps and illustrations where appropriate, it is not included in the listing that appears in each May issue of *Social Education.*

Historical fiction, nonfiction, biography—somewhere there's a trade book that applies to whatever your class is studying. To assess the quality of books for children, McGowan (1987) has recommended the following criteria:

© Elizabeth Crews

Ethnic literature

1. Decide whether the book is *developmentally appropriate*. Can the prose be understood by its intended audience, and are the setting, plot, and themes familiar to young readers?

2. Determine whether the book has *literary value*. Is it meaningful and enjoyable to read, and has the author written with attention to character development, dialogue, plot, imagery, and message?

3. Determine whether the book presents *valid information*. Is the story told with reasonable accuracy and in a "true-to-life" fashion?

4. Determine whether the book has *a message of value*. Does the author examine an issue worthy of the reader's attention, or does the story involve values that the reader should eventually assimilate?

An area of children's fiction particularly appropriate to social studies is ethnic literature. For example, *The Big Push* by Betty Baker (1972), based on a historical incident that occurred when the Hopi Indian children were forced to go to school, is almost guaranteed to generate an active discussion. Likewise, children are likely to enjoy *The Hundred Penny Box* by Sharon Bell Mathis (1975), a poignant story about a young boy who convinces his mother not to throw out all the old things that belong to his great-great-great-aunt, who lives with them.

You might consider using trade books in one or more of the following ways:

- As supplementary reading for children

- As background reading for yourself

- As reference material for children to use

- As a springboard for writing activities

- As the vehicle for units or lessons

- As the basis for an individualized reading program that parallels whatever you are dealing with in social studies

Trade Books for Teachers.   There are countless trade books for teachers, most of which could also be called activity books. They are typically aimed at teachers and are filled with potential social studies activities, usually accompanied by cute illustrations and easily reproducible materials. As you might guess, the quality of these materials can vary tremendously. All are available on-line at Amazon.com or Barnes & Noble (**www.barnesandnoble.com**) or can be ordered from your local bookstore. Here is a sampling:

Activity books for teachers

Tracey Ann Schofield. (2000). *101 Social Studies Activities for Curious Kids.* Carthage, IL: Teaching & Learning Company.

Betsy Burgess & Laurie Swiryn. (2001). *Web Activities Across the Curriculum (intermediate).* Westminister, CA: Teacher Created Materials, Inc. Comes with a CD-ROM.

Elizabeth Van Tine, Shirley Lee, Camille Cooper, & Barbara White. (1999). *Super Social Studies.* New York: Scholastic.

Marilyn Kretzer, Marlene Slobin, & Madella William. (1996). *Making Social Studies Come Alive.* New York: Scholastic Professional Books.

Max W. Fischer. (1993). *American History Simulations*. Huntington Beach, CA: Teacher Created Materials.

In addition to general activity books such as those in the preceding list, there are more specialized reference books available on selected topics. For example, if you are interested in creating food-related experiences that will go along with whatever your class is studying, consider Suzanne Barchers and Patricia Marden's *Cooking Up U.S. History*. (Englewood, CO: Teachers Idea Press, 1999, 2nd ed.). This book contains recipes from historical periods (colonial, revolutionary, civil war, etc.) as well as for various regions of the country (the Pacific Northwest, the Midwest, and Prairies, etc.). Some of the historic recipes are simple and could be made in the classroom, but others are more complicated and really require a kitchen.

A second volume in this category could be useful for teachers who want to incorporate children's literature into their social studies program. Consider Shan Glandon's *Caldecott Connections to Social Studies* (Englewood, CO: Libraries Unlimited, 2000). This book includes techniques and activity sheets for correlating twelve Caldecott winners including Paul Goble's *The Girl Who Loved Wild Horses* (Scarsdale, NY: Bradbury Press, 1978), Chris Van Allsburg's *Jumanji* (Boston: Houghton Mifflin, 1981), and Maurice Sendak's *Where the Wild Things Are* (New York: Harper & Row, 1963*)*. The activities that accompany each of the Caldecott books are thought provoking and are clearly tied to social studies.

Teaching Kits

Self-contained kits Teaching kits are self-contained packages of instructional materials. We have long been fascinated by David Macaulay's wonderful series of books: *Cathedral* (1973), *Pyramid* (1975), *Castle* (1979), *The Way Things Work* (1988), and others. PBS Video (1420 Braddock Place, Alexandria, VA 22314-1698) has now developed multimedia teaching kits based on Macaulay's books. The kits, "Middle Ages" (which combines *Cathedral* and *Castle*) and "Pyramid," cost approximately $200 and include videotapes, teaching modules, and related material. *The Way Things Work* is now available on CD-ROM.

Materials for loan or rent Many museums and state departments of education offer specialized teaching kits on a loan or rental basis. The Institute for Texan Cultures in San Antonio, for example, offers rental kits on "The Indians of Texas." If that topic is not something your students might study, consider the "Mysteries in History" toolbox available from the Indianapolis Children's Museum. Or contact the education coordinator at the nearest historical museum of reconstructed settlements (e.g., Old Sturbridge Village in Massachusetts, Connor Prairie Settlement in Indiana) or your state department of education to find whether they have instructional materials available for loan or rent. Addresses for these sources are in the Resource Handbook.

Self-contained teaching kits can cost upward of $750. As a result, the lower cost of loan or rental kits (approximately $25 plus shipping) often makes them more attractive to cost-conscious administrators. On the other hand, however, most kits last for years. If four teachers at a grade level share a teaching kit and use it for five years, the per-use cost of a $750 kit would be $37.50, which is not much more than the rental costs.

Workbooks

Consumable material

Most social studies textbook series have workbooks that are correlated with them, but these must be ordered separately each year; they don't just come with the texts. These materials are called *pupil study guides, activity guides,* or something similar, but they are *workbooks* nonetheless. If you teach in a program that demands the kind of reinforcement that workbooks offer, you may find them helpful.

Computer-Based Resources

Computer-based resources

Like many teachers, I use my computer extensively. All my course syllabi, most of my instructional materials (class handouts), and many of my examinations are now created and stored on the computer. If I were teaching in a school where I had to keep lots of student records, I would use a computer-based grade-book program. Considering the amount of information and routine paperwork that teachers must deal with, computers have proven to be wonderful tools for managing classroom-related tasks.

Instructional Applications

TECHNOLOGY

The six basic modes of computer-assisted instruction (CAI) are (1) tutorial, (2) drill and practice, (3) simulation, (4) integrated application programs, (5) problem solving, and (6) hypermedia environments (Braun, Fernlund, & White, 1998). Each of these is described next.

Tutorial Mode. Tutorial programs are available for a variety of topics, including basic economics, introductory history and geography, and, in some cases, nonsubject-related topics. Tutorial programs were among the earliest forms of social studies software. They are designed to present information to students, usually step by step and in sequential chunks, and are often accompanied by colorful graphics. In a tutorial program, the computer takes the place of the teacher, the textbook, or another source as the provider of information. Most tu-

Mastery learning

torial programs also use a form of branching or mastery learning. This means that when the students respond correctly to a series of questions the program will move them into new material. However, if students respond incorrectly, the computer will recycle them until they can demonstrate mastery.

Drill-and-Practice Mode. Drill-and-practice programs are designed to reinforce prior learning through repetitive practice. If you wish your students to learn the states and capitals or to practice locating places using latitude or longitude, for example, there are several programs that can help them. In fact, most social studies software falls into the drill-and-practice mode.

Electronic workbook

Drill-and-practice programs have been likened to electronic workbooks. But unlike traditional workbooks, the material is often presented randomly rather than sequentially. This means that students do not interact with the same series of questions and activities each time they use the software. In addition, drill-and-practice programs often use a gamelike format that, when combined with superb graphics, color, and sound, can make them appealing and almost painless.

TECHNOLOGY

A major asset of drill-and-practice programs is their ability to provide immediate feedback. For example, wherever students enter an incorrect answer, the program typically responds with an encouraging "Try again, Zack." Unfortunately,

Immediate feedback

most computer-based programs do not recognize or give credit for partially correct or misspelled answers, as human graders might. Some drill-and-practice programs avoid this limitation by asking questions in a multiple-choice format, so that students need enter only the letter (A, B, C, or D) for the correct response. Despite these limitations, the interactive nature of drill-and-practice programs can add life to what might otherwise be dull stuff.

Simulation Mode. The simulation mode was described in some detail in Chapter 9, so we will say little more about it here. Using simulations, children can place themselves into lifelike situations in which they must make decisions similar to those that had to be made in whatever real-life situation the simulation depicts. Those decisions may relate to traveling westward on the *Oregon Trail* (or its newer siblings, *Yukon Trail* and *Amazon Trail,* MECC, 1996), building and operating a dinosaur theme park (*DinoPark Tycoon,* MECC, 1995), or operating a school store (*Classroom StoreWorks,* Tom Snyder, 1997).

Beating the computer

Computer-based simulations are very popular but can also be very time consuming. In addition, children sometimes approach simulations as they do video games, where their objective is to outwit the program so they can "win." Such situations may require human intervention—a teacher-led discussion, perhaps—that refocuses students' attention on the content being simulated, and not just the outcome.

Integrated Application Programs. Databases, spreadsheets, and word-processing programs have been available for at least a decade, but integrated application programs incorporate these formerly separate entities into a single powerful program. Examples include *Appleworks* (Claris), *Microsoft Word* (Microsoft), *Clarisworks* (Claris), *Greatworks* (Symantec), and *Works for Windows* (Microsoft). Any one of these programs can be useful for developing and presenting data for teacher-developed instructional activities and for upper elementary and

Integrated packages

middle-school students' presentations. For example, Janet Jacobsen's students used the *Works* program to create their reports and the graphics associated with them. More appropriate for lower elementary students are programs like *Magic Slate* (Sunburst), *KidWriter* (Spinnaker), or FrEd Writer (Computer Using Educators). Because even most kindergarten children are able to use computers successfully, any hesitancy in this area probably reflects the teacher's misgivings and not the students' capabilities (cf., Bryant, 1992).

Problem-Solving Mode. Integrated application programs can provide the basis for some fascinating problem-solving activities. For example, consider posing the following question to your students: "How do underdeveloped nations differ from developed nations?" The first step is helping students to decide what characteristics might separate underdeveloped and developed nations. Using a database program, you can easily provide per capita income information for different nations, which students can then use to determine which ones are "developed" or "undeveloped." Once that decision is made, students can use a database program to determine what characteristics are associated with "developed" and "undeveloped" countries.

TECHNOLOGY

Figure 13.1, which shows the age distribution data for the United States and Bangladesh, was generated by the *PC Globe* database program. Other programs

FIGURE 13.1 Age Distribution, United States of America (USA) and Bangladesh

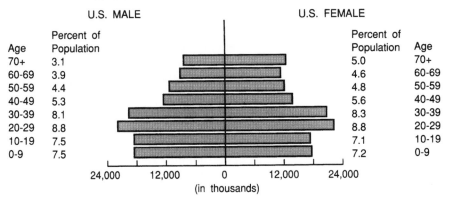

U.S. MALE			U.S. FEMALE	
Age	Percent of Population		Percent of Population	Age
70+	3.1		5.0	70+
60-69	3.9		4.6	60-69
50-59	4.4		4.8	50-59
40-49	5.3		5.6	40-49
30-39	8.1		8.3	30-39
20-29	8.8		8.8	20-29
10-19	7.5		7.1	10-19
0-9	7.5		7.2	0-9

24,000 12,000 0 12,000 24,000
(in thousands)

Total population: 248,231,000
Total male population: 120,640,000
Total female population: 127,591,000

Life expectancy (male): 72 years
Life expectancy (female): 79 years

BANGLADESH MALE			BANGLADESH FEMALE	
Age	Percent of Population		Percent of Population	Age
70+	1.0		0.8	70+
60-69	1.7		1.4	60-69
50-59	2.6		2.3	50-59
40-49	4.0		3.6	40-49
30-39	5.6		5.1	30-39
20-29	7.9		7.6	20-29
10-19	13.2		12.0	10-19
0-9	15.6		15.6	0-9

20,000 10,000 0 10,000 20,000
(in thousands)

Total population: 114,718,000
Total male population: 59,194,000
Total female population: 55,524,000

Life expectancy (male): 54 years
Life expectancy (female): 53 years

offer similar capabilities. By comparing these data for the United States and Bangladesh, students can identify at least one factor, the birth rate, that characterizes the difference between developed and undeveloped nations.

Hypermedia Environments.   There are basically two types of hypermedia programs: (1) Internet browsers, such as *Netscape* and *Microsoft Internet Explorer,* and (2) hypertext programs such as *Hypercard* and *Hyperstudio* (for Apple computers) and *Linkway* (for PCs). All of these programs permit users to navigate interactively through audio, video, and text modes. You must have a modem or be wired directly to a network server to use an Internet browser, but hypertext-based programs have no such requirements.

Interactive navigation

Hypertext programs are assembled much like a deck of index cards—each containing certain information—that can be arranged and rearranged in different ways. By pressing a button located on each card, you can move to the next card or, in some instances, start a CD-ROM or other audiovisual device. When a hypertext program is combined with audiovisual equipment, the result is a hypermedia environment, perhaps even a multimedia extravaganza!

Programs for presentation

Hypertext programs are especially well suited for presentations, either by teachers or students. This is because users can easily alter the sequence of presentation. Unfortunately, the description of hypertext programs is often more imposing than the programs themselves. Most middle-school students can learn to use *Hyperstudio* readily, whereas most primary students often feel more comfortable using a somewhat simpler version called *SlideShow*.

Telecommunications

TECHNOLOGY

More and more elementary classrooms today have computers. However, far fewer classrooms have one or more computers, one or more modems, and one or more telephone lines. All three elements—computer, modem, and telephone line—are needed before your classroom computer can connect to the Internet and on-line information services such as America Online. The key and most costly element in connecting your classroom computer to the outside world is a dedicated telephone line.

Help is in sight

You may remember Janet Jacobsen from an earlier vignette, whose students use the on-line services (e.g., America Online) and communicate via E-mail with individuals around the world. By current standards, her classroom is exceptional, simply because it has its own telephone line. The federal initiative to wire all schools should one day make such facilities commonplace.

Evaluating Software

The quality of social studies software varies tremendously. Sometimes a program's instructions are unclear; in other instances, a program may produce inaccurate stereotypes or require information that students don't have. Such flaws can make the programs unusable or, in the case of inaccurate stereotyping, inappropriate for use with children.

Recommended criteria for evaluating computer software are illustrated in Figure 13.2.

FIGURE 13.2 Computer Software Evaluation Form

Program (title) _____ Grade Level(s) _____

Producer _____ Cost _____

Hardware Required: _____

_____

I. Program Description (describe briefly):

II. General Considerations:
Does the program promote

1. active social studies learning?	Yes _____	No _____
2. meaningful social studies learning?	Yes _____	No _____
3. a pluralistic perspective on our society?	Yes _____	No _____
4. an integrative interdisciplinary perspective?	Yes _____	No _____

III. Instructional Design:
(Briefly summarize any of the following elements that apply; note any problems):

1. Is the content accurate, appropriate, and worthwhile?	Yes _____	No _____
2. Is the content appropriately sequenced and free from stereotyping or biases?	Yes _____	No _____
3. Does the reading level fit the recommended audience?	Yes _____	No _____
4. Does the program make unusual demands of the student, e.g., excessive background knowledge, reading lengthy narratives, etc.?	Yes _____	No _____

IV. Technical Considerations:

1. Are the instructions/documentation well organized, clearly written, and complete?	Yes _____	No _____
2. Are all needed materials included?	Yes _____	No _____
3. Does the program operate as it is supposed to?	Yes _____	No _____

Overall Rating _____ *Evaluated by:* _____

Source: Part II is adapted from Rose & Fernlund, 1997.

● ● ● ● ● Nonprint Materials

Reading and the written word—the print media—have so dominated American schools that nonprint media—videotape, pictures, films, and the like—have a long way to go before they have the educational impact of the printed word. Nevertheless, there have been substantial increases in both the amount of nonprint media available and in the different kinds of nonreading-based materials designed for educational purposes.

Pictures, Films, and Videotapes

The largest and most obvious category of alternatives to the printed word is pictures—those things "worth a thousand words." They come in many forms: collections of study prints, films and filmstrips, videotapes, and paintings and other works of art. Or they can be nothing more than illustrations and advertisements that you have clipped from magazines, calendars, and other sources.

The beauty of photographs as teaching tools lies in their ability to present selected yet uninterpreted data (as described in the section on culture cards, pages 313–314). Yet educators too often tend to interpret the data for viewers almost immediately. Explanatory captions are provided for most photographs and illustrations, and a narration serves this purpose for films. The intent, traditionally, has been to use the narration or picture caption to convey information. However, re-

On removing captions and narrations

moving or eliminating the caption or narration increases viewers' involvement with the picture because it forces them to make their own interpretations.

Videos and films are available for almost any topic you can name. There is also a body of educational films and videos that have no narration, only the natural sound of whatever they depict. For example, more than six hours of nonnarrated film or video beautifully portray the life of the Netselik Eskimos (*Fishing at the Stone Weir; Caribou Hunting at the Crossing Place; Autumn River Camp, Parts I and II;* and *Winter Sea Ice Camp, Parts I and II*) and are available from libraries across the country.

Eliminating the narration automatically eliminates any vocabulary problems the narration could present. So the same nonnarrated film or video can sometimes be used by primary students, twelfth graders, and even adults, usually with a different emphasis at each level.

Making your own videos

As the cost (and size) of camcorders has decreased, more teachers are making their own videotapes. This has been a boon in schools where field trips have been largely eliminated because of policy or budget considerations, or when it would be dangerous to take a large group of students to a site, such as a steel mill. Yet even where field trips are permitted, some teachers videotape them anyhow so that they can call attention to specific elements when they get back to their classroom.

Realia

Remember when a fellow student brought in his "genuine" Indian arrowhead collection to share with the class? Or when someone's relatives had been to the

TECHNOLOGY UPDATE

Virtual Touring on the Internet

Unless you teach in the vicinity of Plimoth Plantation in Massachusetts, or Colonial Williamsburg in Virginia, taking your class on a field trip to either place is probably out of the question. And if you are studying the Middle Ages, you probably don't even think about visiting a medieval castle or cathedral, both of which are in Europe. However, by connecting to the Internet, there are hundreds of places your class can visit via a "virtual tour." Some of these places include:

1. The Plimoth Plantation at:
   http://spirit.lib.uconn.edu/ArchNet/Topical/ Historic/Plimoth/Plimoth.html

2. Colonial Williamsburg at:
   http://www.history.org

3. Old Philadelphia at:
   http://www.ushistory.org/iha/index/html

4. The Museum of Egyptian Antiquities in Cairo, Egypt, at:
   http://interoz.com/egypt/museum

5. The twelfth century Durham Castle and Cathedral in Durham, United Kingdom, at:
   http://www.dur.ac.uk/~dla0www/c_tour/ tour.html

Virtual touring on the Internet is usually interactive. This means you can determine how quickly to progress through the tour and whether you wish to investigate additional areas of interest. For example, the diagram below is the floor plan of Durham Castle. By clicking your mouse on one of the numbers, you will get a photograph and a more detailed explanation of that area.

1. The Gatehouse
2. The Courtyard
3. The Entrance, Buttery and Kitchen
4. The Great Hall
5. The Black Staircase
6. The Norman Gallery
7. The Norman Chapel
8. The State Rooms
9. Bishop Tunstall's Gallery
10. Bishop Tunstall's Chapel

Durham Castle Plan

Source: Reprinted by permission of the University of Durham, Durham, UK.

If you are curious as to whether there is a virtual tour available for a topic that your class is studying, contact the on-line collection of virtual tours at:

http://www.virtualfreesites.com/tours.html. You can also use an on-line search engine to locate similar sites.

Realia: the real thing

Orient and brought back an authentic Japanese fan? These things—the arrowheads, the Japanese fan, and other real objects that might be associated with social studies teaching—are all encompassed by the term *realia*.

Most realia are adjuncts to social studies teaching, primarily because the objects are precious to their owners, often part of a collection, and as such the owner would rather not have them handled and possibly broken. Thus they often become things to be displayed—looked at but not used—during a teaching activity, and perhaps rightfully so. Some realia are probably best handled via display and in a passing fashion, such as when a student brings in a World War II bayonet during your study of colonial America.

Options

Using realia unrelated to whatever your class is studying is difficult to justify on almost any grounds. But assume, for a moment, that somewhere in your travels you have acquired a colonial candle mold and your class will be studying colonial America. What are your options? You have several. First, you could display the device and say, "This is a colonial candle mold." You could then describe how it was used.

Second, you might place the mold in a prominent location but say nothing about it. Questions are going to be asked about it, you can be sure. But to the question "What is it?" you could respond, "What do you think it is?" You might mount a large sheet of paper near the mold and ask the children to list what they think it is. At a convenient time, you might display an illustration of someone using a candle mold, again saying nothing about it. Someone will soon notice it, and you may not even need to say anything else at all. Or you might pose the question "How are candles made today?," which will initiate another adventure.

As springboards to inquiry

If the function of the realia is obvious, you might wish to take a different tack. For the Japanese fan mentioned earlier, you might want to ask who uses fans in Japan and why. Are they necessarily to keep Japanese women cool? If you pursue this line of questioning, identify—in advance—some sources the students can use to validate their answers. They may find that fans are a normal part of a Japanese dancer's equipment.

● ● ● ● Community Resources

Every community everywhere has someone who has been somewhere or who knows something that can be useful in your social studies program. And almost every community also has places you can visit that will also be an asset to your program.

Resource Persons

Using resource people effectively

Identifying individuals in the community who have specialized knowledge or experience is not especially difficult. The list can go from authors to zookeepers. The more challenging task is using those resource people effectively.

Part of the problem occurs because resource people are, by definition, specialists. As such, they are familiar with the intricacies, the nuances, and the jargon of their specialization. Your students, however, may be at a level where their main concern is with the most fundamental aspects of a specialized area.

The local history buff who, for example, gets enmeshed in the minutiae of who married whom in the early 1840s can't count on keeping your students' interest for very long. Once their interest is lost, your students may begin to get restless, and your guest speaker may take their behavior as a personal affront.

Clarify expectations ahead of time

Therefore, even though it may seem an imposition, clarify in advance exactly what you want the speaker to cover to ensure a successful experience for both the resource person *and* your class.

A related problem arises because resource people are sometimes ill equipped to do more than talk to students. Unless they deal with young children regularly, they are unlikely to have audiovisual aids or other media to enliven their presentations. Even if they have such media, you will need to have worked with your class to establish a need or desire for whatever information the resource person can provide. One of the most helpful things you can do is provide the resource person with a list of questions or topics that your class has developed before the presentation. This helps ensure that (1) the class has at least a passing acquaintance with whatever the resource person will cover (otherwise students won't be able to frame intelligent questions) and (2) the resource person has an idea of the level of the class's concerns and can prepare accordingly.

Lay the necessary groundwork

A final suggestion about using resource people: be wary of people who *insist* on talking to your class. Among the people who willingly volunteer their services, there are always some who would use the schools as a platform for their special causes. Even if you are sympathetic to the cause, whatever it may be, you may risk your professional future by honoring their offer. Before issuing an invitation, be certain to check school policies and inform the appropriate administrative personnel (principal, etc.) of your intentions.

Caution

Oral History

Oral history refers to written histories that are produced primarily from spoken (or oral) sources. When students get involved in oral history projects, they usually do so on a cooperative learning basis. Several students working together develop a written history using data they have gathered by interviewing individuals from the community who have firsthand knowledge of historically interesting events or ways of life. The interviews are tape-recorded and then converted into transcripts that provide the basis for the written history. The resulting document, probably the only one of its kind in existence, is usually placed in the school library.

Using community resources to create history

Oral history is ideally suited to the study of recent local history. The key element is that there must be people around who know something about the period or topic in question and are willing to be interviewed. Grandparents and senior citizens are frequent and often willing subjects for oral history projects.

Plan interviews in advance

A key aspect of oral history activities involves helping students to plan and structure their interviews. If they don't plan carefully, they can easily end up with random conversations of little historic value. Student interviewers must be clear about what information they are after, who is going to ask which questions, and so forth. Their purpose may be to get a local resident's account of the day the old courthouse burned down, someone's views on how population growth has affected the community, or almost anything else that might be of interest. The students' purpose is to conduct an interview *about something*. It doesn't matter so much what that "something" is as long as students understand what kind of information they are after.

Here are some guidelines for conducting oral history activities:

Suggested guidelines

1. The focus should be on one manageable topic, especially in the lower elementary grades.

2. Prepare carefully for the interview, including helping students to "bone up" on the topic by using other sources—wills, diaries, other accounts. On the other hand, don't do so much preparation that your students lose interest.

3. Equipment for the interview may include props like an old photograph or picture, but a tape recorder is essential.

4. Appointments for interviews should be made through official sources so that students don't face the burden of explaining the entire project. Interviews should be restricted to one hour or less.

5. Send students in interview teams of two or three.

6. Contact the computer teacher for possible assistance in putting the transcripts on a word processor.

Logistics   The logistics of oral history combined with the mechanics of producing transcripts from several dozen tape-recorded interviews can sometimes become so cumbersome that the project may not seem worth the effort. At the same time, students involved in an oral history project are actually creating history. In the process, they can also be developing skills in listening, observing, and asking questions; organizing information; and distinguishing fact from opinion and relevant from irrelevant information. If they do nothing else, oral history activities may lead students to a better understanding and appreciation of the older generation. That alone may make oral history projects worth the effort.

Field Trips and Tours

Some teachers take their students on tours of museums, bakeries, fire stations, and the like, which can provide enriching, hands-on experiences that would be impossible to duplicate in a classroom. Other teachers, however, take their students on field trips to the same places. The distinction between *tours* and *field trips* is based on (1) the activities that take place in the classroom prior to the trip and (2) the students' perceptions about why they are going.

KEY IDEA

Identifying community resources is often less difficult than using those resources effectively.

Before scientists "go out into the field," they usually identify their purpose for going. When archaeologists decide to dig at a particular site, for example, their decision is usually based on (1) prior research, (2) a clear sense of purpose (for digging), and (3) previously identified questions or problems that they hope to answer. Likewise, if your students were going on a field trip to a bakery, they should arrive armed with *previously identified* questions that they want answers for: "Do bakeries grind their own flour?" "Do bakeries use the same kind of flour available in supermarkets?" In other words, because of the students' previous classroom experience, they arrive at the site with a clear sense of why they are there. Students will probably enjoy the experience and learn things they didn't have questions about, but this is simply extra frosting on the cake.

Logistics.   Although tours and field trips can add immeasurable value to education, most experienced teachers can also tell horror stories about things that went wrong on a field trip or tour: kids who got lost, children who spent all their lunch money at the souvenir stand, and so forth. The logistical problems can have you tearing your hair out in short order.

In addition, students sometimes assume that rules for classroom conduct don't apply to outside-of-school activities, as on a field trip or tour, which then leads to discipline problems. Although there is certainly no guarantee, the clearer sense of purpose associated with field trips will probably result in fewer discipline problems. Likewise, preplanning can eliminate some of the logistical and discipline-related problems associated with field trips and tours. Consider the following suggestions:

- Obtain administrative approval before announcing the trip to students. (On the application form, always use "field trip," even if you're planning a tour to the zoo—it sounds better and may be easier for the administrator to justify.)

- Avoid going anywhere on Mondays and Fridays. Over the weekend (for a Monday trip), kids often forget to bring their lunches, spending money, and so on. Friday trips deny the opportunity for immediate follow-up.

- Recruit, screen, and instruct parent chaperons so that they can contribute significantly to the trip. Don't wait until just before leaving to tell parents what you expect of them. Send a note home beforehand that outlines (1) what you expect parents to do, (2) rules you have discussed with students, and (3) any other pertinent information.

- Create task groups with specific responsibilities before the trip takes place. For example, there can be recorders (keep records and journals), collectors (obtain necessary items for or from the trip), photographers, public relations people (thank-you-note writers), and maintenance people (clean up).

- If you are taking a tour, select an impressive place. If you were bored on your last trip to the sewage-treatment plant, your students probably will be bored too.

- Take everyone, including your troublemakers. Leaving them behind could lead to deep-seated resentment you can never overcome.

- Send parental permission slips home even if the school uses a blanket permission form covering all field trips for the year.

- Even with signed permission slips, you may be legally liable if you agree to supervise students in too large an area. We're not talking about the Superdome here. Trying to supervise students in two large halls of a museum could make you liable if something happened to someone. Err on the safe side, and *take one adult for each group of five children*. If you plan to videotape the trip, take

How tours and field trips differ

Avoiding logistical problems

Recommendations

Communicate with parents in advance

Take everyone

along a parent to do that so you remain free to devote your complete attention to leading the expedition.

Use name tags

- Use name tags (including the school name). This is essential for young children; for older students it enables chaperons to call them by name.

- Avoid going in private cars whenever possible; the legal hazards (insurance coverage, etc.) are considerable.

- Be sure to take a first-aid kit, a summary of students' medical information, especially allergies, and a list of the children's home and emergency phone numbers.

- Prepare a guidesheet for students to complete while at the museum or other resource.

- Be certain to debrief the activity. As is true of most things educational, what happens after a field trip is as important as what takes place during or before it.

- Be sure to send thank-you notes to all parents who assist you.

Don't overlook walking field trips to nearby locations. Supermarkets, banks, bakeries, and those old standbys, the post office and fire station, often welcome visits from schoolchildren. Whether you walk or take a bus, the crucial element is that your students understand why they are going on the field trip. Otherwise, field trips and tours may be seen as just another day off from school.

Using Community Resources

Using community resources—either resource persons or field trips—involves both a logistical and a substantive dimension. The logistical side includes such things as contacting individuals and arranging for buses (and rest stops, parental approval and assistance, etc.). The substantive dimension relates to the content that you and your class (and perhaps a resource person) will be studying.

Related issues

Many school districts have specific guidelines for the logistical (and legal) considerations concerning resource persons and field trips. Sometimes they also cover substantive questions. Could you, for example, invite an avowed white supremacist to speak to your class? Could you take your students on a field trip to a slaughterhouse or a funeral home? Consider how you would respond if you were an elementary principal and a teacher came to you with such a request. If the teacher could show a clear relationship between the slaughterhouse (or the funeral home) and whatever the class was studying, would it make any difference to your decision? The issues here are far from simple.

Once you have gotten the necessary permissions, the success of the experience will probably depend on the preliminary work you do before a resource person enters your classroom or before your class leaves on the field trip. The basic questions you need to ask yourself include the following:

Basic considerations

- Is a community resource appropriate for the purposes of my group?

- Have I planned preliminary activities that provide a context within which my class can interpret whatever they hear or see?

- Have I identified appropriate follow-up activities?
- Does my class have an identifiable need for the information that the resource can provide?
- Do my students understand what is expected of them—both in terms of their conduct and in terms of what they are to learn?

If you can answer these questions in the positive, you'll be on the way to making effective use of the resources that your community can provide. If you cannot, keep your aspirin handy.

● ● ● ● Acquiring Instructional Resources

Determining what is available

Where do teachers get the things they teach with? Many school systems provide a budget from which teachers purchase teaching materials. Where such budgets exist, they are almost always small. In acquiring instructional resources, your first step is to identify what is available from commercial publishers or other sources. You can usually find catalogs of educational materials somewhere in the school—the library, the resource center, or the teachers' lounge. The names and addresses of the major teachers' magazines and social studies journals are located in the Resource Handbook.

Many school systems accept teachers' requests for materials in the spring and purchase the materials the following summer. This may mean that you don't have the opportunity to purchase materials during your first year of teaching. In that event, you will be forced to do what hundreds of other teachers do—buy materials yourself. But before doing that, you have a couple of other options. First, find out if there is something you can use that is free (or inexpensive). The quality of free and inexpensive materials can vary tremendously, however, so be selective. Evaluate why various concerns are willing to sell materials inexpensively or give them away. Many schools subscribe to one or more guides to free and inexpensive materials. Sources and addresses are listed in the Resource Handbook.

Second, consider making your own materials. Some of the best teaching resources are those that teachers have developed themselves. For example, teachers created most of the student activities in this book. Most of them went through some refining—that is, they were tried out with students and then revised—but once developed, they become a resource to be used in future years.

The process of developing teaching materials is not as difficult as you might suspect (a large dose of common sense is about as helpful as anything). Typically, you do the following:

1. Identify (a) the major concept(s) you want to teach and (b) the major question(s), issue(s), or skill(s) you want the children to deal with. (Note: This is sometimes the most difficult step of all.)
2. Decide what kind of format you want to use—a fact sheet, role-playing, limited-choice decision making, and so on.
3. Create the activity (and duplicate as needed).
4. Use the activity with your students.
5. Revise as needed, based on what you found in Step 4.

 SUGGESTED ACTIVITY

Congratulations! Your budget request has been approved and the board of education has authorized $250 per teacher for social studies teaching materials other than textbooks. How will you spend your funds?

It's sometimes wise to add a Step 3(a): before you duplicate an activity for students, share it with someone you can rely on for honest feedback—a colleague, a fellow student teacher, or someone else. You are almost certain to find that something you thought was perfectly obvious isn't, and thus you will gain a chance to make appropriate adjustments before using the activity with your students.

SUMMARY

There are countless resources teachers can use for teaching social studies, including a can of corn, as noted earlier, a colonial candle mold perhaps, or even a telephone directory. Determining what is or is not a potential teaching resource is primarily a matter of perception, a matter of asking yourself what you could teach by using "that." The second key is one stressed throughout this book; that is, a resource is something you use to teach, as opposed to something you teach about.

The one resource available almost everywhere is the textbook. Using a textbook as your primary resource during your first year of teaching is understandable and, in some cases, politically expedient. But as you become more familiar with the terrain you are expected to cover, consider integrating some of the other resources available to you. These may include daily newspapers, children's books—both informational and fictional—and perhaps one of the current events publications. They may also include computer-based resources, such as tutorials, drill-and-practice programs, simulations, integrated application programs that incorporate databases, spread-

sheets, and word-processing programs, and, if you have the necessary hardware, programs that allow your students to connect to the Internet or develop presentation materials using one of the hypertext-based programs.

Even if you do not have sophisticated computer equipment, there are other traditional resources that can add to your program. These include individuals in the community who can provide expertise on particular subjects, as well as field trips and tours to places that your students might not otherwise visit. However, the key to using community resource people, field trips, or tours successfully lies in the kind of preliminary work you do before the event occurs. Students who understand why they are listening to a resource person or visiting a particular site are much less likely to regard the event as a lark.

Regardless of what resources for teaching social studies you choose to use, the basic expectation is that they reflect accurate and unbiased, quality "stuff." In addition, the resources must be used in ways that capture the students' attention. Unless they can fulfill that requirement, the quality issue becomes irrelevant.

SUGGESTED READINGS AND RESOURCES

Print Resources

Michael J. Berson, Barbara C. Cruz, James A. Duplass, & J. Howard Johnson. (2001). *Social studies on the Internet.* Upper Saddle River, NJ: Prentice Hall. This little volume is filled with Internet addresses along with short descriptions of what each site offers. Its organization follows an eclectic but useful pattern—subjects commonly taught in social studies, planning and instruction, controversial issues, and so on.

J. A. Braun, Jr., P. Fernlund, & C. S. White. (1998). *Technology tools in the social studies curriculum.* Wilsonville, OR: Franklin-Beedle and Associates. This book provides an excellent overview of the latest technology-related options available to teachers. Also includes reprints of articles.

Shan Glanon. (2000). *Caldecott connections to social studies.* Englewood, CO: Libraries Unlimited. This wonderful volume contains lesson plans and teaching materials for using twelve Caldecott medal-winning children's book. Among the books are *The Girl Who Loved Wild Horses, The Little House, Jumanji, Grandfather's Journey,* and *The Oxcart Man.*

Mildred Knight Laughlin & Patricia Payne Kardaleff. (1991). *Literature-based social studies: Children's books & activities to enrich the K–5 curriculum.* Phoenix, AZ: Oryx Press. Although I have cited this volume previously, I repeat it here because it contains exemplary units that are based on children's books and that are keyed to topics common to many social studies programs.

Internet Resources

Introductory Note: Web sites sometimes change their Internet addresses or cease operating entirely. All the addresses supplied here were operating when this book was printed, but if any of them fails to work properly, enter the desired topic or organization into any standard search engine.

SOFTWARE AND SOFTWARE REVIEWS

SuperKids Software Reviews

http://www.superkids.com/aweb/pages/reviews/socstudl/sw_sum 1.shtml

Parents, teachers, and children do reviews of social studies software at this site. Very useful.

Technology and Learning Online

http://www.techlearning.com/

This highly recommended site is the home page of the journal *Technology and Learning*. A notable feature is its software review search engine, which permits you to search for reviews of software related to social studies or the other subjects taught in elementary and middle schools.

ADDITIONAL RESOURCES

Information about Islam and Muslims

www.islamicity.org

This site offers a wealth of readily understandable information about Islamic culture. It is suitable for both students and teachers.

Teaching Tolerance

www.tolerance.org/teach

This site is maintained by the Southern Poverty Law Center, whose main focus is on hate groups and intolerance in the United States. Offers excellent background materials and lesson plans on teaching tolerance.

OTHER SOCIAL-STUDIES–RELATED MATERIALS

Sources

http://www.intel.com/intelleducate/teacher/links

This extremely useful site is maintained by the Intel Corporation and offers links to resources for classroom teachers. These include professional organizations, the ERIC Clearinghouses, specialty Internet publications, and numerous other areas that involve technology and education. **Bookmark quality.**

Social Studies Software

http://ed.info.apple.corn/education/techlearn/sp/socstsoft.html

Apple Computer maintains this site, which includes listings of social studies software titles that are organized by categories. These include: (1) simulation software, (2) historical software, and (3) reference software. Useful.

Epilogue

REMEMBER WHEN YOU

- Couldn't understand why Australia was a continent but Greenland wasn't?
- Thought Paris, Boston, and Chicago were states?
- Memorized the Preamble to the Constitution, the Gettysburg Address, or the presidents of the United States in order?
- Were taught that "mail carriers deliver the mail" when you already knew it? . . .

Introduction: Reflecting on Things Past

This book began by asking whether you remembered some of the things listed above. It ends with the hope that you have a better context for explaining and interpreting those things you remembered. Hopefully, you understand that the perspective from which some maps are drawn makes Australia appear smaller than Greenland (even though it is actually about three times larger) and that young children often have difficulty distinguishing among cities, states, and countries until they gain more experience with their world.

Many changes have occurred in social studies education over the years, ranging from efforts to teach "history as history" and "geography as geography," through attempts to teach children to use the social and behavioral sciences as they deal with the worlds in which they live. To whatever extent I have an opportunity to influence the direction that social studies education in the future may take, I wish to suggest the following as possible emphases that can assist us in the twenty-first century.

Instructional Premises for the Twenty-first Century

- Observation and listening should receive increased emphasis as skills for gaining access to information.
- There should be increased emphasis on helping students become more aware of the thinking processes they use.

- There should be increased awareness of how mathematics can be a tool for communicating social information.

- There should be an increased use of fiction and nonfiction literature in teaching social studies.

Desirable directions

- There should be increased recognition of the power of technology to place a world of data at students' fingertips.

- From the primary grades onward, students should be increasingly involved in designing and conducting their own investigations—their own "social studies," if you will.

- Social studies programs and teaching should emphasize systems of relationships among social phenomena rather than learning isolated pieces of information.

- Increased emphasis should be placed on helping students become skillful in making and testing social ideas.

- The assessment of students' performance will be increasingly based on portfolios and specific examples of student achievement.

- The trend toward "less is more"—that is, helping students to develop in-depth understanding of fewer significant topics, with correspondingly less superficial coverage—should continue.

A never-ending problem

From time to time, various individuals and organizations release reports intent on showing what students don't know. Most of those reports are accompanied by claims that we need to teach more of "this" and more of "that" to rectify the apparent crisis. I am not trying to excuse the many problems in schools today, but *so long as the reservoir of knowledge continues to grow, there will always be things that students don't know.*

Efforts to teach children everything they might ever be expected to know may have contributed to the problem. The time available for teaching has not increased significantly over the last century, whereas the reservoir of knowledge grows larger with each passing day. By trying to cram everything into the limited time available, many social studies (and other school) programs have opted for breadth—for covering large amounts of information in a comparatively short time—instead of focusing in depth on significant understandings, ideas, and skills. The superficial skimming that occurs in "trying to cover everything" has too often resulted in mere exposure and the knowledge of a few facts and names, but at the cost of in-depth understanding.

Living in an information-rich world

Clearly all students should know certain basics, certain fundamental ideas and skills. How you identify *which* fundamentals those are depends on your view of the world for which you are educating children. Sometimes this may mean placing more emphasis on information like "Columbus voyaged to America" and "New Delhi is the capital of India," assuming, of course, that social studies programs have ceased emphasizing such information. But also we need to ask ourselves how such information will help students to function in an increasingly information-rich world—a world of computers and other electronic media. In other cases, the fundamentals can include powerful questions and ideas that are drawn from the human experience—questions like "What makes us human?" and "How did we get this way?" and ideas like "Change begets change" and "All people define the world from their own frame of reference." In still other cases, the fundamentals can include skills—the process (critical thinking) skills identified earlier.

To deal with either the content or process to the exclusion of the other is to deal with neither well. Skills taught in isolation can be forgotten as quickly as facts taught in isolation. Teaching social studies should not be a matter of teaching content *or* teaching information-processing skills, for the two are reciprocal and inseparable. As we move further into this century, social studies teaching must reflect content *with* process, and process *with* content, for these, I think, are children's keys to their world.

As a kind of benediction, here is an old proverb that has served well over those years:

> Give a man a fish
> and you feed him for one day.
> Teach him how to fish, and
> he feeds himself for a lifetime.

In many respects, teaching social studies is indeed like teaching children how "to fish." I hope that this book will serve as your guide to opening the fascinating world of social studies to the children you teach. Best wishes!

D. A. W.

Resource Handbook Contents

Introduction

This handbook has been designed as something you can turn to when you want additional information on a social studies–related topic.

The Resource Handbook has four parts. Part 1 includes materials that are detailed extensions of topics discussed in the text itself. If you are interested in the answers to some of the activities in the text, or if you want to examine the national standards for social studies, look in Part 1 of the Handbook.

Part 2 of the Handbook includes (1) an annotated lesson planning guide, and (2) Alleman and Brophy's guidelines for designing teaching activities. Part 3 of the Handbook provides listings of sources for a variety of teaching and resource materials. If you are interested in looking for living history sites or sources for in-expensive instructional materials, for example, look for these in Part 3.

Part 4 of the Handbook provides annotated bibliographies of children's literature. This section has four parts: (1) children's books that are useful for teaching character and selected morals and values, (2) children's historical fiction and folk literature for common social studies topics, (3) nonfiction books you might use to teach about topics commonly taught in social studies, and (4) children's books for teaching about women's roles throughout history. With the multitude of children's literature available for teaching social studies, and considering the broad range of topics that social studies encompasses, I trust that you will find these bibliographies useful.

Part 1 Materials Related to Activities in the Text

1.1 Data Cards for the "Presidency" Activity

Card 1

Data About Benedict Arnold, as of 1801. Before he joined the British in their attempt to defeat the rebels during the American Revolution, Arnold had served George Washington with distinction during military campaigns from 1776 to 1779. Distressed with financial worries and feeling that he was not receiving adequate recognition from the Continental Congress for his services, he abandoned the American cause and became one of the best-known traitors in American history.

Card 2

Data About Franklin D. Roosevelt, as of 1945. The American people elected Roosevelt president four times. Because of his New Deal programs designed to combat the severe financial depression of the 1930s and his leadership during World War II, many historians have classified him as one of the most effective chief executives ever to hold the office. Some of Roosevelt's critics, however, have felt that he misused the power of the presidency by exerting extensive political pressure on Congress to secure passage of the New Deal legislation. He served as president from 1933 until his death in 1945. An attack of polio in the early 1920s left Roosevelt's legs partially paralyzed for the remainder of his life.

Card 3

Data About Martin Luther King, Jr., as of 1968. Before he was assassinated in 1968, the Reverend Martin Luther King, Jr., had become one of the most active champions of the nonviolent civil rights movement. Beginning with his successful boycott of segregated city buses in Birmingham, Alabama, King rose to become leader of the Southern Christian Leadership Conference, one of the most effective organizations to lobby for federal civil rights legislation during the 1960s.

Card 4

Data About Alexander Hamilton, as of 1804. Until his death in a duel with Aaron Burr, Hamilton served his country as an adviser to George Washington. His arguments for adoption of the federal Constitution were instrumental in its final approval. His financial genius helped to establish the United States on a firm financial footing during its early years.

Card 5

Data About Hilary Rodham Clinton, as of 2002. Hillary Clinton, wife of former President Bill Clinton, was the first First Lady ever elected to the United States Senate, and the first woman elected statewide in New York. Almost immediately after her husband's election, he appointed her to chair the Task Force on Health Care Reform, a role in which she became the target of significant criticism that sometimes spilled over into her later activities. Nevertheless, she has continued to be a leading advocate for women's rights and children's issues.

Card 6

Data About Henry G. Cisneros, as of 2002. During President Clinton's first term in office, Cisneros served as Secretary of Housing and Urban Development. As such, he was America's foremost federal housing and economic development official. He was responsible for administering federally assisted housing and economic development programs throughout the nation. In 1981, Henry Cisneros became the first Hispanic mayor of a major U.S. city, San Antonio, Texas. Both as mayor and in his later activities, Cisneros has received numerous awards and honors. These include selection as one of the "Ten Outstanding Young Men of America" by the U.S. Jaycees, selection as Outstanding Mayor by *City and State* magazine, and the Hispanic Man of the Year by *Vista* magazine. Cisneros's departure from public service was hastened when a long-standing, extramarital affair was publicized in the media, and by his desire to improve his economic circumstances by working in the private sector.

Card 7

Data About Abraham Lincoln, as of 1865. With the exception of George Washington and Franklin D. Roosevelt, probably no other president ever entered office facing such immense problems as did Abraham Lincoln. Historians of Lincoln's life generally agree that he did as much as any chief executive could have done to lead the Union to victory in the Civil War and to attempt to heal the wounds of that conflict in both the North and the South. On numerous occasions before and during his presidency, Lincoln suffered periods of severe mental depression. His untimely assassination occurred in 1865.

Source: Adapted from Marsha Hobin, "Clarifying What Is Important," in Allan O. Kownslar, Ed., *Teaching American History: The Quest for Relevancy.* © National Council for the Social Studies. Reprinted by permission.

1.2 NCSS Standards for Social Studies (Abridged)

The NCSS standards are organized around ten thematic strands that correspond with one or more relevant disciplines and that span the educational levels from the early and middle grades to high school. The standards are expressed in statements that begin with "Social studies programs should include experiences that provide for the study of"—for instance, culture. The thematic strands are as follows.

Culture

The study of culture prepares students to answer questions such as: What are the common characteristics of different cultures? How do belief systems, such as religion or political ideals, influence other parts of the culture? How does the culture change to accommodate different ideas and beliefs? What does language tell us about the culture? Relevant courses and disciplines include geography, history, sociology, and anthropology, as well as multicultural topics across the curriculum.

Time, Continuity, and Change

Human beings seek to understand their historical roots and to locate themselves in time. Knowing how to read and reconstruct the past allows one to develop a historical perspective and to answer questions such as: Who am I? What happened in the past? How am I connected to those in the past? How has the world changed, and how might it change in the future? Why does our personal sense of relatedness to the past change? Relevant courses and disciplines include history.

People, Places, and Environment

The study of people, places, and human-environment interactions assists students as they create their spatial views and geographic perspectives of the world beyond their personal locations. Students need the knowledge, skills, and understanding to answer questions such as: Where are things located? Why are they located where they are? What do we mean by "region"? How do landforms change? What implications do these changes have for people? Relevant courses and disciplines include geography and areas studies.

Individual Development and Identity

Personal identity is shaped by one's culture, by groups, and by institutional influences. Students should consider such questions as: How do people learn? Why do people behave as they do? What influences how people learn, perceive, and grow? How do people meet their basic needs in a variety of contexts? How do individuals develop from youth to adulthood? Relevant courses and disciplines include psychology and anthropology.

Individuals, Groups, and Institutions

Institutions such as schools, churches, families, government agencies, and the courts play an integral role in people's lives. It is important that students learn how institutions are formed, what controls and influences them, how they influence individuals and culture, and how they are maintained or changed. Students may address questions such as: What is the role of institutions in this and other societies? How am I influenced by institutions? How do institutions change? What is my role in institutional change? Relevant courses and disciplines include sociology, anthropology, psychology, political science, and history.

Power, Authority, and Governance

Understanding the historical development of structures of power, authority, and governance and their evolving functions in contemporary U.S. society and other parts of the world is essential for developing civic competence. In exploring this theme, students confront questions such as: What is power? What forms does it take? Who holds it? How is it gained, used, and justified? What is legitimate authority? How are governments created, structured, maintained, and changed? How can individual rights be protected within the context of majority rule? Relevant courses and disciplines include government, politics, political science, history, law, and other social sciences.

Production, Distribution, and Consumption

Because people have wants that often exceed the resources available to them, a variety of ways have evolved to answer such questions as: What is to be produced? How is production to be organized? How are goods and services to be distributed? What is the most effective allocation of the factors of production (land, labor, capital, and management)? Relevant courses and disciplines include economics.

Science, Technology, and Society

Modern life as we know it would be impossible without technology and the science that supports it. But technology brings with it many questions: Is new technology always better than old? What can we learn from the past about how new technologies result in broader social change, some of which is unanticipated? How can we cope with the ever-increasing pace of change? How can we manage technology so that the greatest number of people benefit from it? How can we preserve our fundamental values and beliefs in the midst of technological change? This theme draws upon the natural and physical sciences, social sciences, and the humanities. Relevant courses and disciplines include history, geography, economics, civics, and government.

Global Connections

The realities of global interdependence require understanding the increasingly important and diverse global connections among world societies and the frequent tension between national interests and global priorities. Students will need to be able to address such international issues as health care, the environment, human rights, economic competition and interdependence, age-old ethnic enmities, and political and military alliances. Relevant courses and disciplines include geography, culture, and economics; may also draw upon the natural and physical sciences and the humanities.

Civic Ideals and Practices

An understanding of civic ideals and practices of citizenship is critical to full participation in society and is a central purpose of social studies. Students confront such questions as: What is civic participation and how can I be involved? How has the meaning of citizenship evolved? What is the balance between rights and responsibilities? What is the role of the citizen in the community and the nation, and as a member of the world community? How can I make a positive difference? Relevant courses and disciplines include history, political science, cultural anthropology, and fields such as global studies, law-related education, and the humanities.

Abridged from the Executive Summary of *Expect Excellence: Curriculum Standards for Social Studies Electronic Edition* (1996), 2–4.

1.3 K–4 Standards for Historical Thinking

Standard 1. Chronological Thinking, which includes the following performance indicators: (a) distinguishing between past, present, and future time, (b) identifying in historical narratives the temporal structure of a historical narrative or story, (c) establishing temporal order in constructing their [students'] own historical narratives, (d) measuring and calculating calendar time, (e) interpreting data presented in time lines, (f) creating time lines, and (g) explaining change and continuity over time.

Standard 2. Historical Comprehension, which includes (a) reconstructing the literal meaning of a historical passage, (b) identifying the central question(s) the historical narrative addresses, (c) reading historical narratives imaginatively, (d) providing evidence of historical perspectives, (e) drawing upon the data in historical maps, (f) drawing upon visual and mathematical data presented in graphics, and (g) drawing upon the visual data presented in photographs, paintings, cartoons, and architectural drawings.

Standard 3. Historical Analysis and Interpretation, which includes (a) formulating questions to focus their inquiry or analysis, (b) identifying the author or source of the historical document or narrative, (c) comparing and contrasting differing sets of ideas, values, personalities, behaviors, and institutions, (d) analyzing historical fiction, (e) distinguishing between fact and fiction, (f) comparing different stories about a historical figure, era, or event, (g) analyzing illustrations in historical stories, (h) considering multiple perspectives, (i) explaining causes in analyzing historical actions, (j) challenging arguments of historical inevitability, and (k) hypothesizing influences of the past.

Standard 4. Historical Research Capabilities, which include the following performance indicators: (a) formulating historical questions, (b) obtaining historical data, (c) interrogating historical data, and (d) marshaling needed knowledge of the time and place and constructing a story, explanation, or historical narrative.

Standard 5. Historical Issues—Analysis and Decision-Making, which includes the following performance indicators: (a) identifying issues and problems in the past, (b) comparing the interests and values of the various people involved, (c) suggesting alternative choices for addressing the problem, (d) evaluating alternative courses of action, (e) preparing a position or course of action on an issue, and (f) evaluating the consequences of a decision.

Source: K–4 Standards for Historical Thinking, National Center for History in the Schools (1995). Reprinted by permission.

1.4 The Essential Elements of Geography

The following are the six "essential elements" and eighteen related standards developed by the Geography Education Standards Project (1994).

Element One: The World in Spatial Terms

Geography focuses on the relationships between people, places, and environments by mapping information about them in a spatial context. The geographically informed person knows and understands:

1. How to use maps and other geographic representations, tools, and technologies to acquire, process, and report information from a spatial perspective.
2. How to use mental maps to organize information about people, places, and environments in a spatial context.
3. How to analyze the spatial organization of people, places, and environments on the earth's surface.

Element Two: Places and Regions

The identities and lives of people are rooted in particular places, and in those human constructs called regions. The geographically informed person knows and understands:

4. The physical and human characteristics of place.
5. That people create regions to interpret the earth's complexity.
6. How culture and experience influence people's perceptions of places and regions.

Element Three: Physical Systems

Physical processes shape the earth's surface and interact with plant and animal life to create, sustain, and modify ecosystems. The geographically informed person knows and understands:

7. The physical processes that shape the patterns of the earth's surface.
8. The characteristics and spatial distribution of ecosystems on the earth's surface.

Element Four: Human Systems

People are central to geography in that human activities help to shape the earth's surface. Human settlements and structures are also part of the earth's surfaces that human beings compete to control. The geographically informed person knows and understands:

9. The characteristics, distribution, and migration of human populations on the earth's surface.
10. The characteristics, distribution, and complexity of the earth's cultural mosaics.
11. The patterns and networks of economic interdependence on the earth's surface.
12. The processes, patterns, and functions of human settlements.
13. How the forces of cooperation and conflict among people influence the division and control of the earth's surface.

Element Five: Environment and Society

The physical environment is modified by human activities, largely as a consequence of the ways in which human societies value and use the earth's natural resources. Human activities are also influenced by the earth's physical features and processes. The geographically informed person knows and understands:

14. How human actions modify the physical environment.
15. How physical systems affect human systems.
16. The changes that occur in the meaning, use, distribution, and importance of resources.

Element Six: The Uses of Geography

The knowledge of geography enables people to develop an understanding of the relationships between people, places, and environments over time—that is, of the earth as it was, is, and might be. The geographically informed person knows and understands:

17. How to apply geography to interpret the past.
18. How to apply geography to interpret the present and plan for the future.

Source: Geography Education Standards Project (1994). *Geography for Life: National Geography Standards 1994.* Washington, DC: National Geographic Society. Reprinted by permission.

1.5 Sample Learning Style Inventory

Place the letter that best reflects your preference in the blank provided.

____ 1. When you really want to study something and learn it well, would you rather (a) work alone, (b) study with others having similar interests, (c) work by yourself but in a setting where there are other people around?

____ 2. Assuming that each of the following modes is effective and that you have a choice, would you most prefer to learn something by (a) reading, (b) listening, (c) observing?

____ 3. Learning situations that cause you the most concern are those that appear to be (a) ambiguous, (b) rather closely defined as to the desired outcome, (c) without guidelines, where you are completely on your own.

____ 4. Do you have most trouble learning things that (a) use abstract symbols, (b) use diagrams and charts, (c) use mathematical numbers and figures?

____ 5. When you are not really interested in something you are studying, do you find yourself (a) able to discipline yourself to study, (b) easily distracted by other things, (c) going through the motions to look as though you are studying?

____ 6. When memorizing something, do you find yourself (a) developing a theme within which to relate the parts, (b) creating a pattern that cues the parts, (c) trying to picture the thing in your mind?

____ 7. Would you prefer to study something that (a) involves some creative effort of your own, (b) calls for you to apply analytical and critical skills, (c) lays out all the points in front of you so you have a chance to understand it?

____ 8. When do you find that you do your best learning? (a) in the early morning, (b) around midday, (c) in the afternoon, (d) during an "all nighter."

____ 9. When studying, do you find that you (a) create relationships without being told, (b) understand the material but have some difficulty putting it together, (c) must be given the "whole" before the "parts" make sense?

1

_____ 10. In most classes, would you rather be taught by someone who (a) knows the material and can tell it to you clearly and precisely, (b) knows the material and teases and leads you to conclusions, (c) knows the material but primarily raises questions?

_____ 11. Do you feel most comfortable when asked (a) to analyze the material studied, (b) to report on the material studied, (c) to summarize the material studied?

_____ 12. When studying something completely new, do you (a) need someone around to encourage your efforts, (b) prefer to figure it out for yourself, (c) tend to give up easily even if encouraged?

_____ 13. Do you consider yourself as a student who (a) grasps new ideas quickly, (b) goes at a slightly slower pace, yet masters ideas well, (c) deals with new material so thoroughly that you are able to identify new ideas and/or relationships that extend beyond those explicit in the original materials?

_____ 14. When studying with a particular instructor, are you (a) very conscious of the teacher's reaction to how you are doing, (b) indifferent to what the teacher thinks about your progress, (c) interested in the teacher's response but only after you have completed the task on your own?

_____ 15. If taking a class in which there were no grades or other rewards, would you probably (a) work just as hard as you would if there were grades, (b) end up doing something else you really wanted to do, (c) exert minimal effort?

_____ 16. Do you like taking courses where (a) both the objectives and procedures are clearly spelled out, (b) the procedures are fairly clear but the objectives are vague, (c) both the objectives and procedures are vague but there is a lot of excitement and drive on the part of the instructor?

_____ 17. When studying something new, would you say your attention span is (a) continuous, (b) irregular, (c) short but concentrated, (d) without a particular pattern?

_____ 18. Do you sense the most satisfaction when (a) you've been able to figure out and repair something using your hands and your mind, (b) you've been able to conceptualize or see some meaning in academic work, (c) other people say they think you've done a good piece of work, regardless of what that work is?

_____ 19. When you find yourself in a situation determined by the clock, do you usually (a) start making all sorts of mistakes under pressure, (b) slow down and do what you can, (c) speed up and surprise yourself at how much you can do when the heat is on?

_____ 20. If you asked those people who know you best, they would probably say that (a) you are usually level-headed and have a lot of common sense, (b) it takes you a long time to get an idea but when you do you hang on to it, (c) you are always coming up with far-out ideas that sometimes work?

_____ 21. When bored in a class, do you usually (a) daydream, but of things related to what you are studying, (b) daydream of things seldom related to what you are studying, (c) pay attention even though it doesn't mean very much?

_____ 22. Do you find that when something new comes up you (a) adapt rather easily, (b) fight it for a while but are willing, usually, to give it a try, (c) make darn well sure it makes sense and/or is right before making any effort to accept it?

_____ 23. When in a classroom with other students and observing a teacher teaching, do you (a) think of other ways to present the material and to teach, (b) listen to what the teacher is saying rather than watch how he or she is teaching, (c) wonder what the teacher wants and how you can deliver?

_____ 24. If you don't like the instructor, for whatever reason, do you (a) tend not to do well, (b) find reasons for not studying and learning, (c) not let it affect how hard you try?

_____ 25. Do you get upset when studying something that (a) has no immediate and practical application, (b) appears to have some application but you are not sure just what, (c) is too darn practical and immediate?

_____ 26. When a teacher fails to "come across," do you have a tendency to blame (a) the teacher who, after all, is responsible for the class, (b) the subject matter—especially if the teacher tries, (c) both the teacher and yourself for not making it worthwhile?

_____ 27. If you took a course in social studies, would you want it to (a) focus primarily upon the facts, (b) pose some insight into contemporary problems of society, (c) have some payoff in your daily life?

___ 28. The problem with many teachers is that they (a) overkill, that is, teach too much of the same thing, (b) try to cover too much, (c) do not allow the student to really wrestle with the content.

___ 29. Do you believe that most students gain confidence through (a) having rather well-established objectives and procedures, (b) being allowed to try different things, (c) psyching out the reward system and playing the game?

___ 30. When studying, do you prefer (a) absolute silence, (b) low background noise, including music, (c) relative quiet, (d) loud conversation or music, etc., (e) sometimes one way, sometimes another?

___ 31. Where do you prefer to study? (a) in your own room, (b) in a learning center, (c) at the library, (d) at a media center.

___ 32. What types of assignments do you most prefer? (a) teacher-directed, (b) projects by contracts, (c) self-directed projects, (d) a combination of these.

___ 33. How do you most prefer to be evaluated on something? (a) by formal tests, (b) through teacher conferences, (c) on research papers or other written projects, (d) on the amount of your class discussion.

___ 34. Which of the following is most likely to bring forth your best performance? (a) self-satisfaction, (b) clearly defined teacher expectations and deadlines, (c) public recognition of your achievement, (d) working in a subject area with which you are quite comfortable and familiar.

Summary

Instructional modes. Determine your preferred instructional mode from responses to questions 2, 4, 7, 8, 11, 17, 19.

_____

_____

Structure. Determine the degree of structuring from responses to questions 3, 6, 9, 12, 13, 16, 20, 22, 23, and 32.

High	Medium	Low

_____

Social context of learning. Determine the general expectations for the way in which teachers handle their authority from questions 1, 10, 19, and 24.

_____

_____

Group-related activities. Determine your preference for group-related activities from responses to questions 1, 12, 30, 31, and 34.

_____

_____

Physical context of learning. Determine your preferences regarding the physical environment from the responses to questions 8, 17, 30, and 31.

_____

_____

Reward/praise. Determine preferences for reward/praise from responses to questions 14, 15, 26, 29, 33, and 34.

_____

_____

Goal preferences. Determine your general goal preferences from the responses to questions 5, 18, 25, and 27.

Longer range	Shorter range

_____

1.6 Sources of Commercially Available Learning Style Measures Include:

• •

- Learning Style Inventory, Price Systems, Box 1818, Lawrence, KS 66044-1818
- Learning Style Profile. National Association of Secondary School Principals, 1904 Association Dr., Reston, VA 22091-1598.

1.7 Recipes/Directions

• •

1.7.1. Recipes for Relief Maps

Papier-Mâché. Tear newspapers into strips and soak in water overnight. Mix wheat paste (wallpaper paste) with warm water to the consistency of thin cream. Squeeze water out of the newspaper strips, dip into the paste, remove the excess, and then apply to the map form.

Salt and Flour. Mix four cups flour, two cups salt, and approximately two cups water. Knead thoroughly. Food coloring may be added to the water, or tempera paint can be kneaded into the mixture. The mixture may require from two to three days to dry completely.

Sawdust and Glue. Mix slightly thinned white glue with dampened, fine sawdust until it reaches a workable consistency.

Once the relief maps have dried, they can be coated with a thin mixture of plaster of Paris and water and then allowed to dry overnight. This coating will keep paint from soaking in as much as it otherwise would.

1.7.2 Directions for Making Paper

Introduction. This recipe produces a very rough paper similar to papyrus. Before you begin this activity, you might ask for parent volunteers who will make several, small wooden frames (open rectangles), about 6 by 9 inches, with old window screening attached to the bottom. Old picture frames also work well.

Materials List

One blender, to mix the ingredients
Several clean sponges
A tub or container large enough to hold the screened frames
Grass (or cattails—leaves only, no heads)
Water
One or two old bedsheets
Torn pieces of old, used, lightweight paper (not newsprint)
One bottle laundry starch

Procedure. Place equal amounts of torn paper and the grass or cattail leaves into the blender, and cover with water to make a pulp. Turn blender to high and mix thoroughly. Make several batches, adding about 1 tablespoon of laundry starch to each batch. Put the pulp into a tub that is large enough to accommodate the screen. Add as little water to the tub as necessary to create a fluid mixture, and stir. Insert the screen into the water until it is covered with a layer of the pulp mixture, then pull up and out. Lay the screen on the old bedsheet, and use sponges to soak up some of the excess water from the pulp, but do not let it get so dry that the pulp sticks to the screen. Place a dry area of the sheet over the screen, and then flip so the pulp falls out of the screen onto the sheet. Place on a flat surface, remove the screen, and let the paper dry overnight.

This paper that you produce will be rough, fragile, and difficult to write on. In addition, it may not be even at the edges. Help students to understand that the 8½ × 11 paper we are all familiar with is a convention of modern life and is the result of advanced paper-making techniques.

Part 2 Planning Resources

2.1 Alternative Lesson Planning Guide

This planning guide is designed to serve different kinds of lessons. Therefore some elements, like motivation and establishing set, will apply to all lessons, but other components may not. At times, you may teach lessons that don't use guided practice or review, for example, or where there is no need to state assumptions. Skip the sections that don't apply to the kind of lesson you are teaching. Note also that because this guide is designed to communicate your lesson to someone else, such as a cooperating teacher or a university supervisor, it is necessarily more comprehensive and specific than the day-to-day plans that most teachers use. Most teachers will have usually thought about the following planning elements, even if they don't write them in their plan books.

I. *Overview*/Rationale/Justification. Provide a brief overview of this lesson and why it is something that students should experience or learn.

The key questions here are the following: What's going to happen in this lesson? What is the main idea(s) you are driving at? How will this lesson pertain to something your students will use in the future?

II. State *Objectives*. List at least two objectives for this lesson.

Objectives should be stated in terms of behaviors or knowledge that students will demonstrate at the end of the lesson.

III. *Assumptions*. Identify specific skills or knowledge that students must have *prior* to lesson.

This section of the planning guide pertains primarily to skill- and concept-oriented lessons and may not be relevant to other kinds of lessons. State prerequisite knowledge/skills specifically, such as the ability to count by fives or to identify the symbols used to show cities on a map. Do not identify global skills, such as reading, the ability to multiply, how to use a map, and so on.

IV. Review, Developing Motivation, and Setting the Focus.

In most cases, the following elements can be described in a sentence or two.

A. *Review.* Describe how you will relate this lesson to students' prior learning experiences.

Identify how you will make connections with previous learning in ways that have meaning for students.

B. Develop *Motivation and Setting the Focus* (Establishing Set). This planning element has three components: a description of (1) how you will get students interested in this lesson, (2) how you will introduce the content/skills, and (3) how you will make students aware of the objectives for the lesson.

Your introduction or beginning activity should be content centered and tied to the purpose of the lesson. Be especially cautious about using seemingly obvious questions for "motivational" purposes— that is, "Has anyone ever seen television? or an elephant? etc." (everyone has). Be equally careful about your terminology. For example, a "discussion" involves the identification and assessment of different points of view on an issue; it is not a random sharing of opinions or question-and-answer. Most children can readily tell you about the time they went to Disneyland, for example, but this is more likely to be recitation, not a discussion. Having children share their perspectives on abortion could provide a legitimate (though unlikely) basis for a discussion. The point is that having children share their prior experiences may be desirable—even if no one listens to them—but such activities should not be presented as discussions.

V. Develop the *Lesson*.

A. Provide *Instructional Input*. Outline and describe the content and skills included in the main body of the lesson and how you will present them.

In this part of the lesson you will present content, use manipulatives, give examples, explain, define, read, model, and provide directions for activities, and so on. You may wish to write a script for portions of this section as long as you recognize that scripts can be confining and destroy spontaneity.

B. *Modeling* the Content and Skills. Describe how you will model or demonstrate the content and skills introduced in Part V-A.

Modeling is among the most important parts of the lesson and refers to doing, explicitly demonstrating, talking through, and thinking aloud. Modeling should afford students an opportunity to "see" your reasoning process, to see how you attack a problem. Note that showing the children a completed model, of a narrative story for example, is not modeling.

C. Check for Student Understanding (*Assessment*). Describe how you will assess students' understanding to make sure they have mastered the content and skills introduced in Part V-A.

Use oral, written, or signal responses to check for students' understanding before moving on to application or guided practice. Signal responses can include raising hands, crossing arms, putting a hand on the head, and so on.

VI. *Guided Practice.* Describe the guided practice you will provide relating to the content and skills developed in Part V-A.

This aspect of the lesson cycle is most appropriate, even essential, to certain subjects like mathematics and may be less appropriate to other subjects, like literature. Guided practice is usually called for if you ask students to apply something that you have taught.

VII. *Closure* (and Assign Individual Practice or Homework as Appropriate). Describe how you will close the lesson. Describe the individual practice or homework you will assign, if appropriate, to this lesson.

The purpose of closure is to "lock in" the learning ex-

perience. You might summarize the main points of the lesson, or have students do so, explain how the content and skills will be needed in the future, or have students do something "one more time." The closure should have substance; it cannot be a hasty review of the lesson or an administrative end, for example, "Close your books."

VIII. *Follow-up* Activities. Briefly describe other activities or lessons that logically follow from this lesson, or how you would integrate the "big ideas" from this lesson into other subject areas.

Few lessons contain elements that cannot be followed up on. Sometimes it may be the content of the lesson— what it is like to live in different climates, for example. At other times, the process that students used in this lesson can apply to other lessons—practice with a model for writing descriptive narratives, for example. In this section, you should indicate how you will tie this lesson into future lessons. The question to ask yourself here is, How does this lesson tie into other things I might teach?

2.2 Principles for the Design, Selection, and Evaluation of Instructional Activities (Abridged)

Criteria	Response		
A. Primary Principles	Yes	No	NA
A1.　　Goal Relevance			
A1.1 Does the activity address worthwhile curricular goals?	—	—	—
A1.1a Is the activity's primary goal an important one?	—	—	—
A1.1b Is there a clear relationship between what students will be doing and the activity's primary goal?	—	—	—
A1.2 Does the activity deal with (a) powerful ideas that are (b) represented accurately?	—	—	—

Criteria	Response			B. Secondary Principles	Yes	No	NA
A. Primary Principles **(cont.)**	Yes	No	NA	The following are desirable but not essential.			
A1.3 Is the format of the activity clear and uncomplicated?	—	—	—	B1. *Multiple Goals*			
A2. *Appropriate Difficulty Level*				B1.1 Does the activity accommodate multiple goals (e.g., content and process, etc.) as opposed to just a few goals?	—	—	—
A2.1 Is the activity difficult enough to challenge students but not so difficult that it confuses or frustrates them?	—	—	—	B1.2 Does the activity call for integration across subjects or for inclusion of special topics?	—	—	—
A2.2 Do students have the relevant prior knowledge or skills that the activity requires?	—	—	—	B2. *Motivational Value.* All things considered, is the activity one that students will enjoy or at least find meaningful and worthwhile?	—	—	—
A2.3 Does the activity provide enough structuring that students can complete it with reasonable effort?	—	—	—	B3. *Topic Currency*			
A2.4 Does the activity *not* combine difficult new processes and difficult new content?	—	—	—	B3.1 Does the activity deal with recently taught major ideas (as opposed to minor details or isolated content)?	—	—	—
A3. *Feasibility*				B3.2 Are skills incorporated for authentically applying current knowledge (as opposed to isolated skill exercises)?	—	—	—
A3.1 Is the activity feasible in terms of (a) normal constraints (space, time, equipment, etc.) (b) the possibility for students to carry out instructions unambiguously and complete the activity with a sense of closure and accomplishment?	—	—	—	B4. *Whole-Task Completion.* Does the activity provide for the completion of a meaningful task (as opposed to isolated skill practice)?	—	—	—
A4. *Cost Effectiveness*				B5. *Higher-Order Thinking*			
A4.1 Does the activity justify its costs in time and trouble for both teachers and students?	—	—	—	B5.1 Does the activity provide opportunities to process information (interpret, analyze, etc.) (as opposed to just locating and reproducing information)?	—	—	—
A4.2 Will the structure of the activity (e.g., closed vs. open-ended, etc.) accomplish the goal directly and without needless complications?	—	—	—	B5.2 Does the activity provide opportunities for genuine discourse and discussion (as opposed to recitation)?	—	—	—
A4.3 Can students who lack prior knowledge or skills be accommodated?	—	—	—	B5.3 If the activity involves writing, does it call for coherent written explanations or arguments (as opposed to filling in blanks or copying)?	—	—	—
A4.4 If the activity cuts across subject lines, does it (a) address major goals in those subjects, and (b) still reflect time allotments for those subjects?	—	—	—				

Criteria	*Response*		
B. Secondary Principles **(cont.)**	Yes	No	NA
B6. *Adaptability.* Can the activity be adapted to accommodate individual differences among students?	—	—	—

Source: Abridged from Jere Brophy and Janet Alleman, "Activities as Instructional Tools: A Framework for Analysis and Evaluation," *Educational Researcher,* Vol. 20, No. 4 (May 1991), pp. 15–19.

2

Part 3 Instructional Resources

3.1 Sources for Teaching Materials

1. Social Studies Journals

1. *Social Studies and the Young Learner,* which is available from the National Council for the Social Studies, 3501 Newark Street NW, Washington, DC 20016. This is the only journal that deals specifically with elementary- and middle-school social studies.
2. *Social Education,* the K–12 journal of the National Council for the Social Studies. Address: 3501 Newark Street, NW, Washington, DC 20016.
3. *The Social Studies,* also a K–12 journal. Published by Heldref Publications, 1319 Eighteenth Street, NW, Washington, DC 20036-1802.

2. Social Studies Publications for Children

Write (or call) the publishers listed here for examination copies of these materials.

2.1 General

> *Calliope: World History for Young People*
> Cobblestone Publishing Inc.
> 7 School Street
> Peterborough, NH 03458
> (800) 821-0115

Calliope is published five times during the school year and is for students in Grades 4–8. Each issue features in-depth information and activities on a single topic.

> *Cobblestone: The History Magazine for Young People*
> Cobblestone Publishing Inc.
> 7 School Street
> Peterborough, NH 03458
> (800) 821-0115

Cobblestone is appropriate for students in Grades 4–8 and is published ten times a year. Each issue features an episode of historical interest, such as the Underground Railroad or the Roaring Twenties.

> *National Geographic World*
> National Geographic Society
> Dept. 01090
> 17th and M Streets NW
> Washington, DC 20036

This monthly magazine is appropriate for eight- to twelve-year-olds (or older). Each issue contains articles on a variety of social studies topics.

2.2 Current Events Publications

> *My Weekly Reader*
> American Education Publications
> 245 Long Hill Road, P.O. Box 360
> Middletown, CT 06457

> *Let's Find Out* (kindergarten) or *Scholastic News* (Grades 1–6)
> Scholastic, Inc.
> 730 Broadway
> New York, NY 10003-9538

> *Junior Review* (Grades 6–9)
> Civic Education Service
> 1733 K Street NW
> Washington, DC 20006

> *ABC New 4 Kids Online*
> http://abcnews.go.com/abcnews4kids/kids/index.html

ABC News 4 Kids posts interactive, animated new stories every Tuesday and Thursday appropriate for elementary- and middle-school students.

> *Children's Express Online*
> http://www.childrens-express.org/

Children's Express (UK) is a British program for young people aged 8–18.

> *Time for Kids*
> http://timeforkids.com/TFK/

Three editions for elementary grades are available by subscription.

3. Resources for Global Education

Two excellent sources of information about global education are:

1. The American Forum for Global Education, 45 John Street, New York, NY 10038, and
2. The Stanford Program on International and Cross-Cultural Education (SPICE), Littlefield Center, Room 15, 300 Lassen Street, Stanford, CA 94305-5013.

4. Resources for Law-Related Education

Center for Civic Education
5146 Douglas Fir Road
Calabasas, CA 91302

Materials include student books (e.g., *We the People,* and *With Liberty and Justice for All*), teachers' guides, and resource materials.

Constitutional Rights Foundation
6310 San Vincente Boulevard
Los Angeles, CA 90048

Materials, primarily for Grades 7–12, include simulations, lesson plans, student resources, a *Bill of Rights Newsletter,* and other materials.

American Bar Association
Special Committee on Youth Education for Citizenship
1155 East 60th Street
Chicago, IL 60637

Materials include a newsletter for teachers, *Update on Law-Related Education,* classroom materials, and a catalog of law-related audiovisual materials.

Law in a Free Society
606 Wilshire Boulevard
Santa Monica, CA 90101

Materials include case studies and lesson plans for Grades K–12, and in-service training.

Law in Action Units
West Publishing Company, Inc.
50 West Kellogg Boulevard
St. Paul, MN 55165

Materials include units and lesson plans for Grades 5–9.

National Institute for Citizen Education in the Law
605 G Street NW, Suite 401
Washington, DC 20001

Materials focus primarily on teacher training and the development of law-related curriculum materials.

Opposing Viewpoints Series
Greenhaven Press
Box 831
Anoka, MN 55303

Materials offer opposing points of view on a variety of law-related issues.

5. Resources for Character Education

American Institute for Character Education
A nonprofit educational research foundation that offers a K–9 character education curriculum. Dimension II Building, 8918 Tesoro, Suite 220, San Antonio, TX 78217. Phone: (512) 829-1727 or (800) 284-0499.

Center for the Advancement of Ethics and Character
Dedicated to helping schools recapture their role as moral educators, the Center has developed a model that emphasizes the curriculum as the primary vehicle for transmitting moral values to the young. The Center publicizes this model through its teacher academics for public school teachers and administrators. A similar program is directed toward college and university faculty responsible for the preparation of future teachers. The Center is also involved in researching and developing curricular materials for use by schools, teachers, and parents. Kevin Ryan, Boston University, School of Education, 605 Commonwealth Avenue, Boston, MA 02215. Phone: (617) 353-3262.

Center for Character Education
An academic alliance of schools and universities that brings together educators interested in implementing the Integrated Character Model for moral education. This model reflects the view that knowledge, affect, and action are integrated in persons of mature character. Duquesne University, School of Education, 410 Canevin Hall, Pittsburgh, PA 15282. Phone: (412) 434-5191.

Center for Civic Education
This Web site is sponsored by the Center for Civic Education, a nonpartisan corporation dedicated to fos-

tering the development of responsible participation in civic life. The Center specializes in civic/citizenship education, law-related education, and international educational exchange programs for developing democracies. The CCE Web site has curriculum materials, sample lesson plans, and related children's literature bibliographies as well as a comprehensive on-line catalog, a good listing of available papers and articles on civic education, and a wonderful annotated list of Internet resources. **www.civiced.org**

The Character Counts Coalition

This project of the Josephson Institute represents a national partnership of organizations and individuals involved in the education, training, or care of youth. It reflects a collaborative effort to improve the character of America's young people by focusing on the six pillars of character: trustworthiness, respect, responsibility, fairness, caring, and citizenship. It aims to combat violence, dishonesty, and irresponsibility by strengthening the moral fiber of the next generation. 4640 Admiralty Way, Suite 1001, Marina del Rey, CA 90292. Phone: (310) 306-1868.

The Character Education Partnership

A nonpartisan coalition of organizations and individuals concerned about the moral crisis confronting America's youth and dedicated to developing moral character and civic virtue in young people as a way of promoting a more compassionate and responsible society. Activities include a national clearinghouse, community programs, school support, publications, annual and regional forums, and a national awards and media campaign. John A. Martin, Executive Director, The Character Education Partnership, 1250 North Pitt Street, Alexandria, VA 22314. Fax: (703) 739-4967. **www.character.org**

Ethics Resource Center

This center is working toward restoring our society's ethical foundations by strengthening the capacity of our institutions to foster integrity, encourage ethical conduct, and support basic values. Established in 1977 as a nonprofit, nonpartisan, and nonsectarian organization, the Ethics Resource Center has developed practical and effective programs that address the needs of the education, business, and govern-

ment communities. Resources include research support, curricular materials, workshops, and conference sponsorship. 1120 G Street NW, Washington, DC 20005. Phone: (202) 737-2258.

Exploring Ethics Through Children's Literature

This organization offers a literature-based program for Grades 2–6. Critical Thinking Press, P.O. Box 448, Dept. 4, Pacific Grove, CA 93950-0448. Phone: (800) 458-4849. Fax: (408) 372-3230.

The Giraffe Project

This is a nonprofit literature project devoted to spreading the word about people who "stick their necks out for the common good." Its various programs include the Giraffe Heroes Program, a story-based curriculum that teaches "courageous compassion and active citizenship"; the Giraffe Heroes Training Program; and a variety of public information and awareness programs. **www.giraffe.org**

International Center for Character Education

The International Center for Character Education (ICCE), housed at the University of San Diego, has as its purpose to "enable school personnel, parents, teacher educators, faith community members . . . to come together to study, discuss . . . the character education of children and youth." The ICCE offers the only Certificate and MA programs in character education and a variety of other services and awards. **www.teachvalues.org**

The Jefferson Center for Character Education

This organization was formed in 1963 to publish and promote programs for schools that teach sound character values and personal responsibility. 202 South Lake Avenue, #240, Pasadena, CA 91101. Phone: (818) 792-8130.

Project Wisdom

A for-profit organization that is "committed to providing schools with Character Education materials that encourage students to reflect" on values and their application. The centerpiece of the program is a collection of thought-provoking messages to be read over the PA system. The program also includes a reproducible set of weekly themes, weekly journals, classroom discussion guides, and a booklet of quotations for the classroom. **www.entech.com/projectwisdom**

WiseSkills

This organization offers a community-based character-building program for Grades K–8. Legacy Learning, P.O. Box 3213, South Pasadena, CA 91031-6213. Phone: (818) 441-7944.

Source Note: This listing is abridged and adapted from "The Bonner Center for Character Education Web Links," at the California State University, Fresno, and from "Character Education Organizations and Publications," maintained by the Center for the Fourth and Fifth Rs, Dr. Thomas Lickona, Director, Education Department, SUNY Cortland, Cortland, NY 13045. Used by permission.

6. Other Sources of Materials

Social Studies School Service Catalog (free)
10000 Culver Boulevard, P.O. Box 802
Culver City, CA 90230

Where to Find It Guide (published annually in a fall issue of *Scholastic Teacher*)

Scholastic Magazines, Inc., 50 W. 44th Street
New York, NY 10036.

6.1 Teachers' Magazines

1. *Teaching-PreK–8.* Address: P.O. Box 54805, Boulder, CO 80323-4805.
2. *Teacher.* Address: 4301 Connecticut Avenue NW, Suite 432, Washington, DC 20077-3522.
3. *Learning* (the year varies with the current year). Address: 1111 Bethlehem Pike, Springhouse, PA 19477.
4. *Instructor.* Address: 7 Bank Street, Dansville, NY 14437.

6.2 Guides to Free or Inexpensive Materials

Educator's Guide to Free Social Studies Materials, edited by Patricia H. Suttles and William H. Hartley. Educators Progress Service, Inc., Randolph, WI 53956. *Note:* Guides to other free and inexpensive material are also available.

Free and Inexpensive Materials on World Affairs, by Leonard S. Kenworthy. Teachers College Press, 1234 Amsterdam Avenue, New York, NY 10027.

Free and Inexpensive Teaching Aids, by Bruce Miller. Box 369, Riverside, CA 92502.

Free and Inexpensive Learning Materials (updated annually). George Peabody College of Vanderbilt University, Nashville, TN 37203.

Selected Free Materials for Classroom Teachers, by Ruth H. Aubrey. Fearon Publishers, 6 Davis Drive, Belmont, CA 94002.

6.3 Newspaper-Related Materials

Many local newspapers maintain a "Newspaper in Education" department that will provide teaching tips and other aids for integrating newspapers into the curriculum. If your local paper does not offer such a service, contact the American Newspaper Publishers Association Foundation (The Newspaper Center, Box 17407, Dulles International Airport, Washington, DC 20041) for information.

3.2 Directory of Living History Museums

Alabama

Constitution Hall Village
404 Madison Street
Huntsville, AL 35801
(800) 678-1819

Constitution Hall Village is located at the site of the drafting of Alabama's 1819 constitution. Both single-day and five-day educational programs are available.

Alaska

Eklutna Village Historical Park
510 L Street, Suite 200
Anchorage, AK 99501
(907) 276-5701

Eklutna is the oldest continuously inhabited Athapaskan site in Alaska. Its cemetery contains spirit houses that were built to protect the spirits of the deceased, and the park has two Russian Orthodox churches built by missionaries in the 1830s.

Native Village of Alaskaland
Fairbanks Native Association
201 First Avenue, 2nd Floor
Fairbanks, AK 99701
(907) 452-1648

This village contains a variety of different types of housing used by Native American Alaskans, including sod dwellings and plank houses.

Arizona

Pioneer Arizona
3901 West Pioneer Road
Phoenix, AZ 85027
(602) 993-0212

Descendants of the horses that Columbus brought to North America on his second voyage in 1493 are raised at Pioneer Arizona. The museum also includes more than twenty buildings that reflect the influences of Native American, Spanish, and Mexican cultures.

Arkansas

Arkansas Territorial Restoration
200 East 3rd Street
Little Rock, AR 72201
(501) 324-9351

This museum reflects frontier life in Arkansas from 1819 to 1870.

California

El Pueblo de Los Angeles Historic Monument
125 Paseo de la Plaza, Suite 400
Los Angeles, CA 90012
(213) 628-0605

This community, which later became known simply as Los Angeles, has twenty-seven reconstructed buildings.

Mission San Juan Capistrano
31882 Camino Capistrano #107
San Juan Capistrano, CA 92675
(714) 248-2048

Franciscan padres founded the Mission of San Juan Capistrano in 1776. The Serra Chapel is the oldest continuously inhabited building in the state of California. The mission is also famous for the annual migration of swallows each spring.

Colorado

Bent's Old Fort National Historic Site
35110 Highway 194 East
La Junta, CO 81050
(719) 384-2596

This reconstructed frontier fur trading post features blacksmithing and frontier medicine.

Connecticut

Mystic Seaport and Maritime Museum
50 Greenmanville Avenue
Mystic, CT 06355
(203) 572-0711

The Mystic Seaport and Preservation Shipyard is home to nineteenth-century tall ships and schooners. The maritime museum contains antique navigational equipment. The accompanying planetarium has programs explaining how sea captains relied on the stars to determine their location at sea.

Delaware

Delaware Agricultural Museum
866 North DuPont Highway
Dover, DE 19901
(302) 734-1618

Historic activities and demonstrations vary depending on the season. During the summer, children can experience schooling from that period of our history. Lessons are taught from the McGuffey Reader and Noah Webster's Blue Backed Speller with "ciphering" done on a slate. During July and August, children can dress in clothing of the period, churn butter, feed the chickens and cow, and enjoy a storyteller. During the winter months, guides provide interpretations of rural life in the 1850s.

Hagley Museum and Library
P.O. Box 3630

Wilmington, DE 19807
(302) 658-2400

The Hagley Museum and Library focuses on the E. I. du Pont family's role and history in the nineteenth century. Tours include the du Ponts' Georgian mansion and gardens, workers' quarters, and gunpowder mills.

Florida

Historic Saint Augustine Spanish Quarter
P.O. Box 1987
Saint Augustine, FL 32085
(904) 825-6830

Saint Augustine was founded more than 470 years ago and is the oldest continuously inhabited European settlement in North America. Life during the Spanish colonial period of the 1740s is portrayed in restored buildings and gardens.

Georgia

Agrirama
P.O. Box Q
Tifton, GA 31793
(912) 386-3344

This museum consists of almost forty restored buildings that illustrate traditional and progressive farming.

Idaho

Pioneer Village and Idaho Historical Museum
610 North Julia Davis Drive
Boise, ID 83702
(208) 334-2120

This museum village consists of restored and reconstructed log cabins and adobes that may be toured by school groups.

Illinois

Lincoln's New Salem State Historic Site
R.R. #1, Box 244A
Petersburg, IL 62675
(217) 632-4000

Abraham Lincoln first stopped at New Salem when he and a friend copiloted a flatboat down the Sangamon River to the Ohio and Mississippi Rivers. He later re-

turned there to settle and study law. The re-created village provides demonstrations of activities common to daily living during Lincoln's lifetime.

Naper Settlement
210 West Porter
Naperville, IL 60540
(708) 420-6010

This mid- to late-nineteenth-century settlement features historic games and crafts, soap making, and open-hearth cooking.

Indiana

Conner Prairie
13400 Allisonville Road
Fishers, IN 46038
(317) 776-6000

Conner Prairie presents three historically accurate areas, each with its own costumed interpreters. Prairietown is an 1836 Indiana village; the second area features the nineteenth-century home of William Conner, a land developer and politician; and the third area is a Pioneer Adventure Area where children are encouraged to participate in dipping candles, soap making, weaving, and wood carving.

Historic New Harmony
506 1/2 Main St.
P.O. Box 579
New Harmony, IN 47631
(812) 682-4488

The Harmonie Society fled Germany because of religious persecution and ultimately developed a utopian community that later failed.

Iowa

Living History Farms
2600 NW 111th Street
Urbandale, IA 50322
(515) 278-2400

This museum depicts agrarian culture from the sixteenth century through to the 1850s.

Amana Colonies
P.O. Box 303

Amana, IA 52203
(800) 245-5465

In 1855 a group of separatists from Germany settled on 27,000 acres in Amana. The community features three furniture factories and several craft shops.

Kansas

Old Cowtown Museum
1871 Sim Park Drive
Wichita, KS 67203
(316) 264-0671

This museum features thirty buildings from an authentic cow town of the Old West.

Kentucky

Shaker Village of Pleasant Hill
3500 Lexington Road
Harrodsburg, KY 40330
(606) 734-5411

This nineteenth-century Shaker village has more than thirty original buildings, each furnished with Shaker furniture.

Louisiana

Acadian Village
200 Greenleaf Road
Lafayette, LA 70506
(800) 962-9133

This museum features a general store and houses from nineteenth-century Acadiana.

Maine

Norlands Living History Center
R.R. #2 Box 3395
Livermore Falls, ME 04254
(207) 897-2236

This center has two programs, one that depicts the post–Revolutionary War period and the other that portrays the post–Civil War era.

Maryland

Baltimore City Life Museums
800 East Lombard Street
Baltimore, MD 21202
(410) 396-3279

Six different museums portray life in nineteenth-century Baltimore.

Massachusetts

Hancock Shaker Village
P.O. Box 898
Pittsfield, MA 01202
(413) 443-0188

The Hancock Shaker Village features more than twenty restored buildings, and demonstrations of furniture and textile making.

Plimoth Plantation
P.O. Box 1620
Plymouth, MA 02362
(508) 746-1622

The Plimoth Plantation features a reconstructed village and a replica of the Mayflower.

Michigan

Colonial Michilimackinac
P.O. Box 873
Mackinaw City, MI 49701
(616) 436-5563

This former military outpost and fur trading center has re-created a 1770s Native American encampment, complete with wigwams.

Troy Museum and Historic Village
60 West Wattles Road
Troy, MI 48098
(313) 524-3570

This museum presents a program in which children reenact chores that were common to pioneer families.

Minnesota

Oliver H. Kelley Farm
15788 Kelley Farm Road
Elk River, MN 55330
(612) 441-6896

This farm depicts life in 1860s Minnesota.

3

Missouri

Arrow Rock State Historic Site
P.O. Box 1
Arrow Rock, MO 65320
(816) 837-3330

Located near the beginning of the Santa Fe Trail, this nineteenth-century village includes a restored church, tavern, courthouse, and newspaper office.

Nebraska

Stuhr Museum of the Prairie Pioneer
3133 West Highway 34
Grand Island, NE 68801
(308) 381-5316

This museum features a Pawnee lodge (replica) and a collection of Native American and Old West artifacts.

New Hampshire

Strawbery Banke
P.O. Box 300
Portsmouth, NH 03802
(603) 433-1100

Strawbery Banke, which was once a colonial seaport, depicts four centuries of history and culture.

New Jersey

Historic Batso Village
Wharton State Forest
Route #9 Batso
Hammonton, NJ 08037
(609) 561-3262

Batso Village was a nineteenth-century ironworking and glassmaking center.

New Mexico

El Rancho de Las Golondrinas
Route 14, P.O. Box 214
Santa Fe, NM 87505
(505) 471-2261

This town was founded by the Spanish as an overnight stop on the Royal Road to Mexico City.

New York

Museum Village
Museum Village Road
Monroe, NY 10950
(914) 782-8247

This village depicts agrarian life in the 1880s.

Old Bethpage Village Restoration
Nassau County Department of Recreation
 and Parks
Round Swarp Road
Old Bethpage, NY 11804
(516) 572-8400

This reconstructed village reflects agricultural, domestic, and trade activities from the pre–Civil War period.

North Carolina

Oconaluftee Indian Village
P.O. Box 398
Cherokee, NC 28719
(704) 497-2111

This village, which is located on the Cherokee Reservation, shows the history and traditions of the Cherokee Nation.

Ohio

Hale Farm and Village
P.O. Box 296
Bath, OH 44210
(216) 666-3711

This living museum depicts life in the 1850s. Demonstrations include glassblowing, candlemaking, blacksmithing, and maple sugaring (in season).

Ohio Village
1982 Velma Ave.
Columbus, OH 43211
(614) 297-2439

This museum portrays problems encountered by African-Americans during the early 1800s.

Pennsylvania

Historic Fallsington
4 Yardley Ave.

Fallsington, PA 19054
(215) 295-6567

This 300-year-old village was founded as a haven for Quakers and features a garden containing plants common to colonial America.

South Carolina

Middleton Place
Ashley River Road
Charleston, SC 29414
(803) 556-6020

At this restored eighteenth-century plantation, guides demonstrate woodworking and blacksmithing.

Tennessee

Museum of Appalachia
P.O. Box 0318
Highway 61
Norris, TN 37828
(615) 494-7680

The best time to visit is during the Fall Homecoming, in October, when demonstrations of goat milking, molasses-making, and spinning dog hair into thread are featured.

Texas

Old City Park
1717 Gano Street
Dallas, TX 75215
(214) 421-5141

This city park contains thirty-five restored buildings, from a log cabin to an antebellum mansion.

The Ranching Heritage Center
4th & Indiana
Lubbock, TX 79409
(806) 742-2498

This facility traces the history of ranching from the days of dugout homes to the early 1900s. It features over twenty restored buildings and railroad facilities.

Utah

Ronald V. Jensen Living Historical Farm
4025 South Highway 89-91

Welsville, UT 84339
(801) 245-4064

Interpreters demonstrate how family members on a Mormon farm in the early 1900s did their daily chores.

Virginia

Colonial Williamsburg
P.O. Box 1776
Williamsburg, VA 23187
(804) 229-1000

Among the largest and most famous of the living history museums in the United States, Colonial Williamsburg contains more than 100 restored or reconstructed buildings. A variety of educational programs are available.

Washington

Fort Nisqually Historic Site
Point Defiance Park
5400 North Pearl
Tacoma, WA 98405
(206) 591-5339

This living museum re-creates a former fort and Hudson Bay Company trading post.

Rainier Legacy
Pioneer Farm/Ohop Indian Village
7716 Ohop Valley Road
Eatonville, WA 98328
(206) 832-6300

This museum, which is open between early March and late November, contrasts a Native American settlement with that of European pioneers.

Wisconsin

Old World Wisconsin
South 103 West 37890
Highway 67
Eagle, WI 53119
(414) 594-2116

This living history museum shows nineteenth- and twentieth-century farmsteads for a variety of Scandinavian cultures.

Part 4 Annotated Bibliographies of Selected Children's Books

4.1 Children's Books for Teaching Character, Morals, and Values

In the following bibliographies, the grade-level designation "P" means the book might be more valuable for the primary grades, kindergarten to Grade 3; the designation "I" means the intermediate grades, 3–8.

A. Self-Esteem

Adoff, Arnold. (1991). *Hard to Be Six.* Illus. by Cheryl Hanna. Lothrop, Lee & Shepard. P, 32 pages.

> On the occasion of his sister's tenth birthday, a six-year-old boy reflects on how tough it is to be just six.

Allinson, Beverley. (1990). *Elfie.* Scholastic. P, 32 pages.

> Elfie has the loudest voice of any ant you will ever meet, so loud, in fact, that all the other ants in the community run away from her. Elfie feels (and is) rejected for a voice that she can't seem to control. When an emergency arises, Elfie's bellowing voice saves the lives of the rest of her family, and they come to accept her for what she is.

Browner, Anthony. (1985). *Willie the Champ.* Knopf. P, 32 pages.

> Willie is a sensitive boy who likes to read, listen to music, and take walks in the park but isn't any good at activities like soccer, swimming, or bike racing. One day when Willie encounters the neighborhood bully, Buster Nose, he doesn't run away as the other kids do. Instead, he defends himself against Buster and is declared a hero by the other children.

Bryan, Ashley. (1989). *Turtle Knows Your Name.* Atheneum. P, I, 32 pages.

> This West Indian tale is about a boy with a very long name, Upsilimana Tumpalerado. He works diligently just to pronounce his name, and when he finally succeeds, he and his grandmother celebrate. Unfortunately, only one of his friends, Turtle, can remember and pronounce his name, but Turtle's effort makes Upsilimana Tumpalerado feel good.

Carle, Eric. (1984). *The Mixed-Up Chameleon.* Harper. P, 32 pages.

> Sometimes he is green and sometimes he's brown, but this poor chameleon doesn't know who he is or what color he ought to be.

Cohen, Barbara. (1991). *213 Valentines.* Illus. by Wit Clay. Holt. P, I, 55 pages.

> Wade is an African-American boy who has transferred to Kennedy School to participate in its gifted and talented program. At the new school, Wade feels so unpopular that he is sure he will not receive any valentine cards—except from the one person who drew his name. To avoid this, Wade buys 200 valentines, which he sends to himself and a friend under the names of famous people.

Glenn, Maggie. (1990). *Ruby.* Putnam. P, 32 pages.

> Ruby, a teddy bear, thinks that the "S" stamped on her paw at the toy factory means "special." The other teddy bears tell her that it means "second" and that she is a mistake. To avoid being thrown out, Ruby escapes from the factory and makes her way to the best toy shop in town. A little girl then selects Ruby because she is different from all the others; Ruby has character.

Graham, Amanda. (1987). *Who Wants Arthur?* Gareth Stevens. P, 32 pages.

> Arthur, a dog who has been in the pet shop for what seems like forever, decides that for someone to want him, he will need to act like other popular animals. For example, when Arthur sees that fish are popular, he tries to act like a fish, but to no avail. Only after Arthur becomes himself does someone buy him.

Hooks, William H. (1989). *The Three Little Pigs and the Fox.* Illus. by S. D. Schindler. Macmillan. P, I, 32 pages.

In this version of the classic tale, the smallest pig, the female runt of the litter, outwits the fox and saves her bigger brothers.

Klass, Sheila Solomon. (1991). *Kool Ada.* Scholastic. I, 176 pages.

Ada is a strong-willed girl with adjustment problems. Not only is she new to her northern school, but she has recently moved from a home in the rural, southern mountains. A compassionate teacher finally helps Ada understand that her rough exterior and quick temper are only compounding her problems.

Lane, Megan Halsey. (1990). *Something to Crow About.* Dial. P, 32 pages.

In this predictable book, Randall is a rooster who wants to lay eggs, and Cassie is a chicken who would like to cock-a-doodle-do. They both eventually realize that being different is what they should crow about.

Leaf, Munro. (1936). *The Story of Ferdinand.* Illus. by Robert Lawson. Viking. P, 48 pages.

In this classic story, Ferdinand is a bull who would rather smell the flowers than butt horns with the other bulls. When it comes time to select new candidates for the bull ring, Ferdinand goes off by himself and sits next to some flowers. Unfortunately, Ferdinand sits on a bee, which results in a demonstration of jumping and wild movements that convinces the judges that he belongs in the bull ring. When Ferdinand finally enters the ring for his "big event," all he does is smell the flowers in the ladies' hats.

Levine, Ellen. (1989). *I Hate English.* Illus. by Steve Bjorkman. Scholastic. P, I, 32 pages.

Every non-native speaker of English knows what a hard language it is to learn. This is the case in this story of a young girl who is being tutored in English but sees little need to learn it. Eventually she begins to feel better about speaking her native tongue and about acquiring a second language.

Lionni, Leo. (1969). *Alexander and the Wind-Up Mouse.* Random House. P, 32 pages.

Alexander is a real mouse who meets Willie, a wind-up mouse. Alexander tries to transform himself into a mechanical mouse like Willie, who is loved by a human, only to find that Willie has been discarded by his owner. Alexander then realizes that being a real mouse isn't so bad after all.

Milhouse, Katherine, & Dalgiesh, Alice. (1990). *The Turnip, an Old Russian Tale.* Putnam. P, 32 pages.

Mice are among the most powerful literary creatures, and so it is in this tale. Everyone who tries to pull a turnip from the ground is unsuccessful until the mouse finally lends a hand.

Peet, Bill. (1986). *Pamela Camel.* Houghton Mifflin. P, 48 pages.

Poor Pamela Camel thinks that she is the dumbest animal in the circus. Pamela feels so bad that she runs away, but in the process she saves a train from destruction. For her heroism, she is given first place in the circus parade.

Polacco, Patricia. (1990). *Just Plain Fancy.* Bantam. P, 32 pages.

Naomi is an Amish girl, one of the plain people. Amid all the plainness, Naomi complains to her little sister that just once she would like to have something fancy. One day as Naomi is collecting eggs, she notices one that is different and fancier than the rest. She places it under a hen, and when it hatches it produces an unusual-looking bird. Naomi fears that her fancy bird, a peacock, will be shunned. Instead, the elders view Naomi's peacock as a miracle.

Rodgers, Frank. (1988). *Who's Afraid of the Ghost Train?* Harcourt Brace Jovanovich. P, 32 pages.

Robert is afraid of almost everything and gets teased by his friends accordingly. One day his grandpa, a former lion tamer, gives him an idea for handling his fears. He tells Robert to pretend that the lions are just big babies. Robert tries this technique when riding the Ghost Train at the carnival the next day.

Thomas, Patricia. (1971/1990). *"Stand Back," Said the Elephant, "I'm Going to Sneeze!"* Illus. by Wallace Trip. Lothrop. P, 48 pages.

When an elephant sneezes, all kinds of unexpected things can happen—and do in this story. But once again, a mouse surprises the elephant and keeps him from sneezing, thus saving the other animals from their embarrassing responses to his sneeze. Unfortunately, the elephant ends up laughing, the effects of which are almost as bad as sneezing.

Yorinks, Arthur. (1988). *Bravo Minski.* Illus. by Richard Egielski. Farrar, Straus & Giroux. P, 32 pages.

It is difficult to be a scientific genius, especially when your father hauls you around Europe showing off your talents, but this is Minski's fate. But one day, when Minski hears an opera star, he determines to find a way to get the same kind of beautiful voice. Although his father thinks that Minski's musical intentions are impractical and unworthy of a scientific genius, Minski pursues his quest to become a musical performer.

Zolotow, Charlotte. (1972). *William's Doll.* Illus. by William Pene du Bois. Harper. P, I, 32 pages.

William has a basketball and a train set, but what he really wants is a doll. It doesn't matter that his brother thinks he is a creep, and the boy next door calls him a sissy; they just don't understand. William's grandmother is apparently the only person who understands how he feels and is willing to give him the doll he seeks.

B. Respect for Others

Anholt, Lawrence. (1991). *What I Like.* Illus. by Catherine Anholt. Putnam. P, 32 pages.

In simple rhyming text, six children share the different things they like to do. They eventually join hands and chant, "What we all like is . . . making a friend."

Brewster, Patience. (1991). *Rabbit Inn.* Little, Brown. P, I, 32 pages.

Some unexpected guests are coming to Rabbit Inn, so all the other animal guests cooperate to help the rabbit owners to clean up the place. On the last page of the book, they find out who the special guests are.

Herman, Charlotte. (1991). *Max Malone Makes a Million.* Illus. by Cat Bowman Smith. Henry Holt. P, I, 64 pages.

After Max reads about a get-rich-quick scheme, he sets out on one of his own. A six-year-old neighbor volunteers to help him, but Max just scoffs at him. In this instance, the younger child (the six-year-old) is successful and Max is not.

Hoffman, Mary. (1991). *Amazing Grace.* Illus. by Caroline Binch. Dial. P, 32 pages.

This is one of the growing number of books, like Spinelli's *Maniac Magee,* that addresses prejudice and bias directly. In this case, Grace, a truly talented dancer, wants the role of Peter Pan in a school play. But because she is both a black and a female, her classmates decide it would be inappropriate for her to play that role. Fortunately, Grace's grandmother is able to help her deal with her disappointment.

Isadora, Rachel. (1991). *At the Crossroads.* Greenwillow. P, I, 32 pages.

This book is about the children from a segregated South African township who gather at a crossroads to await their father's return from ten months in the mines. The African experience on which this book is based is real, and the underlying emotion—jubilation at the return of a loved one—is universal.

Johnston, Tony. (1986). *Pages of Music.* Illus. by Tomie dePaola. Putnam. P, I, 32 pages.

An artist and her son visit the island of Sardinia, where the poor shepherds share their bread with them. The son, who never forgets the sound of shepherd's pipes, returns years later as a composer and conductor. With him he brings his entire orchestra and an orchestral piece he has composed especially for the shepherds of Sardinia.

Kline, Suzy. (1991). *Mary Marony and the Snake.* Illus. by Blanche Sims. Putnam. P, I, 64 pages.

Mary Marony stutters and her second-grade classmates, especially Marvin Higgins, tease her. Mary earns the respect of her fellow students when Marvin's father brings a snake to school and Mary rescues it when it gets loose.

Morris, Ann. (1990). *On the Go.* Lothrop, Lee & Shepard. P, I, 32 pages.

The photographs in this nonfiction book show how people move themselves and things from one place to another in various parts of the world. Children learn that it is normal for people in some parts of the world to carry things on their heads or use various pack animals.

Shelby, Anne. (1991). *Potluck.* Illus. by Irene Trivas. Orchard. P, 32 pages.

> Potluck is an alphabet book. For each letter of the alphabet, a child whose name begins with that letter uses an action that begins with that letter to bring a food that begins with that letter to a potluck meal. The illustrations depict children of all racial and cultural backgrounds, and the foods they bring come from around the world.

Spinelli, Jerry. (1990). *Maniac Magee.* Little, Brown. I, 154 pages.

> This Newbery Award winner involves a white, homeless school dropout who lives for a time with a black family, then teaches an illiterate former minor league baseball player how to read, and finally makes friends with Mars Bars, the "baddest" black kid in town. The human relationships and the caring are both touching and profound.

Stevenson, James. (1991). *The Worst Person's Christmas.* Greenwillow. P, I, 32 pages.

> This book uses a cartoon format to show a Scrooge-like person who refuses to celebrate Christmas until some neighborhood children give him a present. He is ultimately forced to be jovial for the holidays.

Williams, Karen Lynn. (1991). *When Africa Was Home.* Orchard. P, I, 32 pages.

> Peter, a white child, was raised by an African nanny while his parents were working for the Peace Corps in Malawi. Peter has no desire to return to the United States, but he must say goodbye to his African extended family and friends. In the United States, he hates the cold snow and dreams of his former home in Africa. At the end of the story, the family returns to Africa and Peter is happy to be home again.

This bibliography is adapted from *Literature-Based Moral Education: Children's Books & Activities for Teaching Values, Responsibility, & Good Judgment in the Elementary School,* by

Linda Leonard Lamme, Suzanne Lowell Krogh, and Kathy A. Yachmetz. (1992). Used by permission of The Oryx Press, 4041 North Central at Indian School Road, Phoenix, AZ.

4.2 Historical Fiction and Folk Literature for Common Social Studies Topics

A. PRIMARY GRADES (K–3)

1. Prehistory Through A.D. 1

Literature Reflecting African or Egyptian Perspectives

Araujo, F. P. (1994). *The Perfect Orange: A Tale from Ethiopia.* Illus. by Xiao Jun Li. Rayve.

> An orphan girl gives the King an orange and accepts a donkey in return; only then does she learn that its bags are full of riches.

Bryan, A. (1989). *Turtle Knows Your Name.* Atheneum.

> This folktale from the West Indies is about the importance of names to family members.

Kimmel, E. A. (1994). *Anansi and the Talking Melon.* Illus. by J. Stevens. Holiday.

> Anansi, who has eaten Elephant's melon, tries to trick Elephant into believing it was a talking melon. Elephant shares his news with others, but King Monkey is insulted by the melon and disorder ensues.

Maddern, E. (1993). *The Fire Children: A West African Creation Tale.* Illus. by F. Lessac. Dial.

> This tale explains the origin of people who have different skin tones.

Souhami, J. (1996). *The Leopard's Drum: An Ashante Tale from West Africa.* Illus. by author. Little, Brown.

> Osebo, the leopard, refuses to give Nyame, the Sky God, a drum that Nyame envies. Nyame offers to reward the animal that can bring it to him, and although many animals try, only Achicheri, the tortoise, succeeds.

Walsh, J. P. (1995). *Pepi and the Secret Names.* Illus. by F. French. Lothrop, Lee & Shepard.

Pepi assists his father in decorating a royal tomb, makes friends with animals, guesses their secret names, and then gets them to pose for his father.

Literature Reflecting Asian Perspectives

Hong, L. T. (1995). *The Empress and the Silkworm.* Illus. by the author. Albert Whitman.

Set in China nearly 5,000 years ago, Si Ling-chi, the Empress, unwinds the thread of a cocoon that falls from a mulberry tree. She creates the first silk material that becomes a robe for the Emperor.

Jaffe, N. (1995). *Older Brother, Younger Brother: A Korean Folktale.* Illus. by W. Ma. Viking.

A young brother cares for an injured baby sparrow, which returns with a gift of wealth.

McDermott, G. (1981). *The Stone-Cutter: A Japanese Folk Tale.* Illus. by the author. Puffin Books.

This tale from Japan is about a boy who wanted to be stronger than the sun and mightier than a cloud.

Shute, L. (1986). *Momotaro, the Peach Boy: A Traditional Japanese Tale.* Lothrop, Lee & Shepard.

A small boy, who was born inside a peach, grows to challenge the evil *oni* who threaten his community.

Uchida, Y. (1986). *The Dancing Kettle.* Creative Arts Books.

The legends and myths in this Japanese collection all relate to the principles of Shintoism.

Van de Wetering, J. (1978). *Little Owl: An Eightfold Buddhist Admonition.* Houghton Mifflin.

Stories about animal characters introduce different aspects of the Buddhist religion.

Wells, R. (1996). *The Farmer and the Poor God: A Folktale from Japan.* Illus. by Yoshi. Simon & Schuster.

A farmer and his wife who have been impoverished by the Poor God, who lives in their attic, plan to escape their curse by running away. The god hears them and weaves sandals to follow them. The couple change their minds about going, and the sandals make them rich and happy.

Yep, L. (1993). *The Man Who Tricked a Ghost.* Bridgewater Books.

Young Sung makes himself rich by learning the secret of a fierce warrior ghost, and then using this to defeat him.

Young, E. (1995). *Cat and Rat: The Legend of the Chinese Zodiac.* Illus. by the author. Holt, Rinehart & Winston.

The Emperor announces that the winners of a race through the forest will have one of the years in the zodiac named after them.

Literature Reflecting European Perspectives

Turner, A. (1987). *Time of the Bison.* Illus. by B. Peck. Macmillan.

This fictional tale is set in prehistoric times and tells about how Scar Boy wants to earn a new name.

Literature Reflecting Hispanic Perspectives

Blackmore, V. (1984). *Why Corn Is Golden: Stories about Plants.* Illus. by S. Martinez-Ostos. Little, Brown.

This collection of folk stories is about corn and other plants.

Greger, C. S. (1994). *The Fifth and Final Sun: An Ancient Aztec Myth of the Sun's Origin.* Houghton Mifflin.

This folktale tells why humans live in the Age of the Fifth Sun—the first four suns were destroyed by jealous gods.

Kurtz, J. (1996). *Miro in the Kingdom of the Sun.* Illus. by D. Frampton. Houghton Mifflin.

This Incan folktale is the story of Miro, a girl who can run swiftly and understand the language of the birds. She is able to free her imprisoned brothers and find a cure for the ailing son of the Incan king.

Mora, P. (1995). *The Race of Toad and Deer.* Illus. by M. Itzna Brooks. Orchard.

In this Guatemalan tale, a deer challenges a toad in a race similar to that of "The Tortoise and the Hare."

Pitre, F. (1995). *Paco and the Witch.* Illus. by C. Hale. Lodestar.

A witch has cast a spell on a Puerto Rican boy that can be broken only if he can guess her name. A

4

crab teaches Paco a song to remember the name and the boy is saved. The witch goes looking for the animal that betrayed her, so the crab hides whenever he see a human.

Literature Reflecting Biblical, Mediterranean, or Middle Eastern Perspectives

Aesop (1985). *Aesop's Fables.* Illus. by M. Hague. Holt, Rinehart & Winston.

> This book includes thirteen fables.

Aroner, M. (1993). *The Kingdom of Singing Birds.* Kar-Ben.

> This classic Hasidic tale is about making one's own choices. When the King calls Rabbi Zusya to make his silent birds sing, Zusya tells him that he must set the birds free.

Bahous, S. (1993). *Sitti and the Cats.* Illus. by N. Malick. Roberts Rinehart.

> This Palestinian fairy tale focuses on the harshness of village life.

Hort, L. (1995). *The Goatherd and the Shepherdess: A Tale from Ancient Greece.* Illus. by L. Bloom. Dial.

> In this classic Greek myth, a shepherdess, Chloe, saves her lover, Daphnis, from kidnappers by blowing on a dying cowherder's pipes.

Hutton, W. (1991). *The Trojan Horse.* McElderry.

> This is the classic Greek tale about how Greek soldiers, hidden inside a huge horse, capture the city of Troy.

Kimmel, E. A. (1994). *The Three Princes: A Tale from the Middle East.* Illus. by L. E. Fisher. Holiday.

> A princess says that she will marry whichever suitor returns from a quest with the most magnificent wonder. She marries the one who sacrifices his treasure for her.

Kuskin, K. (1993). *A Great Miracle Happened There: A Chanukah Story.* HarperCollins.

> A mother tells her son about the origins of Chanukah.

MacGill-Callahan, S. (1995). *When Solomon Was King.* Illus. by S. T. Johnson. Dial.

King Solomon's life is saved by a lioness that Solomon had restored to health.

Rockwell, A. (1996). *The One-Eyed Giant and Other Monsters from the Greek Myths.* Illus. by the author. Greenwillow.

> This book presents ten myths about such monsters as Typhon, Echidna, Hydra, Cyclopes, and Medusa.

Literature Reflecting Native American Perspectives

Bania, M. (2002). *Kumak's House: A Tale of the Far North.* Illus. by the author. Alaska Northwest Books/Graphic Arts Center Publishing.

> A wise village elder helps Kumak and his family learn a lesson about contentment.

Bushyhead, R. H., & Bannon, K. T. (2002). *Yonder Mountain: A Cherokee Legend.* Illus. by K. Rodanas. Cavendish.

> In this retelling of a traditional Cherokee tale, three young men compete to become the tribe's new leader.

de Armond, D. (1988). *The Seal Oil Lamp.* Sierra/Little.

> This ancient Inuit tale tells about Allugua, a child who is born blind and, at age seven, is going to be abandoned until the Mouse Woman intervenes to save him.

de Paola, T. (1988). *The Legend of the Indian Paintbrush.* Putnam's.

> This is the story of Little Gopher, a child who cannot be like other children, and why the wildflowers bloom with such brilliant colors.

Gates, F., reteller. (1994). *Owl Eyes.* Illus. by Y. Miyake. Lothrop.

> This Mohawk legend tells how Raweno, the creator, gives each animal its traits. Because Owl pesters everyone as Raweno is trying to do this, he gives him big eyes and ears, to see only what is in front of him and hear what is he is told.

Hausman, G., reteller. (1996). *Eagle Boy: A Traditional Navajo Legend.* Illus. by C. and B. Moser. HarperCollins.

> Learning about the Eagle Way, which is culturally significant to the Navajo, is the focus of this legend

4

about a young boy who dreams of eagles and is taken up to the clouds to meet Eagle Chief.

McDermott, G. (1974). *Arrow to the Sun.* Viking.

This Pueblo Indian tale tells about the people's beliefs about the sun.

Stevens, J. (1996). *Old Bag of Bones: A Coyote Tale.* Holiday.

This retelling of a Shoshoni tale is about the trials of Old Coyote when he asks Buffalo to share his strength, youth, and power.

Young, E. (1993). *Moon Mother: A Native American Creation Tale.* Illus. by the author. HarperCollins.

This tale explains how people and tribes came to be, and why newborn babies cry.

Literature Reflecting Pacific and Australian Perspectives

Maddern, E. (1993). *Rainbow Bird: An Aboriginal Folktale from Northern Australia.* Illus. by A. Kennaway. Little, Brown.

Bird Woman snatches fire from Crocodile Man and then flies around putting fire into the heart of every tree. Thereafter, people can make flames from dry wood.

2. Early History A.D. 1 Through A.D. 1700

Literature Reflecting African Perspectives

Aardema, V. (1995). *Anansi Finds a Fool: An Ashanti Tale.* Illus. by B. Waldman. Dial.

In this amusing folktale, Anansi is outfoxed while trying to trick someone else.

Bryan, A. (1986). *Lion and the Ostrich Chicks and Other African Folk Tales.* Atheneum.

This is a collection of Hausa folktales.

Wisniewski, D. (1992). *Sundiata: Lion King of Mali.* Clarion.

This biography relates the life of Sundiata, who overcomes the inability to speak or walk, to become the Lion King of the Mali Empire.

Literature Reflecting Asian Perspectives

Han, S. C. (1995). *The Rabbit's Escape.* Illus. by Y. Heo. Holt.

This Korean folktale is about Rabbit's escape from a turtle that intends to deliver him to the Dragon King of the East Sea.

Uchida, Y. (1993). *The Magic Purse.* Illus. by K. Narahashi. McElderry.

When a poor man does an errand for a beautiful woman he meets, she gives him a magic purse of gold coins that support him through his life. Each year, the man follows the woman's instructions and leaves one coin in the purse.

_____. (1995). *The Wise Old Woman.* Illus. by M. Springett. McElderry.

When a cruel lord in medieval Japan decrees that the elderly at age seventy must be abandoned in the mountains, a young farmer hides his elderly mother to protect her.

Early Life in the American Colonies

Bulla, C. (1981). *A Lion to Guard Us.* Crowell.

This is the touching story of how three motherless children keep their lion's head door knocker as they sail from London to Jamestown to find their father in the new colony.

_____. (1988). *Squanto, Friend of the Pilgrims.* Scholastic.

This is the biography of Squanto, the Native American who befriended and offered immeasurable aid to the Pilgrims at the Plymouth Colony.

Good, M. (1993). *Reuben and the Fire.* Illus. by P. B. Moss. Good Books.

This is a fictionalized account of Amish life depicted through the activities of Reuben and his sisters. When Reuben sees his neighbor's barn burn down, the entire Amish community gathers for a barn raising.

Walters, K. (1993). *Samuel Eaton's Day: A Day in the Life of a Pilgrim Boy.* Scholastic.

This fictionalized account describes the daily life of seven-year-old Samuel Eaton in the Plimouth Colony.

4

Literature Reflecting European, Mediterranean, or Middle Eastern Perspectives

Adler, D. (1991). *A Picture Book of Christopher Columbus.* Illus. by J. Wallner & A. Wallner. Holiday.

This biographical picture book focuses on the life and time of Columbus.

Conrad, P. (1991). *Pedro's Journal.* Illus. by P. Koeppen. Caroline House.

This is the fictionalized diary of twelve-year-old Pedro, a ship's boy, who sails on Columbus's first voyage. Unfortunately, he is at the helm of the *Santa Maria* when he sails into a reef and sinks the ship.

Hodges, M. (1993). *The Hero of Bremen.* Holiday.

In this tale, Roland, a legendary hero, assists the crippled Hans to get land needed by the town of Bremen.

Pushkin, A. (n.d.). *The Fisherman and the Goldfish.* Illus. by V. Konashevich. Trans. by P. Tempest. Moscow Progress Publishers.

This is the Russian version of "The Fisherman and His Wife," in which an old man asks a goldfish for favors.

Talbott, H., reteller. (1995). *King Arthur and the Round Table.* Illus. by the reteller. Morrow.

This story follows King Arthur and his establishment of the Round Table.

Literature Reflecting Hispanic Perspectives

Marzollo, J. (1991). *In 1492.* Illus. by S. Bjorkman. Scholastic.

The rhyming text in this book depicts Columbus and his arrival in the new world.

Literature Reflecting Native American Perspectives

Brebeuf, Father Jean de. (1993). *The Huron Carol.* Dutton.

This is the story of the birth of Christ as set in the Huron world. It was written in the 1600s by a missionary, Father Jean de Brebeufin.

Fradin, D. (1992). *Hiawatha: Messenger of Peace.* Margaret K. McElderry/Macmillan.

This is the biography of Hiawatha, an Iroquois, who helped unite the seven Iroquois tribes into the Iroquois Confederacy.

Kessel, J. K. (1983). *Squanto and the First Thanksgiving.* Illus. by L. Donze. Carolrhoda.

This is the biography of Squanto, the last of the Paatuxet Indians, who helps the Pilgrims survive the harsh winter of 1620.

Sage, J. (1995). *Coyote Makes Man.* Illus. by B. Techentrup. Simon & Schuster.

In this Crow legend, a coyote creates a new creature.

Sewall, M. (1995). *King Philip's War.* Atheneum.

This fictionalized story is told in two voices: the Wampanoag and Pilgrim. The different points of view explain how relations between the colonists and the Native People eventually led to King Philip's War and, ultimately, to the destruction of the Wampanoags and their allies.

Swamp, C. J. (1995). *Giving Thanks: A Native American Good Morning Message.* Illus. by E. Printup, Jr. Lee & Low.

The words in this text, which give thanks to Mother Earth and the Great Spirit, are taken from Iroquois ceremonies.

Talashoema, H. (1991). *Coyote and Little Turtle: A Traditional Hopi Tale.* Trans. from Hopi by E. Sekaquaptewa and B. Pepper.

In another of the Coyote legends, Little Turtle tricks Coyote into throwing him into the pond.

3. 1700 Through 1900

Famous Americans

Adler, D. A. (1996). *A Picture Book of Davy Crockett.* Illus. by J. and A. Wallner. Holiday.

This brief biography chronicles Crockett's life from his birth in Tennessee to his death at the Alamo.

Aliki. (1988). *A Weed Is a Flower: The Life of George Washington Carver.* Illus. by the author. Simon & Schuster.

4

This biography relates the life and achievements of George Washington Carver.

Giblin, J. C. (1992). *George Washington: A Picture Book Biography.* Illus. by M. Dooling. Scholastic.

This biography follows events in Washington's life from childhood onward.

_____. (1995). *Thomas Jefferson: A Picture Book Biography.* Illus. by M. Dooling. Scholastic.

This pictorial biography chronicles events in Jefferson's life from childhood onward.

Walter, R. (1992). *The Story of Daniel Boone.* Dell.

This biography highlights the exploits of this famous Kentucky frontiersman.

Literature with African or African-American Themes

Barrett, T. (1993). *Nat Turner and the Slave Revolt.* Millbrook.

This is a fictionalized account of the rebellion that Nat Turner led against slave holders in Hampton, Virginia.

Bennett, E. (1992). *Frederick Douglass and the War Against Slavery.* Millbrook.

This is a biography of Frederick Douglass, who was born into slavery, but who became one of the foremost writers and speakers in the abolitionist movement.

Johnson, D. (1994). *Seminole Diary: Remembrances of a Slave.* Macmillan.

This fictional story is in a diary format and tells how Libbie and her family escape from slavery and join with the Seminole Indian tribe for safety.

Stanley, S. (2002). *Monkey for Sale.* Illus. by the author. Farrar, Straus & Giroux.

This story describes the complex chain of barters that two girls must make in order to rescue a monkey from a market in the Congo.

Wright, C. C. (1995). *Wagon Train: A Family Goes West in 1865.* Illus. by G. Griffith. Holiday.

This fictional story portrays the hardships that an African-American family faces when they travel west.

Literature Reflecting Asian Perspectives

Brett, J. (2002). *Daisy Comes Home.* Illus. by the author. G.P. Putnam's Sons/Puffin.

Set in China, this charming picture book is about bravery and bullying.

Coerr, E. (1988). *Chang's Paper Pony.* Illus. by D. K. Ray. Harper & Row.

This is the fictional story of Chang, who works in the kitchen of a gold mining camp in California. Chang finds gold nuggets under the floor in a cabin, returns them to their owner, and is rewarded with the pony he has always wanted.

Conger, D. (1987). *Many Lands, Many Stories: Asian Folk Tales for Children.* Illus. by R. Ra. Tuttle.

This is a collection of fifteen folktales from various countries in Asia.

Literature Reflecting European Perspectives

Conway, C. (1994). *Where Is Papa Now?* Illus. by author. Caroline House/Boyds Mills Press.

The fictional story of the daughter of a New England ship's captain who wonders where he is as his ship travels around the world.

Penn, M. (1994). *The Miracle of the Potato Latkes: A Hanukkah Story.* Illus. by G. Carrni. Holiday.

One potato that Tante Golda shares with an old beggar during a potato famine multiplies until she has enough to serve potato pancakes (latkes) to her guests.

Literature Reflecting Hispanic Perspectives

Crandel, R. (2002). *Hands of the Maya: Villagers at Work and Play.* Photographs by the author. Holt.

This book focuses on the hands of Mayans as they work making tortillas, carving stone, weaving, and washing, and other traditional activities.

Gray, G. (1978). *How Far, Felipe?* Harper.

This fictional story is about Felipe and his family as they move from Mexico to California with Colonel Juan de Anza's expedition in 1775.

Living in the Era 1700 to 1900

Hall, Donald. (1979). *Ox-Cart Man.* Illus. by B. Cooney. Viking.

> This story follows a New England family in the nineteenth century as the father takes their year's farm products to sell in the city.

Kam Mak, K. (2002). *My Chinatown: One Year in Poems.* Illus. by the author. HarperCollins.

> This stunning picture book uses poems to describe a young immigrant's life in New York City's Chinatown.

Saunders, S. R. (1995). *The Floating House.* Illus. by H. Cogancherry. Macmillan.

> This is a fictional story about the McClure family's journey down the Ohio River en route to new land in Indiana.

Shelby, A. (1995). *Homeplace.* Illus. by W. A. Halperin. Orchard.

> This fictional story traces a family's history in the same house that began as a log cabin built by an ancestor in 1810.

Smiler, N. (1992). *Snowshoe Thompson.* Illus. by J. Sandin. HarperCollins.

> This is the fictionalized story of John Thompson, who moves to northern California from Scandinavia in the early 1850s and becomes a mailperson.

Smucker, B. (1996). *Selina and the Bear Paw Quilt.* Illus. by J. Wilson. Crown.

> When a Mennonite family decides to flee to Canada just before the Civil War, the grandmother gives her granddaughter a handmade bear-paw-patterned quilt.

Yezerski, T. F. (2002). *A Full Hand.* Illus. by the author. Farrar, Straus & Giroux.

> This book tells the exciting story of nine-year-old Asa, as he learns to navigate a canal boat in the American northeast more than one hundred years ago.

Life on the Frontier

Brenner, Barbara. (1978). *Wagon Wheels.* Illus. by D. Bolognese. Harper & Row.

> This is a fictionalized account of a true story of a black pioneer family who sought free land offered in Kansas.

Coerr, Eleanor. (1986). *The Josefina Story Quilt.* Illus. by B. Degen. Harper & Row.

> This story is about a young girl who makes quilt squares to record her travels west in a covered wagon.

Harvey, Brett. (1988). *Cassie's Journey.* Illus. by D. K. Ray. Holiday.

> Cassie describes the problems her family encounters traveling by covered wagon from Illinois to California in the 1860s.

Holling, Clancy. (1942). *Tree in the Trail.* Houghton Mifflin.

> This old but fascinating account describes events that occurred around a cottonwood tree in Kansas that eventually became a yoke for a team of oxen.

Hooks, William H. (1988). *Pioneer Cat.* Random House.

> The story of a young girl who smuggles a cat on a wagon train to Oregon.

Levinson, Nancy S. (1988). *Clara and the Bookwagon.* Illus. by C. Croll. Harper & Row.

> Clara learns to read after the first traveling library visits her father's farm.

Rounds, Glen. (1983). *Mr. Yowder and the Windwagon.* Holiday.

> This delightful book describes Mr. Yowder's fruitless attempt to use wind power to drive a prairie schooner.

4. 1900 to the Present

Noted Americans

West, A. (1992). *Roberto Clemente: Baseball Legend.* Millbrook.

> This is a biography of Roberto Clemente, the Puerto Rican boy who became an outfielder for the Pittsburgh Pirates.

Literature Reflecting African or African-American Perspectives

Aardema, Verna. (1981). *Bringing the Rain to Kapiti Plain.* Illus. by B. Vidal. Dial.

4

This African folktale tells how Ki-pat brings rain to end the drought.

Hamilton, Virginia. (1985). *The People Could Fly.* Illus. by L. and D. Dillon. Knopf.

This collection of African-American folktales is about animals, the supernatural, and striving for freedom.

Pomerantz, Charlotte. (1989). *The Chalk Doll.* Illus. by F. Lessac. Lippincott.

Rosa's mother describes her life and childhood in Jamaica.

Literature Reflecting Asian Perspectives

Lewin, T. (2002). *Big Jimmy's Kaum Kau Chinese Take Out.* Illus. by the author. HarperCollins.

This story provides lively behind-the-scenes views of a contemporary Chinese restaurant through the eyes of the owner's son.

Rattigan, J. K. (1993). *Dumpling Soup.* Illus. by L. Hsu-Flanders. Little, Brown.

This is an account of seven-year-old Marisa, a Hawaiian girl who celebrates New Year's with her extended family.

Say, Allen. (1982). *The Bicycle Man.* Houghton Mifflin.

In postwar-occupied Japan, a group of schoolchildren are amazed by an American soldier's bicycle tricks.

Literature Reflecting European Perspectives

Joosse, B. M. (1995). *The Morning Chair.* Illus. by M. Sewall. Clarion.

When a young boy and his parents leave Holland for New York City, the boy is comforted by the fact that the family is bringing some of its rituals with them.

Polacco, P. (1990). *Thunder Cake.* Philomel.

In this tale of Russian origin, a little girl's Babushka (grandmother) helps her to overcome her fear of thunderstorms by baking a Thunder Cake, which they eat during the storm.

Schwartz, D. M. (1991). *Supergrandpa.* Illus. by B. Dodson. Lothrop, Lee & Shepard.

This is the fictionalized story of a sixty-three-year-old man who enters the Tour of Sweden, a 1,000-mile bicycle race.

Life in the Twentieth Century

Baker, S. A. (1995). *Grandpa Is a Flyer.* Illus. by B. Farnsworth. Albert Whitman.

This is a fictionalized account of a grandfather who shares his love for flying with his granddaughter.

Caseley, J. (2002). *On the Town: A Community Adventure.* Illus. by the author. Greenwillow.

While working on a class assignment, a young boy discovers his community.

Good, M. (1982). *Nicole Visits an Amish Farm.* Walker.

This is a story of how a child from the city spends her summer on an Amish farm.

_____. (1995). *Reuben and the Blizzard.* Illus. by P. B. Moss. Good Books.

This is a story of how Reuben and his Amish family are affected by a blizzard.

Harvey, B. (1987). *Immigrant Girl: Becky of Eldridge Street.* Holiday.

This story about Russian immigrants living in New York City is based on a young girl's diary.

Schertle, A. (1995). *Maisie.* Illus. by L. Dabovich. Lothrop, Lee & Shepard.

This is a fictional account of a farm girl who shares events from her life up to her ninetieth birthday.

Family Life/Problems

Aliki. (1979). *The Two of Them.* Greenwillow.

A little girl's grandfather cares for her until she grows up; then she cares for him until he dies.

Blaine, Marge. (1975). *Terrible Thing That Happened at Our House.* Illus. by J. Wallner. Parents Magazine.

Children may need to accept new responsibilities when Mother goes back to work.

Brown, Laurie Krashy, & Brown, Marc. (1986). *Dinosaurs Divorce.* Little, Brown.

This account may help to offset some of the anxieties that children feel when their parents are going through a divorce.

Clifton, Lucille. (1983). *Everett Anderson's Goodbye.* Illus. by A. Grifalconi. Henry Holt.

This is the story of a boy who goes through several stages in coming to accept his father's death.

Drescher, Joan. (1980). *Your Family, My Family.* Walker.

This story shows how family units are often made up of different combinations of people.

Hazen, Barbara Shook. (1979). *Tight Times.* Illus. by T. Hyman. Viking.

A family living in poverty supports one another even though the father has lost his job.

Hutchins, Pat. (1985). *The Very Worst Monster.* William Morrow.

This account tells about Hazel's effort to overcome her jealousy when her baby brother arrives.

MacLachlan, Patricia. (1982). *Mama One, Mama Two.* Illus. by R. Bornstein. Harper & Row.

This is the story of a little girl who must live with foster parents while her mother recovers from a mental illness.

Roy, Ron. (1980). *Breakfast with My Father.* Illus. by T. Howell. Houghton Mifflin.

David is disappointed when his father, who is separated from his mother, does not take him to their usual Saturday breakfast.

Rylant, Cynthia. (1984). *This Year's Garden.* Illus. by M. Salagyi. Bradbury.

A family's responsibilities for caring for a garden change with the seasons.

Smith, Miriam. (1989). *Annie and Moon.* Illus. by L. Moyes. Gareth Stevens.

Moon, the cat, must adjust to living in new places, just as do Annie and her mother.

Wells, R., & Wells, T. (2002). *The House in the Mall.* Illus. by D. Andreasen. Viking/Puffin.

Emily's diary describes events of 1927 when her Enfield, Kentucky, family decides to order a house from a catalog.

World War II

Ahlberg, J., & Ahlberg, A. (1981). *Peek-A-Boo!* Puffin.

This book offers a delightful account of a day in the life of a British toddler during World War II.

Bishop, Claire H. (1952). *Twenty and Ten.* Viking.

This is a story of how twenty Gentile children hide and protect ten Jewish children from the Nazis in occupied France.

Innocenti, Roberto. (1985). *Rose Blanche.* Creative Education.

This is the story of Rose Blanche, who lives in a small German town where the war doesn't seem to cause many changes in her life—until she discovers a concentration camp outside of town.

Leitner, Isabella. (1992). *The Big Lie.* Scholastic.

Isabella and her family are taken to Auschwitz, but not all of them survive the ordeal.

Spiegelman, Art. (1986). *Maus 1: A Survivor's Tale.* Scholastic.

This is a comic book with Polish mice and Nazi cats, in which an old Jewish mouse tells his son the story of his life during the war.

Tsuchya, Yukio. (1988). *Faithful Elephants: A True Story of Animals, People, and War,* translated by Tomoko Dykes. Trumpet.

This is the story of how the keepers at the Tokyo Zoo must kill the wild animals because the army fears that bombs may hit the zoo and permit the animals to escape.

Literature Reflecting Mediterranean or Middle Eastern Perspectives

Heide, F. P., & Gilliland, J. H. (1990). *The Day of Ahmed's Secret.* Lothrop, Lee & Shepard.

This first-person story tells of one day in the life of a young boy, Ahmed, who lives in a Middle Eastern city.

Oberman, S. (1994). *The Always Prayer Shawl.* Illus. by T. Lewin. Caroline House/Boyds Mills.

This is the story of how a prayer shawl passes down through the generations.

4

Portnoy, M. A. (1994). *Matzah Ball: A Passover Story.* Illus. by K. J. Kahn. Kar-Ben.

> At a baseball game, Aaron's mother reminds him that he cannot eat certain foods because it is Passover. Aaron is unhappy but an elderly man sitting beside him gives a special piece of matzah.

Segal, Sheila F. (1994). *Joshua's Dream: A Journey to the Land of Israel.* Illus. by J. Iskowitz. Roberts Rhinehart.

> This is a fictionalized account of how Joshua and his family go to Israel and plant a tree in the desert.

Literature About Native American Peoples

Martin, Bill, Jr., & Archambault, John. (1987). *Knots on a Counting Rope.* Illus. by T. Rand. Henry Holt.

> A Native American boy and his grandfather recall his birth, his first horse, and an amazing race.

Rogers, Jean. (1988). *Runaway Mittens.* Illus. by Rio Munoz. Greenwillow.

> A young Eskimo boy continually loses his mittens until newborn puppies find a use for them.

Von Ahnen, K. (1994). *Charlie Young Bear.* Illus. by P. Livers Lambert. Council for Indian Education Series/ Roberts Rinehart.

> In this fictional account, Charlie, a young Mesquakie boy, dreams of buying a bicycle with money that his people will get for past treaty violations.

Whitehorse, B. (1994). *Sunpainters: Eclipse of the Navajo Sun.* Northland.

> A contemporary Native American listens to his grandfather's story about the little people who repaint the world during an eclipse of the sun.

Literature Reflecting Hispanic Perspectives

Thomas, J. R. (1994). *Lights on the River.* Illus. by M. Dooling. Hyperion.

> Teresa and her family remember how they celebrated Christmas in their village in Mexico before they left to become migrant workers.

Williams, V. B. (1984). *A Chair for My Mother.* Greenwillow.

> This is the story of a family saving money to buy a new chair after a fire in their apartment.

Contemporary Concerns

Elys, S. M. (2002). *Home At Last.* Illus. by F. Davalos. Lee & Low.

> This story uses realistic examples to capture the difficulties that immigrant families encounter because of limited skills in speaking English.

Heard, G. (Ed.). (2002). *This Place I Know: Poems of Comfort.* Illus. by eighteen renowned artists. Candlewick.

> The events of September 11, 2001, inspired this collection of "words of comfort."

McPhail, D. (2002). *The Teddy Bear.* Illus. by author. Henry Holt.

> Readers of all ages will delight in this book, while young readers will understand the significance of giving and having compassion for others.

Okimoto, J. D., & Aoki, E. M. (2002). *The White Swan: A Story About Adoption.* Illus. by M. So. Clarion.

> Four American families awake one day to meet their new Chinese daughters in the city of Guangzhou, China.

O'Neill, A. (2002). *The Recess Queen.* Illus. by L. Huliska-Beith. Scholastic.

> This book tackles the very serious and important topic of bullying but in a lighthearted way.

Salat, C. (2002). *Peanut's Emergency.* Illus. by T. Lyon. Charlesbridge.

> This story focuses on the importance of following preestablished instructions in case of an emergency. In this instance, Peanut experiences a "scary emergency" when no one arrives to pick her up from school.

B. INTERMEDIATE GRADES (3–6)

1. Prehistory Through A.D. 1

Living in the Times Before Christ

Fahs, S., & Spoerl, D. (1988). *Earth Sky Life Death.* Starr King Press.

This collection includes some creation stories from various cultures, including Adam and Eve, the creation of humans by Prometheus, and Odin's ancestors.

Literature Reflecting African or Egyptian Perspectives

Anderson, D. A. (1993). *The Origin of Life on Earth: An African Creation Myth.* Sights Productions.

This myth, which presents an African version of how life originated, emphasizes the sacredness of life and the need for determination and generosity.

Giblin, J. C. (1990). *The Riddle of the Rosetta Stone: Key to Ancient Egypt.* Crowell.

This is the story of how the Rosetta Stone's message was deciphered, and how it has influenced our knowledge of the Egyptian civilization.

Greger, C. S. (1996). *Cry of the Benu Bird: An Egyptian Creation Story.* Illus. by adapter/author. Houghton Mifflin.

This story explains how the Benu bird arises from an ocean surrounded and starts time on earth while another being, Atum, creates life and order.

Nevin, T. (1996). *Zamani: African Tales from Long Ago.* Jacaranda.

These folktales from various African countries involve humans talking with animals.

Stanley, D., & Vennema, P. (1994). *Cleopatra.* Illus. by D. Stanley. Morrow.

This account portrays Cleopatra as a brilliant and daring ruler.

Literature Reflecting Asian Perspectives

Hong, L. T. (1995). *The Empress and the Silkworm.* Illus. by the author. Albert Whitman.

Set in China nearly 5,000 years ago, Si Ling-chi, the Empress, unwinds the thread of a cocoon that falls from a mulberry tree. She then creates the first silk material that becomes a robe for the Emperor.

Tata, M. (1995). *The Geese and the Tortoise and Other Stories.* Illus. by H. Benton. Tata.

The three stories in this volume were originally written in Sanskrit. "The Crows and the Snake" deals with peace, "The Four Friends" with friendship, and "The Geese and the Tortoise" with vanity.

Literature Reflecting European Perspectives

Bilenko, A. (1974). *Ukranian Folk Tales.* Illus. by R. Adamovich. Dnipro Publishing of Kiev.

This collection of twenty tales shows how good deeds are rewarded and wicked deeds are punished.

Osborne, M. P. (1996). *Favorite Norse Myths.* Illus. by T. Howell. Scholastic.

This collection includes myths such as "How Thor Got His Hammer" and "The Golden Apples."

Smimova, G. (1993). *Fairy-Tales of Siberian Folks.* Trans. from Russian by O. Myazina and G. Shchitnikova. Vital.

The sixty animal fables in this collection represent fifteen ethnic groups in Siberia.

Literature Reflecting Hispanic Perspectives

Baquedano, E. (1993). *Aztec, Inca & Maya.* Knopf.

This account contrasts three major civilizations.

Flor, A. A. (1989). *Feathers Like a Rainbow: An Amazon Indian Tale.* Harper.

This tale, set in the Amazon rain forest, explains how the birds got their colors.

Gaudiano, A. (1972). *Azteca: The Story of a Jaguar Warrior.* Roberts Rinehart/Denver Museum of Natural History.

This story about an Aztec warrior shows how his beliefs in the power of the jaguar influenced his life.

Literature Reflecting Greek, Mediterrean, or Middle Eastern Perspectives

Climo, S. (1995). *Atalanta's Race: A Greek Myth.* Illus. by A. Koshkin. Clarion.

After Atalanta races her lover, Melanion, they face Aphrodite's revenge.

4

Coolidge, O. (1949). *Greek Myths*. Illus. by E. Sandoz. Houghton Mifflin.

> An excellent collection of Greek myths.

Eisler, C. (1992). *David's Songs; His Psalms and Their Story*. Illus. by J. Pinkney. Dial.

> A young shepherd, David, who eventually became King of Israel, wrote forty-two Psalms that have endured for over 2,000 years.

Hutton, W. (1991). *The Trojan Horse*. McElderry.

> This is the classic Greek tale about how Greek soldiers hidden inside a huge horse were able to capture the city of Troy.

Lasky, K. (1994). *The Librarian Who Measured the Earth*. Illus. by K. Hawkes. Little, Brown.

> This is the biography of Eratosthenes of Cyrene, a librarian and geographer who estimated the circumference of the earth.

Literature Reflecting Native American Perspectives

Ehlers, S. (1979). *The Bossy Hawaiian Moon*. Illus. by W. H. Kiyabu. Edward Enterprises of Honolulu.

> This is a tale of how the stars and clouds show the bossy moon that they too are supposed to live in the sky.

Hodges, M. (1972). *The Firebringer: A Paiute Indian Legend*. Little, Brown.

> This tale tells how the Native People first obtained fire.

Philip, N. (1995). *Songs Are Thoughts: Poems of the Inuit*. Illus. by M. Foa. Orchard.

> The free-verse selections in this book reflect the happiness and life of the Eskimo people.

2. Early History A.D. 1 Through A.D. 1700

Perspective: Early Life in the American Colonies

Aliki. (1984). *The Story of William Penn*. Prentice-Hall.

> This is a biography of William Penn, the Quaker who established the colony of Pennsylvania as a refuge for religious nonconformists.

Fritz, J. (1980). *Who's That Stepping on Plymouth Rock?* Putnam's.

> This book portrays the history of early settlers landing on Plymouth Rock.

Kagan, M. (1989). *Vision in the Sky: New Haven's Early Years 1638–1783*. Linnet Press.

> This fictional account focuses on the strict Puritan values imposed on the early Colonists, and on their relations with the Native Americans.

Lobel, A. (1971). *On the Day Peter Stuyvesant Sailed into Town*. Illus. by author. Harper & Row.

> When Peter Stuyvesant lands in New Amsterdam (New York), the town is a mess. Stuyvesant leads a massive clean-up effort.

Stone, M. (1989). *Rebellion's Song*. Steck-Vaughn.

> This collection of stories focuses on the lives of six people living in Colonial times.

Van Leeuwen, I. (1996). *Across the Wide Dark Sea: The Mayflower Journey*. Illus. by T. B. Allen. Dial.

> This story is a fictionalized account of a young boy's journey on the Mayflower.

Literature Reflecting European Perspectives

Asimov, I. (1991). *Ferdinand Magellan: Opening the Door to World Exploration*. Illus. by J. R. Karpinski. Gareth Stevens.

> This biography details Magellan's childhood and life as the first explorer to sail around the world.

Asimov, I., & Kaplan, E. (1991). *Henry Hudson: Arctic Explorer and North American Adventurer*. Gareth Stevens.

> This book chronicles the problems that Henry Hudson encountered as he searched for the fabled Northwest passage.

Fisher, L. E. (1992). *Galileo*. Macmillan.

> This is a biography of Galileo, whose astronomical observations were attacked by the Catholic Church and others. Despite the attacks, many of his observations about gravity, magnetism, and motion became the basis for modern scientific thought.

_____. (1993). *Gutenberg.* Illus. by the author. Macmillan.

> This biography focuses on the man whose invention (the printing press) changed the course of history.

Hunt, Jonathan. (1996). *Leif's Saga: A Viking Tale.* Simon & Schuster.

> Sigrid is a young Viking girl whose father tells her the story of Leif Ericson.

Materll, H. M. (1995). *Foods & Feasts with the Vikings.* Silver Burdett.

> This book explores the foods that the Vikings ate and what they drank.

Shafer, A. (2002). *The Fantastic Journey of Pieter Bruegel.* Illus. by the author. Dutton.

> Fabricated diary entries trace Pieter Bruegel's sixteenth-century journey from Antwerp to Rome.

Literature Reflecting Hispanic Perspectives

Foreman, M., & R. Seaver. (1992). *The Boy Who Sailed with Columbus.* Arcade.

> This is the fictional account of Leif, an orphan, who is left behind as punishment after he runs the *Santa Maria* aground.

Rohmer, H., Chow, O. & M. Vidauke. (1987). *The Invisible Hunters.* Children's Book Press.

> This is a fictionalized account of how the first European traders affected the life of the Miskiot Indians in seventeenth-century Nicaragua.

Schlein, M. (1991). *I Sailed with Columbus.* Illus. by T. Newsom. HarperCollins.

> Julio, a ship's boy, befriends a native boy who helps to calm the superstitious crew. Useful information on navigation and measuring distance.

Literature Reflecting Native American Perspectives

Bierhorst, J. (1987). *Doctor Coyote: Native American Aesop's Fables.* Illus. by W. Watson. Macmillan.

> This collection of brief fables has traveled from Aesop to Native Americans.

Nashone. (1988). *Grandmother Stories of the Northwest.* Sierra Oaks Press.

> Some of the stories in this collection show the Native Americans heritage in the west.

3. 1700 Through 1900

Famous Americans

Adler, D. A. (1987). *Thomas Jefferson: Father of Our Democracy.* Holiday.

> This is a biography of Jefferson, his life and times.

Adler, D. A. (2002). *A Picture Book of Dwight David Eisenhower.* Holiday House.

> This illustrated biography of the thirty-fourth president highlights Ike's military career and lifelong commitment to public service.

Fradin, D. B. (2002). *The Signers: The 56 Stories Behind the Declaration of Independence.* Illus. by M. McCurdy. Walker.

> This book offers an excellent reference on the signers of the Declaration of Independence.

Kimmel, F. Cody. (2002). *One Sky Above Us.* (Young Buffalo Bill series) Illus. by S. Snow. HarperCollins.

> This is the second installment in a series of novels based on the childhood adventures of western showman Buffalo Bill.

McDonough, Y. Z. (2002). *Peaceful Protest: The Life of Nelson Mandela.* Illus. by M. Zeldis. Walker.

> This easy-to-read biography traces the life of one of the most important leaders of the twentieth century.

Monjo, F. N. (1974). *Grand Papa and Ellen Aroon.* Dell.

> This fictional account is written from the perspective of Thomas Jefferson's nine-year-old granddaughter.

Vance, M. (1947). *Martha, Daughter of Virginia: The Story of Martha Washington.* Illus. by N. Walker. Dutton.

> This life story chronicles Martha's life from childhood to her widowhood.

Wade, M. D. (1995). *Benedict Arnold.* Watts.

> This biography chronicles the life of one of America's most famous traitors.

4

Literature Reflecting African or African-American Perspectives

Everett, G. (1992). *John Brown: One Man Against Slavery.* Illus. by J. Lawrence. Rizzoli.

> This biography of John Brown's raid on the arsenal at Harper's Ferry is written from the perspective of his teenage daughter.

Ferris, J. (1988). *Go Free or Die: A Story about Harriet Tubman.* Carolrhoda.

> This biography is a moving chronicle of the life of Harriet Tubman, an escaped slave who returned to the South to spy for the Union Army and lead people out of slavery.

Johnson, D. (1993). *Now Let Me Fly: The Story of a Slave Family.* Macmillan.

> This is a fictional story of Minna and her family's harsh life on a plantation.

Lester, J. (1987). *The Tale of Uncle Remus: The Adventure of Brer Rabbit.* Dial.

> This collection has over forty tales that are retold in black English.

Lyons, M. E. (1994). *Master of Mahogany: Tom Day, Free Black Cabinetmaker.* Scribner's.

> This is the biography of Tom Day, who eventually becomes one of the largest furniture producers in North Carolina.

Moore, C. (2002). *The Daring Escape of Ellen Craft.* Illus. by M. Young. Lerner Publishing.

> This is the moving story of Ellen Craft's escape from slavery to freedom.

Pelz, R. (1990). *Black Heroes of the Wild West.* Open Yesterday and Today Hand Publishing.

> This is a collection of brief biographies about African-Americans and their journeys to the frontier.

Porter, C. (1992). *Meet Addy.* Pleasant Co.

> Addy Walker is an African-American girl who grows up during the Civil War.

Rappaport, D. (2002). *No More! Stories and Songs of Slave Resistance.* Illus. by S. W. Evans. Candlewick Press.

> This dynamic nonfiction picture book documents various forms of slave resistance: subversion, uprisings, escape, poetry, religion, and song.

Winter, J. (1989). *Follow the Drinking Gourd.* Knopf.

> This is a fictional account of Peg Leg Joe, a one-legged sailor who teaches slaves about the Underground Railroad. Includes the song and music he uses to do this.

Living in America (1700 to 1900)

Revolutionary War Era

Krensky, S. (2002). *Paul Revere's Midnight Ride.* Illus. by G. Harlin. HarperCollins.

> Readers travel with Paul Revere from Boston to Lexington, where he hears the first shots of the American Revolution.

Miller, B. M. (2002). *Growing Up in Revolution and the New Nation, 1775 to 1800.* Lerner Publishing Group.

> This illustrated volume focuses on the daily life of children in America from 1775 to 1800. Excellent illustrations, clear text, and a visually appealing layout.

Murray, S. (2002). *American Revolution.* (Eyewitness Books Series). OK Publishing.

> This is an illustrated and moving guide to the people, battles, and the details of life during the American Revolution.

Life on the Frontier

Alder, E. (2002). *Crossing the Panther's Path.* Farrar, Straus & Giroux.

> This is the true story of a fourteen-year-old, Irish-Mohawk boy who lived at British Fort Malden and of his friendship with Tecumseh and French Jesuits in Detroit.

Lawlor, Laurie. (1986). *Addie Across the Prairie.* Illus. by G. Owens. Albert Whitman.

> Describes the adjustments that a young girl, Addie, must make when her family moves from Iowa to the Dakota territory.

MacLachlan, Patricia. (1985). *Sarah, Plain and Tall.* Harper & Row.

This is the classic tale of a prairie farmer who orders a wife from New England by mail order.

Wilder, Laura Ingalls. (1953). *On the Banks of Plum Creek*. Illus. by G. Williams. Harper & Row.

This story describes the life of a pioneer family along Plum Creek in Minnesota.

The Civil War Era

Beatty, Patricia. (1987). *Turn Homeward, Hannafee*. William Morrow.

This book describes how the Union Army forced two children from Georgia to the north, and of their escape and return home.

_____. (1988). *Walking the Road to Freedom*. Illus. by P. Hanson. Carolrhoda.

The story of a woman who speaks out against slavery and advocates women's rights.

Bolotin, N. (2002). *Civil War A to Z: A Young Readers' Guide to over 100 People, Places, and Points of Importance*. Dutton/Puffin.

With lively segments presented in alphabetical order, this is an excellent source book for stimulating students' interest in the Civil War.

Lester, Julius. (1968). *To Be a Slave*. Illus. by T. Feelings. Dial.

This collection is based on interviews with former slaves.

MacLachlan, P. (1994) *Skylark*. HarperCollins.

This is a sequel to MacLachlan's *Sarah, Plain and Tall* (1985, Harper & Row).

McPherson, J. M. (2002). *Fields of Fury: The American Civil War*. Atheneum.

This is an illustrated and highly readable introduction to the Civil War that grabs children's attention with its vintage photographs, period oil paintings, and campaign and battlefield maps.

Nixon, Joan Lowery. (1987). *A Family Apart*. Bantam.

This is the touching story of six children who are adopted by farm families in the Midwest because their mother cannot support them.

Reit, Seymour. (1988). *Behind Rebel Lines*. Harcourt Brace Jovanovich.

This is a story of the exploits of Emma Edmonds, who spied for the Union Army.

Turner, Ann. (1987). *Nettie's Trip South*. Illus. by R. Himler. Macmillan.

Nettie is a ten-year-old girl who travels to Richmond before the Civil War and is shocked by the aspects of slavery she has seen.

Literature Reflecting European Perspectives

Levinson, R. (1985). *Watch the Stars Come Out*. Dutton.

This fictional story about crossing the Atlantic in the 1890s is told from a child's point of view.

Turner, B. (1991). *The Haunted Igloo*. Houghton Mifflin.

This is the fictional story of Jean-Paul, a French Canadian who walks with a limp because of a birth defect. When the native Inuit boys tease him and exclude him from their activities, Jean-Paul learns to deal with his limitations.

Yoder, J. W. (1996). *Rosanna of the Amish*. Herald Press.

This fictionalized story follows the life of an Irish orphan who was raised by the Amish in central Pennsylvania in the 1800s.

Literature Reflecting Hispanic Perspectives

Meyer, K. A. (1987). *Father Serra: Traveler on the Golden Chain*. Our Sunday Visitor Publishers.

This is a biography of Father Serra, who spent almost thirty years helping to found the missions in California.

Literature Reflecting Mediterrean or Middle Eastern Perspectives

Shepard, A. (1995). *The Enchanted Storks*. Illus. by A. Dianov. Clarion.

This tale set in ancient Baghdad tells about a ruler and his assistant, who are tricked by a magician.

4

Literature Reflecting Native American Perspectives

Young, R., & J. Dockery, editors. (1994). *Race with Buffalo: And Other Native American Stories for Young Readers.* Illus. by W. E. Hall. August House.

> This is a collection of over thirty tales, arranged by subjects, that go back to ancient times.

4. 1900 to the Present

Noted Americans

Cedeno, M. E. (1993). *Cesar Chavez: Labor Leader.* Millbrook.

> This is the biography of Chavez's struggle to improve working conditions for the farm workers in California.

Gutman, B. (1973). *Hank Aaron.* Grosset.

> This is the biography of a baseball superstar.

Haskins, J. (2002). *Champion: The Story of Muhammad Ali.* Illus. by E. Velasquez. Walker.

> This book examines the turbulent voyage of Muhammad Ali's life. It shows both his quick wit and his pensive side.

Old, W. (2002). *To Fly: The Story of the Wright Brothers.* Illus. by R. A. Parker. Clarion.

> Great illustrations and a good story reinforce the lessons of reliance and teamwork.

Literature Reflecting African or African-American Perspectives

Rosen, M. I. (1995). *A School for Pompey Walker.* Illus. by A. B. L. Robinson. Harcourt.

> This is the fictionalized story of a free slave who sold himself into slavery to raise money for a school.

Weatherford, C. B. (2002). *Remember the Bridge: Poems of a People.* Philomel/Puffin.

> This illustrated compilation of original poems commemorates specific African-Americans as well as major obstacles and accomplishments of their lives.

Literature Reflecting Hispanic Perspectives

Mikaelsen, B. (2002). *Red Midnight.* RAYO/Harper.

> Twelve-year-old Santiago and his four-year-old sister flee Guatemala when their village is destroyed, which leads them on an odyssey that ends in a new life in the United States.

Literature Reflecting Asian Perspectives

Graff, N. (1993). *Where the River Runs: A Portrait of a Refugee Family.* Illus. by R. Howard. Little, Brown.

> This fictionalized story tells of the struggles of the Prek family as they escape the civil war in Cambodia and journey to the United States.

Hill, E. S. (2002). *Chang and the Bamboo Flute.* Illus. by L. Liu. Farrar, Straus & Giroux.

> Chang, a mute Chinese boy whose father uses cormorants to fish the Li River of southern China, becomes a hero when heavy rains damage the family's raft home.

Life in Twentieth-Century America

Bial, R. (2002). *Tenement: Immigrant Life on the Lower East Side.* Illus. by the author. Houghton Mifflin.

> This book presents a compelling look at the sounds, sights, and smells of tenement life in New York City during the height of European immigration.

Damon, D. (2002). *Headin' for Better Times: The Arts of the Great Depression.* Lerner Publishing Group.

> This illustrated book examines the prolific artists of the Great Depression, ranging from Isaac Soyer's paintings of the unemployment line to Marc Blitzstein's opera with a pro-labor message.

Dooling, M. (2002). *The Great Horse-less Carriage Race.* Illus. by the author. Holiday House.

> Excellent illustrations help readers relive the excitement of the great 1895 Chicago automobile race.

Foster, S. (1987). *Where Time Stands Still.* Putnam.

> This book shows the life of Amish children today.

Lehrman, Robert. (1992). *The Store That Mama Built.* Macmillan.

This is an account of how a Jewish immigrant woman operates a store in a small town in Pennsylvania at the turn of the nineteenth century.

Matas, C. (2002). *Sparks Fly Upward*. Clarion.

A wise rabbi helps twelve-year-old Rebecca Bernstein resolve conflicting loyalties in this story, set in early twentieth-century Canada, of immigration, cross-cultural friendship, Jewish identity, and personal courage.

Miller, D. S. (2002). *The Great Serum Race: Blazing the Iditarod Trail*. Illus. by J. Van Zyle. Walker.

The illustrations will transport students to the forests of Alaska along the path of the famous dogsled race to Nome.

Taylor, Mildred. (1990). *The Road to Memphis*. Dial.

This story is part of the continuing saga of the Logans, a close-knit African-American family that must deal with white hatred and bigotry in the South. In this account, Stacy Logan is old enough to join the army, and the war is never far from anyone's mind.

Thoreau, Henry. D. S. Schnur (Ed.). *Henry David's House*. Illus. by P. Fiore. Charlesbridge.

Extracts from *Walden Pond* are complemented by sensitive illustrations to introduce readers to this major figure in American literature.

West, T. (1993). *Fire in the Valley*. Silver Moon Press.

Early in the twentieth century, eleven-year-old Sarah Jefferson and her family protest Los Angeles's desire to divert water from their valley.

Wyman, Andrea. (1991). *Red Sky at Morning*. Holiday.

This is a fictional account of the struggles that a twelve-year-old girl, Callie Common, and her grandfather face trying to run a farm in Indiana by themselves.

Yep, L. (2002). *When the Circus Came to Town*. Illus. by S. Wang. HarperCollins.

This storybook is based on actual events that occurred in the early twentieth century and features a young girl who catches smallpox. It also captures the pain of being different.

World War II

Degens, T. (1974). *Transport 7-41-R*. Viking.

This story describes a thirteen-year-old girl's journey from the Russian sector of defeated Germany to Cologne on a train carrying returning refugees in 1946.

Garrigue, Sheila. (1985). *The Eternal Spring of Mr. Ito*. Bradbury.

This is the account of a young English girl who is sent to stay with relatives in Canada and learns about racism and hysteria toward Japanese citizens.

Levitin, Sonia. (1970). *Journey to America*. Atheneum.

Lisa and her family leave Berlin to escape the Nazis in 1938. After many hardships they are reunited in America.

Lowry, Lois. (1989). *Number the Stars*. Dell.

A ten-year-old girl and her family use courage and cunning to help their Jewish friends escape the Nazis in German-occupied Denmark.

Maruki, Toshi. (1980). *Hiroshima No Pika*. Lothrop.

This work chronicles the ordeal of Young Mii, who is eating breakfast at home in Hiroshima when the atom bomb is dropped.

Yolen, Jane. (1988). *The Devil's Arithmetic*. Viking Kestrel.

During one Passover celebration, Hannah opens the door and finds herself transported to a Polish village during the war. After she is placed in a concentration camp, she understands why no one should ever forget the Holocaust.

Literature Reflecting Mediterranean or Middle Eastern Perspectives

Heide, F. P., & Gilliland, I. H. (1992). *Sami and the Time of the Troubles*. Illus. by T. Lewin. Clarion.

This fictionalized account is set in Beirut, Lebanon, and describes what it is like to live amid sporadic warfare.

4

Literature Reflecting Native American Perspectives

Chandonnet, A. (1993). *Chief Stephen's Parka.* Roberts Rinehart.

> Chief Stephen's wife is preparing to sew a parka for her husband, which will enable him to be a successful hunter and leader.

George, J. C. (1995). *Everglades.* Illus. by W. Minor. HarperCollins.

> As they tour the Everglades in a dugout canoe, a Native American storyteller tells children about how people have affected the original inhabitants.

Gilliland, H. (1994). *Flint's Rock.* Roberts Rinehart.

> A young Cheyenne is devastated when he learns that he must leave his dog, his village, and his grandfather to live with his sister in the city.

Contemporary Concerns

In association with UNICEF. (2002). *A Life Like Mine: How Children Live Around the World.* OK Publishing.

> This book explores the rights of children and their living situations in different countries. Fabulous multicultural photographs.

Myers, W. D. (2002). *Patrol: An American Soldier in Vietnam.* Illus. by A. Crifalconi. HarperCollins.

> This is the haunting story of Walter Meyers, who joined the army at seventeen, served in Vietnam, and lost his brother there in 1968.

Woodson, J. (2002). *Our Gracie Aunt.* Illus. by J. J. Muth. Hyperion.

> This story explores issues of family and love through the eyes of a young boy struggling to understand his absentee mother's behavior.

C. MIDDLE-SCHOOL GRADES (6–8)

1. Prehistory Through A.D. 1

Literature Reflecting African or African-American Perspectives

Aardema, V., reteller. (1994). *Misoso: Once upon a Time Tales from Africa.* Illus. by R. Ruffins. Knopf.

> This is a varied collection of folktales.

Literature About Early People of North America and Europe

Bruchac, J. (1995). *Gluskabe and the Four Wishes.* Illus. by C. Nyburg Shrader. Cobblehill.

> This Abenaki folktale is about four men who are given wishes, but with "strings" attached.

Dyer, T. A. (1981). *A Way of His Own.* Houghton Mifflin.

> A band of hunters and gatherers abandons Shutok because they believed his crippled back held an evil spirit that gave them bad luck.

Lopez, B. (1990). *Crow and Weasel.* North Point Press.

> A fictionalized account of the first meeting of humans.

Literature Reflecting European or Mediterranean Perspectives

Craig, R. (1995). *Malu's Wolf.* Orchard.

> This account focuses on the life, beliefs, and taboos of Malu, whose Cro-Magnon tribe lives in southern Europe.

Dillon, E. (1974). *Rome Under the Emperors.* Thomas Nelson.

> This is a fictional tale of four boys who live during the days of the Roman Empire.

Getz, D. (1994). *Frozen Man.* Illus. by P. McCarty. Holt.

> This is an illustrated account of the frozen body of a man who died 5,000 years ago.

Martell, H. M. (1992). *Over 6,000 Years Ago: In the Stone Age.* Macmillan.

> This account portrays Stone Age culture based on archaeological evidence found mainly in Europe.

Moessinger, P. (1994). *Socrates.* Creative Education.

> This account takes the form of a (fictional) letter from Socrates to his sons explaining his philosophy.

Walsh, J. P. (1922). *Crossing to Salamis.* Heinemann.

> This fictional story tells of a family's flight from Athens to Salamis to escape an invading army.

2. Early History A.D. 1 Through 1700

Literature Reflecting African or African-American Perspectives

Hamilton, V. (1969). *The Time-Ago Tales of Jadhu.* Illus. by N. Hogrogian. Macmillan.

> This is a collection of folk literature.

Literature Reflecting Asian Perspectives

Haugaard, E. C. (1984) *The Samurai's Tale.* Houghton Mifflin.

> This fictional tale describes the life of the samurai, the professional soldiers of Japan.

McCaughrean, G. (2002). *The Kite Rider.* HarperCollins.

> This adventure story, set in thirteenth-century China, focuses on a Chinese boy who expriences betrayal, family problems, and sacrifice as he travels with the great Mongol conqueror Kublai Khan.

Miller, L. (1987). *The Black Hat Dances: Two Buddhist Boys in the Himalayas.* Putnam's.

> This is a fictionalized account of a novice in a monastery in Sikkim whose lifestyle differs markedly from a typical person in that culture.

Namioka, L. (1992). *The Coming of the Bear.* HarperCollins.

> This is a fictionalized account from the 1600s about Japanese colonists, who were trying to settle the island of Ezo (Hokkaido), and their problems with the original, Aimu inhabitants.

San Souci, R. D. (1992). *The Samurai's Daughter.* Illus. by S. T. Johnson. Dial.

> This fictional account of a samurai's daughter's search for her banished father provides excellent insights into the life of the samurai in Japan.

Literature Reflecting European or Mediterranean Perspectives

Fritz, J. (1994). *Around the World in a Hundred Years: From Henry the Navigator to Magellan.* Illus. by A. B. Venti. Putnam's.

> This is a fictionalized account of the explorer's voyages.

_____. (1980). *Where Do You Think You Are Going, Christopher Columbus?* Illus. by M. Tomes. Putnam's.

> This is a fictionalized biography of the famous explorer.

Hunter, M. (1981). *You Never Knew Her as I Did!* Harper.

> This is the fictionalized biography of Mary, Queen of Scots that is written by a page in her court.

O'Dell, S. (1981). *The Feathered Serpent.* Houghton Mifflin.

> This is the fictional story of the conflict that a young priest, who is working with the Mayan people, feels between his beliefs and the Mayan's beliefs in worshiping idols and offering sacrifices.

Early Life in the American Colonies

Bowen, G. (1994). *Stranded at Plimoth Plantation, 1626.* HarperCollins.

> This story of daily life in the Plimoth colony is based on the fictional diary of Christopher Sears, a young settler.

Levitin, S. (1973). *Roanoke: A Novel of the Lost Colony.* Atheneum.

> This fictionalized account describes relationships between the colonists and the Native People.

Literature Reflecting Hispanic Perspectives

Rohmer, H., Chow, O., & Vidauke, M. (1987). *The Invisible Hunters.* Children's Book Press.

> This fictionalized account describes the impact that the first European traders had on the Miskiot Indians in seventeenth-century Nicaragua.

Marvin, I. R. (1993). *Shipwrecked on Padre Island.* Illus. by L. Miller. Hendrick-Long.

> In this fictional story, a young girl loses her bracelet on Padre Island in 1554; 400 years later it is found by another girl.

3. 1700 Through 1900

Living in the Eighteenth and Nineteenth Centuries

Banim, L. (1994). A *Spy in the King's Colony.* Illus. by T. Yuditskaya. Silver Moon Press.

4

This story, set in Boston in 1775, involves eleven-year-old Emily Parker, who suspects someone of being a spy for the Loyalists. She gets involved in delivering a secret-coded note to General Washington.

Fix, P. (1994). *Not So Very Long Ago: Life in a Small Country Village.* Dutton.

This is a fictionalized account of daily life in a European village.

Haley, A. (1988). *A Different Kind of Christmas.* Doubleday.

This fictional story relates to the Christmas season on the Underground Railroad.

Philbrick, N. (2002). *Revenge of the Whale: The True Story of the Whale Ship Essex.* Putnam's Sons/Puffin.

This is an unforgettable account of twenty men who were stranded in the remote South Pacific after an angry whale sank their ship.

Riskind, M. (1981). *Apple Is My Sign.* Houghton Mifflin.

This is the fictionalized story of Harry Berger, nicknamed "Apple" because his family tends orchards, who attends a school for the deaf.

West, T. (1994). *Mr. Peale's Bones.* Silver Moon Press.

This is the fictionalized account of a young boy and his father who help to excavate mammoth bones in upstate New York.

Literature Reflecting Asian Perspectives

Yep, L. (1993). *Dragon's Gate.* HarperCollins.

This is a fictionalized account of experiences of the Chinese immigrants who built the transcontinental railroad.

_____. (1985). *Mountain's Light.* Harper.

This is a fictionalized account of Chinese immigrants during the days of the California Gold Rush.

Literature Reflecting Hispanic Perspectives

Finley, M. P. (1993). *Soaring Eagle.* Simon & Schuster.

This is an account of how rumors of war between Mexico and the United States affect a young boy and his father.

Krumgold, J. (1953). *And Now Miguel.* Illus. by J. Chariot. Crowell.

This is a fictional story about how Miguel looks forward to the time when he is old enough to join the men who work on a ranch.

O' Dell, S. (1981). *Carlota.* Houghton Mifflin.

This is a fictional tale of how Carlota and her father ambush settlers who are trying to annex California to the United States.

Literature Reflecting Native American Perspectives

Hudson, J. (1990). *Dawn Rider.* Putnam's.

This is the fictional story of a teenage Blackfoot girl, Kit Fox, who, although forbidden to ride horses, disobeys and helps her people when their camp is attacked.

_____. (1989). *Sweetgrass.* Philomel.

This is a fictionalized account of how a fifteen-year-old Blackfoot girl dealt with the effects of smallpox in her family.

Wallin, L. (1984). *In the Shadow of the Wind.* Macmillan.

This is the fictionalized story of a white boy and Native American girl who fall in love at a time when the Creek People were trying to save their lands from settlers.

4. 1900 to the Present

Living in the Twentieth Century

Armstrong, W. (1969). *Sounder.* Illus. by J. Barkley. Harper.

This is a fictional account of the hardships faced by a black sharecropper and his family.

Blue, R. (1979). *Cold Rain on the Water.* McGraw.

This fictionalized story tells of a Jewish family's journey from Russia to the United States.

Kerr, R. (1994). *The Texas Orphans: A Story of the Orphan Train Children.* Eakin Press.

This is a fictionalized account of orphans from New York City who are put on a train to Sequin, Texas, where they start new lives with new families.

World War II

Sook, N. C. (1991). *The Year of Impossible Goodbyes.* Houghton Mifflin.

> This fictionalized account describes how a family dealt with the Japanese occupation during World War II.

Literature Reflecting African or African-American Perspectives

Asgedom, M. (2002). *Of Beetles and Angels: A Boy's Remarkable Journey from a Refugee Camp to Harvard.* Little Brown.

> This powerful survival story traces a family's flight from war-torn Ethiopia in 1980 to its 1983 resettlement in Chicago. The story also involves the horrors of civil war and how refugees battle prejudice, language barriers, and poverty to survive.

Walter, M. P. (1982). *The Girl on the Outside.* Lothrop, Lee & Shepard.

> This is a fictionalized story of two students who set out to desegregate Central High School in Little Rock, Arkansas.

Literature Reflecting Asian Perspectives

Huong, D. T. (1988). *Paradise of the Blind.* Morrow.

> This fictionalized account describes life in Vietnam under Communist rule in the 1970s through the eyes of a teenage girl.

Yep, L. (1991). *The Star Fisher.* Morrow.

> This is a fictional account of a Chinese-American teenager living in West Virginia, who quarrels with her parents about their adherence to Chinese traditions.

Literature Reflecting European or Mediterranean Perspectives

Skurynski, G. (1992). *Good-Bye, Billy Radish.* Bradbury Press.

> This is the fictional story of two best friends, Hank Kerner and Billy Radish (really Bazyli Radichevych),

who have different points of view about working in the steel mills.

4.3 Annotated Bibliography of Nonfiction Books for Common Social Studies Topics

A. Primary Grades (K–3)

Noted Americans, Legendary

Kellogg, Steven. (1984). *Paul Bunyan.* Morrow.

> Presents incidents in the life of this legendary hero.

———. (1986). *Pecos Bill.* Morrow.

> Presents incidents in the life of this legendary Texas hero.

———. (1988). *Johnny Appleseed.* Morrow.

> Presents the real life and legends of Jonathan Chapman, alias Johnny Appleseed, who helped build the orchards of the Midwest.

Le Sueur, Meridel. (1947). *Little Brother of the Wilderness.* Knopf.

> This is another of several biographies of Jonathan Chapman (Johnny Appleseed).

Noted Americans, Real

Adler, David A. (1989). *A Picture Book of Abraham Lincoln.* Illus. by John and Alexandra Wallner. Holiday.

> Follows Lincoln from log cabin to the White House.

———. (1989). *A Picture Book of George Washington.* Illus. by John and Alexandra Wallner. Holiday.

> Follows Washington's rise to become the "Father of Our Country."

———. (1989). *A Picture Book of Martin Luther King, Jr.* Illus. by Robert Casilla. Holiday.

> Follows King's contributions to civil rights.

Blue, R., & Naden, C. (1991). *Colin Powell: Straight to the Top.* Millbrook.

> This biography chronicles the life of Colin Powell.

4

Cavan, S. (1992). *Thurgood Marshall and Equal Rights.* Millbrook.

> This biography is the life story of the first black justice to serve on the U.S. Supreme Court.

_____. (1992). *W. E. B. Du Bois and Racial Relations.* Millbrook.

> This account is about W. E. B. Du Bois, one of the founders of the NAACP.

Freedman, Russell. (1987). *Lincoln, A Photobiography.* Clarion.

> Presents the life of Abraham Lincoln in text and pictures.

Roberts, N. (1988). *Henry Cisneros.* Children's Book Press.

> This biography chronicles the life of Henry Cisneros, a noted San Antonio mayor and former cabinet officer.

Smith, K. B. (1987). *Martin Luther King, Jr.* Messner.

> This account of King's life uses illustrations from the Smithsonian Institution and the National Portrait Gallery.

Literature Reflecting African or African-American Perspectives

Bradby, M. (1995). *More Than Anything Else.* Illus. by C. K. Soentpiet. Orchard.

> This is a fictionalized biography of Booker T. Washington, a former slave with an overwhelming desire to learn how to read and write.

Coles, R. (1995). *The Story of Ruby Bridges.* Illus. by A. Ford. Scholastic.

> This is a biography about a six-year-old who enters a whites-only school in New Orleans in 1960.

Cwiklik, R. (1992). *A. Phillip Randolph and the Labor Movement.* Millbrook.

> This account is about a civil rights crusader.

Musgrove, M. (1976). *Ashanti to Zulu.* Dial.

> This award-winning alphabet book shows customs from twenty-six African cultures.

Saint James, S. (1994). *The Gifts of Kwaanzaa.* Albert Whitman.

> A family's preparation for the African-American Harvest Festival is described through the eyes of a child.

Walker, A. (1974). *Langston Hughes, American Poet.* Illus. by D. Miller. Crowell.

> This biography chronicles the life of one of America's greatest African-American poets.

Archaeology

Dragonwagon, Crescent. (1990). *Home Place.* Macmillan.

> This story tells what it is like for an early family to live in modern times.

Pickering, R. B. (1987). *I Can Be an Archaeologist.* Children's Book Press.

> This book also suggests how children can use artifacts as clues to the past.

Pryor, B. (1992). *The House on Maple Street.* Mulberry.

> An arrowhead is lost hundreds of years ago but is found as the years go by.

Ancient Egypt

Courtalon, C. (1988). *On the Banks of the Pharaoh's Nile.* Young Discovery Library.

> This text introduces children to the culture through illustrations and a text that should be read aloud by an adult.

Maestro, B. (1991). *The Discovery of the Americas.* Lothrop.

> This text details the travels of the Stone Age people across the Bering Land bridge to North America.

Metropolitan Museum of Art. (1991). *The Giant Book of the Mummy.* New York, Metropolitan Museum.

> This huge book focuses on the discovery of the tomb of Tutankhamen, the Boy King.

Early Life in the American Colonies

Sewall, M. (1990). *People of the Breaking Day.* Atheneum.

> The book provides a detailed account of the daily life of the Wampanoag people prior to the arrival of the colonists.

Water, K. (1996). *Tapenum's Day: A Wampanoag Boy in Pilgrim Times.* Illus. by R. Kendall. Scholastic.

> A fictionalized person, Tapenum, describes the daily life of the Wampanoag people. Also includes photographs from the re-created Native American home site at the Plimouth Plantation.

Life in the Colonies

Costabel, E. D. (1988). *The Jews of New Amsterdam.* Atheneum.

> This is an account of Jews who journeyed to America during the Colonial period, and their discovery that life in the colonies did not value equality for everyone.

Life in the Twentieth Century

Baer, E. (1984). *This Is the Way We Go to School.* Scholastic.

> Written in a simple rhyming pattern, this book depicts the modes of transportation that children around the world use to get to school.

Brandenberg, A. (1984). *Feelings.* Greenwillow.

> Different feelings generated by everyday situations are presented in a manner with which children can identify.

Gray, N. (1988). A *Country Far Away.* Orchard Books.

> Two young boys, one of whom lives in an American suburb and the other in a village by the ocean, share similar experiences.

Kandoian, E. (1989). *Is Anybody Up?* Putnam's.

> As Molly starts to prepare her breakfast, many people in other parts of the world are doing the same thing.

Masoff, J. (2002). *Everest: Reaching for the Sky.* Scholastic.

> In this illustrated account, readers relive the ascent to Everest, and the help that climbers Edmund Hillary and Tenzig Morgay provided to the Himalayan people.

Morris, A. (1989). *Bread, Bread, Bread.* Lothrop, Lee & Shepard.

> The photographs in this book show that people all over the world eat bread or something similar to it.

Spier, P. (1980). *People.* Doubleday.

> This book describes the appearance, customs, food, traditions, and people from all areas of the world.

Life on the Frontier

Freedman, Russell. (1988). *Buffalo Hunt.* Holiday.

> This is an illustrated account of the life of Native Americans on the Great Plains, and the importance of the buffalo to their lives.

————. (1985). *Cowboys of the Wild West.* Clarion.

> This account focuses on the day-to-day life of cowboys and the hardships they faced on a trail drive.

Jakes, John. (1986). *Susanna of the Alamo.* Illus. by P. Bacon. Harcourt Brace Jovanovich.

> This account focuses on Susanna Dickinson, one of the few survivors of the Battle of the Alamo.

Literature Reflecting Asian Perspectives

Haskins, Jim. (1987). *Count Your Way Through Japan.* Illus. by Martin Skoro. Carolrhoda.

> Life in Japan is depicted using the Japanese words and symbols for numbers one through ten.

Mannis, C. D. (2002). *One Leaf Rides the Wind: Counting in a Japanese Garden.* Illus. by S. K. Hartung. Viking/Puffin.

> The author uses haikus to count the objects in a Japanese garden (three bonsai, ten lanterns, etc.). Notes on Japanese gardens are also included.

Weston, Reiko. *Cooking the Japanese Way.* Lerner.

> Describes Japanese food habits and recipes.

4

Literature Reflecting European Perspectives

Beirne, B. (1992). *Siobhand's Journey: A Belfast Girl Visits the United States.* Illus. First Avenue Ed.

> This photo essay is about a young Irish girl, Siobhand McNulty, who leaves the religious/political conflict of Northern Ireland to spend a summer with an American family.

Fisher, L. E. (1994). *Kinderdike.* Illus. by the author. Macmillan.

> This poem is a tribute to a Dutch town that rebuilt after a devastating flood.

Kalman, B. (1992). *We Celebrate Hanukkah.* Crabtree.

> This book explains the origins of Hanukkah.

Mitchell, B. (1993). *Down Buttermilk Lane.* Illus. by J. Sandford. Lothrop, Lee & Shepard.

> This account shows one day in the life of an Amish family.

Stanley, D. (1996). *The True Adventure of Daniel Hall.* Illus. by the author. Dial.

> This is the biography of Hall's four-year journey on a whaling ship.

Wildsmith, B. (1996). *Saint Francis.* Eerdmans.

> This book focuses on the major events of the life of St. Francis of Assisi.

Literature About Native American Peoples

Costable, E. D. (1992). *The Early People of Florida.* Illus. by the author. Atheneum.

> This book details the life of the indigenous people of Florida from prehistoric times to 1845 (statehood).

Driving Hawk, V. (1993). *The Sioux.* Illus. by R. Himler. Holiday.

> This book describes the history, culture, and present-day life of the Sioux.

Gnese, A. (1995). *Anna's Athabaskan Summer.* Illus. by C. Ragins. Caroline House/Boyds Mills Press.

> This is an account of the activities at a midsummer fish camp along a river in Alaska.

Hoyt-Goldsmith, D. (1992). *Arctic Hunter.* Holiday.

> This account follows Reggie and his family from the Alaskan town north of the Arctic Circle, where they live in the winter, to the fishing and hunting camp where they go in the summer.

Sneve, V. D. H. (1996). *The Cherokees.* Illus. by R. Himler. Holiday.

> This picture book history shows what has happened to the Oklahoma and North Carolina bands in the last 200 years since the Trail of Tears.

Literature Reflecting Hispanic Perspectives

Adler, D. A. (1992). *A Picture Book on Simon Bolivar.* Illus. by R. Casilia. Holiday.

> This illustrated biography chronicles Bolivar's life and accomplishments.

Anderson, J. (1992). *Miguel Hidalgo Costilla: Father of Mexican Independence.* Milbrook.

> This is the biography of Father Hidalgo, the Catholic priest who called his parishioners to rebel against the Spanish colonial government.

————. (1992). *Simon Bolivar: Latin American Liberator.* Milbrook.

> This biography traces the life of Simon Bolivar, who was instrumental in overthrowing Spanish rule in Central and South America.

Jacobs, F. (1992). *The Tainos: The People Who Welcomed Columbus.* Putnam's.

> This book describes the life of native people on a Bahamian island in the late fifteenth century.

Palacios, A. (1993). *Viva Mexico!: A Story of Benito Juarez and Cinco de Mayo.* Illus. by H. Berelson. Steck-Vaughn.

> This biography follows the life of Benito Juarez until his presidency in 1816 and explains the Battle of Puebla, which was the basis for the annual May 5th celebration.

Reed, L. R. (1995). *Pedro, His Perro, and the Alphabet Sombrero.* Illus. by the author. Hyperion.

> In this modified alphabet book, Pedro celebrates his birthday by decorating a sombrero with objects

from A (avion/airplane) to Z (zorillo/skunk). (Pronunciation guide included).

Literature Reflecting Mediterranean or Middle Eastern Perspectives

Fleetwood, J. (1992). *While the Shepherds Watched.* Illus. by P. Melnucsuk. Lothrop, Lee & Shepard.

> A young boy participates in a night filled with wonder as he sees the birth of a lamb, is visited by an angel, and visits a stable in Bethlehem.

Matthews, M. (1996). *Magid Fasts for Ramadan.* Illus. by E. B. Lewis. Clarion.

> Fasting is a common practice for Islamic families celebrating Ramadan, but eight-year-old Magid is considered too young.

Yolen, J. (1996). *O Jerusalem.* Illus. by J. Thompson. Scholastic.

> This is the story of how Jerusalem has dealt with three religions.

B. INTERMEDIATE GRADES (3–6)

Noted Americans, Real

D'Aulaire, I., & D'Aulaire, E. P. (1952). *Buffalo Bill.* Doubleday.

> This biography chronicles events in the life of Buffalo Bill.

Johnston, J. (1977). *Harriet and the Runaway Book: The Story of Harriet Beecher Stowe and Uncle Tom's Cabin.* Illus. by R. Himler. Harper.

> This is a biography of Harriet Beecher Stowe, a New Englander, who writes one of the most famous books opposing slavery.

Murphy, J. (1995). *Into the Deep Forest with Henry David Thoreau.* Illus. by K. Kisler. Clarion.

> This biography is based on entries in Thoreau's journal.

Stanley, D., & Vennema, P. (1993). *Charles Dickens: The Man Who Had Great Expectations.* Illus. by D. Stanley. Morrow.

> This biography chronicles highlights from Dickens's life.

Rome

Cohen, D. (1992). *Ancient Rome.* Illus. by H. Bond. Bantam.

> This book offers a concise overview of the history of ancient Rome. It includes the conflict with Carthage, the activities of Hannibal, gladiator contests, and the emperors, and the destruction of Pompeii.

MacDonald, F. (1993). *A Roman Fort.* Peter Bedrick.

> This book uses drawings and diagrams to show how a Roman fort was constructed. It also includes living conditions and soldiers' weapons.

Literature Reflecting African or African-American Perspectives

Ferris, J. (1988). *Go Free or Die.* Illus. by K. Ritz. Carolrhoda.

> This is the biography of Harriet Tubman, the former slave who became a legendary figure on the Underground Railroad by helping almost 300 other slaves (including her parents) gain their freedom.

Lawrence, I. (1993). *The Great Migration: An American Story.* HarperCollins.

> This pictorial account shows the migration of African-Americans from the South in 1916–1919.

Ritter, L. S. (1995). *Leagues Apart: The Men and Times of the Negro Baseball Leagues.* Illus. by R. Merkin. Morrow.

> This is the story of baseball's Negro League and some of its stars.

Africa and Egypt

Giblin, J. C. (1990). *The Riddle of the Rosetta Stone: Key to Ancient Egypt.* Crowell.

> This is the story of how the message of the Rosetta Stone was deciphered and how it has influenced our knowledge of the Egyptian civilization.

Harris, N. (1995). *Everyday Life in Ancient Egypt.* Illus. by K. Maddison. Watts.

> This book offers an illustrated overview of the history of Egypt. Includes topics such as food, clothing, shelter, and religion.

4

Archaeology

Hooper, M. (1996). *The Pebble in My Hand: A History of Our Earth.* Viking.

> Finding a pebble on the ground leads a child to speculate on where it came from.

Hoopes, L. L. (1989) *Half a Button.* Harper & Row.

> Suggests how artifacts serve as clues to the past.

Early Colonial Period

Anderson, I. (1984). *The First Thanksgiving Feast.* Illus. by G. Ancona. Clarion.

> This book, with photographs from the Plimouth Plantation, offers a first-person account of life in the 1620s.

Sewall, M. (1986). *The Pilgrims of Plimoth.* Atheneum.

> This book, which describes the lives of people living in the Plymouth Colony, is based on the writings of Governor William Bradford.

China

Fisher, L. E. (1986). *The Great Wall of China.* Illus. by the author. Macmillan.

> This account covers all facets of the building of the Great Wall of China.

Civil War

Johnson, Neil. (1989). *The Battle of Gettysburg.* Four Winds.

> This account is based on photographs from the 125th anniversary reenactment of the Battle of Gettysburg.

Literature Reflecting Asian Perspectives

Brown, T. (1995). *Konnichiwa! I Am a Japanese American Girl.* Photographs by Kazuyoshi Arai. Holt.

> This book describes a young girl's life in San Francisco.

Cha, D. (1996). *Dia's Story Cloth: The Hmong People's Journey of Freedom.* Illus. by C. Cha and N. T. Cha. Lee & Low.

> This is the autobiography of a young girl and her family who flee from Laos in the 1960s, spend time in a refugee camp in Thailand, and then emigrate to the United States.

McMahon, P. (1993). *Chi-Hoon: A Korean Girl.* Illus. by M. O'Brien. Caroline House/Boyds Mills Press.

> This is an account of an eight-year-old's life in modern Seoul.

Schmidt, J., & Wood, T. (1995). *Two Lands, One Heart: An American Boy's Journey to His Mother's Vietnam.* Illus. by T. Wood. Walker.

> This is a touching story of how a refugee from Vietnam takes her son back for a visit to her homeland.

Theunissen, S. (2002). *The Maori of New Zealand.* Lerner Group.

> Using two-page spreads of drawings and photographs, this book introduces readers to the history, culture, and economy of the Maori people of New Zealand.

Literature Reflecting European Perspectives

Carrick, C. (1993). *Whaling Days.* Illus. by D. Frampton. Clarion.

> This book traces whaling from twelfth-century Basque whalers through modern whaling methods.

Lauber, P. (1970). *Who Discovered America? Settlers and Explorers of the New World Before the Times of Columbus.* Random House.

> This text is an overview of exploration in pre-Columbian times.

Moscinski, S. (1993). *Tracing Our Irish Roots.* John Muir.

> This book describes the potato famine and other conditions in Ireland, as well as the prejudice the Irish encountered when they arrived in the United States.

Greece

Asimov, I., & Reddy, F. (1995). *Astronomy in Ancient Times.* Gareth Stevens.

> This book focuses on astronomy at the time of the ancient Greeks.

4

Pearson, A. (1995). *Everyday Life in Ancient Greece.* Illus. by E. Dovey. Watts.

This book offers an illustrated overview of life in ancient Greece, including food, clothing, housing, and religion.

Literature Reflecting Hispanic Perspectives

Anderson J. (1989). *Spanish Pioneers of the Southwest.* Illus. by G. Ancona. Dutton.

This book portrays the life of a Spanish pioneer family in eighteenth-century New Mexico.

Hoyt-Goldsmith, D. (2002). *Celebrating a Quinceanera: A Latina's 15th Birthday Celebration.* Illus. by L. Migdale. Holiday House.

This book explains the Quinceanera as an important rite of passage in a modern Hispanic society.

Lasky, K. (1994). *Days of the Dead.* Photographs by C. G. Knight. Hyperion.

This book shows how a rural family prepares for traditional Mexican celebrations.

Westridge Young Writers Workshop. (1992). *Kids Explore America's Hispanic Heritage.* John Muir.

This text presents the Mexican side of the Battle of the Alamo.

Living in America

Ammon, R. (1989). *Growing Up Amish.* Atheneum.

This account explains the Amish movement and its associated lifestyle.

Bial, R. (1994). *Shaker Home.* Houghton Mifflin.

The text focuses on life in communal Shaker communities.

Rappaport, D. (1987). *Trouble at the Mines.* Crowell.

This is a fictionalized account of the coal strike in Pennsylvania in 1899, as recounted by a coal miner's daughter.

Smith, D. J. (2002). *If the World Were a Village: A Book About the World's People.* Illus. by S. Armstrong. Kids Can Press.

Imagine the 6.2 billion people on our planet reduced to a village of 100. This book provides information on who the villagers are, how they live, as well as information on languages, nationalities, ages, religions, and food.

Life on the Frontier

Anderson, Joan. (1986). *Pioneer Children of Appalachia.* Illus. by G. Ancona. Clarion.

This photo-essay of Appalachian pioneer life between 1790 and 1830 was made at a living history museum in West Virginia.

Cooper, Michael. (1989). *Klondike Fever.* Clarion.

This photo-essay focuses on the founding of the city of Dawson during the Alaskan gold rush.

Fisher, Leonard E. (1987). *The Alamo.* Holiday.

This book presents the history of the Alamo, site of the famous battle in which Jim Bowie, Davey Crockett, and other famous frontier figures died.

World War II

Bergman, Tamar. (1991). *Along the Tracks.* Trans. from the Hebrew by Michael Swirsky. Houghton Mifflin.

This is the true story of a young Jewish boy who flees Nazi-occupied Poland but is separated from his family and becomes one of the thousands of abandoned children wandering through Russia.

Dahl, Roald. (1986). *Going Solo.* Penguin.

This is the story of Dahl's experience as a fighter pilot in Africa, Greece, and the Middle East.

Mochizuki, Ken. (1993). *Baseball Saved Us.* Lee & Low.

This is a touching account of how Japanese-Americans imprisoned in a desert internment camp build a baseball field to relieve the monotony of their imprisonment.

Uchida, Yoshiko. (1971). *Journey to Topaz: A Story of the Japanese-American Evacuation.* Scribner's.

This is a moving account of how Japanese-American families were moved to internment camps during World War II.

4

Literature Reflecting Mediterranean or Middle Eastern Perspectives

Fisher, L. E. (1989). *The Wailing Wall.* Illus. by the author. Macmillan.

> The author traces the history of the Wailing Wall in Jerusalem, where Jews have long gathered before their Sabbath and Feast Days.

Howard, G. (2002). *A Basket of Bangles: How a Business Begins.* Illus. by C. K. Noll. Millbrook Press.

> This picture book, set in Bangladesh, provides an easy-to-understand economics lesson involving the idea of co-ops.

Lee, K. (1993). *Tracing Our Italian Roots.* John Muir.

> This book describes the hardships of life in Italy, and the prejudice that people who emigrated to the United States faced when they got here.

Paris, A. (1995). *Jerusalem 3000: Kids Discover the City of Gold.* Pitspopany Press.

> This is the story of the city of Jerusalem from its earliest days to the present time.

Schur, M. R. (1996). *When I Left My Village.* Illus. by B. Pinkney. Dial.

> This is the account of a family of Ethiopian Jews who escape persecution and a drought by walking through the desert at night.

Mexico, Aztecs, Incas, and Mayans

Baquedano, E. (1993). *Aztec, Inca and Maya.* Knopf.

> This text uses a compare and contrast approach to introduce the three civilizations—Aztec, Inca, and Mayan.

de Trevino, E. B. (1980). *Here Is Mexico.* Farrar, Straus & Giroux.

> This book traces Mexican history from pre-Columbian times to the colonial period.

Glubok, S. (1968). *The Art of Ancient Mexico.* Harper.

> This book focuses on Mexico prior to the arrival of the Spaniards. Includes pre-Columbian cultures such as the Aztec, Mixtec, Toltec, and Zapotec.

Martinez, G., & Edwards, J. (1973). *The Mexican Americans.* Houghton Mifflin.

> This book focuses on pre-Columbian Mexico but extends to the mission period in California and Mexican independence.

Literature Reflecting Native American Perspectives

Arnold, C. (1992). *The Ancient Cliff Dwellers of Mesa Verde.* Illus. by R. Hewett. Clarion.

> This book describes the history of the Anasazi, who disappeared from southwest Colorado after they constructed magnificent cliff dwellings.

McLerran, A. (1995). *The Ghost Dance.* Illus. by P. Morin. Clarion.

> This book describes the impact that the westward expansion had on the resources needed by Native Americans.

Roop, P., & Roop, C. (1992). *Ahyoka and the Talking Leaves.* Illus. by Y. Miyake. Lothrop, Lee & Shepard.

> This is the biography of Ahyoka, a Cherokee girl, who discovers that letters relate to sounds. Ahyoka and her father create an alphabet and written language for their people.

Warren, S. (1992). *Cities in the Sand: The Ancient Cities of the Southwest.* Chronicle.

> This book explores life in the Anasazi cliff dwellings, the irrigation canals of the Hohokarn, and the pottery of the Mogollon.

C. MIDDLE-SCHOOL GRADES (6–8)

Ancient Egypt

Macdonald, F. (1993). *Ancient Egyptians.* Barron's.

> This illustrated account covers most aspects of this civilization.

Literature Reflecting Asian Perspectives

Fagan, B. M. (1987). *The Great Journey: The Peopling of Ancient America.* Thames & Hudson.

> This account focuses on the arrival of peoples in North America.

Satder, H. R. (1992). *The Earliest Americans.* Illus. by J. D. Zallinger. Clarion.

> This account tells about the humans who came to North America across the land bridge between Siberia and Alaska.

Literature Reflecting Hispanic Perspectives

Bendick, J. (1993). *Tombs of the Ancient Americas.* Watts.

> This text, with photographs, focuses on the Incas.

Jimenez, C. M. (1993). *The Mexican American Heritage.* COSMEP.

> History from prehistoric times to present day.

Literature Reflecting Native American Perspectives

Ayeer, E. J. (1993). *The Anasazi.* Walker.

> The text focuses on the Anasazi Pueblo people, and the methods that archaeologists use to learn about their lifestyles.

Monroe, J. G., & Williamson, R. A. (1993). *First Houses: Native American Homes and Sacred Structures.* Houghton Mifflin.

> This text explores a variety of Native American dwellings—longhouses, hogans, earth lodges, tipis, and kivas.

Yue, C., & Yue, D. (1988). *The Igloo.* Houghton Mifflin.

> This account portrays the Thule People, the ancestors of the Inuit.

History, Life, and Culture in the Americas

Auch, M. J. (2002). *Sashes of Roses.* Holt.

> Readers get a real picture of the travails of Irish immigration to New York City, the working conditions in sweatshops, and a first-person account of the Triangle Shirtwaist Fire.

Blumenthal, K. (2002). *Six Days in October: The Stock Market Crash of 1929.* Atheneum.

> This illustrated book provides an overview of the 1929 stock market crash and also serves as a primer on the stock market itself.

Crowe, C. (2002). *Mississippi Trial, 1955.* Pogelman Books/Penguin Group USA.

> This book describes the racially motivated murder of Emmett Till and the aftermath of that crime on a Mississippi Delta town in the 1950s.

Davies, J. (2002). *Where the Ground Meets the Sky.* Cavendish.

> This book focuses on the scientists and their families who live in a climate of secrecy in New Mexico in 1944 during the creation of the atomic bomb.

Rice, B. F. (2002). *The Place at the Edge of the Earth.* Clarion.

> This engrossing story reveals the harsh reality of Indian boarding schools.

Rinaldi, A. (2002). *Numbering all the Bones.* Hyperion Books.

> Eulinda, a thirteen-year-old former slave and unacknowledged child of the man who was her master, searches for her brother lost in the Civil War. She teams up with a former Confederate officer and Clara Barton to clean up and identify those who died at Andersonville prison.

World War II

Forman, James. (1970). *Ceremony of Innocence.* Hawthorne.

> Until they were executed by the Gestapo, Hans and Sophie Scholl published the "White Rose" leaflets that denounced Nazism.

Biographies

Delano, M. F. (2002). *Inventing the Future: A Photobiography of Thomas Alva Edison.* National Geographic.

> Delano tells the story of Edison's life through richly illustrated period photographs.

Gherman, B. (2002). *Ansel Adams: America's Photographer.* Photographs by Ansel Adams. Little, Brown.

> This book traces the milestones of Ansel Adams's life and depicts his development as a renowned photographer.

Hill, C. M. (2002). *John Lewis: From Freedom Rider to Congressman.* (African-American Biographies series). Illus. by author. Enslow.

> This is the illustrated story of John Lewis's involvement with the civil rights movement.

Landau, F. E. (2002). *Osama Bin Laden: A War Against the West.* Twenty-First Century.

> The text presents biographical information about the militant Islamic leader Osama bin Laden, including his role in international terrorism and the beliefs that fuel his actions.

Marrin A. (2002). *Secrets from the Rocks: Dinosaur Hunting with Roy Chapman Andrews.* Dutton.

> This fabulous story about Roy Chapman Andrews, together with photographs and drawings of animals, includes commentary about the senselessness of killing animals for sport, and the perils of the field.

Meltzer, M. (2002). *Ten Kings and the Worlds They Ruled.* Illus. by B. Andersen. Orchard Books/Scholastic.

> The author examines how leaders have historically used power by providing brief descriptions of the lives of Kings Hammurabi, David, Alexander the Great, Attila, Charlemagne, Kublai Kahn, Atahualpa, Mansa Musa, Louis XIV, and Peter the Great.

Partridge, E. (2003). *This Land Was Made for You and Me: The Life and Songs of Woody Guthrie*. Viking/Puffin.

> This gritty biography profiles the life of Woody Guthrie, the creative but troubled folksinger.

Contemporary Concerns

Armstrong, J. (Ed.). (2002). *Shattered: Stories of Children and War.* Knopf.

> Although some children may imagine war as exciting, this powerful book tells how a wide range of wars can destroy the world's youngest citizens.

Cart, M., Aronson, M., & Carus, M. (Eds.). (2002). *911 The Book of Help.* Illus. by C. Raschka. Cricket Books/Marcato.

> This sensitive and timely book is a collection of essays that deal with how young people coped with the tragedy of September 11, 2001.

Draper, S. M. (2002). *Double Dutch.* Atheneum/Simon & Schuster.

> This intriguing novel will keep young readers turning the pages in order to learn the secret that haunts Delia.

Frank, M. (2002). *Understanding September 11th: Answering Questions About the Attacks on America.* Viking.

> This illustrated reference book is organized in a question/answer format.

Hooper, M. (2002). *Amy.* Bloomsbury.

> Amy is not naive about meeting people on the Internet, but she becomes a victim nonetheless.

Martin, A. M. (2002). *A Corner of the Universe.* Scholastic.

> This is a moving story about twelve-year-old Hattie, whose world is expanded with the arrival of her mentally disabled uncle.

Myers, A. (2002). *Tulsa Burning.* Walker.

> This book is less about the 1921 Tulsa race riots than it is a story about relationships between fathers and sons and between the races in rural Oklahoma.

Nelson, P. (2002). *Left for Dead: A Young Man's Search for the USS Indianapolis*. Delacorte.

> This is the true story of how eleven-year-old Hunter Scott uncovered the real story behind the World War II sinking of the *USS Indianapolis,* and how his discovery led to the reversal of a wrongful court-martial against the ship's captain.

Young, M. B., Fitzgerald, J. J., & Grunfeld, A. T. (2002). *The Vietnam War: A History in Documents.* (Pages from History series). Oxford.

> This collection of original documents and photographs details both the war in Vietnam and parallel events occurring in the United States and in Asia.

Zephaniah, B. (2002). *Refugee Boy.* Bloomsbury.

> This realistic portrayal deals with the hopelessness of civil war by focusing on Alem, a young boy who survives the war between Ethiopians and Eritreans and becomes a refugee in England.

4.4 Annotated Bibliography of Children's Books for Teaching About Women and Women's Roles Throughout History

A. Prehistory to A.D. 1

1. Primary Grades (1–3)

Bernhard, E., reteller. (1994). *The Girl Who Wanted to Hunt: A Siberian Tale.* Holiday.

> Anga, a young girl, wants to be a hunter like her father, but she must somehow escape a demanding stepmother.

Gerson, M. (1994). *How Night Came from the Sea: A Story from Brazil.* Illus. by C. Golembe. Little, Brown.

> An African sea goddess, Jemanja, allows people to escape the scorching sun by bringing them the gift of night.

Gerspem. (1995). *People of the Corn: A Mayan Story.* Illus. by Carla Golembe. Little, Brown.

> This is a creation myth about the role of corn in the Mayan civilization.

Jiang, W. (1992). *La Heroina Hua Mulan: The Legend of Mu Lan.* Illus. by the author and Xing Gen. Victory Press T. R. Books.

> This story, which is set in ancient China, tells how Mu Lan fights for her country disguised as a boy.

Kimmel, E. (1995). *Rimonah of the Flashing Sword: A North African Tale.* Illus. by O. Rayan. Holiday.

> Princess Rimonah joins a band of forty thieves and rides with them against her jealous stepmother, the queen.

Yep, Lawrence. (1990). *The Shell Woman and the King.* Dial.

> This is the story of a young Chinese girl who outsmarts a selfish king.

2. Intermediate Grades (3–6)

Lee, J. M. (1995). *The Song of Mu Lan.* Illus. by the author. Front Street.

> Set in China around 400 B.C., this is the story of Mu Lan, who, for ten years, takes the place of her father in battle.

3. Middle-School Grades (6–8)

Brennan, J. H. (1992). *Shiva's Challenge: An Adventure of the Ice Age.* HarperCollins.

> In this fictional account, Shiva, who lived around 14,000 B.C., finds her way home from an icebound wasteland.

McGraw, E. J. (1990). *Mara, Daughter of the Nile.* Coward.

> This is the fictional story of Mara, a slave whose mixed loyalties allow her to spy for both the king and queen.

B. Early History A.D. 1 Through A.D. 1700

1. Primary Grades (K–3)

Accorsi, W. (1992). *My Name Is Pocahontas.* Illus. by the author. Holiday.

> This is a fascinating biography of Pocahontas, the daughter of the Native American chief Powhatan.

Raphael, E., & Bolognese, D. (1993). *Pocahontas: Princess of the River Tribes.* Illus. by the authors. Scholastic.

> This is a brief biography of selected events in the life of Pocahontas.

Van Woerkom, D. (1975). *Becky and the Bear.* Illus. by M. Tomes. Putnam's.

> This is a fictionalized account about Becky, a young girl who lives in Maine, whose father and brother refuse to allow her to hunt with them. When Becky encounters a bear, she feeds it molasses and rum to make it fall asleep; then she and her grandmother tie the bear to a tree.

2. Intermediate Grades (3–6)

Christian, M. B. (1990). *Goody Sherman's Pig.* Macmillan.

> This is a fictionalized account of Goody Sherman's 1636 battle with church elders and the courts over

4

her runaway pig. This battle is said to have caused the colony to create two legislative branches of government.

Fisher, A. (1970). *Jeanne d'Arc.* Illus. by A. Fortenberg. Crowell.

> This biography depicts the life of Joan of Arc, the nineteen-year-old girl who led the French Army and became the national heroine of France. (Read aloud to young children.)

Fradin, D. B. (1990). *Anne Hutchinson.* Enslow.

> This is a biography of Anne Hutchinson, who preached that people with true religion would follow God's guidance through an "Inner Light." Brought to court, Anne is found guilty of "traducing" the ministers and ordered to leave the colony. She ultimately founds a settlement at Portsmouth that offers religious freedom.

Fritz, E. I. (1991). *Anne Hutchinson.* Chelsea.

> This biography also traces events in the life of Anne Hutchinson, who was banished from the colony in New England.

Garden, N. (1995). *Dove and Sword: A Novel of Joan of Arc.* Illus. by the author. Farrar, Straus & Giroux.

> This is the fictionalized story of Gabrielle, a young girl who goes to war. (Read excerpts aloud to young children.)

3. Middle-School Grades (6–8)

Brooks, P. S. (1983). *Queen Eleanor: Independent Spirit of the Medieval World.* Lippincott.

> This is a biography of the twelfth-century queen, Eleanor of Aquitane.

Burch, J. J. (1991). *Isabella of Castile: Queen on Horseback.* Watts.

> This biography tells the story of the Queen of Spain who, with her husband, Ferdinand, financed Columbus's voyages to the New World.

Churchill, W. (1969). *Joan of Arc: Her Life as Told by Winston Churchill.* Dodd.

> This is the biography of Joan of Arc, the heroine of France, who was eventually condemned and burned at the stake.

Duran, G. (1992). *Malinche. Slave Princess of Cortez.* Linnet/Shoe String Press.

> This is the biography of Malinali/La Malinche, an Aztec princess who was a slave and interpreter for Cortez during his conquest of Mexico.

Nichols, J. K. (1993). *A Matter of Conscience: The Trial of Anne Hutchinson.* Illus. by D. Krovatin. Steck-Vaughn.

> This biography describes the religious climate in Salem, Massachusetts.

C. 1700 Through 1900

1. Primary Grades (1–3)

Adler, D. A. (1995). *A Picture Book of Sojourner Truth.* Holiday.

> This is the story of Sojourner Truth, a former slave who becomes a passionate advocate against slavery.

Blumberg, R. (1993). *Bloomers!* Bradbury.

> In this fictionalized story, Libby intrigues her cousin, Elizabeth Cady Stanton, when she comes to town wearing an outrageous costume for the times—bloomers. The costume soon becomes the uniform of the women's movement.

McCully, E. A. (1996). *The Bobbin Girl.* Illus. by the author. Dial.

> This is the fictionalized story of Harriet Hanson Robinson, whose home becomes a meeting place for women who walk out from their jobs in textile mills in protest of a pay cut.

McKissack, P. and F. (1993). *Sojourner Truth, Ain't I a Woman?* Scholastic.

> This biography describes Sojourner Truth's trial when she sues in court to regain her son.

Miller, R. H. (1995). *The Story of Stagecoach Mary.* Illus. by C. Hanna. Silver Burdett Press.

> This is a fictionalized account of Mary Fields, the first African-American woman to drive a stagecoach that carries the mail.

Raphael, E., & Bolognese, D. (1994). *Sacajawea: The Journey West.* Scholastic.

This biography is about the Native American girl who accompanied the Lewis and Clark expedition.

Roop, P., & Roop, C. (1987). *Keep the Lights Burning, Abbie.* Illus. by P. Hanson. Lathrop, Lee & Shepard.

This is a fictionalized story of Abbie, the daughter of a lighthouse keeper in Maine, who must take over during a storm when her father leaves and her mother becomes ill.

St. George, J. (1989). *By George, Bloomers!* Shoe Tree.

This is a fictionalized story of how bloomers came to be a symbol of the women's rights movement.

2. Intermediate Grades (3–6)

Berleth, R. (1994). *Mary Patten's Voyage.* Albert Whitman.

This is a fictionalized account of how a ship captain's eighteen-year-old wife took over and sailed the ship around Cape Horn.

Dalgliesh, A. (1987). *The Courage of Sarah Noble.* Macmillan.

This fictionalized account is based on the true story of eight-year-old Sarah Noble, who goes into the wilderness with her father to cook and care for him.

Fritz, J. (1995). *You Want Women to Vote, Lizzie Stanton?* Illus. by D. Disalvo-Ryan. Putnam's.

This biography depicts Elizabeth Cady Stanton's efforts for women's rights.

McGovern, A. (1975). *Secret Soldier: The Story of Deborah Sampson.* Scholastic.

This is a biography of a young woman who disguises herself as a boy and joins the army in the Revolutionary War.

Jordan, D. (1994). *Susie King Taylor: Destined to be Free.* Illus. by H. Bond. Just Us Books.

This is a biography of a slave who learns to read and write, escapes from slavery, and becomes a teacher of black children and adults. She then becomes a nurse in the Union Army.

San Souci, R. (1993). *Cut from the Same Cloth: American Women of Myth, Legend, and Tall Tale.* Philomel.

This book is a collection of stories about women from different cultures whose heroic actions and deeds often saved themselves, and their families and friends.

3. Middle-School Grades (6–8)

Atkinson, L. (1978). *Mary Jones: The Most Dangerous Woman in America.* Crown.

This biography is about an early supporter of the labor movement.

DePauw, L. G. (1975). *Founding Mothers: Women in America in the Revolutionary Era.* Houghton Mifflin.

This account focuses on women's contributions to the Revolutionary War.

Hoople, C. G. (1978). *As I Saw It: Women Who Loved the American Adventure.* Dial.

This account describes the struggles and contributions of colonial and pioneer women.

Levenson, D. (1973). *Women of the West.* Watts.

This is a collection of brief biographies about the lives of Native American, African-American, and European-American women.

Markham, L. (1992). *Helen Keller.* Watts.

This is a biography of Helen Keller.

Meade, M. (1976). *Free Woman: The Life and Times of Victoria Woodhull.* Knopf.

This is the biography of the first woman to run for president of the United States.

Meigs, C. L. (1970). *Jane Addams: Pioneer for Social Justice.* Little.

This is the biography of social reformer Jane Addams, the founder of Hull House.

D. 1900 to the Present

1. Primary Grades (1–3)

Gonzalez, F. (1992). *Gloria Estefan: Cuban-American Singing Star.* Millbrook.

This is a biography of Gloria Estefan, who enters the United States as a Cuban exile and becomes an international star in the music world.

4

Hawxhurst, I. C. (1993). *Antonia Novello: U.S. Surgeon General.* Millbrook.

> This is the biography of the Puerto Rican girl who became the Surgeon General of the United States.

2. Intermediate Grades (3–6)

Giblin, J. C. (1992). *Edith Wilson: The Woman Who Ran the United States.* Viking.

> This is the biography of the life of Edith, who supported President Wilson when he became ill during World War I.

Igus, T. (1991). *Great Women in the Struggle.* Just Us Books.

> This is a collection of brief profiles of eighty-plus African-American women.

Kerby, M. (1990). *Amelia Earhart: Courage in the Sky.* Illus. by E. McKeating. Puffin.

> This is the biography of the noted aviator, Amelia Earhart, who disappeared on an around-the-world flight.

Orgill, R. (2002). *Mahalia: A Life in Gospel Music.* Candlewick.

> Singer Mahalia Jackson grew up in poverty but fulfilled her aunt's prophecy that she would someday "walk with kings and queens."

Ransom, C. F. (1993). *Listening to the Crickets: A Story About Rachel Carson.* Carolrhoda.

> This is the biography of the biologist whose book, *Silent Spring,* played a major role in banning the use of the insecticide DDT.

Veglahn, N. (1977). *The Mysterious Rays: Marie Curie's World.* Illus. by V. Juhasz. Coward.

> This biography chronicles the later life of Marie Curie, the French chemist who discovered radium.

3. Middle-School Grades (6–8)

Fisher, M. P. (1989). *Women in the Third World.* Watts.

> This account provides profiles of women involved in contemporary issues.

Freedman, R. (1993). *Eleanor Roosevelt: A Life of Discovery.* Clarion.

> This is a biography of Eleanor Roosevelt.

Hull, M. (1994). *Rosa Parks: Civil Rights Leader.* Chelsea.

> This biography describes how Parks's refusal to give up her bus seat sparked the Montgomery Boycott and led to subsequent civil rights actions.

Roosevelt, E. (1984). *Eleanor Roosevelt, with Love: A Centenary Remembrance.* Dutton/Lodestar.

> This biography is by Roosevelt's son, Eliot.

Ryan, P. M. (2002). *When Marian Sang: The True Recital of Marian Anderson.* Illus. by B. Selznick. Scholastic.

> This is a breathtaking account of Marian Anderson, the black American opera singer, who was famous in Europe before facing the racism that barred the door of opera houses in the United States.

Schneider, D. (1993). *American Women in the Progressive Era, 1900–1920.* Facts on File.

> This account, which includes primary sources, describes women's struggle for equality.

Stanley, S. C. (1993). *Women in the Military.* Messner.

> This account describes women who have served in wartime as well as the establishment of women's branches of the armed forces.

References

Prologue: Reflecting on What's Ahead, p. 1

Alter, J., & Denworth, L. (1990). A (vague) sense of history. *Newsweek*, Special Issue, 31–33.

Garrison, W. H. (2003). Democracy, experience, and education: Promoting a continued capacity for growth. *Phi Delta Kappan*, 84, 525–529.

Schaps, E., & Solomon, D. (1990). Schools and classrooms as caring communities. *Educational Leadership*, 48, 38–42.

1. The Dynamics of Social Studies, p. 8

Arendt, H. (1961). *Between past and future*. New York: Viking.

Banks, J. A. (1997). *Educating citizens in a multicultural society*. New York: Teachers College Press.

Bruner, J. (1996). *The culture of education*. Cambridge, MA: Harvard University Press.

Dewey, John. (1938). What is social study? *Progressive Education*, 15 (May), 367–369.

Lindquist, T. (1998). *Ways that work*. Portsmouth, NH: Heinemann.

_____.(2002). *Seeing the whole through social studies* (2nd ed.). Portsmouth, NH: Heinemann.

MacIntyre, A. (1990). How to be a North American. In J. Quay & J. Veninga (Eds.), *Making connections: The humanities, culture, and community* (pp. 1–25). Occasional Paper No. 1. American Council of Learned Societies and the Federation of State Humanities Councils.

McGoogan, Gail. (2002). Around the word in 24 hours. *Educational Leadership*, 60, 44–46.

National Council for the Social Studies. (1994). *Expect excellence: Curriculum standards for social studies*. Executive Summary. Washington, DC.

Ravitch, D. (2002). September 11: Seven lessons for schools. *Educational Leadership*, 60, 6–9.

Salinas, P. D. (1997). *Assimilation, American style*. New York: Basic Books.

Tocqueville, Alexis de. (1947). *Democracy in America*, ed. Henry Steele Commager, tr. H. Reeve. Oxford: Oxford University Press.

Welton, D. (1999). Integrating technology in elementary classrooms. *Social Studies and the Young Learner*, 12.

Zemelman, S., Daniels, H., & Hyde, A. (1998). *Best practice: New standards for teaching and learning in America's schools* (2nd ed.). Portsmouth, NH: Heinemann.

2. History and the Social Sciences: The Knowledge Base for Social Studies, p. 42

Arendt, H. (1961). *Between past and future*. New York: Viking Press.

Bednarz, S. (1997). Using the geographic perspective to enrich history. *Social Education*, 61, 139–145.

Brody, R. A. (1989). Why study politics? In National Commission, *Charting a course: Social studies for the 21st century* (pp. 59–63). Washington, DC: National Commission on Social Studies in the Schools.

Brophy, J. E., & VanSledright, B. A. (1997). *Teaching and learning history in elementary schools*. New York: Teachers College Press.

Bruer, J. (1993). *Schools for thought: A science of learning in the classroom*. Cambridge, MA: Harvard University Press.

Bruner, J. (1986). *Actual minds, possible worlds*. Cambridge, MA: Harvard University Press.

Caine, R. N., & Caine, G. (1994). *Making connections: Teaching and the human brain*. New York: Addison-Wesley.

Commager, H. S., & Muessig, R. (1980). *The nature and study of history*. Columbus, OH: Merrill.

Dawson, E. (1929). *Teaching the social studies*. New York: Macmillan.

Egan, K. (1979). What children know best. *Social Education*, 43, 130–134.

Elkind, D. (1982). *The hurried child*. Reading, MA: Addison-Wesley.

Gardner, H. (1991). *The unschooled mind: How children think and schools should teach.* New York: Basic Books.

Good, T. L., & Brophy, J. E. (1994). *Looking in classrooms* (6th ed.). New York: HarperCollins.

Henry, T. (1994). Mapping out geography plan. *USA Today,* 21 October, 4D.

Joint Committee on Geographic Education. (1984). *Guidelines for Geographic Education.* Washington, DC: National Council for Geographic Education and the Association of American Geographers.

Levstik, L., & Barton, K. (1997). *Doing history: Investigating with children in elementary and middle schools.* Mahwah, NJ: Lawrence Erlbaum Associates.

Momigliano, A. (1982). History in an age of ideologies. *The American Scholar,* 51, 495–507.

Piaget, J. (1950). *The psychology of intelligence.* New York: Harcourt Brace.

Postman, N., & Weingartner, C. (1969). *Teaching as a subversive activity.* New York: Dell.

Schug, M. C., Lopus, J. S., Morton, J. S., Reinke, R., Wentworth, D. R., & Western, R. D. (2003). Is economics your worst nightmare? *Social Education,* 67, 73–78.

Theroux, P. (1997). Letter from Hong Kong. *New Yorker,* 12 May, 54–65.

3. How Social Studies Programs Are Organized, p. 68

Apple, M. (1993). *Official knowledge: Democratic education in a conservative age.* New York: Routledge.

Cornbleth, C., & Waugh, D. (1995). *The great speckled bird: Multicultural politics and educational policymaking.* New York: St. Martin's Press.

Hirsch, E. D. (1988). *Cultural literacy.* New York: Vintage Books.

_____. (1991–1993). *What your kindergarten [through sixth] grader needs to know.* New York: Doubleday.

_____. (2001). Seeking breadth *and* depth in the curriculum. *Educational Leadership,* 59, 22–25.

Larkins, G., Hawkins, M. L., & Gilmore, A. (1987). Trivial and noninformative content of elementary social studies: A review of primary texts in four series. *Theory and Research in Social Education,* 15 (Fall), 299–311.

Marshall, M. (1996). Disadvantaged students narrow gap. *Common Knowledge,* 9, 3 & 5.

National Council for the Social Studies (NCSS), Task Force on Scope and Sequence. (1989). In search of a scope and sequence for social studies. *Social Education,* 53, 380–382.

Pappas, C. C., Keifer, B., & Levstik, L. (1995). *An integrated language perspective in elementary school: Theory into action.* White Plains, NY: Longman.

Peterson, B. (1995). What should children learn? A teacher looks at E. D. Hirsch. In D. Levine, R. Lowe, B. Peterson, & R. Tenorio (Eds.), *Rethinking schools: An agenda for change* (pp. 74–88). New York: New Press.

Taba, H., Durkin, M. C., McNaughton, A. H., & Fraenkel, J. R. (1967). *Teacher's handbook for elementary social studies* (introductory ed.). Menlo Park, CA: Addison-Wesley.

Toppo, G. (2003). Textbook examples of PC. *USA Today,* 17 April, 7D.

Weatherford, J. (1988). *Indian givers: How the Indians of America transformed the world.* New York: Crown.

Whitmire, R. (2000). Core knowledge boosts scores. *USA Today,* 30 May, 8D.

4. The Dimensions of Cultural Diversity, p. 94

Ayers, S. (2003). Teaching about religion in the elementary grades. *Social Studies and the Young Learner,* 15, 27–29.

Banks, J. (1989). Approaches to multicultural curriculum reform. In J. Banks & C. McGee Banks (Eds.), *Multicultural education: Issues and perspectives* (pp. 189–207). Boston: Allyn & Bacon.

Barber, B. R. (1992). *An aristocracy for everyone: The politics of education and the future of America.* New York: Ballantine Books.

Bigelow, B. (1996). On the road to cultural bias: A critique of the Oregon Trail CD-ROM. *Rethinking Schools.* 10, Milwaukee, WI: Rethinking Schools.

Christensen, L. (1994). Unlearning the myths that bind us. In B. Bigelow, L. Christensen, S. Karp, B. Miner, & B. Petersen (Eds.), *Rethinking our classrooms: Teaching for equity and justice.* Milwaukee, WI: Rethinking Schools.

Delpit, L. (1995). *Other people's children.* New York: New Press.

Douglass, S. L. (2002). Teaching about religion. *Educational Leadership, 60,* 32–27.

Elnour, A., & Bashi-Ali, K. (2003). Teaching Muslim girls in American Schools. *Social Education, 67,* 62–64.

Elrich, M. (1994). The stereotype within. *Educational Leadership, 51,* 12–15.

Flynn, V., & Chambers, R. D. (1994). Promoting gender equity: What you can do? *Learning 94, 22* (5), 58–59.

Gay, G. (1991). Culturally diverse students and social studies. In J. Shaver (Ed.), *Handbook of research on social studies teaching and learning* (pp. 154–174). New York: Macmillan.

_____. (1997). Educational equity for students of color. In J. A. Banks & C. A. M. Banks (Eds.), *Multicultural education: Issues and perspectives* (pp. 171–194). Boston: Allyn & Bacon.

Grant, C. A., & Sleeter, C. E. (1989). *Turning on learning.* New York: Merrill.

Haynes, C. C., & Thomas, O. (2000) *Finding common ground: A guide to religious liberty in public schools.* Freedom Forum, 75–76.

Kames, M. (2000). Girls can be president. *Middle-Level Learning.* An occasional publication of the National Council for the Social Studies. January/February 2000, M5–M8.

Lee, E. (1994). Taking multicultural, anti-racist education seriously. In B. Bigelow et al. (Eds.), *Rethinking our classrooms: Teaching for equity and justice.* Milwaukee, WI: Rethinking Schools.

Orfield, G., Frakenberg, E. D., & Lee, C. (2003). The resurgence of school segregation. *Educational Leadership, 60,* 16–20.

Sadker, M., & Sadker, D. (1994). *Failing at fairness: How America's schools cheat girls.* New York: Macmillan.

Shade, B. J., & New, C. A. (1993). Cultural influences on learning: Teaching implications. In J. A. Banks & C. A. Banks (Eds.), *Multicultural education: Issues and perspectives* (pp. 317–331). Boston: Allyn & Bacon.

Stokes, S. S. (1997). Curriculum for Native American students: Using Native American values. *The Reading Teacher, 50,* 576–584.

Children's Literature

Mochizuki, K. (1993). *Baseball saved us.* New York: Lee & Lowe.

Uchida, Y. (1971). *Journey to Topaz: A story of the Japanese-American evacuation.* New York: Scribners.

5. The Dimensions of Instructional Diversity, p. 124

Allen, R. (2003). Maximizing learning in inclusinve classrooms. *Curriculum Update.* Association for Supervision and Curriculum Development, Spring, 1–6.

Gardner, H. (2000). *Intelligence reframed: Multiple intelligences for the 21st century.* New York: Basic Books.

_____ & Checkley, K. (1997). The first seven . . . and the eighth. *Educational Leadership, 55,* 8–13.

Good, T., & Brophy, J. (2000). *Looking in classrooms* (8th ed.). New York: Longman.

Johnson, D., & Johnson, R. (1998). *Learning together and alone: Cooperative, competitive and individualistic learning* (5th ed.). Boston: Pearson Allyn & Bacon.

King-Sears, M. (2003). Three steps for gaining access to the general education curriculum for learners with disabilities. Electronic Edition at: http://ldonline. org/ld_indepth/general_info/three_steps.html.

Mooney, J., & Cole, D. (2000). *Learning outside the lines.* New York: Simon & Schuster.

Riding, R. (2002). *School learning and cognitive styles.* London: Fulton.

Rosenthal, B. (1971). *The images of man.* New York: Basic Books.

Spolsky, B. (1998). *Sociolinguistics.* Oxford, UK: Oxford University Press.

Temple, L. (2000). Disputed health duties injected into teaching of disabled. *USA Today,* 15 February, 9D.

Thomas, K. (2000). Let's talk about what I can do. *USA Today,* 15 August, D1–2, 7.

Turnbull, A., Turnbull, R., Shank, M., & Leal, D. (1999). *Exceptional lives: Special education in today's schools* (2nd ed.). Upper Saddle River, NJ: Merrill/Prentice Hall.

Children's Literature

Kraus, R. (1998). *Leo the late bloomer.* Illustrated by J. Aruegho. New York: HarperCollins Juvenile Books.

Lyon, G. (1994). *Mama is a miner.* New York: Orchard Books.

Priceman, M. (1994). *How to make an apple pie and see the world.* New York: Alfred Knopf.

6. Developing Character and Values, p. 144

Allen, R. (2003). The democratic aims of service learning. *Educational Leadership,* 60, 511–55.

Bennett, W. J. (1994). *The book of virtues.* New York: Simon & Schuster.

Billig, S. H. (August, 2000). The effects of service learning. *School Administrator.* (Web Edition) American Association of School Administrators at: http://www.aasa.org/publications/sa/2000_08/billig.htm

Bloom, E. (2003). Service learning and social studies: A natural fit. *Middle Level Learning,* a supplement to NCSS publications. 17 May/June, M4–M7.

Boyle-Baise M. (Winter, 2003). Doing democracy in social studies methods. *Theory and Research in Social Education,* 31, 50–71.

Brogmann, A. (1992). *Crossing the postmodern divide.* Chicago: University of Chicago Press.

Canter, L. (September, 1989). Assertive discipline: More than names on the board and marbles in a jar. *Phi Delta Kappan,* 70, 57–60.

Cooper, D., & Snell, J. (March, 2003). Bullying—Not just a kid thing. *Educational Leadership,* 60, 22–25.

Doyle, D. P. (February, 1997). Education and character. *Phi Delta Kappan,* 78, 440–443.

Fabes, R. A., et al. (1989). Effective rewards on children's prosocial motivation: A socialization study. *Developmental Psychology,* 25, 509–515.

Gilligan, C. C. (1977). In a different voice: Women's conceptions of the self and morality. *Harvard Educational Review,* 49, 481–517.

_____. (1982). *In a different voice: Psychological theory and women's development.* Cambridge, MA: Harvard University Press, 25–32.

Glasser, W. (1990). *The quality school.* New York: Harper & Row.

Grusec, J. (1991). Socializing concerns for others in the home. *Developmental Psychology,* 27, 338–342.

Himmelfarb, G. (1995). *The demoralization of society.* New York: Knopf.

Kilpatrick, W. (1992). *Why Johnny can't tell right from wrong.* New York: Simon and Schuster.

Kohn, A. (February, 1997). How not to teach values. *Phi Delta Kappan,* 78, 429–439.

_____. (2003). Almost there, but not quite. *Educational Leadership,* 60, 26–30.

Leming, J. S. (1985). Research on social studies curriculum and instruction: Interventions and outcomes in the socio-moral domain. In William B. Stanley (Ed.), *Review of research in social studies education, 1976–1983.* Washington, DC: National Council for the Social Studies, and the Boulder, CO: ERIC Clearinghouse for Social Studies/Social Science Education, and the Social Science Education Consortium, 123–213.

_____. (November, 1993). In search of effective character education. *Educational Leadership,* 51, 63–71.

Lickona, T. (March, 1977). How to encourage moral development. *Learning,* 5, 37–43.

_____. (November, 1993). The return of character education. *Educational Leadership,* 51, 6–11.

Morris, R. (March/April, 2003). Colonial America and service learning in the fifth grade. *Social Studies and the Young Learner,* 15, 11–14.

Mussen, P., & Eisenberg-Berg, N. (1977). *Roots of caring, sharing, and helping: The development of prosocial behavior in children.* New York: Freeman.

Olweus, D. (2003). A profile of bullying at school. *Educational Leadership,* 60, 12–17.

Peterson, K. (2002). Parents feel they're failing to teach values. *USA Today,* 30 October, D1.

Raths, L. E., Harmin, M., & Simon, S. B. (1978). *Values and teaching* (2nd ed.). Columbus, OH: Charles E. Merrill.

Ryan, K. (1993). Doing half the job. *Houghton Mifflin/ Educators' Forum,* Fall, 12.

Simon, S., Howe, L. & Kirschenbaum H. (1992). *Values clarification: A handbook of practical strategies for teachers and students.* New York: Dodd Mead.

Children's Literature

McMullen, K. (1991). *The great eggspectations of Lila Fenwick.* New York: Farrar Straus & Giroux.

Piper, W. (1930/1954). *The little engine that could.* New York: Grosset & Dunlap, Penguin Group.

Van Allsburg, C. (1988). *Two bad ants.* Boston: Houghton Mifflin.

7. Social Studies: Gateway to Literacy, p. 172

Beck, I., & McKeown, M. (2002). Questioning the author: Making sense of social studies. *Educational Leadership, 70,* 44–47.

Button, K., Johnson, M., & Furgeson, P. (1996). Interactive writing in a primary classroom. *The Reading Teacher, 49,* 2–10.

Chadwell, G. (1992). *Developing an effective writing program for the elementary grades.* Andover, MA: The Network.

Chall, J. S., & Conard, S. (1991). *Should textbooks challenge students?* New York: Teachers College Press.

Christiansen, L. (1998). Whose standard? Teaching standard English. *Rethinking our classrooms: Teaching for equity and justice.* Milwaukee, WI: Rethinking Schools.

Cooper, J. D. (2003). *Literacy: Helping children construct meaning* (4th ed.) Boston: Houghton Mifflin.

Flood, J., & Lapp, D. (1987). Reading and writing relations: Assumptions and directions. In J. Squires (Ed.), *Dynamics of language learning.* Urbana, IL: National Council of Teachers of English.

Hennings, D. (2002). *Communication in action* (8th ed.) Boston: Houghton Mifflin.

Hymes, L., & Hymes, J. (1960). *Hooray for chocolate.* Reading, MA: Addison-Wesley.

Irvin, J. L., Lunstrum, J. P., Lynch-Brown, C., & Shepard, M. F. (1995). *Enhancing social studies through literacy strategies.* Washington, DC: National Council for the Social Studies.

McAuley, K., & Wilson, R. H. (1985). *The United States past to present.* Lexington, MA: Heath.

McCoy, M. M. (May/June 2003). Incorporating effective writing strategies. *Social Education, 67,* 200–202.

Morrow, L. M. (1989). *Literacy development in the early years: Helping children read and write.* Englewood Cliffs, NJ: Prentice Hall.

Pinnell, G. S., & McCarrier, A. (1994). Interactive writing: A transition tool for assisting children in learning to read and write. In E. Hiebert & B. Taylor (Eds.), *Getting reading right from the start: Effective early literacy interventions* (pp. 149–170). Needham, MA: Allyn & Bacon.

Robinson, F. (1962). *Effective study.* New York: Harper & Row.

Taba, H., Durkin, M., Frankel, J. R., & McNaughton, A. (1967). *Teacher's handbook for elementary social studies* (introductory ed.). Reading, MA: Addison-Wesley.

8. Planning and Orchestrating Instruction, p. 208

Anderson, L. W., & Krathwohl, D. R. (Eds.). (2001). *A taxonomy for learning, teaching, and assessment: A revision of Bloom's taxonomy of educational objectives.* New York: Longman.

Bloom, B. S., et al. (1956). *Taxonomy of educational objectives: The classification of educational goals, handbook I: Cognitive domain.* New York: Longman.

Brophy, J., & Alleman, J. (May, 1991). Activities as instructional tools: A framework for analysis and evaluation. *Educational Research, 20,* 9–22.

Brophy, J., Alleman, J., & O'Mahony, C. R. (Winter, 2003). Primary-grade students' knowledge and thinking about food production and the origins of common foods. *Theory and Research in Social Education, 31,* 10–50.

Egan, K. (February, 2003). Start with what the students knows or with what the student can imagine? *Phi Delta Kappan, 84,* 443–445.

Krathwohl, D. R., et al. (1964). *Taxonomy of educational objectives: The classification of educational goals, handbook II: Affective domain.* New York: Longman.

Leavell, J., Hatcher, B., Battle J., & Ramos-Michail, N. (May/June, 2002). Exploring Hispanic culture through trade books. *Social Education, 66,* 210–215.

NCSS (1994). *Curriculum standards for social studies: Expectations of excellence.* Washington, DC: National Council for the Social Studies.

Children's Literature

Bunting, E. (1991). *Fly away home.* Boston: Houghton Mifflin.

Burton, V. L. (1939). *Mike Mulligan and his steam shovel.* Boston: Houghton Mifflin.

Hoyt-Goldsmith, D. (1996). *Migrant worker: A boy from the Rio Grande Valley.* New York: Holiday House.

Jiménez, F. (2000). *La mariposa.* Illustrated by Simon Silva. Boston: Houghton Mifflin.

Mora, P. (1997). *Tomas and the library lady.* Illustrated by Raul Colon. New York: Knopf.

9. Assessing Learning, p. 241

Alleman, J., & Brophy, J. (1998). Assessment in a social constructivist classroom. *Social Education,* 62, 32–42.

ASCD. (1996). Designing rubrics for authentic assessment. *ASCD Education Update,* 38 (December), 7.

O'Neil, J. (1994). Making assessment meaningful. *ASCD Curriculum Update,* 36, 3–5.

_____. (1996). Teaching for performance. *ASCD Education Update,* 38, 8, 1, 6.

Parker, W. C. (1991). *Renewing the social studies curriculum.* Alexandria, VA: Association for Supervision and Curriculum Development.

Spady, W. G. (1994). Choosing outcomes of significance. *Educational Leadership,* 51 (6), 18–22.

Wiggins, G. (1989). Teaching to the authentic test. *Educational Leadership,* 46 (April), 41–47.

Children's Literature

Fritz, J. (1987). *Shh! We're writing the constitution.* Illustrated by Tomie de Paola. New York: G. Putnam's Sons.

10. Strategies and Activities for Effective Teaching, p. 272

Brophy, J., & Alleman, J. (1990). Activities as instructional tools: A framework for analysis and evaluation. Occasional Paper No. 132. East Lansing: Michigan State University, Institute for Research on Teaching.

Johonnot, J. (1887). *Stories of our country.* New York: D. Appleton.

Kellogg, S. (1988). *Johnny Appleseed.* New York: Morrow.

Lauritzen, C., & Jaeger, M. (1994). Language arts teacher education within a transdisciplinary curriculum. *Language Arts,* 71 (8), 581–587.

National Council for the Social Studies. (1994). *Expectations of excellence: Curriculum standards for social studies.* Washington, DC: National Council for the Social Studies.

Silverstein, S. (1964). *The giving tree.* New York: Harper & Row.

Walker, B. M. (1979). *The little house cookbook.* New York: Harper & Row.

11. Nurturing Critical and Reflective Thinking, p. 303

Anderson, L. W., & Krathwohl, D. R. (Eds.). (2001). *A taxonomy for learning, teaching, and assessment: A revision of Bloom's taxonomy of educational objectives.* New York: Longman.

Beyer, B. K. (Ed.). (1987). *Practical strategies for the teaching of thinking.* Boston: Allyn & Bacon.

Bloom, B. S., et al. (1956). *Taxonomy of educational objectives: The classification of educational goals, handbook I: Cognitive domain.* New York: Longman.

Rowe, Mary Budd. (1969). Science, silence, and sanctions. *Science and Children,* 6, 11–13.

12. Helping Students Understand Maps, Globes, and Graphics, p. 329

Joint Committee on Geographic Education. (1984). *Guidelines for geographic education.* Washington, DC: National Council for Geographic Education and the Association of American Geographers.

Monmonier, M. (1991). *How to lie with maps.* Chicago: University of Chicago Press.

Pritchard, S. F. (1989). Using picture books to teach geography in the primary grades. *Journal of Geography,* 88, 126–136.

Children's Literature

Burton, V. L. (1943). *Katy and the big snow.* Boston: Houghton Mifflin.

Freschet, B. (1977). *Little black bear goes for a walk.* New York: Scribner's.

Hutchins, P. (1968). *Rosie's walk.* New York: Macmillan.

McCloskey, R. (1941). *Make way for ducklings.* New York: Viking.

Potter, Beatrix. (1995). *Peter rabbit.* Dover.

Schwartz, D. M. (1985). *How much is a million?* Illustrations by S. Kellogg. New York: Lothrop, Lee & Shepard.

Taylor, M. (1968). *Henry explores the jungle.* New York: Atheneum.

13. Using Instructional Tools: Print, Multimedia, and Community Resources, p. 356

Braun, J. A., Jr., Fernlund, P., & White, C. S. (1998). *Technology tools in the social studies curriculum.* Wilsonville, OR: Franklin, Beedle & Associates.

Bryant, K. (1992, September). Apply early language connections. *The explorer,* 1–2.

Ellerbee, L. (1995). What shall we tell the kids? *Liberal Opinion Week,* 6 (May 1), p. 7.

Macaulay, D. (1973). *Cathedral.* Boston: Houghton Mifflin.

_____. (1975). *Pyramid.* Boston: Houghton Mifflin.

_____. (1979). *Castle.* Boston: Houghton Mifflin.

_____. (1988). *The way things work.* Boston: Houghton Mifflin.

McGowan, T. M. (1987). Children's fiction as a source for social studies skill-building. *ERIC Digest* (No. 37). Bloomington, IN: Clearinghouse for Social Studies/Social Science Education.

Reiss, F. (2001). *Terrorism and kids.* Boston: Peanut and Jelly Press.

Rose, S. A., & Fernlund, P. M. (1997). Using technology for powerful social studies learning. *Social Education,* 61, 160–166.

Children's Literature

Baker, B. (1972). *The big push.* New York: Coward, McCann & Geoghegan.

Burton, V. L. (1939). *Mike Mulligan and his steam shovel.* Boston: Houghton Mifflin.

Grahame, K. (1954). *The wind in the willows.* New York: Scribners. (Originally published in 1908.)

Mathis, S. B. (1975). *The hundred penny box.* New York: Viking Press.

Index

• • • • About the Author

David A. Welton, an Ohio native, is Professor
Emeritus of Elementary Education at Texas Tech
University. After earning bachelors degrees from
Western Reserve and Kent State Universities, and a
masters and doctorate from Ohio University (Athens,
Ohio, not Columbus!), Dr. Welton taught at Syracuse
University before settling at Texas Tech, where he
remained for 25 years until his retirement in 2001.

Dr. Welton is active in the National Council for the
Social Studies and other professional organizations.
The former editor of the Elementary Section of *Social
Education*, he is also the author of numerous articles
on the teaching of social studies, and has directed
several funded projects that focused on developing
field-based teacher training programs.

Dr. Welton and his wife, Kathleen, now reside in the
Piedmont of North Carolina. They have three sons, all
of whom have also left the high desert of West Texas
for the mountains of Colorado and New Mexico. In
their absence, their parents are once again enjoying
the unhindered use of their automobiles and telephone.